ADVANCE PRAISE FOR

Here Where We Live Is Our Country

"Molly Crabapple's words are as glorious as her colors, her writing as vivid as her painting. Reading her *Here Where We Live Is Our Country* today, with Gaza in ruins and the rest of the world seemingly on the road to ruin, is revelatory, a reminder that even in the most dehumanizing of times a loving humanity might endure, even if only fleetingly."
—Greg Grandin, author of *The End of the Myth*

"*Here Where We Live Is Our Country* is a captivating and meticulously researched story of family, community, and solidarity. Molly Crabapple takes us through decades of forgotten memories to rediscover an essential part of Jewish history and a revolutionary movement whose organization and ideals are more relevant than ever, and which may yet point the way toward a better future."
—Mike Duncan, author of *Hero of Two Worlds*

"At a time when racism and xenophobia are being institutionalized in the United States and are once again sweeping Europe, *Here Where We Live Is Our Country* should give succor to those seeking inspiration for their own forms of resistance today. Molly Crabapple is a masterful storyteller who possesses an admirable sense of history and writes with verve and wit. In this book, she tells the fascinating, long-neglected story of the socialist fighters of the Jewish Bund—as well as those of Zionism, Soviet communism, fascism, the plague of antisemitism—and explains how it has all fueled the unfinished duels of the present day in Israel and Palestine. Remarkable for its historical sweep as well as its timeliness, *Here Where We Live Is Our Country* is a true tour de force." —Jon Lee Anderson, author of *Che: A Revolutionary Life*

ALSO BY MOLLY CRABAPPLE

Tiger Slayer
(illustrator; written by Ruby Lal)

Brothers of the Gun
(with Marwan Hisham)

Drawing Blood

HERE WHERE WE LIVE IS OUR COUNTRY

HERE WHERE WE LIVE IS OUR COUNTRY

The Story of the JEWISH BUND

MOLLY CRABAPPLE

ONE WORLD
NEW YORK

One World
An imprint of Random House
A division of Penguin Random House LLC
1745 Broadway, New York, NY 10019
oneworldlit.com
penguinrandomhouse.com

Portions of this work were originally published in the article "My Great Grandfather the Bundist," by Molly Crabapple, published in *The New York Review of Books* on October 6, 2018.

Grateful acknowledgment is made to the following for permission to use the following material:
Madeleine Atkins Cohen: English translation of Yiddish text by Leivick Hodes. Used by permission.
Brian Gocial: Excerpts from the English translation of *Social Democracy and the National Question* by Vladimir Medem, translated by James Conway, commissioned by Brian Gocial. Used by permission.
Mark Erlich, Executor of the Estate of Victor Erlich: Excerpts from *Bread and Matzoh* by Sophia Dubnova-Erlich, translated by Alan Shaw. Used by permission.

Library of Congress Cataloging-in-Publication Data

Names: Crabapple, Molly, author
Title: Here where we live is our country / by Molly Crabapple.
Description: First edition. | New York, NY: One World, 2026.
Identifiers: LCCN 2025049704 (print) | LCCN 2025049705 (ebook) | ISBN 9780593229453 hardcover | ISBN 9780593229460 ebook
Subjects: LCSH: Allgemeyner Idisher arbayṭerbund in Liṭa, Poylen un Rusland | Jewish socialists—History—20th century. | Labor movement—History—20th century.
Classification: LCC HD6305.J3 C73 2026 (print) | LCC HD6305.J3 (ebook)
LC record available at lccn.loc.gov/2025049704
LC ebook record available at lccn.loc.gov/2025049705

Printed in the United States of America

5th Printing

FIRST EDITION

Book Team: production editor: *Evan Camfield* • managing editor: *Rebecca Berlant* • production manager: *Mark Maguire* • copy editor: *Mimi Lipson* • proofreaders: *Christopher Ross, Barbara Stussy, Susan Gutentag* • indexer: *Ina Gravitz*

Book design by Barbara M. Bachman

The authorized representative in the EU for product safety and compliance is Penguin Random House Ireland, Morrison Chambers, 32 Nassau Street, Dublin D02 YH68, Ireland. https://eu-contact.penguin.ie

For my mother, Janice

Soon we will search in the margins of *your*
history, in distant countries, for what was
once our history.

—MAHMOUD DARWISH,
ELEVEN STARS OVER ANDALUSIA
(TRANSLATED BY AGHA SHAHID ALI)

Tradition is not the worship of ashes.
It is the preservation of fire.

—GUSTAV MAHLER

CONTENTS

Part Three
THE ALTERNATE WORLD
(1917–1939)

Part Four
FIRE
(1939–1948)

A NOTE ON NAMES

THE BORDERLANDS OF EASTERN EUROPE CHANGED HANDS THROUGHOUT the twentieth century, and each new regime brought a new set of place names. Additionally, the borderlands' Yiddish-speaking Jews had their own names for the towns and cities they inhabited. To choose a place name is thus to reveal one's partialities. In general, I chose the name used in the time period I was writing about, unless there was a Yiddish version that I found more congenial. For Ukrainian cities, I use Ukrainian rather than Russian spellings, out of gratitude to the Ukrainians I met when I visited their country in 2022 during the Russian invasion. I do not use diacritic marks in Polish words, since they are unfamiliar to American readers.

With personal names, I use the version most familiar to Americans—Viktor, not Wiktor—unless a person was famous under a less facile spelling.

Identity is unruly, morphing based on self-definition and societal acceptance, but for simplicity's sake, a few rules hold true.

After 1917, a "communist" refers specifically to a supporter of the Communist Party of the Soviet Union.

Notwithstanding the vast Muslim population of the tsarist empire, a Russian, Pole or Ukrainian can be assumed to be Christian unless otherwise noted. Notwithstanding the diversity of our global diaspora, unless otherwise specified, "Jews" refers to the Yiddish-speaking Jews of Eastern Europe.

CAST OF CHARACTERS

(in order of appearance)

PART ONE: UNDERGROUND (1772–1905)

Samuel Rothbort: Bundist leatherworker from Volkovysk. Later, an artist in New York City. My great-grandfather.

Pavel Axelrod and Georgi Plekhanov: co-founders of the Emancipation of Labor group, the first Russian Marxist organization.

Pati Kremer: unofficial co-founder of the Bund in Vilna and wife of Arkady Kremer. Later, spiritual leader of the resistance in the Vilna ghetto.

Arkady Kremer: co-founder of the Bund in Vilna.

Liuba Levinson: early leader of the Bund in Vilna.

Julius Martov: socialist activist who helped create the theoretical basis for the Bund. Later, leader of the Menshevik-Internationalists.

Vladimir Ilyich Ulyanov: communist theorist, newspaper editor, orator, and founder of the Bolshevik Party. Later, the first leader of the Soviet Union, under his nom de guerre, **Lenin**.

Vladimir Medem: Bundist leader, writer, and theoretician.

Raphael Abramovich: Bundist and Menshevik-Internationalist leader.

Mark Liber: Bundist orator, right-wing Menshevik leader, and member of the Petrograd Soviet in 1917.

Leon Trotsky: communist theorist, orator, political leader, and commander of the Red Army. Later, a refugee.

Meyer London: fundraiser for the Bund and labor lawyer in New York City. Later, a socialist congressman.

Anna Lipshitz: Bundist orator, nicknamed "The Fury" for her speeches in Odesa during the revolution of 1905.

PART TWO: REVOLUTION (1906–1918)

Gina Medem: Bundist activist from Lodz and wife of Vladimir Medem.

Sophia Dubnova: poet, sex columnist, and Bundist revolutionary. Wife of

Bundist leader Henryk Erlich. Mother of Alexander and Victor Erlich.

Simon Dubnov: eminent Jewish historian of the diaspora. Father of Sophia Dubnova.

Henryk Erlich: Bundist and Menshevik leader on the Petrograd Soviet in 1917. Lawyer and journalist. Later, leader of the Bund in interwar Poland. Husband of Sophia Dubnova. Father of Alexander and Victor Erlich.

Alexander Kerensky: leftist lawyer, orator, parliamentarian, and leader of the Russian Empire for several months during 1917. Later, a New Yorker.

Esther Frumkin: only woman on Bund's central committee in Minsk. Later a leader in the Jewish Section of the Communist Party of the Soviet Union.

PART THREE: THE ALTERNATE WORLD (1917–1939)

Moishe Rafes: Bundist leader in Kyiv and delegate to the Ukrainian Central Rada. Later a leader in the Jewish Section of the Communist Party of the Soviet Union.

David Lipetz: Bundist mayor of Berdichev, Ukraine. Later, a general in the Red Army under the name of **David Petrovsky.**

Bernard Goldstein: head of the Bund's self-defense militia in Warsaw.

Józef Pilsudski: Polish socialist. Military leader. Later, the father of independent Poland.

Viktor Alter: leader of the Bund in interwar Poland.

Vladimir Jabotinsky: leader of Revisionist Zionism.

David Ben-Gurion: Labor Zionist leader, chief of the Histadrut and the Jewish Agency. Later, the first prime minister of Israel.

Avram Markus: Bundist newspaper editor in Volkovysk. Father of communist activist **Shlomo Markus.**

Meir Zeleviansky: elderly shoemaker and Bundist in Volkovysk.

David Dubinsky: secretary for a Bundist bakers union in Lodz. Later, head of the Ladies' Garment Workers Union in New York City and co-founder of the Jewish Labor Committee.

Baruch Charney Vladeck: Bundist orator who fled to New York and became a socialist alderman. Later, co-founder of the Jewish Labor Committee.

Hugon Tyminski: Polish pharmacist and nationalist agitator in Volkovysk.

Marek Edelman: Bundist youth activist whose mother, **Tsipie,** ran the

Bundist women's movement. Later, the second commander of the Warsaw Ghetto Uprising.

PART FOUR: FIRE (1939–1948)

Zygmunt Zaremba: leader in the Polish Socialist Party. Founder of the Workers Brigades for the Defense of Warsaw alongside his comrade, Mieczyslaw "Mek" Niedzialkowski.

Maurycy Orzech: head of the Bundist union of artisans.

Arthur Zygielbojm: Bundist councilman from Lodz. Later, representative to the Polish Government in Exile in London.

Sonia Nowogrodska: Bundist teacher and political prisoner. After the Nazi invasion, leader in the party underground.

Jacob Celemenski: Bundist tailor from Krakow. Later an underground courier.

Ignacy Samsonowicz: Bundist journalist.

Stefan Rowecki: general and first commander of the Polish Home Army.

Zivia "Celina" Lubetkin and Yitzhak "Antek" Zuckerman: Leaders in the left-Zionist youth movement Dror. Later, founders of the Jewish Combat Organization in the Warsaw ghetto.

Zalman Friedrich: Bundist youth activist and ghetto fighter.

Leon Feiner: lawyer and Bundist leader from Krakow. Later the Bund's representative on the Aryan side of Warsaw.

Michal Klepfisz: Bundist athlete and engineer. Later a bomb maker.

Gina Klepfisz: Bundist athlete and nurse. Sister of Michal Klepfisz.

Vladka Peltel: member of the Bund's youth movement Tsukunft in Warsaw. Later a weapons smuggler.

Maria Sawicka: Polish socialist, athlete, and resistance fighter.

Jan Karski: courier for the Polish Home Army.

Mordechai Anielewicz: activist with the left-Zionist youth movement Hashomer Hatzair. Later, the first commander of the Warsaw Ghetto Revolt.

Jurgen Stroop: German SS commander responsible for suppressing the Warsaw Ghetto Revolt.

Adina Blady: Bundist and pediatrician at the Bersohn and Bauman Children's Hospital in Warsaw. Later an underground courier.

INTRODUCTION

During his elder years, my great-grandfather, the post-Impressionist artist Sam Rothbort, tried to paint back into existence the murdered world of his shtetl childhood. Amid the hundreds of watercolors that he called "memory paintings," one stood out. A girl silhouetted against some cottages, her dress the same color as the crepuscular sky above. A moment before, she'd hurled a rock through one now-shattered cottage window. On the painting's margin, her boyfriend offers more rocks.

"Itka the Bundist, Breaking Windows," Sam captioned the work.

I may have been fifteen, seventeen, or twenty when I saw the watercolor, in my great-aunt's sunbaked living room or my mother's apartment; I don't recall exactly. What sticks with me is the old-world awkwardness of the heroine's name. *Itka.* I turned the Yiddish syllables on my tongue. And *Bundist.* What was that?

This question became a thread that led me to the Bund, a revolutionary society of which my great-grandfather had been a member, whose story was interwoven with the agonies and triumphs of Jews in eastern Europe, and whose name has all but been erased. But this thread did not merely draw me back into the vanished past. It became a guide for our moment, in all its horror and possibility, in all its repression, courage, and loss.

Founded in 1897 in the city of Vilna in the Russian Empire, and reaching its height in interwar Poland, the Bund was a sometimes-clandestine political party whose tenets were humane, socialist, secular, and defiantly Jewish. Bundists fought the tsar, battled pogroms, exalted the Yiddish language, and built vast networks of political and cultural institutions out of little more than love and grit. Seeking to liberate Jews from the poverty and violence of interwar Poland, they raised their children on the radical ethos of working-class solidarity and subaltern pride. Ultimately, these youth helped lead the Warsaw Ghetto Revolt. Though the Bund was largely obliterated by Nazi Germany and the Soviet Union, the group's opposition to Zionism better explains its absence from current consciousness. Though the Bund celebrated eastern European Jews as a people, they irreconcilably opposed the establishment of a Jewish state in Palestine. The diaspora *was* home, the Bund argued. Jews could never escape their problems by the dispossession of others. Instead, Bundists created the doctrine of *do'ikayt*, or "Hereness." Jews had the right to live in freedom and dignity wherever it was they stood. They would fight for a better and more beautiful world, even alongside people they had been raised to see as enemies.

The Bund's philosophy spoke to my sense of Jewishness in a way neither the synagogue nor Israel ever had. Maybe this had to do with my upbringing. My Jewish mother, a gifted illustrator, taught me to paint when I was four. My Puerto Rican father, a professor of political economy, introduced me to Marxism when I was six. I grew into an incorrigible artist with a commitment to leftist politics. In 2011, when the anticapitalist Occupy Wall Street protests broke out near my Manhattan apartment, I hurried downstairs to draw them. This would be my gateway to journalism. For the next decade, I traveled around the world covering demonstrations, war zones, and refugee camps. I watched the Arab Spring, and other idealistic mass movements like it, buckle under state violence, and I saw how the mass arrival of refugees was seized by the international far right to catapult itself to power.

All of this drew me toward the party that my great-grandfather referenced in that evocative watercolor. In my free time, I began to read about the Bund. Despite vast differences in the worlds that we inhabited, Bundists seemed to me like kin. Like them, I knew the floor of a police cell, the boredom of a leftist meeting, the electric charge of passing a pamphlet to a stranger, the high of believing, rightly or wrongly, that you are about to change the world. In 2018, I wrote an article about the Bund for *The New York Review of Books*. It remains the most popular piece I have ever done. Afterward, hundreds of young Jews sent me messages to say the essay healed a wound within them. They had never known their ancestors had fought back. I also received notes from the elderly descendants of Bundist leaders, each bearing anecdotes more precious than rubies. These convinced me that Bund's story was too big for a single article. I needed to write a book.

For the next six years, I lost myself in research. In order to read the words of Bundist activists, I studied Yiddish, the once nearly extinct language of the eastern European Jewish working class that the Bund had championed, even though its Germanic syntax tortured me and its vagabond vocabulary, garbed in Hebrew letters, laid constant traps for my tongue. This allowed me to dive into dusty archives, decipher forgotten pamphlets, and commune, unmediated, with the Bund's rebel dead.

But I didn't content myself with text. Revolutionary life is far richer than the words in a propaganda pamphlet. To discover the sensual reality of the Bund's world, I traveled to the former Pale of Settlement. I laid daffodils on the graves of ghetto fighters and took night trains through a Ukraine battered by the Russian invasion. In a Los Angeles parking lot, I listened to an octogenarian Yiddish scholar sing me partisan hymns, and I translated Bundist literature while stuck at Israeli army checkpoints in the occupied West Bank.

As the poet Irena Klepfisz wrote, "History stops for no one," least of all a writer. Over the course of my making this book, millions died in a global pandemic. Far-right parties rose in Europe. Israel embarked upon a genocide in Gaza. The weakness and hypocrisies of the Democratic Party paved the way for the sadistic revanchism of a second Trump term. Horrors multiply. In the America of today, just as in the Bund's interwar Poland, state security men lock immigrants in concentration camps and kidnap dissidents for the crime of speech. As I wrote this book in the New York Public Library, chants for Palestine resounded outside the windows. Often, I went down to join the protesters.

The more I dug into the Bundist past, the more I realized it was not past at all. It was, rather, a candle to illuminate the tumultuous present. Despite war, state collapse, and genocidal repression, the Bund fought for the very multiracial, democratic socialism that a new generation now champions at the ballot box. The Bundists built alternate worlds of beauty, of courage, and of hope, which allowed their people to persevere even in the midst of an apocalypse. Their ideas are still vital today. The Bund was a Jewish group, but its history is not for Jews alone. It belongs to all of us who believe in the necessity of human solidarity. In the story of the Bund—across decades and geographies, ages and faiths—I found the story of our own time, a blueprint for survival, a cautionary tale of death, and a philosophy that might yet save us.

Part One

UNDERGROUND

1772–1905

Sam Rothbort as a
young man in Volkovysk

CHAPTER 1

ORIGINS

(1772–1897)

EVERY FAMILY HAS ITS LEGENDS.

My mother brought me up on stories of her family's nonconformity. We came from a line of grand and impecunious artists. There was Cousin Jack Lush, a militant vegetarian long before it was en vogue. Cousin Jack walked across America to prove the health benefits of his diet. When he finally reached the East Coast, some mayor came out to present him with the key to his city, but Jack could not stop walking and passed him by. Eventually he walked off the entire continent, into the Caribbean, where he retired as the battery king of Trinidad. Or so my mother said. His sister, the dark beauty Vivian, was a sculptress, the sole protégée of Attilio Piccirilli, the Bronx's "master of stone," and carved her own sister, naked, for the doors of Rockefeller Center. Another relative, back in the 1930s, dreamed of buying a van and driving it down South to sell Theosophical pamphlets, and thus deliver a message of peace to Alabama in his thick Jewish accent. This cousin wrote to my great-grandfather Sam to raise funds but was not, I presume, successful. His was only one of the fascinating letters addressed to Sam. There are piles of these, crammed with spiraling Yiddish script—reminiscences of Paris, notes from famous writers, Rosh Hashanah cards with art nouveau type pressed into the luxuriant cardstock—that my mother kept in shoeboxes in her closet.

If Jack and Vivian were stars in my mother's recounting of family lore, my great-grandfather Sam Rothbort was the moon and sun combined. He was an artist whose thousands of sculptures filled the storage room for which my mother begrudgingly paid. He was the humanist who thought all men were brothers, and the prankster who could eat fire and hang by his feet from a chin-up bar well into his eighties. He was an autodidact whose daughter, my glamorous grandmother Ruth, stewed in resentment because he would not send her to college, and he was a monomaniac who took back his paintings from the Brooklyn Museum in a fit of pique, only to spread them out on the lawn of his humble house in Sheepshead Bay, dubbed "the Rothbort Home Museum of Direct Art," in an effort to impress his genius directly upon the masses. He was a Great Man, in his mind and our minds, unrecognized by this selfish city. He was New York. He was ours.

My mother grew up close to her grandfather. When she was sick, Sam spooned honey in her mouth and called it medicine. He taught her to paint, just as she taught me. Falling asleep each night surrounded by his art, I tried to absorb his gift by proxy. I would stare at the wood frames he carved himself, each Yiddish letter gouged with a chisel, and imagine that someday I would paint something good enough to hang inside them. I read Sam's self-published book of essays, *Out of Wood and Stone,* and I listened eagerly to my mother's stories. I never met Sam Rothbort, but I might as well have. I knew him. He spoke to me through countless mediums, his smile wry, his black eyes mischievous. He had made himself an artist. This meant I could do the same.

In the myriad photos Sam Rothbort left, he appears in many guises. In one, taken during his twenties, when he had just arrived in America, he stands awkwardly, his head pinched by a derby a size too small. In another, he balances on a scaffold and applies swirls of plaster to a ceiling. There he is in his Brooklyn garden, and in the pages of a long-out-of-print New York art magazine. These photos, as much as his paintings, fleshed out his image as Artist Progenitor, who brought the family line to the New World in 1904 and remained alive long enough to see my parents wed. Occasionally, my mother would find a photo of the family that he had left behind in Volkovysk, his hometown in the old country. Was it Russia or Poland? Our notions were vague. I could divine no resemblance between the family members in the photos and my jovial great-grandpa. His relatives were skinny, religious Jews, men in black coats and women with wigs, like the Williamsburg Hasidim. They didn't smile, because life was hard in the Old World. Their pinched mouths seemed to whisper a warning.

You might have made it in America, kid. But it's different back in Europe. Poverty. Shacks. Cholera. In the end we all were gassed.

No need to look back.

THE PAST

As a kid, I never felt at home in the present. I loathed school, loathed my peers, loathed my own awkward inability to speak. I imagined that I would have done splendidly elsewhere, in a bohemia from long ago and far away. My great-grandfather was one thread to this imagined future-past. The biography section of my local library provided others. I took out fat volumes on Lola Montez and Oscar Wilde and tried to scry my own future in their stories. I bought armfuls of thrift store paperbacks for similar reasons. The past soaked my art. I copied Goya and memorized the poems of Edna St. Vincent Millay. After I left home at seventeen, I tried to live like I was some mashup of Anaïs Nin and Toulouse-Lautrec, often to comic effect. I posed for art classes for cash. I hid myself in the corners of burlesque clubs, where I drew fan dancers and fire-eaters who were themselves trying to resurrect a half-fictitious Paris. After I moved into a squalid little tenement in Williamsburg, I hung Sam's paintings on my walls. But my fascination with my great-grandfather didn't extend to the place he came from. I imagined myself in lavish capital cities—Paris, Mexico City, Saint Petersburg, built by people who were not his people—and never in the Volkovysk of his birth. A darker history loomed in the background of the family photos he brought from Russia, one that I declined to research further. I papered over the ignorance with stereotype. I didn't look back.

Only later did I ask myself about the history that had shaped Sam Rothbort. I was a journalist by then. I had traveled to war zones and interviewed refugees in camps that disgraced the European continent. I had sat on a balcony in Gaza and listened to Israeli bombs fall in the distance until, at last, the muezzin called in the dawn. Used to asking questions about others, I now began to wonder about my own family's past. Sam's unconventionality had paved the way for mine, but why was he himself so different from how the world intended him to be? Why was he, the son of a Talmudic scholar, never seen inside a synagogue? Why did he sculpt a communist fist, then add rueful commentary in his notebooks? Why did he denounce war? At a time when intermarriage was taboo, why did he accept my Puerto Rican father? Why did he never mention Israel?

What was the nature of his bond to Volkovysk, his hometown, which he immortalized in six hundred loving watercolors? How did he create himself in a place as grindingly oppressive as his birthplace? Then my mother gave me one of his notes, found in a shoebox, with these enigmatic words: "I belonged to the underground." And for the first time, I realized that Sam Rothbort had not just been shaped by the Pale of Settlement. He had tried to shape it in turn.

THE PALE

"Everyone makes mistakes, even God," says Benya Krik, the Jewish gangster king of Isaac Babel's *Odessa Stories.* "Was it not a mistake on

The Pale of Settlement, circa 1900

Moscow
Smolensk
Gomel
THE RUSSIAN EMPIRE
Dnipro River
Sea of AZOV
BLACK SEA

God's part to settle the Jews in Russia, where they have been tormented as if in hell?" Of course, Jews had settled themselves in those lands long before the Russian Empire claimed them for herself.

In the mid-1300s, as the Black Death burned across Western Europe, Jews became scapegoats, booted from one fiefdom to the next, until the Kingdom of Poland saw an opportunity for economic development: in 1343, King Casimir the Great granted Jews legal protections. Nobles invited them to establish towns on the banks of the country's many rivers, to run liquor monopolies, and to collect taxes from peasants. So Sam's ancestors came.

Centuries passed, times of strife and times of acceptance, until this world shattered in 1772. That August, Prussian, Russian, and Austrian troops simultaneously invaded the Polish-Lithuanian Commonwealth and sliced it up amongst themselves. Sam's ancestors ended up on the Russian side.

The partition brought more than a million Jews under the control of the Russian Empire. Immediately, the Russian nobility fretted about what this would do to their Orthodox Christian kingdom. Worried that these rapacious infidels would prey upon the peasantry, Catherine the Great drew a border around her newly conquered portion of Poland and declared it to be the Pale of Settlement, the place Jews could not leave. Things got worse with each tsar that followed. By the time Catherine's great-grandson, Tsar Nicholas I, took the throne, whole bodies of law had been written to restrict the empire's Jewish subjects. Tsar Nicholas I wrote his policies with the declared aim of forcing a third of Jews to die, a third to emigrate, and a third to convert to Christianity. Most Jews were already banned from the great cities of Saint Petersburg and Moscow, but he expelled them from the countryside, barred them from all manner of professions, and harshly restricted their admission to universities. Jewish boys became eligible for military conscription at age twelve, with the term lasting twenty-five years. Bigotry was constant and mob attacks a regular occurrence.

Life in these Jewish communities was confined as much from within as from without. We are the people of the book—or books, rather: a library of legal texts that stretch back to Babylonian exile and cover everything from the rules around menstruation to the permissibility of tying different types of knots on days of rest. Time was religious time, set in an eternal cycle of holidays, the mikvah, and sabbath. Life was hierarchical, with the rabbi at the top. Daily affairs were dictated by a *kehillah*, a council of pious notables who dealt with tsarist officials through bribes and supplication. Sometimes, they did the government's dirty work. It was the kehillah who provided the quota of Jewish kids for military service, and it was the kehillah who hired kidnappers to snatch poor children for the army and thus keep the rich kids safe at home.

In the late 1700s, a group of young Jewish men rose up against this thicket of legal constraint and communal obligation. At the end of the eighteenth century, the Jewish Enlightenment—the *Haskalah*—swept through central and eastern Europe, a century after the Christian Enlightenment had so inadequately sundered Church and State. A *maskil*—or follower of the *Haskalah*—sneered at the bearded shtetl traditionalists. While maskilim approved of modernized religious practice and glorified Hebrew as a "great" language on par with Russian or French, everything else about being Jewish had to go. Ditch your insular ways, the maskil said—your yeshivas, your arranged marriages, your special haircuts, your Yiddish. Prove that you are civilized enough to deserve some civil rights. In Germany, Jews like the philosopher Moses Mendelssohn and the saloniste Rahel Varnhagen sought to slay Christian prejudice through urbane intellect, social glitter, and commercial triumph. Germany freed Jews of their last legal restrictions in 1871.

Things didn't work that way in the Russian Empire. A backward autocracy that drew its legitimacy from the powerful Russian Orthodox Church, the empire defined Russian identity as Slavic and Orthodox Christian, casting Jews as the eternal racialized others. There was no free press, no parliament, and no legal outlet for dissent. The government put down street demonstrations with elite mounted troops drawn from Ukrainian Cossack communities, and a secret police force called the Okhrana suppressed potential subversion with floggings, public executions, and Siberian exile.

Out of this morass, Tsar Alexander II emerged in 1855 as a bearer of modernity. He freed Russia's serfs in 1861 (forcing them to pay back the costs incurred by their emancipation) and eased some of the old antisemitic laws, including the university quotas and the childhood military conscription. Russian maskilim hailed him as their champion.

PROPAGANDA OF THE DEED

"Be a man in the streets and a Jew at home," wrote Judah Leib Gordin, a maskil poet in Vilna, in the 1860s. The implication here was of mutual exclusivity. But why were only Christians men? Why must you cut off pieces of yourself in an attempt to squash your soul, like an ugly stepsister's foot, into a glass slipper that was not cast for you? Though I sympathize with the maskilim, I do not wonder why so many young Jews chose to join their Christian peers in other, more militant ideologies.

Take the populist Narodnik movement—romantic socialists who believed Russia would be redeemed by its noble peasantry. In 1874, Jewish and Christian Narodniks abandoned the cities for the countryside, where these mostly middle-class kids imagined they could incite a peasant uprising. The peasants promptly reported them to the police. After this failure, some Narodniks grew more extreme. Were these rebellious youth the first people to refer to themselves, and not merely their enemies, as terrorists? Believing exemplary violence could provoke a mass uprising against the tsar, they swore themselves to the propaganda of the deed.

In the late 1870s, a legion of violent Narodnik-inspired groups emerged in the Russian Empire. They were comprised of university boys—like Vladimir Lenin's idolized elder brother—and, even more famously, of girls, the nihilist pinups who glared out from illegal political postcards. It is from this group that the bohemian Vera Zasulich emerged. She shot her way into history with a bulldog revolver, even if the bullet she fired merely wounded Saint Petersburg's governor. In 1881, the aristocratic Sophia Perovskaya did Zasulich one better and masterminded the death of Tsar Alexander II.

On a chilly March afternoon in Saint Petersburg, Perovskaya watched the tsar's imperial cortege turn onto Catherine Canal's embankment, then took out her handkerchief and blew her nose. At this signal, a young man threw a bomb beneath the bulletproof royal carriage. It exploded, killing a Cossack guard. The dazed Alexander emerged from his battered carriage, incredulous at his own survival. Moments later, another young man threw a bomb at the monarch's feet. Shrapnel tore apart both assassin and tsar.

The government sentenced Perovskaya to hang, along with her five accomplices. One of them was Hesya Helfman, a beautiful Jewish seamstress who had fled an arranged marriage for Kyiv's revolutionary underground, then run the safe house where Perovskaya and her co-conspirators plotted the tsar's assassination. Helfman died of blood poisoning in the Peter and Paul Fortress, shortly after giving birth to a little girl.

Alexander II's son, now crowned Alexander III, watched blithely as pogroms swept the Pale in the wake of his father's murder, which many blamed on the Jews. The pogroms hit all classes of Jewish society, regardless of dress, piety, or politics. Pogromists beat the clean-shaven elite and the bearded poor alike. The attacks shattered the maskilim's faith in integration. In the aftermath of the 1881 pogroms, an Odesa physician named Leon Pinsker began to advance the new idea that Jews could only be safe in an independent Jewish state. In a few years, this would be known as Zionism.

Tsar Alexander III drew several lessons from his father's murder: Crush dissent. Reforms indicate weakness. Never trust the Jews. In 1882, the new tsar brought back the old antisemitic laws that his father had overturned. These May Laws set off the first great Jewish exodus from the empire. Villages emptied out as gangs of young people slung bags over their backs and walked together, borders be damned, all the way to Antwerp, to sleep on the streets and wait for the steamships that would take them anywhere. Johannesburg. Buenos Aires. Orchard Street.

PAVEL AXELROD

If desire to escape the Old World's hatred sent Jews across the oceans, Geneva was where revolutionaries—Jewish and not—gathered to keep the Old World close enough to kiss. A rich, modern city in politically neutral Switzerland with thriving universities, a free press, and convenient transport to London, Paris, and Berlin, Geneva was the perfect place for a wanted man—or woman—to raise funds, gather disciples, and prepare herself for a return to the fray. Marxists, nihilists, populists, and anarchists gathered together to dream great dreams of the incipient twentieth century. What cataclysms would shake it? What utopias would they build from the ash?

Pavel Axelrod was one such rebel. Jewish by birth, Axelrod rejected any pull of the particular. "How senseless then and indeed how criminal to devote oneself to the Jews, who are only a small part of the vast Russian empire," he wrote. Back in Russia, he had been a Narodnik sympathizer who ran a safe house, just like Hesya Helfman, but he had fled years before Tsar Alexander's II's murder and now ran a successful dairy business in Switzerland that financially supported other revolutionaries. As Axelrod watched the 1881 pogroms back home with horror, one revolutionary proclamation issued by the Narodnik terrorist group People's Will made him pause. "People in the Ukraine suffer most of all from the kikes," the pamphlet read. "The kike curses the peasant, cheats him, drinks his blood."

Axelrod's Jewishness meant little to him, but now he began to wonder what it meant to everyone else. Some Russian revolutionaries cheered the pogroms as an uprising by the dispossessed. In an essay he wrote in their aftermath, Axelrod described the pain of the Jewish student who realizes that "the majority of this Russian society . . . considered all Jews—the pious Jewish worker, a petit bourgeois, a moneylender, an assimilated lawyer, a socialist prepared for prison or deportation—as kikes, harmful to Russia, whom Russia should get rid of by any or all means." This held true even among the "socialist-minded Russian students" who were Axelrod's comrades. Few Russian socialists wanted to hear this critique, and they deemed Axelrod's thoughts too controversial to be published.

This was Axelrod's last foray into what would later be labeled identity politics. He soon put aside the "senseless and criminal" pull of his own ethnicity in favor of the wide world where history could be so thrillingly made. In Geneva, he reconnected with an old comrade from the Narodnik underground, a patrician rabble-rouser named Georgi Plekhanov. Together, they discarded their Narodnik faith in favor of the scientific certainties of Marx and Engels. In 1883, Axelrod, Plekhanov, their fellow revolutionary Leo Deutsch, and the would-be assassin Vera Zasulich founded Emancipation of Labor, the first Russian Marxist group, which, after four decades of improbable events, would lead to the creation of the Soviet Union. Like Marx, and many Marxists, Axelrod made a choice that superficially seemed like an abandonment of his people. The revolution would wipe away race hatred, these rebels believed. All men would live as brothers once they remade the world.

VOLKOVYSK

My great-grandfather Samuel Rothbort was born on November 25, 1882, a year after Tsar Alexander II's murder. As luck would have it, the pogrom wave that followed never hit his hometown.

Volkovysk is a place that appears only passingly in history books. Smack in the middle of the Grodno Governorate in the Pale of Settlement, Volkovysk was a picturesque stop on the railway line that ran between Bialystok and Slonim. It was ringed by fir forests, bisected by the Nieman River. Outside the town, the sun shone over the chalk quarry, whose white cliffs reflected into a miraculous turquoise lake. The old watermill churned beside the Polish church, and by the river sat two prisons. The Black prison held ordinary criminals, and the White prison was for radicals. Jews made up just under half of the latter's eight thousand residents.

Volkovysk's houses were wooden, decimated by fires with such regularity that townsfolk marked the years by how long it had been since a conflagration; a fire destroyed much of the town when Sam was four. It was a religious place, well stocked with synagogues that, decades later, Sam would paint from memory—the cupolas, the carved white bimah, the frescoes and stained glass, the men beneath their prayer shawls, swaying as one. Such piety only complemented the striving of the town's Jewish bourgeoisie—the *balebatim* in Yiddish—who founded scores of communal self-help institutions, including an orphanage, a hospital, and an old-age home. When the workers dug the foundation for the railway station, they found a mammoth tusk. The balebatim crowed with delight. The ancient beast must have ridden the ark with Noah, they reckoned. After the waters subsided, the mammoth would have walked all the way from Mount Ararat to their Volkovysk. And why not? It was such a fine place, almost as good as Bialystok, and maybe one day it would grow just as big. The balebatim proudly hung the tusk in the railway office.

One night when I visited my mother's apartment on New York's Upper West Side, she dug through her shoeboxes of family papers until she unearthed a small rectangle of paper that must have come from the dawn of photography. It was a picture of Sam's grandparents. In the photo, the old man, a horse doctor by trade, wore a caftan and yarmulke, and ruefully arched his left eyebrow. The woman rested her hand on his shoulder. She was corseted in dowdy black, with a pious woman's wig to cover her shaved head. Further shoebox investigations turned up photos of Sam's father, Reb Hersch. He wore a skullcap and Ottoman-style waistcoat and held his handsome head proudly, his skin stretched tight over angular bone. A baker's son who had transcended his father's humble profession to become a Talmudic scholar, Reb Hersch left Volkovysk in 1884 and spent most of Sam's childhood in America, a country he detested for its cheerful impiety and lack of kosher food.

We have no photo of Sam's mother, Chaya Ruchl—only images painted from memory by her son. In one watercolor, Chaya Ruchl runs over to the men's section of the synagogue and halts the Sabbath services—a time-honored way for the shtetl's powerless to get a hearing for their grievances. What her problem was I don't know, but in her defiant bearing I see a spark that would later manifest in Sam Rothbort, and perhaps, later still, in me. This single insurrection aside, Chaya Ruchl's life followed the standard script. She married at twelve, after which she toiled to run a religious home, raise her children, and earn enough money to support her husband as he analyzed Talmudic minutiae with the men. The last part she accomplished by means of a tiny flour mill, whose products she sold at the market that sprung up in Volkovysk during fair days, when peasants streamed in from surrounding villages. Before heading to the market, Chaya Ruchl prepared her bread. As she kneaded the dough, bits fell beneath the table, which Sam, her toddler son, pilfered. He molded the dough into lions. These would be Sam's first works as an artist.

From deeper inside her shoebox, my mother pulled out her only photo of Sam as a child. He is a sharp-boned waif in a sailor suit next to a fey little sister named Ruchl, who is garbed like a harlequin. His smooth cheeks show that the photo was taken before his bout of smallpox. But this boy seems less real than the child Sam portrayed in his autobiographical watercolors, and it is through these painted memories that I understand his early life. I see him as a baby, rocked by Chaya Ruchl beneath a photograph of his absent father. Or at age five, as he listened to his uncle Simcha the shoemaker weave fantastical tales. I see him during the harsh Volkovysk winters, when he sketched with his fingers on the frosty windowpanes. I see him during green summer days, a little boy who rolled up his pants and waded into the marshes to make flutes from the reeds. He climbed trees to spy on the girls as they swam naked in the river. He ran with a gang of boys as mischievous as he. Once, Sam's grandfather caught him shimmying down a neighbor's cherry tree. His fingers were stained red, his mouth purple. His pockets bulged with pits. "Search me," Sam bluffed. The old man reached for his belt, then shrugged and walked away.

Beyond the Jewish neighborhood lay rye fields, full of "fearful poetry and strange beauty," Sam later wrote, and beyond that the Christian part of town. "I began to understand that I am a Jewish child, surrounded by strange neighbors, speaking a strange language, with a cold look in their eyes," Sam wrote in an autobiographical sketch my mother found in a shoebox. When Sam and his friends ventured over to Volkovysk's Christian side, boys their age chased them with dogs. The Jewish boys hurled rocks back. Later, Sam took revenge in his watercolors, caricaturing his Christian neighbors as ruddy blond giants, dressed in riotous magenta skirts and embroidered rubashkas that contrasted with the black capotes of conservative Jewish men. This sartorial flamboyance only highlighted the slack stupidity that Sam gave their faces.

An army garrison was quartered outside Volkovysk. On their days off, the soldiers drank, then staggered into the streets, where they squeezed accordions, bellowed army songs, and merrily smashed the Jewish shops until local heroes like nine-fingered Shmuel Dovid and his sons grabbed iron bars and chased them away. Though the town had been spared during the death-soaked year of 1881, Sam painted another pogrom that took place at some point during his youth. Blond oafs tore apart a feather bed. Beneath the goose feathers lay a battered child.

Sam's childhood freedom ended when his grandparents consigned him to a cheder—a traditional religious school. Sam hated cheder, just as I hated school, for its boredom and constraint. He glared at the walls and plotted his insurrection.

Sam began to draw in class. He had no sketchpad, so he used his prayer books, hidden beneath his desk—the same maneuver I mastered as a recalcitrant student a century later. He drew Reb Herschel, his frumpy wife, and his fellow cheder inmates. He sketched mean and fast. When Reb Herschel found the book, he beat Sam's ass, but Sam kept drawing. Soon, he earned a nickname: Shmuel Chudozhnik—Shmuel the Artist.

SAM WAS NINE YEARS old in 1891, when the great famine hit Russia. His watercolors do not show the skeletal peasant families who were forced to remain in their villages by Cossacks, while the tsar stole their grain so that exports could continue apace. Next year came cholera. By the end of 1892, five hundred thousand residents of the Russian Empire were dead. Sam's mother, Chaya Ruchl, was one of them. She must have been younger than I am now. She had married at twelve, to a man who returned home only to fill her with another pregnancy, and she had seen nothing of the world except a few miles of muddy streets. That was all life offered to a woman who knew her place. There she remained, in her place, the section of Volkovysk's Jewish cemetery reserved for cholera victims.

Soon after his mother's death, Sam's grandparents apprenticed him to a cantor. Sam would have joined one of the innumerable troupes of boy singers who trailed their masters around the Pale, trilling folk songs and passing the plate at synagogues after big holiday gigs. Then puberty hit, and his clear voice became a ranine croak. With his showbiz career done, he took on a less glamorous apprenticeship at Bloch's tannery, one of Volkovysk's largest industrial concerns.

"The Russian Jewish proletariat is the pariah among pariahs," wrote the Marxist theoretician Karl Kautsky in 1901. Banned from seeking better prospects in Saint Petersburg or Moscow, Jewish workers were trapped in a spiral of unemployment and poverty. Kept out of the best-paying jobs in heavy industry by racism, by their observance of Sabbath, and by owners' belief in their troublesome natures, most Jewish workers toiled for Jewish artisans nearly as impoverished as themselves, in homes or suffocating sweatshops too small to fall under the meager rubric of tsarist employment law. They worked at least sixteen hours a day—men, women, and children as young as six—for pay so low they could hardly afford to die. Theirs was an almost entirely Jewish world, held together by pseudofamilial solidarity. Your boss might punch you, but you'd still sit together at synagogue on Friday. And above your boss squatted the tsarist legal code, predicated on your, and his, unworthiness. You were both Jews. That identity mattered more than your status as exploiter or exploited. You lived together under a discriminatory legal regime and the floating morass of racism it enabled.

Russian revolutionaries didn't think about Jewish workers like Sam

Rothbort. These workers didn't till the land, like the peasantry that the Narodniks idolized, and were not members of the industrial proletariat in whom Marx's disciples placed their hopes. The Jewish worker made stockings, not railway track. He manufactured brushes, not steel. He could strike, and what would it matter? You can't stop an empire by refusing to tailor a dress. He didn't even have the courtesy to stay in a single class. Instead, ever precarious, he slipped from town to city in search of work, from "boss" to "employee" and back again. Yiddish had a word for these workers: *luftmenschen*. They owned nothing and belonged nowhere. Rootless, they wandered, as if they themselves were made of air.

THE TANNERY

Production in the Bloch tannery took place beneath racks of dripping skin. The workday began before dawn, when the skins arrived from the slaughterhouse, and lasted till late at night. The factory had no windows, and the rooms reeked of burned hair, birch oil, dead animal, and piss. Many tanners died by forty—some from "Siberian plague," the excruciating black sores now known as anthrax poisoning. Bloch's leather had buyers in Europe and even New York City. This earned his workers nearly nothing but made the old proprietor rich enough to spend his days studying Talmudic law.

Sam later wrote that when his voice cracked, it sealed his destiny as a painter. About this I have my doubts. A twenty-hour workday has a way of depleting one's energy, and had things continued as intended, Sam's true talents might never have been expressed. No, something else tipped the scales in favor of my great-grandfather. Call it what you will. God, or chance, or the dialectical forces of history. But it would greet Sam Rothbort in the summer of 1898.

Pati Kremer
(maiden name
Srednitskaya)

CHAPTER 2

THE PARTY

(1890–1898)

PATI KREMER

THE EVENTS THAT WOULD CHANGE MY GREAT-GRANDFATHER'S LIFE—and the history of Europe—began 130 miles to the north, in the walled medieval city of Vilna. Vilna was home to 154,000 people—about half of them Jews—and was a center of Talmudic scholarship. Polish, Russian, and Yiddish jostled on hand-lettered storefronts. The city's apartments clustered around private courtyards in which roving theater troupes performed. This was the hometown to which a young Jewish woman named Pati Srednitskaya returned in 1890, to begin her sentence of internal exile under the watchful eyes of the Okhrana—the Russian Empire's secret police.

I picture Pati as she was at twenty-three, when she stepped down from the locomotive into the jewel box of the Vilna train station, the strain of her months' imprisonment in the empire's heartland still visible on her lovely fairy face. Perhaps she wore the black then favored by radicals, or perhaps some corseted confection more befitting of the wealthy merchant's daughter that she was. And who waited for her at the station? Her doting family? Or her lover, whom she had followed to Saint Petersburg—and whose influence her family no doubt blamed for her arrest?

Pati was quite capable of getting into trouble on her own. She had the trait most common in revolutionaries—the inability to take the world before her as a given—combined with a dazzling energy that made her try to fix things, no matter how quixotic her quest. When Pati was fifteen, the lady who sold her parents sauerkraut mentioned she had an illiterate daughter in Novgorod, six hundred miles away. Within a week, our heroine had stowed away on a train, blackboard under her arm, intent on teaching the girl how to read. Pati tracked the girl down to a sweatshop, but she and her fellow workers cared more about their future marriages than Pati's academic ministrations. Soon their mothers ran Pati out of town. The mission failed, but the missionary impulse remained. A few years later, a musician acquaintance told her parents about an unusual boarder to whom he rented a corner of his attic, a poor, friendless teenager from the shtetl. He never smiled. He spoke with no one except stray cats. He sat in the corner all day with his head buried in a book, and pity the fool who interrupted him. "Pati, you're so happy," the musician wheedled. Couldn't she stop by and cheer his wretched tenant up?

Pati climbed up to the tiny attic on Zavalne Street and squinted in the dim light. The tenant sat reading in the corner. When she entered, he raised his curly black head and regarded her with hostile curiosity. He was the most handsome boy she had ever seen.

"What is your name?" she asked, trying to compose herself.

"Arkady." He didn't ask her name in return.

She looked at the dingy room and the words poured out of her, stupid and heartfelt. "It's so dark here! Come! Stay with my family! There everything is beautiful!" His glare stopped her.

"Tell me," asked Arkady Kremer, "have you ever seen how poor children live?" The words hung in the air like a reproach, and suddenly she was ashamed of her nice dress, of her happiness.

"I guess I'll go," she whispered, turning to hide her tears. He grabbed her wrist and pulled her back. "Stay," Arkady demanded. "I'll talk with you. Maybe then you'll understand."

How many girls like Pati—pretty, vivacious—have fallen for cold, ironic boys like Arkady Kremer? How many have tried to save those boys through the energetic bounty of their love? You can't rescue the world one man at a time, I told my friends when they fell in love with New York's angry radicals—the mean, Derrida-quoting grad students, the pouty anarchists fresh out of lockup, the supposedly brilliant writers who preferred video games to writing—but they fell hard anyway. It seldom ended well. Trysts at squats left them covered in spider bites. The boys drained their bank accounts for experimental magazines that never materialized, then hopped freight trains down South to disappear into the latest protest encampment. Sometimes, more dangerously, they stayed.

So it was for Pati. Arkady was a provincial tutor's son with a temperament so ascetic that he refused to replace his decaying shoes. "They're full of holes!" Pati pleaded and offered to buy replacements for him. He countered as he always did. "Who am I to act like I'm better than anyone else?" Over the years, she followed Arkady through a series of miserable rooms with pipes that froze, while he scratched out a living tutoring yeshiva boys in math, secretly introducing them to the scandalous secular world. When he left to study engineering in Saint Petersburg, Pati followed, taking up dentistry, one of the few trades that earned a Jew the right to live in the capital. In Petersburg they had everything two radical young lovers might need, including an apartment shared with a friend and Arkady's sister, where they sat all night at the samovar trying to figure out the best ways to remake the world. Once, they tried to educate some sex workers about socialism. Arkady was too awkward to approach the women, but his friend came home with two, who pretended to listen to their lectures, sweet-talked Pati out of money, and disappeared. Their idyll ended when Arkady refused to inform on fellow students to the university administration. Expelled from school and thus deprived of his Saint Petersburg residency permit, he left to study in Riga. With him away, Pati joined an illegal Narodnik reading group. Before long, she was arrested as a terrorist.

THE VILNA GROUP

Vilna street

In Vilna, Pati reunited with Arkady Kremer. Like her, he had a rap sheet. Things had not gone as planned for him in Riga, where he had dabbled in socialist politics, been arrested, and spent six months in jail before being exiled from the city. Together again, the couple ensconced themselves in a garret just big enough to fit their books. After prison, the idealistic all-night discussions they enjoyed in Saint Petersburg must have taken on a sharper edge. Prison taught a person how a stone floor felt against their cheek when they tried to sleep before their next interrogation. Or how much blood could pour from a person's mouth if a guard hit them right. The tsarist empire may have lagged behind the rest of Europe in other areas of industrial production, but it sure knew how to manufacture its own enemies. For little more than joining a discussion group, generations of bookish youth were jailed, tortured, and exiled to Siberia. They came back as enemies of the state.

It didn't take long for Arkady and Pati to find their people: four educated Jewish idealists like themselves who already had their first arrests behind them. They met John Mill and Timofey Kopelzon, two schoolboys who snuck off together to study Marx, then Shmuel Gozhansky, a young teacher who had helped plot a tailors' strike; and then Liuba Levinson joined their reading circle. Liuba's father had forbidden her to study abroad, but she ran off to Geneva anyway. There, she joined the Marxist disciples of Plekhanov and returned home carrying suitcases packed with illicit pamphlets spelling out the workers' revolution to come. Cops grabbed her on the Russian side of the border. (Something terrible had happened to Liuba in prison, but the sources I read didn't go into specifics. It could have been anything, from rape by guards to the torture of solitary confinement. She was never the same afterward.)

Now known as the Vilna Group, this clique accepted Arkady Kremer as their leader. They were all in their early twenties and had wrecked their lives well enough to free themselves from the prospect of a future. Their loyalties lay with each other, their bonds cemented in unheated rooms where they drafted pamphlets while listening for the policeman's knock at the door. In a different country, they might have dissipated their energies on sex or drugs or electoral politics, but in Russia, they threw everything into laying the groundwork for a revolution they doubted they'd ever see. They called themselves "pioneers," and indeed they were—explorers who built outposts in their own hometowns, dedicated to converting their communities to a foreign faith.

Anyone might be a traitor, and a radical's only protection was mastery of the conspiratorial arts. The rules were strict. Choose a pseudonym. Write in code. Don't ask unnecessary questions. Speak in whispers, even in your own home. They used disguise, trickery, and pretexts. Pati opened a dental office that doubled as a conspiratorial center. Revolutionaries came and went with their faces bandaged, as if with toothache, to hide their identities from the police.

At first, the Vilna Group devoted itself to setting up "circles"—free classes where educated revolutionaries taught uneducated workers, intending to transform seamstresses and leatherworkers into a revolutionary vanguard. That vanguard would train their fellow workers, who would then train more workers, until, one far-off day, they would constitute a working class educated enough to topple the tsar and build a socialist utopia.

There were some obvious problems with this plan, not the least of which was language. The Vilna Group might have been Jews, but they were also members of the intellectual middle class. As such, they spoke Russian. Yet in the Pale, three quarters of Jewish workers spoke Yiddish, a language that only Pati and Shmuel Gozhansky could manage. How could the Vilna Group organize the proletariat if the proletariat didn't even understand what they said?

What the Vilna Group didn't count on was the workers' own gluttony for knowledge. Jews fetishized books, but because of the strict quotas that kept them out of university, the best a poor kid could hope for was a few years of rote memorization at cheder. Education (especially in Russian, the language of state power) gave these workers a chance at something more. They were tanners like Sam, factory girls who had abandoned shtetl life for the yoke of the big city sweatshop, escaped yeshiva students who already doubted God. On a blackboard, Pati would write out the Cyrillic letters. *Ahh. Beh. Veh.* She pronounced. They imitated.

Once workers had basic Russian, a plethora of topics opened up. Physics, economics. Surplus value. Life in other lands. The teacher offered them Marx like a prize. Nothing felt more modern than Uncle Karl, an insurrectionist with a prophet's beard. To be a Marxist was to become a citizen of the dawning century, at least until the lecture wrapped up. Afterward, the exhausted workers walked back to their tenements, where their religious parents rebuked them for staying out late.

Over time, the Vilna Group's popularity grew. Pati helped workers start their own circles. She ran from a conspiratorial meeting to a rich supporter's house and shamelessly hustled up funds. Our girl could not sit still. She was a *tuer*, a doer, as practical activists were charmingly called in Yiddish—not a theorist like Liuba Levinson, and not a leader like Arkady. But for all the Vilna Group's success in starting lecture circles, after four years, they had to admit they were no closer to the revolution. The workers who attended their circles hadn't used what they learned to organize their factories. Instead, they put on airs. Peppering their speech with mispronounced Russian phrases, lugging Russian books they could barely read, the Vilna Group's pet workers mocked their shop-floor colleagues as hopelessly unsophisticated hicks. *They* were meant for better. Some even began to prep for their gymnasium exams. Why shouldn't they go to university like their teachers, Arkady and Pati, and leave the wretched Pale behind?

The Vilna Group had aimed to produce revolutionaries. Mostly, they'd created hipsters.

They'd have to try a different tack.

THE PEOPLE

For decades, Jewish workers in Vilna had been creating their own trouble. The first strikes broke out in 1871 among the teenage girls who rolled cigarettes and sewed socks in the city's factories. By the 1880s, workers across the Pale had built themselves the rudiments of a trade union movement. They created mutual aid funds to sustain their strikes, and organized militias to defend picket lines and punish strikebreakers. These were the workers the Vilna Group needed to reach.

Jewish workers suffered both ethnic bigotry and brute economic exploitation, a dual oppression that the Vilna Group was the first to put into words. Concepts like intersectionality (coined more than a century later by the scholar Kimberlé Crenshaw to describe the ways a person's various identities subject them to interlocking systems of oppression) and identity politics (a phrase first used by the Combahee River Collective to name "the most profound and potentially most radical politics" that came when they, Black lesbian socialists, fought for their own liberation) are commonplace in American intellectual circles today, even if they're mostly misunderstood. In the fin-de-siècle Russian Empire, they had not even been dreamed of. That's why an 1894 May Day speech by the Vilna Group's Julius Martov had such a bracing effect. The scion of a wealthy Jewish family in Saint Petersburg, Martov was a brilliant, sensitive writer of twenty-three sentenced to serve out a stint of political exile in Vilna. His outsider's perspective gave him an insight that would prove formative for his comrades.

Jewish workers were oppressed both as workers and as Jews, as a race and a class, Martov said. They could not "rely solely on the Russian or Polish proletariat," who might sell them out for profit or under duress. Instead, they must "fight as an organized Jewish group alongside the other groups for economic, civic and political liberty." While Martov would renounce his words as he rose through the ranks of international socialism, the idea that one should fight as both a Jew and a worker became the Vilna Group's lodestar.

Tuers like Pati put Martov's ideas into practice, in the language that workers spoke. I see her squint as she translates a Marxist pamphlet into Yiddish. How would she turn this argle-bargle into something the factory girls would understand? She reproduced each pamphlet by hectograph. For hour after hour, she pressed each Yiddish master sheet into the hectograph's gelatin, rubbed it with alcohol to transfer the words onto the gel, then smoothed down the pamphlet paper until her text appeared. She could earn a prison term for each phrase. She put on her worst dress and snuck past the factory gates to slip a pamphlet into a teenager's hand. Later, she met the girls who ran workers' mutual aid funds. Did they look at her with the same curious hostility as Arkady once did, when she first met him in that attic on Zavalne Street? Did they wonder what she could possibly know about their lives? I think about the time I spent canvassing housing projects in New York for socialist political candidates. I knocked on doors whose buzzers read Cabán, the same Puerto Rican last name I was born with, and I tried to overcome all their well-founded skepticism about politicians, and about pale bourgeoise women like me. We all deserve better, I told them, repeating the campaign talking points. We can have better. Together we are strong. I often worried that these were lies, but I reproached myself for my cynicism, because sometimes, intoxicatingly, we would win. Pati must have felt the same.

The Vilna Group's new strategy was simple. Talk plainly. Listen. Make things better in the here and now. Shmuel Gozhansky scored their first victory. When workers complained about long hours, he uncovered a law dating back to Catherine the Great that guaranteed a twelve-hour workday. Through a combination of strikes and legal know-how, the Vilna Group got the law enforced. After that, the workers saw these radicals as more than bizarre rich kids. Suddenly, they were useful.

ON AGITATION

The Vilna Group's conspiracy spread across the Pale of Settlement. John Mill carried it to Warsaw, Liuba Levinson to Bialystok, others to Minsk and Lodz. In cities across the Pale, they supplied preexisting mutual aid groups with literature and cash. Thousands of workers joined the Vilna Group's unions. Strikes spread. Wages climbed. Hours fell. In 1893, as the movement flourished, Arkady decided to write up the conclusions he drew from its success.

A slim pamphlet in his native Russian, Kremer's *On Agitation* has received none of the laurels owed to such a foundational text. In English, it exists in a single academic anthology, rather than in the sort of gilt-edged volumes dedicated to the collected works of Kremer's future enemies. Intended as a manual for aspiring revolutionaries, its ideas were soon used, then condemned, by more brilliant and ruthless men. Forgotten or not, *On Agitation* remains an unpretentious, practical text that promises no utopias. Instead, there are strikes, pickets, petitions, street canvasing—a grind well known to any activist. It is an invitation to work.

Kremer held that illegal educational circles didn't work. You might teach a few dozen workers to speak the jargon of scientific socialism, but this just made them seem like freaks to their follow workers, whom you, the putative revolutionary, needed to organize. Outside your pretentious little circles, workers were already launching strikes for wages, hours, dignity. The revolutionary just had to listen. As he organized with workers around issues they cared about, the revolutionary's insights would "teach workers to stand up for their interests, . . . raise their courage, . . . give them confidence in their own strength, [and] make them realize the need to unite." With unions banned, the workers' fight for a raise would bring with it split skulls and prison terms, and so would naturally grow into a struggle for free speech, free association, and other political rights. With each casualty they suffered and each victory they won, the workers would grow more radical, and the revolutionary would egg them on. The capacity for revolt was like a muscle that they'd build through constant use. At last, when no more economic concessions could be wrung from the bosses, the class struggle would transform into a revolution.

On Agitation does not mention Jewish workers. Arkady Kremer wrote for workers. Full stop.

ULYANOV

Words travel. They are tapped in Morse code on the walls of jail cells, concealed in false-bottomed suitcases, wedged beneath a woman's corset. In the spring of 1894, *On Agitation* began to move. A copy reached Moscow, where it was immediately hectographed and distributed to radicals around the empire. Before Arkady Kremer ever set foot abroad, *On Agitation* made its way to the Geneva offices of the Emancipation of Labor group, where it was read by Georgi Plekhanov, Pavel Axelrod, Leo Deutsch, and Vera Zasulich, the four founders of Russian Marxism, who had spent the last decade in fractious exile. They printed their own edition in 1896.

Arkady's words flew farther. It was in Saint Petersburg that *On Agi-*

tation found its most influential reader. In 1895, police had allowed Julius Martov, the young writer whose May Day speech did so much to chart the Vilna Group's course, to return to his close-knit family in Saint Petersburg. Unreformed, Martov resolved to bring the skills he'd learned in exile to the capital's industrial districts. He gathered a crew. Some were old comrades from Saint Petersburg, some were newer comrades from Vilna, and some were intellectuals who ran illegal study circles of the sort that Kremer dismissed. Their clunkily named Union of Struggle for the Emancipation of the Working Class was the first Marxist group to form inside Russia proper. Its leaders were Martov and a single-minded, prematurely balding young aristocrat named Vladimir Ilych Ulyanov. With *On Agitation* as a guide, they set to work.

Vilna was one thing, and Saint Petersburg another. The Okhrana could hardly allow revolutionaries to infiltrate the empire's economic core. In December, they arrested the entire group and exiled Ulyanov and Martov to Siberia.

Six years later, after he was safely settled into London exile, Ulyanov wrote a short book that praised *On Agitation* for its usefulness to his generation of organizers. Unlike Kremer's words, Ulyanov's are easy to find today. Translated into countless languages, *What Is to Be Done* has been kept continuously in print for over a century. It's published under Ulyanov's pen name: Lenin.

THE ORGANIZATION

The year 1896 was delicious. Despite the arrests of its leaders, the Saint Petersburg Union of Struggle flourished using the Vilna Group's techniques. Mass strikes spread, and new social democratic groups established themselves from Moscow to Kyiv. That summer, Georgi Plekhanov led a delegation of exiled Russian socialists to the fourth congress of the Second International, held in London—the main gathering for socialist parties from around the world. It was the first time Russian socialists had been represented at the international event. There, Plekhanov praised the Vilna Group's efforts. "These pariahs, destitute even of those pitiable rights which are the heritage of the Christian subjects of the tsar . . . [are entitled to be] ranked as the avant-garde of the Russian Labor movement," he said. He ended his speech with a stirring call to unite Russia's scattered Marxist groups into a single Russian social democratic party.

Back in Vilna, Plekhanov's call forced Arkady and his comrades to think. Where would the loose network that the Vilna Group had organized fit into a party that spanned the entire Russian Empire? How could they hold their own and represent themselves at the congresses that defined international socialism? They needed to transform themselves into something more formal, not quite a party, perhaps, but an organization—in Yiddish, the word was *Bund.*

Arkady set the Bund's founding conference for October 5, 1897, on the evening of Yom Kippur. Invitations arrived by various means: encoded in a Warsaw newspaper classified, or delivered by anonymous courier, scrawled in invisible ink. However they came, all carried the same promise. At a safe-house attic in the suburb of Lukiskes, Pati, her now-husband Arkady, and their friends would remake the world.

Then, in late September the police arrested Pati Kremer.

Despite his wife's arrest, Arkady Kremer met with twelve comrades in the safe-house attic. They were five intellectuals and eight workers, all veterans of the Vilna Group. Two were women—a translator named Rosa Greenblat and Maria Zhaludskaia, a brash seamstress who ran the Vilna Group's activities in Warsaw. Like all Marxists, they wanted to overthrow the tsar and bring about socialism. But for Jews like them, the revolution promised something greater: equality. It would not just overturn the laws that restricted their movements and stunted their educations. It would also bring about brotherhood between people formerly divided into oppressed and oppressors. The Bund would fight not just for general Russian political demands but also for the specific interests of Jewish workers, Arkady Kremer said, echoing Martov's 1894 May Day speech. "That is because the Jewish workers suffer not only as workers but also as Jews, and we dare not and cannot remain indifferent at such a time."

Next March, the Russian Social Democratic Labor Party held its first congress in Minsk. The Bund found the safe house, ran the security, and sent three out of the nine attendees. They entered the RSDLP as "an independent organization for the Jewish proletariat." If the RSDLP was meant to represent the entire working class of the vast Russian Empire, the Bund would speak, act, and fight for the Jewish working class of the Pale of Settlement. They joined the party as equals.

CHAIM NEMZER

Though the RSDLP was tiny, the Okhrana moved fast to quash it. Days after the congress, police arrested five hundred members of various Marxist grouplets around the empire.

Three months later, police seized the Bund's printing presses in Minsk and Bobruysk and grabbed at least forty-five members. They found Arkady at his parents' home. As they led him off, his mother ran after them. "Take me," she screamed, but the police threw her to the floor, where she convulsed, in a stroke or heart attack. She would never walk again. By the end of summer, the Okhrana had reduced the RSDLP to a few tiny Bundist cells. Their new leaders were not bookish class traitors like Pati Kremer but, instead, the workers she had educated, a tough, Yiddish-speaking proletariat.

These workers resurrected the Bund after the empire's assault, increasing its fame through strikes, illicit handbills, and newspapers in Polish, Yiddish, and Russian, with propaganda sandwiched in between stories by popular writers. The party's name spread from gangsters to factory workers to itinerant agitators, like a young tutor named Chaim Nemzer, whom the Bund dispatched from Vilna to Volkovysk in the summer of 1898. In Sam Rothbort's hometown, he found surprisingly fertile ground.

THE STRIKE

Sam was fifteen that summer. He was a skinny kid with big ears and smallpox scars who liked to swim in the Neiman River. He drew charcoal portraits for extra money, but talent didn't save him from Bloch's tannery. After work, he would lie down in a corner of the shirt factory where some apprentices slept. He would hide beneath a sheet and try to ignore the rats as they scampered across his face. In sleep, he honed his talent for escape. He had absconded from Christian peasants, from his teacher, from the cantor, and he could flee again into the many-colored dream.

There are many ways Chaim Nemzer could have met my great-grandfather. Perhaps a co-worker slipped Sam a pamphlet at Bloch's tannery. Or perhaps Nemzer accosted Sam on his way back from work and told him there was no God. It was a technique perfected by John Mill. "If God exists, he should prove it," Mill would announce. "He should kill me on the spot." By remaining impudently alive, the agitator laid the groundwork to shatter other convictions.

Regardless of how Sam and Nemzer met, God played his part in bringing Sam to the movement. It was He, after all, who designated a weekly day of rest. Even a lowly apprentice got twenty-five hours off—from Friday's sunset start to Saturday's sunset end—in which to praise the lord and eat his herring, but come Saturday night, it was back to work for him. When Sam saw the sky darken on Saturday, he thought of the dead sinners whose souls Satan released for the span of Sabbath. His respite was also ending. In a few minutes, he would return to the flames.

Apprentices loathed those Saturday nights, and that September of

1898, Volkovysk Bundists decided to take advantage of their hate. Just after Rosh Hashanah, whispers began in the workshops. Everyone wanted Saturday off. The bosses wouldn't give it to them. Together, workers could make them listen.

Strikes had a standard choreography, wrote the revolutionary Hersh Mendel. Organizers planned in secret. On a predetermined day, at a predetermined shop, one guy gave a signal. In unison, workers stormed into the streets, where a group of supporters was waiting. Together, they marched to other shops, where they called for the workers to join them. Once they had collected a critical mass, they smashed the windows, halted the work, and beat any scabs the boss brought in to replace them. At this point, the boss might hire thugs, and the strike would become a battle.

I can picture Sam when he heard the strikers outside Bloch's tannery. He would have smiled as he threw down his scraper, untied his apron, and swaggered out, his boss's curses be damned. These were the Days of Awe, when God inscribes each human's name into the book of life, and the apprentices were determined to write themselves some better entries. They hollered. They threw rocks. They grinned at their own daring.

When the boss brought in strikebreakers, they beat them in the streets.

After Yom Kippur, the bosses agreed to the apprentices' demands. Sam never worked another Saturday night in Volkovysk.

THE DIALECTIC

So it was that my great-grandfather abandoned his place in a secure if circumscribed community and plunged into a modern insurrection. In keeping with the underground's conventions, he took a nom de guerre: Shmuel Chudozhnik. Shmuel the Artist, in Russian. I wonder what this new Chudozhnik had to say to his father, Reb Herschel Rothbort, during the two times the old man returned to Volkovysk before he at last settled in New York and married, abandoning his rebellious son.

Along with Sam's father, God the father slunk away across the ocean. To be a Bundist meant to break with religion. At a Bundist gathering, the pastries might be fried in pig fat, just to prove a point. For the new revolutionary man, the synagogue was only an edifice on which to slap up posters (which they did on Friday nights, knowing the laws of Sabbath forbade the synagogue guardians from removing posters until Saturday at sunset).

For many revolutionaries, History took God's place. According to the Marxist conception of dialectical materialism—an immortal, inescapable, and unfalsifiable science—man shaped history and was shaped by the history he made. History was a train, barreling up and down the rollercoaster track of thesis-antithesis-synthesis until, at last, the train pulled up in front of its final destination, that ill-described heaven known as communism, and the passengers, Sam among them, would step out dizzily into the sun. Until then, the train of history kept moving. Revolutionaries could divine its direction, but only the workers themselves could steer. As for Tsar Nicholas II, or Bloch who owned the tannery? History was merciless here. It barreled forward. All those who stood against it would die beneath its wheels.

Over a century after that Yom Kippur strike, my mother found a note Sam Rothbort had written to himself.

> For a thousand years, the Jewish people lived their own life, which they called Golas—captivity—waiting each day for the messiah to arrive and bring them back to their homeland, the kingdom of Jerusalem. Also to wake up all the dead and bring peace to all nations, and freedom from hate . . .
>
> That was only until the 1890s. Till the revolution movement spread. The new Messiah arrived—no more Jew, no more Goy and no more God. A world of brothers. "Working men from all the nations, be united" was their slogan. Overnight I threw off humble Judaism and became a world brother.

Along with his belief in God, when Sam Rothbort joined the revolution, he lost, or tried to lose, his feeling of separation from the non-Jewish world. For his whole life up until that point, Sam had mocked and feared Volkovysk's Christians. They were the aliens across the rye fields, the stone throwers, the soldiers, the belligerent, dangerous drunks. Now he would have to accept them as comrades. Of all the breaks with his old life, this perhaps was the hardest.

AFTER THE STRIKE, THE Volkovysk Bund grew to seventy members. Like Chaim Nemzer, these young people have mostly vanished into time. If they exist at all, it is on the pages of the *Volkovysk Memorial Book*, an oral history of the town compiled after the Holocaust, but even there they hide behind nicknames, noms de guerre, or spellings transformed by changes of borders and citizenship. Still, I find a few. The smartass shoemaker Meir Zeleviansky. The bricklayer L. Schlossberg. Berl Dzhik, exiled to Siberia and forced to leave his wife behind. There were three girls: Perl, the baker's daughter; the seamstress Beyle Rivkah; and Rosa Einhorn, a dental student. The underground offered these girls something finer than an arranged marriage, a flour stall, and a lifetime tending kids. They could stride out into the night, like Itka in Sam's painting, to hurl rocks through windows and release the new world waiting on the other side of the glass.

As new men and new women, the Bundists needed new knowledge to replace the old. They made a library, which offered Yiddish translations of popular novels to newcomers, but socialist texts to people they knew. Out of these books, a community began to emerge, tied together by ideology, yes, but also by the adrenaline of pent-up youth. Before Chaim Nemzer came, their elders had decided everything. They lived in the shadow of the father/the boss/the teacher who beat them, then the cop/the provincial bureaucrat/the tsar above. Now there was no more shame. They were radicals. They were teenagers. They were breaking the law, and crime tasted as sweet as their neighbor's stolen plums. They met in the Zamkov forest, where they raised the red flag beneath the rustling branches and sang their anthem, "The Oath," written by the poet S. An-sky just for them.

Heaven and earth will hear us,
the bright stars will bear witness,
an oath of blood, an oath of tears—
We swear, we swear, we swear!

Sam stretched out on the grass and listened. Sometimes, he kept watch for cops. He knew the forests well enough to paint them forty years later from memory. No police would catch him there.

Some days, the Bundists tossed illegal flyers like confetti. Others, they fought the bosses' thugs. They held demonstrations, these naughty youth dressed in high-necked shirts like the peasants who once beat them. And why not? The peasants were the people, but so were they. The great earth, whose forests and chalk cliffs Sam had wandered as a child, belonged equally to them all.

On Sabbath nights, when parents slept off their meals, these kids had once snuck off to ice-skate. Now they stole out to the houses of their tribes. The Bundists had the seamstress Beyle Rivkah's house, the Zionists another, and the rich gymnasium students a third. They would sing, each in their own language, in Yiddish, Hebrew, or Russian, the songs floating over the streets where the apolitical boys and girls walked hand in hand, their loyalty not to a party but to each other, and snuck down by the river to kiss. All these young people knew they were creating the world anew. When they parted, the samovar cold, the cigarettes smoked down, the rich to their silken beds and Sam to his rat-infested shirt factory, they were equals, just like the poor Arkady and the rich Pati were equals, because the revolution would make everyone equal, and never again would anyone have to bow their head.

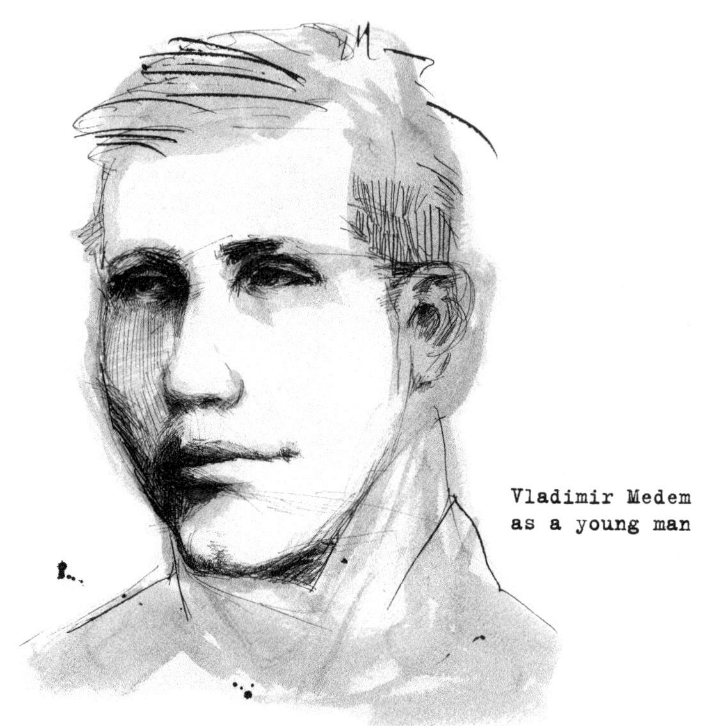

Vladimir Medem
as a young man

CHAPTER 3

QUESTIONS OF IDENTITY

(1897–1902)

VLADIMIR MEDEM

VLADIMIR MEDEM WAS ONLY THREE YEARS OLDER THAN SAM AND MIGHT as well have been his photonegative. Where Sam was a dark little urchin who spoke Yiddish and stank of chemicals, Medem was a rich boy with exquisite Russian, whose class showed in every wave of his flaxen hair. Yet the two were comrades, even if they never met.

Medem's path to the revolution was also distinct. He was born in 1879 in Minsk, where his father, an army doctor who converted to Lutheranism to keep his job, had him baptized to spare him the indignities of anti-Jewish laws. Seeking to conceal the family's ethnicity, his father banned the word "Jew" from being used in the house, lest the servants hear. "My Jewish origin was . . . a degradation, a sort of secret disease about which no one should know," Medem wrote. He grew into a pious, literary Christian. One memory troubled his assimilation: his father, lit by his kerosene lamp, reading from a Hebrew bible he had bought during army service in Constantinople. For Medem, this moment symbolized his Jewishness. Seductive letters he could not understand.

Medem entered medical school at the University of Kyiv in 1897, the year the Bund was born. By that time, he'd lost both his parents and his Christian faith. He began to question his identity. Was he a Russian? Or was he something else, that shameful thing his family only admitted in whispers?

The University of Kyiv was the ideal place to find out. The school was a subversive hotbed, where Narodniks and Marxists argued in smoky student apartments and illegal pamphlets slipped from hand to hand. Every so often, at night, mysterious men dropped by to visit Medem's roommate, only to vanish in the morning. One evening, Medem eavesdropped on their conversation. He heard an unfamiliar word: *Bund.*

Medem's life would soon change. In February 1899, Cossack troops broke up a student street party in Saint Petersburg. The Cossacks' motives were obscure, but the students' bashed skulls and new arrest records delivered a message: the revolutionary organizing happening across the empire was not to be tolerated. Thirty thousand students went on strike in solidarity—those at the University of Kyiv among them. Despite his shyness, Medem's classmates elected him to the strike's central committee. He spent three feverish months dashing off communiqués demanding amnesty for the Saint Petersburg students and his striking classmates until, one June morning, Cossacks arrested them all. A few days later, Medem was exiled back to Minsk and banned from university for life.

Adrift, he haunted the streets of Minsk's Jewish quarter. On Friday nights, he stared longingly at the sabbath candles in his neighbors' windows. In spite of his baptism, he was sure that these were his people. Armed with the Hebrew bible, *Das Kapital*, and story collections by Yiddish writer I. L. Peretz, Medem threw himself into the city's subversive bohemia. That winter, the Bund got in touch. Medem expected to start at the top. Surely his intellectual mien and unfinished medical degree qualified him for a spot on the Bund's central committee. The Bundists told him to organize Christian railway workers instead. Medem donned a peasant blouse and embarked upon a series of ill-fated rendezvous. The workers didn't live up to his expectations. They were better dressed than he was, and their apartments considerably cleaner. Far from wanting his guidance, they mocked and evaded him. Medem had more success as a writer, and on May Day 1900, a Bundist newspaper published his first article.

From there, things moved fast. He joined the editorial board of the Bund's illegal newspaper, *The Minsk Worker*. At night, he snuck past Governor's Street, now transformed into a *birzhe*—a temporary autonomous zone for revolutionaries. It was risky to visit the birzhe, Medem knew. The police had been spying on him since his arrest. Still, he snuck over whenever he could. His comrades might have nicknamed him "the goy," but Medem knew that he had finally found his place.

I recognize something in Medem's awkward groping for an identity that was only imperfectly his own. It's common among children from plural, blended backgrounds, children of immigrants, and children of mixed marriages like me. I remember my own uneasy longing when I attended a concert at El Maestro, a Puerto Rican boxing gym in the Bronx. An aged performer sang "La Borinqueña," the island's revolutionary anthem, and everyone raised their fists. Everyone sang along, except me. Back then, my Spanish was as bad as Medem's Yiddish, and I didn't know the lyrics. Was I even Puerto Rican? Was Medem even a Jew? When I got home, I memorized the words, so I could pass this test if it came up later. Medem had more dramatic options. In 1901, police rounded up a passel of Minsk organizers, Medem among them. At the prison, he wrote down his nationality on the intake form. Jew. He didn't hesitate.

EXILELAND

Switzerland remained the first stop for most revolutionaries fleeing the tsarist empire. In an 1881 letter to Friedrich Engels, the elderly Marx sneered at the luxury exiles had who "in order to carry on propaganda in Russia . . . came to Geneva!" Twenty years later, these troublemakers had fanned out to capitals across Europe. I call this revolutionary diaspora "Exileland"—a country within a continent, as cramped, cosmopolitan, and histrionic as the place from whence it fled. Exileland was the crucible that forged the revolutionaries who defined the twentieth century, as well as a garden in which thousands of grandiose dilettantes squawked like parrots let out of their cages.

Some of Exileland's residents were hunted men like Medem. Others were merely students kept out of Russian universities by various restrictions, whose hearts and allowances became targets for prophets false or true. All hid contraband, begged for loans, and skipped town often, as the local government's forbearance could vanish overnight. Georgians and Latvians honed their nationalism in Exileland, as did Polish socialist bank robbers. Exileland was a place for smugglers. Snitches. Scoundrels. Nihilist poets mooching off their mistresses. Pamphleteers who grifted money for printing presses they never bought. Trust fund boys who wanted to blow up an opera. Girls who planned assassinations to reclaim their good names. Lunatics. Sluts. Queers. Con men. Cop killers. Sublime cynics. Disillusioned workers. A duke pretending to be a laborer. A laborer pretending to be a duke. Every Marxist sect found its followers, from tame social democrats to blood-curdling democratic socialists. Or was it the other way around? Every so often an Exileland murder got written up in the local newspaper. The victim might have been a comrade offed by the Okhrana, or just an informant getting his due.

Above all, Exileland's residents believed they would return. No matter how long someone stayed in Exileland, they felt it was temporary. One day, the revolution would kick off, and they'd return to Russia to die on the barricades or be crowned as messiah—and possibly both at once.

Medem arrived in Exileland in 1901. After his arrest in Minsk, he'd skipped bail and navigated a purgatory of safe houses to escape the Russian Empire, making his way to Berne.

Berne was home to hundreds of Russian Jewish students, who scandalized the stodgy Swiss with their zest for living. "No Russians!" read signs at many boarding houses. They gorged themselves on political tracts forbidden in the homeland and held nightly lectures, for which an escaped activist like Medem was eagerly sought.

From Berne, Medem's relatives wanted him to continue on to Belgium to study engineering, and he might have done just that if not for a devastating discovery. His health had been delicate since a teenage bout of typhus, and his escape from Russia left him in such rough shape that a friend insisted he see a doctor. The prognosis was dire. Incurable kidney disease. The doctor doubted Medem would live past thirty. This news clarified his thoughts. If he had only a few years left, he wanted to spend them with the sort of people he loved. He enrolled in the University of Berne to study Spinoza and sunk into the student colony's embrace. He also rejoined the underground, enlisting in the Bund's foreign committee, a support group for the party that published newspapers and raised funds to be sent back to comrades inside the Russian Empire.

Launched in 1898 in Geneva, the foreign committee quickly attracted a following amongst Exileland's idealistic, footloose Jewish students. Within a few years, these converts had spread the Bund's ideology to European capitals, then across the globe, to Los Angeles and Mexico City, Johannesburg and Melbourne. If a city had Jews from the Pale of Settlement, then it would have a support group for the Bund.

The foreign committee's work was half prosaic paper shuffling, half conspiratorial drama. One day, a tuer like Medem might write an article, send a press release, and continue an epistolary argument with a union boss in Antwerp. The next day, he would spend hours wedging subversive handbills between the pages of scientific catalogs. After meticulously gluing the pages shut, he would pack the catalogs into a false-bottomed suitcase and give it to a student returning home to the Russian Empire, where the handbills would be distributed. Medem and his comrades tracked down political detainees, sent them letters, and organized escapes. When, after two years' imprisonment in Moscow, Arkady Kremer fled Russia, the foreign committee eased his way to London. In 1902, they arranged for Pati to join him. When she arrived, she was horrified by the poverty and clutter of Arkady's leaky flat. "What happened to all the money I sent you?" she demanded. "I gave it to the foreign committee," Arkady drawled, staring at her through glasses held together with tape. "You want to take it back?"

ISTANBUL

The YIVO Institute for Jewish Research in New York holds the archives of the Bund's foreign committee. For two years, I stole away there whenever I had a chance. I wore a good dress, did my hair, and, taking nothing but a pencil and notepad, climbed the steps to the archive's inner sanctum, thoughtless of obligation and of time. I told myself I was hunting ghosts. But was that right? The papers that the archivist spread before me felt as alive as any person.

They didn't look like much—just jumbled scraps—but they were survivors of Medem's world. Sometimes, as I touched the pages, I imagined that my fingerprints lined up with his. More than a century ago, Medem had leafed through these archives in search of a certain sentence, just as I leafed through them in search of him. Pamphlets shouted their slogans. Correspondents bantered in Swedish, Russian, Polish, English, German, French. Yiddish letters swirled, then grew jagged like the lines of a heart-rate monitor. Writers filled each postcard to its edges. They sometimes cut out the stamps, to be cleaned with vinegar and reused. These were the papers of skinflints who employed every trick to survive. A Greek postcard from Brooklyn recalled walks in the hills of Thrace. Another passel of letters bearing the Ottoman script of the Socialist Workers' Federation of Salonica discussed how the Sephardi workers there and the Yiddish workers of the Bund might collaborate to stamp out Zionism. I stopped on one card, postmarked from Constantinople. On it, a new arrival from Jaffa provided an update on the local union scene.

I ran my fingers over the stamp.

Here, Medem's world met mine. I had my own stint in Exileland. For years, I commuted to Istanbul to write a book with a journalist from the ISIS-held fragment of Syria. The worst war in the world was churning just across the border, and the cafés of Istanbul's hipster neighborhood Cihangir were filled with its flotsam—the aid workers, refugees, journalists, lobbyists, and spies—drinking, fighting, and loving beneath the jerry-rigged fairy lights. For many of them, these would be the best years of their lives, built on the hell lived by other people. Ironically, there were few Turks in this story. They were busy dealing with their country's slide into dictatorship. Cihangir was full of foreigners, both the privileged kind and those who adamantly were not.

Sometimes, I hear a bar of Turkish *sanat* music and nostalgia cuts me deep. I remember the parrot in the lobby of the Grand Hotel de Londres whom I tried to teach to say, "Fuck the police." I remember the Syrian guys on Istiklal Avenue singing the anthem of their revolution: "Janna Janna." *My country is heaven.* They belted each line straight from their chests. The Syrian bookstore in the formerly Greek neighborhood. (It is gone now, and the Syrians, like the Greeks before them, have been partially expelled.) One night, the journalist took me to a Kurdish bar. The floor was soaked with beer, a rainbow Pride flag hung from the ceiling, and someone had scrawled tributes to guerrilla movements all over the walls. The patrons stamped through a joyous halay. I drew them, my hands moving to the singer's voice. We staggered out into the sunrise to see the Bosporus topped with domes.

For two years, this journalist and I wrote about the war together, typing all afternoon, then walking to Cihangir, where we smoked Marlboros, drank bitter coffee, and petted cats.

We ran into people from everywhere in Istanbul. Many of them can no longer return. First, the war against the Kurds reopened, like the stitches of a half-healed wound, and those who covered it were arrested and deported. D., whom I planned to spend Thanksgiving with, was bundled into a car in the middle of the night. E. was grabbed while investigating antiquities and spent a week in solitary. R., possessor of a less lucky passport, spent months inside. Then came the passport bans. The names rumored to be on lists. I missed a date with C. in Istanbul, but she fled to Croatia before we could reschedule. The lira plummeted. The border closed. Editors' interest in the war faded. Everyone wanted out.

With each month, more of our Istanbul vanished. Favorite bars became construction pits. The freelancers were replaced by Saudi hair-transplant tourists, bandages still swaddling their heads.

The roundups of Syrians began, and no one except Syrians complained. Police combed the streets, checking IDs, beating up guys, boys even, then throwing them on buses back to the war. The secular opposition politicians said this was a rational response. How else could Turks deal with all the Arabic letters on the shop signs? How else could they process this rude resurgence of their Eastern past? The journalist slipped over the border, back home to Raqqa, unsure of what would come.

Some nights I dream of Istanbul. Did people once dream of Casablanca, of Marseilles? For some, these cities were their last ports of call before they flung themselves out to sea, to test their strength and swim for the rock that was a future. For others, for journalists, for me? We were vultures, circling in a photogenic locale that for a few years felt like the center of the earth. As Trump gained and lost and regained power, as ISIS rose and fell, I thought of the Istanbul I had known. One night, years after the golden days, I sat in a bar in London, drinking with other castoffs from this time. A harsh nostalgia filled the room, and we staggered onto the streets, drunk and angry, because we had lost a city that had never really been ours.

NATION

Medem quickly became a hot ticket on the radical lecture circuit, where the rhetorical skills he'd discovered during the Kyiv student strike now won him the admiration of countless young women. In the overheated back rooms where Medem wowed his acolytes, he liked to dissect Exileland's hottest topics, and at the dawn of the twentieth century, no topic was hotter than the debate between ethnic nationalism and internationalism.

"A people destined to achieve great things for the welfare of humanity must one day or other be constituted a nation," wrote Giuseppe Mazzini, Italy's prophet of nationalism. For the Italian people to seize to their destiny, they needed an Italian state. Ethnic nationalists of other countries agreed. From Greece to Serbia to Poland, these ideologues flogged the causes of their assorted Peoples, whose folktales, embroidery patterns, and glorious, martyr-strewn histories entitled them to ethnically homogenous countries on their God-designated slices of land. European ethnonationalism had little place for Jews or other diasporic peoples, who were viewed as eternal aliens at best and toxic bacilli at worst. Zionism grew alongside it, as both a reaction and, in the writer Naomi Klein's words, a doppelgänger.

Others objected to all this talk of blood and soil. "The working men have no country," wrote Karl Marx and Friedrich Engels in *The Communist Manifesto*. Internationalists to the core, they believed that despite the identities the state foisted upon them, people were people, and workers were, above all, workers. Ethnic divisions amongst them were distractions meant to keep them from toppling their true oppressors. So Marx said, and so Marxists believed.

Arkady Kremer had founded the Bund as an internationalist. For him, a Jewish organization was a defense against the ferocious antisemitism of the Russian Empire, where no matter how secular and assimilated a Jew might be, he still endured legal discrimination and quotidian violence. Kremer believed that Jewish workers needed their own organization because they couldn't trust Christians to fight for their rights, but his attachment to ethnic particularism stopped there.

His co-founder John Mill had a different take. Mill came from Warsaw, where he admired the pride Poles felt for their oppressed country, culture, and language. Why did eastern European Jews deserve anything less? Legal equality was essential but insufficient, Mill thought. Instead, he advocated Jewish self-organization for its own sake, and the preservation and promotion of Yiddish language, literature, and culture. Borrowing the concept of *national cultural autonomy* from the Austrian socialists Otto Bauer and Karl Renner, Mill envisioned a Russian socialist movement, and eventually a Russia, where each region's ethnic groups could keep their own languages, customs, and representative bodies while still fighting side-by-side for a better world. By the time Medem arrived in Exileland, most Bundists supported Mill's ideas.

One of Mill's most passionate young partisans was Mark Liber. Son of an aspiring Hebrew-language poet from Vilna, Liber was the youngest of five radical siblings. One brother had helped start the Union of Struggle for the Working Class with Lenin. Liber had his scars. Traumatized by his experience as a journalist covering a pogrom's aftermath for a Bundist newspaper, he argued obsessively with the assimilationist old guard that the party needed to fight for Jewish autonomy.

Liber and Medem grew close in Exileland, but their attraction was that of opposites. The twenty-three-year-old Raphael Abramovich balanced them out. Witty and affable, Abramovich had a radical pedigree equal to that of Liber. As a schoolboy, he mischievously swiped a classmate's jacket, only to find an illegal Marxist economics pamphlet in the pocket. From then on, he was hooked. At first, he limited his revolutionary activities to participation in socialist discussion groups, but that was enough to earn him expulsion from university in Riga, then arrest and exile. When Abramovich and Medem first met, Abramovich dressed like a hobo. The soles of his shoes flapped, revealing holey socks. The debonair Medem recoiled. For years afterward, Abramovich teased him for his bourgeois airs.

The trio soon became inseparable. Medem used Abramovich and Liber as sounding boards for his ideas about nationality, but talk of identity hit him on a level deeper than it did them. Both of them grew up Jewish in the Pale. Neither ever had to wonder who he was. It was different for Medem. Like many young people raised between cultures, Medem yearned for a simple sense of self and community that he imagined people with less complicated backgrounds possessed.

Medem's ideas got their first major public hearing in 1903 in Zurich, at the Bund's fifth conference. The exact text of Medem's speech has been lost, but it was broadly similar to an essay titled "Social Democracy and the National Question" that he published some months later. He began with a symbolic act of a parricide. Medem described the assimilated Jew of Western Europe, who, "trembling, humiliated, accustomed to have other people spit in his face," could only secure civil rights by erasing his difference. "Make yourself like others! Deny your heritage, mock everything of Jewish character, spit three times whenever you hear the dirty [Yiddish] spoken . . . Because that is the only way you will get an equal fat share like the 'resident' bourgeois . . . and secure for [yourself] a slice of the Leviathan." Medem's target is unmistakable, even though he does not say his name: his father, the convert who banned Yiddish from his household and whispered when he said the word *Jew*. Doctor Medem, who baptized his son in order to give him what in today's America they would call "whiteness." In two brutal pages, Medem exorcised his father's ghost. He then moved on to more current concerns.

Even as he mocked assimilation, Medem loathed nationalism, which he saw as a scam that elites used to justify new wars, corner new markets, and inscribe new borders in blood. The nationalism of the oppressed was no better. If a persecuted minority managed to obtain a country for itself, it still had to deal with the other people living there. For a new state's newly minted minorities, "the old oppressor is simply replaced by a new one," Medem wrote, neatly predicting the eastern European border wars of the next forty years.

Class came first for a socialist like Medem. His sympathies lay with Polish factory workers, not Jewish industrial barons. "Solidarity of the entire nation means giving up the class struggle, [and the] spiritual and material enslavement of the proletariat," he wrote. When, decades later, the Black Panther Party chairman Fred Hampton said, "We say we're not going to fight capitalism with black capitalism, but we're going to fight it with socialism," Medem would have cheered. But class war alone would not eliminate the racism Jews faced in the tsarist empire, nor the self-contempt it had bred, which had made assimilation seem like the price of acceptance.

"Oppression is eliminated not only through the destruction of unjust state forms, but also through the *creation* in their place of certain guarantees," Medem wrote. In other words, it wasn't enough for the Russian government to take its boot off minorities' throats. Jews and other minorities needed government support to build their own cultural institutions, to study and work in their own languages. Only then could assimilation be a choice.

Medem's text was a sensitive exploration of how to build multiracial democracy, but it was too complicated for his audience. It was too assimilationist for some, too identitarian for others. At the 1903 conference, debate grew so violent that the whole matter was struck from the official record.

TUER

The Bund was a practical group whose strength lay in its tuers, not its theoreticians.

A hundred and twenty years later, these tuers are not easy for me to study. They didn't write books, and their cares—the smashed skull, the empty strike fund, the stinking vats at Bloch's tannery—are far from the disputes that Medem was having in Switzerland. Rank-and-file activists only occasionally surface in archives. Their names are more likely to appear in a provincial police report than in a newspaper, in a deportation order than on a banquet invite. Their greatest chance for fame comes if they are murdered during a protest. In that case, they might wind up on a commemorative party postcard. But while I can't flesh out these tuers' lives the way I can with Medem, they were his party's blood and bones.

For this reason, one of my prized possessions is a photographic history of the Bund, *The Bund in Pictures,* published in 1957. Bound in smoke-blue cloth, it resembles a high school yearbook, comprised almost entirely of tuers. I turn to page twenty-one. There he is, in the upper right. Hirsh Lekert, bootmaker, hero, and terrorist.

Lekert made his name in 1902, in Vilna, after Governor Victor von Wahl forbade any May Day celebrations. Polish and Jewish workers marched anyway. Cossacks charged them with whips. Thirty arrests. So far, business as usual. That night, while von Wahl attended the theater, Bundists showered him with flyers. Police arrested these activists too. The next day, von Wahl ordered the detainees to be stripped naked and beaten. Periodically, a doctor checked their pulses. They were not allowed to faint.

Hirsh Lekert was a man of action. Two years before, he had led workers in a mass jailbreak. As punishment, he was jailed and exiled to Ekaterinaslav in Russia's interior, but escaped and arrived back in Vilna just in time for that fateful May Day. When he heard about his comrades' torture, he and five friends decided that something needed to be done.

All good Marxists disapproved of terrorism, so the Bund's central committee forbade their plan. Hirsh Lekert didn't listen. Instead, he bought a pistol. On the night of May 18, von Wahl and his cronies stumbled out of the Lushinka circus. Hirsh Lekert fired twice, but the bullets only grazed von Wahl's leg. Thanks to the intervention of the minister of the interior, Vyacheslav von Plehve, a military court hanged Lekert a few weeks later. On the scaffold, he refused the consolation of a rabbi.

Lekert must have known that there are many sorts of immortality. Despite the failure of his attack, he lived for decades as an icon. He starred in plays and ballads, and was celebrated in the radical press that he, an illiterate shoemaker, would not have been able to read.

After such an outpouring, how could the Bund reject Lekert? Soon, the central committee issued new pamphlets to praise his action. The failed assassination was not terrorism, after all, but "vengeance for a shameful insult," and so in line with official party policy. Safely martyred, Lekert joined the Bund's pantheon.

VOLKOVYSK

By 1902, the Bund was *the* largest revolutionary party in Russia, with thirty thousand members, and Volkovysk hosted an energetic little cell. Volkovysk Bundists robbed the government liquor store to fund their movement. They attacked the wagons that transported political prisoners, threw tobacco in the face of the guards like makeshift pepper spray, and freed their friends. After cops arrested Sam Rothbort's comrade Berl Dzhik, Bundists sawed through the bars of his cell and hid him in Beyle Rivkah's house. When the cops came looking for Berl, Beyle disguised him as an old woman, and he fled into the night.

I try to picture Sam Rothbort as he was then, in the Zamkov forest, sprawled with his friends on a fragrant carpet of pine. Being an artist, he will forgive me if I use imagination to fill the archive's silence. They probably all laughed at Berl Dzhik's escape. Berl in drag? Ridiculous! How did anyone fall for his disguise? Sam would take a pocketknife from his coat. He would find a branch, then begin to carve it. Berl Dzhik, wig, tits, and all, would appear beneath his wiry hands.

CHAPTER 4

RIVALRIES OF EXILE

(1903–1904)

Leon Trotsky in his youth

KISHINEV

THE FIFTH CONGRESS OF THE BUND, IN ZURICH, TOOK PLACE IN THE shadow of a pogrom that had happened a few months earlier in the town of Kishinev. Whipped up by a local newspaper editor, over the course of three days in April 1903, Kishinev Christians raped dozens of Jewish women and murdered forty-five Jews. In and of itself, this was hardly a departure from the past, but unlike other towns where pogroms took place, Kishinev was near Russia's border with the Habsburg Empire. Foreign press flooded in to photograph the rows of shrouded corpses and telegraph rape victims' testimonies across the ocean, and the name *Kishinev* became an international synonym for the massacre of Jews.

Despite its notoriety, Kishinev was unexceptional in its way, parallel to the contemporaneous terrorism of Southern whites on Black enclaves in America. This comparison is not my own. In 1903, Black activists drew immediate parallels between lynch mobs and Russian pogromists. It was not just the brutality. It was the complicity, even connivance, of the state. While Southern sheriffs used lynch mobs to reinforce hierarchies inherited from slavery, the Russian state permitted pogroms as a safety valve for popular rage. Most Jews blamed the Kishinev pogrom on Vyacheslav von Plehve, Russia's notoriously antisemitic minister of the interior, especially after a letter appeared in *The Times* of London that purported to show von Plehve ordering the attacks (historians later proved this letter to be a forgery). For Jewish radicals, Kishinev only strengthened their revolutionary beliefs. One doesn't negotiate with a government helmed by murderers. One overthrows it.

ISKRA

After Kishinev, Medem toured Exileland to speak about the poisonous ideologies that led to the pogrom. In the German city of Karlsruhe, he had scarcely finished his speech when one of the attendees sprung up to disagree. Medem knew the young man by reputation. He was a devotee of *Iskra*, the punchy new newspaper Lenin and Martov had founded to advance their Marxist vision. *Iskra* was already notorious for the rhetorical savagery it used against other socialists, and for its commitment to total centralization.

In his 1902 pamphlet *What Is to Be Done,* Lenin spelled out his belief that only a ruthlessly centralized party of obedient professional revolutionaries had a chance of seizing power in Russia. Meanwhile, the Bund had developed in the opposite direction, preaching that a decentralized coalition of autonomous groups would do the best job at revolution. In this they were consistent. When the Bund co-founded the RSDLP in 1898, they were the largest, best-organized socialist group in the Russian Empire. The Bund entered the new party as an autonomous entity whose turf was the Yiddish working class. They meant to keep their turf exclusive.

Lenin saw this as a recipe for failure. The thirty-three-year-old was already revealing personality traits that would shape the coming century. He was a brilliant tactician, a Machiavellian in the service of utopia, who devoted astounding will, focus, and discipline to pursuit of revolutionary ideals. A man of few scruples, he excelled at backroom bureaucratic maneuvers. He flew into debilitating rages. He shouted curses at rivals he wanted to dominate. He was always right—in his own eyes, at least.

Lenin had long yearned to subordinate the Bund, and he saw his chance in early 1902. After police arrested half of the RSDLP's organizing committee, Lenin decided to shape the new committee to his liking. Mysteriously, the Bund's invitations were never sent. With no Bundist delegates in the room, Lenin stacked the committee with his partisans. *Iskra* attacked the Bund for their absence.

When Medem finally met Lenin in Berne, he was not impressed. He had imagined Lenin would be a giant, but instead, *Iskra*'s leader resembled a "a crafty Russian grain dealer. . . . When you speak to him, he looks at you with his small eyes—eyes directed at you obliquely, from something of an angle, and with a cunning devilish smile, as if to say, 'There's not a word of truth in what you're saying!' " Medem later wrote. He pegged Lenin a tyrant in waiting. For the next year, the Bund and *Iskra* fought in their respective newspapers.

The Bund devoted much of its fifth congress, held in Zurich, to strategizing against the pugnacious Iskrites. They prepared to offer the RSDLP an ultimatum: they would have to recognize the Bund as the sole representatives of the Jewish proletariat during the upcoming party congress, or else the Bund would walk.

But back to that tiny discussion group in Karlsruhe, where Medem and the young *Iskra* devotee first came face-to-face. The Iskrite had a corona of black curls and a mordant mouth that reminded Medem of a bird of prey, but Medem's eyes immediately went to his yellow shoes. They seemed too flamboyant for a political refugee.

The young refugees's comment had nothing to do with Medem's lecture. Instead, he berated the Bund for criticizing the RSDLP over a perceived failure to fight antisemitism. This was just more obsessive fixation on Jewish victimhood, the refugee said. If Russian workers were racist, it was because they were ignorant products of a backward autocracy. Overthrow the tsar and the racism would disappear. The RSDLP was the only group with a plan to do it.

The young man's birth name was Leon Bronstein, but he went by the nom de guerre of Trotsky.

A few months later Medem again crossed Trotsky's path. This time, he demanded to know if Trotsky considered himself a Jew or a Russian.

"I am a social democrat. That's all," Trotsky responded, honestly.

THE CAGE

Even in revolutionary circles, Jews differed over how to protect themselves. Bundists believed that safety came not just from socialist solidarity but from ethnic pride and smuggled handguns. They wrote war ballads in Yiddish and swaggered down the streets of their Jewish neighborhoods, flaunting their Jewish noms de guerre. Other Jewish revolutionaries disagreed. Jewish men and women like Karl Marx, Ferdinand Lasalle, Karl Kautsky, and Rosa Luxemburg make up the honor roll of European socialism. Believers in neither God nor tribe, they denied that there was such a thing as a Jewish people. Lacking their own land or any single language, Jews were not a nation but a caste, created through what the Black Marxist academic Barbara Fields would later call *racecraft*. Once legal oppression ended and medieval prejudice stopped, Jews would cease to exist as a separate group.

They were able to believe this because, despite stereotypes as to their looks, Jews could at least try to pass as ethnic Russians or Germans or Poles. When the Black poet Amiri Baraka wrote about "the ugly silent deaths of Jews under the surgeon's knife, to awake on Sixty-ninth Street with money and a hip nose," he was talking about a capacity to conceal their difference that Black Americans would never have. Bronstein could change his name to Trotsky. He could convince himself that this would work.

Julius Martov (birthname Tsederbaum) was the best critic of the Bund's identity politics, and that's probably because he helped create them. His 1895 speech "The Turning Point" first clearly articulated their intersectional approach. Eight years later, Martov had rejected its content. He saw no point in creating a movement for a tiny minority, and Jews were only 2 percent of the Russian Empire's population.

"However perfect the organization of that relatively insignificant section which the Jews constitute may be—so long as the organization of the vast majority of the proletariat of heavy industry limps on both legs, the most intensive and dedicated work in its own little corner will not yield even a tenth of that result which it could produce," Martov wrote.

To overthrow the tsar, they *needed* Russians.

When the Bund demanded to be considered the sole representatives of the Jewish proletariat, Trotsky and Martov took it as an insult. How could it be otherwise? They aimed for the world. The Bund wanted to shove them back into the Pale of Settlement. If the Bund was a practical impediment for Lenin, for its rival Jewish socialists it was something worse. It was a cage.

THE SECOND CONGRESS

When the Russian Social Democratic Labor Party's second congress began in Brussels on July 17, 1903, few realized it would have cataclysmic effects on the Bund's future.

Every day, Vladimir Medem and Mark Liber joined the dozens of delegates gathered in the back room of a wool worker's cooperative, which they soon realized was infested with fleas. That was the least of their problems. Everything had been stacked against them in advance. Plekhanov was chairman, and Lenin vice-chairman. Every important delegate was with *Iskra*, and *Iskra* drafted the agenda. Though the Bund was overwhelmingly the largest revolutionary group in the Russian Empire, out of the conference's fifty-one delegates, only five, thanks to Lenin's maneuverings, were Bundists. Standing astride a makeshift dais draped in red cloth, Plekhanov scolded the Bund, whose status was the first item on the agenda. Within days, Trotsky, Martov, and Medem's friend Mark Liber were engaged in open war.

MEETINGS

Scholars have analyzed the minutes of the second congress at length, but it's hard for me to do justice to the tendentious hellscape of those weeks. I could lay out every motion or objection, but that wouldn't evoke the misery of a leftist meeting, a torment you must live through to grasp. When I read the minutes, I am there. In Brussels, yes. But also in New York, at the monthly meeting for a socialist group held in an airless library basement, where I watch two graduate students wrangle over the creation of bylaws no one bothers to read. It's hour three. The air is hot. "Stack!" Comrade A. screams. His Adam's apple bobs with fury. "Point of order!" hisses Comrade B. I want to squeeze through the walls and escape into the clean sunlight. Time is the only thing we can't replace, and I feel each second slip away. I can't count how many hours I've spent like this, convinced that this was how we build an organization, and from there a future. It's a conviction I still hold. So much of our past has been shaped by this petty proceduralism. You could draw a straight line between an amendment in Brussels and a mass grave in Kazakhstan. But I'm getting ahead of myself.

LONDON

After three itchy days spent arguing at the Belgian wool cooperative, the delegates in their hotel rooms were awakened by knocks. The political police had arrived to question them as foreign subversives.

After some unpleasant nocturnal interrogations, the delegates fled to London, where they booked meeting rooms under the pretense that they were members of a fishing club. The congress mercilessly resumed. Medem immediately loathed the British megapolis. When the steam-powered metro stalled, which it often did, its cars filled with black soot. Above ground, Medem wandered helplessly between identical apartment blocks while street kids, recognizing him as a foreigner, lobbed rotten vegetables at his back.

The congress had dragged on for six weeks when Martov put the Bund out of its misery. He demanded the Bund delete a paragraph of its rules that gave it the right to organize Jewish workers wherever it liked. It was a referendum on the party's autonomy. When the vote came, the Bund lost, 41–5.

There was nothing left to say. Liber announced the Bund's withdrawal from the RSDLP. The stunned delegates marched out, as lost, Medem wrote, as a "piece of flesh" torn from a living body.

MAJORITY

From the Bund's foreign committee headquarters in London, Medem ruefully listened to rumors that the Iskrites had begun to fracture over the question of party membership. Should the RSDLP be a mass party of workers, as Martov envisioned? Or should it be the top-down conspiracy Lenin wanted, in which a central committee commanded and a full-time cadre obeyed? "Lenin had bared his teeth," Medem wrote. "A section of his comrades of yesterday had failed to dance to his tune on even the smallest point of statute;—presto!—they had already become personae non grata."

Lenin won, and though he didn't admit it, Medem had played a part in his victory. The Bundists had had five delegates, whose votes they could have used to extract concessions. Instead, when the moment called for ruthlessness, Bundists made speeches, then showily left the room. They kept their principles but frittered away their power. Lenin himself was baffled by the Bund's exit. "They were actually masters of the situation," he later wrote.

With the Bund gone, Lenin had just enough delegates to win. Ever astute on matters of branding, Lenin labeled Martov's crew "Minorityites," or *Mensheviks*. He seized the term "Majorityite" for his side. In Russian, the word is *Bolshevik*.

BASEL

On the way home from one interminable political gathering full of enemies, Medem stopped by Basel, Switzerland, to observe another group of antagonists—the Zionists, who were in the midst of their sixth world congress.

Political Zionism had made its global debut in 1897, the same year as the Bund, and the two groups had been enemies from the start. They couldn't have been more different. While the Bund's first congress comprised a few fugitives in a Vilna attic, the inaugural Zionist congress filled a posh Swiss casino and turned Theodor Herzl, its founder, into a superstar. A journalist from Vienna, Herzl had once thought Jews could win acceptance through assimilation; he even proposed mass conversion to Christianity. Then he covered the Dreyfus affair. In sophisticated France, Herzl watched the courts condemn a Jewish army lieutenant named Alfred Dreyfus on obviously fake charges of espionage, then sentence him to life imprisonment on Devil's Island. Dreyfus was loyal. He had fought for France. He had assimilated. He had done everything right. It didn't matter in the end. After the trial, French crowds beat Jews and burned Jewish shops.

The Dreyfus trial convinced Herzl that hatred was baked into the bread of Europe. Jews couldn't fix it. No matter how patriotic they were, Europeans would loathe them, and before long, the old European lust for ethnic slaughter would return. Jews needed a state of their own as a refuge, Herzl thought. At first, he didn't care where it was. More crucially, he didn't care how they got it.

Herzl settled on Palestine, then part of the Ottoman Empire. An atheist himself, he was driven not by religious faith but by the force of biblical branding. Neither he nor any other Zionist leader cared about the Palestinian Arabs who made up the vast majority of the land's inhabitants. Initially, Herzl pitched his potential Jewish state as an outpost of European civilization that would somehow benefit Palestinians. (In his private journals, he was franker and wrote that they should be stripped of their land and coerced to leave.) This attitude was typical. When Zionist leaders bothered to mention Palestinians at all, their approaches ranged from condescension to calls for ethnic cleansing.

The Bund found the entire idea delusional. How would Zionists convince Europe's nine million Jews to move to tiny Palestine? And what would they do with the people living there? The whole project was a fanciful distraction from the real battles that Jewish workers faced in eastern Europe. Chaim Weizmann, the Zionist leader who later became the first president of Israel, wrote in 1903 that "our hardest struggle everywhere is conducted against [the Jewish Labor Bund]," while the Bund described Zionism as "the most evil enemy of the organized Jewish proletariat." The Bund banned Zionists from membership, and the two groups tussled on the lecture podium and in the streets. Medem himself spent many nights arguing with Zionist orators in various student colonies. He stopped by Basel anyway, driven by curiosity about Herzl.

When Medem squeezed himself into the Basel casino, the whole crowd seemed to be suffering from mass hypnosis. The audience moaned and writhed when Herzl appeared onstage, waving their handkerchiefs and unleashing thunderous applause. A tall man with a regal beard, Herzl proudly spoke about his meeting with the notorious Russian minister of the interior, Vyacheslav von Plehve, whom Jews held responsible for the Kishinev pogrom. Like Herzl, von Plehve thought that Jews needed to abandon Europe. When Herzl asked von Plehve to pressure the Ottoman sultan to turn over land in Palestine for settlement, the minister had generously agreed. The crowd cheered. Medem was appalled.

Medem's disgust grew when a writer he knew told him the price for von Plehve's acquiescence. Von Plehve promised to support the colonization of Palestine if, in return, Herzl convinced the Jewish Labor Bund to stop its activities against the tsarist state.

The conversation between Herzl and von Plehve illustrates the Bund's problem with Zionism. Zionism was not just impractical, in Bundists' eyes. It was submission to the same bigots who wanted to kick Jews out of their homes. The Bund believed that Jews belonged in eastern Europe. "We are not strangers here and not guests, even though the Russian government considers us as such," one local Bund committee wrote. "The richness of the land is soaked through with our blood. . . . We demand and fight for that which belongs to us, for human, civil and political rights." To leave meant letting their tormenters win. The Bund coined a word for this stubborn insistence on staying: *do'ikayt.* Hereness, as opposed to the There of Palestine. Bundists would fight for freedom and dignity in the place where they lived.

Hereness was hard-won in eastern Europe. It had nothing in common with the fuzzy tolerance beloved by liberals. Do'ikayt meant defiance, backed by arms. In 1906, the *American Jewish Yearbook* published a table of forty-seven pogroms that took place in the year after Kishinev. In three cities, the table notes, "riots were suppressed by Self Defense."

In *The Bund in Pictures,* these self-defense groups pose as if for a high school yearbook. The young men crane their skinny necks to show their good sides to the camera. They wear black. They angle their weapons in parallel. They pose in front of a studio backdrop. In a forest. Next to the corpses of their friends. In September 1903, two hundred of these youth beat back a pogrom in Gomel, a mostly Jewish town not far from Kishinev, which was carried out by Christian railway workers who were supposed to be their proletarian brothers. The pogromists only managed to kill seven Jews.

The purpose of these self-defense squads was never merely practical.

They were also a way for young Jews to re-create themselves. Gone was the humiliating past, when their fathers bowed their heads before the Russian Bigmen and paid fat bribes to avert calamity—not that it always worked. When a Jewish kid picked up a gun, she cast herself as a subject of history, not its object. She did not need to plead for sufferance from anyone. She was an equal in her own land. "Killing a European is killing two birds with one stone, eliminating in one go oppressor and oppressed: leaving one man dead and the other man free," wrote Jean-Paul Sartre about anticolonial violence in his preface to Frantz Fanon's *Wretched of the Earth.* He could have been speaking about the young fighters of the Bund.

Over the next years, the Bund turned self-defense into a science. During Easter, a group's blond members might attend church services, to see the mood of the parishioners. When funds from abroad didn't suffice, fighters "asked" wealthy Jews for contributions, then bought knives, whips, handguns, and metal bats. They organized neighborhoods to fight back. Chemists made bombs. Girls learned first aid and women boiled water to throw at attackers. Families turned their homes into barracks. Teenage seamstresses lobbed rocks, and big-eared youths, twins of Sam Rothbort, gulped as strangers shoved pistols in their hands.

VOLKOVYSK

My mother always told me Sam Rothbort left Volkovysk because of trouble. She regretted that she had never asked about specifics. When I researched the self-defense groups, I found a likely answer.

In an essay titled "Self-Defense as an Emotional Experience," the historian Inna Shtakser dove deeply into the testimonials of tsarist-era political prisoners who sought pensions from the new Bolshevik government. I skimmed the endnotes. My eye caught on the name *Volkovysk.*

The endnote contained the pension application of one Naum L'vovich, member of the Volkovysk self-defense militia. The militia protected the city on market days, when farmers poured in by thousands to sell their crops to Jewish traders and get good and drunk at local taverns afterward. The market was a tinderbox in which hard bargaining turned easily into violence.

In his application, L'vovich described a pogrom in Volkovysk that took place at the end of 1903. L'vovich wrote that he had commanded a unit of ten fighters in the defense of one of Volkovysk's main squares. Two policemen led a crowd hunting for Jewish stalls to plunder. Details about the two men are scarce. One was the chief. The other had a nickname, Chugunchik—Little Cast Iron—that hinted at his disposition. The defenders opened fire. Both cops died on the spot.

After the pogrom, police began to hunt for socialists. Naum L'vovich was soon in jail. A few months later, my great-grandfather Sam smuggled himself out of the empire.

IN 2020, MY MOTHER found a piece of paper on which Sam Rothbort had written an outline of his life. In it, he said he had been "involved in a shooting" on behalf of the underground in Volkovysk. With these four words he confirmed what I can only assume was his involvement in Officer Chugunchik's death. He never said anything else, but the Bund had only seventy members in Volkovysk, and Sam was one of the most active. Whether or not he pulled the trigger, he would have been a target for retribution.

What had Sam done on the afternoon of the pogrom? Had he held a pistol, or merely a metal bat? What did he think as he watched Chugunchik's blood seep into the market dirt where he had sat as a child? He never said.

During one of her shoebox excavations, my mother found another note. In it, Sam describes himself as a young revolutionary, whose dignity recoiled when he smashed his "goyish brother" with his fists. It is the "Christian world that cuts each other's throats with the blessing of Christ, and blames the Jews for their troubles," Sam wrote. For two thousand years, Jews had not involved themselves in war. How could they now make bloody revolution? Sam's comrades did. He hints darkly at the price.

In his words I see the seeds of a pacifism—exemplary, inflexible, and self-defeating—that he clung to through the next half century. I read and reread the note, trying to divine the meaning behind his awkward grammar. He had fought, yes, but violence was not his nature. "It had come from their side first."

FLIGHT

Sam must have spent his last days in Volkovysk in a state somewhere between excitement and fear. There would have been money to be gathered and telegrams to be sent. I don't know how long Sam stuck around after Officer Chugunchik's death, but thanks to one of his watercolors, I have an image of his final moments. In *Grandmother's Last Goodbye (to America)*, an aged woman screams. Her upflung arms mirror the narrow dirt street on which she stands, the narrow houses, the narrow, blighted life that the boy in the foreground is about to put behind him, just as his father had done. Two generations had abandoned her. On a winter day when Sam Rothbort stepped into some train station on the line between Bialystok and Slonim, he was trailed by his grandmother's reproach.

Sam made the three-hundred-mile journey to Germany by train, horse cart, and foot. He had no passport, and often no ticket. In one watercolor, he painted himself hiding from conductors beneath a woman's skirt. As the Polish-German border got closer, he would have encountered other Jews headed for America. By day, they would have crammed together in peasant safe houses, and by night, smugglers would have taken their cash, rounded them up like cattle, brought them to a field, and told them to run, dammit, because the cops were behind them and Germany was on the other side. Liars. How many fields had they crossed, only to find themselves still inside Russia?

At last, Sam made it into Germany. From there he rode the rails 625 miles to the port city of Antwerp. On March 19, he boarded his ship.

CHAPTER 5

THE GOLDEN LAND

(1904–1905)

NEW YORK CITY

SAM'S SHIP DOCKED ON MARCH 30, 1904.

Twenty million immigrants would arrive in the United States before the country's entry into World War I, the majority of whom passed into New York City through Castle and Ellis islands. They were Irish, Italians, Germans, Jews, Chinese, Syrians, Greeks. In New York, refugees, fugitives, immigrants, and exiles intermingled, intermarried, and swapped roles. They created new dance forms and new political machines, invented new creole languages of capitalism and corruption. The vast majority of immigrants planned to stay, but a good number longed to return to their homelands once the occupier had been kicked out, the king killed, and a new, more agreeable, ideology adopted.

New York was the world capital of radical diasporas at the turn of the century. A visitor could drop by the headquarters of the Irish nationalist Clan na Gael to help buy guns for the precursor to the IRA, then swing downtown to Little Syria, where the nation's first Arabic newspaper, *Kawkab Amreeka,* excoriated Ottoman oppression of minorities. Armenians and Filipinos, Koreans and Czechs, all used New York to hone their anti-imperialist arguments and build their fundraising networks. Here, the great Cuban poet José Martí drew up plans to rid his island of Spanish domination, and here was his last port of call before he boarded the boat that took him to die in battle in Contramaestre. The Puerto Rican flag first flew in 1895, not in San Juan but at Chimney Corner Hall, on the intersection of Broadway and Wall Street, at a meeting of the Revolutionary Committee of Puerto Rico. Two years later, with the committee's assistance, Antonio Mattei Lluberas would purchase thirty thousand machetes and, waving that new flag, set out to lead an uprising in Yabucoa. (Spoiler: he failed.) New York hosted two Italian branches of the Socialist Party, as well as the anarchist Bresci Circle, named for the assassin of King Umberto I. On the Lower East Side, Russian Narodniks shared café tables with German socialists booted by Bismarck, while, a few blocks over in Chinatown, residents refused to acknowledge their membership in the secretive Revive China Society, helmed by the revolutionary Sun Yat-sen. Forget Exileland. New York was Exile Galaxy. It had Geneva's political freedom combined with America's economic might. Here, cash was so plentiful that a few coins could shake loose into the hands of even the poorest immigrant to fund an insurrection somewhere else.

Like most of these immigrants, Sam didn't know it, but when he came to America, he had entered an even more vicious human hierarchy—and radically improved his place. In Russia, Jews had been the prime targets for state persecution. In America, they were merely discriminated against and disdained. Sam would soon learn he had other identities here, and that, like all countries, America was built on someone's blood.

At the turn of the century, New York was home to tens of thousands of African Americans. Most were internal refugees from Southern lynch mobs and Jim Crow–inflicted poverty. The city was less of a refuge than they had hoped. 1900 was the year of the so-called New York City Race Riot, when, for five days, Irish mobs attacked Black neighborhoods, furious because a Black man named Arthur Harris had defended his wife from an undercover cop. Irish, Jewish, Italian, Greek—no matter who an immigrant was back home, once he got here, he was better off than Black Americans. Sam had left Russia as a hated Yid. At Ellis Island, the immigration officer listed his nationality as "Hebrew." In 1917, on his naturalization papers, the official merely described him as "white."

THE EAST SIDE

At Ellis Island, a bureaucrat filled in Sam Rothbort's details. No money. Leather tanner. Closest relative? His father.

Harris Rotbarth, once Reb Hersch, lived in a tenement on 97 Forsyth Street. It would have been the same sort of place in which I spent my early twenties, a lightless railroad apartment with an air shaft for ventilation, where the sounds of child abuse mingled with the scuttling of rats. At least I had my own room. In Sam's day, the Lower East Side was one of the most densely populated places on earth, where a family of ten might share three hundred square feet in an apartment that was at once laundry room, cafeteria, garment factory, and hostel for a rotating cast of new arrivals from eastern Europe. This was Sam's first place to crash.

Back in Volkovysk, Reb Hersch had been a Talmudic scholar, but in New York he worked in the remnants business. With his new wife, Celia, the new American Harris picked through the trash to find fabric that his neighbors discarded after doing piecework. He smoothed out the scraps and sold them on a pushcart, likely on nearby Orchard Street. Sam found the street's name ironic. He didn't see a single tree.

To reconstruct the next four years of Sam's life, I have only his recollections, as well as the studio portraits he took with his New World friends. My mother pulls these from her shoebox. "A trumbonik," she calls him. A troublemaker. Sam is five foot four, his slight frame filled out with muscles, his jaw clenched, a bowler hat perched atop his head.

Years later, Sam wrote some doggerel about his time on the Lower East Side. The Grand Street mademoiselles (seamstresses decked out for their day off). The Yiddish theaters where the audiences laughed so hard they choked on their peanuts. The rush-hour delis full of cheap pastrami sandwiches. The bedbugs and lice. The big talkers, like "Uncle David with a clean shave/Fell from heaven/in America he was months—six, seven"—a sweatshop worker whose ulcer didn't dull his enthusiasm for the "wonders of Columbus' land."

In thousands of garrets, thousands of Davids spun their improbable dreams. A greenhorn might live in shit, but if he worked hard enough, the city dangled promises of plenty. Sam's first job was as a house painter. Companies made paint out of white lead mixed with linseed oil, and if the chemicals made him puke, well, that was just "painters' colic," which is to say, a normal part of the job.

The Lower East Side was home to 290,000 Jews, enough to constitute their own cohesive world. Jewish landlords fought Jewish tenants, and Jewish sweatshop bosses fought Jewish workers. Everyone kept their grudges against Christians for old times' sake. Italian guys hassled Jewish girls, and Jewish guys beat Italians for their effrontery. It was rough, but it was nothing like the pogroms back home. For white immigrants across New York, street violence was a game of equals, and Jews gave as good as they got.

A few weeks after Sam arrived in New York, two drunk marines stumbled into a Jewish neighborhood for some old-fashioned harassment. One had a revolver, the other a bayonet. When the pair tried to pull the beard of a man named Sam Stein, it became clear that Brooklyn had different rules. Stein fought back. The marine with the gun tried to shoot Stein but missed. The bullet shattered a shop window instead. The whole neighborhood poured onto the street, and only police intervention saved the two marines from mob justice. Afterward, they were court-martialed. There were plenty of antisemites in America, but in 1904 there was little in the way of state antisemitism. Sure, Christians attacked Jews, but those Christians might go to jail. Local newspapers gave significant space to the persecution of Jews in tsarist Russia, even as they justified or glossed over the persecution of Black people at home.

Goaded by homesickness, Sam began to draw the town he had left behind. None of these drawings survive, but based on Sam's autobiographical writings, I can guess that he drew Volkovysk with a love that was at once pagan and biblical. "The nearby little river was my Jordan. The synagogue with its cupolas was the temple that Solomon had built." These watercolors became his respite from the New York present.

SOCIALISM IN YIDDISH

It didn't take Sam long to find his people.

He had landed in the largest Jewish city on earth, home to the largest, most radical Jewish proletariat in history. "From the margins of Europe Jews had moved to the very heart of the world's new economic colossus, 'the capital of capitalism, the capital of the twentieth century, and the capital of the world,' " wrote the historian Tony Michels. By the late nineteenth century, these poor youth packed into the sweatshops of the titanic New York garment industry. Educated radicals like Mikhael Zametkin and Abraham Cahan also toiled in the shops. They had fled the police roundups that followed Tsar Alexander II's assassination in 1882 and now found themselves condemned to live as part of the masses that they preferred to fetishize from afar. Like Arkady Kremer, these radicals spoke Russian (if they knew Yiddish, they preferred to hide it), and so formed a pretentious little circle they called the Russian Colony, which devoted itself to speeches about revolution in the motherland.

Cahan and the rest of the Russian Colony might have stayed stuck in impotent nostalgia if not for encounters with their exiled German neighbors. Heirs to the most advanced socialist tradition in Europe, these Germans convinced their Jewish peers to move beyond their insular circles of declassed intellectuals and speak to the actual workers toiling alongside them, using Yiddish, the language these workers spoke. Cahan's cohort took this advice to heart, and the Russian Colony succeeded wildly. It organized trade unions, self-education societies, libraries, strikes, and boycotts. In 1886, years before Pati Kremer had started educating her small groups of workers in Vilna, a strike by New York Jews brought the entire garment industry to a halt.

The Russian Colony created the modern Yiddish press. Back in Russia, censors had permitted a single, stultifying Yiddish weekly, but in New York there were no such restrictions. The city had papers to represent every tendency, from highbrow socialism to insurrectionary anarchism to the comfortable Orthodox middle class. Inevitably, these newspapers made their way back home. In 1886, radicals shipped copies of the socialist *Folkstsaytung* to the Pale of Settlement, where it was immediately banned by tsarist censors. It didn't work. Smugglers snuck more New York Yiddish newspapers into the Pale, where revolutionaries like Arkady Kremer used them as inspiration for their own, underground Yiddish press. In 1897, the year the Bund was born, Abe Cahan launched *The Forward* in New York City. It would become America's most popular Yiddish newspaper. Like the early Bundists, Cahan was internationalist in theory. He wrote in Yiddish because Yiddish was the language that Jewish workers spoke, but he wanted to "erase all boundaries between Jew and non-Jew in the labor world." Instead, like the Bund, he ended up creating a secular, socialist, but specifically Jewish world.

By the time Sam arrived in New York, this sort of socialism was alive on every East Side street—in the mutual aid societies, debate clubs, picket lines, night schools, and the lectures that Jewish workers obsessively attended. (Utopia, for them, might have been one long lecture series.) Socialist Yiddish papers sold 120,000 copies a day. Socialism filled the mouths of the soapbox speakers at Rutgers Square, who worked their crowds like old-school village preachers, shifting from topic to topic until one caught the imagination of the exhausted humans shuffling by. Wham. Hook. Bam. Make 'em stop. Cry. Believe. On the Lower East Side, socialism meant more than Marx. It was the idiom of something broad, free, and generous—the fight for a Better and More Beautiful World. To be a socialist meant to be a human, to affirm that there was more to life than the brutish quest for coin. Back in Volkovysk, the Bundist Chaim Nemzer had helped Sam survive Bloch's leather tannery. In New York, socialism did the same for hundreds of thousands of Jews.

Dozens of strikes took place during Sam's first year in the city. There were strikes by butchers, bricklayers, elevator operators, and the kids who made boxes at Cohen's factory, during which little girls attacked child scab laborers and made hideous faces at the cops. In April 1904, on Orchard Street, a hundred asphalt workers threw rocks at scabs. In July, fifty thousand garment workers struck, with *The New York Times* remarking that the seamstresses "get into all sorts of arguments with the men strikers when they meet in the little coffee shops of Ludlow, Suffolk and Forsyth." Then, in August, forty thousand members of the Structural Building Trades Alliance unions walked off the job. Sam would have walked off too—except he wasn't in the union. The Alliance's painters' union had banned all Jews from membership.

PATI KREMER AND LIUBA LEVINSON

Naturally, all this ferment attracted Bundist visitors. In December 1903, Arkady Kremer arrived from London. Pati was already in town making arrangements. Thanks to her work, Arkady would be greeted by a rally organized by the labor lawyer Meyer London and would go on to give spare, ironic speeches at private gatherings arranged by *The Forward.* Pati saw little of the city. She may have been a revolutionary, but by now she was also the mother of a little girl named Vera. Parenthood came first. In her memoirs, she insists this was her choice, which she made despite Arkady's protests. "I will do your share of the work for our child, you do my share of the work for the party," she told him, comparing the division of labor to military discipline. Over the next eight months, Arkady met with small groups of workers while Meyer London set up the Bund's U.S. fundraising operation and Pati subsumed herself in the domestic sphere that takes so many women out of historical record, while sometimes compensating them with private joys.

That same year, another of the Bund's pioneers, the brilliant, morose Liuba Levinson, sailed for New York City, where her sister lived. Like Pati, she had her baby with her, but she lacked Pati's commitment to family life. Liuba had given birth in Siberian exile, which wrecked her health, though her nerves had been shot even earlier, as a teenager, after some unspecified incident during her imprisonment. Liuba intended to dump her baby with her sister, sneak back into Russia, and return to the revolution unencumbered. It was not to be. During the heat wave of 1903, Liuba drew herself a bath. Once in the tub, she grew dizzy. Her head slipped below the water. Liuba Levinson was thirty-seven years old when she drowned in that kitchen bathtub. She must have looked like the Ophelia of Orchard Street.

VOLKOVYSK REVOLUTIONARY UNION

On November 11, 1903, a small group of Bundist immigrants gathered in a tenement on 56 Orchard Street and founded the Volkovysk Revolutionary Union. They printed up membership cards and elected a board. They also addressed more practical matters. When a woman comrade was arrested in Berdichev, in northern Ukraine, the Volkovysk Revolutionary Union sent cash.

At some point after his arrival in New York, Sam joined the Volkovysk Revolutionary Union. It was not a powerful group, to put it kindly. They were broke young people, lost, like him, in a selfish city, struggling to support each other while they kept their connections to the past. To keep the old spirit alive, they held picnics, ran lectures, and sold tickets to the endless series of balls where the Lower East Side workers passed their time. They sent letters to Bundists back in Volkovysk to announce their endeavors and took out ads in *The Forward* when they got letters in reply. They talked big, as if to compensate for the inadequacy of their actions. From their workbenches they would free first their hometown, then Russia, then the world.

In November, the Volkovysk Revolutionary Union held a masquerade ball at New Irving Hall, with cash prizes for the best costumes. Decades later, Sam would paint himself in myriad disguises—as a pirate, as a sorceress, as Rembrandt. I wonder if the habit dated back to this event. In the one costumed photo I have of him from the era, Sam wears a tiny derby. His two friends wear top hats. They glower like vaudeville thugs. Perhaps he dressed like this when at one of the Volkovysk Revolutionary Union's masquerade balls. Once past Irving Place Theatre's Moorish doorways, the workaday world would have disappeared into a fantasia of self-creation. At a masquerade, it didn't matter how poor you were. A rag seller could be the Angel of Socialism. A pattern cutter could be a Cossack, and a factory girl an acrobat. Corsets nipped waists. Rouge brightened pallid cheeks. Someone passed out glasses of schnapps. The band played their hometown songs. Couples whirled through the violent new Bowery waltz. Like a revolution, a party is an attempt at utopia. The revolutionaries savored it. They danced long into the night.

At their tenement clubhouse, the Volkovysk Revolutionary Union devoured *Forward* articles chronicling the ferment back in Russia. They read about rebellions in Siberia, strikes in the Lena goldfields. In July 1904, they would have joined the spontaneous celebrations that broke out when a terrorist belonging to the peasant-populist Socialist Revolutionary Party killed that arch-antisemite, the minister of the interior Vyacheslav von Plehve. "Von Plehve Dead!" crowed *The Forward* in its largest typeface, so that the headline took up half the page. Abe Cahan threw a party the next day at the newspaper's office and invited readers to bring along their American friends. The East Side danced in the streets.

The Jewish Labor Bund held weekly picnics at the pleasure parks in the Glendale section of Queens, a five-cent ride on the streetcar from the Lower East Side. Jostled by beery Germans, the Bundists staked out their spot of grass and toasted the death of von Plehve. They riffed on *The Forward* headlines to one another. *The tsar's nuts! He's locked himself inside his palace!* They knocked back their beers, then sang their anthem.

Heaven and earth will hear us,
the bright stars will bear witness,
an oath of blood, an oath of tears—
We swear, we swear, we swear!

Buoyed by the lyrics, they felt their loyalty anew. Maybe the movement had seemed insignificant when they were bent over their sewing machines, but in the park, they could allow themselves to indulge in the exile's vice—the fantasy of return.

As the months passed, memories of Volkovysk dimmed beside the struggle for subsistence. Then, on the morning of January 23, 1905, Sam looked at the front page of *The Forward,* and his old home, with all its idealism and carnage, came crashing back.

A BLOODBATH.

St. Petersburg Strikers Murdered
by the Thousands . . .
Women and Children Among the Victims . . .
Bloody Revolution Breaks Out.

The Volkovysk Revolutionary Union would have scoured the papers for details of the events that would later be known as Bloody Sunday. Beyond the thrill, they must have felt the certainty that Marxism always promised. History was not merely a corpse, dissected upon the table of the academy, but a secret and mighty current whose course they too could shape. Were they not also the proletariat? For a house painter named Sam Rothbort, the revolution had finally come.

CHAPTER 6

REVOLUTIONARY PREQUEL

(January–September 1905)

BLOODY SUNDAY

VLADIMIR MEDEM WAS BLASÉ AS HE WALKED THE SWARMED STREETS of the Russian colony in Zurich, where it seemed that all of Exileland was gathered around copies of the *Neue Züricher Zeitung*. In Saint Petersburg, the paper revealed, workers had decided to take matters into their own hands.

Marxist schematics said that Russia was not ripe for revolution, Medem thought, and he had never heard of Father Gapon, the former priest who, the night before, on January 22, 1905, had led fifty thousand workers on a march toward the Winter Palace, home of Tsar Nicholas II. Gapon had advised the authorities that the march would be peaceful. Workers and their families, dressed in their Sunday best, marched with the utmost faith that the government would listen to their requests for better working conditions. They sang songs of praise to the tsar they called their Little Father. The tsar was a good man, they thought. He wanted what was best for his children.

When they approached the palace, soldiers opened fire, murdering at least 130 people within minutes. Tsar Nicholas was at his vacation palace at the time.

The workers who survived would never forget the sight of the children strewn like broken dolls over the cobblestones, the wives whose tidy, much-mended dresses bloomed with dirt and gore. The betrayal twisted within them, until it became a weapon. The next morning 160,000 Saint Petersburg workers walked out on strike.

During a lecture to student groups a few days later, Medem continued to shrug off the events. Maybe the uprising represented progress, but, as an atheist and a Marxist, he couldn't imagine a real revolution springing from the actions of a priest. Inside the empire, in the Latvian industrial city of Dvinsk, Medem's Exileland friend Raphael Abramovich saw things more accurately. Now a prominent Bundist orator, days after the massacre, he dashed off a pamphlet called *To Arms:*

> The Great Day has come! The revolution has come! . . . We will gain our freedom, or we will die! Let everyone go into the street and unfurl the red flag! Attack the stores where arms are sold! Everyone get a gun, a revolver, a sword, an ax, a knife! . . . Let every street become a battlefield! Let us give up the blood of our hearts and receive the rights of human beings!

REVOLT

The Bund's foreign committee printed two hundred thousand copies of *To Arms,* in three languages, which they then mailed to over a hundred cities inside Russia. Activists passed out the pamphlets at the birzhes, dropped them from theater balconies, and scattered them in factory courtyards where workers could find them in the morning.

Within a week, strikes wracked the Pale of Settlement, as two hundred thousand workers walked off their jobs. Whether in swish provincial capitals or muddy shtetlach, workers thronged into the streets, where Cossacks cut them down with bullets and whips. As Arkady Kremer had predicted a decade earlier in *On Agitation,* this repression was clarifying. As the dead piled up, demands quickly leapt from the economic to the political: not just a pay raise but the end of autocracy.

Even having withdrawn from the RSDLP, the Bund's thirty thousand members still made it the largest Marxist party in the empire, but as representatives of an ethnic minority, they knew they couldn't work alone. They needed to unite with their rivals. There were many to choose from around the empire. The Russian Social Democratic Labor Party, split into Menshevik and Bolshevik factions since the congress of 1903, had twelve thousand members. Latvia, Lithuania, and Ukraine each had its own social democratic party. Poland had two: the pro-independence Polish Socialist Party (PPS) and the anti-independence Social Democratic Party of the Kingdom of Poland and Lithuania (SDKPiL). With great difficulty, the Bund persuaded this alphabet soup of groups to hold a conference in Riga in February, where they agreed on a list of liberal demands including the right to vote, freedom for political prisoners, an eight-hour workday, free speech, a free press, the separation of church and state, and, the most cherished demand of revolutionaries, a freely elected constituent assembly. Without dropping their theoretical and personal disputes, the groups agreed to work together in the streets.

Here, I want to put myself into a protester's skin. The closest I've known to 1905 is the summer of 2020, after the police murdered George Floyd, when the sickly silence of lockdown New York was shattered by a mass uprising. Still, the past is a foreign country, and I need a guide. Itka, the girl who shattered a window in Sam's watercolor that so affected me as a teenager—what was she doing during the revolution's early days? Let's light a candle to her. I hold her hand as she leads me through some Pale of Settlement slum shuttered tight on the Bund's orders. We come upon a cordon of thugs in flat-caps, members of the party battle squad. Some of them have scars earned fighting pogroms. Itka nods. They let us pass. We slip into the stream. Red rags wave. Songs sound in multilingual cacophony. Everyone is here—the grandmothers, the brats from the block, the boy who called Itka a whore. Our bodies move with theirs. Our feet carry us into rich neighborhoods we never dared enter. They're ours. We float in disbelief. It happened. We broke open the world. Despite our century of distance, Itka and I share a few common experiences. We both have taken over a street and mistaken it for a country, both grabbed hands with a stranger and mistaken it for a vow. I remember the Black kids who marched into the Financial District that hot 2020 summer. They stood next to the statue of a man who owned their ancestors and said that this was their land, then danced down the steps of the New York Stock Exchange with joyous rage. The same joy and rage played out in 1905, throughout the Pale of Settlement.

KRYNKI

Three weeks after Bloody Sunday, Bundists and socialists in the Polish town of Krynki called a mass meeting in a synagogue to incite a general strike. With the 1,500 people who showed up, they proceeded to take over the city. As they marched through the city streets, police fled in their wake. The revolutionaries looted the post office and trashed the police station, destroying the records but confiscating the weapons. They poured all the liquor into the street to avoid drunken fiascos and set up armed patrols to keep order in the city. The next day, the Russian military marched in. In the melee that followed, soldiers shot forty-two workers and arrested several hundred more, but not before Bundists had sampled a drug that revolutions unreliably deliver. For twenty-four hours, they had held power, hand in hand with their Christian brother workers. They were not outsiders, nor were they victims. They were equals. The Here they had so precariously inhabited became, for a moment, home.

NEW YORK CITY

News of the Russian uprising electrified New York. Uptown, in the splendid new St. Nicholas Cathedral, the Russian Orthodox archpriest prayed for the survival of the "well-loved" tsar. The Lower East Side was a different story. *The New York Times* reported: "All the highways and byways of that crowded section of the city at once became filled with . . . a series of unbroken processions converging on the offices of the Jewish newspapers." At *The Forward*, the staff scrambled to produce bulletins of the latest information, but this only excited the crowd further. They shoved their way into the newsrooms and demanded, *now*, to know what was going on.

Meetings began that night. Sam and the rest of the Volkovysk Revolutionaries might have crowded into Clinton Hall, where delegates from the Bund's twenty-six American branches listened to the poet Morris Winchevsky read the latest dispatches. When Winchevsky told the audience that troops in several cities had refused to fire on protesters, a veteran Bundist named Jenny Horowitch dissolved into tears. "They are our brothers too! I knew it all the time!"

Revolutionaries held multiple meetings each night. Some devolved into riots. In the Brooklyn neighborhood of Brownsville, hundreds packed the American Star Hall and, to the bemusement of a *Brooklyn Daily Eagle* reporter, chanted "Hurrah for the terrorist organization."

(By this they meant the Socialist Revolutionaries, who had blown up Interior Minister von Plehve.) When the first round of fundraising proved disappointing, labor lawyer Meyer London berated the crowd. How dare they fritter away their paychecks gambling on boxing matches when a great drama was taking place back home? The time for forbearance was over. Their brothers needed arms. London demanded a week's wages from every attendee. They'd thank themselves next year when they were marching in a parade to celebrate Free Russia. The donations flowed. A local real estate developer even ponied up one hundred dollars, as long as eighty dollars went to "the terrorists."

As I read London's speech, a pair of sentences struck me.

> Are you aware that in Russian Poland, thousands of our Jewish boys and girls are giving their lives . . . for liberty? They . . . pray to God, not to lead them again out of Egypt, but to help them to free Egypt.

Egypt, the site of Jews' Old Testament enslavement, was a metaphor for tyranny, in the American South as well as Russia's Pale. In Egypt, Egyptians cracked the whips. When Moses led the Jews to the promised land, Egyptian armies pursued him, until God drowned them in the Red Sea. London's speech offered no such escape. These kids would stay and fight there, amongst the Egyptians, until they won a freedom that encompassed even their oppressors.

DVINSK

On February 15, on the other side of the world, twenty Bundists gathered in Dvinsk, where the central committee had set up its secret headquarters inside a covertly rented apartment. The delegates analyzed the course and future of the uprising. How could they turn an outburst into a revolution? They planned more strikes and protests, guarded by workers organized into battle squads. They discussed how to deal with their newfound financial bounty: a Friends of the Bund branch in New York had raised a thousand dollars, the equivalent of twenty-four thousand dollars in today's money. This cash would be sent to Belgium, where comrades would acquire pistols that young women would then smuggle into the Pale, border guards being less suspicious of girls. Inside the empire, legions of small-town chemistry students turned themselves into bomb makers—"Nobels," in party slang. In his memoirs, Abramovich recalled a shtetl rabbi who proudly presented the central committee with his homemade hand grenades.

Despite their skill with weapons trafficking, the Bundists knew that armed civilians were no match for the power of a state. They pinned their hopes on the army, which was comprised of conscripts, and already demoralized from the wretched war with Japan. To win over the troops, thousands of Bundist pamphlets found their way into soldiers' barracks, where they were hidden in toilets, or left at canteen samovars. All had the same message: Shoot your officers. Protect the people. Join us.

"Patrol!" the lookout screamed. The delegates inside the Dvinsk apartment shoved their notes into the oven. Just before lighting the match, they realized it was a false alarm. The police were on the hunt for an illegal liquor distillery in the building's basement. Finding nothing, they trotted past their actual enemies.

MARTYRS

Arkady Kremer missed the Bund's conference in Dvinsk, but he was likely there two weeks later when the party proclaimed a general strike, one of hundreds they would call in the coming months. Over the next five days, mobs of mostly Jewish workers shuttered the factories, then battled the cops their bosses called for help. When soldiers cordoned off the city center, three thousand Jewish and Christian workers, marching beneath the red Bundist banners of revolution, tried to force their way past the wall of bayonets. The bayonet blades slashed at workers' flesh, and the workers responded with rocks, sticks, and fists. Young Bundist men fired from the courtyards, disappeared into tenements, then fired again from the balconies. Within days, one Dvinsk resident in five was in the streets. When soldiers shot a teenage worker named Aba Reich in the clashes, protesters carried him to the cemetery on their shoulders. A young girl waved his bloody shirt like a flag.

Reich's death couldn't go unanswered. By the end of March, a growing number of police officials would be gunned down by Bundist battle squads, or dispatched by clever little explosives, nicknamed "matzoh balls," hurled by guys who turned up later in Brooklyn under unassuming American names. Aba Reich was neither the first nor the last protester killed in 1905. Martyrs need funerals, and funerals become protests, which produce more martyrs, more vengeance, more state retaliation, more martyrs again.

PATI KREMER

Pati had spent the first months of the revolution in Vilna, under police surveillance, raising her daughter, Vera, alone. She seized a brief break between protests to smuggle herself and her child to Dvinsk, where Arkady toiled on the central committee. It had been fifteen years since Pati's first arrest. In that decade and a half of poverty and exile, she and Arkady had been apart more often than they had been together, but she never wavered from their path. They had aged. Pati was thin and dry, Arkady mustachioed and stout. As she watched him hug their child, she was filled with a terrible tenderness. He was the same boy she had discovered in the attic on Zavalne Street, marooned amongst his thoughts. Was she marooned in him? Pati's memoirs say little of the cities beyond their apartment, where the seeds that they had once so quixotically planted had at last burst into bloom.

NEW YORK

I know just as little about Sam's thoughts during this revolutionary year. He painted walls. The white lead got in his mouth, into the corners of his eyes. It mingled with his sweat. On the scaffolding, his head reeled. He choked down the vomit, then steadied himself. He went on. After work, he drank a beer in the tenement at 56 Orchard Street where the Volkovysk Revolutionary Union met. Perhaps they had a letter from home. From Moishe Katriel, Beyle Rivkah, Chaim Nemzer. Whoever it was, the revolutionaries tore open the note. Thrilling tales came from their no-longer-sleepy hometown, about smuggled guns and mutinous soldiers in the local garrison, where officers had ordered five men shot for insubordination. After these executions, the Volkovysk Revolutionary Union held a special meeting, with a fifty-cent fine for not attending.

SOLIDARITY

From the uprising's first days, the Russian government sought to make the word *Jew* synonymous with *revolutionary*. Undercover agents circulated pamphlets that called for genocide, and police spread rumors that Jews would torch the churches, believers inside, then launch the "kike revolution" for their "kike kingdom"—to use the authorities' words.

Their efforts were augmented by nearly two hundred far-right groups who bore the collective nickname the Black Hundreds. With their secretive membership, government connections, and flagrant murders of ethnic minorities, the Black Hundreds came to resemble a Russian version of the KKK. Cops and Hundreds worked hand in hand, while unaffiliated racists—whether criminals, peasants, or college kids—were always available to help.

Though they liked their guns, the Bundists believed that solidarity was their greatest weapon. If they liberated Egypt alongside the Egyptians, they wouldn't need to flee across the sea. Bundists raised strike funds for Christian workers and loaned them their printing presses. In the Grodno, they led strikes amongst Christian brick workers. In Riga, they organized draft riots. In Ukraine, they created parallel organizations. In the tsarist empire's rural Belarusian borderlands, they worked with local peasant groups to publish pamphlets that described how the peasants' true enemies, "the military, the rich, and the uncaring regime," used Jews as their scapegoat.

LODZ

This solidarity reached its apex in industrial Lodz, the tsarist empire's answer to Manchester. In mills that resembled miniature cities, a multiethnic workforce of Poles, Russians, Germans and Jews wove textiles for industrial barons like Izrael Poznanski, who constructed neoclassical palaces with the profits.

The Russo-Japanese war was wrecking the Lodz economy, and after strikes broke out at Grohman's textile factory on May 16, 1905, Cossacks shot three workers. Fifty thousand people attended their funeral. The cycle was set into motion.

It was a fifteen-minute walk from Grohman's factory to Wschodnia Street, the Bundist birzhe. For years, Wschodnia Street had come alive each Saturday at sunset when members of the Little Bund, the party's unauthorized kiddie affiliate, came out to play. Despite the prohibitions of older activists, these preteen hellions organized themselves into a Little Rascals–style gang with socialist trappings. They walked out of cheder, smashed bosses' windows, bullied Zionist youth groups, and paraded with sticks they held like guns.

On May 27, the conflict escalated when the police turned their attention to Wschodnia Street and to the Little Bund, which was enjoying their weekly parade. Cops stormed into the crowd of kids, swinging their clubs and, eventually, shooting their pistols. The bullets found their marks. Two little boys fell to the pavement, blood gushing from their shocked mouths. Impatient to leave, an officer kicked another boy. His boot shattered the child's fragile ribs, puncturing his lung. The child died in the gutter.

The Bund organized a funeral for the murdered children. The victims' ragged friends led ten thousand workers toward the cemetery. The marchers were Polish, German, Jewish, but it didn't matter. As James

Baldwin wrote, "The children are always ours, every single one of them, all over the globe."

BY MAY 30, THIRTY-FIVE thousand people were out on strike. Crowds wandered the city, red flags in hand, until police dispersed them. Once night fell, cops retreated to their stations, and the workers ruled the streets.

On June 18, the Bund and Lodz's two Polish socialist parties hosted a joint picnic in the nearby forest. Thousands of Jewish and Polish workers came. They spent the afternoon drinking booze and listening to rabble-rousers, so when they marched back to town, they were high on the idea of their own power. On Lagiewnicka Street, they ran into an army detachment. Someone shot a pistol—each side blamed the other—and by the time the chaos stopped, five Polish and Jewish protesters were dead.

Troops took the protesters' corpses to the gray stone monolith of Poznanski Hospital. Crowds gathered outside the iron gates. Within a few hours, orderlies brought out the shrouded corpses of the Polish victims. Workers carried their bodies to the Catholic cemetery and buried them in the black summer earth, without a single cop daring to make a peep. The Jewish bodies remained inside Poznanski Hospital.

The sun set. Outside the hospital, the crowds muttered darkly about the delay. The Poles had already buried their people. Why was the hospital holding onto the corpses of the Jewish victims? Jews and Poles waited together till dawn. At sunrise, their patience broke. They stormed the hospital, only to find the bodies gone. Police had smuggled their dead friends through a side door and buried them in secret graves. The crowd would not even be permitted the opportunity to grieve.

From the hospital, the crowd marched toward Piotrkowska Street in fury. Soon, they were fifty thousand strong. Fortified by looted liquor, they shouted slogans against tyranny and belted out banned subversive ballads. Sympathizers flew revolutionary banners from the windows. Terrified cops fled their posts, but the protesters pursued them. Crowds crammed into Old Market Square, beneath the Andalusian arches of the Old Synagogue. Speakers from each party climbed atop boxes and hollered out paeans to the workers' bravery. They'd kicked out the cops. They'd seized the streets. Next, they'd seize the world.

The workers lingered for an hour, cheering the speakers, growing braver from one another's chants. At nine in the evening, they reformed into a protest line and began to march down Glowna Street. "Down with despotism," they shouted. Without warning, Cossacks rode in from the side streets, firing volleys of bullets into the crowd. Hundreds screamed as the bullets entered bellies, knees, shoulders. Eighteen workers fell down dead. The panicked crowd scattered, leaving the victims behind.

The next morning, workers began building barricades on the Bundist birzhes on Wschodnia and Poludniowe streets, under the leadership of the twenty-two-year-old Virgil Kahan. They used trash cans, overturned wagons, poles, girders, sand barrels, signboards, cobblestones, lashed together with telegraph wire. The three parties proclaimed a general strike. "The fury of the mob found full vent, and even children, caught by the contagion, were . . . heard swearing they were ready to die for liberty," reported *The New York Times*. In Old Market Square, a Bundist girl mounted a crate to address the people. A police sniper eyed her, aimed, then pulled the trigger. Her head snapped back. Blood poured from her shattered skull.

From there, the rebellion exploded too quickly for any party to claim it as their own. For a few heady days, Lodz belonged to its multiethnic working class, united across race and ideology.

Dozens of infantry battalions marched into Lodz. On shuttered streets, the clip-clop of Cossack ponies mixed with rebel rifle fire, directed at anyone foolish enough to break the strike. "Every alley must be a fortress," read one Bundist broadsheet. "You must shower bullets on the servants of tyranny from every rooftop, balcony and window." Workers stripped guns from the bodies of dead soldiers. They threw sulfuric acid, petrol bombs, and rocks. Barricades spread from Jewish neighborhoods to the Polish and German ones, until they had cut off a hundred streets. Beneath constant gunfire, government sappers blew up the barricades. Once a barricade fell, Cossacks invaded, to steal and murder as they pleased; witnesses watched them snatch baubles from dead women's necks. In Baluty, the workers' neighborhood, Cossacks gunned down an entire Jewish family as they attempted to catch a train out of town. Later that day, revolutionaries threw a bomb into the Cossacks' barracks.

Prominent citizens begged the governor general for protection. On June 26, Lodz came under martial law. The prisons overflowed with Jewish socialists. Over eight days, authorities killed 561 people to put down the rebellion. Most of them were Jews.

ODESA

Rebellion was spreading across the empire, and the Bund followed its currents. That summer, the party sent their top orator, Anna Lipshitz, south to Odesa, the empire's fourth largest city, to win converts. A corrupt, cosmopolitan boomtown lounging on the Black Sea, Odesa lured ambitious poor from throughout the empire, especially from the Pale of Settlement. But bosses paid low and played rough; when girls in Popov's factory went on strike in 1902, police broke down the doors of their apartments and dragged them back to work by their hair. No wonder the city was on edge.

Lipshitz, who traveled under the false name Maryushka, was only twenty-two. She was literary and romantic, to the point that fellow revolutionaries chided her for her decadent tastes. She was tiny, with massive black eyes and a long nose that a male comrade mentioned unkindly in his memoirs. But even he had to admit that she was the best speaker of their group. Lipshitz was a born street orator. Her sister Esther had been tortured to death by the police, and this loss must have given her words an extra weight.

She came at the right time. In early June, workers in the Peresyp industrial district planned a general strike. After informants tipped off the police, the government ordered a clampdown. On June 13, protesters gathered at Henn's factory. Cossacks fired into the crowd. When the news spread, workers across Odesa walked off their jobs.

Soon, to move between neighborhoods, Anna would have had to weave around overturned tramcars and slip behind barricades jerry-rigged from telephone poles, all while teen girls hurled cobblestones at Cossack patrols. She would have witnessed the beatings of police officers who strayed from their units and likely heard the explosion of anarchist bombs. It must have thrilled her. This moment was meant to be hers.

On June 15, in the opal hour before sunrise, Anna Lipshitz heard the news, alongside the rest of the city. A battleship named *Potemkin* had just dropped anchor in Odesa's port. It was flying a red flag.

Hoarse, bleary, her dress stiff with dried sweat, Lipshitz would have pulled herself off the floor of her safe house and joined the crowds clambering toward the port. The ship gleamed like a dream.

About a week earlier, a *Potemkin* sailor named Vakulenchuk had protested the maggoty meat that the crew received for rations. When officers executed him, it triggered a mutiny. Sailors shot the captain, threw a few officers overboard, locked the rest below deck, and seized control of the ship. They sailed for Odesa, where they hoped to contact local revolutionaries while waiting for other ships in the Black Sea Fleet to join them.

The sailors had deposited Vakulenchuk's body on a pier. A sign on his chest explained he had been killed over wormy meat. Crowds knelt before the dead man, kissing his hands, surrounding him with flowers.

Lipshitz would have seen the battleship towering above this tableau of Christian reverence: its hull armored with Krupp cement, the twin gun turrets on its fore and aft, the sixteen quick-firing guns in casements, the four Hotchkiss guns—all pointed at the city. Here was a tool of violence—modern and powerful. For the first time, it was on her side.

The *Potemkin* sailors warned Odesa's authorities that their battleship would bombard the city if they interfered with the protests, so cops and military kept their distance from the port. Thus protected, every revolutionary party called its people down. Lipshitz mounted the Bund's platform. Beneath a black banner that read HONOR THE FALLEN COMRADES, she began to speak. Her words have been lost, but they must have been powerful; newspapers nicknamed her the Fury.

As Lipshitz inflamed the crowds, two Mensheviks and a Bundist rowed out to the *Potemkin* to try to persuade the sailors to lead an uprising. They just had to come ashore, distribute guns, seize the city's arsenal, and call on the restive Odesa garrison to side with them. If they did, one of the empire's largest cities would be theirs. This was their moment, the Menshevik Constantine Feldmann shouted, his voice hoarse from overuse. They just had to seize it.

Irresolute and impressionable, the *Potemkin*'s crew rejected his proposal. They wanted to wait for the rest of the Black Sea Fleet to mutiny. They believed that time was on their side.

Tens of thousands of people wandered on the wooden boardwalk of the port beside the sea. There were many speakers, but accounts paint Anna Lipshitz as their queen. In his book on the events of 1905 in Odesa, historian Robert Weinberg sketches the following story. An undercover cop tried to heckle a Bundist woman speaker. He called her a kike, thinking that would turn the audience against her. Instead, the woman incited the crowd against the provocateur, until they set upon him and smashed his skull.

The woman is not identified in Weinberg's text, but the moment is shown in Sergei Eisenstein's pioneering silent film, *Battleship Potemkin*. His script identifies the orator as a "Bundist," and for her party comrades who saw the film, she was unmistakably Anna Lipshitz.

By afternoon, people started to loot the harbor's warehouses. Soon the kegs were freed. Pricey wine burned mouths that had never tasted the like before and would never taste it again. Revelers drank all they could, then hauled the rest to the city center. The looting wasn't universal. One sailor pleaded, "We need freedom, not vodka." Some workers guarded the warehouses. Others threw the kegs into the sea, shouting curses at the alcohol whose convenient appearance would derail so many revolutionary moments. But few listened.

No one knows who started the fires, but they spread quickly, since Odesa's warehouses were built from wood. Soon, flames were everywhere, eating the loot, the port, and its people. Blinded by smoke, the revelers tried to escape the port, but it had been cordoned off by the military in an attempt to contain the day's disorders, and those whom the fire spared, the soldiers didn't. Nearly 1,300 people died that night. The crew of the battleship *Potemkin* watched it all, unable or unwilling to help.

The next afternoon in Odesa's ruined port, the bodies lay swelling in the summer heat. The whole city was rotten with fear. Soldiers attacked a funeral procession to bury the now putrid corpse of Vakulenchuk, the *Potemkin*'s martyr. Worried when their crewmates didn't return on time from the funeral, the *Potemkin* finally fired on the city. They aimed for the opera house, where officers were meeting, but the gunner deliberately missed. Like many of his fellow sailors, the previous night had convinced him that revolution was less seductive in practice. Two days later, the battleship *Potemkin* abandoned Odesa, having failed to either spark a mutiny or protect an uprising. After months of wandering, it finally surrendered in Romania.

As in Lodz, tsarist officials blamed the whole Odesa business on the Jews.

CHAPTER 7

REACTION

(October 1905–January 1906)

ZURICH

THE TROUBLE IN ODESA NOTWITHSTANDING, BY AUTUMN, THE BUND HAD achieved some of its most cherished goals. On the Lodz barricades, they had proven themselves as fighters against the empire. Through their battle squads, they had shown they could defend their people. Above all, they had changed how Jews saw themselves. For centuries, Jews had cowered before the representatives of tsarist power. Now they stood upright as armed, equal citizens of the land. The Pale became the Bund's kingdom. As Raphael Abramovich traveled from town to town, he felt like the ambassador of a great power.

At the beginning of October, Medem awaited Abramovich's arrival in Zurich. For months, he and the rest of the Bund's foreign committee had been preparing for the sixth party congress—a momentous occasion in these revolutionary times—and at last they had succeeded in smuggling most of their leaders over the border. But just as the Bund's top leaders had crossed into Switzerland, papers arrived from Russia with news that a massive general strike was underway.

It had started in Saint Petersburg, when the printers' union went on strike for higher wages. The railway and telegraph workers joined, bringing transport and communications to a halt. Soon, millions of workers had walked off their jobs, and the dead could not be buried due to lack of undertakers. All of this was being organized by soviets—committees of factory workers, union leaders, and delegates from revolutionary groups that had sprung up in cities across the empire.

This was not the time to have a party congress, but what could the Bundists do? They were stuck in Switzerland. With telegrams from Russia cut off, they had no real knowledge of the situation on the ground. Separated from the revolution to which they devoted their lives, they decided to pretend that nothing had changed. The revolutionaries would not discuss the tumult in Russia but instead slogged through a list of topics that grew less relevant by the hour. Who cared about theoretical questions of school autonomy when, back home, the workers ran the cities, when activists from the factory committees traveled the empire on locomotives with red flags?

Resentful and on edge, the Bundists debated, but the words did nothing to still their anxiety. One night, Medem sat down at the piano to play the party anthems. They sang the words from memory.

Heaven and earth will hear us,
the bright stars will bear witness,
an oath of blood, an oath of tears—
We swear, we swear, we swear!

For years, the Bundists had considered Jewish workers the avant-garde of revolution in backward Russia. Now it was reversed. Seemingly in a day, the revolution had moved out of the Bund's borderlands to Saint Petersburg and Moscow, great cities that banned most Jews from residence, and to the trains and telegraphs, vital infrastructure where Jews were not permitted to work. "When strikes involve millions of workers; when the movement has pulled warships into its wake—what significance does your Bund have with its handful of would-be 'proletarians'? It's all so small, so pathetic and wretched," says a young revolutionary in S. An-sky's 1907 novella *In Shtrom*. History was being made, and as the party of the Jewish working class, the Bund was condemned to the periphery, just like the men and women it represented.

BLOOD ON THE PAVEMENT

The tsar's ministers could ignore many things, but not the economic paralysis of the empire. After four days of general strike, the technocratic minister of finance, Count Sergei Witte, convinced Tsar Nicholas II to offer meager concessions in the form of his October Manifesto. In it, the tsar legalized several political parties, made it easier to publish a newspaper, and established a duma, or elected legislature, with paltry powers. The manifesto's importance came from the fact the tsar had offered it against his will. The revolution had forced the absolute autocrat to acknowledge his people. The palace published the manifesto on October 17.

In Exileland, Bundists celebrated the manifesto as a victory. "A mighty new crack . . . has shaken the rotting edifice of the autocracy to its foundations. . . . The proletariat showed that a general uprising is not a dream but a reality." But even as they tried to grapple with the implications of the new political freedoms now on offer, terrifying telegrams began to arrive from home.

Within hours of the manifesto's publication, street celebrations turned to horror as police opened fire on protesters in cities around the empire. Their whips slashed protesters' faces. Their truncheons broke protesters' bones. Police gunned down protesters in Saint Petersburg and Warsaw and Minsk. Even Volkovysk got a martyr, a Bundist named Yossel the Guts. The party called for a funeral parade. Sam's hoodlum friends hoisted Yossel's body on their shoulders and walked silently down shuttered Broad Street, behind the black and red flags that Beyle Rivkah had sewn. It felt like all Volkovysk was behind them. The cell's leader, baby-faced Yudel Likovsky, spoke at the cemetery. Though his words have been lost to time, the impression they made lingered in the town's memory long after the facts of Yossel's death had been forgotten.

From there, news got worse. Over twelve days, pogroms broke out in 690 towns and cities across the Russian Empire, as supporters of the tsar took out their anger and confusion on the Jews. Medem read the telegrams, and he imagined blood rising like a tidal wave, carrying away his beloved streets.

Pogrom is a vague word, so let's describe specifics. In less than two weeks, in nearly seven hundred places, humans—formerly complex individuals, but now uninhibited members of a mob—invaded the homes of their Jewish neighbors, ignored their appeals to sentiment or shared history, and gleefully beat them to death. They cut open the bellies of old men and stuffed them with the feathers from their goose-down comforters. Swollen with booze, righteous with reactionary politics, they raped teenage girls, then threw them out windows. When Jewish families offered them bribes in exchange for their lives, they laughed, took the money, and killed them anyway. Police only encouraged the attackers.

Jews who survived pogroms seldom did so unscathed. They lost legs, eyes, life savings, parents, sweethearts, sanity, and above all, the belief that the towns where their families had lived for centuries had ever been their homes.

In Odesa, the pogrom began on October 18. Young radicals had gathered in the dusty streets of the city's Jewish Moldavanka district to celebrate the October Manifesto. They waved red flags and carried desecrated portraits of the tsar. High on unexpected victory, the radicals passed a group of Russian workers. One of the radicals demanded the Russians remove their hats.

The two groups began to brawl. Soon an ethnic riot engulfed the

Moldavanka. Christians looted Jewish shops and attacked Jewish passersby, some of whom fought back. By the end of the night, four Christians and an unknown number of Jews were dead.

The next day, Odesa conservatives called a patriotic demonstration in support of the tsar. Toward the end of the march, gunfire broke out. No one can agree on where the bullets came from, though two eyewitnesses later testified that they saw some demonstrators fire into the air. It didn't really matter. Self-defense fighters, who had been hiding on rooftops to protect Jews from another pogrom, thought they were under attack and showered the nationalist crowd with homemade bombs. The marchers headed to the Moldavanka shouting, "Death to kikes."

For four days, Christian Odesa pillaged Jewish Odesa in a festival of destruction helped by the smirking indifference of the state. City Governor Dimitri Niedhardt even told a delegation of Jewish leaders that since they had wanted "freedom," this was the freedom they were going to get. Pogromists murdered Jews with sadistic hysteria. According to historian Robert Weinberg, one girl watched as a "neat, delicate" youth of her acquaintance was dragged from their hiding place and had his skull smashed in with a table leg. Just like lynchings in the American South, pogroms were family affairs. Blood-smeared Russian mothers loaded their pushcarts with the spoils from looted Jewish houses, then had their kids torch the homes behind them as they left.

Jews and socialists fought back as best they could. The Bundist self-defense militia, led by a self-possessed young woman named Nadezhda Grinfeld, battled the mobs, dragging captive pogromists back to the university, where law students did interrogations. But despite their bravery, these militias were outnumbered and outgunned—especially since both police and soldiers helped their attackers. Within a day they had been overcome, and Grinfeld had a bullet in her leg. Twenty-two Bundists died fighting the mobs.

By October 22, pogromists had murdered eight hundred Odesa Jews, and left perhaps a hundred thousand more homeless.

While mob violence can only happen if enough people are prepared to kill their neighbors, most Jews thought the real culprit was the state. In 1904, the Bund had written that "pogroms exist only where the government wants them," and the events of 1905 proved them right. Pogromists rampaged under police protection. Police and conservative journalists had blamed Jews for Russia's military defeats, so troops fresh from Japan—the same soldiers the Bund had put their faith in—joined the murders.

Then there were the multitudinous Black Hundreds groups, the most famous of which was the Union of the Russian People. Founded by physician Alexander Dubrovin and boasting three hundred thousand members, the union was Europe's first fascist political party. Believers in a pure Russian empire helmed by an omnipotent Russian tsar, the union denounced Jews in genocidal terms as "the root of all evil," who should be wiped from the face of the earth. The union played a key role in Odesa's mass murders.

Tsar Nicholas II might not have planned pogroms himself, but he adored Dubrovin's pogromists. He sported the union badge at events and hosted Dubrovin's friends at his vacation palace in Tsarskoye Selo. He personally pardoned every Dubrovin follower that his courts managed to convict. A few days after the Odesa pogroms, Nicholas wrote to his mother that, since "nine-tenths of the revolutionaries [were] Jews," Jews had brought the pogroms upon themselves. He even telegrammed Dubrovin to thank him for his service.

All this would have seemed familiar to anyone who had watched the local sheriff put on a Klan hood in the American South, so it's not surprising that in the early years of the twentieth century, America's preeminent Black newspaper, *The New York Age,* devoted significant column space to attacks on Russia's Jews. By the winter of 1905, it was running nearly a condemnation a week.

On November 23: "The Jewish people have been persecuted more than any other people since the crucifixion of Jesus Christ. . . . Our sympathies are with the persecuted of all races and lands."

On November 30, they decried the fact that "no nation has yet interfered on behalf of Odessa's butchered thousands."

One December 7, they wrote: "The civilized world has never witnessed anything quite so horrible as the massacres of Jews, which are daily taking place in Russia. With the Ku Kluxism, peonage and chain-gang systems in the South, we have believed that the American negro endured the hardest lot of all mankind. We must revise our judgement."

These are generous statements from people facing similar attacks in the blood-soaked turn of the century. Oppressed themselves, the *Age*'s writers sought solidarity with oppressed people elsewhere. Though I do not believe that oppression gives anyone the power of prophecy, it can sharpen analysis, leading to predictions more astute than anything put out by comfortable columnists at *The New York Times.* "The crime of the century is being committed in Russia," the *Age* wrote at the end of 1905, by which point thousands of Jews had been murdered. "According to the inexorable law of compensation, it must be paid for in years to come at a terrible price."

SAINT PETERSBURG

Always one to seize a moment, Trotsky had smuggled himself back into Russia not long after Bloody Sunday and wasted no time transforming himself into a star. Living under a fake name, with old arrest warrants hanging over his head, Trotsky swaggered through the capital, conscious of the role he would play in the drama around him. Trotsky had broken with Lenin during the tumultuous second RSDLP congress of 1903, but he soon split as well from Julius Martov's Mensheviks, who dominated the Saint Petersburg Soviet, the revolution's organizing body in the capital. He was now a party of one. Words were the source of Trotsky's power. He churned out pamphlets and spoke constantly, to every sort of audience, honing his rhetoric and switching his codes. With the soldiers he talked as brashly and simply as they did. Amongst the beau monde, no radical was more chic.

If Medem had turned his back on a posh upbringing to devote his life to a small and persecuted people, Trotsky took a different tack. For him, there were no people, and no nations. His loyalty was to history, and his stage was the entire world. Wildly arrogant, indifferent to identity, impervious to fear, Trotsky rushed to wherever the action was happening, and he spoke to the largest crowd he could, in whatever terms it took to move them. You can see the results. On October 17, the day of the Manifesto, Medem was stuck in Exileland, playing the Bund's anthem on the piano of Café Terese. Trotsky was at a Saint Petersburg demonstration, with hundreds of thousands of protesters at his feet. He knew exactly what to say.

He warned them not to trust this moment. The tsar had granted them nothing. They, the workers, had taken their rights by force, and so could rely only on their own strength to protect them. The manifesto was just a piece of paper, Trotsky said. He took out a copy and dramatically tore it to shreds.

DVINSK

After the October Manifesto was announced, the Saint Petersburg Soviet told the unions to end their general strike. With rail service resumed, the Bundists cut their conference short and boarded trains packed with political exiles headed toward Russia. Raphael Abramovich set off for the Saint Petersburg Soviet, where he would serve as the Bund's delegate. The party sent Medem to Dvinsk, where the Bund had its headquarters. From there, leaders would assign him to where he was needed.

Before Medem caught his train to Dvinsk, he sat in his rented room and burned letters from the last four years. Silently, he said goodbye to Exileland. He imagined the lakes, the snow-covered trees of Berne, the nights in London, Brussels, Paris, Amsterdam, and Berlin. Maybe he thought of the girl from summer. She was a medical student, a comrade. For her, he was a god. For him, she was just a fling. She'd gotten pregnant. He didn't want a baby. She decided to give birth anyway. Did this weigh on his decision to leave? One by one, he consigned each letter to the fireplace. He wouldn't need them where he was going.

In late November, Medem and his comrade Vladimir Kossovsky stopped by the Bund's office in Geneva to grab fake passports and pistols that they barely knew how to shoot. Disguised in derby hats and fancy suits, they arrived at the Russian border on November 27. When they switched trains, Medem noticed how shabby the Russian cars were compared to the German ones. He settled into his seat and tried to sleep. In the next compartment, two military officers ranted about the kikes. He shut his eyes, but "the constant return of the angry hissing of the malicious word. Kike. Kike Kike" kept him awake until the train arrived in Dvinsk. Kossovsky and Medem stepped out into the mud of the provincial city. They stumbled through the rundown streets until they spotted a particular door. They knocked. An eye appeared in the peephole. Medem whispered two Hebrew words, "Gam tsu," that formed the first half of a passphrase. "Le'tovah," the man on the other side responded, completing the sentence. *This too is for the best.* The door opened. His friends embraced him.

When Medem walked through Dvinsk, all he could think about was a past visit to Berlin. Memories of those grand boulevards only emphasized the poverty of the present. Why had he come back? Between shabby houses, a band of Jewish children play-acted revolution. They marched in ranks and shouted "hurrah," then broke into a run, as if fleeing from the cops. On the next block, a Zionist speaker harangued a crowd. "Proletarianization! Emigration! Colonization!" "Silly boys," Medem's companion smirked. When Medem returned to his hotel that night, the streetlights were all broken. He remembered the pogroms and felt grateful for the gun in his pocket.

VILNA

A few weeks later, the party assigned Medem to Vilna.

In the winding stone streets of the Jerusalem of Lithuania, the Bund seemed to run the show. This was due to a twenty-seven-year-old playwright named A. Vayter, the head of the local self-defense squad. After cops gunned down protesters in early October, Vayter had refused to be cowed. He demanded the city remove police from the route of the funeral procession. For reasons lost to history, they agreed. The next day, thousands of Jews and Christians marched behind Vayter to the cemetery, their silence more threatening than any chant. Not a single cop dared to show his face along the way. From then on, cops hid in their stations, leaving security to Vayter.

Walking down the street on his first day in Vilna, Medem heard someone shout his name, in flagrant violation of conspiratorial protocol. He forced himself not to turn. Out of the corner of his eye, he saw a student who'd attended one of his speeches back in Switzerland. "Medem!" hollered another voice, then another. How did so many people know who he was? He tried to ignore them, but soon the calls overwhelmed him, and his fans bore him to the Bund's office, where the secretary was so busy signing up new members that he barely had time to mutter hello. Medem embraced old friends. His doubts faded. Of course he was right to come back.

The savagery of tsarist repression hadn't dimmed the revolutionary fervor of the streets. Radicals had seen, and sacrificed, too much. They had experienced the spontaneous brotherhood of barricade fights. They had seized neighborhoods—even whole towns, like Krynki. They had wrung concessions from a monarch who thought himself appointed by God. They had also watched their friends bleed out from gunshot wounds and didn't want to imagine those deaths had been in vain. They told themselves that the massacres were merely the system's death spasms. They just needed to keep struggling and, inevitably, they would triumph.

Vilna's old city functioned as a temporary autonomous zone, and those of us who have known such zones can still feel their magic at the distance of a century.

In 2011, the anticapitalist protesters of Occupy Wall Street set up camp in downtown Manhattan, a block from my apartment. They turned a sterile concrete square into a mini city, complete with a gourmet kitchen, a library, even a table to get free hand-rolled cigarettes. Occupy's wild generosity was meant to prefigure a different world. For fifty-nine days, the square evolved into a stage for art projects, theoretical experiments, lunatic feuds, moments of failure and grace, until police batons drove us out. After the mayor destroyed the Occupy encampment, the city scrubbed off every trace of us, as if soaping out the mouth of a defiant child. It wasn't just our ideas, which were a mixed bag at best. They hated us because we had claimed the streets as ours.

The anarchists who founded Occupy hobbled it with a cumbersome form of direct democracy in which anyone could veto any proposal (a method that favored its most bumptious participants). The Bundists, however, were comfortable wielding power over neighborhoods they controlled. In cities throughout the Pale, they levied taxes and used the money to fund soup kitchens for strikers. They forced bosses to close early, creating an eight-hour day in practice where it didn't yet exist in law. In many towns, the mere mention of the Bund's name was enough to make an employer fold. In their birzhes, Bundists set up courts that took over the roles once played by rabbis; they mediated business disputes and ruled on broken engagements. When streets were too small, they commandeered the synagogues. They bolted the doors, elbowed their way to the front, and spoke to their captive audience. Who would stop them?

Medem savored his first days in Vilna. He would stride into the Intellectuals' Club on Gedimino Avenue, the unofficial headquarters from which the Bund ruled the city, and watch the urgent debates, the writers pounding out proclamations. He visited the secret apartment where the Bund's provincial representatives met. He'd cross the courtyard of some nondescript tenement, climb a harrowing staircase, and walk into a room filled with people clamoring, arguing, demanding a fake name, a fake passport, justice for a failed romance. Conversation stopped when Medem entered. Some of the guests had seen him in the student clubs in Exileland. Others had heard his story. Here he was in the flesh, a blond and elegant young man, baptized as a Christian, who could have done anything but chose to live as a member of the oppressed.

A few days after his arrival, Medem's comrades took him to the circus grounds, the same place where, two years prior, Hirsh Lekert had tried to shoot Governor von Wahl. Medem climbed the rickety stage, looked at the thousands of faces gathered beneath him, and gave his first public speech inside the Russian Empire. Afterward, the gang ambled over to the theater. Before the curtain went up, the audience demanded the orchestra play "The Marseillaise." When it finished, they demanded an encore, then another. To hell with the play, Medem thought. Our revolution is still alive.

AUTUMN

The Bund's fervid activity in the Pale soon compelled Abramovich to leave Saint Petersburg, ceding his spot on the soviet to Mark Liber, and join Medem in Vilna. Together, the two friends set up the Russian-language journal they'd imagined back in Zurich, but as the days grew colder, they began to notice a change in Vilna's mood. The air felt raw, ugly. Cops returned to the streets. There was no question of Medem speaking at the circus where he had made his triumphant homecoming address; police had padlocked the building.

The Bund planned street demonstrations against the tsar. Expecting bloodshed, they set up first-aid stations for their protesters. When he went outside, Medem carried a pistol. He and Abramovich made regular trips to the railway station, awaiting the arrival of newspapers from the capital. Every issue brought worse news. Even Medem's landlord was getting nervous. He pleaded with his tenant, "When the moment comes for new 'events' to break, let me know, so I can hide myself abroad."

In the papers, Medem learned of strikes and more strikes, each of which only impoverished workers further. In the wake of the October Manifesto, the revolution's supports started to fragment as middle-class liberals peeled away, satisfied with the new rights promised to them. The Saint Petersburg Soviet organized a worker's militia to protect workers from the police. The Bund's self-defense squads drilled to defend their communities from pogroms.

By November 22, the authorities had had enough. That day, police arrested the soviet's ostensible leader, leaving Trotsky in charge. On December 2, the soviet issued a financial manifesto, urging everyone to withdraw their money from banks and refuse to pay taxes, to starve the tsar of the cash he needed to buy guns. The next day, soldiers stormed the soviet's headquarters at the Technological Institute. When they entered the soviet's meeting room, Trotsky coolly scolded them for their interruption. He declared the session closed, as was his prerogative, then allowed himself to be arrested with a smile. In the wake of this news, Medem advised his landlord to flee.

ODESA

The arrests in Saint Petersburg infuriated revolutionaries across the empire. In response, the Moscow Soviet called for a general strike. Within ten days, thousands of armed Moscow workers took to the barricades.

"This time we're not alone," read one pamphlet issued by the Bund, with an optimism verging on delusion. "The army is not against the people. . . . Whole battalions and regiments are aligned with us."

The Odesa Soviet planned a solidarity strike for the Moscow uprising, and the party dispatched Medem to the city. He found Odesa's grand avenues hostile, its people still reeling from the pogroms that had left eight hundred dead. At the Bund's canteen, Medem's comrades prepared for the strike without enthusiasm. The memory of October's bloodshed was too fresh. The Odesa Soviet turned out to be a dozen Jewish nerds who gave passionate speeches about how Russian factory workers would walk off their jobs and join an armed demonstration in the heart of the city, but when the soviet called the strike, few workers listened. The strike fizzled. The city went under martial law.

Hunger stalked Odesa that winter. In workers' neighborhoods, Medem saw the ashen faces, with cheekbones that were too sharp. "The famished people would drop into a coffeehouse; the proprietor would allow them to warm themselves while they huddled in the corners and stared at food with hungry eyes," he wrote. The revolutionary meetings stopped. The days drifted by, empty and futile, until the news came that the army had killed over a thousand workers to crush the Moscow rising.

Governments are machines far sturdier than most radicals imagine. The ecstasy of the street fades quickly. Cold sets in. Intellectuals dither. Respectable folk long for order. Daily life resumes, with its petty joys and wearisome practicalities. People need to eat. With the Saint Petersburg Soviet's leaders in prison, workers were adrift. They had a year of unemployment behind them, and the defeated Moscow uprising was a grim example of where armed resistance led. The uprising also scared the well-heeled liberals who once paid radicals like Trotsky to dazzle their party guests. For them, the existing regime was preferable to an anarchic uprising—especially now that Count Witte, ghostwriter of the October Manifesto, had been elevated to the role of de facto prime minister. Once the revolution's supporters split, the government swooped in to arrest, flog, and execute hundreds of suspected rebels.

Medem returned to Vilna. Only two weeks had passed, but the city was no longer his. The Intellectuals' Club closed its doors to the Bund, and the same crowds that had once fêted them now snubbed them as failures. A coachman explained it to Abramovich like so: "We understand the tsar, socialism, and solidarity, but a horse is still a horse. A horse wants oats, and the strike committee has no oats to give him."

Medem got to work on his newspaper. He tried to ignore the obvious. The revolution was dead.

DEAD MAN'S MARCH

On Monday, December 4, 1905, 125,000 eastern-European Jews converged on Rutgers Square, on the Lower East Side, to mourn their families murdered in Russian pogroms. They had walked for hours, in long columns, from the synagogues of Brownsville and Bushwick. They had sung their dirges on Meserole Street. They howled the whole length of the Williamsburg Bridge. Guys climbed the lampposts to get a better view. They would have seen an ocean of funeral black dotted with upside-down American flags and mourning banners. Led by the socialist congressional candidate Joseph Barondess, the mourners surged west to Broadway, where they shut down traffic, then north to Union Square. Thirteen hundred cops couldn't control them. Along the way, the band played the Dead Man's March. Every few blocks, they stopped to pray. This time, they didn't pray to free Egypt, as Meyer London had had them do a few months earlier. They prayed for their family and their friends. Their cries echoed for blocks.

"For many Jews inclined to socialism, [the pogroms] constituted a blow that tended to disorient them completely. They had awaited for years the advent of the great day of jubilee, and when it finally came it found itself drenched in rivers of innocent Jewish blood," wrote Medem.

The pogroms forced Jewish socialists to face the hostility of much of the Christian working class. Jews and Christians had struck, demonstrated, and died together in 1905. They draped their friends' coffins in red flags and marched to the cemetery together, where they gave speeches together about the international brotherhood of working men. Then the pogroms began, and the Christian workers vanished or joined in. Historian Simon Dubnov described a sense of betrayal that the Bund's ideologues barely dared articulate. The workers and peasants across the Russian Empire who "broke Jewish heads, tore out children's eyes, raped women and cut them to pieces, were doing what their fathers and brothers did in years past and will do again in favorable circumstances." As for the Christian radicals who died defending Jewish neighborhoods? They were, Dubnov wrote, merely "wonderful exceptions to the miserable rule."

I saw a glimpse of this when I walked around Lodz on a frigid Easter in 2022. The city was shut as tightly as it would have been for a general strike. When I turned down Revolution of 1905 Street, named for the moment when the Bund came closest to reaching its dreams, I noticed the buildings had been graffitied with dozens of six-pointed stars. I saw more stars in Baluty, the old Jewish workers' district, and over the streets that had once been the Bundist birzhes. The stars had been scrawled over Polish words I didn't understand, in such density and profusion that I soon lost count. Google told me what was going on. Before the war, Lodz's two football teams, Widzew and LKS, both had Jewish players. The Jews are gone now, but their memory remains, and each team's fans calls the others' fans "Jews" as an insult. When they see their rivals' graffiti, they paint a Jewish star over it. Sometimes the fans just spray-paint the star all by itself and write the Polish word for *fuck* next to it.

Fuck [Jewish Star]. Fuck [Jewish Star]. The city does not bother to paint them over.

"I cannot but emphasize the great respect in which . . . Christian Lodz holds the Jews," a correspondent from *Iskra* had written after the revolution of 1905. A lot can change in a century. I walked down Wschodnia street, my hands shoved in my pockets. I counted the six-pointed stars.

If this was eastern Europe, no wonder so many of us had decided to leave. Only a fool would try to free Egypt, many Jews reckoned. It was, after all, filled with drunken, violent Egyptians. New York beckoned from across the sea. One hundred twenty-five thousand Jews from the Russian Empire arrived in America in 1906. They filled the Lower East Side and Williamsburg, then overflowed east, turning Brownsville into a boomtown. In muddy Brooklyn lots, real estate hustlers threw up shacks to house these refugees. The next year, official efforts to restrict Jewish immigration began.

Around this time, Sam received a photo from his comrades back in Volkovysk. It was a beautiful thing, on embossed cardstock, and when I was a teenager, I hung it in my bedroom. I liked to make up stories about its subjects. The photo showed two rows of nerds, posed awkwardly in front of an ornate studio backdrop. They were not imposing figures, to say the least. They wore black peasant blouses that, when draped over their sloping shoulders, made them resemble seals. Their eyes crackled with mischief. Arrests dogged them. The police had shot their friend. The governor of their district decried the "endless looting and terrorist acts" done by Jewish criminals just like them. Judging from that photo, they remained unbowed. Soon, even these true believers were skipping town. Isadore Cohen and handsome Moishe Katriel both turned up on the East Side before the decade's end. The Volkovysk Revolutionary Union hobbled along, and even managed a costume ball in the winter of 1906, but their hearts were not in it. The New York present, of garment sweatshops and modest union victories, held more promise than the fight for paradise in a Russian Empire that wanted them dead. The last mention I could find of the Volkovysk Revolutionary Union was in 1907, in *The Forward*. It was on a list of organizations who gave money to a strike fund. It didn't contribute much.

Sam was also coming apart. His stomach screamed. His joints ached. At first, he thought it was tuberculosis, but like most painters, he had lead poisoning. Too sick to work, he left for Norwich, Connecticut, where he got a job in the Davenport gun factory. He slipped from the record.

Part Two

REVOLUTION

1906–1918

CHAPTER 8

INTERREGNUM

(1906–1914)

ARKADY KREMER

"I HAVE BEEN STRUCK BY HOW HARD IT IS, FROM INSIDE AN UPRISING'S nucleus, to even know when a revolutionary moment has passed," wrote Naomi Klein in her foreword to a book by the Egyptian revolutionary Alaa Abd El-Fattah. "Among core organizers there are still meetings, still strategy sessions, still hopes for a new opening just around the corner—it's only the masses of supporters who are mysteriously absent." She could have been speaking about what happened after the revolution of 1905.

In the two years that followed the October Manifesto, the tsarist government arrested thousands of people. One of them was the Bund's founder, Arkady Kremer. In 1907, a decade after he had launched the Bund in a safe-house attic, a Vilna court charged Arkady as leader of an illegal political organization. Pati stepped in to save him. A wealthy family friend presented the judge with an affidavit, swearing that Arkady was an itinerant salesman for his dental equipment company and not the wandering revolutionary that they imagined. She offered a bribe to assuage any last-minute doubts. Her maneuvering worked. After a few months of pretrial detention, Arkady was free. As he stepped past the stone walls of Lukiskes prison, he might have taken stock of his life. He was middle-aged, with a wife he seldom saw and a young daughter he barely knew. He had given the last two decades to a revolution that had failed. With a self-awareness rare in leaders, Kremer understood that he had little to offer in whatever battles would come next. In his speech resigning from the Bund's central committee, he said that the new era needed an orator, a great intellectual, or a military man. He was none of the above. He asked to resume the trade that he had learned as a young outlaw. Arkady Kremer became a typesetter for a Bundist newspaper. He and Pati would never live apart again.

The party tried to keep going, even as its best leaders quit or fled to New York. Frustrated young people picked up the guns they had been sent for self-defense and instead embarked on countless robberies—*expropriations*, in revolutionary parlance. Leadership disapproved, but the kids did it anyway. Who could blame them? They wanted to bring the exhilaration of the past into their drab and compromised present. Mostly, people quit. The Bund had thirty thousand members in 1906. By 1910, this number had plummeted to 609.

VLADIMIR MEDEM

Medem had not imagined things going like this in 1906, when the Bund appointed him to the central committee. Then, he had relished the convivial warmth of the Bund's Vilna office on Chopin Street, where he edited a newspaper with Abramovich. But after the government began to yank back the meager freedoms that the October Manifesto promised, things soured fast.

Funds ran out. Subscribers dwindled. Writers couldn't be paid. Despite the supposed freedom of the press that followed the October Manifesto, police shut down each Bundist paper after a few issues. Once, Medem arrived late to an editorial meeting, only to find that cops had arrested his entire staff. Pushed by police repression on one side and the competition from Zionist and Orthodox Jewish parties on the other, the Bund turned away from thoughts of revolution and instead tried to organize and elevate ordinary life. They set up unions, which engaged in a series of disastrous strikes that failed to win any pay raises. They stood candidates for local elections, which they mostly lost to their more religious rivals. They worked with aid societies. They helped build secular Jewish schools. They participated in Yiddish conferences. With the support of their old enemies, the Bolsheviks, they even rejoined the RSDLP. None of this helped them hold on to their membership.

With most of his friends abroad or in jail, Medem was often alone in Vilna. He sat in the empty safe house that had once swarmed with comrades from other cities. He was broke. The party had no money to support him, and he couldn't get a job, since he was living on false papers. He felt like a burden. His memories of Western Europe beckoned him back.

When Medem arrived in Berlin in 1908, he expected his trip to last the summer. He ended up staying in Exileland for years. Hundreds of Russian radicals did the same. Why not? It was a good time for a breather. Europe had been at peace for decades. The old cosmopolitan empires held sway. In countries grown prosperous with wealth stolen from their colonies, taboos were shattered, and culture reached a dazzling refinement. The old coexisted with the new. Gustave Klimt painted golden vamps in the Habsburg capital. In Paris, Picasso and Braque violently deconstructed bodies into cubes. Their figures' painted contortions echoed those of the dancers in Diaghilev's Ballet Russes. A thousand isms bloomed. Literary. Artistic. Political. On a single street, Freud could squeeze past Trotsky. At the British Library, Aleister Crowley and Lenin might have battled for a chair.

When I read memoirs of this time, life seems rich as molten chocolate. Why would anyone want to change anything, I asked myself, even if they were a revolutionary? If I were in Medem's place, I would have sunk into those European days, like I sank into the subversive bohemias of New York, London, and Istanbul. I would have forgone all utopian aspirations for the actual paradise right there, in, say, Vienna. Fuck the dialectic. Give me fine words and coffee topped with whipped cream, radical journals spread over the bar of an underground nightclub, speeches whose primary purpose was to impress a fan dancer, not a gaggle of the most disagreeable men in the world. That would have been enough for me.

Medem shared my hunger for beauty. "I would hurl myself like a ravenous creature, at . . . the cultural riches of those European capitals," he wrote. Opera, theater, galleries, yes, but other entertainments as well. In Berlin, he saw a poster for an appearance by Saharat, one of the faux-Oriental dancers popular at the time. He rushed off to the Wintergarten to watch her. Upon returning home, he said, in awe, "I went. I saw. Let men make speeches later." Yet it was never enough. He was a star speaker, an idol for the students in the Russian colonies that he toured, but beneath this, he was deeply depressed. Though the Bund had rejoined the RSDLP, most of the larger party's energy was taken up with verbal knife fights between Mensheviks and Bolsheviks, or between Lenin and other Bolsheviks, or between Trotsky and everyone else. Rumors and counteraccusations flew. It all disgusted Medem. His kidney disease worsened. Still young, he felt the paralyzing imminence of death. He pictured his future self, poisoned by his own body. More and more, he locked himself in his room.

Perhaps there was additional reason for his sadness. Nothing is more temporary than a paradise, and there is no garden without a snake. Writers like to trot out the Gramsci quote: "The Old World is dying, and the new world waiting to be born. The interregnum is the time of monsters." Maybe, when Medem looked out at the hopeful faces that filled the lecture halls of Exileland outposts from Paris to Berne to Berlin, he realized that none of it could last. This was the interregnum. The monsters may not have been obvious, what with the chestnut trees, the sunlight, and the Seine, but they would reveal themselves soon enough. And they would not be strangers either.

BROOKLYN

Sam did not last long at the Davenport gun factory. After two years of Connecticut exile, he returned to New York around 1908 and planted himself in the East Side's overflow room—the recently Jewish neighborhood of Williamsburg.

Sam took up residence in the very neighborhood, South Williamsburg, where I write these words. He sauntered beneath the same elevated train tracks that I do, squeezed past the same sorts of hawkers, and sidestepped similar piles of trash. As soon as Sam snagged a room, the quest for rent began. First, he found a plumber to take him on as an apprentice. When union members ran him off the job, he tried his hand at day labor. Armed with a wheelbarrow, he hauled bricks on construction sites in Harlem. This time, he had better luck and was promoted to watchman.

At night, in mansions still coated with construction dust, Sam finally had space to draw. He was alone. No one could tell him to stop. He used scrap lumber for paper, a burned stick for a pen. He carved creatures from wood. He doodled into wet plaster. He discovered his artistic voice. After a year of Sam's solitary practice, the master builder found his graffiti. It must have been good. Rather than kick him off the job, he told Sam he was wasting his talent. "You're an artist, Rothbort," he said. Overhearing the master builder's praise, a Hungarian painter named Stein asked Sam if he'd like to become his apprentice. You can carry my bag, Stein offered. Sam enthusiastically agreed.

SAM AND ROSE

Not long afterward, Sam met Rose Kravitz at a friend's house in Williamsburg. She was only eighteen, a sweatshop seamstress, and had arrived two years earlier, from a shtetl not far from Volkovysk called Lunna Wola. As a child, I marveled at the romance of her hometown's name. Luna. Moon. I imagined a Marc Chagall sort of wonderland, celestial, pearlescent—not the cluster of dilapidated shacks that I later found in old photos. Years later, I learned Lunna's name came not from the moon but from *lunas*, an old Baltic word for mud. In comparison, Volkovysk might as well have been Constantinople. Rose would have known about the Bund, since their battle squad attacked the Lunna post office a year before she left for America.

Rose had flushed cheeks, luxuriant hair, and the round black eyes of a Scottish Fold cat. Sam looked at her breasts. He thought of an afternoon, years earlier, after he finished a mural in the office of a Lower East Side fortune teller. The man offered to tell his future. "There's a girl for you with beautiful *mamtakim*"—Yiddish for sweets, money, or tits—the fortune teller pronounced. Rose had no sweets, and no money, but otherwise, she fit the description.

At twenty-six, Sam at last had something to offer. His apprenticeship with Stein led to a stint with a legendary decorator, Gordon the Bum. The name was fitting. Gordon, Sam wrote, "worked me for eight months but only paid me for three weeks." Still, the exposure led to better things. Soon, Sam was climbing forty-foot extension ladders to adorn the ceilings of mansions all over East Harlem. He painted George Washingtons, grapes, nymphs. He copied Michelangelo. He filled a pastry bag with plaster and squeezed out rosettes in rococo efflorescence. It was a time before "the beautiful classic disappeared, and the modern went to a world unknown," he later wrote.

Rose's family quickly arranged a marriage.

VLADIMIR AND GINA

So much about Vladimir Medem's marriage to Gina Bizenzwieg remains a mystery. Daughter of a wealthy Lodz family, Gina joined the Bund in her teens. She first heard Medem speak during a visit to Switzerland in 1903, but groupies surrounded him, and she couldn't get close. They ran into each other over the years at parties, where they flirted audaciously. She relished his attention—he was, after all, a star—but the thought of getting close frightened her. Marriage to a famous man meant endless sacrifice, and she had no desire to subdue her own confident vivacity. One afternoon the pair sat at a café in the mountains outside Geneva. For the first time, Medem revealed the gravity of his kidney disease, telling her he only had a few more years to live. She didn't know what to say. "I will never let you be alone," she had blurted out. The 1905 revolution came, as if to save her from her hasty promise. They both returned to the Russian Empire, where she organized factories, was arrested, and spent eight months in a Lodz jail.

She ran into Medem again four years later, in 1909, at Lake Maggiore, in southern Switzerland. She was on vacation with her student friends, and he, fresh off the Vilna disaster, asked to join them. The pair strolled through vineyards heavy with blood-dark grapes. They rowed a sailboat out to islands with musical names, like Isola Madre and Isola Bella, and watched the white peacocks strut over the steps of ancient palaces beneath the harvest moon.

On the boat back to Geneva, Medem's illness returned. This, more than the lakeside romance, set Gina down her path. Like so many formidable women in eras hostile to female ambition, she decided to make Medem her project. He could "give so much to the world if there was someone else who would renounce a normal, healthy life, and all the experiments and journeys," she later wrote. That someone would be her.

Everyone opposed their marriage. "You're too young to end up a nurse," warned a mutual friend. Medem's family was still Christian and didn't want him to marry a Jew. Nor did her family want a "goyish" revolutionary for a son-in-law. Medem's father had baptized him into the Russian Orthodox Church, which didn't permit intermarriage. To marry Gina, the famous orator of the Jewish Labor Bund converted to Lutheranism.

For Medem, these were years of fervent productivity, when he made his name as a theoretician. He churned out essays on Jewish history, identity, and the Yiddish language. In response to both Zionism and the demands of European societies that Jews assimilate completely to earn acceptance, he defined the Bund's philosophy of diasporic nationalism, in which Jews could preserve their cultures in the countries where they lived, rather than building a far-off ethnostate in Palestine. Inevitably, his kidney disease attacked. More doctors. More bills. All the things that made Gina herself—her revolutionary activities, her flirtations, her friends and family—became subservient to caring for the Great Man. While Medem posed at the podiums of innumerable party conferences, she tried to scrape together rent. She grew to dislike the Bund, though her memoirs do not specify the reasons—beyond claiming a certain coldness on the party's part, incidents of carelessness or selfishness. Perhaps they just treated her like Medem's wife.

In the spring of 1912, the party sent Medem to Vienna to edit a new newspaper called *Lebens-Fragen* that would be published out of Warsaw. Though the Bund intended *Lebens-Fragen* to be a legal periodical, Warsaw police quickly arrested its entire staff. Medem didn't think much of it at the time. He was too enraptured with the Habsburg capital. It appeared to him a cosmopolitan wonderland. The city's Germans, Czechs, Poles, Italians, Bosnians, and Jews seemed to live together in idyllic harmony, the peace barely ruffled by the occasional protests held by insignificant groups of racists, who, Medem imagined, would never attain power.

Thanks to government missteps, the Bund was on the rise again. That year, tsarist troops massacred over two hundred striking workers at the Lena goldfields, and the public outrage that followed brought new members to the party. The next year, in 1913, a Kyiv court tried a Jewish factory foreman named Mendel Beilis on the sensational charge of ritual murder. On the orders of the justice minister Ivan Shcheglovitov, the empire's top prosecutors claimed Beilis had stabbed an adolescent Christian boy in order to use his blood for sinister religious rites that their star witness, an alcoholic Lithuanian priest, claimed were mandated by the Talmud. Shcheglovitov hoped the Beilis trial would redirect popular anger toward pogroms. It backfired. On the trial's first day, the Bund launched protest strikes across the empire. Their defense of the innocent Beilis won them thousands of new recruits. The foreign press saw the trial as a classic example of Russia's medieval backwardness. Their articles made the tsarist regime into the laughingstock of Western Europe and America. Brilliant defense lawyers browbeat the prosecution's witnesses, trapping them in webs of contradictions. After a few hours' deliberation, the jury acquitted Beilis, who quickly fled to New York.

In Vienna, Medem sat at the legendary cafés, contentedly writing up the Bund's latest victories and translating articles on the Balkan Wars across the border. Gina didn't share his enchantment. She had no friends in Vienna. Her whole family was in Lodz, where Medem, with his open warrant, could not travel, and where he, ill and needy, would not even permit her to visit. At last, the isolation was too much. She gave him an ultimatum. She would kill herself unless they returned to the Russian Empire.

Abramovich warned Medem not to cross the border, saying that when the police caught him, they'd ship him to Siberia. But Medem ignored his old friend. He and Gina boarded a train toward the Russian Empire at the end of 1913. Maybe this time things would work out better. Maybe this time it would feel like home.

NEW YORK

I have a photo of Sam and Rose from the early days of their marriage hanging in my bedroom. They are glamorous, as people from the past often are. She wears a stole of murdered minks, heads and all, around her slender shoulders, and her face is topped with a plumed picture hat. With his bowler, Sam looks almost bourgeois. This photo would have been taken during the years when they hopscotched through tenements around Brooklyn's chaotic Broadway Triangle.

In 1911, Rose gave birth to their first child, a boy named Henry. She persuaded Sam to leave their pestilent little apartment behind and go in with three other families on a dairy farm in the Catskills. A few notes left by Sam reveal that the land provided none of the consolations he had hoped for. With forty cows to milk each day, the couples began to bicker, and within a few years, the farming experiment collapsed. The Rothborts returned to Brooklyn in 1913. Rose may have been pregnant again, this time with my great-aunt Ida.

By then, New York's Jewish left was teeming with Sam's old comrades. The failed 1905 revolution had pushed thousands of Bundist refugees to the city, and in the intervening years, they'd managed to find their legs. Bundists dominated the Workmen's Circle, a socialist mutual aid society. With fifty-nine thousand members in hundreds of branches across America and Canada, the Workmen's Circle catered to every aspect of life—cultural, economic, and social. They provided medical insurance, old age homes, and burial plots. Thousands of children studied at their secular Yiddish schools. Flush with success, the Workmen's Circle swallowed up radical grouplets like the Volkovysk Revolutionary Union, which celebrated its induction as an official Workmen's Circle branch by printing new membership cards in gold.

Other former Bundists rose to lead equally powerful organizations. Sidney Hillman, boss of the Amalgamated Clothing Workers, had led the Bund's first May Day demonstration in Kovno. David Dubinsky, boss of the International Ladies Garment Workers Union, had helmed the Bundist bakers' union in Lodz before moving to America. Trained since their teens in the discipline of smuggled pamphlets, illegal marches, and prison cells, they found conditions more congenial in America. By 1914, their two groups represented over a hundred thousand workers between them and had wrung concessions from employers through massive strikes. Victory had a moderating effect. Revolution might have been the only choice when they lived under the hemophiliac Romanov autocracy. In America, they could strike and vote. For the moment, this seemed sufficient. Here where they lived was their country.

That is not to say that New York's socialist Jews forgot about the There of Russia. It was their birthplace, after all. They supported Russian insurrectionists with such brio that the Okhrana sent secret agents to monitor their activities. Hundreds attended the Bund's annual summer picnic in Liberty Park. Thousands marched on the anniversary of Bloody Sunday. When Russian revolutionaries visited New York, they were received ecstatically. People packed lecture halls to see the Bundist orator Maxime, a bookworm who had won over Riga's railway workers and so seized control of the city during the 1905 revolution. They applied their values to their new home; in 1908, when a white mob attacked Black people in Springfield, Illinois, Yiddish dailies didn't merely condemn the "pogrom"; they urged street protests and collected donations for survivors. But their milieu combined radical beliefs with a surprising American patriotism. Old Glory waved alongside the red flag. Street parades marked May Day and the anniversaries of the French Revolution, the Paris Commune, and the assassination of Alexander II, as well as the Fourth of July. They sang their ballad, "Women Workers," which implored women to emulate Hesya Helfman, the seamstress who helped to kill Tsar Alexander II, then followed up with "The Star-Spangled Banner."

In these years, Jews flocked to the powerful Socialist Party of America, whose 113,000 members made it one of the largest socialist movements in the world. In the 1912 presidential election, its candidate, Eugene V. Debs, received nine hundred thousand votes, an astounding 6 percent of the popular vote. Over the next few years, Jewish districts in New York elected ten socialist assemblymen, seven socialist city councilmen, and one socialist municipal judge.

By the time the 1914 congressional elections rolled around, excitement among New York's Jewish neighborhoods was at a boil. The last time, Tammany Hall's man, Henry Goldfogle, had managed to squeak into office through a combination of ballot forgery and physical attacks on rival organizers, but Jewish leftists resolved not to let him win again. The socialist candidate was Meyer London, now a beloved labor lawyer, who had represented fifty thousand cloak makers during their victorious strike of 1910. To defend London's voters, the unions organized their workers to fight off Tammany thugs at the poll sites. "Don't worry about Goldfogle's pathetic little gang," promised *The Forward*. "It's all been taken care of. [They] won't dare to make a peep."

On election night, fifty thousand people gathered in front of the new Forward Building at 175 East Broadway to wait for the results. The building itself seemed like a harbinger of triumph. Constructed only two years before, the beaux arts wonder towered over the surrounding slums like a narrow wedding cake. It was the first skyscraper on the Lower East Side. Above the doorway glowered carved busts of Marx, Engels, Lasalle, and a bearded man who could have been either August Bebel or Karl Liebknecht, but no one was quite sure. The Workmen's Circle, the Farband, and the United Hebrew Trades all had offices there. "Where is the synagogue of our Jewish workers? Where is the temple of freedom, of equality, of brotherhood?" Abe Cahan had asked. This was it. *Forward* staffers used a magic lantern to project the election results from each district on the building's walls. Each time London's tally rose, the crowd broke into cheers. A *Forward* writer spotted many Bundists among the crowd. One said to another it felt "exactly like the October days" of the revolution nine years prior, which is to say, the days before the defeat. At two A.M., there were no more districts to count. London had won. Screams, kisses, the chords of "The Marseillaise." In the stinking East Side, the air itself seemed perfumed with victory.

When London arrived at four A.M., supporters carried him on their shoulders to the Forward Building, where he addressed the crowds. He was a small, bespectacled man with a professorial mien, but in the sketch that appeared the next morning on the front page of *The Forward,* he towered over Rutgers Square like the colossus.

SAM ROTHBORT

When Sam came back to New York, he turned his full attention to art. He seldom slept more than four hours a night. He began painting the city in a postimpressionist impasto. The bathers in Coney Island. The ice skaters. Rose's profile, her chin now round from motherhood. She encouraged his art. Paints came before shoes, she said.

He began to exhibit his work at the Forward Building. When the Brotherhood of Painters and Decorators at last permitted Jewish members, Sam joined Local 992 in Brownsville, where he took newly arrived Bundists under his wing. He made his living painting murals in bordellos and funeral parlors, mansions and Williamsburg slums. Cupids flew in lazy circles. Sometimes he gave them his daughter Ida's face. As he painted, he wondered how such delicate wings could hold aloft the tubby cupids. Then again, these were the golden days of the interregnum, a time when even fat little babies could fly.

CHAPTER 9

COLLAPSE

(1914–1916)

HOMECOMING

MEDEM CROSSED THE BORDER WITHOUT INCIDENT. GINA HAD GONE ahead to Warsaw, and he was probably grateful for the time alone. He stopped in Kovno, where his brother lived, and where he hoped to put his papers in order. He was happy to be back. As he rested at his brother's flat, he realized the weight of his homesickness, and his relief to have it gone. The fifth day after his arrival, he attended a lavish party thrown by his brother's in-laws. It was a vodka-soaked debauch, where celebrants gorged themselves, danced, and toasted long into the night. Medem staggered to bed just before dawn, hoping to pass out for eternity.

His brother woke him up an hour later. The cops were outside, and they had a warrant.

The police led Medem through the sleeping city. It was too bright. He shut his eyes, but the sun pounded on his eyelids. He wasn't afraid. This wasn't his first ride. What was the worst they could do? Kick him out of Russia? Only one detail of the warrant made him pause: it was signed by a magistrate in Warsaw.

What did they want with him in Warsaw? His mind went back to the previous year, when Warsaw cops had raided the Bund's newspaper, *Lebens-Fragen,* which Medem edited from Vienna. They had arrested the staff, but arrests were so frequent that he hadn't given it much thought at the time. He didn't know about the letters police had discovered in one of the defendants' homes. She must have saved them out of sentimentality. A decade old, they detailed every drama, feud, and fuck among the radical set in the Swiss student colonies, with special attention to Vladimir Medem, whom she identified by his legal name as a leader of the Bund. The Warsaw magistrate sent out orders for Medem's arrest on charges of membership to an illegal organization.

When Medem had come back to Kovno, his brother wasn't the only one waiting.

Medem entered the cell. The iron door clanged shut behind him. He let himself collapse onto the cot. Head pounding, mouth still dry from last night's vodka, he fell into an unquiet sleep.

He passed the next five months in cells like this, first in Kovno, then inside the whitewashed walls of the Tenth Pavilion, a prison housed in the Warsaw Citadel, in a monotony that was only tolerable because he forced himself to conform to its rhythms. Ritual was the key to sanity, Medem knew. He would be disciplined. He would not think about the future. He would take each day as if it were his first and his last. Straighten up the cell. Guard your clothes so no one steals them during bath time. Preserve any small object—soap sliver, button—like it was a diamond. Tolerate the morons. Watch the snitches. Organize a protest for the poor guy stuck in solitary. Find your comrades—one of his cellmates was a barely educated young Bundist named Bernard Goldstein who bore a terrifying scar across his face. Eavesdrop on the conversations that prisoners tap out on walls in their special prisoners' morse code. One tap means *a*. Two taps mean *b*. Each tap is a second. Sixty taps in a minute. Three hundred and sixty taps in an hour. Eight thousand six hundred forty taps in a day. *Tap tap tap.*

The lawyer came every other week, with cheerful updates about his prospects.

Gina came every other week. She blamed everyone but herself.

So it went. *Tap tap tap.* Seconds. Minutes. Hours. Days. Until one balmy afternoon in June, when Gina told him that Austria's archduke, Franz Ferdinand, had taken a wrong turn in Sarajevo, into an unplanned encounter with Gavrilo Princip, teenage assassin for Serbia's ultranationalist Black Hand Society.

Medem closed his eyes. The snares of alliances and counteralliances, pan-Slavic loyalties and mutual defense pacts, appeared with all their idiot logic, leading to a conclusion so obvious that he didn't need to wait for whatever pompous announcement the government would issue later.

Three shots. Russia was at war.

THE GREAT WAR

The Great War began with all the inevitability of a Grecian play. After Princip assassinated Franz Ferdinand, Austria-Hungary attacked Serbia, with the help of its ally Germany. Bristling from defeats in the Balkan Wars, Bulgaria and the Ottoman Empire soon joined up on Austria's side. These four states comprised the Central Powers. Meanwhile, mutual defense pacts with Serbia pulled England, France, and the tsarist empire into the war. They were known as the Allies.

Most Europeans thought the conflict would be over by Christmas.

They had not yet been on the receiving end of industrial warfare. For decades, they had done their killing in the colonies—turning their poison gas and machine guns on Africans armed with ancient rifles. Now everyone—banker and trashman, poet and line cook—itched to bring that murder home. War would be an adventure, Europeans thought. It would wipe out the decadence. Make men manly. Put women in their place. Even European workers thought this way. European workers' parties followed.

The Second International, the worldwide organization of socialist parties, of which the Bund was a member, was supposed to prevent wars like this. Yet it collapsed like a meringue on a humid day. First, the Social Democratic Party of Germany, the biggest, most powerful socialist party in Europe, betrayed Marx's adage that the working man had no country and voted to fund *their* country's war. Socialist parties in the other belligerent countries followed. In France, England, Belgium, Austria, and so on, socialists turned their backs on long-held ideals of international brotherhood and instead threw themselves into nationalist hallucinations, somehow blind to where they would lead.

Things didn't go well for socialists who foresaw the coming catastrophe. Some antiwar intellectuals were merely kicked out of their current countries of exile. Take Leon Trotsky, who had settled in Paris after a dramatic escape from Siberian exile. After the war, the French government deported him; our man landed in the Bronx. Others, like the brilliant critic of the Bund Rosa Luxemburg, were locked in jail for pacifism. And these were the lucky ones. The famed socialist leader Jean Jaurès had sought to avert France's entry into the conflict. He was dining at Montmartre's Café du Croissant when a nationalist shot him in the back; a Parisian jury declared his murderer innocent of any crime.

The war divided Russian socialists into three camps. There were the defencists, who believed Russia needed to be defended against Germany, and thus wanted to continue the war. There were the internationalists, who called for an immediate end to the war, without victors or victims, but had only vague ideas on how to get there. The Bund's 1914 statement is typical of this view. "International socialists must strive to put an end to this bloodbath" by putting pressure on the warring governments to make a peace without annexations or indemnities. "Down with the war. Long live international brotherhood."

Finally, revolutionary defeatists wanted Russia to lose so the war between nations would become a war between classes. This unpopular approach was championed by Vladimir Lenin.

The war spelled the end of the freewheeling Exileland in which

Medem had come of age. His Vienna was gone. No coffeehouse, no polyglot spread of newspapers, no Kaiserschmarrn, no espresso topped with crème Chantilly. A wartime capital had no place for rootless radicals like his friends. Bundists fled Austria for neutral countries. Those who stayed ended up in prison camps. As the weeks passed, the carefully constructed idylls of retired revolutionaries turned into cages. Take the Kremers, now a decade into a new life in Provence. Arkady was an engineer. Pati raised their daughter, Vera, a precocious teenaged artist, *comme une française*. When they had begun their life in France, they were only a train ride from their Vilna family, but the war began, and the borders rose like brambles. They and their loved ones might as well have been on opposite sides of the earth.

These were metaphorical prisons, while Medem sat in the real thing. His thoughts didn't revolve around geopolitics or international brotherhood, but around a single question: Would the war set him free?

THE PALE

The war was a disaster for every Russian revolutionary party, but it hit the Bund hardest.

Overnight, the government banned the Yiddish press. The military drafted four hundred thousand Jews, including many of the Bund's best activists, while police rounded up leaders like Mark Liber in the wave of arrests that accompanied mobilization.

The Pale of Settlement was now a front line, and the military viewed its five million Jewish inhabitants as potential spies. Fearing Jews would assist the advancing enemy armies, the empire's top general ordered mass deportations east, to central Russia. Within months, over two hundred thousand people were made homeless. Often, they had as little as twelve hours to pack and could take only what they could carry. "Go to Palestine" jeered their Christian neighbors as the Jews waited at the rail stations. These neighbors then looted their homes.

Jews were emptied from Grodno, from Dvinsk, from Kovno, onto cattle cars moving east. They were disgorged into towns in central Russia, far outside their former area of confinement. Though they were impoverished and despised by their new neighbors, they might have noticed one ironic upside to current events. For two hundred years, Jews had been trapped in the Pale of Settlement. Now, by order of Tsar Nicholas II, the borders of the Pale had been demolished, if not in law, then in reality.

POGROM

Through the autumn of 1914, the Russian army advanced into the Austro-Hungarian Empire. They marched into the provinces of Galicia and Bukovina, where nine hundred thousand Jews had enjoyed quasi-equality for the past two centuries under liberal Habsburg rule. This ended overnight. Jews were fired from their government jobs, their land stolen, and their businesses sacked. The poet S. An-sky used his job as an aid worker to chronicle the atrocities. In one torched synagogue, An-sky wrote, "the corners of the room and the adjoining chapels were fouled, not by horses but by people. They turned a temple into a latrine."

Most Russian army pogroms started with an accusation. A Jew fired at soldiers from his window. A Jew communicated with the Austrians via a radio hidden inside his beard. Murder, rape, and robbery followed. In Volkovysk, survivors told S. An-sky that the army had driven Jews into the market square—the same market square where Sam Rothbort watched his mother sell her wares—and forced them to strip naked and ride on pigs. Soldiers finished them off with machine guns.

I don't know if Volkovysk's Christians took part in these amusements, but in village after town after bustling city, pogroms unfolded with local help. Christians told the army which property belonged to Jews. They watched their neighbors, who bought their grain and mended their pants and flirted with their brothers, get their teeth knocked out with rifle butts, and after the army took their neighbors hostage, these Christians walked through the busted doors of their vacant homes and loaded their bags with as much loot as they could carry.

Austrian Jews fled en masse from the conquered provinces: to Vienna and Budapest.

Hobbled by wartime repression, its local branches isolated from each other by the shifting front, the Bund tried to protest. On hidden printing presses, they churned out illicit broadsheets to condemn the massacres. In free Geneva, the Bund's foreign committee appealed to socialist parties and to the citizens of the world for solidarity against the violence. They got some statements of support, but little else. Inside Russia, party activists threw themselves into aid for the displaced. They set up tea houses, canteens, and work bureaus. These were not only for Jews. Longstanding German communities were also deported under suspicion of espionage, and the Bund extended them help. When Yiddish schools sprang up to educate displaced kids, Bundists signed on as teachers. Twenty-five thousand children were enrolled in these schools over the next few years. Despite their socialist, secular ideology, the Bund took part in the larger Jewish aid organizations alongside Zionists and rich businessmen. Here where they lived was their country, they said, no matter how much events tested this conviction.

EVACUATION

Despite his hopes, the war didn't bring Medem freedom. A few days after mobilization began, a guard told Medem to collect his things. The Tenth Pavilion was being vacated. Prisoners would be sent to the interior. Medem boarded the prison wagon to a fortress in another city. Then another. Then another.

Through smuggled newspapers, guards' chatter, and the reports of new detainees, Medem began to grasp what had befallen his country. In sweltering cattle cars too crowded to sit or lie down in, the men gossiped to distract themselves from thirst. What was happening outside? Stories flew about barricades in Saint Petersburg and labor disturbances in Berlin. Could this be a revolutionary moment bigger than 1905? The train stopped at a station jammed with soldiers, as unfree and interchangeable as the prisoners themselves. When the soldiers filed past, one prisoner whispered, "Comrades! The German workers don't want to fight! They've already gone on strike." "Let them strike . . . We'll march to Berlin and finish them off," the soldier laughed. *No,* Medem thought, *revolution is not in the cards.*

OREL

When Medem arrived in Orel prison, it was already packed with hundreds of men like him taken from Polish prisons near the front. At first, he bristled at the company. He was a political prisoner, and thus slightly higher in the prison hierarchy, yet he was forced to share a cell with hooligans so filthy they could pull clumps of lice out of their pockets. But prison exerts an equalizing effect. Those men had nothing, and neither did he. Guards had long since stolen their money. Medem had prepared for this eventuality by hiding a roll of bills inside his shoe, but the guards stole his shoes.

Every few weeks, they moved him on. Sometimes east, sometimes west toward Warsaw. The cycle pointlessly repeated. The men lined up for transfer. The warden barked. The men stripped. The guards' fingers went on his dick, in his ass. They searched his clothes for cigarettes. Then came slaps. Then shackles. Then the trip to nowhere, to do it all again. "One became a minuscule element in the vast pile of gray human dust. . . . As if by a gigantic steam shovel, this dust pile was scooped into an amorphous heap . . . shoved into filthy prison cars . . . swept apart, lumped together in a new pile," Medem wrote. He tried to cling to his old self—the star orator, the aristocratic aesthete, the radical students' idol—but each day it slipped further away.

To keep sane, he tried to control what he could. He was one of thirty-five men in a cell made for nine, and bedbugs carpeted the floor. The old-timers just let the bugs suck their sores, but Medem refused. Twice a day, he stripped naked and crushed any eggs they had laid in his clothing. These bug hunts improved his spirits. Many prisoners have told me that the key to survival is the achievement of small goals.

PEREGRINATIONS

Smolensk. Orel. Orel. Smolensk. Back to Warsaw. The authorities shuffled Vladimir Medem this way and that. Slowly the superiority he felt as a political prisoner disappeared, and he began to realize he was just a victim among victims, snatched capriciously by a machine. He listened to his cellmates' stories. The authorities told some Polish peasants to form a militia against the Germans, then arrested them for forming a militia. They held Ukrainian day laborers over expired passports. They picked up lunatics for no reason and held them until they'd accumulated enough lunatics to justify hiring a specialist to take them all to an asylum in Moscow. They carted off little boys as enemy combatants, just because of their German ethnicity. Medem didn't favor the innocent over the guilty. One of his best friends was a Persian murderer who played a good game of dominos. Medem admired the professional thieves for their camaraderie and dash. Unlike the innocents, they entered the cells with their heads high and immediately divvied up their tobacco according to strict codes of solidarity. They saw theft as a trade like any other. "Someone's got to steal," one said. "And here I am. That someone is me." Medem found them more moral than most respectable people. No prisoner ever cared that he was a Jew.

His kidneys got worse. He could no longer hold down prison food. When it was time to scrub the floors, he sat in bed and smoked, and his weakness was so obvious that his cellmates picked up the slack. Or perhaps it was the force of his personality. "Style can become a sort of moral courage," Edmund White wrote of Jean Cocteau, and I would say the same about Vladimir Medem. Fellow prisoners described him as an aristocrat, so determined was he to cling to any bit of culture that survived in the archipelago of cages. Somehow, he procured literary magazines from avant-garde Saint Petersburg. He played chess expertly with pieces made from chewed-up bread, and he sang Russian duets from memory with the communists. He gave fabulous lectures in which he detailed the proposals from the last congress of the Bund in Vilna. Perhaps he read their statements aloud. "The fight against tsarist reaction is, for the Jewish worker, a fight for life, in the purest sense of the word," etc. The imprisoned workers were so impressed that they wouldn't even let him carry the toilet bucket.

WARSAW

In May 1915, nearly two years after his arrest, the Warsaw judge gave him a sentence. Four years' hard labor in leg irons. The amount of time didn't matter, Medem knew. With his disease, he'd never leave prison alive.

Medem's only hope was the Germans. That summer, they were moving fast. The German army booted Russia out of Galicia and Bukovina, then kept going until they had pushed into Poland. The Russian press blamed Jews for the defeats, and the Russian military pogromed as it retreated.

Each day, the Germans moved closer to Warsaw, bringing with them Medem's chance of freedom. Each day, the Russians shipped more prisoners to the interior. Medem watched these men line up by the hundreds in the prison courtyard. Some were his friends. But sick prisoners were not supposed to travel, and Medem was sicker than ever. Thanks to Gina's bribes, he lay alone in the nearly vacant prison hospital. Just when he let himself hope he'd outlast the Russian army, guards threw him on a wagon to another Warsaw prison. *This time,* they promised, they'd send him somewhere he'd never escape.

Medem and his cellmates became experts in divination, scrying meaning in the mysterious rumbles that might have been artillery shells. The Russian guards left, to be replaced by a Polish citizens committee, but they could still come back. Vladimir Medem pictured the bridges over Warsaw's Vistula River. Prisoners crossed those bridges to get to the train station. As long as they stood, he wasn't free.

The night of August 4, pandemonium broke out. Gunfire. Cannon shriek. Medem, a revolutionary who plotted to bring down the state but who mostly wrote pamphlets, had never heard such fury in his life. Despite the instinctual horror in his body, he was seized with desperate joy. He grabbed his cellmate's hands so tightly he could feel the other man's pulse. They waited to hear the mines planted on bridges across the Vistula River that the Russian army would detonate behind them when they fled. The sun rose. The mines boomed. The bridges collapsed into the water. There was no way back to Russia.

The Polish guards put on civilian clothes. Shrapnel whistled overhead as the Russians fired from the other side of the river. A shell hit near the prison. The walls shook. Medem braced. Would the machine get him in the end? It would not. Call it God, or chance, or the dialectical forces of history, but for the first time in his life, Medem was exactly where he needed to be. The shells stopped. The prison administrator came in and told the men that the Germans had ordered their release. "Gentlemen, you are free."

Medem walked out the open gates. Except for a few German military trucks, the streets were empty. A drizzle fell. The patter of raindrops mixed with gunfire. Gina was there waiting for him.

Later, at a sumptuous dinner with her family, he looked out the window and thought how miraculous it was that there was no one to prevent him from escaping into the streets of Warsaw. He took Gina's arm. They walked out the door, into the occupied city, the Paris of the East, guarded by a mermaid with a sword. By this time, millions had died in the war, and Medem owed his freedom to the occupation army. It didn't matter. The pair would seize delight, even in the midst of the apocalypse. They walked wherever they wanted. They walked until they could walk no more.

Sophia Dubnova
סאָפיע
דובנאָװע
ערליך
הענריק ערליך
Henryk Erlich

CHAPTER 10

REVOLUTIONARY ECSTASIES

(January–April 1917)

SOPHIA DUBNOVA

SOPHIA DUBNOVA BEGAN THE YEAR 1917 IN A STATE OF FRAUGHT EXpectation. At thirty-two, she lived the delicious but sometimes contradictory life of an artist revolutionary. The favorite daughter of the renowned Jewish historian Simon Dubnov, Sophia grew up in Vilna. She had scored a lucky university placement in Saint Petersburg, only to be expelled for signing a petition against the war with Japan. At nineteen, she joined the Bund. She agitated in small towns under false identities, smuggled pamphlets between cities by taping them to her body to mimic a pregnant belly, and incited mutiny in the Grodno army garrison. (Her soldier boys were later shot.) She spent the halcyon year of 1910 in Parisian Exileland, where she studied literature at the Sorbonne and participated in the internecine political dramas that played out across the tables of the Taverne du Panthéon. The Bund once chose her to speak at a memorial for the Paris Commune. Lenin preceded her on the podium. He didn't speak about the commune, but instead about the mechanics of revolution. An uprising might break out from the unthinking energies of millions of people, he said, but to become something more, it needed to be shaped by history's priests—career revolutionaries like himself. At the time, Sophia didn't dwell on his words.

In Paris, she reunited with an old flame. She'd met Henryk Erlich years before, in the microscopic Saint Petersburg Bund, which was more of a debate society than a revolutionary cell. Henryk, the only son of a rich, religious family in Lublin, was tall and thin, with hollow cheeks, and sad, hooded eyes beneath heavy brows. First arrested at twenty during brawls over the performance of a racist play, he was halfway through his law degree when they met, and the pair spent nights wrapped in intellectual conversation. Once Henryk finished his degree, the two parted ways. When Sophia saw him again in Paris, he was fresh off a three-month prison stint in Warsaw. They wandered the Left Bank together. The booksellers by the Seine had never been so charming, the lilacs of Boulevard Arago never so sweet. You can love a city through a man, Sophia learned. They married in Saint Petersburg the next year, in 1911, with no family and little fuss. She wore a gray overcoat. Henryk messed up the vows. She resolved to keep using her maiden name.

In the years that followed, they settled in Saint Petersburg and had two sons. Henryk was in and out of jail but rose through the ranks of the party and, in 1915, became a member of the Bund's central committee. During these years, the Bund became close to the Mensheviks, with top Bundists like Henryk taking prominent roles in the Menshevik party. He often visited the Duma at Tauride Palace, where several Menshevik deputies served. When his cab pulled up before its splendid bulk, he would gather the pages of whatever speech he or Sophia had written and shove them into his briefcase, then walk down the colonnaded hallways into the domed hall where near-powerless delegates sat stacked in semicircles, their faces turned toward a portrait of Tsar Nicholas II. Outside the palace, Henryk managed brutal electoral campaigns and edited the Bund's Russian-language newspaper, all while practicing law in the office of a famous defense attorney. He worked late and was seldom home. Politics was his life.

Her husband may have been a party man, but Marxist dogmatism fit Sophia like an itchy dress. She was a socialist aware of the movement's absurdity, and an artist who couldn't resign herself to the injustice of the world. In youth, she crushed on the family maid with sapphic fervor. She briefly dated the right-wing Zionist journalist Vladimir Jabotinsky, who organized self-defense squads after the Kishinev pogrom, until her liberal father banned him from their house. Sharp-eyed and bohemian, she shunned revolutionary asceticism. She read Nietzsche—too decadent, said her comrades—and dressed in lavish costumes for the artists' balls she attended during an Arcadian few months in Munich. (Henryk had to be bullied to participate.) After her return to Saint Petersburg in 1911, Sophia had made a name for herself in the feverish artistic world of the capital, reading her verses in the smoky basement cabarets and blue-curtained salons that defined the Russian Silver Age. Her work soon caught the eye of Russia's most famous leftist writer, Maxim Gorky, who invited her to contribute to his celebrated literary journal, *Chronicle.*

In Petersburg, the Erlichs lived on the quiet Bolshaya Monetnaya Street, next to *Chronicle*'s cramped offices. "Here you could meet the beginning writer nervously kneading his manuscript, the party activist just returned from exile," Sophia wrote. Even the Odesa prodigy Isaac Babel came through. Then the war came, and the city's name changed to the more Russian-sounding Petrograd.

The army conscripted Sophia's friends. The censors sliced her poetry apart. The Germans advanced, taking Lublin, where Henryk's parents lived. The *Chronicle* office became her retreat. There, wartime privations seemed to disappear amidst the cigarette smoke and talk and clack of the secretary's typewriter.

As the twelfth anniversary of Bloody Sunday neared, Henryk busied himself with crafting statements for the Workers' Group of the War Industries Committee.* "Our urgent task is to destroy autocracy, to bring full democracy to the country. . . . The whole Petrograd working class must head for Tauride Palace." Two days later, the government arrested most of the Workers' Group.

"Not everything can be foretold and foreseen. Blood and fire can give voice when no one expects them to," wrote Sophia's acquaintance, the poet Alexander Blok, in 1913. As 1917 began, his words took on a prophetic resonance. As the Russian Empire entered its fourth year of war, it had nothing to show for it except lost territory and over a million dead soldiers. The economy collapsed. Food prices climbed. In front of bakeries, lines of women stood until icicles formed on their faces while, far away, their men died for nothing. Sophia sensed that something was about to happen, but she didn't know what.

WOMEN'S DAY

On the miserable gray morning of International Women's Day, March 8, 1917,† working women of Petrograd took to the streets. It was not the first protest that year—the city's metal workers were also on strike—but the women were furious from hunger and grief. They began in the Vyborgsky factory district, where they screamed for their men to join them, then poured into the posh parts of Petrograd—like Bolshaya Monetnaya Street, where Sophia Dubnova and her family lived. She watched the crowds gather, the "workers in long vests, women in shawls, members of the intelligentsia in lambskin hats." The red flag appeared. First, they called for bread. Next, they called for the death of the regime.

The tsar ordered police to suppress the protests. Mounted police charged the crowds, slashing with their whips. But the crowds stood firm. They shouted curses and pelted the cops with hunks of ice.

By March 11, over two hundred thousand people were on strike. Stores shuttered. Streetcars lay on their sides, the windows smashed.

* An organization of worker-delegates from factories that supplied the military.

† The Russian Empire used the Julian calendar, which is thirteen days behind the Gregorian calendar used by Western countries. Women's Day fell on February 23 inside Russia and March 8 outside it. Soviet Russia switched to the Gregorian calendar in early 1918.

The air was livid with chants and the sound of bullets, as police, protesters, and soldiers clashed in a war whose battle lines shifted by the hour. Sometimes the soldiers obeyed orders to shoot into the crowds, but mostly they hesitated to fire bullets at women who could have been their mothers. Most of them agreed with the protesters. They also wanted bread and peace.

That night Henryk Erlich received an invitation to a gathering of leftist activists at the home of a flamboyant young Duma deputy named Alexander Kerensky. A celebrated defense lawyer and self-described socialist, Kerensky bubbled with enthusiasm about the possible beginnings of a revolution. "Characteristic hysteria," smirked another guest, who assured the room that this so-called revolution was going nowhere.

The next afternoon, the Fourth Company of the Imperial Guard's Pavlovsky Regiment mutinied. They marched out of their barracks, opened fire on a mounted police patrol, and disappeared into the streets. After this first revolt, a dam broke, and whole units began to defect, taking their weapons with them. Desperate reports piled up at the Petrograd office of the Okhrana. The Litovsky Regiment had plundered the arsenal at Kirochnaya Street, hauling off rifles in stolen automobiles. Soldiers from the Preobrazhensky Regiment had lynched their commander when he refused to give them weapons. "They sent soldiers by horse and by car to all the other military units for the purpose of inciting mutiny. Shooting has started. The crowds . . . are very large." After that, the tsar's secret police went silent.

Insurgent troops marched toward Tauride Palace, where the Duma was holding an emergency session. Though the Duma's delegates had been chosen in an election in which most people were not permitted to vote, they formed the closest thing the Russian Empire had to a parliament, and so protesters looked to them for leadership. Kerensky was happy to oblige. This was their moment, he thought. The Duma should lead the revolution. When he heard shouts from Tauride's entrance signaling the mutinous soldiers' arrival, he knew exactly the pose to strike. He ran to the center gate. With a flair for the dramatic that would define his role in coming days, Kerensky greeted the mutineers as heroes.

At the same time, another crowd attacked Kresty prison and released the prisoners, among them Erlich's comrades, the leaders of the Workers' Group. These activists also headed to Tauride Palace.

That afternoon, in room 12 in the left wing of Tauride, these prisoners joined several dozen representatives of radical parties, including Henryk Erlich. Together, they took up an idea from the revolution of 1905 and declared themselves the Temporary Executive Committee of the Soviet of Workers' and Soldiers' Deputies. Inspired by the Saint Petersburg Soviet of 1905, and with the help of several of that original soviet's leaders, the Petrograd Soviet was created to represent the capital's workers and soldiers. It would be a grassroots forum for direct democracy. By the people. For the people.

To make this vision a reality, the Soviet's leaders dispatched messengers to Petrograd's factories and barracks, seeking delegates for their first session at Tauride Palace that night. Two hundred and fifty people showed up. After hours of feverish chatter, they elected an old Georgian Menshevik named Nikolai Chkheidze as president of the Soviet, with the magnetic young Kerensky as a vice president. Kerensky, though, had grander dreams. After a passionate homily to revolution, he disappeared into the right wing of Tauride Palace, where he and thirteen other progressive Duma delegates formed the Provisional Government of Revolutionary Russia.

Meanwhile, Erlich and the rest of the executive committee worked through the night. When dawn came, each man staggered off to find a spot of floor on which to sleep. I imagine Erlich spread his fur coat between a box of bullets and a stranger's feet. As he stared at the topless nymphs who capered across Tauride's ceiling, contradictory thoughts must have filled his mind. The bloodlust of the streets would likely have disgusted Erlich, who was a refined, gentle man. He would have worried that a tsarist general might attack the city. Every tendon would have ached. But, exhausted as he was, perhaps Erlich didn't want to let himself slip into unconsciousness, because that would have meant the revolution's first day was over. When someone has waited for something their entire life, and it arrives at last, they never want it to end.

Outside, teenagers tied red rags around their arms and loaded guns onto trucks they barely knew how to drive. Fire rouged the sky. When Erlich woke up, he might have seen soldiers bayonetting portraits of Tsar Nicholas, the Last.

THE FIRST DAYS

In Petrograd, there were now two centers of power—the Duma on the right side of Tauride Palace and the Soviet on the left. While foreign states recognized the Duma as Russia's government, the Soviet ran the city. By this I mean the Soviet's temporary executive committee, otherwise known as Erlich and his comrades.

Chaos defined Erlich's first days in revolutionary Petrograd. The temporary executive committee had few resources and immense responsibilities. Crowds burst in constantly with news of real and fictitious emergencies. The tsar's loyalists holed up in church belfries, taking potshots at members of the newly formed People's Militia. Freed criminals robbed houses. Rioters torched the Okhrana office; the lists of informants went up in smoke. Military deserters wandered, confused, homeless, and hungry, threatening at any moment to erupt into pointless violence. There was no bread. The trams didn't work. Everything was a ruin, and the executive committee knew they had to fix things fast.

As the Soviet struggled to establish order, the capital's people took their vengeance. Mobs hunted representatives of the old regime. Among their first catches was Ivan Shcheglovitov, former chairman of the state council. Four years earlier, Shcheglovitov had ordered Kyiv police to frame the innocent Jewish factory foreman Mendel Beilis on charges of ritual murder. Now Shcheglovitov was the wanted man. Soldiers broke into his apartment and marched him at gunpoint to Tauride, where, in the name of the people, Kerensky put him under arrest.

NEW YORK CITY

On March 15, the tsar signed his abdication papers; with that, 450 years of autocracy were over. You go bankrupt gradually, then suddenly, Hemingway wrote. He might have been talking about the Romanovs.

When the news reached New York, residents of Jewish neighborhoods flooded the streets. "Almost a million men, women and children turned the day into a festival of rejoicing," wrote the *New York Tribune*. In Café Monopole, at Leavitt's, in Little Hungary, former prisoners raised glasses of Schnapps to the revolution's leaders. Crowds smashed every window at the corner of Clinton and Houston streets, just from a surplus of delight.

Thousands gathered in front of the Forward Building for updates on the thrilling events back in Russia. The paper's city editor, former Bundist Baruch Charney Vladeck, addressed the crowd from the balcony. "I was a Russian prisoner in 1905. It was right after a revolution, but such a puny, strengthless revolution it was. Today is different." When rumors spread that the tsar had been killed, the crowds burst into hurrahs.

Blindsided by the uprising in Petrograd, American journalists turned to emigres for expertise. Journalists besieged the offices of *Novy Mir*, an obscure Russian paper on Saint Marks Place, to get the analysis of its pugnacious editor, Leon Trotsky. They mingled with the crowds on Orchard Street and jotted down quotes that compared the revolution to the coming of the messiah and Petrograd to a new Jerusalem. One old professor told them, "Do you wonder at our happiness? We are to be restored from exile, just as we were two thousand years ago." For the moment, the media seemed to agree.

One American journalist struck a more sober note. In *The New York Age,* the country's preeminent Black newspaper, NAACP activist James Weldon Johnson described the celebrations sympathetically, noting that Black people were the only Americans who could truly understand the East Side's joy. After all, they had partied the same way when Lincoln announced emancipation, only to learn bitterly that democracy on paper was far from democracy in practice. After fifty years of betrayal by their white fellow citizens, they'd grown disillusioned, and Jews would be too if they trusted the Christians of the Russian Empire. The revolution might remove some hated laws, but it didn't change society. At best, it had given Jews the opportunity to fight.

THE PETROGRAD SOVIET OF WORKERS' AND SOLDIERS' DEPUTIES

Overwhelmed with work on the Soviet, Henryk moved into Tauride Palace. He telephoned Sophia a few times a day to give her updates, which she passed on to the gaggle of acquaintances who converged at their apartment for advance news of the Soviet's decisions. With most newspapers still shut, Petrograd's people watched the walls for pasted-up Soviet decrees. They listened for gunfire dispatching this alleged reactionary or that. They lived on rumor.

One morning, Sophia woke up to banging on her door. She opened it to see Henryk's sister and her husband, a military doctor at the naval base in Kronstadt, nineteen miles west of Petrograd. Built by Peter the Great on an island in the Gulf of Finland, Kronstadt was home to the Russian Empire's Baltic Fleet. Its tens of thousands of sailors constituted a veritable city and were some of the revolution's most enthusiastic participants.

Behind Sophia's in-laws sat a cart piled with hastily grabbed possessions. The sister's usually vivacious face was haggard, and she had a horrified look in her eyes. Her husband told Sophia that Kronstadt sailors had torn their admiral to pieces with their bayonets.

This is a revolutionary moment, Sophia told herself that night, and many nights afterward. She thought of the French Revolution. This wasn't any different. She tried to suppress the nausea in her gut.

Sophia often braved the snowdrifts to walk three miles to Tauride Palace, to attend meetings of the Soviet in the palace's Catherine Hall. By then the Soviet had swollen to thousands of delegates, and Sophia sweated from the heat of their combined bodies. Beneath gold chandeliers and friezes of Grecian heroes, journalists stalked diplomats, Kronstadt sailors slurped tea, and representatives of political factions competed in noisy grandiloquence. The Soviet measured votes by the volume of the cheers. When the Soviet's leaders tried to talk, no one listened. "People had come not to hear speeches but to claim their right to rule the country," Sophia later wrote.

This experiment in direct democracy quickly spread across the Russian Empire, including to the former Pale of Settlement. Workers and soldiers set up their own soviets, with countless Bundists among the leaders. I think of Leivik Hodis, a military mechanic stationed in Smolensk. When news of Petrograd's revolution came, he joined some Christian socialists in his unit, arrested his officers, and seized control of the city, where he now represented the Bund in the local soviet. He had gone from pariah to power.

When I imagine Hodis that February, I think back to twelve years prior, at the American Star Hall in Brownsville, when socialist orator Meyer London told the crowd: "Are you aware that in Russian Poland, thousands of our Jewish boys and girls . . . pray to God, not to lead them again out of Egypt, but to help them to free Egypt?" For Hodis, and for thousands of other Bundists spread across the empire's borderlands, it seemed like their prayers had been answered. The revolution flamed, and they threw themselves into it, as both participants and offerings. By their actions, they sought to make good on the Bund's redemptive credo. Here where they lived was their country. They had liberated it, alongside their Christian brothers. Egypt was now free.

THE PROVISIONAL GOVERNMENT

On March 15, the day of the tsar's abdication, the first cabinet of the Provisional Government of Revolutionary Russia was appointed. Its members immediately set about trying to make Russia the freest country on earth. In rapid succession, they abolished the death penalty, banned torture, and gave women legal equality. Free speech, free press, and universal suffrage were the laws of the land. Soon, the provisional government promised, a freely elected Constituent Assembly would be convened to determine Russia's ultimate form of government.

Among the most eloquent exponents of liberty was the newly appointed justice minister, the dashing young lawyer Alexander Kerensky. He was a magnetic figure, so beloved that crowds wept at his speeches. Clearly, the future belonged to him.

In his first act as justice minister, Kerensky freed all political prisoners, including the hundred thousand troublemakers confined in Siberia. Immediately, these exiles embarked on a race against time. They had to get to the train stations before spring came, thawing the ice and turning the roads into impassable mud. Anyone who could commandeered reindeer sleighs. Those who couldn't walked. Twenty Bundists joined a band of political convicts who stumbled upon a reporter from the Associated Press. After ten days on the road, the group was "shaggy, uncouth, unwashed, emaciated. Two had lost hands and feet from frostbite, and one had been shot in the leg." Some wore rags, others fur coats donated by sympathizers, one "the gold braided uniform tunic of the dismissed governor under a ragged and greasy overcoat." Many were chained hand and foot, but the blacksmiths were on strike, so no one could be found to free them. At the former governor's mansion, sympathetic locals held a banquet in the prisoners' honor. The clang of their shackles nearly drowned out the toasts.

RETURN

In Bronx tenements, Swiss cafés, and Austrian detention camps, exiled Russian radicals learned they could come home. At New York rallies in support of the revolution, marchers raised money to buy steamship tickets back to the motherland. In the following year, eight thousand people returned to the Russian Empire, in perhaps the largest voluntary reverse migration in American history. One of them was Leon Trotsky.

Vladimir Medem was among those who could not return. Thirty-eight years old and living in Warsaw at the time of the revolution, Medem had emerged from prison in 1915 as a legend on both sides of the Atlantic. He had made good use of the years since. Taking advantage of the tolerance for Jewish political activity shown by Warsaw's German occupiers, he restarted the Bund's newspaper, *Lebens-Fragen,* and set up the foundations of a thriving subculture, including Yiddish schools, orphanages, libraries, and soup kitchens. But Medem soon found the limits of German tolerance. Appalled by the starvation and forced labor that the occupation imposed, Medem wrote a series of critical pamphlets. As punishment, the Germans locked him briefly in a concentration camp.*

Medem never stopped longing for Russia. Then the revolution came,

* Pioneered by the British in South Africa during the Second Boer War, concentration camps imprisoned minorities and dissidents rather than criminals, and were soon taken up by governments across Europe.

bringing with it the fulfillment of his life's work. What did Warsaw soup kitchens mean when, back in Russia, the Bund had helped topple a dynasty; when his old underground friends were now reshaping their homeland? In Russia, hundreds of Bundists now served on kehillahs (Jewish communal councils), city councils, and soviets. Party membership exploded until it reached thirty-three thousand members, and new Bundist branches sprang up from Crimea to the Siberian city of Irkutsk. The Russian Bund was building the future. Soon, friends' surreptitious messages began to arrive in Warsaw, pleading for Medem to join them in revolutionary Petrograd. But with Germany and Russia at war, the border remained unbreachable. History beckoned, and Vladimir Medem was trapped outside.

THE JEWISH NATION IN THE HANDS OF THE RUSSIAN NATION

On March 22, 1917, the provisional government announced the abolition of all restrictions based on nationality, religion, and class in the Russian Empire. After 126 years of government oppression, Jews were now officially equal.

The tsarist race laws had choked ambitions and stifled lives. As a girl, Sophia Dubnova had watched her father study bookbinding in a futile attempt to qualify as one of the categories of Jewish tradesmen permitted to live in Saint Petersburg. Glue-smeared practice volumes sat on his bookshelf as a testament to his failure. After Sophia's radical clique was expelled from university, one Jewish girlfriend even registered as a prostitute, just to retain her right to live in the capital. Now, before Sophia's eyes, the bureaucratic walls of the Pale of Settlement fell forever. Universities opened. Jews could enter government service. The *New York Tribune* reported, with astonishment, that one Mr. Epstein had even become the police commissioner of Minsk.

If the Bund's founders had once said that "Jewish workers suffer not only as workers but also as Jews," such suffering now seemed like a thing of the past.

From their commandeered office on the posh Nevsky Prospect, the Bund sent a communiqué to *The New York Times* to celebrate legal equality. It was a document full of swagger, as befitting a party that had won. It closed with a statement of trust in Russian society that is all the more remarkable because it contradicted their foundational beliefs. In 1897, Martov wrote that Jews could not "rely solely on the Russian . . .

proletariat," who might sell them out for profit or under duress. Twenty years later, the Bund thought otherwise. "The liberation of the Jewish nation is in the faithful hands of the Russian nation," they wrote. They allowed themselves to believe.

Sophia also allowed herself to believe. On March 23, she was one of the million Petrograd residents to make their way to the Field of Mars for the funeral of protesters killed in the first days of the revolution. Columns from factories, trade unions, and political parties marched behind two hundred red-draped coffins. Among them marched the Bund. They held their banner high, its gold Yiddish letters shimmering in the sunlight. This was no longer the flag of despised criminals. It flew openly in the capital, held by equal citizens of a revolutionary state. At the Field of Mars, Sophia saw S. An-sky, the poet who'd penned "The Oath," the Bund's anthem. She took the old man's arm. The spring air, the old friend, the crush of silent mourners, all conspired to overwhelm her. She had never felt such brotherhood in her life.

MARK LIBER

On April 27, 1917, in Petrograd, the Bund opened the first conference it ever legally held inside the Russian Empire. Beneath banners reading LONG LIVE THE REVOLUTION, old friends embraced as if their years of exile had never happened. They teased one another about their gray hair and wandered timidly amongst the unfamiliar hordes of new recruits to their party. Who were all these people, the old-timers asked themselves. No matter. Life was starting afresh.

They took their seats in a massive auditorium and looked up at the presidium, where the Bund's central committee sat surrounded by crimson flowers. Among the elderly pioneers from the Vilna days, they would have recognized a younger face, that of Mark Liber. By 1917, Medem's Exileland best friend had grown into a star. He had spent years touring Russia, America, and Europe, living on fake papers, addressing illegal meetings, and escaping jails. When the revolution hit, he was two years into a sentence of administrative exile in Kazakhstan. He hurried back to Petrograd, where he joined Henryk Erlich in the Soviet. In no time, he had become the city's most famous orator. Most nights found Liber at Ciniselli Circus, where he spoke about the revolution's glories as if possessed. Kronstadt sailors carried him out on their shoulders afterward.

"His talent was created for meetings of thousands of workers, for a parliament," wrote one admiring journalist. "His hour has come."

While maintaining his role in the Bund, Liber threw his energies into their sister party, the Mensheviks, quickly rising to leadership. In Petrograd, this made sense. Russia's capital might have been the center of world revolution, but it was far from the Bundist base.

Due to laws that had, until a month earlier, locked Jews out of the capital, Petrograd had few Jewish workers, and the local Bund branch was really just a club for a few hundred well-off professionals. But if Mark Liber missed the scrappy counterculture of the Pale of Settlement, he didn't show it. As a Menshevik leader, he could shape policy for the entire Russian Empire—especially now that the Mensheviks had teamed up with the Socialist Revolutionaries to rule the Soviet. That spring, Liber was the most powerful Bundist in history.

After the fraternal greetings and theoretical debates that lard all leftist conferences, the Bundists moved to a crucial question: Should their party participate in the provisional government?

This seemingly obvious question was more fraught then we might guess. For Bundists to join the government would mean tearing up Marx's theory of historical development, which foresaw inevitable progress from feudalism, to capitalism, to socialism, to communism, with each stage following the last, much as, at a formal dinner party, the seafood follows the soup. As orthodox Marxists, the Bundists believed that a socialist revolution could not take place in a backward country like Russia, which needed a few centuries of capitalist industrialization and parliamentary democracy to set the stage. Only then could socialist parties dream of taking power. That was what the laws of dialectical materialism said—by the Bund's reckoning, anyway—and they were committed to following their theory to the end. I wonder too if power felt dirty for these lifelong underdogs. Maybe they wanted to remain pure. Whatever the reason, in the name of Marxism, the Bund resolved to sit on the sidelines.

The Bund then turned their attention to the war.

Here, Mark Liber took the stage.

Before the revolution, most Bundist leaders had opposed World War I, but with the tsar gone, things took on a different cast. Russia was no longer an autocracy run by inbred aristocrats. It was *theirs*. By April 1917, most Bundist leaders believed that Russia should keep fighting alongside her allies until they all made a joint peace deal. What better way for Russia to join the club of Western democracies? Besides, Germany and Austria now occupied most of the former Pale of Settlement, the Bund's heartland, where they forced Bundists onto labor gangs and imprisoned party activists. They had to rescue their people. They had to defend the world.

That was the case Mark Liber made.

(Can I be surprised? How often have I seen the powerful politely justify mass murder, and otherwise decent people go along with it because it seems like the responsible, respectable thing to do? And despite everything, Liber was a decent man.)

Liber erred in one regard. You can't fight a war without an army. By 1917, Russian soldiers were starving conscripts, so badly armed they had to take guns off their comrades' corpses. Caught in a blind machine of mechanized slaughter, they simply wanted to survive. Soldiers in Petrograd overthrew the tsar for one reason: to stop the war. If the revolutionary government wouldn't stop the war, soldiers would overthrow them too.

Liber mentioned none of this. After a fervent denunciation of German aggression, he proposed a resolution to "fight for peace and defend the land." It passed with a healthy majority.

FINLAND STATION

Liber's speech must have been influenced by the arrival two weeks prior of a man he loathed from his own Exileland past.

As soon as news of the revolution reached Switzerland, the country's eight hundred Russian political exiles elected a committee to negotiate their return to Petrograd with the British government (which would have transported them home on military ships). This proved difficult, however, since, due to their antiwar activities, British intelligence services had put many of the exiles on a travel blacklist. Negotiations went nowhere. At last, one person decided to make separate arrangements. On April 9, 1917, Vladimir Lenin, joined by six Bundists and thirty-one other socialists, boarded a private train in Zurich. They traveled through Germany, with the permission of the German government, to arrive in Petrograd on April 16. Though many in the Soviet viewed this trip through an enemy country as an act of treason, they knew Lenin from abroad and, more out of protocol than enthusiasm, organized a delegation to greet him. Late that night, Erlich joined his fellow representatives at Finland Station.

Masters of the visual, the Bolsheviks had organized a crowd to greet their leader. Lenin stepped out into a sea of flags and flowers. Erlich saw a man of medium height, broad shouldered, with a bald head and the "small, sprightly, crafty eyes" that Medem had remarked upon over a decade earlier, which reminded them both of a tricky salesman. Erlich noted the strength in Lenin's back.

The Soviet's chairman offered some cautious greetings, but for

Lenin, the old man might as well have stayed home. The moment the speech ended, Lenin turned his back on the delegates. He walked out of the reception room and into the square, climbed atop an armored car, faced the crowd, and launched into a pitiless denunciation of the Soviet.

"The people need peace; the people need bread; the people need land. And they give you war, hunger, no bread. . . . We must fight for the socialist revolution, fight to the end, until the complete victory of the proletariat."

The delegates were dumbfounded. The war was *their* fault? The hunger was *their* fault? They, lifelong socialists, survivors of prison and exile, were obstacles to a socialist revolution? Them? None of the Bolsheviks in Petrograd talked this way. The speech didn't correspond to the orderly progression of development that Marx laid out in *Das Kapital.* It was not comradely. It was not nice. Had Lenin gone nuts?

The crowds cheered like he was the messiah.

CHAPTER 11

REVOLUTIONARY DISCONTENTS

(May–October 1917)

MAY DAY

MAY 1, 1917, MARKED THE FIRST LEGAL CELEBRATIONS OF MAY DAY inside the Russian Empire. On that bright, chilly Tuesday, hundreds of thousands of people streamed through Petrograd's boulevards to the Field of Mars. Marchers pulled their coats tight as they walked behind their hand-sewn banners. Socialist red dominated, dotted here and there with anarchist black. Walking beside her husband and father, Sophia Dubnova held on to her sons' hands. Her boys wore red ribbons pinned to their lapels, and they were proud to look like men.

On the river, the sunlight melted the ice floes. Sophia listened to the pieces crack. Years later, she recalled the moment in a poem.

Oh distant First of May,
The bridge humming in spring apparel,
The Neva, the golden Neva
Under the swelling drift ice!
Sun transparent chunks
Were borne off in foam and spray,
The ice was helpless and fragile
Like your freedom, my fatherland

Sophia must have cherished the day as a respite from the tumult of the previous weeks. After Lenin's arrival at Finland Station, Petrograd's formerly congenial revolutionary milieu had shattered into warring camps. From his first day in town, when he strode into Tauride Palace to inform the socialist delegates that they had done everything wrong, Lenin insisted that his party's job was to overthrow the "government of capitalists and landowners" and give all power to the soviets. He quickly marginalized any Bolshevik dissenters, as he had done in Exileland.

Just as quickly, his ideas became inescapable.

The Bolsheviks commandeered a palace belonging to the tsar's ballerina-mistress Mathilde Kshesinskaya for their headquarters, and Lenin often harangued the crowds from its balcony. He spoke in terms simple enough for a five-year-old to understand, even if that five-year-old was Sophia's son Alex. The boy first saw Lenin thanks to his nanny, who mooned around the palace looking for a Kronstadt sailor of her own. While his nanny cased the crowd, Alex listened to the bald little man on the balcony, who said the war was stupid, the government's plan to retake Constantinople was stupid, and that troops should turn their bayonets on their officers. Alex thought that baldie had a point.

"I don't care about Constantinople," he proclaimed one night.

"Where did you hear that?" Sophia asked.

"That's what the uncle says," he answered. She knew immediately who uncle was.

THE TRIALS OF GOVERNANCE

Winter blossomed into spring. The ice floes melted along the Neva. Fissures grew in the revolutionary homeland, threatening to crack it apart.

It turned out that the people who had just overthrown their autocrat nourished even more dangerous dreams. Around the empire, long-suppressed nationalist movements raised their heads. In Ukraine of the golden sunflowers, intellectuals had put together a parliament—the Rada—whose calls for autonomy scandalized Petrograd politicians. *Wasn't Ukraine a Russian possession?* Workers too shook off their fear. Demanding higher wages, an eight-hour workday, and respect as equals, over half a million people went on strike. Wages went up, but prices climbed higher. To cover the deficit, the government printed money. Inflation soared.

Peasants itched to evict their aristocratic landlords and divide up the land for themselves. Soldiers wanted to return to their villages, not die in a pointless war. The revolution was nine weeks old, and patience was running out for the politicians in Petrograd.

THE END OF EXILE

Back in Switzerland, Bundist Raphael Abramovich was furious when he read about the splash Lenin made in the capital. Back in 1905, Abramovich had been among the revolution's most enthusiastic agitators, but after several arrests, he mellowed, got an office job, and urged the party to turn its back on its illicit past by forming legal trade unions and running in elections.

Then came the revolution of 1917. Now Lenin was in Petrograd making history, and the rest of the exiles were sitting on their asses in Switzerland. Abramovich had one thought. They needed to get home.

At last, the great day arrived. On May 13, two hundred and eight exiled revolutionaries boarded the train toward Petrograd to the sounds of brass bands and the cheers of hundreds of Swiss workers. Among these exiles were Polish socialists, *Iskra* editors, and gray-bearded Narodniks who had once conspired to kill Tsar Nicholas II's grandfather. The sarcastic Bolshevik journalist Karl Radek grinned, showing a gap where German police had knocked out his front teeth. Menshevik leader Julius Martov nursed a cough. Abramovich and his family boarded the Bundist wagon. From the window, he watched Exileland load itself into the train cars. *I will never forget this,* he thought.

Even as they barreled toward the homeland, the exiles couldn't help but get into the squabbles that marked their previous lives. At a German border town, one grouplet staged a sit-down strike to demand a dedicated railway car like the other parties. They refused to move until Abramovich surrendered half the Bund's wagon to them. Abramovich spent so much time like this—smoothing egos, finding seats, and warming milk for babies—that he never had a chance to look out the window, at the dark track guarded by enemy soldiers, and think about the step he had taken. In Sweden, his baby daughter got sick, so while the rest of the exiles proceeded to Petrograd, the Abramovichs stayed behind to find doctors. When their train finally pulled into Finland Station, Abramovich expected no one to be waiting, but his Exileland crew organized a welcoming party several hundred strong. Henryk Erlich stepped forward to give him the official greetings of the Bund and the Menshevik party.

They embraced. Abramovich knew that he was home.

RAPHAEL ABRAMOVICH

In Petrograd, Abramovich quickly found himself at odds with Bundist leadership over the issue of World War I—especially with his old friend Mark Liber, who had become one of the war's most strident supporters. Abramovich had always opposed the war, and the revolution had done nothing to change his views. A slaughterhouse was a slaughterhouse, he knew. It didn't matter who owned the building. Alienated from his comrades, Abramovich drew closer to the brilliant Menshevik leader Julius Martov, who now helmed a dissident antiwar faction called the Menshevik-Internationalists.

Despite his deviation from the official line, the Bund valued Abramovich's long service to the party. They appointed him as editor of their Petrograd newspaper, *Workers' Voice,* where he compiled stories about Bundist groups around the empire. While the Petrograd Bund might have been peripheral in the capital, local Bundist groups in the former Pale were transforming Jewish life through vivid networks of culture and mutual aid, while also arming up to defend their communities against pogroms that they hoped were the last gasps of the hateful old regime.

But Abramovich did not merely use his platform to glorify his party. He lobbied relentlessly for peace.

As much as he opposed the war on moral terms, Abramovich was painfully aware of how the continued slaughter empowered the Bolsheviks—the one group to speak out definitively against it. Lenin's party might have been a small minority in the Soviet, but they were a rising power on the streets. They organized relentlessly in barracks, in factories, and on the front. For muscle they had Kronstadt sailors and brigades of armed workers called the Red Guards.

But instead of sensing the popular mood, Liber and his fellow socialists who ran the Soviet grew more conservative, hewing ever more closely to Kerensky's provisional government. These former radicals now spoke of patriotism and moderation and postponed their old promises of world peace and eight-hour workdays to an ever more distant tomorrow. This earned them the ironic nickname "right-wing socialists." Obliviously, most Bundist leaders did the same. If Marxist theory told them that Russia needed a capitalist government, and that socialists could not seize power in Russia in 1917, they would follow that theory to the end.

Liber soon lost his star spot at Ciniselli Circus, where, every night, Bolshevik orators incited the crowds against the capitalists and landlords in government. Within weeks of Abramovich's arrival, an incident showed him how deeply these speeches resonated. He was on a packed tram passing through Vyborg, the factory district that was now a Bolshevik stronghold. A woman worker entered the car and squeezed her way next to him. She elbowed him the entire ride. When they reached their stop, he smiled at her. "Why did you shove me?" he asked.

She sneered. "Why shouldn't I shove you?" she answered, with unmistakable menace in her voice.

Abramovich was about to respond when he felt the eyes of the other passengers on him. He was suddenly aware of his suit, which he'd brought from Switzerland, of his fedora and glasses. All of it was perfectly normal over there, but here, he realized, it looked provocatively ostentatious, like the sort of thing a capitalist or landlord might wear. He wanted to defend himself to these workers. After all, he'd spent time in prison for their sake. The hatred in their eyes stopped him. He stared at the floor in silence until he reached his stop.

THE FIRST CONGRESS OF THE SOVIETS

On June 16, the First All-Russia Congress of the Soviet of Workers' and Soldiers' Deputies opened at the building of the First Cadet Corps on Petrograd's Vasilyevsky Island. In what was the first real test of mass democracy in the former Russian Empire, twenty million people had cast their ballots to choose eight hundred delegates, including the Bundists Henryk Erlich, Mark Liber, and Raphael Abramovich. Abramovich could not help but marvel at the clamorous Cadet School hallways, which were packed with innumerable political factions, trade unions, and freelance orators, all talking as if they could make up for centuries of enforced silence in a single day.

At the congress, the most pressing issue should have been a new military offensive championed by Alexander Kerensky, who had recently been appointed minister of war. Against the advice of the army's general staff, the government mobilized hundreds of thousands of reserve soldiers in a last-ditch attempt to turn things around on the Western Front. Many were middle-aged farmers, ripped from their villages at the start of summer planting. They marched through Petrograd under banners that read LET US MAKE BREAD FOR THE PEOPLE, well within the delegates' sight. Yet when Bolsheviks proposed a debate about the upcoming offensive, Mark Liber's bloc of right-wing Mensheviks and Socialist Revolutionaries refused to consider it.

Four days into the conference, Liber ran into the Cadet Corps building red with rage. He held proofs for an upcoming edition of the Bolshevik newspaper *Pravda*, whose front page called for an armed demonstration against the provisional government. Liber had always believed Lenin was a dictator in waiting. Now he had proof. There it was, plain as day, Liber shouted. Lenin was plotting a coup.

Liber's announcement threw the congress into a tumult. The Soviet quickly banned the Bolshevik demonstration and instead organized a counterdemonstration to support the provisional government.

The next day Raphael Abramovich watched as Liber marched down Nevsky Prospect alongside the rest of the Soviet's executive committee, with five hundred thousand people behind them. But though it ought to have been a triumph, Abramovich could not help but notice that Bolshevik banners far outnumbered Menshevik flags.

In the sea of Cyrillic signage, Abramovich spotted the Yiddish flag of the Petrograd Bund. Its leader, Virgil Kahan, also held a banner, reading ALL CONFIDENCE TO THE PROVISIONAL GOVERNMENT! that was painfully out of touch with the crowd's mood. Abramovich felt a terrible tenderness as the little crew passed from his sight.

Later, Virgil would tell Abramovich how his comrades ended their day. They had thoughtlessly wandered into a group of thousands of burly Bolshevik steelworkers, who did not appreciate the Bund's pro-government banner. Words were exchanged. A steelworker tore the Bund's flag from its pole. Virgil dove to retrieve it.

During the revolution of 1905, Virgil had been fighter-king on the Lodz barricade, but things can change in a dozen years. The contrast between former strength and current frailty feels ever greater when one is surrounded by younger men, their boots, and their fists. The Bund's torn flag told Abramovich one story, but a detail Virgil added made his stomach sink. During the scuffle, the workers called him a kike.

HENRYK ERLICH

After two days at the first congress of the Soviets, Henryk Erlich had had his fill of demagogues. At one point, he listened incredulously while Lenin spat out un-Marxist nonsense about ending capitalism by forcing all the capitalists to reveal their hidden gold (which, Erlich mused, the learned Lenin could not possibly have believed!). Worse, the soldiers had cheered. Enough! Everyone wanted to talk about the war, but Erlich was poised to do something about it. The Soviet planned to set up an international peace conference, and thanks to his German-language skills, Henryk Erlich would be the only Bundist taking part.

The idea seemed logical. They would get unions and socialist parties from the warring countries to meet in neutral Sweden, put out a collective peace appeal, and pressure their governments to end the war that, in the span of three years, had already killed over ten million people. When Erlich departed Russia that June, he had every reason to hope. But these were not logical times. The tour, which began with speeches before ecstatic crowds in Italy, quickly devolved into a gauntlet of humiliations. French papers called him a Jewish agent of the Kaiser. When Erlich and his colleagues reached London, the press smeared them as German spies.

Erlich soon realized that there would be no peace conference in Stockholm. Even if individuals wanted to attend, the French and British governments had blocked their exit visas. Thanks to the Allies' stubbornness, the Soviet's efforts for "a democratic peace without annexations and indemnities" ended in total defeat.

When Erlich returned in August, Russia seemed ready to disintegrate. Workers struck constantly, and robbers prowled the Petrograd streets. Things were worse at the front, where the debacle of Kerensky's offensive had taken four hundred thousand soldiers' lives. Hundreds of thousands more soldiers simply demobilized themselves, lynching their officers, grabbing their weapons, and fleeing home to their villages. Kerensky too had lost his youthful shine. After violent antiwar demonstrations by Bolshevik soldiers, he appointed himself prime minister in a bid to keep order, then moved into the Winter Palace, where he fired off increasingly authoritarian dictates while swanning around in robes once worn by Tsar Alexander III. In September, he secretly got involved with a coup attempt, led by the army's new commander in chief, Lavr Kornilov. Or not so secretly. When Kornilov's coup collapsed, rumors spread that Kerensky was in on the conspiracy.

As Kerensky's fortunes fell, those of the Bolsheviks soared. For the working people of Petrograd, they seemed like the only option. Other parties had discredited themselves by supporting the war and Kerensky's foibles. The Bolsheviks, at least, promised peace, land, and bread. Each night, crowds jammed Ciniselli Circus to hear Trotsky speak. With scathing wit and prophetic power, Trotsky denounced the provisional government, along with his special scapegoats, the right-wing socialists like Mark Liber, who prevented the Soviet from seizing power to serve as the true tribune of the people. Trotsky's words echoed on every street.

When Erlich walked through the crowds on his way to the Soviet, he felt like his city had gone insane. Who were these people? Were these *the People*, the agents of history? He could no longer recognize them. His mouth could not form words that they would hear. If only he could lie or play on their emotions. If only he could recite the simple slogans that moved their hearts. But he couldn't. He was helpless. The masses were a foreign country. He walked by the speakers without having the heart to challenge them.

REVOLUTIONARY RUSSIA

The Bund's official history of this time, when the Russian Revolution was hurtling toward its denouement, devotes itself to lists of conferences. Abramovich, Erlich, Liber, and their comrades spent the eight months of Russia's democratic experiment traveling around the empire attending conferences on languages, unions, schools, and cultural work. In August, Abramovich went to Kyiv to attend a conference for the Ukrainian Bund, where they released an enlightened platform that called for public bakeries, better sanitation, free healthcare, as well as unpopular positions like "Jewish schools without god." At the same conference, Abramovich finally induced the Bund to pass a resolution in support of peace. It took them long enough.

Words, and more words. That was it. I can see all these delegates on all these podiums, passing all these motions about eight-hour workdays and the dignity of Yiddish, committed to the belief that they were building a new world and closing their eyes to the world around them. They read off the fraternal greetings from this or that socialist splinter group from this or that London neighborhood—and the tectonic plates were shifting beneath their feet.

When I try to picture the Bund in the summer of 1917, I think of a crumbling Yiddish anthology called *Revolutionary Russia*, published in New York to raise funds for the Bund's Petrograd newspaper. The anthology's editor, A. Litvak, had arrived from New York in July. When Abramovich saw Litvak at the door of the Bund's office, he could barely recognize the tattered vagabond he'd once known. An American gentleman stood before him. The pleats in Litvak's pants were razor sharp. His shoes twinkled. His collar was white as cocaine. Filthy and sleep-deprived, Abramovich merely gawped.

"Chaim Yank?" Abramovich asked, calling Litvak by the name he'd used in Vilna. A childlike smile broke out across Litvak's chubby face. Proudly, Litvak presented the Petrograd Bundists with treasures from the Big Apple. A wristwatch. A fountain pen inscribed with his name. Several dozen American dollars to contribute to the party treasury. Immediately upon arrival, Litvak began compiling *Revolutionary Russia*.

It was a beautiful volume, with an art nouveau cover, reports from the March uprising, analysis of power dynamics in the provisional government, and stirring poems with titles like "My Sharpened Song, My Singing Sword." Financial contributors were in the back. More than once, I ran my finger down the list in search of Sam Rothbort's name. It was not there. Instead, I found the Radical Pinsk Workmen's Circle branch 210. Anna Kishin of Omaha. Jack Zilberknapf (formerly Warsaw's Yakov the Bootmaker). There were many Harrys, Loises, and Beatrices who garbed their insurrectionary politics in bland American names. Each gave a dollar to support the Bundist press in Russia.

The most touching part was Litvak's foreword. It was full of the same idealism that induced him to leave New York, that rich city where he had carved out a literary career, for hungry and threadbare Petrograd. How could he do otherwise? He was a Bundist, and this was the greatest event of the century. He wanted to convey every detail to the "the revolution's far-flung children": Sam and his fellow Jewish workers in America. Things could be different. The future had not been written. They could change the world. "Through the cold ink and arid pages of this collection," Litvak would deliver them a gospel from their comrades back in Russia, their "old, long enslaved, but finally liberated home."

CHAPTER 12

DENOUEMENT

(November 1917)

MINSK

ON OCTOBER 7, THE BUND CELEBRATED ITS TWENTIETH BIRTHDAY. WITH both Warsaw and Vilna under German occupation, the party chose Minsk, home to their central committee, to host their jubilee. If the Bund was insignificant in Petrograd, in Minsk they were a people's party, with 3,500 local members. They ran the local soviet alongside their Menshevik allies and controlled the central bureau of trade unions, and the Bundist Aron Vaynshteyn chaired the city council.

Abramovich began the five-hundred-mile journey from Petrograd to Minsk in an ominous mood. His train car was packed with soldiers shuttling to and from various collapsing fronts. The brotherliness of the revolution's early days was a distant memory. Faces were drawn and skinny—food was growing harder to find in the cities. As the train lurched along the battered tracks, the miserable passengers cursed each other and elbowed for more room.

Only thirty miles from the front line, Minsk hosted the headquarters of the empire's Western Army. Everything showed the marks of war. Many factories were dismantled and shipped east to prevent them from falling into German hands. Thousands of wounded soldiers filled the hospitals. Streets swarmed with refugees. Even so, when Abramovich stepped out of his train car, the city felt like a celebration. The Minsk branch of the Bund spared no expense in celebrating their movement's birthday. Hawkers offered commemorative issues of their newspaper, printed in red ink. Five thousand workers marched in their parade. For three days, Minsk's Bundist leadership gathered with thousands of well-wishers in the lemon-drop splendor of the City Theater. Singers serenaded them, poets recited odes, and every party, except the Bolsheviks, sent their greetings.

At a soirée for leaders, Esther Frumkin led the songs. Frumkin was the only woman on the Bund's central committee. She was a single mother with a spartan work ethic, a ferocious intellect, and a jealous fixation on Yiddish, whose supremacy against Hebrew she had famously fought for at the first international Yiddish conference in Czernowitz in 1908. (Famous in the small world of Yiddish scholars, at least.) At Bund conferences, she argued with equal passion for Russia to continue the war.

Frumkin and Abramovich might have spent the last months in political combat, but that night, they put their knives away in favor of fragile comradery. Outside, the world fell to pieces, but here, the Bundists were among family. They papered over differences, like they always did. They toasted their old leaders, who had founded the party and led it to victory in their revolutionary homeland, then belted the words of their latest song, an impudent parody of a song from the Passover Haggadah set to a folk tune made for dancing.

What is one?
The Bund is One
And more is none . . .

The night passed too quickly.

The next day, they returned to the City Theater to give their talks. Liber, of course, was the star. He didn't rain insults on the Bolsheviks as he usually did. Instead, he gave a panegyric to his party. "We were always democratic," Liber told the crowd. "Though our work was underground, our leaders always lived amongst the people. We had battles of ideas but never split into warring factions. We cherished our party unity above all else, and so we remained as one." The audience sang "The Oath." Their voices rose in a wave.

PETROGRAD

Abramovich arrived back in Petrograd in a vile mood. After a glorious opening, the Bund's jubilee had collapsed into rhetorical battles over the war; the arguments grew so sharp he feared that his party would split.

He returned to a city ready to boil. There were violent strikes and attacks on bakeries. Gangs searched the houses of anyone accused of hoarding food. Breadlines stretched as long as they had in February. Eight months after they had overthrown Tsar Nicholas II, ordinary people felt like they had little to show for it.

Disgusted with the war, Kerensky, and his socialist enablers like Mark Liber, the people of Petrograd turned toward the Bolsheviks as the only party promising to give all power to the soviets. Bolsheviks swept the municipal elections and, after a feverish get-out-the-vote campaign, won majorities in the Moscow Soviet and the Petrograd Soviet, which Kerensky had exiled to Smolny Institute, an aristocratic girls' school on the city's outskirts.

This move didn't faze Trotsky, the Petrograd Soviet's new chairman-in-waiting. He strode through Smolny in a black leather jacket with the air of one anointed. Which, in a way, he was. His Military Revolutionary Committee controlled forty thousand armed Red Guards and had the allegiances of the Petrograd and Kronstadt garrisons.

In *Workers' Voice*, Abramovich warned of an imminent Bolshevik coup, but no one in the government had the will to intervene.

NOVEMBER 7

Later, Abramovich would bemoan that he moved through November 7 like an automaton, oblivious to the details. He didn't realize he was living through history—we seldom do—so the day's texture was lost. This was only one of his regrets.

His morning started like always. At ten, he slogged through the rain to Mariinsky Palace, where he served on the newly convened pre-parliament—one of the several pointless pseudo-institutions that Kerensky cobbled together to shore up his government's legitimacy that fall. Abramovich and his fellow delegates were due to meet before the second congress of the Soviets that night. He could see Mariinsky's columns from blocks away, arranged like soldiers in ceremonial dress. As he got closer, he noticed a tank blocking the palace doorway. It was topped with a red flag.

"You can't go in!" barked a boy soldier, pointing his machine gun toward Abramovich.

"There's a session of pre-parliament." Abramovich responded.

"Pre-parliament has been arrested," the boy insolently replied.

Abramovich backed away.

In the four miles between Mariinsky and Smolny Institute, Abramovich would have seen trucks taking Red Guards from the factory districts. He would have heard the thwack of paper pasted against buildings as teenagers hung posters to announce the transfer of power to the soviets.

Tanks blocked Smolny's entrance, but when Abramovich proffered his delegate's pass, a soldier waved him through.

He ran through crammed and reeking hallways, to the repurposed classroom that he and Julius Martov used for their Menshevik and Bundist internationalist groups. There, he learned that the previous night, Bolshevik detachments had seized most strategic points in the city, even encircling the Winter Palace, the headquarters of the provisional government, which was meeting there that night. Kerensky had escaped the city in a car flying the American Embassy's flag.

When the second congress of the Soviets opened that night, the Bolsheviks and their allies, the Socialist Revolutionary breakoff group called the Left SRs, would hold the majority. They would rubber-stamp the seizure of power.

Unwilling to either fight Lenin or submit to him, the Menshevik-Internationalists decided to send a delegation to the Bolsheviks—maybe they could convince them to create a power-sharing agreement with the other socialist parties. Abramovich and two comrades trudged to the Bolshevik headquarters in classroom 36.

Inside, top Bolshevik Felix Dzerzhinsky lounged at a table with his friends. Dzerzhinsky had a long history with the Bund. He had been Liber's schoolmate, Medem's cellmate, and fiancé to Liber's sister, who died of tuberculosis in his arms. Prison changed him. When the wounds from his shackles festered, doctors nearly had to amputate his legs. Guards beat him so badly that his jaw was permanently broken, jutting to one side. He had a fanatical mien that disconcerted Abramovich; at the Smolny buffet a few weeks prior, he had fantasized about shooting every last member of the bourgeoisie.

Dzerzhinsky icily rejected Abramovich's requests. No, the Bolsheviks would not hold fire until after the congress of the Soviets. No, they were not particularly interested in making a government with other socialist parties.

Abramovich tried some arguments about the Marxist progression of history, but he could see he'd lost his case. He felt a sharp pain in his belly and realized he hadn't eaten since the previous evening. He decided to go home and prepare for the congress that night.

SMOLNY

Abramovich returned to Smolny around nine P.M. He took a second to appreciate the tableau. Before the revolution, aristocratic belles had practiced waltzes in Smolny's ballroom. They whirled in circles, their pale skirts like petals around them, while oil paintings of long-dead duchesses stared down. "Be pretty, be useless," the duchesses commanded, and the girls prepared themselves for a world they imagined would last forever. They revolved, their hands outstretched, to brush each other's fingertips, while radicals like Abramovich planned a revolution that would sweep them from the floor. Now the revolution had spun beyond him. On the presidium sat six members of the Soviet's old executive committee, including Mark Liber, who had an ashen face and indignant, sunken eyes. Two thousand soldiers, sailors, and factory workers jammed the ballroom. They clambered up the columns, hung off the ledges, filled the air with their cigarette smoke and sweat.

The Soviet's old chairman, the Menshevik Fyodor Dan, opened the congress with a declaration that the Winter Palace was under siege. He and the rest of the Soviet's former leaders left the stage, to be replaced by twenty-one Bolsheviks and Left SRs, including Leon Trotsky.

On the floor, the delegates screamed, hooted, and traded insults until an explosion shut them up. It was the *Aurora*, the Bolshevik gunship, firing on the Winter Palace.

A frail figure fought his way to the stage: Martov, the leader of the Menshevik-Internationalists.

In the bombardment of the Winter Palace, Martov heard the first shots of what would become a civil war. Believing that unity was the only way to forestall grave violence, he implored the Soviet's socialist parties to form a government together, before the workers they represented started slaughtering each other in the streets. In the name of the Bundist Internationalists, Abramovich backed him up. The Soviet unanimously accepted.

I can imagine a future in which Martov's proposal had won, and the other socialist parties had built a government alongside the Bolsheviks, with all the compromises this implied. Their presence might have forestalled Lenin's worst instincts, letting Russia develop into a flawed, impoverished, but somewhat functional democracy. But this was not to be, because of right-wing socialists like the Bundist Mark Liber.

These men would never compromise with the Bolsheviks, whom they saw as a pack of coup plotters and demagogues. The assault on the Winter Palace was only the latest proof. Some of these men were members of the provisional government while others loathed it, but all viewed it as a legitimate institution. No one had the right to overthrow the provisional government, least of all that scumbag Lenin.

One after the other, these right-wing socialists fought their way to the ballroom stage and righteously declared that they would have nothing to do with the Bolsheviks.

Henryk Erlich got the final word. American journalist John Reed transcribed his speech in his classic work of reportage, *Ten Days That Shook the World*, though he confused him with Abramovich, an error Abramovich bemoaned in his memoirs. Reed described Erlich's "eyes snapping behind thick glasses, trembling with rage" as he took the podium.

> What is taking place now in Petrograd is a monstrous calamity! . . . Our duty to the Russian proletariat doesn't permit us to remain here and be responsible for these crimes. Because the firing on the Winter Palace doesn't cease, the Municipal Duma together with the Mensheviki and Socialist Revolutionaries, and the Executive Committee of the Peasants' Soviet, has decided to perish with the Provisional Government, and we are going with them! Unarmed we will expose our breasts to the machine guns of the Terrorists.

The Bolshevik Lev Kamenev cut him off, jingling a bell. "Keep your seats and we'll go on with our business!" he sneered.

Erlich led fifty delegates toward the door. I doubt he realized he was giving in to the same tendency that the Bund had shown fourteen years before, when Medem and Liber walked out of the third conference of the RSDLP and left the floor clear for Lenin's takeover. It was the fatal impulse to value principle over power, to leave the battlefield at the very moment they most needed to stay and fight. Amidst curses, threats, and distant gunfire, they marched out of Smolny, into a future shaped by violence and a Russia in which they would no longer play a part.

Erlich and the rest made one last effort to save the provisional government. Three hundred socialists, including the elderly mayor of Petrograd, marched four abreast down Nevsky Prospect toward the Winter Palace, defiantly singing "The Marseillaise." After a block, they ran into a cordon of sailors who would not let them pass. The group insisted. "We are ready to die, if you have the heart to fire on Russians and on comrades." The sailors would not give them the satisfaction. "We will spank you! And if necessary, we will shoot you too. Go home now and leave us in peace!" one said, laughing. Offered slapstick rather than sublime martyrdom, the group retreated, still four abreast, in silent, dignified defeat.

RAPHAEL ABRAMOVICH

After Erlich's group of socialists left the Soviet, the rest of the delegates were in no mood to hear Martov's call for unity. Why should the Bolsheviks form a government with a bunch of losers? To the Mensheviks, Socialist Revolutionaries, and Bundists, Trotsky declared: "You are miserable bankrupts. Your role is played out; go where you ought to go—into the dustbin of history."

Martov stormed out. Loyally, Abramovich followed.

NEW YORK

History keeps moving, and we all wind up in the dustbin at the end.

Once, over egg salad sandwiches in his Inwood apartment, Bundist historian Jack Jacobs told me he had met Alexander Kerensky. I was flabbergasted. Kerensky? The leader of Russia in 1917? Was Jack older than I thought?

Jack told me the story. As a teenager, he worked in the Bund's archives, and Kerensky would visit his colleague, the chain-smoking Polish-born Bundist Hillel Kempinski. After Kerensky fled Petrograd in a car flying the American flag, he'd followed the path of so many political exiles, to New York City, where he settled until his death in 1970. Jack recalled how the one-time leader of revolutionary Russia would ask Kempinski to dig out yellowed party texts, undoubtedly for one of his many diatribes against Lenin. When Trotsky sent the Bundists off to the dustbin of history, this must have been what he meant.

They were losers, yes, but what about the people who won? Within two decades, Kamenev would be shot by the state he helped build. Trotsky? Murdered in Mexico. And Lenin, whose indomitable will brought the Bolshevik Revolution into being, would scarcely have time to enjoy it. He was dead a few years later. His body was embalmed, against his wife's wishes, then displayed like a wax doll in a mausoleum meant to legitimize the rule of Stalin, a man he had hated. Meanwhile, Alexander Kerensky was alive in New York City. He could see the sky, smell the subway stink, grab some borscht at B&H, then stop by the Bund's archives, where someone from the old world was there to greet him.

Who's to say who came out worse?

CHAPTER 13

AFTER OCTOBER

(November 1917–August 1918)

SOPHIA DUBNOVA

"THE COUP!" BLARED THE FRONT PAGE OF THE BUNDIST NEWSPAPER *Workers' Voice* in its first issue after the Bolshevik seizure of power. It was not a revolution, the writers said, but a crazy escapade by Lenin and Trotsky. But, for all the Bund's diatribes, a reader who skipped the newspaper's first two pages might not have realized that anything had changed. The issue was filled with discussions of the Bund's usual concerns, like cultural work, pogroms in Ukraine, and the recently announced Balfour Declaration, in which Britain promised Jews a national home, whatever that meant, in Palestine. Like most observers, the Bund didn't imagine that the Bolsheviks would stay in power.

During its first weeks in control, Lenin's government weathered several threats. In Petrograd, it crushed a revolt at a school for military cadets, then suppressed a potential railway strike.

White-collar employees went on strike, creating chaos at government ministries. When the Bolsheviks set up new departments, liberal intellectuals refused to apply for jobs. One day Sophia received a letter with the unfamiliar signature of Vladimirov Sheinfinkel, inviting her to visit a department in charge of the distribution of manufactured goods. When she entered their offices, she didn't recognize the stooped man at the desk, until a memory from a dozen years before flashed through her mind.

She had been a revolutionary in the Gomel underground. He was one of the fugitives who sought shelter in her flat. When he took her copy of Lermontov off the bookshelf, it fell open to her favorite poem. He swore it was his favorite too. They stayed up all night reading to each other. When the sleigh bells rang in the morning to signal his departure, he kissed her hand, in defiance of revolutionary mores.

Here he was, behind the desk of power.

After complimenting the poems she published in Gorky's *Chronicle*,

Vladimirov got down to business. He wanted her to run a new production department for children's goods.

"I've never organized anything," she replied.

"Who among us has?" he answered. "What were we taught? Conspiracy. And now the time has come to run a government whose like has never been seen anywhere. We'll stumble, make a heap of errors, but we'll learn."

She told him she couldn't work for the Bolshevik government as a matter of principle.

To her surprise, he quoted a poem she had written after the birth of her son Victor. "There is a terrible force in the pitiful call of a child's hands." All the job entailed was helping hungry children, he said. She could call him if she changed her mind.

After she left, she walked down Nevsky Prospect feeling feverish. She knew she would not call.

The streets were dark, but not quiet. They echoed with shots, screams, and the songs of sailors drunk from the tsar's looted wine cellars. The only light came from bonfires. It was dangerous to walk outside in a fur coat. One of her friends had recently been stripped by a pair of deserters.

At home, Sophia returned to her well-worn copy of Victor Hugo's *Contemplations*. She had underlined a sentence: "The revolution that comes to avenge all creates an eternal good from a transient evil." The evil didn't feel transient.

ELECTIONS

A new slogan went up on the front pages of Bundist newspapers: "The Constituent Assembly is the only hope."

Russian intellectuals had long cherished the ideal of the Constituent Assembly: a democratic body, elected by universal suffrage, that would settle the issues that had bedeviled Russia since March: national independence movements, the division of land to peasants, and the end of the war. The Bund threw itself into the electoral fray. There was a new competitor for the Jewish vote—the Zionists. This movement exploded in popularity after the Balfour Declaration, which gave the previously implausible idea of Jewish statehood the backing of an imperial power. Weeks before the election, 150,000 Jews demonstrated in front of Odesa's British consulate in gratitude. Even though most of these celebrants had no intention of going to Palestine, they hoped a Jewish state might advocate for their rights in Russia.

The Bund chose Raphael Abramovich and Esther Frumkin as candidates for the Constituent Assembly. Their first campaign stop was the impoverished Belarusian town of Vitebsk, where Jewish residents apologetically told the two candidates that they were voting Bolshevik because they wanted their sons to come home from the war.

Abramovich heard the same in the city of Polotsk on the Dvina River, when he made his case at meetings of the town's twenty-thousand-man garrison held in the circus every night. He told the soldiers that his party also wanted to make peace—they just didn't want soldiers to lynch their commanders and flee the front in chaos. German shells punctuated his remarks. He swore that the Bund had wanted to form a unified socialist government, but that Bolsheviks backstabbed them when they tried to negotiate. The crowd applauded. They gave more applause to the Bolshevik speaker who followed him.

Voting began on November 25 and stretched over two weeks. Abramovich and Frumkin lost their races. All the Bund had to show for themselves was a single delegate.

CRACKDOWN

Despite the Bolsheviks' seizure of power, they still had a rival—the Socialist Revolutionaries, a party of agrarian populists with a long record of peasant activism and an even longer list of tsarist officials they had assassinated. In the elections for the Constituent Assembly, the Socialist Revolutionaries won a plurality of the votes. Shocked and humiliated to have come in second, the Bolsheviks launched a campaign to discredit the election results. Simultaneously, they put Petrograd and Moscow under martial law. To enforce this repression, they created a new secret police organization, the Cheka, helmed by Felix Dzerzhinsky, who brought the lessons he learned as a prisoner to bear in his new office.

In the leadup to the Constituent Assembly, the Bolsheviks cracked down on the opposition press. They ordered the closure of the main Menshevik paper, *Workers' Gazette*, where Henryk Erlich was co-editor, then sent detachments of sailors to smash the printing shop. The Mensheviks resurrected their papers with new names to stay ahead of the bans, but the Bolsheviks arrested their editors.

At a December meeting of the Menshevik central committee, Liber vented his contempt for anyone who still advocated compromise. The Bolshevik usurpers shut down more newspapers and arrested more socialists than any tsar ever dared, he said. They were preparing an attack on the Constituent Assembly. It was time for armed revolt, not playing nice on the soviets. When Martov argued that they could work with the new government while keeping their principles, Liber threatened to quit the party.

From then on, the Mensheviks would be split between Liber's and Martov's followers. Each side ran their own electoral slates, advocated contradictory policies on everything from participation in the soviets to collaboration with armed uprisings, and engaged in mutual recrimination. Once among the most popular parties in the empire, the Mensheviks bled members.

THE CONSTITUENT ASSEMBLY

On January 18, 1918, came the long-awaited day of the Constituent Assembly. Inside Tauride Palace, over four hundred delegates, from Irkutsk to Tiflis, converged to decide the most important questions of their revolutionary homeland.

Though they had spent the last months working to discredit the assembly, the Bolsheviks grudgingly allowed it to go ahead—not that they intended to permit its Socialist Revolutionary plurality to accomplish much. To intimidate delegates, they encircled Tauride Palace with thousands of Red Guards. Machine guns pointed threateningly from adjoining rooftops.

Despite these attempts at suppression, tens of thousands of white-collar workers and intellectuals gathered in the Field of Mars, under banners that read, LONG LIVE THE CONSTITUENT ASSEMBLY. Sophia marched alongside Henryk, looking cautiously from side to side. A protester struck up an old revolutionary song. Around her, marchers whispered that soldiers were waiting a few blocks away to ambush them. They sang louder in defiance. "We'll push our way into the kingdom of freedom," Sophia sang, walking forward even as she heard the gunfire. Then she heard a scream. Images slid before her eyes like slideshow frames. A sailor, cap turned sideways, gun in hand. An old man on his knees. Shots. The crowd shoved apart, tearing her hand from Henryk's. His coat disappeared behind strangers' bodies. Someone pushed her. She tumbled onto the sidewalk. A building caretaker pulled her into a dim passageway filled with protesters, then bolted the gate. "Until they stop shooting, I won't let anyone out," he barked. "Afterward, good riddance."

Bolshevik forces killed twenty-one people that day.

While Sophia was dodging bullets, the Constituent Assembly met for a single session at Tauride Palace. When the Socialist Revolutionaries refused to ratify Lenin's latest manifesto, the Bolsheviks and Left SRs walked out. The remaining delegates spent the day giving meandering speeches until, a few hours after midnight, Bolshevik sailors forced them out at gunpoint. When they arrived the next morning, they found Tauride's gates padlocked.

"The best among the Russian people have for almost a hundred years lived for the idea of a constituent assembly. . . . Yet now the 'people's commissars' gave the order to shoot down the crowd demonstrating in honor of this idea," wrote Sophia's friend Maxim Gorky. But though the Constituent Assembly might have been the ideal for intellectuals like Sophia Dubnova, it meant little to the average Russian. They didn't protest when it was destroyed.

KYIV

The dispersal of the Constituent Assembly might have been a nonevent in most of Russia proper, but it horrified the leaders of the Ukrainian Central Rada.

For the past year, the Rada's leaders, socialist intellectuals Mykhailo Hrushevsky and Volodymyr Vynnychenko, had wrangled for Ukrainian autonomy, only to be met with contemptuous dismissals. Even for liberal Russians, Ukraine was a prized possession. They did not intend to give it up. When Red Guard gunmen shot up pro–Constituent Assembly protests in Petrograd, it was the final straw. If the Bolsheviks would shut down the most cherished organ of revolutionary democracy, Vynnychenko wrote, then they were "the same Russian chauvinists and imperialists" as the last regime. On January 22, 1918, the Rada declared Ukrainian independence.

The Rada's leaders were enlightened, humanistic men who envisioned a multicultural, socialist Ukraine. In keeping with these ideals, the Rada adopted the Law of National-Personal Autonomy, which provided government funding for Jews and other minorities to run their own cultural institutions. They set up a ministry of Jewish affairs and proclaimed Yiddish an official language, to appear on street signs and exquisite new banknotes.

But despite the Rada's liberal gestures, Bundists remained deeply suspicious of Ukraine's national movement, even voting against Ukrainian independence in the Rada. This was probably inevitable. Though generations of tsars had oppressed both Ukrainians and Jews, there was little love lost between the groups. Many Jews viewed Ukrainians as violent peasants, and many Ukrainians viewed Jews as usurious collaborators of foreign tyrants. The history went deep: between 1648 and 1657, Ukrainian Cossacks led by Bohdon Khmelnytsky had slaughtered twenty thousand Jews as part of their uprising against Polish rule. (Khmelnytsky remains a national hero.) Intellectuals in Kyiv might have issued earnest proclamations about multiculturalism, but in the countryside, old hatreds burbled like lava, always ready to erupt. When the Rada's minister of military affairs, Symon Petliura, left his post to create a Cossack-inspired militia called the Haidamaks, it seemed to validate the Bundists' worst fears about armed ultranationalists. Pogroms broke out. When Moishe Rafes, the Bund's delegate to the Rada, tried to pass a resolution condemning the attacks, his fellow delegates voted it down.

Five days after the Rada declared independence, Russian soldiers laid siege to Kyiv, and on January 29, hundreds of pro-Bolshevik workers launched an uprising at the city's arsenal. Some of these workers were Jews. Petliura's Haidamaks quickly crushed the rebellion. Afterward, they marched through the cobblestone streets of the Jewish neighborhood of Podil screaming, "We will slaughter all the yids." They slaughtered twenty-two Jews, two of them Bundists. After death threats from Petliura's men, Moishe Rafes went into hiding.

Petliura's victory was short-lived. On February 9, the Russians took Kyiv. Despite their skepticism about Ukrainian independence, local Bundist leadership was horrified by the invasion. They condemned the Russians as "an occupation army" who "bombed out all the national achievements of the revolution in Ukraine"—and refused to recognize the Bolshevik government.

As the Reds instituted their own reign of terror against Kyiv's citizens, rumors spread that Jews had welcomed the invasion. As vengeance, Petliura's Haidamaks rampaged through the countryside murdering Jews who they claimed were communists.

Desperate to free themselves from their Russian invaders, on February 9, Ukraine's leaders signed a defense treaty with Germany and Austria. Three weeks later, Haidamaks and their German backers booted the Reds from Kyiv. More pogroms followed, carried out by Ukrainians who blamed the Jews for the Bolshevik invasion.

On March 3, after months of wrangling, the Bolsheviks signed their own treaty with Germany and Austria in the city of Brest-Litovsk, ending Russia's role in World War I. In exchange, Russia gave up control of most of the former Pale of Settlement and over half of its industrial land. Russians of all political stripes considered the Brest-Litovsk treaty a humiliating capitulation. Lenin forced it through anyway. Only he seemed to realize the basic truth that you can't fight a war without an army.

The Brest-Litovsk treaty rid Ukraine of Russia—for the moment, at least. But their German defenders were beginning to act a lot like occupiers. The Germans took over railroads, looted state warehouses, and even hauled away Ukraine's famous black earth to fertilize German fields. Rebellion grew against the Germans, and against the Rada who had welcomed them.

Despite the violence, Rafes and his fellow Bundists added their voices to a new constitution, which, after weeks of haggling, contained enlightened laws on national autonomy. On the afternoon of April 28, Rada delegates gathered in their headquarters at Kyiv's Pedagogical Lyceum to discuss the increasingly tyrannical German rule. Rafes had just started to speak when a German officer burst in, barked that the building was surrounded, and put the entire government under arrest.

HUNGER

Half of the former Russian Empire's wheat fields were behind enemy lines. The war destroyed the rest. The earth was blasted, the silos torched, the horses shot, even the seeds stolen by this army or that. Peasants refused to sell their crops to the government for worthless paper money, notwithstanding the commissars and their pious exhortations to feed their brothers in Petrograd. They buried the surpluses or used them to make vodka.

Factories laid off their workers. Starving workers fled to the countryside.

The Bolsheviks called on workers to abandon their quest for the eight-hour day, to accept wages at a third of their prewar level, to toil and shut up. When persuasion failed, the Bolsheviks gunned down their protests.

Seeking to channel the popular discontent, Bundists ran candidates for local soviets. On the rare occasions when they won, the Bolsheviks either falsified results or arrested their delegates.

That spring in Petrograd, the great hunger began. Breadlines became melees, and black-market prices soared. Writing grew harder for Henryk Erlich. After he edited an issue of his newspaper, he lay on the couch for hours with his eyes closed. Hunger made it impossible to think.

In May, Erlich went to Moscow to represent the Bund at a Menshevik conference. The party was more divided than ever, unsure if they should keep running candidates for the soviets, despite repression, or forgo what Liber called "Bonapartist clubs that gather together around these déclassé dregs" and instead join armed anti-Bolshevik uprisings. While the two sides bickered, Erlich's neighbor whispered that there was black-market flour available for purchase somewhere on Moscow's outskirts. When Erlich returned to Petrograd, Sophia asked the results of the conference. He dropped a sack of flour on the table by way of reply.

Horses collapsed from hunger, and dogs picked at their bodies. Impoverished members of the old elite sold their possessions on the side of the road. After hours in line, all Sophia could manage was a ration of salted fish so hard she needed to beat it into dust to make it edible. As she pounded the fish on the counter, she imagined she could hear all the other women in their kitchens, pounding the same fish, the beat of their efforts hammering through the revolutionary slogans until nothing was left but this metronome of survival.

BELLUM OMNIUM CONTRA OMNES

The situation grew darker for Bundists in Kyiv, where the German occupiers installed an aristocratic Ukrainian general named Pavlo Skoropadskyi as the country's dictator; he preferred the traditional Cossack title: hetman. Hetman Skoropadskyi undid the social reforms of his predecessors, dissolving the Ministry of Jewish Affairs and overturning laws allowing for Jewish cultural autonomy. With German help, he brought back the old elites to suck more money from the impoverished populace. Ukrainians responded with a guerrilla insurgency. The hetman blamed the Jews.

Kyiv soon filled with anti-Bolshevik refugees. Flush with cash they had smuggled out of revolutionary Russia, aristocrats and business magnates partook in orgiastic self-indulgence. More menacing were the young military officers whom the revolution had stripped of family estates and career prospects, and who hated the Bolsheviks with a nauseous fury. These men would flock to the fledgling Volunteer Army, soon known as the Whites.

Founded by tsarist generals who had fled Russia just weeks after the Bolshevik takeover, the Whites fought to restore some version of the old regime that had so richly benefited their families. As Whites battled Reds across the Russian steppes, each side left a trail of war crimes behind them. The Whites relished pogroms—vengeance, they said, for the prominence of Jews amongst the Bolsheviks. They emphasized this point by cutting Bolshevik stars into the corpses of their Jewish victims. But Reds also carried out pogroms, most notably in the Ukrainian city of Hlukhiv, where, under the cry of "Eliminate the bourgeoisie and the Yids," they murdered over a hundred Jews. After the massacre, the Bundist leader Vladimir Kossovsky saw the street outside the Soviet "literally sodden" with victims' blood.

By summer, much of the former Russian Empire fell out of Soviet control. Across the shattered corpse of this empire, nationalist independence movements, foreign proxies, Allied expeditionary forces, megalomaniacal warlords, forest robbers, and peasant bands all trained their guns on the new government. The term *civil war* does not do justice to the chaos. It was the *bellum omnium contra omnes* that Thomas Hobbes invokes in *Leviathan*. The war of all against all.

SOPHIA DUBNOVA

"The summer was dusty and torrid," Sophia wrote. "In the piles of trash scattered on the street, mangy stray cats rooted about persistently, in hopeless search for something edible, and filled the air with their cross meows. In well-to-do houses people cautiously chewed hard horse meat."

Repression reverberated around Russia. The Cheka arrested the Bund's local leaders in Bogorodsk, and in Vitebsk they publicly executed a Bundist for smuggling a comrade's letters out of prison, then refused to give his family his body. A Menshevik report in June 1918 noted that in Minsk, "the persecution of socialists has reached such proportions that they had to go underground, just like under czarism."

All of this must have weighed on Sophia's mind when she and Henryk contemplated a painful decision. At the start of the year, a letter arrived from her in-laws begging them to return to Henryk's Polish hometown, Lublin, which was then under Austrian occupation. Their steam mill was back up, the authorities left them alone, and best of all, they had plenty to eat. Sophia's boys were so skinny that she could encircle their upper arms with her middle finger and thumb. They followed her from room to room with sing-song supplications for food. If they stayed in Russia, she worried they would starve to death.

When their travel permits arrived that August, Henryk and Sophia swore that the move would not be final. They would stay in Lublin just long enough for their sons to put on weight, then resume their lives in Petrograd. On the freight train west, Sophia heard guns rumble in the distance; they were not far from a front line of the civil war. They rode in semidarkness, sitting on their bags to protect them from thieves. When Henryk bought bread at the Minsk station, the boys ripped into it like animals. They got out at Orsha, a small city at the fork of the Dnipro River, where the Austrian-occupied zone began. As they went through passport control, a sharp pain overtook Sophia. Terrified she would lose her sons in the crowd, she grabbed their hands so hard that they yelped. From the train window she watched as the letters on the signs went from Cyrillic to Latin. She began to cry uncontrollably—ugly, choking tears that Henryk would not understand. Where had this come from? She seemed so calm before. She swallowed hard, forcing herself to be silent. She knew her Polish-born husband could never feel as she did then. Her old life, with her family, her friends, poetry in her own language, in her own familiar country, passed irrevocably into the distance. In a later poem, she wrote that she was "a daughter/Torn away from her mother."

Part Three

THE ALTERNATE WORLD

1917–1939

CHAPTER 14

THE CHAOS

(1917–1921)

SAM ROTHBORT

THE YEAR 1917 BROUGHT CHAOS TO RUSSIA, BUT ON THE OTHER SIDE OF the world, my great-grandfather's art career was on the rise. That was the year he first exhibited with the Society of Brooklyn Artists in the glittery Abraham & Straus department store (a palace of commerce whose white-gloved attendants spoke twenty-three languages, from Gaelic to Arabic), and at the Pouch Mansion in Prospect Heights. The *Brooklyn Daily Eagle* began to mention his work. He painted Rose, his kids, and the streets outside their Bushwick tenement, in a postimpressionist impasto that he called "direct art." His canvases were bold, modernist, New York. In May 1917, one month after the United States joined World War I, he finally applied for American citizenship. Samuel Rothbort, age thirty-four, renounced forever his allegiance to any foreign prince, potentate, state, or sovereign. He was neither an anarchist nor a polygamist. It was his intention to become a citizen of the United States of America, so help him God.

It was a good time to cement his status. After America entered World War I in April 1917, it began to look less kindly on European Jewish radicals, many of whom opposed the conflict. The American government would target them with the Espionage Act that June. The prominence of Trotsky and other Jewish Bolsheviks turned this state scrutiny into an obsession. The FBI's precursor, the Bureau of Investigation, sent spies to radical haunts, like the evocatively named Golden Rooster, where they tried to comprehend the ornate factionalism of socialist politics, imagining a network that connected Trotsky to Hindu priests and the Jewish Labor Bund. They got most things wrong but managed to ruin lives all the same.

In my mother's shoebox we found a faded card from the Bureau of Investigation acknowledging an interaction with Sam Rothbort. It was filled out with his 1918 address. I wrote to the FBI asking for any records pertaining to my great-grandfather, but they claimed that none existed.

Then I looked at the signature on the Bureau of Investigation card. Chas. De Woodey, district supervisor. I contemplated the name's Knickerbocker etymology, the waspish abbreviation of Charles to Chas. I had found my antagonist.

De Woodey, it turned out, was J. Edgar Hoover's boy, a hunter of German spies and other subversives who sent undercovers to arrest any immigrant drunk enough to publicly doubt American military might. He made his career persecuting Wobblies, Indian freedom fighters, and a famous Turkish dancing girl, but his path crossed Sam's during the "slacker raids" of September 1918. With the help of a jingoistic quasi-civilian spy group called the American Protective League, de Woodey's officers poured into immigrant neighborhoods to demand draft cards. Officers herded sixty thousand men who could not produce cards into horse carts and dragged them off to the Fifth Avenue Armory, where draft dodgers were set up with registration appointments at their local boards. Anyone who refused was shipped to a concentration camp upstate.

So it was that on September 12, 1918, fourteen years after he escaped conscription into the tsarist army, Sam stood at Local Board 75 in Greenpoint, to be registered to fight in someone else's war.

SOPHIA DUBNOVA

While my great-grandfather was cursing his luck in a Brooklyn draft office, Sophia Dubnova was going crazy in Lublin. She hated the overstuffed, overfed Erlich family home, where her mother-in-law nagged her to get Henryk to take up work as a pricey lawyer, and where the prosaic nattering of her father-in-law's business acquaintances constantly interrupted her thoughts. She was a poet, dammit. She needed space. To keep her cool, she buried herself in Russian newspapers. Things were going to hell, as usual. The civil war raged in the south. Sophia lived for the occasional letter from her father.

Henryk was equally miserable in his childhood home, but he had the party as an escape. The Bund flourished in occupied Poland. Cut off from the old intelligentsia in Russia, confronted with mass unemployment and starvation, the party turned away from the theoretical cul-de-sacs of its early days toward its true strength, practical organizing. With money provided by the Jewish socialist diaspora, tuers set up trade unions, economic cooperatives, and soup kitchens that fed hundreds of thousands of workers. Built on the principle of mutual aid rather than top-down charity, members elected their own leadership and settled their own disputes. The Bundist Emanuel Nowogrodski would later call these institutions "universities of socialist self-management" that trained the next generation of leaders. The Bund's city committees stood up to the forced labor regime imposed by the German occupation. Under Vladimir Medem's leadership, the party wove itself into the fabric of daily life.

When Medem arrived at the Erlich home in Lublin that autumn, he was like a visitor from another planet. Prison had not damaged his good looks. "Oy, he looks like a real count," sighed Sophia's mother-in-law, and the Erlich women flirtatiously proffered delicacies for him to sample. Only Sophia recognized the pain in Medem's eyes. His three-year-old daughter, Natasha, had recently died of meningitis. Medem implored Henryk to stay in Poland rather than returning to Petrograd. "We are in greater need of living leaders than of prisoners languishing in Russian jails," he told them. Sophia knew her exile would be permanent.

GEOPOLITICS

Events in nearby Germany shook the world. A mutiny amongst sailors on a doomed naval campaign broke out in Kiel. Uprisings spread to Munich and Berlin. Soon Germany was in the midst of a full-scale revolution. Kaiser Wilhelm fled, and the social democrats proclaimed a republic. For socialists around the world, Germany offered an unexpected hope. Perhaps the events in Russia were the start of a worldwide revolution. Perhaps Lenin and Trotsky were right.

On November 11, 1918, the Republic of Germany signed an armistice. The First World War ended before America could send Sam Rothbort to fight. For Russia, its costs were incalculable. Russian casualties included the Romanov dynasty, the March Revolution, and three million human beings. Things went better on Sophia's side of the border. After 130 years of partition, Poland stood united and independent under the leadership of general Józef Pilsudski, aristocrat, revolutionary bank robber, war hero, and longtime acquaintance of the Bund, whose leaders he befriended during a stint hiding out in Vilna.

By 1918, Pilsudski was no longer the fiery leftist of his youth. "I took the red tram of socialism to the stop called Independence, and that's where I got off," he told an old underground acquaintance who greeted him as "comrade."

Pilsudski may have been an authoritarian nationalist, but he differed in one respect from others who wore this label. He envisioned a multi-ethnic Poland, like the old Polish-Lithuanian Commonwealth, which would include Jews and other minorities as equals. When he came to power, he invited the Bund to join his government. The Bund declined, declaring that, for them to participate, Pilsudski would need to grant

Jews, Germans, Ukrainians, Lithuanians, and all the rest their national-cultural autonomy. Bundists were also furious because Polish soldiers kept smashing up their clubs.

As Medem wrote, every nation-state creates its own minorities, and this was especially true in Poland; ethnic Poles barely constituted a majority within the borders of the newborn state. This demography gave right-wing Polish nationalism an insecure, paranoid disposition, especially with regard to the Jews, who made up 13 percent of the population. Jews' numerousness made them "the worst enemies" of Poland, according to one pamphlet published by the National Democrats, an economically conservative, Catholic, and luridly racist political party that would become the Bund's most dangerous Polish antagonists.

Co-founded by right-wing pamphleteer Roman Dmowski in 1897, the National Democrats, or Endeks, had spent the last twenty years building their Polish nationalism not upon the armed struggle for independence but upon genocidal antipathy toward the country's Jews. In the now-independent Poland, they enjoyed terrorizing Jewish neighborhoods while nourishing grand dreams of mass ethnic cleansing. They yearned for a Poland free of Jews.

This sort of racism wasn't confined to nationalists—it even infected members of the Polish left. Days after independence, workers' parties formed soviets in most major Polish cities. Erlich joined the Lublin Soviet as the Bund's delegate. At the first meeting, Polish socialist delegates announced that if they served alongside Jews, their own constituents would reject them. "The Polish proletariat still isn't adult enough to understand that we need a united front" to fight the capitalists, Erlich shot back. The soviet kicked out the Jewish parties anyway.

All this depressed Sophia Dubnova further. She spoke Polish, adored Polish poets, supported their country's struggle, and would have liked to celebrate their independence alongside them, but after months in Lublin, her sympathies were wearing thin. She realized that many of the Poles who had so recently freed themselves from Russian oppression were all too eager to take on the role of oppressors. "For the first time in my life, I felt compelled to breathe the stuffy air of the ghetto," she later wrote.

The Bund sent Henryk Erlich to Warsaw, where the soviet accepted Jewish parties. He could not afford to bring Sophia with him. To escape the claustrophobic Erlich home, she would wander Lublin's old city. In the gothic church, she watched the worshippers prostrate themselves, while the saints glowered at her from the frescoes, their pinched mouths seeming to whisper, "You have no place in this place."

When Henryk visited from Warsaw, he was full of excitement at the

Bund's success. She said nothing about her homesickness. Why cause her husband more pain?

LVIV

Borders were ill-defined in the former Pale of Settlement. They leapt forward and backward, squiggled and curved. They melted like slush in the springtime. They dissolved beneath the boots of passing armies, like Trotsky's Reds and Anton Denikin's Whites, Petliura's Haidamaks, the Black anarchist armies of Nestor Makhno, the peasant Greens, and the armies of newly minted nation-states whose mutually contradictory revanchist claims would, in the coming years, turn the region into a killing field.

Now free of the Russian Empire, Poland immediately embarked on its own imperial wars of conquest, starting with the exquisite, formerly Habsburg city of Lviv.

Beautiful Lviv, I first saw you in 2022, almost a year into the Russian invasion. I remember your stone nymphs, the grace of your squares, the tart sea buckthorn tea served in your cafés, the girls with glass-smooth blow-outs, their sexiness a middle finger to the air raid sirens. I remember the exhibit of destroyed Russian military hardware. You had to walk on a Russian flag to enter, and a mannequin in a Russian uniform hung over the doorway from a noose. You were Ukrainian Ukrainian when I visited, but this had not always been the case. You once were called *Lwow* by your Polish majority. In Yiddish—your population was one-third Jewish—you went by *Lemberg*.

After the Germans left in November 1918, Ukrainian fighters declared Lviv the capital of their short-lived West Ukrainian People's Republic. Pilsudski differed. With over half the population being Polish, Lwow clearly belonged to him.

When Polish troops took Lviv (or was it Lwow?), Lemberg was the place that suffered. The soldiers burned the Jewish neighborhoods, pillaged their stores, broke down their doors with hand grenades, raped women and forced them to stand naked in front of mobs, which, it must be said, contained many members of the local Christian elite. This was not the drunken bloodlust of the Russian countryside but, rather, a massacre carried out by a professional army in a city they had secured, in front of the approving gaze of local residents. The Polish army murdered at least seventy-three Jews. When Jewish newspapers reported on the pogrom, the Polish government blamed the victims.

The Lviv massacre was the among the first of over a thousand pogroms that took place between November 1918 and March 1921 within the former Pale of Settlement. They were of a ferocity and sadism never before experienced in eastern Europe. Almost everyone took part. Ukrainians, Lithuanians, Russians, Poles. Cossacks, criminals, warlords, aristocrats, soldiers, deserters. Whites, Greens, monarchists, reactionaries, nationalists, people with no ideology whatsoever, and even units that were ostensibly communist.

It didn't matter who one was, or what one believed. Everyone killed Jews. Everyone raped Jews, burned their houses, threw them out of trains. When Jews tried to form self-defense units, they were outnumbered, and the sight of Jews with weapons only provoked their attackers more. Each pogrom aimed not just to kill but to humiliate, to prove the victims' subhumanity, to them and to an audience, often made up of the victims' acquaintances. Pogromists—drunk, singing, laughing—slit open their neighbors' bellies, burned their children's babysitters alive, forced their classmates to dig their own graves. Pogromists rewarded themselves by filling their carts with so much loot it made their horses groan and selling it cheaply in the bazaars that sprung up around killing sites. Sometimes, they just left it in the gutter. Why not? They'd gotten it for free.

Everyone claimed these massacres were justified. Poles said Jews sided with Ukrainians. Ukrainians said they sided with Russians. Russian Whites said they sided with Russian Reds. Russian Reds said they were capitalist exploiters. Jews were spies for every side, Christ killers, traitors, internationalist financiers, unscrupulous speculators, and, above all, revolutionaries. Everyone agreed they had it coming.

WARSAW

Poland began 1919 in turmoil. On January 4, the racist Endek party tried to overthrow the government. The coup failed, but Pilsudski refused to charge the conspirators, afraid this would make them martyrs. In parliamentary elections later that month, Endeks won a plurality of the vote.

Sophia joined Henryk in Warsaw. The Erlich family moved into a cheap apartment near the *Lebens-Fragen* offices, where Henryk worked alongside Medem as an editor. At the paper, one hot topic was the rise of Zionism. Since the Balfour Declaration, the movement had exploded, siphoning resources from Poland's exhausted Jewish community. In one article, Medem described a Jewish man fainting from hunger beneath a Zionist poster that called, with "fat, black, screaming letters" for money to be sent to Palestine.

Medem found Zionist ambitions ridiculous. For the Bund, the fight for Jewish life was in Poland, and Erlich joined Medem at its center. He got elected to the Warsaw city council, supervised union work, and stayed up late writing urgent editorials denouncing government repression. The Warsaw police often confiscated the Bund's newspaper, which only egged Erlich on.

In their cramped apartment with its peeling wallpaper, Sophia strove to convey the beauty of Russian literature to her boys. Despite their age, she gave them Gogol and Turgenev. She took them on walks to Saxon Gardens, where they discussed poetry in her native language, indifferent to the shouts of passersby. "Speak Polish!" they sniped. "I speak it as well as you," she quipped back, whereupon they'd say that Jews like her ought to get out while the going was good, back to "her" Trotsky's Russia, or, inevitably, to Palestine.

BERNARD GOLDSTEIN

Days after the end of World War I, posters went up around Kyiv calling on the population to overthrow the hated regime of Hetman Skoropadskyi and to restore the Ukrainian People's Republic—the democratic government German occupiers had overthrown back in April. These posters were issued in the name of an underground organization called the Directorate, which had been founded by the Rada's former leader, Volodymyr Vynnychenko, with Petliura's troops for muscle. Since they hated the hetman as much as anyone, Kyiv Bundists heeded the call.

Bernard Goldstein led their fighters. Born in an impoverished shtetl in eastern Poland, Bernard joined the party at age thirteen. By sixteen, he had already survived one prison term; for a keepsake a guard left a saber scar across his face. A quiet bruiser who spoke in a mangled mixture of three languages, Bernard spent the next decade escaping jails and organizing unions. He once shared a cell with Vladimir Medem. In

1915, during a stint in Siberia, Bernard earned his place in legend. During a routine checkup, the police commissioner flipped Bernard's eyelids up to check for trachoma. "Are you a doctor?" Bernard sneered. The commissioner slapped him across the face. Not one to be insulted, Bernard slammed a kerosene lamp over the commissioner's head. The commissioner retaliated harshly. But Bernard had a compassionate streak. When the Revolution broke out in March 1917, the prisoners overthrew their guards, tied the commissioner to a tree, and presented him to Bernard to execute. Bernard refused. The revolution, he declared, must be humane. From Siberia, he made his way to Kyiv, where he served on the city's soviet during the brief days of revolutionary democracy.

When the 1918 uprising against the hetman began, Bernard's two hundred fighters took over the elegant streets around the Bessarabian Market, in the city center. They might have set up snipers' nests amidst the market's wooden stalls, lit bonfires, or gotten boot prints all over counters that once groaned with sturgeon and champagne. When they guarded Khreshchatyk Street, the archangel atop City Hall must have seemed to raise her arm in benediction.

UKRAINE

In late December, Vynnychenko and his Directorate returned to power in Kyiv, with a little bit of help from the Bund.

This time, it would be different, Vynnychenko swore. He offered promises of autonomy and condemnations of pogroms. But there were menacing signs. The Directorate barely controlled its own troops outside of Kyiv. What troops it did control were under the ostensible command of Petliura. Over the next year, these troops would carry out pogroms of world-shattering violence.

Berdichev's Bundist mayor, David Lipetz, quickly learned about the gulf between the Directorate's lofty words and the actions of its soldiers. Lipetz was not naïve; he even helped found self-defense squads. Yet, when pogromists gathered outside his house in January screaming, "Give us the Yid who runs this city," he was as helpless as any old-time shtetl victim. The pogromists lined up his family, put guns to their heads, and would have pulled the triggers if Lipetz hadn't managed to bribe them with some valuables. Pogromists murdered seventeen Jews that day. When Lipetz and other Jewish leaders tried to bury their dead, the pogromists attacked the funeral and killed two more. Lipetz and Moishe Rafes led a Bundist delegation to Kyiv to demand they stop the pogroms. The Directorate did nothing.

The pogrom wave grew after Petliura took over the Directorate in February. A few days later, a division of Petliura's troops led by Ivan Semesenko rode their horses through the main drag of the small town of Proskurov and murdered 1,500 people in Petliura's name.

The Polish army was hardly better. "In order to deflect the attention of the masses from their real needs, and to drown the revolutionary struggle of the proletariat in a wave of race-hatred . . . the reactionary forces organized a series of anti-Jewish pogroms," Erlich told the Warsaw Soviet in March. In early April, in Pinsk, the Polish army arrested thirty-five Jews at a meeting about aid distribution and gunned them down against the wall of a nearby monastery. Two victims were Bundists: the municipal worker Moishe Glauberman and the teacher Abraham Chaim Haltsman. At a parliamentary inquest later, the army justified themselves by exhibiting a photograph of Jewish men armed with pistols, meant to be proof that their victims were a threat to Polish security. It was a photograph of a Bundist self-defense squad taken during the revolution of 1905.

After Erlich denounced the Pinsk pogrom in the Bund's Polish-language paper, the Warsaw police hauled him to court on accusations of attempting to "abolish the social order of Poland."

On April 19, Pilsudski led Polish forces into Vilna. In the days that followed, his soldiers murdered eighty-five Jews. Two days into their rampage, Polish legionnaires broke down the door of an apartment that the famed playwright A. Vayter shared with two poets. Vayter had been the leader of the Bund's Vilna self-defense group during the 1905 revolution but, disillusioned by the October pogroms, had turned to literature. When the Red Army seized Vilna, they appointed Vayter as head of a Yiddish publishing house. Now his body lay in the gutter, one of the many Jewish corpses scattered around Vilna's old town.

"The Polish Army brings Liberty and Freedom to you all," Pilsudski declared once he had secured the city.

KOMBUND

In the first twenty years of their existence, the Bund had accomplished many things in the areas of mutual aid, cultural production, and armed self-defense. But there was one thing that the Bund had neglected: the necessity of taking power.

As armed bands ravaged the former Pale of Settlement, Bundists got a brutal lesson in their own helplessness. They represented a small minority. For their communities to survive, they needed allies, but every armed group in Ukraine had carried out pogroms. Only two groups even tried to stop the violence: forces led by the Ukrainian anarchist Nestor Makhno and the Bund's enemies, the Red Army.

For the Bolsheviks, stopping pogroms was a matter of self-interest as well as ethics. They had long known that the conflation of Jew and revolutionary would redound against them, and Trotsky's role as leader of the Red Army brought these slanders to a fever pitch. In the spring of 1919, they began to view pogroms as an existential threat to themselves. They published antipogrom leaflets, and imprisoned or shot instigators. Lenin himself made a gramophone recording to convince soldiers that antisemitism was a tool of the bourgeoisie. Sometimes Red Army units got drunk and murdered Jews anyway, but whatever atrocities they committed paled in comparison to those done by Petliura's Haidamaks, the Polish army, and the Whites.

Unsurprisingly, Bundists in Ukraine began to take a second look at the Bolsheviks. When the Red Army appealed for Jewish recruits, many Bundist pogrom survivors signed up—including the Bundist mayor of Berdichev, David Lipetz. After a second pogrom rocked his city, he lost all faith in the Ukrainian government, quit his post, and enlisted in the Red Army under the goyish pseudonym of Petrovsky.

In February 1919, in Kyiv, Moishe Rafes inaugurated a new group, the Communist Bund, or Kombund. (The Bolsheviks had changed their name to the Communist Party a year before.) The Kombund would ally with the Red Army, which Rafes saw as the only force that could protect Jewish workers from what he described as "mass annihilation." Bundist groups around Ukraine followed his lead and transformed into Kombunds.

Did Rafes and Lipetz have a choice? Poles, Ukrainians, and Whites murdered Jews en masse. Bundists had turned to the Ukrainian government for help, only to be ignored. The Red Army* was the only group even claiming to defend them. In the words of one Bundist survivor, "For us there is no other way."

SARAH FUCHS

Despite the multidirectional terror they lived under, not every Bundist agreed with the choice that Lipetz and Rafes made. I think of Sarah Fuchs. In her photograph in *The Bund in Pictures,* her hollow eyes evoke the intensity of her belief. She'd been a sweatshop seamstress since fourteen. The Bund gave her a union, an education, a family, and a method-

* In January 1919, Nestor Makhno's forces were integrated into the Red Army.

ology to analyze the world. In return, she gave them everything she had. She never married. She had no lovers. She just worked for the Bund. She rotted in jail cells. She organized soldiers on the front lines. At a circus in Berdichev, she promoted the Bundist candidate for the Soviet before an audience of thousands. At a Jewish convention in Kyiv, she explained the party's platform with cool self-assurance while rabbis heckled her for daring, as a woman, to stand so shamelessly onstage. Fuchs could not reconcile herself to the terror that followed Lenin's Revolution. "I do not imagine any social democracy without democracy," she wrote to Rafes a few months after the Bolsheviks took power.

In June 1919, the Cheka stormed Berdichev's Bundist cultural club, where Fuchs spent much of her time. "Where is the counterrevolutionary Sarah Fuchs?" one agent demanded. "I am the counterrevolutionary Sarah Fuchs," she replied. She was interrogated for twenty-four hours straight by a Cheka agent who once had been her party comrade. This made up her mind. She was sick of betrayed trust, of strangers' slogans spoken by her friends' familiar lips. She bought a train ticket to Kyiv. She told her friends she was going for party business, but her smile was too tight. When she arrived, she walked toward the Jewish neighborhood of Podil. The streets were empty except for a few militiamen. She stopped on the bridge over the Dnipro River. She climbed awkwardly atop the railing. She took a breath. Kyiv is beautiful in June, when the air feels floral, electric. Perhaps she paused to enjoy the summer breeze on her face before stepping out, right foot then left, into the sunshine.

She slammed into the water. For a second, her skirt billowed around her like a bell. Did she reconsider her choice? Or did she remember her letter to Rafes: "I know that people with opinions and spirits such as these will now be stoned or (in the best-case scenario) spat upon. I know that there is no place among the living for people of my type. They are superfluous." Her clothes became saturated with water, pulling her to the river bottom.

GOMEL

In April 1920, at the Bund's twelfth congress, in Gomel, the disagreements between the party's pro- and anti-Soviet factions led to a final rupture. A majority of delegates, led by Esther Frumkin, voted to have the Bund enter the Communist Party as an autonomous organization, just as they had entered the RSDLP in 1903. They had little choice. The Bolsheviks might have been bastards, but they were bastards the Bund knew. Soviet rule seemed like the only protection Jews had against the murderous depredations of the Polish army, Ukrainian warlords, and the Whites. And for the moment, the Soviets seemed inclined to be generous, allowing Bundists in Minsk to keep publishing their newspaper and running their clubs, even as they shut down similar efforts by other leftist groups. By Frumkin's reckoning, it was time for the Bund to get on board with the world's first socialist state. When she announced her faction's decision, she no longer spoke in the poetic register of previous years, but with the pseudoscientific jargon of the newborn Soviet state.

This decision was the last straw for Raphael Abramovich, who was fresh out of jail after a hunger strike. He didn't see why his party should fight some murderers by submitting themselves to others. Rather than capitulate, he and his followers left to form the Social Democratic Bund, which, he swore, would uphold the true spirit of the party.

"The existing government demands unquestioning, silent, and *total submission*," Abramovich wrote in a letter to his Menshevik comrade Pavel Axelrod. He was right. The Soviets banned Abramovich's speeches as counterrevolutionary, and the Cheka ransacked his apartment. He lived in fear of another arrest. After much wrangling, Abramovich obtained a visa to accompany his dying friend, Menshevik leader Julius Martov, to Germany.

Shortly after Abramovich's departure, the Cheka arrested the entire Social Democratic Bund committee in Mogilev and sent the leaders to concentration camps. More arrests of Bundist leaders across Russia followed. The Social Democratic Bund issued its last illegal bulletin in 1923. After that, silence.

POLAND, SEA TO SEA

After a year of war with the Soviets, Polish nationalism mutated into a fever dream of empire. *Polska od mirza do morza!* the slogan went. Poland from the Black Sea to the Baltic! With more expansion in mind, Pilsudski signed an alliance with Petliura. They would kick out the Reds, retake Kyiv, and divide Ukraine between them.

In Warsaw, the atmosphere was stifling. On May Day of 1920, after Medem spoke before twenty thousand people in Iron Gate Square, police sealed the side streets and beat the celebrants to a pulp. Cops wrecked the Bund's club in Praga, a suburb on the opposite side of the Vistula River. They shut down *Lebens-Fragen* and arrested its editors. That month, with Petliura's help, Poland took Kyiv and Pilsudski returned to Warsaw as a hero.

The Soviet counteroffensive was savage, spearheaded by the First Cavalry Army—the Red Cossacks immortalized by Sophia Dubnova's old acquaintance Isaac Babel, who served as their political commissar.

Babel fetishized these manly men who had once tormented his family ("his long legs were like girls clad to the shoulders in shining jackboots," Babel wrote of one officer), then snuck off to celebrate Jewish holidays with mournful intellectuals who dreamed of revolutions without bullets and of Internationals of good men. As the Red Army advanced, Babel recorded a war fought in both the future and the deep past, with bombers and armored trains, with machine guns hauled by horse carts, with a Scythian cavalry, with sticks and rocks. The Red Army moved through mud-dark rivers, over fields red with poppies and livid with decayed hunks of human flesh. The Reds retook Kyiv, then Minsk, then Vilna, then crossed the Bug River to reach Bialystok, where Cheka boss Felix Dzerzhinsky set up shop as the future leader of Poland.

SOPHIA DUBNOVA

On July 8, 1920, at an emergency meeting of the Warsaw city council, Henryk Erlich demanded immediate peace and an end to Polish imperial ambitions. "What are we fighting for?" he asked. "Land which doesn't belong to us." He was the only councilman who raised his voice. Hysterical demonization followed. Newspapers smeared the Bund as Soviet traitors, and the government banned the party. Soldiers smashed their union halls and shut down their meetings. The Bundist press went underground. Sympathetic printers typeset their newspapers after work and ran them off on the presses of mainstream newspapers that Bundists commandeered at gunpoint.

Police sealed Warsaw's Jewish districts and hunted leftists house-to-house. They arrested hundreds of Bundists, shipping many off to a concentration camp near Krakow. When undercover cops began to watch his home, Erlich went into hiding.

Sophia was with her maid when the cops broke down her door to demand her husband's whereabouts. "He's away in the provinces," she lied. They tore through the house, overturning drawers, knocking down books, jeering that Yids like her were out to ruin Poland. One policeman picked up a German economics pamphlet. "Communist stuff!" he crowed. His chief, an ashen anorexic with drug-blurred eyes, complimented Sophia on her taste in literature. "You live in modest surroundings," he said. "The Bolsheviks pay meagerly for the services Mr. Erlich renders them." As he interrogated her, she realized that the police knew every detail of the Bund's acrimonious debates about Soviet Russia. Their party was clearly infiltrated with spies. After the police left, Sophia stood in the middle of her scattered papers. Her head raced. She couldn't move for a long time.

By August, the Red Army was a few miles outside of Warsaw. The Communist Party of Poland promised Lenin they would "unfurl the Red Banner of Revolution inside this Fortress of Imperialism." Inside the city, the Polish army hunted draft dodgers for immediate conscription, and the Polish Socialist Party raised battalions of workers armed with scythes. Then, on August 15, Polish forces counterattacked in a little town called Izabelin, forcing the Soviets into a shambolic retreat. Wherever the Polish army went, soldiers carried out pogroms to avenge themselves upon the Jews who they believed were traitors.

The police caught Henryk Erlich in September. Bored with hiding at his friend's place, he shaved off his signature beard in a half-assed effort to conceal his identity and went for a walk. Cops grabbed him within minutes.

Erlich's arrest thrust Sophia into the ranks of women who love imprisoned men. This sisterhood is familiar to me from the times I've taken the visitors' bus to the jail at Rikers Island. You rarely see men onboard. Only women seem to visit Rikers. Once there, these wives, sisters, daughters, mothers, and lovers wait for hours to have guards take their fingerprints, shine flashlights beneath their tongues, and watch them shake out their bras. They pay this price to see their men. In Sophia's Warsaw, women waited the same wait beside the blank brick walls of Mokotow prison. Sophia observed them. They were every age. Some wore fur coats, some tattered sheepskin. Some cried. Others kept a stony silence. All of them had the same bewilderment in their eyes. How could they navigate this bureaucracy? How could they get lawyers for their men, or even permission to visit? Everything was against them.

Sophia knew what to do. After fifteen years in radical circles, she'd been around this block before. She explained the visiting procedure. A crowd gathered around her. She passed out her address so she could help the women file paperwork. Sophia Dubnova may have lost her country, but she hadn't lost her sense of self. She was still the same girl who had incited a military mutiny in Grodno, who smuggled pamphlets taped to her body. She was a revolutionary. She would do what revolutionaries did. She organized.

VOLKOVYSK

The Polish army took Volkovysk in February 1919, and the town had been in bad straits ever since. In April 1920, after rumors spread about matzoh made with babies' blood, soldiers smashed up the Jewish neighborhood. That summer a group of Volkovysk immigrants in New York scraped together eighty thousand dollars to help their families back home. They dispatched two representatives to deliver money to the town rabbi, who intended to use it to buy off the next round of pogromists, whoever they might be.

Shortly after the money arrived, the Red Army took back Volkovysk. With them came one of Sam's old Bundist comrades, Berl Dzhik. The boyish radical who had escaped the cops dressed in drag back in 1903 returned wearing a secret policeman's leather jacket.

With Berl and his men searching Volkovysk door to door, the rabbi knew it was a matter of time until they found the New York cash. Rather than trying to hide, the rabbi summoned Berl for a meeting, to remind him of how the Jewish community had cared for his family during his Siberian imprisonment. Now it was Berl's turn to save them. Berl agreed, despite his alleged ideology, and the two came up with a plan. The rabbi showed Berl where he had concealed the money beneath his floorboards. When Berl supervised a search of the rabbi's house, he made sure to stand on that exact spot so that it, and it alone, remained untouched. Berl knew there were debts to be paid, even in the brand-new Bolshevik state.

In October 1920, the Polish army invaded, retook, liberated, and/or occupied Volkovysk. When a well-known captain died in the battle, the Poles announced they would retaliate by slaughtering the entire Jewish population. The only thing that stopped them was a payment from the rabbi, using the New York cash that Berl Dzhik had helped him conceal.

No matter how I searched, I never found another word about Berl Dzhik, though perhaps his name is hiding in archives in Minsk or Moscow. I don't know if he died in the war, in the purges, in the Nazi invasion, or even, improbably, as an old pensioner in his bed. However it was, a secret policeman like him would have deserved it. Every secret policemen committed his share of murders, and Berl's quotidian workday involved the imprisonment, interrogation, and torture of other human beings. Yet Berl was not foreordained to be a murderer. God and chance and the Dialectical Forces of History all had their parts to play. If events had occurred in a different sequence, Berl might have taken a boat to New York, gotten a job in a sweatshop, and joined a Workmen's Circle branch like my great-grandfather Sam Rothbort. He could have taken Sam's path, and if Sam had stayed in Volkovysk, who's to say he would not have taken Berl's?

REFUGEE

Around two hundred thousand Jews were murdered in the pogroms that took place between 1918 and 1921. The chaos forced six hundred thousand more to flee to Western Europe, America, and Palestine. Governments tried to keep them out with immigration laws, but regulations are no match for the human will to move. The refugees crowded into synagogue basements, into camps filled with dysentery and typhus, and into cities like Vienna, Paris, and lurid, inflationary Weimar Berlin. There, they joined Jewish political exiles from the former Russian Empire, like Raphael Abramovich.

Refugees lead to reaction, as we Americans should know. These Jews were "the world's foremost problem" in the words of Henry Ford, a mass of swarthy subversives who brought with them the whiff of hectographed manuscripts and homemade bombs. Everywhere they went, the right-wing press followed. The venerable *New York Times* listed the Jewish birth names of the "Former East Siders Responsible for Bolshevism." Even if Jews fled Soviet Russia, their countries of refuge saw them as Bolsheviks, just as the world saw the Syrian refugees who fled ISIS in 2015 as terrorists. Their arrival caused a panic in the good citizens of Western Europe—one that men like the young Nazi newspaper editor Alfred Rosenberg were only too eager to exploit.

SOPHIA DUBNOVA

Poland and Soviet Russia signed a ceasefire agreement in October 1920, though official peace would have to wait till the Treaty of Riga the following spring.

From her dining room table Sophia ran an office to help the prisoners' wives, while undercover cops paced the street below. Every day, the women lined up by Mokotow prison. They were whipped by wind, soaked by fat November snowflakes. When Sophia met with Polish Socialist minister Ignacy Daszynski to plead her husband's case, she also appealed for her "nameless sisters," like the nursing mother arrested and separated from her baby because she wouldn't give police the names of her husband's friends. While Sophia spoke, Daszynski fiddled with his silver cigar box. What was he supposed to do? he asked. The woman's husband was a communist. Even the babies of communists need their mother's milk, Sophia answered.

The government threatened Erlich with an eight-year sentence for subversion. When Sophia visited her husband, he passed her fistfuls of notes his fellow prisoners had slipped him during walks around the exercise yard, which she then gave to their wives. After she put her boys to bed, she sat awake. Her thoughts circled each other. Was she still a poet? Or had she forgotten? If she could no longer write, how could she live? Finally, she had enough. She sat down at her desk. She wrote about the prisoners' wives, the tortured, steadfast women who had become her friends. It was nearly sunrise when she put down the pen. Relief flooded her. She could write.

They released Erlich from prison in November. He was thinner, Sophia wrote, "with little tufts of stubble on his sallow face." Other Bundists trickled out of the jails and concentration camps. They came home to a fractured political landscape in a poor and wounded country. They had enemies everywhere. Their party tore itself apart over Soviet Russia. Poland would never welcome them. But this was the first place the Bund landed where they had the freedom to build institutions. Over eighteen years, the span of one generation, they would create an alternate world.

CHAPTER 15

THE COMMUNIST ROMANCE

(1921–1923)

Viktor Alter

POLAND

POLAND EMERGED FROM THE WAR WITH ITS INDUSTRY IN SHAMBLES AND its farmland poisoned by bombs. During the occupation, Germany had dismantled the factories of Lodz and Bialystok and carted their machinery back home. To avoid starvation, the Polish government had bought massive amounts of food from America on credit. Now the bill was coming due.

Poverty exacerbates divisions. It forces people to compete over who deserves survival on such-and-such piece of land. Yet, amidst the hunger, bigotry, and bloodshed of interwar Poland, the Bund staked their claim of Hereness—their right to exist as equals in the places where they lived. To stay was not an act of naïveté, nor of weakness. "Here where I live is my country," the Bund wrote. They accepted all the struggle this implied.

Over the next two decades, the Bund would show Jewish workers that they were a people as worthy as any other. Their methods remind me of those of America's Black Panther Party, another group of young radicals who carried guns and started free breakfast programs and asserted their people's beauty in a country that wanted them dead. Like the Panthers, the Bund was a Marxist party built by and for oppressed and racialized others, who created a network of communal care and cultural uplift, of schools, clinics, mutual aid centers, and youth groups, backed with weapons and branded with militant chic.

Both parties published newspapers that became gateways to capacious intellectual worlds. The Bundist *Folkstsaytung* ran international reporting, sandwiched between ads for handguns, face powder, and nightclubs offering dances with pretty girls. One issue might contain a dispatch from their comrade Pedro Wald in Buenos Aires. (In 1919, Argentine police arrested Wald on accusations of attempting to overthrow the government and form a Patagonian Soviet Republic.) Or they might print a blistering indictment of the state-backed mob murders of Black people in Missouri, writing that "the 'civilized' American lynches with the sort of pleasure one would find among . . . wild beasts." *Folkstsaytung*'s internationalism connected small-town Jewish workers to far-flung struggles. Activist Yonia Fain recalled visiting a tiny shtetl where his shoemaker host asked how he could help the socialists of China.

The Bund created a youth movement, Tsukunft (the Future), for teenagers who worked ten hours a day and lived five to a tenement room but still dreamed of a better and more beautiful world.

Bundist teachers dominated the new, secular Yiddish school system, TSYSHO (Central Yiddish School System). These schools directly challenged the traditional cheders that my great-grandfather endured—which Bundists described as filthy holes where subliterate old men "filled [a child's] small brain with nonsense," using a cat-o'-nine-tails to reinforce their points.

The Bund helped transform Yiddish, the language of the Jewish Street, into a vehicle for transnational literary culture. When they fled disaster, Yiddish became a portable homeland that Bundists carried on their tongues. Secular Yiddish literature and the Bund grew together, until Bundists became the literature's greatest champions. Bundists devoted themselves to the perpetuation of Yiddish long after they had been forced to abandon everything else.

BERNARD GOLDSTEIN

Like the Panthers, the Bund worked in gang-ridden neighborhoods that the state both neglected and surveilled. Jewish Warsaw was a rough place by any measure, with enough crimes to fill the pages of the city's hundred Polish and Yiddish newspapers. Pimps whisked poor girls off to Argentine brothels. Gangs terrorized shopkeepers. Scorned wives threw acid in rivals' faces. When a "cannibal" bit off an enemy's nose in the courtyard of 29 Smocza Street, it was just a blip in the news. To organize this chaos, the Bund tapped Bernard Goldstein, the scar-faced leader of their Kyiv militia, who had recently returned to Warsaw.

The criminality of Bernard's milieu often disgusted him. He struggled against it and tried to get kids out of it, but ultimately, it was what he knew. Since youth, Bernard had been an enforcer. He got on easily with thugs, like the teamster brothers known as the Seven Lions of Praga. When the eldest Lion, Yankl Scarface, married into robber royalty, Goldstein earned an invite to the wedding. He was at the synagogue when Yankl Scarface read the Torah, and he was at the afterparty at their Zygmuntowska Street garret, where they gorged on herring and whisky, and a chanteuse sang gangster ballads till sunrise.

Bernard knew the secret argot of the child bagel hawkers—the codes by which they warned each other of the arrival of the police. He slurped tea at the union buffets with the unemployed. At the thieves' synagogue behind the Gesia Cemetery, where all the Warsaw cutthroats prayed, Bernard chatted up back porters (lawless men who hauled the city's goods in huge wicker boxes lashed to their shoulders). He converted them to Bundism one by one, until his party dominated their union. When the Jewish and Polish slaughterhouse workers were fighting over the allocation of jobs, the party sent Bernard to mediate. He arrived to find the two groups circling each other, knives in hand. When he told them they should refer their disputes to their respective unions, they hurled their knives at the concrete floor with such force that sparks flew from the ground, but they listened to Comrade Bernard.

THE COMINTERN

The same questions that split the Russian Bund threatened to tear the Polish Bund apart when, in 1919, Soviet Russia announced the creation of the Communist International, or Comintern, an international organization of labor parties intended to replace the discredited Second International. The Comintern believed that any day now, capitalism was about to crumble beneath the boots of a global communist revolution. It was time for socialist parties around the world to unite and seize the moment.

The idea of the Comintern attracted Polish Bundists, just as Soviet Russia enchanted leftists the world over. It was, after all, the first country in history to put socialism into practice. But for Polish Jews, it had a special resonance. After the unspeakable massacres of the last two decades, Soviet Russia was the one place in eastern Europe where Jews could ostensibly live as equals. Or even become leaders, like David Petrovsky, formerly David Lipetz, the Bundist mayor of Berdichev. After joining the Red Army, he moved to Moscow and rebuilt the Soviet military education system from the ground up. When Bundist writer Moyshe Olgin visited Moscow in 1921, he watched the old tsarist general Aleksei Brusilov salute Petrovsky at a military parade in Red Square. The sight moved him nearly to tears. If an aristocratic general saluted a Jew in Soviet Russia, then the country must have abolished racism, Olgin reckoned. He returned to New York a committed communist.

Then there was Trotsky, the most famous Jewish revolutionary on earth, though he loathed being identified as such. In Soviet Russia, Trotsky was a hero, the first Jew to command a nation's army since 1037, when Samuel ha-Nagid led the troops of the Emirate of Granada. Even Bundists were impressed. "I wish that more radical Jews like Trotsky were heads of government," wrote one Bundist journalist in New York. "Our foes would not have dared touch us, let alone perpetrate massacres and pogroms against us. . . . If a people can still produce men that can undermine the foundations of the world, [that is] a clear sign of its youthfulness, vitality and stamina." For many Jews, Trotsky was proof that in Soviet Russia, they could do anything.

In April 1920, at the Bund's Krakow convention, a majority of delegates voted to join the Comintern. The main dissenter was Vladimir Medem. He had made up his mind about Lenin in 1903, and every step the Bolsheviks had taken since only strengthened Medem's convictions. In 1918, he predicted that the terror Bolsheviks wielded against their rivals would soon turn inward, to be used against each other. "The day is not far off when we will see revolutionary tribunals in which the more kosher Bolsheviks will execute the more suspect; the circle of 'kosher' or 'authentic' socialists grows narrower," he wrote. Few wanted to listen. The Soviet Union, for all its flaws, was a living socialist state. Most Bundists wanted to be its ally.

When Medem failed to convince his comrades, he resigned from the central committee. Exhausted and disillusioned, he asked American garment unions to send him steamship tickets to New York. He and Gina arrived at Ellis Island in January 1921. He would never see Poland again.

THE TWENTY-ONE CONDITIONS

Only one thing stood in the way of the Bund's entry into the Comintern: a list of rules, called the Twenty-one Conditions. Most of the conditions were fine—the Bund was happy to agitate amongst soldiers, organize peasants, and condemn European imperialism—but a few were intolerable: for instance, the requirement that parties belonging to the Comintern purge themselves of moderate socialists and kick out any leader who disobeyed the dictates of Moscow. Despite these onerous terms, the Bund wanted to find a way to make things work. Perhaps the Soviets would make an exception for them.

Around the time Medem sailed for New York, the Bund dispatched an envoy to Moscow. No documents list this secret agent's name, so I'll call him X. The trip was illegal, and X carried no passport, so that if the Polish authorities caught him, they would not discover his identity. The war had not officially ended, and the borders bristled with armed and jumpy men. Over six perilous weeks, X crossed into Lithuania disguised as a mushroom merchant and, from there, joined a convoy of Latvian prisoners of war. In Riga, the Russian ambassador put him on a train to Moscow.

While still in transit, he received a telegram from the Russian Bund to let him know that the Soviet government had ordered the party's liquidation. As soon as he arrived in Moscow, he got on a train to Minsk to watch their funeral.

X joined the hundreds of people who gathered to hear the Russian Bundists' tormented final speeches. "Comrades, what this has cost each of us will perhaps one day inspire an artistic genius to create a great tragedy. But let us rather be silent about this, friends," cried Esther Frumkin. After voting to dissolve the party, her friend Aaron Vaynshteyn shouted "Long live the Bund!" No one applauded. The next month, Frumkin, Vaynshteyn and their comrades marched to Minsk's State Theater, where, just four years before, they'd celebrated the Bund's future in revolutionary Russia and turned over their banners to the local Communist party.

The Comintern sent X back to Warsaw with a letter for the Bund's central committee. Its contents shocked them. To join the Comintern, the Bund would have to purge their leadership, change their name, and eventually dissolve themselves into the Polish Communist Party. In other words, they would cease to exist.

Clinging to hope, the Bund sent two local leaders, Chaim Wasser and Viktor Alter, to plead their case at the Third Comintern Congress in Moscow.

At thirty-one, Alter, who had been born rich in small-town Poland, was a ladies' man whom friends later nicknamed "the Cary Grant of labor." He had a crackling wit and an explosive amount of energy; he liked to fight with nationalists at the Saxon Gardens for fun. Alter had joined the Bund during the 1905 revolution at age fifteen. His leadership of a student strike earned him a lifetime ban from Russian universities. The next year, a cache of illegal guns exploded in his parents' attic. After that, he thought it would be prudent to skip town. He studied engineering in Belgium, married a Belgian socialist, and returned to Poland on party work in 1912. The Okhrana quickly exiled him to Siberia. He escaped and snuck back into Belgium with a fake passport he'd artfully concealed inside the sole of his shoe. The World War saw him in the Belgian resistance, then as a refugee in London, where he got a factory job, joined the British Socialist Party, and campaigned for Jews to resist the draft. The revolution brought him to Moscow, where he earned a seat on the Bund's central committee. The Bolsheviks jailed him after October. Upon his release, he settled in Warsaw, where he was elected to the city council alongside Henryk Erlich. With his razor-sharp cheekbones, his wave of dark hair, and his collar upturned like a film noir detective, he became a bona fide celebrity—instantly recognizable in City Hall, at a protest in support of the anarchist death-row prisoners Sacco and Vanzetti, or at an eviction on Niska Street, hauling the poor family's furniture back up the stairs. He seemed like the perfect person to plead the Bund's case in Moscow.

When Alter and Wasser arrived in Moscow, they received a chilly reception from the Jewish Section of the Communist Party, which many Russian Bundists had joined after their own party's dissolution. As if to draw a distinction between themselves and their old comrades, the Jewish Section's newspaper berated the Polish Bund for its weak-kneed and "slovenly" refusal to expel more moderate members. Former Bundist Moishe Rafes went one step further and publicly denounced Alter as a spy.

For Alter, Moscow seemed even more oppressive than it had during his last visit, especially when he learned that old comrades were rotting in jail cells on spurious charges. Two weeks after the congress concluded, he tried to help one of these imprisoned socialists by passing their smuggled letter to the British communist leader Sylvia Pankhurst. When the Cheka found out about Alter's role in this illicit communication, they threw him into the notorious Butyrka prison on accusations of espionage. Eleven days' hunger strike nearly killed him, but in the end, the Soviets let him go. They still feared international opinion.

Alter's arrest finally ended the Bund's doomed courtship of the Comintern. In December 1921, at an underground conference held in the Free City of Danzig, Bundists voted to reject the Twenty-One Conditions. A splinter sect of Soviet fanboys flounced out and quit the party.

BERNARD GOLDSTEIN

From then on, communists would be the Bund's mortal enemies, and the labor movement was the front line of their fight. Jewish communists fought Bundists for control of tiny workshops in penny-ante industries like matzoh, candy wrappers, and ladies' shoes—demonstrating their dominance with guns and razor blades as well as the more traditional fists. In this farcical struggle, left-wing Jewish workers in run-down Warsaw districts—many of them literal cousins—bludgeoned one another senseless because of the ideological swerves of Moscow.

Attacked by nationalist thugs outside their neighborhoods and fellow Jewish leftists within them, the Bund decided they needed a more formal means of protection. Enter comrade Bernard. Using his experience running a paramilitary in Kyiv, Bernard Goldstein organized Warsaw union workers into a self-defense militia. Militiamen fought with lead-tipped walking sticks, brass knuckles, and spring-loaded retractable steel rods. He limited gun ownership to a few trusted leaders; the point was to teach a lesson, not leave a trail of murdered enemies. To this end, he forbade his fighters to drink on the job. Most importantly, Bernard created a culture that blended verbal secrecy with visual menace. Armed, uniformed militiamen paraded each May Day, but when asked about their exploits, they said nothing. Silence creates legends.

ELECTION SEASON

In the autumn of 1922, the Bund plunged into their first ever election campaign for the parliament in Poland. Their candidates offered a social-democratic platform of eight-hour workdays, unemployment benefits, peace, equality, and minority cultural rights. They held innumerable rallies in union halls guarded by Bernard's militia, with police bribed to make themselves scarce. They drove trucks emblazoned with their slogans, distributed hundreds of thousands of leaflets, knocked on hundreds of thousands of doors. Late at night, their kids fanned out in cities across Poland to glue posters to courtyard walls. A photo of these boys electioneering in a northeast mill town shows a gang in flat caps, sneering back at the camera. All the while, Bernard's militia protected campaigners from attacks by Endeks and communists.

When the votes came in, the right triumphed; Endeks won 40 percent of deputies. The Left had split itself between the Polish Socialist Party, the Bund, and the communists. The Bund didn't win a single seat.

A friend of Pilsudski's, the liberal populist Gabriel Narutowicz, was elected president, thanks in part to Jewish votes. This exercise of the franchise enraged the Endeks. Hours after Narutowicz's election, nationalist mobs rioted in Warsaw, chanting, "Narutowicz, president of the Jews." On inauguration day, rioters barricaded Ujazdów Avenue, pelted Narutowicz's carriage with snowballs, and beat leftists, journalists, and Jews. A few days later, a nationalist painter shot Narutowicz dead at an art exhibition. The Endek press fêted the assassin as a hero.

THE ENDEKS

After President Narutowicz's assassination, a peasant populist named Wincenty Witos took office as prime minister. Disgusted with the nationalists he held responsible for his friend Narutowicz's murder, Pilsudski retired from politics. While he stewed at his country home, Poland's economy tanked. It became terribly convenient to blame the Jews.

Endek leader Roman Dmowski fulminated about the need to deport all Jews from Poland, and his newspapers called for "a wholesome struggle for [the Jews'] elimination." Attacks ravaged Jewish communities across the country, from Vilna and Lviv to Bialystok and Pinsk. Suffice it to say, these were not good years for the Bund's base in Poland. It was a time of smashed synagogues, blockaded shops, plundered neighborhoods, and broken skulls, when Jews were blamed for every offensive aspect of Soviet policy. When Jewish parliamentarians tried to protest, their Endek colleagues beat them bloody. Endek students petitioned the government to keep Jews out of universities, then went home for summer vacation and beat more Jews for fun.

The government targeted the Bund for both bureaucratic and kinetic repression, banning their unions, strangling their schools in red tape, and shutting down *Folkstsaytung* right before May Day; Erlich reopened the paper the next day, to show that his party would not be intimidated.

On May Day 1923, the Bund organized a massive procession, flanked by a thousand militiamen holding wooden bats. The marchers wove their way to Theater Square, where the Polish Socialist Party had saved them a spot. Fighting started before Erlich even had a chance to speak. Cops attacked communists gathered at nearby Trebacka Street, and within minutes, Theater Square transformed into a whirlpool of knives, sticks, and screams. Nationalists tried to grab the Bund's banner, but Bernard tore the fabric from its pole and hid it beneath his shirt. He saw old Benish Michaelwisz from the central committee swinging his cane at nationalists until it snapped. At the Bund's afterparty at Nowosci Theater, Bernard counted the black eyes. This satisfied him. They had taught both themselves and the government a lesson. They had showed they would fight back.

VLADIMIR MEDEM

Medem got to America just in time. A few months after his arrival, Congress passed the Emergency Quota Act, which radically slashed immigration from the Middle East and from eastern and southern Europe. The main targets were those people that the bill's author, Albert Johnson, called "filthy, un-American, and often dangerous in their habits," which is to say the Jews.

The Red Scare was well underway, so, perhaps out of caution, Medem confined himself to cultural writings. Though he loathed their Soviet flirtation, Medem didn't leave the Bund. The party, he wrote, "was cemented by the blood and tears of its martyrs . . . [which] are thicker than the ink with which platforms are written." Though his politics were out of touch, the East Side never forsook him. He would always be their prince who had given up a life of privilege to fight alongside them, as a fellow member of the oppressed.

Medem died of nephritis on January 9, 1923, in Brooklyn, at the age of fourty-four. Despite the snowstorm, ten thousand people came to his funeral. Over his coffin, Baruch Charney Vladeck said his death was like the passing of a world.

CHAPTER 16

ENEMY OF ZION

(1923–1926)

Vladimir Jabotinsky

BER, DAVID, AND VLADIMIR

ON DECEMBER 23, 1923, ENDEK ECONOMIST WLADYSLAW GRABSKI became prime minister of Poland. Granted near-dictatorial powers by parliament, Grabski immediately began to slash and burn. In the name of balancing the budget, he sold off industries and cut wages. When workers went on strike, cops shot up their protests. Three thousand political prisoners crowded Poland's jails.

Grabski's reforms devastated the Bund's base. When the government launched new public works projects to help the jobless, they turned away Jewish applicants. Parliament rescinded Jews' permits to sell tobacco and alcohol and dismissed Jewish workers from nationalized industries. Grabski raised taxes to perilous heights, targeting Jews the hardest. As much as the violence, Grabski's taxes provoked another wave of Jewish emigration. With the doors to America shut, Polish Jews began to look toward Palestine, which the U.K. ruled under the so-called British Mandate, with the explicit aim of helping Zionists set up a Jewish national home.

There was only one problem. Palestinian Arabs made up the vast majority of the land's population, and the Zionist movement had already set about turning them into enemies. Unlike immigrants, who generally try to integrate into their new countries, the Zionists aimed to supplant Palestinian society. With British support, they set up a quasi-governmental body called the Palestine Zionist Executive (later the Jewish Agency for Palestine) to represent Jews inside Palestine and encourage more Jewish immigration. (Britain forbade Palestinians to create similar institutions.) New Zionist immigrants bought land from Palestinian feudal leaders, brutally expelled farmers who had lived there for generations, and used these dispossessed farmers' labor to build up a parallel society of Jewish-only collective farms, towns, and even a city, Tel Aviv, right next to the graceful Levantine port of Jaffa. They referred to themselves as settlers, or colonists, but they also considered themselves to be the land's native people, returning home.

The Jewish Agency answered to the Zionist Congress, that same body that Theodor Herzl set up in a Basel casino in 1897. Many parties jostled beneath its umbrella. Their philosophies ranged from secular to religious, socialist to fascist, ostentatiously proletarian to snottily bourgeois. In Poland, the Bund's main adversaries were the Labor Zionists and the Revisionist Zionists.

The Marxist Dov Ber Borochov developed the Labor Zionist philosophy in the same late-nineteenth-century ferment that produced the Bund and organized the political party Poale Tsion to carry out his ideas. According to Borochov, Jews' minority status in Europe prevented them from embarking on productive work (by this he meant shirtless hammer-swinging) and relegated them to their stereotypical roles of tailors and money lenders. Jews could only become proper proletarians if they established a Jewish state in Palestine, where Jewish capitalists would exploit Jewish proletarians until class war broke out and the Jewish proletarians gloriously created communism. Borochov thought that since Jews and Arabs were cousins, Palestinians would be perfectly happy with this plan. To back up this dubious point, he brought up the friendship between African Americans in Liberia and the Kru people they colonized. (These African American settlers would later bring plantation slavery to their new West African home.)

By the 1920s, David Ben-Gurion, né Grun, had emerged as Poale Tsion's most important leader in Palestine. A short, squeaky-voiced admirer of Lenin, Ben-Gurion had spent his formative activist years brawling with Bundists in his Polish hometown, Plonsk. After losing one particularly vigorous debate in a synagogue, he had screamed at his Bundist opponent, "We have weapons, and we will kill you all like dogs."

In Palestine, Labor Zionists like Ben-Gurion paid lip service to the idea of brotherhood with the Palestinian masses while enforcing racial segregation in practice. The new Labor Zionist paramilitary, the Haganah, sometimes kidnapped and sexually tortured Jewish women who dated Palestinian men. In 1920, Ben-Gurion was elected secretary general of the Histadrut, a Jewish-only labor union that locked Palestinians out of the Zionist economy in the same way Polish labor policy locked Jews out of jobs in Warsaw.

Labor Zionism's main rival was Revisionist Zionism, which, as propounded by its founder, the Odesa-born journalist Vladimir Jabotinsky, wanted a Jewish state that didn't just stretch from the river to the sea but even encompassed contemporary Jordan. Like Borochov and Ben-Gurion, Jabotinsky came up in the same milieu as the Bund. He even briefly dated the young Sophia Dubnova before her marriage to Henryk Erlich. During the revolution of 1905, the Bund's self-defense militias impressed Jabotinsky, leading him to view Bundists as his greatest rivals. In one polemic, he wrote that the Bund's heroism was a waste. Jewish revolutionaries died to make history on behalf of an alien people—Russians, who would just as soon have them dead. Once the revolution spread, Jews were doomed to be forgotten. "The Jewish revolt was only terrifying to the government because it was a match which could set the Russian heartland afire," Jabotinsky wrote. "When all Russia is ablaze, who remembers the match?"

Jabotinsky was a fascist, in the original meaning of the word. He admired Mussolini. His followers called him Il Duce. He loved a shiny jackboot, a snappy military march. In 1923, he wrote an essay called "The Iron Wall" that shattered the genteel doublespeak of the Zionist Congress. In it he said that, like all colonies, Israel could only be built by subjugating the native people. Palestinians would resist, as all native people do, and one had to either accept this or give up on Zionism and remain powerless and doomed in the diaspora.

PALESTINE

To advance their project, Zionists collaborated with antisemites, among them Arthur Balfour himself, the conservative politician who hoped his Declaration would "mitigate the age-long miseries created for Western civilization by the presence in its midst of a Body which it too long regarded as alien and even hostile, but which it was equally unable to expel or to absorb." Theodor Herzl tried to cut deals with the notorious tsarist minister Vyacheslav von Plehve. During the Ukrainian massacres, Jabotinsky cozied up to Petliura, and right-wing Polish newspapers praised him as a "Jewish Endek" who would remove "millions of destructive microbes" to the Levant.

The Bund considered these alliances acts of treachery. Throughout the twenties, Zionists and Bundists battled one another in newspapers, in city councils, and with their fists.

But while Revisionists and Bundists were like oil and water, the beef between Bundists and Labor Zionists was more intimate. They were fighting for the souls of the Jewish working class. A young person looking for pride, purpose, and community could easily go either way; many switched between groups. Young Labor Zionists in Poland generally had little idea about the brutal evictions that Zionism entailed. Their press either ignored Palestinians entirely or painted a rosy picture of friendship between Jewish kibbutzniks and the grateful Arab villagers nearby. They would only learn the reality upon arrival in Palestine.

The darker things got for Jews in Poland, the more seductive Palestine seemed. While some potential immigrants were drawn by visions of national rebirth in their biblical homeland, for many others, it was merely a way out of Dodge. "Zionism drew its vital juices from defeats and catastrophes," wrote the Bundist leader Emanuel Nowogrodski. With immigration to America cut off and Poland averaging an outbreak of violence a week, even apolitical Jews turned up at the Warsaw offices of the Jewish Agency, the Zionist organization that chose amongst prospective immigrants to Palestine, to apply for a coveted entry permit.

In 1924, Viktor Alter sailed for Jaffa to see the Zionist endeavor up close. He chronicled the trip in *The Truth About Palestine*, a pamphlet he published upon his return to Warsaw.

Palestine didn't impress Alter. No matter how many times he heard American tourists hee-haw the words "holy land," he felt no sense of the divine. The place seemed downright shabby. Everything felt small. Culture, politics, horizons. On a boat ride through the Suez Canal, a Polish merchant told him that he didn't understand why a man as smart as Moses had led the Jews into the land of Canaan. He should have sent the Egyptians across the Red Sea and left Jews to enjoy the splendors of Thebes.

Alter had a typical European attitude of superiority. He looked down on the hundreds-of-years-old Sephardic community—elegant urbanites, integrated into Palestinian society, who spoke the same Arabic and wore the same tarbooshes as their neighbors. "I have more in common with a radical Russian student than a hundred Arab Jews," Alter sniffed. He quickly saw through Zionist marketing. At the time of his arrival, less than a hundred thousand Jews lived in Palestine, where they formed 11 percent of the population. Fewer than ten thousand Jewish immigrants arrived each year. Most lived in cities and did the same sorts of jobs they had in Europe. Despite the Labor Zionist promise of transforming shtetl nerds into muscular kibbutzniks, Palestinian workers powered Zionist collective farms. Zionists' new, Jewish-only communities were underwritten by British guns and the charity of rich Jews in the West.

Allergic to the very idea of assimilation, most Zionists interacted as little as possible with the larger Palestinian society. "There is almost no relation between these two people, and no shared cultural life," Alter wrote. Jewish immigrants didn't learn Arabic, and when they built new neighborhoods, they banned Palestinians from residence. "They are two worlds, frightful strangers to each other," and when trouble broke out, it did so with pyrotechnic brutality.

I could not pinpoint the Jerusalem mansion where Viktor Alter met Musa Kazim Pasha al-Husseini, president of the Palestinian Arab Congress, but I can guess what it looked like. It was probably built of golden stone, like the rest of the old city, with stained-glass windows and jasmine-covered walls. At seventy-five, Musa Kazim was witty and aristocratic, patriarch of one of the city's most prominent families, and in every way Alter's social superior. I can picture his luxurious hospitality, with tulip tea glasses, Egyptian cigarettes, and silver plates of baklawa. Nothing European could compare. Since the Mandate began, Musa Kazim had had a tumultuous relationship with the British authorities. In 1918, the British had appointed him as mayor of Jerusalem, only to fire him in 1921 after he delivered a passionate speech at the anti-occupation riots that broke out at the city's Nabi Musa festival. He had spent the years that followed leading a diplomatic struggle against the Mandate. While Musa Kazim initially sympathized with Jewish immigration, by the time Alter visited, he was fed up. "The immigrants dumped upon the country from different parts of the world are ignorant of the language, customs and character of the Arabs and enter Palestine by the might of England against the will of the people," he wrote in a 1922 letter to Palestine's British occupiers.

"Palestine will be a free country that rules itself alone, exactly as other countries in the world do," Musa Kazim told Alter in his erudite English. He explained that the Palestinian Arab Congress aspired to a democracy that represented Christians, Jews, and Muslims, with full equality for Jews, and even free Jewish immigration if the economic situation permitted. "We are not fighting against Jews, but only for our freedom," he said. Alter wondered who could object to such a program. But outside the plush confines of Musa Kazim's reception room, he sensed a more violent sort of Palestinian nationalism, one that the Zionist movement was doing everything to provoke.

"We feel this is our country," eastern European immigrants assured

Alter. He wanted to laugh at their naïveté. Jews might have bible stories about Abraham, Isaac, and Jacob, he wrote, but Palestinians had lived on the land for a thousand years. If a claim to a country was decided by longevity of continuous residence, the Palestinians were indisputably in the right. Not that Alter believed in this sort of blood-and-soil logic. It reminded him of Polish nationalists, who excelled in "antisemitic agitation which, in the name of Historic Right, tries to divide the population into Masters of the Land and foreigners."

"The right of people to live and work in the land where they are born is independent of whether their forefathers were born there," he wrote. Here where I live is my country.

As for a Jewish state in Palestine? The whole enterprise was doomed. Jews made up a smaller percentage of the population in Palestine than they did in Poland, and the trickle of new immigrants would never add up to a majority. Palestine was Arab, Alter wrote, and Arab it would remain.

"The great majority of the local population views Jewish immigrants with hostility, as foreigners. The anti-Jewish agitation grows stronger by the day. Why will Zionists fight in Palestine, but not in Poland?" Alter asked. "It's because they hope they can vanquish the Arabs." Alter was certain that they would fail.

POLAND

Grabski's reforms didn't work, and by 1926, Poland was in a major economic depression, with a third of the workforce unemployed. Nationalists continued their attempts to drive Jews out of Poland. Despite everything, the Bund fought for their place in their country.

They threw themselves into labor organizing, uniting Jewish trade unions into a single body, the National Council of Jewish Trade Unions, chaired by Viktor Alter, which fought not just for higher pay and shorter hours but for the right to use Yiddish, and for freedom from racist abuse. They created campaigns to combat anti-Jewish discrimination in government employment and held mass meetings to demand state support for the jobless.

They challenged their own community's religious conservatism. The Bund's struggle with Orthodox Jews began in 1922, when the party decided to publish a Saturday edition of *Folkstsaytung*, deliberately flouting rules that forbade work on the Sabbath and infuriating religious Jews. After enough of the Bund's newsboys showed up at the *Folkstsaytung* offices with black eyes, Bernard Goldstein sent in the militia to protect them. This escalated matters. Soon, the Warsaw rabbinate excommunicated *Folkstsaytung*'s entire staff. Yeshiva students and Jewish workers squared off in brawls that filled whole city blocks. In retaliation, Henryk Erlich ran a raucous campaign to get on the Warsaw kehillah. It was a longshot. The kehillah was so conservative that women were not allowed to vote in its elections. But Erlich's charisma and the Bund's relentless social organizing paid off. Despite being dubbed "the enemy of Zion and the enemy of learning," and despite telling a heckler that his party opposed circumcision, Erlich won his race. More Bundists followed him onto the kehillah. And if things didn't always go smoothly—once, a session closed when a Bundist delegate threw a chair at an Orthodox delegate's head—the Bund had another way to serve their people.

Bundist women founded their own organization, YAF (*Yidishe Arbeter Froyen*, or Jewish Working Women), which set up day care centers, disseminated birth control information, and campaigned for free childcare and equal pay. In the summer, Tsukunft boys and girls pitched their tents in the forests. They hoisted red flags, argued socialism, then snuck away to hook up on the meadow grass. Bundist workers gathered in resort towns and went on mountain hikes. Yiddish writers published their oeuvres on Bundist presses. In 1925, the Bundist Max Weinreich founded the YIVO Institute for Jewish Research in Vilna to study the culture of eastern European Jews. Created by working-class intellectuals who had been kept out of universities by racist quotas, YIVO's scholarship was imbued with a defiant insistence that the oppressed should write their own histories. This same spirit led young radicals like my father to fight for the creation of Black and Puerto Rican Studies departments in 1970s New York.

In January 1926, the Bund opened the crown jewel of their network: the Medem Sanatorium, built on four acres of forest in Miedzeszyn, near Warsaw, for poor children at risk of tuberculosis, and named after their legendary leader. Inspired by Rousseau's ideas on education, Medem's director, the Vilna-born educator Shloyme Gilinsky, said that nothing was too good for Warsaw's slum kids. Each day, he tried to prove it.

Medem Sanatorium was a fantasy, a respite for kids who lived seven to a room, who had no electricity, no running water, no bed of their own. Some Bundists even worried that the hoity-toity-ness of the place, with newfangled baths and toothpaste, would alienate children from their parents, but Gilinsky insisted that they'd bring back the good influence. Gilinsky believed that kids and adults were equal, so, contrary to the era's norms, the staff at the Medem Sanatorium didn't beat children. Kids needed to laugh. The hellions played amidst Miedzeszyn's wildflowers, the forget-me-nots, buttercups, and gaudy thistles that blossomed beneath the spruce and pine. They plucked apples from the orchards, inspected snails in the biological museum, raised geese, sunned themselves on the deck, and felt the clean country dirt beneath their feet. Children governed themselves; they made their own newspaper and elected their own parliament. They didn't keep kosher or pray. They observed Jewish holidays in their own heterodox manner. When they put out Elijah's cup at the first Passover seder, Medem's ghost might have taken a sip.

A decade later, the Bund released a film about the Medem Sanatorium, showing the how the place transformed its children. Mischievous Lazar, tormenter of chickens, thief of bread rolls, slowly softened when he realized that, for the first time in his life, there was enough to eat. The yeshiva boy, prissy little Zalman, shed his long Orthodox coat to play. They were happy, because for one summer they experienced the world their party fought for. Here where they lived was their country, the Bund promised. In Medem Sanatorium, they could believe it.

CHAPTER 17

HERE WHERE WE LIVE IS OUR COUNTRY

(1926–1933)

COUP

ON MAY 12, 1926, THE BUND'S LEADERS WOKE UP TO THE NEWS THAT Józef Pilsudski was overthrowing the Polish government. Sick of the economic collapse and the right-wing parties whom he blamed for his friend Narutowicz's murder, Pilsudski massed two thousand troops in Praga, marched over the Kierbedz Bridge into Warsaw proper, and seized the most important points of the city. From his apartment on Nowolipie Street, Bernard Goldstein heard the bullets. He was overcome with relief, mixed with self-criticism. "There is shooting in the fortress of reaction and oppression," he later wrote, "and I'm not there, taking part?" That evening, he grabbed two friends and headed to the front lines around Theater Square. The once-quick walk took hours. Bodies covered the streets. Bernard saw a soldier lying next to the Kierbedz Bridge's aqueduct, brains sprayed across the cobblestones. He went for the dead man's rifle. "Are you crazy?" his friend screamed. "You don't have a permit!" Bernard sheepishly returned the rifle to its place.

At the *Folkstsaytung* office, editors rushed out an emergency issue. "Jewish workers have too much at stake to stand aside during this uprising. . . . You must demand the overthrow of the anti-people's-government," one editorial read. Henryk Erlich grabbed his fellow city councilman, Viktor Alter, and hurried to the Warsaw Town Hall for a press conference to announce their support of the coup. Guns were everywhere. Everyone was a target. They walked carefully, weaving, dodging, running through the intersections with their heads down. A machine gun sprayed. Stone splintered from buildings. Tenements had bolted their courtyard gates, so there was nowhere to run. Alter grabbed Erlich and pressed him against a wall, shielding him with his body.

To support the coup, the Polish Socialist Party and the Bund declared a general strike. Bundists lined up at Pilsudski's field headquarters in Belvedere Palace and offered to enlist, while the Polish Socialist–led railway workers' union tore up the tracks to keep government reinforcements from reaching Warsaw. After two days, the government submitted its resignation. Pilsudski was in charge.

Despite their uneasiness about coups, the Bund gave Pilsudski their support. How could they not? The old government had gunned down workers and deliberately impoverished their community. Meanwhile, Pilsudski was a lifelong radical with a celebrated socialist past. He promised to quash corruption, to stop extremism both left and right, and to unite the country like a tough but benevolent grandfather.

WARSAW

Bundists soon realized that no politician can ever offer salvation. Though Pilsudski declined to serve as president, he stayed on as minister of war and was in every way the actual head of state. Monomaniacal and hot-tempered, Pilsudski loathed the garrulous ineffectuality of electoral politics. Over the next six years, he would jail opponents, confiscate newspapers, and undermine parliament whenever his rivals threatened to get too much power.

Still, it was a good time, at least by the standards of the former Pale of Settlement. The government cracked down on nationalists, and America extended Poland generous credit. The economy improved, even in the slums of Jewish Warsaw. Poland was now a country where the Bund could build a future.

Build they did. *The Bund in Pictures* has dozens of photographs of the innumerable committees by which the Bund organized working-class Jewish life. These diligent men and women set up economic cooperatives to help artisans weather discriminatory tax laws. They created stores, eateries, and workshops. Under Viktor Alter's leadership, the National Council of Jewish Trade Unions became a branch of the powerful International Federation of Trade Unions. Its membership tripled. The Bund set up day care centers, libraries, and drama clubs. Both independently and through the Bundist-dominated TSYSHO school system, the party ran nearly two hundred schools, from kindergartens to a teachers' college to night schools for Jewish workers barely into their teens. In the words of Victor Gilinsky, son of Bundist leader Shloyme Gilinsky, "The Bund was your union, your education, your church."

The Bund had high hopes for the next generation. They would raise their kids to be free and unafraid. These kids would take care of one another, like socialists did. They would fight back, because they came from a lineage of fighters. They would never doubt that this country was their home.

In 1926, the same year as Pilsudski's coup, the Bund created SKIF, the Socialist Children's Union. "We are young, and the world is open," their anthem went. I look through photos of SKIF's mandolin orchestras and summer camps, and I see the wholesome, conventional childhoods that these kids would otherwise have been denied. Marek Edelman, son of the former self-defense fighter Tsipie Edelman, had a typical SKIF childhood. His widowed mother served as secretary for YAF, the Bundist women's movement, so the party helped raise her boy. Marek grew up at protests, where he rode on the shoulders of comrades, red flag in his tiny fist. At ten, he helped run a SKIF group in a Praga homeless shelter. The next year, Medem Sanitarium admitted him on suspicion of tuberculosis. There were Polish and German children among the patients. He learned that the fight wasn't Christian versus Jew but democracy versus fascism. All kids were family in Medem's paradise.

The same year, the Bund founded their sports club, Morgenstern. They had hikes and bike races, gymnastics and boxing matches. In summer, they rented pools to teach kids to swim. In winter, hundreds of workers twirled on their ice-skating rinks. In Warsaw, thousands watched soccer tournaments that *Naye Folkstsaytung** sponsored. The Bund's sports magazine, *Worker Athlete*, breathlessly covered each play.

I leaf through the Morgenstern section of *The Bund in Pictures*. Girls in booty shorts stretch their legs in Lublin. Each has a black heart pinned to her middy blouse. Laughing teens lounge on a riverbank. Two guys mime a boxing match. Big smiles. A perfect punch. On a cobblestone street, boys prep for a footrace. A man braces himself on parallel bars. He throws himself in the air, reaches, flies.

In April 1927, Morgenstern took over a Warsaw circus for a mass acrobatic display. Hundreds of gymnasts performed. In the photos, young men raise their hands. Their chests are broad. Their white shorts show muscular thighs. Young women lean their heads back. Their bodies move together like a symphony. At the end of the show, Morgenstern paraded, each age group in its own distinct uniform. To Bernard in the audience, they looked like a field of flowers. He remembered the prison damp, the cellar safe houses. His generation had suffered. These kids were their reward.

On their first May Day in Pilsudski's Poland, the Bund displayed the richness of their world. Beneath a satin banner lined with braid, Henryk Erlich and Viktor Alter led tens of thousands of marchers. They had their unions, their brass band, their athletes, their motorcade of militiamen, their Tsukunft groups with fighting pennants—red linen bands

* *Folkstsaytung* changed its name to *Naye* [New] *Folkstsaytung* in 1927.

attached to poles they could use as clubs. Then the SKIF kids, each waving a little triangle flag. The Bund marched down the ritziest Polish boulevards. They sang Yiddish songs, to the fury of the onlookers. Let them seethe. These were the Bund's streets. This was their city. To Bernard Goldstein, the procession seemed to stretch for miles.

Banners flew, each embroidered with demands they had debated over endless mass meetings, but the sole real demand was the unwritten statement: Here where we live is our country.

In October, the Bund celebrated their thirtieth anniversary in the largest hall in Jewish Warsaw. Sophia Dubnova and her thirteen-year-old son Victor watched from a balcony bedecked with flowers. Henryk Erlich's speech was the center of the event. Victor's Yiddish was not good enough to understand his father's words, but he saw how dashing he looked on the podium, how he captivated the audience. *That's my dad,* he thought proudly.

I notice something else in the photos of the Bund's anniversary: the girls. They don't resemble Itka the Bundist. They don't wear corsets, these girls. They wear drop-waist dresses and arrange their bobbed hair beneath cloche hats. They are sleek babes of the jazz age, red-lipped flappers whom I might pass in a New York nightclub. They make out with guys. They drink vodka and talk back in three languages. They seize the stage at meetings. They hold their own in a street fight. They belong to themselves.

Unlike the Bund's founders, their political compass didn't point to Russia. They came of age in independent Poland, and they lived in a Warsaw that was worthy of them. If she had the cash, our girl could have snuck into the famous basement cabaret, Qui Pro Quo, where Artur Gold conducted the band and the blond goddess Hanka Ordonówna starred. The ballerina turned showgirl might sing "Mein Yiddishe Momme," then segue to a breathy tango. Our girl might watch some of the poet Julian Tuwim's scandalous political skits, if the joint wasn't raided by the police.

Down the street, our girl could have caught a performance by the Nigerian jazz percussionist August Agbola O'Browne. The city was a diverse place. In the artistic world, Poles and Jews and everyone else mingled easily, like discs in the multilingual catalog from Syrena Record.

Right next to the Great Synagogue, at the Association of Jewish Writers and Journalists at 13 Tlomackie Street, our heroine could avert the advances of the prematurely balding young satyr Isaac Bashevis Singer, listen to editors at impecunious literary magazines heap scorn on the established poets they corrected, then beat every last one of them at chess. She could watch the diva Ida Kaminska play a doomed revolutionary at the Warsaw Yiddish Art Theatre. She could get a ham sandwich by Tabachinsky's coffeehouse, downstairs from the Bund club, where workers stuffed their faces in front of the plate-glass windows on Yom Kippur just to annoy the pious. And she could stop by Fat Yosl's tavern, where Bernard Goldstein organized his teamsters for attack. She was a socialist. She was young. The twenties were roaring.

VOLKOVYSK

The optimism of the twenties spread to backwaters like Volkovysk. By 1926, Sam's hometown was being modernized, the wood shacks replaced with multistory buildings. Two train stations connected it to the rest of the country, attracting Poles who wanted government jobs, and free farmland was parceled out to the Polish military veterans. Neither of these enticements was available to local Jews.

Still, Volkovysk was a Jewish town. Jews thrived in large part because of the mutual aid institutions—orphanages, old-age homes, co-ops, free clinics, and credit unions—that they used to keep each other afloat in a hostile world. The volunteer fire brigade was still Jewish, despite the efforts of the Polish government to disband it, and their orchestra was so popular that girls swarmed their concerts. You could still gather mushrooms in the forest, still hang a hammock beside the river and watch the boats float slowly by. There were no streetlights, so you could still see the stars.

There was trouble too, just like there had always been. The *Volkovysk Memorial Book* uses the word *squatters* to describe the new arrivals from western Poland, who came to take advantage of the government's offers of land. Longtime Jewish and Christian residents didn't view their new neighbors kindly. Perhaps they had their own claims on the land that the state so freely handed out. And despite the relative calm, pogroms still broke out on market days, incited by the newcomers, according to the *Volkovysk Memorial Book.*

As the factories grew in Volkovysk, the Bund grew with them. They set up a secular Yiddish school and a Yiddish library. Their top local activist, leatherworker Avram Markus, ran their newspaper, filling its pages with impudent journalistic campaigns against the town's Zionist elite; the Jewish factory bosses and landlords; and the Orthodox, whom he mocked as "black crows."

The Bund launched a theater troupe and held election meetings at Polonia Cinema. They paraded down Broad Street on May Days.

As this free generation marched, they would have passed by Kanoval home, where Sam's relatives still lived. Their chants might have echoed in their neighbor Moshe Rutchik's house, where Rutchik's friend, the sarcastic Bundist shoemaker Meir Zeleviansky, a man of Sam's generation, liked to sit in the corner parsing obscure points of dialectical materialism until Rutchik snapped, "enough!" Then the two old men might have reminisced about the days of the tsar, when they were just dumb kids who had formed little gangs to fight the soldiers—may their names be erased from the book of life—and about all their friends who had sailed to strange America. Perhaps they remembered the artist Shmuel Chudozhnik, Zeleviansky's comrade. What was Shmuel doing across the sea?

SAM ROTHBORT

The past decade had had its ups and downs for my great-grandfather. In 1919, Sam Rothbort finally found a patron: Hamilton Easter Field. Born into an aristocratic Quaker family and educated in Parisian ateliers, Field was a prominent art critic and collector who championed modernists in his home gallery. Sam Rothbort caught his eye. My great-grandfather needed it. Though Sam exhibited in the Brooklyn gallery world, he never got the hang of social climbing. He was congenitally unable to kiss ass, and so curators relegated his work to the margins of shows. He quit or was shoved out of this artistic society or that, until Field swept in like Prince Charming.

In Sam's work Field found the most fragile of qualities—authenticity. Sam worked directly from life, finishing what he started the same day. This was the real, Sam thought, uncorrupted by memory. Field agreed. "My feeling is that the antipathy against Rothbort's art is the antipathy which most men and women feel against a plain unvarnished tale of truth. . . . They dream of lords and ladies, and do not wish to have their dreams disturbed," Field wrote, comparing Sam's work to the poetry of Walt Whitman. Field hung Sam's paintings at his home exhibitions, and before long, his new discovery was showing in the Brooklyn Museum. Sam had breezed past the gatekeepers and seemed headed to a secure place in the world of High Art.

Or that's how it should have gone, but on April 10, 1922, Field died of pneumonia. He was only forty-nine. Sam stood with Field's other artists in the Quaker cemetery in Prospect Park and watched gravediggers shovel dirt on his patron's coffin. On the subway ride back, another artist turned to him. "Rothbort, you don't know what you lost, but you'll soon find out."

The artist's words were prophetic. Things went south for Sam after Field's death. He bounced around New York artist groups but found a chilly reception wherever he went. "The laymen dream of lords and ladies" and could not stand the unvarnished truth of Rothbort's work. Maybe Field was right.

Embittered, Sam turned his back on the city. "Don't let inept authorities bulldoze you with spineless culture," he wrote on an undated notecard. In 1924, he moved the family to two acres of land in Uniondale on Long Island, where he set up a no-kill egg farm. (A few years earlier, he had become a vegetarian, for moral reasons.) This left the problem of what to do with male chicks. While he worked on his art, Rose cared for three thousand chickens and an unknown number of murderous roosters.

Sam loved the land. It was his provider of sustenance, his guarantee of freedom. In 1925, he took up the hammer and chisel. He preferred fieldstone and scavenged fenceposts, battered materials that hid stories. On a stained lunch counter, he carved a relief of a bull staring down at the victims of pogroms. Above them the moon laughed at mankind's violence. He sculpted the prophets: "Moses, standing and holding his hand with sympathy on the shoulder of the fallen Christ, as if he would say, 'My son, men will have to accept 'thou shalt not kill' before they can accept 'love,' " Sam later wrote. A wry philosophy emerged from these sculptures, one that was witty, earthy, that mocked and yet accepted human frailty. It had been a bad career move to leave New York, but in Uniondale, on a failing farm amidst stunted birch trees, he found his artistic voice.

SOCIAL FASCISM

Were he alive, Medem would have congratulated himself for his foresight. In 1918, at the height of Trotsky's power, he had written, "The day is not far off when we will see revolutionary tribunals in which the more kosher Bolsheviks will execute the more suspect. . . . If today Lenin desires to shoot Abramovich, who can tell that tomorrow he will not shoot Trotsky?" Lenin was nearly four years dead in November 1927 when his party, now helmed by the former bank robber Joseph Stalin, expelled Trotsky and banished him to a remote backwater in Kazakhstan.

At the Comintern's sixth world congress, which closed in September 1928, Stalin announced a new theory called social fascism. In his telling, democratic socialist parties were as bad as, if not worse than, the real fascists who currently ran Italy. These socialists worked as fascism's handmaidens, leading workers away from communism while hiding their villainy behind red banners and Marxist catchphrases. They were the main obstacles to worldwide revolution and needed to be destroyed.

High on the doctrine of social fascism, Poland's Jewish communists escalated their attacks against the Bund. To prosecute their jeremiad, they enlisted the underworld: men like Hershel the Fighter, kneecap-smashing debt collector Dovid Milner, cross-eyed pimp Simkhe Macz, and the dapper Maier Chmopel, who could knife a man as easily as he combed his hair. Communists gave gangsters cover for their rackets, and gangsters gave communists an army.

Communists broke into the Bund's night schools, grabbed students, and pelted teachers with rocks. They interrupted Bundist meetings with jeers. Once, a gang stormed into the Bund club, grabbed the shoemaker Black-Haired Khatskl, and used a cigarette to burn a hole clean through his lip. Communists in Bundist-led unions declared wildcat strikes, not to win higher wages but to force the unions to split. When workers refused to strike against their unions' orders, communists attacked them with clubs and knives.

Bernard tried to speak to the communist workers directly. Flanked by militiamen, he descended into the smoke-filled cellar where communists held meetings to plan their assaults. His appearance stunned the attendees into silence. When he walked to the podium, the chairman gave permission for him to speak.

He said that the war between communists and Bundists had gone on long enough. Communists would no longer beat up workers who stayed loyal to his party's unions. It was time to strike a deal. As labor organizers, they could arrange matters amongst themselves, but if communists kept up their assaults, his men would defend their shops.

The audience said nothing.

Bernard's proposal failed. Embarrassed that a rival had crashed their meeting without consequences, the communists redoubled their attacks. They passed a death sentence on Bernard Goldstein, the worst social fascist of them all, and sent fanatical teenagers to fire revolvers at the cottage where he stayed for summer vacations. Another communist tried to assassinate Bernard outside his apartment. Bernard shot back, wounding the communist, who left a trail of blood across the pavement. When the cops showed up, Bernard refused to reveal the identity of his attacker. For each attack, the Bund's militia meted out revenge in the form of split skulls and shattered rib cages, which only escalated the conflict. Violence took on its own logic. In the years that followed, communists would murder several Bundist workers. They even shot up Medem Sanatorium, terrifying the kids but fortunately killing no one.

Victory against fascism achieved.

BETAR

On New Year's Day 1929, Warsaw watched with astonishment as hundreds of young Jews clad in brown military shirts marched to the Great Synagogue on Tlomackie Street for the first international conference of Vladimir Jabotinsky's Betar youth movement.

Naye Folkstsaytung described the display as "a parade of little Jewish fascists."

Preaching strength, cruelty, and conquest of both banks of the river Jordan, Betar drew inspiration from the same brutish Polish nationalists that the Bund fought in Saxon Gardens. In Poland, its forty thousand members learned to shoot guns and use hand grenades. They promised to die for a Jewish state. If Betar were just "little fascists" in Poland, in Palestine, where a hundred thousand Jews had immigrated since the Mandate began, they were growing into something more akin to Mussolini's *squadristi*. To enforce Hebrew language use, Betar members raided Yiddish cultural events, and they destroyed the property of Jews who hired Palestinian, rather than Jewish, workers. But Palestinians were their primary target. These attacks served the dual purpose of enforcing supremacy upon the other and of re-creating the Jewish self. If Jews were to transform themselves from the emasculated "Yids" of the diaspora, whom Jabotinsky criticized, into his macho "Hebrews," they needed to show the uppity natives that they were boss.

PALESTINE

Jabotinsky fixated on East Jerusalem's Wailing Wall as a casus belli. Believed to be a remnant of the destroyed second temple, the wall was the holiest site in Judaism, positioned directly below the Al-Aqsa Mosque, the third-holiest site in Islam, and flanked by a bustling eight-hundred-year-old Moroccan Quarter. When Jabotinsky returned to Palestine in 1928 to set up a newspaper, he took up Zionist calls to buy and bulldoze adjoining Muslim homes. During that year's Yom Kippur service, Orthodox worshippers tried to put up the screen that traditionally divides men and women during services, only to have it removed by British policemen. This seemingly minor incident became the pretext for Jabotinsky to agitate for full Jewish control of the site. After a year of stupid squabbles, tit-for-tat dick waving, and identitarian provocation, things finally exploded in 1929, when, on the Jewish mourning day of Tisha b'Av, thousands of Jabotinsky's followers raised the Zionist movement's flag and chanted that the wall was theirs. For the next ten days, Jews and

Palestinians murdered each other in a carnival of brutality whose cruelty was worse because, in many cases, it took place between neighbors. Most of the perpetrators were Palestinians, and most of the victims were Jews, particularly Arabic-speaking Sephardic Jews who rejected offers of protection from the Haganah. But Jews also lynched Palestinians, and one Jewish policeman gunned down an entire Palestinian family. The most notorious massacre took place in Hebron, where a Palestinian mob murdered sixty-seven Jews, among them young Lithuanian yeshiva students and a dozen members of the longstanding Sephardic community. (Hundreds of Jews survived by hiding in the homes of their Palestinian neighbors.)

Photos of the victims' mutilated bodies appeared in the international press.

These murders set off a worldwide explosion of Jewish anguish that quickly morphed into calls for bloody vengeance. With this came a suffocating demand for conformity. Any Jew who sought to understand the causes of the violence was a traitor, an apologist for their people's murders.

Days after the riots, Jabotinsky stood in front of six thousand Jews in Tel Aviv and called for war in the name of Zionism, shouting, "Arabia for the Arabs and the land of Israel for the Jews." Dissatisfied with the Haganah's alleged restraint, Jabotinsky's followers founded the ultraviolent Irgun, which would murder hundreds of Palestinians in car bombings and mass shootings in the years that followed.

Protests against the Palestine riots broke out immediately in Poland. At Warsaw's British embassy, police dispersed furious crowds at sword point. Jewish shops shuttered, and worshippers flocked to the Great Synagogue on Tlomackie Street, where the rabbi declared an official fast for the victims. Thousands marched under banners that read, THE WAILING WALL WILL BE OURS. Betar's Polish membership soared, even in tiny Volkovysk, where street mobs chanted, "Jabotinsky was right."

The Bund refused to join this public mourning. They saw too clearly where it would lead. Eternal skeptics of nationalism, the Bund's journalists had covered Palestinian politics with such care that Zionist newspapers called the party "an enemy of the Jews" and claimed it was not a Jewish party but an Arab one. The Bund knew that the British occupation ignored the efforts of Palestinian notables like Musa Kazim Pasha to achieve basic self-determination, as well as the needs and desires of the entire Palestinian population. In 1928, *Naye Folkstsaytung* covered the seventh Palestine Arab Congress in Jerusalem, which demanded a democratic parliament, an end to the British occupation, and a halt on Zionist immigration. It got nothing.

The Bund had no problem with emigration, to Palestine or elsewhere. Believers in more-or-less open borders, they understood that poor people would always seek better lives where they could. They even ran a bureau to help prospective emigrants deal with the bureaucracies of western Europe and the Americas. The Bund believed that people should live where they wanted, Palestine included. The problem was the Zionist demand for Jewish supremacy.

Days after the riots, the Bundist leader J. Khmurner responded to the anti-Palestinian protests in *Naye Folkstsaytung:*

> Following the latest bloody events in Palestine, the Zionists organized demonstrations of mourning; they used the immediate feelings of hurt and rage that had enveloped the Jewish masses... to deflect the thoughts of the masses from the roots of the tragedy. For this reason, the Bund chose not to participate. . . . We consider it our duty to the victims in the Land of Israel and to the Jewish masses here to say the whole truth about the events and their causes. . . . The horrific events show that Jewish labor is absolutely correct to fight against Zionism. . . . We oppose any nationalism, any chauvinism, be it Arab or Jewish.

The Bund said the same to the three thousand workers who packed into Warsaw's Egyptian-styled Splendid Theatre to hear them talk about "the liquidation of Zionism." That night, they passed a resolution:

> The most important condition for a peaceful life together, for the entire population of Palestine, is the renunciation of the Zionist plan to rule the land against the will of the majority.
>
> Zionists have built all their hopes on stripping away the political rights of Palestine's existing Arab population, who constitute the oppressed majority . . . and on forcing them from all positions of power. . . . [Zionists] have stood with every occupying power in Palestine—first Turkey, now England—and have used every means to make sure that Arabs are not granted their most minimal demands for political freedom and self-government. The Arab hatred of the Jewish population is a direct result of Zionist politics. Zionism has poisoned the atmosphere and put the Jewish population of Palestine in danger. . . .
>
> The nationalist demonstrations that Zionists have organized exploit the victims of these tragic events and the understandable upset of the Jewish community. . . . This meeting calls on Jewish workers to fight the storm of nationalism and chauvinism that

> Zionists are unleashing on the Jewish Street. The answer to tragically but pointlessly spilled blood cannot lie in more national hatred, which will inevitably lead to more communal clashes, but in international solidarity and the growth of the socialist movement.

To educate its readers, *Naye Folkstsaytung* published Palestinian perspectives. In one piece reprinted from a Berlin newspaper, an unnamed Arab journalist described how the British high commissioner rejected Palestinian demands for a parliament, and how the occupation shut down every avenue for Palestinian self-expression. He exposed British double standards. When Palestinians tried to hold a peaceful protest in Jaffa, Zionists denounced them to the police as Bolsheviks, but when Jabotinsky toured yeshivas giving far more incendiary speeches, the police looked the other way. "Nothing is more hideous than a bloody civil war, but when an entire population is forced to take up arms, one can't just dismiss it with a quick condemnation. It's rather the duty of every cultured person to examine the causes of this desperate struggle," the journalist wrote.

In "Who Are the Arabs and What Do They Stand For?" *Naye Folkstsaytung* printed a blistering satire of anti-Palestinian racism:

> Arabs are a savage people . . . proven by the fact that they go around with savage ideas, like needing a parliament. . . . Arabs discovered the numeral zero, but they don't use it. They can't even understand the simple fact that 100,000 Jews is a bigger number than 700,000 Arabs . . .

In 1929, Bundist speakers toured Poland, giving hundreds of lectures on Palestinians, Zionism, and the British Mandate. When the Bundist leader G. Zeibert traveled to New York for the Jewish Socialist Federation's national convention later that year, he took the opportunity to denounce the "sentimental mass hysteria" over the Palestine riots, and to place their ultimate blame on political Zionism. The Bund even published a short book by their journalist Yoysef Khmurner titled *What Can the Events in Palestine Teach Us?* The answer to the title's question was this: By collaborating with the British Empire to suppress Palestinian rights to their own country, Zionists had brought the violence on the entire Jewish community.

The Zionists hit back. In a statement sent from Tel Aviv, Histadrut leader David Ben-Gurion wrote that the Bund gave "ideological justification for robbery and murder" and decried their "filthy partnership" with Palestinian leaders whom he held responsible for the riots. In Vilna, Zionists vowed to fight for "the final elimination of the shameful anti-Jewish microbe" of Bundism, and hooligans attacked a Bundist kehillah member with bats.

In Warsaw, the Zionist daily *Haynt* decried "Bundism's disgrace." After having "lost its revolutionary fire," they wrote, the party tried to justify its existence by "spitting on, undermining, and smearing our heroic builders in the land of Israel" and by siding with Palestinian "pogromists." They called for Bundists to be expelled from "the table of the Jewish community," with their funding cut off and their reputation destroyed amongst their American donors. *Haynt* began a jeremiad against the secular Yiddish TSYSHO schools where many Bundists taught. The schools raised "enemies of Zion," *Haynt* alleged. In other words, self-hating Jews.

DICTATORSHIP

After the American stock market crashed in the fall of 1929, the reverberations devastated the Polish economy. Bristling under Pilsudski's authoritarianism, in June 1930, center and left parties met in Krakow to form a new electoral bloc to oppose the country's descent into dictatorship. Furious at the challenge, Pilsudski dissolved parliament and had fifteen opposition deputies thrown into a concentration camp. Pilsudski's supporters won the next elections, thanks to arrests, censorship, and mild voter fraud.

Pilsudski then "instituted a de facto dictatorship papered over with the appearance of democracy," wrote Bernard Goldstein. His government viciously repressed the Left. Police confiscated the Bund's newspapers and banned their meetings on phony pretexts. Cops and Endeks battered their marchers each May Day. Bernard planned his marches like military campaigns. Blond Tsukunft girls hung out in Polish neighborhoods before protests, trying to see what the Endeks were up to. Once the march began, Bernard's militiamen were everywhere. They led the protest, trailed behind, filled the neighboring streets. Militiamen on bicycles formed a wall on either side of the marchers. Slavic-looking Bundist men went undercover, mingling with suspicious groups of hooligans. One May Day, Tsukunft member Josef Gutgold saw nationalist students gather in front of Warsaw University to prepare an attack on comrades. Gutgold tricked them into running down a side street.

Government repression drew the Polish Socialist Party and the Bund together. In 1931, the two parties marched together for the first time in a joint May Day parade. The Polish socialists even volunteered to exchange their militias, so that Poles would protect Jewish marchers and Jews would protect Poles. Bernard touchily declined. To earn respect, he said, Jews needed to protect themselves.

KROCHMALNA STREET

In poor Jewish neighborhoods, the Bund were public servants, with an emphasis on *servant*. They got sick relatives into hospitals and helped small shopkeepers negotiate their back taxes—even if it meant that Henryk Erlich had to leave his desk at *Naye Folkstsaytung* right before a deadline. The Bund mediated private disputes as well. Did a landlord steal the money his tenants gave him for repairs? The Bund's city councilwoman Esther Iwinska filed a lawsuit. If the butcher stole meat from the slaughterhouse where he worked and ended up in jail, the Bund showed up with bail money and a lawyer. Did some rich kid marry a sex worker, then ditch her with nothing? Comrade Bernard made sure she got a big enough payout to open her own shop. Were the pimps and porters fighting? Comrade Bernard stepped in to make peace. In the Kercelak Market, the Bund defended Jewish vendors from gangers' predations. When a landlord tried to evict a tenant, Bernard's militia was there as well. The guys waited till after the bailiff left, then busted open the doors of the evicted family's old apartment and put their furniture back in place. They told the landlord not to bother filing more eviction suits. They'd just keep coming back.

The Bund launched a campaign to infiltrate Krochmalna Street, a communist stronghold nicknamed the Kremlin. Eternal mud ate Krochmalna's pavement, lapping up against the scabrous flophouse walls and encircling the wretched little plazas where sharpsters like Puny Hannah and Chaim-Yosl Jackass ran their scams. On Krochmalna, a Bundist couldn't even hang their party posters without risking a beatdown. The Bund vowed it would be theirs.

Comrade Bernard recruited local delinquents as his foot soldiers. He saw the potential in them, hidden by mute rage and too much liquor, so he shaped them up and taught them how to read and write. "Without Bernard I would probably have sunk into the underworld," one of these men later recalled. The Bund opened a Yiddish school in the neighborhood, which ran activities for the children. On summer days, a crooked-shouldered militiaman dubbed Khaskele Hunchback would summon swarms of kids with a single whistle. He marched them to the forest outside Warsaw, where they'd hike all day, then return tanned and sleepy to mothers so grateful that they wished Khaskele eternal life. At the Bund's new Krochmalna Street clubhouse, their activists exposed porters, butchers, and street peddlers to new worlds of literature and art. The men began to read Yiddish newspapers, even books. They became bona fide intellectuals—in their own eyes, at least.

A new problem emerged in the form of Krochmalna wives. Each day, furious women stormed into the Bund's office and demanded to speak to Bernard Goldstein. What the hell had he done to their men? Ever since their husbands joined the Bund, they barely came home, and when they did, they talked to their wives like they were idiots. When Bernard Goldstein suggested they read a bit to keep up with their husbands' interests, the women burst out laughing. Who would have taught them to read?

The Bund began to enlist these women in the party. They taught them to read and encouraged them to escape their domestic prisons by inviting them to meetings and concerts. Their husbands could pick up the slack. "Let him sometimes sit home at night with the children!" said one newly literate housewife. When the men complained, Bernard chided them. Socialists support women's equality, he said. That meant your equality with your wife.

These activities won the Bund so much love that when a group of communists tried to jump Bernard on Smocza Street, nearby housewives threw themselves on top of the attackers, using their brooms as bludgeons, and would have murdered them if the communists hadn't managed to escape.

RED VIENNA

In July 1931, three hundred athletes from the Bundist sports club Morgenstern prepared to leave for the third Workers' Olympiad in Vienna. They had spent the last two years saving up money to participate, and it promised to be the trip of a lifetime.

With a hundred thousand athletes and over two hundred thousand spectators, the Vienna Workers' Olympiad dwarfed the official Olympics held the next summer in Los Angeles. Organized by the Socialist Workers' Sport International, these olympiads meant to provide a socialist counterpoint to the "capitalist" Olympic Games. The athletes were all workers, and the focus was world peace, not nationalist competition. Red Vienna was the perfect city to host the games.

In the thirteen years that the Social Democratic Workers' Party of Austria had run Vienna, they achieved many extraordinary things. They built airy, avant-garde apartment blocks that housed over a hundred thousand workers. They started free cafeterias, public baths, and after-school programs. They cut infant mortality in half. Committed to roses as well as bread, they lavished money on theaters, libraries, workers' education. The charismatic sports instructor Julius Deutsch led their militia, the Schutzbund, which would inspire the Bund's own youth militia.

Not everyone liked Red Vienna. In Austria's conservative countryside, Catholic politicians grumbled that the city's policies were a decadent Jewish plot. Things had gotten worse since the political rise of the failed Austrian painter across the border; the Nazis were now the second-largest party in the German Reichstag. All of this weighed on Bernard as he boarded a railway car that the Bund and the Polish Socialist Party had rented for their athletes. During the overnight journey, young people danced and passed the vodka. Bernard tried to lose himself in their enjoyment.

As the train approached Vienna, Bernard saw red flags hanging from houses along the tracks. A socialist delegation met them at a station done up entirely in red.

The sense of brotherhood shocked him. A hundred thousand workers, from twenty-six nations itching to start stupid border wars, had biked, walked, rowed boats, motorcycled, and crammed into overstuffed train cars to travel to Vienna, and the city welcomed them so warmly that hotelkeepers didn't try to rip them off. Locals opened their homes to foreign athletes. Bernard crashed with a railway worker whose spacious apartment reminded him of the homes of wealthy professionals in Warsaw. His hosts' hospitality disconcerted him. In the morning, the railway worker's wife served him hot cocoa in bed. When he got back from the games, he found his dirty boxers had been washed and pressed.

At the opening ceremony, the Italian flags flew at half mast, to acknowledge Mussolini's attacks on the labor movement. The flag bearers of each nation saluted each other, until the French and German athletes came face-to-face. They paused—tensions were high between their countries—then stepped forward and gripped each other's hands in friendship. Visitors filled their days with bike races, powerlifting competitions, and chess at the famous Viennese cafés. On the last night, three hundred Morgenstern athletes took their place beside the white-clad Czechs and the azure-uniformed Finns in the final torchlight parade. Yiddish banner high, they strode down the grand Ringstrasse, past the baroque edifice of parliament, and chanted the parade's slogans: "For world disarmament! For general peace!" They belonged there, equal in the family of nations.

World disarmament and general peace were the themes of the Congress of the Labor and Socialist International, a grouping of democratic socialist parties that the Bund had joined two years before, and which opened in Vienna right after the 1931 olympiad. Photos show Henryk Erlich next to future French president Léon Blum. He is a bit hunched, as if the present weighs on him. As editor of *Naye Folkstsaytung*, he kept a close eye on the rise of fascism in Europe, and he was horrified at the seeming obliviousness of Western socialist parties. In his speech at the congress, he saved special ire for the German Social Democratic Party. Where was their sense of fight? he asked. Their independence? Their militancy? Why did they rely on alliances with industrial barons and discredited, centrist politicians whose cruel austerity policies immiserated the workers they were supposed to represent? This sort of spinelessness had already led a chunk of Polish workers to turn to fascism. The same would happen in Germany unless the Social Democrats changed course. They were still the largest party in the Reichstag. They ought to seize power and create a socialist government, before disillusioned workers went over to Hitler for good.

German Social Democratic Party chairman Otto Wels could barely contain his laughter. The nerve of this Erlich, leader of a powerless little party, thinking he could offer his advice. "It has been barely five months since the 'Bund' found its way into the International, but that is enough for it to act as the schoolmaster of German social democracy," Wels sneered. The German social democrats had everything under control. They would proceed as they always had throughout their long and glorious history. If it the came time for a fight, Wels condescendingly welcomed the Bund's "assault battalions" to join them.

THE UNIVERSITY

After the congress, Bernard Goldstein stuck around Vienna to get some tactical training from Red Vienna's militia, the Schutzbund. When he got home, he would need it. The Nazis' victory in the Reichstag elections had stoked the ambitions of Poland's hardcore nationalists. Brutal Polish youth movements sprung up like mushrooms after the rain. Inspired by Hitler's Brownshirts, these young nationalists aimed to strip Jews of their civil rights and evict them from the country. Polish universities became their battlegrounds.

It started that fall semester at the Krakow University, where young nationalist rioters expelled their Jewish classmates. At the University of Warsaw, bat-wielding nationalists drove out Jewish law students in imitation. The Jewish students fought back, helped by Polish socialist friends. The next day, Endeks guarded the gates, promising not to let in a single Jew until the government put harsh limits on their admission to university.

Within a week, riots forced the government to shutter every college in Warsaw. The riots spread to Lomza, Sosnowiec, Poznan, Lviv, and Vilna. In Lowicz, a small town outside Warsaw, high school teachers led their students in the destruction of the Jewish commercial district. With classes canceled, nationalist students lurked around train stations, looking to beat Jewish passengers. They demolished Jewish graves in Sochaczew and ransacked the Jewish library in Pruszkow. In Vilna, Jewish students held back their pogromist classmates by throwing rocks. After a rock killed one nationalist student, his buddies turned his death into a day of mourning. The government arrested hundreds of rioters, but when it came time to press charges, they confined themselves to expelling one Jewish and four Polish students. They were afraid to come out too strongly in defense of Jews, Bernard Goldstein thought. It would make them look bad to their base.

The Bund preferred more direct means of dissuasion. To combat the riots, Bernard inducted hundreds of union guys into his militia. They patrolled parks and swimming spots beside the Vistula River. When nationalist students tried to attack the covered market in Mirowska Square, Comrade Bernard organized hulking porters to greet them.

When the University of Warsaw reopened, nationalist students staked out the right side of their classrooms, forcing Jews to sit on the left, in what they called the "ghetto benches." At student restaurants, new noticeboards forbade Jews to enter, and after school, nationalist youth donned uniforms to enforce a commercial boycott. They surrounded Jewish shops on Nalewki Street, dragged out the customers, and covered the walls with their posters. DON'T BUY FROM JEWS. DON'T SELL TO JEWS. POLAND FOR POLES. JEWS TO PALESTINE.

Nationalist newspapers thanked these students for their service. Endek politicians promised to continue their fight in parliament.

SOPHIA DUBNOVA

In the summer of 1932, Sophia Dubnova took her son Victor to visit her parents in Berlin. She had been in the city six years before, when the Bund hired her to make sense of their voluminous archives. Those were the days of fragile Weimar democracy—the fertile moment of monetary inflation, polymorphous sexuality, and political factionalism that most Americans only know from the movie *Cabaret*—and she had relished them. So had her sons. When it was time for university, Alexander Erlich chose to study in Berlin.

Now, in 1932, she arrived in a different city. The newly legalized Brownshirts filled the streets. Drunk proto–frat boys bonded over the thrill of mob murder, the Brownshirts beat Jews at the subway stations and fought the communist Red Front Fighters with bullets and paving stones. By mid-July, these political clashes had left over a hundred people dead. The cops always took the Brownshirts' side. As for the social democrats, Erlich's comments at the International had been prescient. When President Hindenburg kicked out the Social Democratic leadership of Prussia, Germany's largest state, and installed a conservative aristocrat named Franz von Papen as chancellor, Social Democratic Party chairman Otto Wels declined to call a general strike. His party's paramilitary, the Iron Front, sometimes fought the Nazis, but communists and social democrats regarded each other as the real enemies. After the July elections, the Nazis were the largest party in the Reichstag.

In the Bund's Berlin offices in a dark little wing of the Social Democratic Party's headquarters at 68 Lindenstrasse, old revolutionaries began to consider skipping town. They'd already fled Soviet Russia. What's a city when you've lost a homeland? Paris looked lovely in the fall. In the Menshevik club down the hall, where Raphael Abramovich now led a powerless, righteous, and argumentative little court, the losers of Smolny were equally pessimistic. In their smuggled proclamations, they still held out the hope they would return to a Russia that needed them. Germany, however, was on its own. In Grunewald, a leafy Berlin suburb, Sophia's father, Simon Dubnov, reluctantly packed his library. After so many moves, he dreaded another displacement.

Sophia and Victor returned to Poland, where Victor prepared to start his first term at the Free Polish University. As usual, the semester began bloodily. A thousand nationalist students crowded into a church to mourn their confrere killed in Vilna the prior autumn. Afterward, they marched on Jewish Warsaw, bludgeoning and stabbing whomever they caught. At Warsaw University, nationalist students screamed, "Revenge yourselves on the Jews!" before they threw their female Jewish classmates out of windows. The government closed the university. When young Bundists and Polish Socialists set up a meeting to plan resistance, the police it shut down.

Worse violence broke out in Lviv, when, during a student-led pogrom, drunk nationalist students decided to pick a fight with Jewish gangsters. One of the gangsters stabbed the student Jan Gratowski in the neck. Sixty thousand Christians marched in Gratowski's funeral procession. During the march, a bomb went off, tearing a nationalist student into pieces. The cause turned out to be a hand grenade the student had illicitly stowed in his pocket, but the mobs blamed the Jews anyway. After that, the city exploded. Bat-wielding mobs ransacked Jewish stores, placed bombs in the synagogue, and wounded hundreds of people, including a Jewish parliamentarian. Nationalist student riots spread throughout Poland. They persisted into winter, despite the government's efforts at repression. By then, the Bund had another problem to deal with.

BERLIN

In November, Germany held elections. The Left was split between social democrats and communists, but together, they had enough seats to form a powerful anti-Nazi block. When the social democrats proposed joining forces, the communists refused. Why should they work with social fascists? They weren't worried about Hitler. A brief stint of Nazi rule would teach the masses their mistake. "After Hitler, our turn!" the communist slogan went. Things were all going according to plan.

Champagne corks popped on the first midnight of 1933. At the end of January, Hindenburg appointed Hitler the chancellor of Germany. Hitler may not have been respectable, but he fought communists, and in the eyes of the aristocratic junkers around Hindenburg, that was enough. These serious men were sure they could keep this Nazi clown in check. The social democrats decided that since Hitler had been appointed fair and square, they'd suck it up and wait till the next election, in the name of democracy. When the communists proposed a general strike, the social democrats refused. Why should they work with the party that called them social fascists?

One month after Hitler's appointment, on February 27, the crew at the Bund Archives in Berlin would have found their evening interrupted by the smell of smoke. From their windows, they could have looked west, toward the Brandenburg Gate, to see the sky stained a baneful red. If they followed the crowds down to the police cordons, they would have grasped the cause. The Reichstag was on fire.

CHAPTER 18

DANGEROUS SOLIDARITIES

(1933–1938)

BERLIN

ON THE NIGHT OF FEBRUARY 28, WHEN *NAYE FOLKSTSAYTUNG*'S ANONYMOUS Berlin correspondent telegraphed his copy to Warsaw, he must have known that a fundamental rupture had taken place between the future and the past. He had seen the Reichstag's glass dome shatter. He watched the flames reach high enough to lick the sky. He had heard the police reports about the communist arsonist they found in the wreckage. Even so, he still would have struggled to convey the speed of everything that followed. In a single day, Hitler convinced Hindenburg to sign a decree suspending civil liberties. The government banned the leftist press. Police arrested hundreds of communists, including every delegate to the Reichstag. Their social democratic foes were next in line, since Hermann Göring archly suggested the fire was a joint plot between the parties. The Social Democratic Party protested the "flood of monstrous accusations," but it did them no good. Police invaded the homes of social democratic politicians, tore the doors off their hinges, and dragged them off along with their families.

Storm troopers ransacked the Social Democratic Party's offices at 68 Lindenstrasse, where the Bund had its archives, while more storm troopers were posted out front.

The Bund's archives, lovingly accumulated since the early days of Exileland, told the story of European socialism in all its eloquence, madness, stupidity, and hope. Everything was there. The Menshevik-Bolshevik split. The collapse of the Second International. The rise of Lenin and Trotsky. This vagrant history lay under the guard of Hitler's Brownshirts. Bundists appealed to the Polish embassy for help, but the ambassador refused to get involved. At last, Erlich's friend, the French socialist Léon Blum, arranged for Paris's Bibliothèque Nationale to purchase the collection. For months, the Bund's archivist, Franz Kursky, snuck into 68 Lindenstrasse through a secret side door and packed the documents into crates.

In his youth, Kursky had liked this sort of cloak-and-dagger mischief. He titled a chapter of his memoir "P & S," for his two revolutionary must-haves, the fake (P)assport and the false-bottomed (S)uitcase. But in 1933, he was a paranoid fifty-nine, and these were times of terror. Storm troopers made the laws. They could beat a socialist parliamentarian unconscious and burn his feet with a blowtorch to wake him up. Otto Wels, leader of the Social Democratic Party, who had once condescendingly chided Henryk Erlich for his alarmism, went into exile. The Spandau Citadel filled with political dissidents; the cocky communist leader Ernst Thalmann disappeared into the Reich's dungeons. Kursky could easily have been next.

Thanks to a last-minute intervention by the French ambassador, Kursky and his two rail carriages' worth of archives made their way to Paris. Eighty years later, I would run my fingers across the papers he had saved. Archives are a way for the past to speak directly to the present. The fact that I can write this book owes everything to Kursky's courage.

THE NARAS

As the Brownshirts ravaged Germany, Jews escaped over whatever border they could reach. In Paris, *The New York Times* interviewed traumatized new arrivals. One man watched storm troopers pull a diner from an Alexanderplatz restaurant and beat his face until it resembled beefsteak. A factory owner's wife presented "bloodstained pajamas and a blood-clotted club" as proof of what she endured. Polish Jews beseeched their consulate for help. Within a few weeks of the Reichstag fire, thousands had returned home, with or without the correct paperwork. Their country didn't welcome them. Peasants rioted, afraid of a Jewish invasion, and Endek parliamentarians agitated against the influx of "German fugitive Jews."

The Endeks were no longer the biggest racists in Poland. They had been supplanted by two breakaway youth groups: the National Radical Camp, nicknamed the Naras, and the even more deranged Falanga. Both groups were comprised of rich kids who dressed in gray military blouses and razor-studded shin guards, the better to slice up their victims. In a single night in 1934, Naras wounded thirty people in a raid on a Jewish library on one side of Warsaw, while on the other side of town, they kidnapped a burly porter—leader of a Bundist battle squad—and beat him to death with iron rods.

In Warsaw, the Naras began a new, Nazi-style boycott. Their boys stood in front of the Jewish-owned bookshops on Swietokrzyska Street and passed out pamphlets describing their determination "to clear the country of Jewish parasites," while their girls sang the cheerful ditty "Jews to the Gallows." During Christmas shopping season, Naras lobbed stink bombs into Jewish stores, smashed their windows, pulled their fire alarms, and dragged out their customers. In the old covered markets, they wrecked Jewish stalls, bludgeoned vendors, and declared the place the exclusive property of Poles.

At universities around Poland, every semester began with a bloodbath, as nationalist students attacked Jews with rubber cudgels, revolvers, and firecrackers. At Warsaw University, nationalists even beat the dean of history for failing to sympathize with their crusade. After a few weeks of riots, police shuttered the schools.

Jewish students were not alone. Polish socialist students rescued their classmates from attacks and passed out antiracist leaflets alongside their Bundist comrades. At the main university in Vilna, in the same room where mobs had beaten Jews the previous semester, the Polish Socialist Party organized an evening of poetry to celebrate Jewish-Polish coexistence. In Warsaw, they deployed their men to fight alongside Bernard Goldstein's militia. When Nara thugs beat up Jews in Saxon Gardens, a hundred Polish and Jewish slaughterhouse workers sent them scurrying back to their own neighborhood, where Polish socialists lay in wait to reinforce the lesson. When the Bund needed unregistered handguns, Bernard turned to the Polish Socialist Party, which had members employed in gun shops around Warsaw. One of these workers would order an extra crate of guns. Just before the shipment arrived at the train station in Danzig, another Polish socialist, employed by an exporter, would snatch the guns off the train and conceal them in a crate of deli meat. The guns proceeded safely to Warsaw.

BERNARD GOLDSTEIN

Bernard Goldstein would have liked a different sort of life. Despite his decades-long career in political violence, he was more sensitive than people thought. He loved kids. He cried at sappy songs. As he got older, he realized that the constant bloodshed had taken its toll on him. He walked around with his hand on his revolver, as if every footstep behind him belonged to a nationalist ready to slip a knife between his ribs. He forced himself not to look back. *Toughen up. Get ahold of yourself. You have a job to do.* He choked down his fear.

He was broke. The party had never paid him much. Sometimes he had to ask his brother in America for money, just to make ends meet.

The only fringe benefit he got was when a rich comrade gave him his old shirts. Warsaw gangsters wooed him with offers whose implications were unstated but obvious. "Can I get you a drink, Bernard?" the gangsters asked. "A suit? You look like a bum, Bernard." He was human. He wanted drinks and suits. His union buddies thought he should take the gangsters' offers, but he'd been around long enough to know where such compromises led. Yet he couldn't deny the compulsion he felt to accept them. One night, Bernard begged central committee member Noyakh Portnoy to find him another job in the party. The old man patted Bernard on the shoulder and told him he was the only one they could trust to run their army.

Bernard adored art. At the Yiddish literary club, he let the poetry recitations take him away from the brutal present. He liked to lose himself in the theaters around Leszno Street, where the hit play was a true-crime saga by a master thief turned writer named Urke Nachalnik. He preferred the actors at the corner table at Gertner's restaurant to the beery nights at Fat Yosl's tavern where all gangsters liked to hang. It was at Gertner's that he met his closest friend, the Bundist teacher Shloyme Mendelson. Witty and intellectual, married to a glamorous stage actress, Mendelson was the sort of man Bernard wished he'd had the chance to become. But just like every thug wants to be an artist, every artist wants to be a thug. Mendelson had the same fascination with brawlers that Bernard had with playwrights and poets.

After fights, Bernard often retreated to Mendelson's apartment. "Why do I have to be the enforcer?" he asked one night. Why did he have to break bones, stick guns in people's faces. Each time he bemoaned his life, Mendelson reassured him. He was important. He was a fighter for their people. The intellectuals envied him. "If I was tough like you," Mendelson swore, "I'd gladly take your place."

GOEBBELS

In the summer of 1934, Nazi propaganda minister Joseph Goebbels visited Warsaw, where Pilsudski received him like the representative of any legitimate government. Months earlier, in January, Poland had signed a nonaggression pact with Germany. Now, when *Naye Folkstsaytung* criticized Hitler, cops confiscated the issues and threatened to send the editors to a concentration camp. The government also suppressed a movement by the Bund and other Jewish groups to boycott German goods. It would not do to insult a friendly power.

RED VIENNA

In February, Austria's dictator, Engelbert Dollfuss, came for Red Vienna. The Social Democratic Party of Austria was the most powerful, militant socialist party in Europe, with tens of thousands of armed workers in their Schutzbund militia. After Hitler rose to power across the border, they swore they would not repeat the German Social Democratic Party's mistakes. If fascists tried to destroy democracy, they would call a general strike and, if necessary, take up arms. Yet when Dollfuss seized power in 1933, the Austrian social democrats sat on their hands, letting him chip away at basic freedoms. They hemorrhaged credibility, and their members drifted away. When fascist paramilitaries tried to break into the Social Democratic Party office in February, the party had finally had enough, and the Schutzbund opened fire. The party called a general strike, but their months of inaction had disillusioned their base, and most workers ignored their order. Pursued by the fascists, Schutzbund fighters barricaded themselves inside Karl-Marx-Hof, one of the avant-garde housing estates that were Red Vienna's most famous achievement. They held off government forces for three days, until Dollfuss brought in the artillery and slaughtered the Schutzbund fighters, along with thousands of workers.

For years afterward, the Bund would elegize the valiant fighters of Red Vienna, but poetry can't change the past. When it was time to use force, the Austrian social democrats hesitated, just like their German counterparts, and so they too lost their country.

THE JEWISH LABOR COMMITTEE

On February 25, 1934, days after the fall of Red Vienna, a trio of former Bundists in New York founded the Jewish Labor Committee to help fascism's victims, whether they were Jewish or not.

Despite the Depression, this trio had done well for themselves. David Dubinsky led the powerful International Ladies Garment Workers Union, Baruch Charney Vladeck sat on the board of Mayor La Guardia's housing administration, and Joseph Baskin ran the wildly popular mutual aid society, Workmen's Circle. They represented at least four hundred thousand workers between them. Though they remained socialists, these men were a long way from their insurrectionary pasts. There were no Cossacks in America, no need for jailbreaks or barricades. Through patient organizing, they had built a vibrant union culture, with housing cooperatives in the Bronx and workers' summer resorts. Now they were prominent men in fine suits, New Deal Democrats with a direct line to Roosevelt. The years had faded their scarlet radicalism to a whisper-pink.

The Jewish Labor Committee found their first beneficiary thanks to Abraham Plotkin, an American union organizer unlucky enough to be in Berlin during Hitler's seizure of power. In the chaotic weeks after the Reichstag fire, Plotkin witnessed the brutal Gestapo arrest of his friend, a German union organizer named Martin Plettl. Plotkin had expected such attacks on Jews and communists, but Plettl was a basic-issue Aryan social democrat. Plotkin cabled his friends in the Jewish Labor Committee. After Plettl escaped Berlin to Amsterdam, the Jewish Labor Committee put him on a boat to New York City.

At first, the Jewish Labor Committee stuck to activities like this. They collected money from garment workers, which they used to snatch Europe's trade union aristocracy out of fascist concentration camps. Once they arrived in America, these rescued labor leaders went on lecture tours. Their ticket sales funded the antifascist underground in Europe. But though the Jewish Labor Committee helped many individuals, the American border regime stymied them at every turn. In 1930, Herbert Hoover had radically slashed immigration quotas, then instructed American consulates to issue no more than 10 percent of the meager number of visas allotted to each country. In 1933, the United States accepted less than two thousand immigrants from Germany. Hoover's cruel policy had the support of America's largest union, the American Federation of Labor, which believed that immigrants would steal American jobs. Appeals by Jewish Labor Committee leaders went nowhere. When, at the 1935 American Federation of Labor convention, delegates from Dubinsky's union proposed a resolution to increase quotas for refugees from fascist countries, the federation's leadership shot them down.

THE HOUSE ON AVENUE S

As a Workmen's Circle member, Sam Rothbort fell under the aegis of the Jewish Labor Committee, but I don't know what this meant in practice. In the early thirties, he had his own problems. The farm failed, the art market cratered, and he fell behind on his taxes. Luckily, Rose always had more practical sense than her husband. Over the years, she had squirreled away as much as she could from Sam's sporadic paychecks. When the government finally seized their farm in 1934, she used these savings to buy a house in Brooklyn, at 823 Avenue S.

When I was a child, my great-aunt Ida still lived in the Rothbort home. Every detail of the place evoked a shabby old-world artistry, from the blintzes that Ida baked to Rose's ceramic pitchers to the whimsical stained glass Sam made from broken beer bottles. I loved it in my blood and bones. My great-grandparents' home became my aesthetic lodestar, whose resonances I pursued through underground bookstores and artists' lofts around the world.

In those years, I would sit at the picture window and stare out at the garden, a riot of magnolias, snapdragons, and bowing golden sunflowers that Rose used to arrange into still lifes for Sam to paint. I would descend into the basement that smelled like turpentine, where Ida stored Sam's sculptures. *Stored* is the wrong word, though, for they didn't sit passively but lurked and haunted, like a family of minotaurs carved from wood and stone. Sam's brush still lay in a congealed pool of safflower oil, surrounded by tubes of hand-ground pigment. Perhaps a thousand paintings lined the walls. Two hundred self-portraits, many of them costumed, displayed a talent for disguise he first learned in the underground then honed at the masked balls for the Volkovysk Revolutionary Union, but which would never suffice for the art world to accept him. Sam still sold paintings in the 1930s, though each year his work fell further out of fashion as tastes turned toward abstraction and modernism. He hung at the Brooklyn Museum sometimes, or in the Caz-Delbo Gallery, run by another eastern European Jew who had transited through Geneva's Exileland. He painted murals. His younger son, Lawrence, also wanted to be an artist.

When I was a little girl, I played in the garden with my cousins Barry and Meesha. Barry and I drifted apart over the years, but we reconnected decades later. We sat on the couch in my apartment, not far from the South Williamsburg neighborhood where Sam and Rose made their first home. Barry laid out a stack of black-and-white photographs he had found when clearing out his father's apartment after his death. He wanted me to help identify the people in them.

I looked at a photo of Rose Rothbort and my great-aunt Ida, standing on a boardwalk. Rose seemed to be in her thirties, a bit heavy in the jowls but still attractive in her dark-eyed, pouty way. Ida was a gold-haired sprite of seven or eight. On the back of the photo someone had written: "Coney Island."

Sam Rothbort loved Coney Island. He visited it from his first days in New York. Come June, he could ride the train to Mermaid Avenue, where the tenement dwellers stripped off their clothes and plunged into the gray Atlantic. As a young man, he would mingle beneath the thousand domes, spires, and minarets of the brand-new Luna Park. He would turn the gambling wheel, each spoke a sea lion's head, to try, but fail, to win a prize, then stuff some cotton candy in his mouth as consolation. It was the old market of Volkovysk, with its fire-breathers and acrobats, its violent peasants now transformed by the American gospel of More. He returned each summer with the family and immortalized its pleasure palaces in his paintings.

Every year, he walked by the shore. The ocean stretched before him. If he followed the water to its endpoint, he would have reached Europe, the bloody continent whose union bosses the Jewish Labor Committee now fought to save. How many Europeans would soon throw themselves into the waves? Around him jostled the denizens of New York's megalopolis. They were the lower class of everywhere, born in a thousand warring places, but here, they fought over nothing more consequential than a spot of sand. In this democratic gathering spot, this place of bare bodies and easy solidarity, the storm gathering in Germany must have seemed terribly far away. How could he have imagined that the ravings of a clown with a bristle mustache would ever touch his birthplace?

Driftwood lay on the shore. Sam picked up a piece. The driftwood had come from a tree, he thought, chopped down in some country on the other side of the ocean. It could have been his Zamkov forest. Like him, it had traveled across the world only to wash up, discarded, on this dirty beach. No matter. He was an artist. Even in trash he saw the glowing filaments of divinity, to be revealed by his chisel. He stroked the driftwood, looking for stories hidden in the grain.

SOPHIA DUBNOVA

In 1934, Sophia Dubnova had just turned fifty, and the family was together again. German universities had expelled their Jewish students, so her eldest son, Alexander, returned from Berlin to join his brother, Victor, at the progressive Free Polish University in Warsaw.

With her boys grown, she was also a writer in search of a muse. She found it in the blossoming feminist movement of thirties Poland. Intellectuals like Tadeusz Boy-Zelenski challenged the taboos of conservative Catholic society to demand secular divorce and gender equality. The Society for Conscious Motherhood advocated for a woman's right to use birth control and abortion as she saw fit. Sophia Dubnova decided to bring these ideas into the Bundist press.

Her articles on the ethics of love and sex caused an immediate sensation amongst party youth, especially young women. These girls had come of age with a level of freedom unimaginable to their mothers. They had ostensible, if imperfect, legal equality. Many studied at coed schools. Orthodox Judaism remained patriarchal, but steely young women could still get jobs, escape home, ditch arranged marriages, and raise their kids themselves. Girls comprised half of Tsukunft's membership. These boys and girls hiked together and argued at meetings together, and both got black eyes in university brawls. Together, they filled the cramped rooms of the Bund's club, tramped up steps polished by footfalls, and flirted across tables filched from the party's wartime soup kitchen. In the back rows of the Fame movie theater across the courtyard, teenagers could paw each other like they just invented sex. Darkness kept their secrets.

The Bund was never a feminist paradise. What was, in 1934? Most Bundist bigwigs were men. In interwar Poland, women made up a smaller share of leadership than they had in the days of the tsar. Tsukunft girls often complained that their male comrades talked over them at meetings, that they stuck them with grunt work, or that made dumb comments about their bodies. The important thing was this: girls and boys were in the same room, no partition between them. This closeness forced them to see each other as humans. They flirted awkwardly, broke things off clumsily, and used ideology to paper over heartbreak, but all the while, they were discovering something unprecedented: the prospect of love between equals.

Sophia Dubnova began to receive invitations to speak at Tsukunft meetings. After her talks, the girls jostled to tell her their problems, grateful that they could speak frankly, without shame. They were tough. Many of them had worked in factories since their early teens, and they had no patience for the failings of their male comrades. The boys talked a big game, they said, but they behaved like pigs. They skulked away after sex or, worse, acted like they owned them. Years later, Sophia recalled a spirited teenager named Gutka. After accidentally becoming pregnant, Gutka procured an illegal abortion with Sophia's help. The operation was painful, and Gutka had no desire to sleep with her boyfriend afterward. He reacted poorly, whining, wheedling, and screaming blue balls, until he made himself so thoroughly unattractive that Gutka broke off their relationship. That might have been the end of things, except that Gutka's boyfriend was also a member of Tsukunft. His friends, her male comrades, barraged her with lectures on her bourgeois callousness. How could she cut off a poor boy's "social energy?" They were Marxists. From each according to her ability to each according to his need.

Sophia covered these sorts of dramas for the Bund's youth newspaper. Soon her desk was filled with invitation letters from Tsukunft groups in shtetls across Poland. On Fridays, just before sunset, her rickety bus would pull up to a market square that smelled of horseshit and tar. Shabbos candles glimmered in the windows. It could have been Volkovysk of forty years prior, and Itka the Bundist might have listened to her speak. Sophia lectured in Polish (her Yiddish was never strong) about modernist literature, revolution, and a woman's right to orgasm, to halls packed with kids so eager for life that they could have cracked open the world. Afterward, they would crowd around Sophia with more questions, grab her arm, and conduct her over to a party in someone's attic. She would always remember how "excited young voices criss-crossed. . . . Little tongues of flame leapt up from person to person, and the whole attic was humming and sizzling like dry birch bark set aflame, throwing into the dark, dense night of the shtetl the voices' challenge and yearning."

Afterward, she sometimes received messages from the provincial administration forbidding her to speak on topics that threatened the borders—political or sexual—of the Polish state.

It was not an easy time. Letters from her brother in Moscow stopped, and issues of Soviet literary journals grew thinner as the names of her favorite writers disappeared. Money was tight. Henryk worked as a defense attorney to make ends meet, but he spent much of his time helping imprisoned communists (he loathed their ideas but would defend their right to express them) who obviously had little money to pay him. Otherwise, they had only his small salary from *Naye Folkstsaytung*. They plugged on. The couple wrote side by side. He sweated words and syntax like she did. He also chased the perfect sentence. Together, they were happy. They understood each other and loved each other, in the mature, steady way of people who have spent many years together but have been deprived of each other's company often enough to still feel lucky to have each other for however long they do.

THE DEATH OF PILSUDSKI

In April 1935, Poland passed a new constitution that did away with the last vestiges of parliamentary democracy. A new election law made it nearly impossible for opposition parties to nominate legislative candidates. The president would appoint the prime minister and dissolve the parliament whenever he saw fit.

All of this would have been bad enough under Pilsudski, but the old marshal was wasting away with stomach cancer. He died on May 12, 1935. Crowds lined up to watch his funeral cortege pass by on the way to the Archcathedral of Saint John, where his coffin lay in state for two days, as befitted the father of modern Poland. Afterward, Bundist newspapers printed blunt assessments of Pilsudski's legacy. Police confiscated the issues. But however critical our Bundists were, they must have guessed this was the end of a tarnished golden age. Everything was about to get much worse.

Like many men who believe themselves indispensable, Pilsudski died without nominating an heir. He left that to a quartet of colonels, led by Edward Rydz-Smigly, a dimwitted military man whose main qualifications were his square jaw and his chest full of medals. Confronted with a brutal economic crisis but lacking even a smidgen of Pilsudski's charisma, Poland's leaders turned to racist demagoguery to shore up their power. From now on, antisemitism would be an official policy of the state.

THE COUNTRYSIDE

The countryside was ready to boil. Since the first days of Poland's independence, every successive government had promised the peasants land. Yet, after fifteen years, most farmland remained concentrated in aristocratic estates, and the poor farmers who made up most of the population found their holdings ever more inadequate.

In traditional rural society, peasants and Jews lived together in a symbiotic coexistence that seldom translated to warmth. Peasants brought their crops to shtetl markets, where petty traders like my great-great-grandmother Chaya Ruchl bought their wheat and fixed their shoes and sold them vodka. The traders always seemed slightly better off than the peasants, in the same way an immigrant bodega owner always seems slightly better off than his customers. The differences in class might have been minute, but they caused resentments far more violent than those felt toward aristocrats or millionaires in distant Warsaw. The most passionate hatreds are always intimate ones. All of this gave the nationalists an opportunity.

Forget the landlords, the nationalists said. Forget the aristocrats and the millionaires in Warsaw. Your real oppressor is the hunched little man in his market stall who sews the lining into your coat each winter. Jews charge too much. They rig their scales. They cheat you with bad merchandise. They own wooden stalls and battered workbenches that should rightfully be yours. Also, they killed Jesus.

To combat nationalist incitement, the Bund enlisted the local branches they had in hundreds of shtetls around Poland. Despite police repression, they passed out over a million Polish-language pamphlets explaining how antisemitism was a tool of the rich to divide and conquer. Their youth groups hiked out to villages each Sunday, where they picked crops, cooked in soup kitchens, and made friends with local peasants. But these efforts were no match for a well-funded hate campaign that was supported by the government, ignored by the police, and backed by the Catholic Church.

On March 9, 1936, a pogrom broke out in Przytyk, a town too poor to even afford vowels. As was often the case, it happened on a market day. The peasants, drunk and exhausted, had sold their crops for prices that felt too low. The Jews, impoverished and tax-burdened, had tried to strike sharp deals. Everyone was irritable, suspicious, and acting their worst. In Przytyk, it started with a shoving match—and probably would have ended there as well, if a group of nationalists hadn't spent the past week distributing pamphlets with the charming counsel, "Hit! Hit steadily! Do not be afraid of blood!" That day, a thousand peasants descended on Przytyk's Jewish stalls, where they hacked the shoemaker Josek apart with axes and bludgeoned his wife, Chaya, to death. Police arrested Jews who tried to resist; courts would sentence one defender to eight years' imprisonment.

The pogrom horrified Polish Jews because of everything that it seemed to foreshadow. A song by the Bundist poet Mordechai Gebirtig captured their mood.

> *And you stand there looking on*
> *With futile, folded arms*
> *And you stand there looking on—*
> *While our village burns!*

The Bund called a half-day general strike, with the support of the Polish Socialist Party. It would not be merely against the murders but against fascism, and not just for Jewish rights but for the rights of everyone to work, bread, and freedom. On March 17, just after sunrise, Bernard Goldstein's militia spread through Warsaw's commercial districts. "Shut it down," they hollered, and the traders complied. Shutters clanked. Bolts locked. Teamsters bellowed, "We're going home." Bundist union reps fanned out across the factories and workshops to spread the order. Jewish students stayed home, despite their administrators' threats. The Praga slaughterhouses ground to a halt as Christian workers heeded the Polish Socialist Party's call for a walkout. By eleven, Warsaw's Jewish quarter had transformed into a mass protest, centered on the Bund club's courtyard. The same scene repeated in every Jewish neighborhood in towns across Poland. The strike succeeded beyond the Bund's wildest hopes, associating their name forever with the willingness to fight back.

More pogroms followed, in more immiserated shtetls across Poland. Mobs emptied towns of their Jewish populations. A report by the Joint Distribution Committee (a New York–based relief organization that aided impoverished Jewish communities around the world) summed it up like so:

> These bands of cutthroats are sent around from town to town to break the windows of Jewish stores and ransack the goods, break up their stands and pushcarts in the market places, break human heads, arms and legs, and when their job is done in one town, they take a train to the next. . . . The police disappear and the Jews are left to the mercy of the armed mob. When the goods and wares are destroyed, some heads broken, some arms and legs maimed, the police appear and say, "Time is up, boys."

The party sent Bernard around the country to organize self-defense. In dingy Minsk Mazowiecki, he won a minor victory. After Endeks lit a Jewish house on fire, the flames spread to nearby Polish homes. Without thinking, Bernard ran into a burning building to rescue an elderly Polish woman abandoned in the flames. Once he had brought the woman to safety, he mounted a roof and began barking orders to form a bucket brigade. His actions shocked the Polish onlookers out of their trance. Why was this Jew helping Poles? They began to listen to the whispers of their socialist neighbors, who pointed out that the Endeks, not Jews, had started the fire that now consumed their homes. What those neighbors said might as well have been a metaphor. Jews and Poles lived side by side. Their fates were intertwined. If one burned, the other would burn with them.

MENDELE THE KING

Bernard ran from town to town putting out both literal and metaphorical fires. In September he was in Lodz, where Endek leaflets appeared warning Jews not to vote in the next municipal election. It was no empty threat; nationalists had murdered five Jews since the year began, and when Bernard arrived, the air felt edgy and sour. In the shabby wood streets of the Baluty neighborhood, he saw shattered market stalls and merchants with black eyes.

Bernard had brought with him sixty militiamen from Warsaw. This was nowhere near enough to secure an election, even with backup from his comrades in Lodz. Reluctantly, he called an old acquaintance from the Jewish mafia, nicknamed Mendele the King. The wizened little mob boss was not a politically conscious man, to say the least, but he agreed with Bernard's argument that the Jews of Lodz should not be fucked with—at least, not by people other than him. When Election Day came, hundreds of Mendele's men spread throughout the city, eager to assure that every citizen could cast a ballot, regardless of their ethnicity. They carried steel bats and revolvers in case anyone was inclined to disagree. The Bund and the Polish Socialist Party won the municipal elections. They ruled Lodz together for five months, until the government dissolved the city council.

MOSCOW

Outside Poland, the world moved on. History progressed. Each second fell, one after the other, like water droplets, until they accumulated into a sea.

In 1936, a grandiose series of show trials rocked the convictions of the worldwide Left. The defendants were Grigori Zinoviev, Lev Kamenev, and other members of the original Bolshevik elite that had helped Lenin orchestrate the October Revolution, then construct the Soviet state.

The trials sprang from the 1934 assassination of Sergei Kirov, an affable communist bureaucrat who was the closest that Stalin had to a friend. Police caught Kirov's murderer immediately, but Stalin refused to believe that the mentally ill nonentity had acted alone. Instead, he blamed his most hated enemy, Leon Trotsky, who was still scribbling away in exile. Worse, Stalin thought, Trotsky couldn't have acted alone. Stalin imagined a conspiracy that reached the highest echelons of the Soviet state. The purges that followed consumed thousands of people, including Moishe Rafes, David Petrovsky, Esther Frumkin, and almost every other Bundist who had joined the communists during the killing years of the Russian Civil War. Security services arrested Lenin's closest intimates. Zinoviev and Kamenev disappeared into secret prisons.

When they reappeared two years later, on the docket of the gracelessly named Trial of Trotskyite-Zinovievite Terrorist Center, Zinoviev and Kamenev were broken men. Tortured and terrified for their families' lives, they confessed to every charge put in front of them. Yes, they were diseased, decayed, and perverted terrorists, sex pests, and gluttons, Nazi spies and agents of Trotsky. Yes, they caused famines. Yes, they sabotaged industries. Yes, they killed Kirov. Yes, they conspired to murder Comrade Stalin. Yes, they deserved to be shot (which they were, immediately after their trial). At the show trials that followed, Karl Radek, Nikolai Bukharin, and other old Bolsheviks denounced themselves in similarly sensational terms.

The Bund's leaders might have hated the defendants, but they never doubted their innocence. They had known each other for too long. Bundists and Bolsheviks had grown up together in Exileland. They had scrapped and mocked and loathed each other, but they came from the same vanished world.

In his coverage of the trial for *Naye Folkstsaytung*, Viktor Alter took note of one old Bolshevik missing from the docket—Trotsky himself. The arrogant young fugitive in yellow shoes who had once interrupted Medem's lecture in Karlsruhe, the orator king of the Saint Petersburg Soviet in 1905, the roving war journalist who became the most popular man in newborn Soviet Russia, Lenin's heir apparent.

If, today, they want to shoot Raphael Abramovich, tomorrow they'll want to shoot Trotsky, Medem had predicted in 1918, when Trotsky was at the height of his power. Where was Trotsky in 1936? Expelled from the party, exiled from the country he helped found. He lived under house arrest in frozen Norway, hunted by Stalin's spies. In Viktor Alter's words, "a helpless refugee."

Alter had a brother, a bon vivant named Jean Arens who had risen far in the Soviet state. When the purges began, Arens lived in New York, ostensibly as a journalist. Moscow summoned him back. On the way home, he passed through Warsaw to see his family. Alter begged him to stay in Poland, but Arens refused, and the conversation devolved into a political argument so bitter that their mother had to separate the men. As Jean Arens's train pulled out of the Warsaw station, Alter screamed after it: "Confess nothing!"

The Soviet secret police arrested Arens shortly after his arrival. He disappeared.

The droplets accumulate.

Drip, drip, drip.

CAMP OF NATIONAL UNITY

In February 1937, top Polish politician Colonel Adam Koc announced a new pro-government organization: the Camp of National Unity, or OZON. An Endek rehash in a flashy new fascist skin, OZON based its ideology on Catholicism, Anti-Communism, Army Worship, and Massive Torchlight Parades. Poland was for Poles, OZON said, not its three-and-a-half-million Jewish citizens, whose culture OZON's leader,

Boguslaw Miedziński, described as "disgusting and ridiculous, [based on] sorcery and superstitions, recalling the practices of Asiatic shamans or black chieftains from the African jungle." Jews should be stripped of citizenship, denuded of their assets, and expelled. The government even tried to set up deals with France to ship Polish Jews to Madagascar. (The Malagasy were not consulted.)

The government levied new taxes on Jewish artisans; by 1939, Jews, who made up 13 percent of Poland, would pay 40 percent of the country's taxes. When the government banned kosher slaughter, the Bund organized general strikes, despite their own atheism.

The government stepped up efforts to ruin Jewish businesses. "We must spare no effort to Polonize the main branches of the national economy," said Colonel Jan Kowalewski of OZON. They stripped Jews of trading licenses. Professional associations introduced bylaws restricting membership to "Aryans." Signs went up around the country urging Poles not to buy from Jewish stores.

The Catholic Church supported the boycott. The Polish Cardinal August Hlond told his flock that Jews constituted "the advance guard of a godless life, of the Bolshevik movement, and of subversive action. . . . Jews are embezzlers and usurers, and they engage in the white slave traffic."

None of this was enough to satisfy the far-right Falanga, who demanded laws modeled on those that the Nazis passed at Nuremberg. Jews should be denied the vote, kicked out of the army, banned from Polish companies, forbidden employ or work for Poles, and finally, entirely eliminated from the country. A few months later, OZON made Falanga an official youth-movement affiliate.

Encouraged by official indulgence, nationalist youth gangs proclaimed "Jew-free days" at universities, when they attacked any Jewish student who dared approach their campus. In a single day at a single school in Warsaw, they put twelve Jewish students in the hospital. Their leaflets read, "When you see a Jew, knock his teeth out. Don't waver even if it's a woman. . . . The only thing to be regretted is that you didn't hit hard enough."

Once authorities closed the schools, nationalist students left the cities to spread the riots to their hometowns. Nationalist bombs demolished homes and shops and shook the Katowice synagogue. "Here and there, a Jew is beaten to death," reported *The New York Times.*

VOLKOVYSK

One morning, huge white letters went up on the wall around Volkovysk's Catholic Church: THE JEW IS THE ENEMY! DO NOT BUY FROM JEWS!

Everyone knew who was responsible. The author of those words was a well-heeled pharmacist named Hugon Tyminski, who held nationalist meetings at his swish shop at 13 Pierackiego Street. Tyminski and his friends often picketed the Jewish shops on Broad Street, shouting slurs, smashing windows, and beating whoever looked like an easy target.

Tyminski was only the most enthusiastic representative of the zeitgeist. Over the last few years, OZON's campaign against the Jews had transformed Volkovysk. Jewish shops went bankrupt and were replaced by Christian businesses. Market stalls shuttered. Young people lucky enough to get papers departed for Palestine or America.

Others chose to stay. And to fight. In *The Bund in Pictures,* I found a photo titled, "The Tsukunft Youth Militia in Volkovysk." Fourteen young men and three young women pose in quasi-military garb, with expressions of barely suppressed ferocity. They bear little resemblance to Sam's comrades of 1906. There are no peasant blouses. No dreamy looks. The young people in the photo are serious, and distinctly modern. To learn more about them, I turned to *The Volkovysk Memorial Book,* which identifies the leader of the group as Yankel Rubinstein, son of a locksmith. He looks proper in his suit and glasses, but his thin, righteous face makes him resemble an aspiring Trotsky. His dark girlfriend, Chana Irmess, glares at the camera like she could kill. In another photo, taken at the local Bundist school, sullen boys and girls pose beneath a marvelous painted banner of a falcon transforming into a woman's face. On it was written: WE BELONG TO THE FUTURE.

Avram Markus, editor of the Bund's defunct local newspaper, was still an active party worker in 1937, despite a stint in a Polish prison. His family lived austerely and hosted itinerant leftists in their humble home. Avram refused to hire employees for his small tannery, since he didn't want to exploit the labor of others, and so he exploited the labor of his son Shlomo to keep things going.

He must have worried about Shlomo, whose ambition and talent bridled against the boundaries the state created to stifle Jewish youth. Racist quotas kept Shlomo out of Polish universities, so he studied medicine in Italy. When he returned to Volkovysk, the government refused to recognize his degree, or to allow him to take an examination to prove his knowledge. Unable to practice medicine, Shlomo helped his father at the tannery and volunteered at the Jewish hospital when he could.

Around this time, he began dating Nechama Schein, who was from a wealthy Zionist family. The couple became self-righteous, dogmatic communists.

PALESTINE

In the Zionist movement, the Polish government found a loyal ally in their plans for ethnic cleansing.

During the same years that the Polish government supported fascist youth gangs terrorizing Jewish neighborhoods, they provided machine guns, Mauser rifles, and military training to three Zionist militias in Palestine—the Haganah, which secretly answered to David Ben-Gurion; Jabotinsky's Irgun; and the fascist Lehi militia—even though all three groups had already murdered countless Palestinians. Prospective fighters signed pledges to leave Poland immediately after training. They could not use their skills to defend their own communities.

During the same years that the Polish government demanded the expulsion of three million Jewish citizens, Jabotinsky toured the country calling for their "evacuation," a fine distinction that the Bund didn't appreciate. When Jabotinsky spoke in Vilna, the Bund was there to picket the man they called "the spiritual father of Jewish fascism." "We are citizens with equal rights in this country!" their pamphlets read. "We shall fight for work and for bread, for life and for rights here in Poland! We do not wish to escape from Poland! We shall not permit charlatans to speak in our name!"

In 1937, the Bund had another reason to shun Zionism: Palestine was on fire. The efforts of well-heeled notables like Musa Kazim Pasha had done nothing to gain Palestinians political rights, nor to stop Zionist land purchases and the subsequent expulsions of Palestinian farmers. As if to underscore their indifference to Palestinian opinion, British police beat Musa Kazim Pasha to death in 1933 at a protest in Jerusalem. The situation grew more volatile after Hitler's ascension to power, when 164,000 new Jewish immigrants flocked to the only place on earth that would accept them. Just as the Bund warned, Zionist politics had poisoned the air, and Palestinians didn't welcome their arrival. These Jews may have been refugees fleeing imminent murder, but for Palestinians, they transformed into colonizers the moment they disembarked at Haifa Port. In 1936, Palestinians declared a general strike to protest the Mandate, Jewish immigration, and the unequal wages paid to Palestinian workers. Within six months, it grew into the Great Palestinian Revolt. This armed uprising targeted the British, Zionist institutions and wealthy Palestinians branded as collaborators.

This time around, *Naye Folkstsaytung* was cooler toward the rebels, whom they often referred to as terrorists. I chalk this up to the fact that the new immigrants were not the ideological settlers of prior years but brutally persecuted people with nowhere else to go. The Bund also had little time for pan-Arab nationalism, which they held in the same low esteem as they did the Jewish sort. They knew that the beliefs of the oppressed can be just as dangerous as those of their oppressors if power should happen to shift. As Henryk Erlich wrote in 1933:

> If Jewish nationalism, as a general rule, is not bloodthirsty, this is only out of necessity, not virtue; if an appropriate opportunity arose, Jewish nationalism would show its sharp teeth and nails no less than the nationalisms of other nations.
>
> To be sure, Jabotinsky is nothing more than a small-scale Hitler, a fascist clown. . . . Of course, Jabotinsky's brown-shirt soldiers are nothing more than a tragicomic caricature of Hitler's SA people. But the only thing missing in order for them to become the same beasts is some muscle strength, some territory, and a political opportunity. . . .
>
> No, we are not a chosen people. Our nationalism is just as ugly, just as harmful, and has the same inclination to fascist debauchery as the nationalisms of all the other nations.

The Bund placed the ultimate blame for the revolt on the Zionist movement, which, as *Naye Folkstsaytung* wrote in 1937, "has taken it upon itself to settle people in a home that is for the most part occupied by others, in order to take control of all of it with the assistance of the house superintendent." To illustrate the reality for its readers, *Naye Folkstsaytung* laid out Zionism's more quotidian cruelties. In one piece, a writer described how Zionists beat a Palestinian girl who dared to sell milk in Tel Aviv, and how a driver threw an upper-class Egyptian Jew off an autobus after confusing him with a Palestinian.

For the Bund, Zionists were ideological twins of the same people trying to force Jews out of Europe. Preserved in YIVO's collection of youth autobiographies, I found the testimony of a girl who had briefly joined a Betar youth group. "[The speaker] keeps saying we have to kick out the Arabs, [but] they are also human beings. . . . People also want to kick Jews out from every country in the exact same way and deny them the capability of living," she wrote. She soon left to join Tsukunft.

WARSAW

One May Day, Bernard Goldstein stood on Gliniana Street, watching the Bund's parade pass by. Suddenly, a crash. Black smoke filled the air, followed by pistol shots, screams, and groans. When the smoke cleared, Bernard saw a woman bent over her toddler. "Avremele!" she howled. The boy had a bullet hole through his chest.

Police didn't find any suspects. The government forbade the little boy's family to give him a funeral.

To avenge Avram Shenker's murder, Goldstein's group linked up with the Polish Socialist Party to raid a posh restaurant frequented by Nara journalists. When Bernard walked in, the journalists' heads swiveled. Their silken companions gasped.

That year's hit song was "Suicide Tango." Mieczyslaw Fogg might have crooned from the gramophone: *Give me this one Sunday, the last Sunday, and . . . then let the world fall apart.*

The journalists lunged for Bernard. His friends rushed in, swinging their steel clubs. When they left a half hour later, the restaurant lay in ruins. Bernard's suit was stained with blood and good champagne.

SPAIN

Ever since July 1936, when General Francisco Franco launched a military uprising against the elected government of Spain, the worldwide Left had been riveted by the peninsula. *Naye Folkstsaytung* reported every development of the first European war between socialism and fascism.

The Spanish government appealed to Western democracies for military aid, but the self-described free world was not interested in another war and declared an arms embargo against both sides. Hitler and Mussolini had no such scruples. The pair lavishly supported Franco. Desperate, the Spanish government turned to the Soviet Union. Stalin was only too happy to oblige.

Comintern agents from as far afield as Puerto Rico and China recruited fighters to defend the Spanish Republic. Most volunteers for the International Brigades were communists, but others joined as well: anarchists, socialists, and unaffiliated idealists of the sort immortalized by Ernest Hemingway in *For Whom the Bell Tolls.* Several Bundists enlisted, including Beniak Livshitz, a Tsukunft militia member from Warsaw. The brigades were a place of dazzling diversity, where Ali Abdel

Khaleq, a Palestinian communist from Jerusalem, could join the Yiddish-speaking Naftali Botwin Company; where Chicago's Oliver Law could become the first Black man to lead white Americans as the commander of the Abraham Lincoln Brigade; where Baghdadi Jew Setty Abraham Horresh could lay his arm over the shoulder of Mack Coad, the grandson of slaves from Alabama. Spain seemed like the furnace in which a new antifascist brotherhood could be forged.

It thrilled Viktor Alter, whose migratory, multilingual background had made him an internationalist to the core. As he wrote in his book *The Jewish Question in Poland*, Jews' "liberation can only be a side product of the universal freeing of all oppressed peoples." In Spain he hoped to see this liberation in action.

In April 1937, Alter was in Paris for a labor conference with his friend the Polish socialist Antoni Zdanowski. The pair decided to take a detour to the Spanish front.

The war seemed far away as Alter and Zdanowski crossed the snow-capped Pyrenees. At the border city of Puigcerdà, armed workers greeted them with shouts of "Camarada!" In anarchist Barcelona, Alter saw a city in the midst of collective self-reinvention. The CNT, an anarcho-syndicalist trade union, ran the taxis, and workers committees took over the hotels. The famous Spanish writer José Ortega y Gasset showed Alter around a palace that activists had converted into a shelter for homeless kids. Workers learned to shoot—not just men, but *milicianas*—housewives, sex workers, and factory girls who battled Catholic conservatism to insist that this was *their* revolution, that they would never be subservient again. Viktor Alter fell in love with wartime Barcelona. Its magic let him ignore the darker currents that pulsed beneath that city's surface—the fratricidal contradictions between an anarchist population and their Soviet backers. Along with the weapons and military advisors that the Soviets gifted the beleaguered republic, they also sent spies, informants, and torturers from the NKVD—the Soviet secret police. Alter's nephew, a leftist radio engineer working for the Spanish Republic, had already survived several NKVD interrogations. Just weeks before Alter's arrival, Raphael Abramovich's son, the journalist Mark Rein, had vanished in Barcelona. Years later, the Bund learned that the NKVD kidnapped and murdered Rein on Stalin's orders.

In Valencia, Zdanowski and Alter drank sherry with Prime Minister Francisco Largo Caballero, who begged them to convince Western democracies to lift their arms embargos. In besieged Madrid, the pair learned to tolerate bombardment. One afternoon, a shell exploded in Plaza del Sol. Shrapnel hit the man beside them. He bled out before their eyes.

One photo remains of Alter and Zdanowksi's trip, taken in the small town of Cabanillas del Campo, an hour outside Madrid. It shows the two men surrounded by filthy fighters from the Dabrowski Battalion, sprawled on the Spanish earth. Alter squints as if unaccustomed to such sunlight.

One night, Alter sat in a posh hotel with the Italian socialist Pietro Nenni. "Every revolution is a series of moments, both sublime and base," Nenni told him. "When we look at a revolution up close, it may sometimes seem to us that the repulsive moments come to the fore. But when we look at it from another perspective, of time, space and thought, we see its beauty."

Alter had the opportunity to reflect on Nenni's words as he traversed the country interviewing anarchists, socialists, and communists for a book he published under the title *Spain in Flames*. When he got back to Warsaw, he organized a week of solidarity with Spain, notwithstanding the smears of pro-government newspapers rabid over the photo he took with fighters at Cabanillas del Campo. Bundist sources claim he organized secret weapons shipments for the Republic.

WARSAW

Back in Poland, the government increased its attacks on the Bund. They confiscated more issues of the group's newspapers. In the *Naye Folkstsaytung* archive, white bars appear on the pages—the work of an energetic censor. That summer, when three hundred Morgenstern athletes applied for passports to attend the Workers' Olympiad in Antwerp, the government refused without explanation. At Warsaw City Hall, nationalist students shouted slurs at the Bundist councilmen from the public galleries; Alter and Erlich left work surrounded by bodyguards.

That summer, nationalists carried out hundreds of assaults against Jews. Nationalists descended on Saxon Gardens, where they threw Jews in the lake, clubbed Jewish mothers, and kicked over baby carriages. In September, hundreds of Falanga members blockaded Warsaw's Jewish neighborhood during the Sukkos holiday, until Jewish and Polish workers drove them off. Naras rigged an IED in the office of a Jewish newspaper and threw a bomb on one of the city's busiest streets. The government banned newspapers from reporting on the attacks.

The Bund plastered Warsaw with handbills: DO NOT LET THEM DRIVE YOU FROM THE STREETS!

On the evening of September 26, two bullets blasted through the walls of the Bund's headquarters on Dluga Street, narrowly missing the head of their secretary Shoshke Erlich. A few seconds later, Bernard Goldstein heard a boom. The windows shattered and the rooms filled with suffocating smoke. Shoshke and Bernard ran into the hallway, where they saw the building's foyer in flames. As the attackers fled, they had fired their pistols, injuring three Bundists and the wife of the building's handyman.

Everyone knew it was the Naras.

VENGEANCE

A few nights later, Bundist tailor Hyman Freeman joined dozens of Jewish and Polish workers outside Luksenburg Gallery, a modernist shopping arcade in central Warsaw. The men packed into automobiles. They passed around brass knuckles and pipes. Through the car window, Freeman would have seen a city that he was too poor to enter, full of bright lights, London suits, and shiny cabarets. The cars stopped near an elegant apartment building at 17 Bracka Street, where the Naras had their headquarters. The workers disembarked and creeped to the entrance. Freeman could hear laughter from inside.

Two Polish socialists found the building's circuit box, flipped it open, and cut the wires. The building plunged into darkness.

Freeman and his comrades stormed up the stairs and kicked open the office door. In the gloom they could make out the silhouettes of a few dozen nationalists, who seemed frozen by shock. The workers didn't wait for them to realize what had happened. Freeman brought down his club on his enemy's skull.

For the next fifteen minutes, the workers smashed everything in their sight. Furniture, windows, bones. They were not tailors and porters anymore but conduits of vengeance, and the ruined faces of their adversaries did nothing to assuage their rage. They bashed the mahogany desks into splinters. They shattered the chandeliers. They stood over the bloody blond men and kicked them in their stomachs, and when the nationalists curled up in agony, they brought their boots down on their heads. Knowing the cops might arrive at any moment, Bernard Goldstein ordered his men to finish, but they didn't want to. They were enjoying it too much. They beat the nationalists mercilessly, until at last Bernard prevailed upon them to run.

That night, Bernard learned that a nationalist had died from his wounds.

GHETTO BENCHES

In October 1937, the nationalists achieved a cherished goal when the government segregated university classrooms across Poland. From then on, Jewish students would be forced to sit on the left side of the class, on so-called ghetto benches. The government justified segregation as the only way to stop the annual student riots, but for the nationalists, the benches were just a start. After a decade of concerted harassment, they had managed to halve the number of Jewish university students. If they kept it up, they hoped to eliminate Jewish students entirely.

"This first attempt to institute the medieval ghetto in independent Poland must be repudiated with the most energetic protest," wrote the Bund. Erlich and Alter met with the education minister to protest, but he told them that Jewish students needed to obey the order.

They would not. Across the country, Jews refused to sit in the benches. They stood for hours-long lectures as a rebuke. Universities forbade them to stand, and even expelled them. Nationalist students attacked them, trying to force them into the seats. The Jewish students refused to submit. Polish socialist students sat in the Jewish benches in solidarity.

With Polish socialist support, the Bund called a two-day general strike against the ghetto benches. In the Jewish neighborhoods, Polish socialists gave fiery speeches on behalf of the students. In front of Warsaw University, Bundist and Polish socialist students passed out literature, while mass promenades of armed Jewish workers guarded the youth. As *The Nation*'s correspondent William Zuckerman wrote: "Never before has the Polish Socialist Party worked so harmoniously with [the Bund] against antisemitism."

Thanks to its proximity to Warsaw Polytechnic, the Erlich apartment became a field hospital. Sophia would return from the library to find battered young people getting their wounds stitched up on her couch. Her son Victor's girlfriend, Iza, showed up one day hunched and weeping. On her way to her law exams, nationalist students had thrown her down the staircase. Another day, a pair of muscular students carried in their unconscious, blood-soaked comrade. Son of a famous Endek politician, the victim had turned his back on his father's beliefs to fight alongside his Jewish classmates. Nationalists broke his skull for treachery.

BERNARD GOLDSTEIN

Bernard Goldstein smuggled himself into Brest-Litovsk in May 1937, days after police had led a pogrom in the city. He found a community paralyzed by the knowledge that, at any moment, the pogrom would explode again. In the deserted Jewish quarter, Goldstein met a Polish socialist comrade, the journalist Jan Dabrowski. As the two worked out a battle plan to deal with future attacks, they saw the glow of Sabbath candles in a window. "I explained to Dabrowski the meaning of the Sabbath candles. . . . Deep in somber thought, we both walked silently through the pogromized, empty streets . . . a Jewish and a Polish Socialist. Perhaps, I thought, hope resides in this, that we two, Dabrowski and I, walk here together with a single purpose."

I agree with Comrade Bernard, despite everything that happened next.

HENRYK ERLICH

On November 17, 1937, Henryk Erlich took the stage in Warsaw's Nowosci Theatre for the fortieth-anniversary celebration of the Bund. Three thousand faces stared up at him from the audience, including, notably, delegates from the Polish Socialist Party.

Erlich was an honest man. He didn't sugarcoat the situation. He spoke about the brutal poverty, the unemployment and hopelessness, the pogroms, and the parties inspired by Hitler who, together, desired "to degrade the human being in you, to trample upon your feeling of self-worth, to turn you into pariahs devoid of legal rights and dignity. . . . They wish to deprive us not only of the right to live but also of the possibility of self-defense and struggle."

He denounced the bourgeois Jewish parties who cut deals with nationalists to protect their bank balances, and the Orthodox who told poor Jews that antisemitism was God's punishment for insufficient piety. He scourged the Zionists, "bankrupt not only here but also there—in Palestine," who stubbornly insisted, "There is a law of some kind: 'gentiles must hate Jews. There is no alternative. It is necessary to flee,' " and so played along with the country's leaders to advocate a mass expulsion of Polish Jews.

Then he told them an extraordinary thing.

> You must briefly step out of the confines of your Jewish misery. . . . Look about you and you will see—the Jews are not the only ones who are suffering. The overwhelming majority in the country, whether Poles, Ukrainians, Jews, or others, is suffering from the economic crisis . . . scarcely able to eke out a daily existence.
>
> Shift your gaze beyond the borders of Poland toward the wide world and you will see: Seventy million people are languishing under the heavy boot of Hitlerism. Not only the 500,000 Jews—the whole German people has been transformed into a nation of slaves. . . . Forty million Italians have been turned into a footstool for the "great" Mussolini. . . . And just as in Germany and Italy,

> millions of working people in other, smaller countries which have become areas of reaction are sunk in privation and bondage.

I read Erlich's call for empathy with the same people who had carried out pogroms across his country, who had dropped mustard gas on Ethiopia and forced refined German Jews to clean the streets with toothbrushes, and I remember words from thirty years before, in the American Star Hall in Brownsville, when the Bundist fundraiser Meyer London called out to the crowd: "Are you aware that in Russian Poland, thousands of our Jewish boys and girls are giving their lives . . . for liberty? They . . . pray to God, not to lead them again out of Egypt, but to help them to free Egypt."

This was it. There was only Egypt, the Bund knew, and they were stuck with the Egyptians. They were people first, not Jews or goys. There was no God to save them, to offer exodus across a bloody sea. All that existed was here, even if here was hell. Jews had nothing but their own strength and the fraught solidarities they built with people they had been raised to see as enemies. As his voice rose, Erlich conjured up the Vilna safe house, the red banners hung in the woods, the self-defense squads who fought the tsar's goons with their Browning pistols, the mythology of his party. A party that would always fight.

"Your liberation lies not in passivity and servility, not in empty dreams built on sand and English guns . . . but in the community of struggle with the working class, in the fight right here where you live, where your grandfathers and fathers lived. . . . Salvation lies here and nowhere else, in untiring struggle for freedom, hand in hand with the working masses of Poland!"

CHAPTER 19

THE EVE

(1938–1939)

REFUGEES

THE BLEED OF REFUGEES CONTINUED. PACIFISTS AND REDS FLED—I don't want to be exclusionary—but above all, *refugee* meant *Jew*. Jews spilled out of Germany and Austria, which Hitler annexed in March 1938. They besieged the closed doors of consulates, filled out paperwork till their hands contorted, not knowing that their visas had been denied in advance. They chartered death boats like the Syrians of 2015, rickety little wrecks with which to reach not Europe but Palestine. The British caught some boats and deported the passengers. Others sank into the sea. Whole scam industries sprung up to exploit these refugees. Visas to Latin America, jobs in India, fake papers in Casablanca, permissions to cross into the Soviet Union (where most travelers ended up in gulags), all available in exchange for their last stores of cash. Celebrity helped a few people find places in the West. We all know about Albert Einstein. Mostly, neither west nor east nor north nor south would take them. Three hundred thousand of the most refined, elegant, assimilated Jews that Christian Europe had ever known had been stripped of their identities, so that nothing remained but the crude facts of their lineage and the irritating urgency of their need. No one wanted them. No one ever wants a refugee. Mexico found them culturally unsuitable. Australia didn't want to "import a race problem." The United States declined a plan to take twenty thousand kids. Even the American Jewish Committee didn't want the borders opened. They were afraid it would cause more antisemitism. The next year, the poet W. H. Auden wrote "Refugee Blues."

Dreamed I saw a building with a thousand floors,
A thousand windows and a thousand doors:
Not one of them was ours, my dear, not one of them was ours.

MAREK EDELMAN

At seventeen, Marek Edelman was alone. His mother, Tsipie, had died of ulcerative colitis right after the Bund's 1937 conference. At her funeral were hundreds of poor women. They had swarmed out of the Krochmalna cellars to pay their respects to the flinty fighter who gave them the notion of a better life. Afterward, Marek went a little crazy. He was seventeen, scrawny, sullen, with the wispy mustache of a boy trying to look grown. A wretched student, he would not have graduated if it was not for the party. The Erlichs took him under their wing, with Sophia's younger son Victor tutoring Marek in Polish literature until he managed to squeak through his exams. The Bund fostered a familial sort of responsibility. They couldn't let Tsipie's son fail.

Warsaw felt smaller. Whole districts were Falanga territory. Marek didn't walk near Theater Square, especially not on Sundays, when Father Trzeciak did his sermons. Trzeciak was an admirer of Hitler who ranted about how Jews invented porn and murdered Jesus. His speeches had already inspired three knife murders. After church, Falanga boys marched with clubs in their razor-studded shin guards to put Trzeciak's teachings into practice. They only caught Marek twice, but each time, they sliced him up badly. The Falanga newspaper incited. "Jews, with the help of communism and freemasonry, murdered a hundred thousand people in Spain," read one headline from April 1938. The back pages advertised guaranteed Christian shops, so Poles could buy from Poles.

Now funded by Christian merchants' associations, anti-Jewish pickets grew in size and fury. In April 1938, there were picketers outside every single Jewish shop in Lodz. In Volkovysk, pharmacist Hugon Tyminski's followers encircled the Jewish shops on Broad Street and wouldn't permit Christians to enter. The courts charged thousands of Jews with "insulting the Polish nation." Bombs went off around the country. On May Day, a nationalist bomb exploded in the main square of Warsaw's Jewish neighborhood, minutes before the Bund's procession was scheduled to pass. Later that month, OZON published their pompously titled *Thirteen Theses on the Jewish Question*, stating that Jews were a tribe of rootless liar-thieves who needed to be forced out of jobs, universities, and public life, until the happy day when the government could finally ship them all to Palestine.

HENRYK ERLICH

Jewish political parties sought different paths to deal with Poland's spiral into fascism. The Orthodox Agudah Yisrael party counseled prayer and patience. Zionist groups proposed a united front in the form of a Jewish self-help congress. The Bund, predictably, refused. For many historians, this was another example of incomprehensible Bundist sectarianism. Here Jews were, on the edge of ruin, and the Bund, as usual, refused to play nice with their own people. Not just that. In the summer of 1938, the Bund attempted to make their own competitive Congress of Jewish Workers. The Polish government soon banned their efforts.

Henryk Erlich's father-in-law, the renowned Jewish historian Simon Dubnov, publicly scolded the Bund for their stubbornness. In Dubnov's view, the Bund had cut themselves off from the Jewish people at the very moment when they most needed to unite. In response, Erlich wrote an open letter that would become the Bund's iconic statement on Zionism.

Of course the Bund didn't cut itself off from the Jewish people, Erlich wrote. They'd fought for the Jewish people for forty years. They organized self-defense squads in tsarist Russia. They defended Mendel Biellis at his famous blood libel trial in Kyiv. In Poland, they built a vibrant counterculture with little more than love and grit, then marshaled it to protest racist violence. Of course they fought for Jews. That was why they refused to ally with Zionists.

While the Bund fought for Jews' place in Poland, the Zionists sided with a government trying to force Jews from their homes. While the Bund called protest strikes against pogroms, Ben-Gurion and Jabotinsky pranced on Polish stages, giving speeches that supported the pogromists' demand for Jews to leave. After Polish foreign minister Józef Beck said that three million Jews must be deported, Zionist leader Chaim Weizmann smiled and shook his hand.

"Zionism, in point of fact, has always been a Siamese twin of antisemitism," Erlich wrote. "Zionism has always regarded the law of force, of nationalistic action, as the normal law of history, and on this law has based its perspectives on Jewish life. In the forty years of its existence, it has always appeared lost and helpless in the presence of any victorious freedom movement. . . . The Zionists regard themselves as second-class citizens in Poland. Their aim is to be first-class citizens in Palestine and make the Arabs second-class citizens."

Erlich spelled out a fatal conflict at the heart of Zionism. The establishment of Israel would lead to perpetual war with its neighbors and the people it had dispossessed. "If a Jewish state should arise in Palestine, its spiritual climate will be: eternal fear of the external enemy (Arabs); eternal struggle for every bit of ground with the internal enemy (Arabs); and an untiring struggle for the extermination of the language and culture of the non-Hebraized Jews of Palestine. . . . Is this a climate in which freedom, democracy and progress can grow?" Erlich asked. "Indeed, is it not the climate in which reaction and chauvinism ordinarily flourish?"

From that same year, I found a faded poster advertising the Bund's candidates for the kehillah elections in Volkovysk. The writer accused Zionists of collaborating with the government campaign to drive Jews out of Poland. "We are not foreigners! We will not leave!" the flyer declared. "We will fight for our freedom, together with Polish workers and peasants! And if Zionists, left or right, try to interfere with our struggle, we will kick them off the Jewish Street!"

Here where we live is our country.

EVIAN

By 1938, over three hundred thousand Jews had fled Hitler's Germany. Inevitably, many sought safety in America. That July, President Franklin Delano Roosevelt called an international conference in the French resort town of Evian-les-Bains to figure out how the world might deal with the burden these refugees represented. Delegates from thirty-two countries attended. For nine days, they swapped business cards, ate steaks, puffed on good cigars, and toasted their own beneficence with flutes of fine champagne. They dodged and dithered. They shed crocodile tears over the three hundred thousand Jews—poor things—brutalized by fascism, and concocted excuses for why their countries could not take a single one.

The Zionist movement sent three Histadrut leaders as observers to Evian; one, named Golda Meir, would become the prime minister of Israel. The observers aimed to paint Palestine as Jews' only possible refuge. For the Histadrut's chief, David Ben-Gurion, refugees were not individuals so much as building blocks for a potential state, and if the conference offered them other places to flee, it might damage his movement. Mounting persecution didn't change his view. A few months later, after Kristallnacht, Ben-Gurion said he preferred that half of all German Jewish children take refuge in Palestine rather than all of them finding safety in England.

Ben-Gurion's concerns proved unjustified. The only country at Evian to make a concrete promise to accept refugees was the Dominican Republic, whose rapacious dictator Raphael Trujillo offered visas for a hundred thousand Jews. Trujillo needed the good press, since in the previous year he had ordered his army to machete murder twenty-five thousand Haitians in an attempted genocide. Trujillo hoped the Jews would bring money, and that their pale skin would racially whiten the Dominican people.

Evian deeply affected Golda Meir. According to historian Seth Anziska, "When she returned to Tel Aviv, Meir stepped up her campaign against British restrictions on Jewish immigration to Palestine. Jews needed a demographic majority because, as she wrote in her memoir, 'only here could Jews live as of right, rather than on sufferance, and only here could Jews be masters, not victims, of their fate.' "

As for the Bund, they viewed the refugees with characteristic internationalism. For them, mass displacement was not a Jewish issue. It affected any person of conscience who lived in a fascist state. Fascism created refugees, *Naye Folkstsaytung* knew, whether they were Jews or Reds or others. Taking a thousand or two refugees was like putting a Band-Aid on a bullet hole. As long as Hitler remained in power, millions would continue to flee.

GERMANY

That August, the Bundist Jacob Pat passed through Berlin on his way home from New York. For a Jew, this was an act of manic daring. He could easily have been arrested or killed. Pat saw a city he once loved covered with shrieking signs. JEW. JEW. ARYANS ONLY. JEW. He sat in forlorn little rooms, bare of furniture, where former grand dames of the Jewish faith lived after their fifth eviction. He learned about the terror of the concentration camps. Ruined businessmen explained the inanities of visa applications. One had an Argentine visa. It had fallen through. "My life hangs by a hair," he said. Pat also heard stories of German customers who still patronized Jewish shops. "Not all of Germany is lost," he wrote hopefully in *Naye Folkstsaytung*. "Germany isn't all Nazi. Not every German is a beast."

More anti-Jewish laws passed in Hungary, Romania, and Italy. In September, Hitler invaded Czechoslovakia's Sudetenland, a German-majority area that contained all of the country's defensive fortifications. Poland tagged along to grab a few hundred miles of borderland for themselves. Instead of helping a fellow League of Nations member, England and France pressured Czechoslovakia to cede their territory to Hitler. When the British prime minister Neville Chamberlain came back from the treaty signing at Munich, he did so with a promise: "I believe it is peace for our time." Jewish refugees poured out of Sudeten land.

The Labor and Socialist International collapsed over the Munich Pact. At the International's next congress in Brussels, French socialists supported the pact, while the British demanded that every effort be made to stop Hitler's expansion. The Czechs withdrew and expelled all Jews from their party. Erlich would undoubtably have agreed with the Brits, but he was not at the congress. The Polish government had refused him a passport.

BERNARD GOLDSTEIN

By the late thirties, Bernard Goldstein was a legend. To the tabloids, he was "ruler of a band who terrorized Warsaw," his mythos burnished with false stories about nights at the lubricious Club Adria, where he supposedly danced the tango and handed out roses to the dames. To the Krochmalna thugs, he was a role model. To the city's Jewish poor, he was a protector. To Chief Runge of the Security Police, he was a menace. Once, after cops arrested Bernard at a street fight, Runge threatened to send him to a notorious concentration camp in Kartuz Bereza.

"Who's the boss of Poland's capital?" Runge screamed. "You or me?"

Bernard sized him up. In a quiet voice he answered, "As long as you refuse to protect the Jewish people, I'll do it. If I am to get Kartuz Bereza for that, go ahead and send me there."

Runge released him.

That fall, Bernard got a tip from his Polish socialist friends that the Naras were plotting to murder Henryk Erlich. Pretending to be defendants in need of legal help, their assassins had set up an appointment with Erlich. When they showed up, they'd shoot him dead.

Erlich lived on the Polish side of town, where the Bund's militia couldn't go without attracting unnecessary attention, so Bernard arranged a gang of Polish workers to assist him. On the appointed morning, Bernard staked out Erlich's building. He stationed one group of workers at the gate, with another hidden inside the courtyard and a third in the stairwell, a half story up from Erlich's apartment, where they could jump the assassins the moment they made it to Erlich's door. The assassins showed up at ten. They were tall and arrogant, in fedoras and bespoke suits, their every step conveying their privileged lives. One rang the bell. Bernard was on them in a second. The assassins tried to back away, with flowery protestations of innocence, but the luxuriance of their elocution only increased Bernard's rage. He marched them downstairs. In the courtyard, Polish workers surrounded them. A worker pressed his revolver to an assassin's forehead, then clicked the safety off. The assassins raised their hands. The Polish workers frisked them, confiscating revolvers from their pockets.

"Give me your passports!" Bernard barked. The pair handed them over. He wrote down their names and addresses. They lived in the nicest part of town.

Bernard raised his handgun, letting them get a good look. He stared at them. His scarred face was like a mask. He spoke slowly, so they could absorb what he said. If anything happened to comrade Erlich, with or without their involvement, he would hunt them down himself and put a bullet through each of their fancy foreheads. For now, they could get the fuck out of his boss's building.

Afterward, Bernard went to breakfast. He was starving.

Later, Bernard's comrades criticized him for not killing the assassins or at least breaking their kneecaps. Bernard shrugged. At nearly fifty, he had seen enough bloodshed for ten lifetimes. He'd avoid it when he could.

ZBASZYN

No one ever wants a refugee. Refugees come in waves, like poisoned water. They are a flood, which drowns. They swarm like insects. They inundate. They swamp. They must be quarantined in camps, like lepers, but they are themselves the leprosy, the virus that rots the body politic.

The more refugees, the greater their need, the less anyone wants them.

Poland didn't want Jewish refugees, even if these refugees were its own citizens. Afraid that Germany might deport Polish Jewish residents en masse, on October 6, 1938, the Polish government announced a decree that stripped the citizenship of anyone who had lived abroad for more than five years, unless the Polish embassy stamped their passports by the end of the month. Inside Germany, Polish embassy staff declined to stamp Jews' passports.

Poland's ambassador to Germany, Józef Lipski, met with Hitler on October 21. The Führer reassured him that now that the issue of Sudetenland was settled, Germany would demand France and Britain grant it colonies of its own, to which eastern Europe could exile its Jews. "If [you] can find such a solution we shall build [you] a beautiful monument in Warsaw," Lipski responded.

On October 28, three days before the deadline set by the Polish government for Poles abroad to have their passports stamped, the Gestapo began to round up Polish Jews. They grabbed sixteen thousand people from their beds and dumped them at the border, with nothing but ten reichsmarks in their pockets and the clothes on their backs. Over the next weeks, thousands more Jews joined them. Rabbis, school kids snatched from class, Jews caught queuing in front of the Polish embassy for their special stamps. After an endless train ride to the border, guards shoved the Jews out of the carriages at bayonet point and told them to run. Machine guns sprayed them from behind. They sank up to their knees in frigid mud, crawled through barbed wire, lost their children, broke their bones. At last, they reached the Polish frontier at Zbaszyn. Though they were Polish citizens, the Polish police refused them entry.

Encircled by police, thousands of deportees camped in fields near the Zbaszyn railway station. They could not enter their country, since, as the pro-government paper *Gazeta Polska* complained, "overpopulated Poland has the largest percentage of Jews in the world and is now . . . menaced by a Jewish invasion."

For days, then weeks, then months, the deportees waited in the frozen mud of Zbaszyn. The elderly began to die.

The Bund formed a help committee. They raised funds, brought in doctors, and organized press delegations to visit the deportees. (When *Naye Folkstsaytung* reported on their conditions, the government confiscated the issues.) Tsukunft kids passed out soup and tea. It reminds me of the solidarity work that today's anarchists do with people trapped by border regimes. How many times have I watched punks hand out coffee to refugees on different continents, because that's what humans do, regardless of papers? We shouldn't have had to, of course. We are only there because of the failures of the state. The Bund shouldn't have had to either, but Poland refused to spend a zloty on these Jewish citizens. The Bund stepped into the breach to do what was needed.

Other people would also take matters into their own hands. On November 7, Herschel Grynszpan, the teenage son of two deportees trapped in Zbaszyn, talked his way into the German embassy in Paris. There, in the name of his countrymen, he shot the Nazi ambassador five times in the stomach.

KRISTALLNACHT

The night of Ambassador vom Rath's death, Nazi government unleashed a series of attacks on the Jewish population that would go down in history as *Kristallnacht,* the Night of Broken Glass. The name obfuscates the savagery of what took place. Around Germany, Austria, and Sudetenland, state-backed mobs torched hundreds of synagogues, destroyed thousands of businesses, and killed hundreds of Jews. They invaded homes, Jews' sole sanctuary from violence, dragged out Berlin hipsters and elderly Viennese professionals and, under hails of blows, forced them to clean the streets with toothbrushes. Then they raped the women. The humiliation was the point. Afterward, hundreds of Jews committed suicide. They would have left if they could have, but no country would accept them. They had nowhere on earth to go.

Germany painted Kristallnacht as a spontaneous response to the ambassador's murder, but it was choreographed by Joseph Goebbels and instigated by the SS and the Hitler Youth.

Unlike most of the Polish press, *Naye Folkstsaytung* covered "the horrifying pogrom" in detail. Readers knew about the thirty thousand Jews shipped off to concentration camps after Kristallnacht, about the one-billion-Reichsmark fine imposed on the Jewish community, and the wealthy couple in Munich who threw themselves out a window because they couldn't continue living after what they'd seen. A week after Kristallnacht, Henryk Erlich wrote an article titled "In the Darkest Night." In it, he berated the Polish nationalists who bayed like "jackals" to repeat Kristallnacht on their own soil, and the feckless Polish government, which flirted with the Nazis, oblivious to the fact that one day, they too might be a target.

SAM ROTHBORT

For Sam Rothbort, Kristallnacht gave him a terrible premonition about his hometown. He realized that his Volkovysk would not last forever. It was not waiting for his glorious homecoming, when he would pass out money and tell tall tales of Columbus's land, like returning immigrants had done throughout his childhood. More than an ocean lay between him and his birthplace. History rushed forward, and against it, art was a fragile refuge. In the late thirties, Sam Rothbort began to paint the world of his childhood. In these memory paintings, patriarchs read the torah. Grandmother circled her hands over the sabbath candles. Boys spied on the women's bathhouse. Tsarist soldiers bared their swords. These paintings showed me another Volkovysk as well, one struggling into the turbulent twentieth century, where young people raised red flags in the woods, burned down factories, beat strike breakers, and snuck across borders in the dead of night on a quixotic quest to reshape the world. I saw Itka the Bundist, a corseted girl in a crepuscular alleyway, who threw rocks through a window as if she could release the future waiting for her on the other side of the glass. Over the next decade, as his hometown's fate became clear, Sam Rothbort would paint 616 of these watercolors. It was there that I discovered the Bund.

ELECTIONS

"We struck back at every action of the Polish anti-Semites, believing that the Jews would retain their civil rights only if they showed that they could protect themselves," wrote Bernard Goldstein. At the same time, the Bund appealed for international intervention against fascism, "but our efforts were too puny to turn back the powerful forces that were pushing an indifferent and unresisting world toward a precipice." Though the Bund's appeals abroad went unheeded, their resistance earned them the loyalty of the Jewish community at home. This love shone when the municipal elections came in December 1938. The weather was icy, but when housewives saw Bundist canvassers from their windows, they ran outside with kettles and poured them steaming glasses of tea. Kids paraded down Smocza Street with red rags tied to sticks as makeshift socialist flags. To suppress the vote, the city had put the Jewish neighborhood's voting place in a rough Polish area that voters had to cross a mud pit to reach. Rumors flew about nationalist attacks, so to forestall any trouble, Bernard organized patrols, and the Bund's militiamen walked voters to the polls.

When the results came in, they were greater than the Bund could have dreamed. They had won victories in almost every major Jewish city in Poland, including sixteen out of the nineteen seats won by Jewish parties on the Warsaw city council.

As of 1938, the Bund was the most popular Jewish party in Poland.

WHEN PARLIAMENT REOPENED A few weeks after the elections, OZON representatives issued plans to divide the country's population into three tiers. Poles would be full citizens. The rights of the German and Slavic minorities would depend on their perceived loyalty. Jews would be stripped of citizenship, then expelled from the country, with their property seized to fund their deportations. OZON warned the world to make space for this newly stateless population. Otherwise, Poland would be forced to resort to "discriminatory measures" to solve what they called "the Jewish Question."

SPAIN

For the Left, calamities accumulated. In February 1939, the Spanish Republic fell to Franco's fascists. As Camus wrote later, "It was in Spain that [my generation] learned that one can be right and yet be beaten, that force can vanquish spirit, that there are times when courage is not its own recompense." Ten thousand International Brigades fighters died in the war, including the young Warsaw Bundist Beniak Livshitz. His comrades buried him in the medieval city of Lérida, under the nom de guerre of Barcelo Lorenzo.

Five hundred thousand people fled across the Pyrenees into France, where the French government locked them in concentration camps.

On March 15, Hitler invaded what was left of Czechoslovakia.

More refugees fled.

GERMANY

While Poland had okayed Hitler's annexation of Sudetenland, they were perturbed when he took over the rest of Czechoslovakia, since Germany now bordered Poland on three sides. Foreign minister Joachim von Ribbentrop took on an increasingly belligerent tone in his dealings with the Polish ambassador. Hitler demanded more concessions, including that Poland give Germany the city of Danzig, where the German minority regularly attacked Jews and Poles. On March 23, Hitler seized Memel, a Lithuanian port city that Poland regarded as its turf. Even the medal-festooned blowhards in government could see where things were headed. The army began a partial mobilization, and Poland signed a mutual defense pact with Britain to bolster the treaty it already had with France. If Hitler invaded, at least they could count on help from the two powerhouses of Western Europe.

On April 28, Hitler told the Reichstag that the Polish-German nonaggression pact was "no longer in existence." The delegates broke into thunderous applause.

PALESTINE

In the spring of 1939, one more country closed to Jewish refugees: Palestine.

After three years of war against Palestinian guerrillas, Britain had crushed the Great Palestinian Revolt with the same cruelty they used from Dublin to Delhi. They had bombed villages, tortured hostages, demolished homes, exiled leaders, and doled out the death penalty for offenses as minor as the possession of a few bullets. Historian Rashid Khalidi estimates that at least 14 percent of the adult male Palestinian population was injured, imprisoned, exiled, or killed. Britain also shaped the Haganah into a vicious counterinsurgency force. (Throughout the revolt, the illegal Irgun also bombed and shot hundreds of Palestinians.) Now that they'd defeated the Palestinian uprising, it was time for Britain to put policies in place that would prevent things from kicking off again. In May, they released the White Paper, which promised an independent Palestine within ten years and severely curtailed Jewish immigration. Britain intended for the White Paper to address the demands that had led to the Great Palestinian Revolt. It also shut the doors of Palestine to Jewish refugees from Hitler exactly when they needed the refuge most. For the Zionist movement, this was a grave betrayal. The militias that Britain armed would soon turn their guns against their benefactors.

CUBA

The same week that the Brits announced their white paper, SS *St. Louis* departed from Hamburg for Havana with a cargo of 937 Jewish refugees. Each held a landing certificate for Cuba. Five days before the ship pulled into the Havana port, forty thousand Cubans staged a rally against the refugees. A spokesman for the former Cuban president told the crowd to "fight the Jews until the last one is driven out." Only 34 passengers were permitted to disembark. The remaining 903 sent desperate supplications to the United States, but Roosevelt, eyeing his election chances, gave his regrets. Several passengers attempted suicide. The boat was forced back to Europe.

In *Naye Folkstsaytung*, Leivik Hodes wrote about the *St. Louis*, and all the other ships that wandered across the oceans filled with German Jews and antifascists whose "good Aryan blood" had been rendered null by their convictions. The ships bobbed helplessly. As long as the world refused to crush fascism, refugees would continue to flee Europe. Their ships would find no port.

POLAND

Everyone knew that war with Germany was inevitable, so the Polish government decided to rearm. To fund a new air force, they forced citizens to buy bonds. Those who resisted might be sent to concentration camps. Jews gave generously to the armament funds, but they were still smeared as misers and war profiteers in the nationalist press. The pro-government newspaper *Gazeta Polska* dismissed Jewish efforts to unite in the face of the Nazis. "The fact that our relations with the Reich are worsening does not in the least deactivate our program in the Jewish question." They threw the Bundist city councilman Leon Feiner into a concentration camp and refused to release him unless his party supported OZON's plan to ship Jews to Palestine.

Despite all this, the Bund was at its peak. In Warsaw, a hundred thousand people marched in their May Day parade. That summer, they swept the next round of municipal elections. They were now the most popular Jewish party in Vilna, Lublin, and Bialystok. Even in little Volkovysk, the Bund got three thousand votes and sent the brick factory owner Schlossberg, the activist Ravitzky, and the teacher Merkin to the city council. Morgenstern was the most popular sports club in the country. A hundred thousand workers belonged to Bundist trade unions. Hundreds of kids recuperated in Medem Sanatorium, where they learned to eat broccoli, peered into fish ponds, and acted out idealistic plays.

Eighty years later, the sanatorium director's son Victor Gilinsky could still recall flashes of that time. He was tiny, the sanatorium's mascot. He could envision the handsome counselor named Batya, who ran up a path while Victor bounced on his shoulders, terrified he would fall. Batya shouted the Bund's greeting: *Khavershaft*. Comradeship.

In Warsaw, the comedienne Ina Benita batted her eyelashes on the silver screen and the hit tango "Golden Chrysanthemums" wafted out of sweetshops. The Yiddish operetta *Shulamith* continued its sold-out run at the palatial Nowosci Theatre. "A Triumph!" wrote *Naye Folkstsaytung*. Every evening, Marek Edelman and the other young Reds gathered on Lezno Street. Communists walked on the left, Bundists on the right. Each group shouted insults at the other. Morgenstern soccer teams played friendly games in city parks. When the new forward Rubinstein scored an epic goal, the Bund's sports correspondent noted his athletic promise.

Those who could retreated to their summer cottages to hike in the forests and swim in the country's many rivers. Viktor Alter's wife took their son back to Belgium for their annual vacation. Sophia joined her father Simon Dubnov in Riga. Tsukunft and SKIF set up their summer camps in the woods outside Wloclawek, on the bank of the Vistula. The two groups used to pitch their tents separately, but racists liked to attack them when they slept, so now they kept together for safety. In July, Bernard Goldstein took a New York comrade to visit them. As their car turned onto the forest road, they saw lines of tanned young people waving red flags to greet them. Bernard felt a flush of pride. Later, as they ate around the campfire, Bernard's New York comrade told him that the summer camps in America might have been fancier, "but what you have here, we don't have." There were tears in his eyes.

On August 23, 1939, Nazi foreign minister Ribbentrop flew to Moscow, where he and the Soviet foreign minister, Vyacheslav Molotov, signed a nonaggression pact. Erlich denounced the pact in *Naye Folkstsaytung,* demanding to know how the workers in German concentration camps felt seeing the Soviets empower their persecutor. He didn't know, of course, about the secret protocol that would split Poland between the two powers, but he would find out soon enough. In response to the pact, Viktor Alter called the Polish prime minister, Felisjan Slawoj Skladkowski, to propose a unity government. The prime minister brushed him off.

The government called the Bund's office and told them to liquidate their summer camp in Wloclawek. They didn't say why, but Bernard knew it was in an area where military fortifications would be built. Sadly, he helped the campers fold up their tents. Henryk called Sophia at her father's home in Riga. The country was mobilizing. She needed to come home.

Even as the Germans readied their panzer tanks, the colonels who ran the Polish government maintained an oblivious sangfroid. Pompous military men who had spent the years since Pilsudski's death creating a cult around their army, they could hardly admit that they were woefully unprepared. They had kicked everyone's ass in the Polish-Soviet war, had they not? Their air force may have been out of date, but they had their cavalry, who had terrorized the Reds less than twenty years before. And they had iron-clad defense treaties with France and Britain. Newspapers repeated the propaganda slogan: "United, Strong and Ready!"

Despite everything that Poland had done to them, the country's three million Jews rose to new heights of loyalty. They enlisted en masse in the military, raised fortunes for the Air Force. "At the hour when the country's fate is to be decided," wrote the Bund in an August 29 proclamation, "we declare once more, in the name of the great Jewish masses, their readiness to make the supreme sacrifice, together with the entire working population of Poland." An organization founded by border-flouting revolutionaries who were critical of all national independence movements had transformed into a party of patriots.

TRENCH

Warsaw was calm, the writers at *Naye Folkstsaytung* noted in their August 30 issue, the final one to make it abroad. The government had advised the population that there was no need to horde food or arrange transport for an evacuation, so there were no longer lines at shops. The weather was lovely. Kids capered around the parks, enjoying the last days of summer. Crime continued as it always had. A railway worker found a beheaded woman's body at 26 Gorczewska Street. A fight broke out between Engineer R. and Madame Wronski over a forty-five-zloty debt. Two women committed suicide around town. Two drowned men were pulled from the Vistula. In their headquarters at 26 Dluga Street, the Bund continued its usual schedule of meetings for Tsukunft, SKIF, YAF, the trade unions, and a division for former Hasidic kids known as the Arkady Group. A children's charity at 30 Nowolipki Street ran a short-story contest for Jewish youth. Entries were due on October 15.

Most of all, *Naye Folkstsaytung* noted the digging. For the last week, thousands of Varsovians had turned up to dig defensive trenches around the city. The Bund organized brigades. Every morning, hundreds of workers marched out of each of the Bundist union locals in military formation, shovels slung over their shoulders, revolutionary ballads on their lips. The YAF women dug. The Morgenstern athletes dug. One *Naye Folkstsaytung* writer, who went by the initial Y., was amidst the throngs at the Gesia Street registration point. At last, Y. found his group, Tsukunft members in blue blouses and red scarves. When they arrived at their worksite in the Polish neighborhood, they found a mob of people already tearing up the earth. Among them Y. might have seen white-blond railway men and their sturdy wives. Criminals. Lawyers. Doctors still wearing their coats. Rabbis heading up lines of yeshiva students in sidelocks and gabardine. Even the same nationalist scum who had once sliced open their faces during battles at the university. All of them were there to dig. Here where they lived was their brutal, fucked, and beloved country, and it belonged to all of them, together. For the first time, Warsaw was united. For once, everyone knew who the enemy was.

Part Four

FIRE

1939–1948

Arthur Zygielbojm

CHAPTER 20

INVASION

(September 1, 1939–October 4, 1939)

DAY ONE

ON SEPTEMBER 1, WARSAW'S YIDDISH DAILY *HAYNT* PUBLISHED ITS FINAL issue. It ran a chess game, noted the mobilization of the British army, and let readers know what to consider when purchasing a gas mask. It also mentioned that German planes had entered Polish airspace. Another provocation.

By the time the issue was released, 1.8 million German troops had already crossed the border into Poland. Nazi bombers clouded the sky, targeting railways, and striking sixty cities at once. Panzers tore up telegraph wires, cutting military leadership off from units in the field. The Wehrmacht poured in from the north, the west, and the south, surrounding the Polish army and sending it into a desperate retreat. In *Naye Folkstsaytung*, Henryk Erlich published an appeal for "unstinting sacrifice and armed resistance," but within a day, it was clear the army would collapse.

Poland's only hope was to hold out long enough for their allies France and England to come to their aid. When the two countries declared war on Germany on September 3, Varsovians marched to the French and British embassies with tricolors and union jacks to honor their saviors. No help came.

The next evening, government ministries began to evacuate Warsaw. They burned their documents and took with them anything that might have been useful during a siege. Lines of limousines crept over the Vistula, filled with the puffed-up mediocrities who constituted Poland's ruling class. Over the next few days, OZON leaders Edward Rydz-Smigly, Józef Beck, and Adam Koc, and even Cardinal August Hlond, would all abandon the capital.

DAY TWO

The luxury shops were still open on Warsaw's grand boulevards, albeit with sandbags in the windows. Women might need evening purses, even at the end of the world. The radio broadcast a torrent of contradictions. The Nazis have arrived! The French are bombing Berlin! The mix of lies and truth only spread more panic.

The government called a press conference to announce their imminent evacuation. *Naye Folkstsaytung*'s correspondent Pinkhos Schwartz was in the audience. He immediately telephoned Henryk Erlich. That night, the Bund's central committee convened to grapple with the news.

Thousands of party activists gathered in the courtyard below *Naye Folkstsaytung*'s offices to await the central committee's decision. Most of the leaders wanted to stay. Warsaw was the largest Jewish city in Europe. How could they abandon their people? The well-heeled union leader Maurycy Orzech insisted that they needed to fight shoulder to shoulder with their comrades in the Polish Socialist Party.

But how could they fight without an army? They had no heavy weapons, just revolvers and brass knuckles. Who would follow them into battle? Voters might have chosen them for city council, but that didn't mean they'd join them in mass suicide. And when Germans bombed Warsaw in reprisal, wouldn't Poles blame the casualties on the Jews?

There was a train headed out of Warsaw, with three seats reserved for the Bund's leaders. Would it be wiser to go east, or would it be betrayal?

They talked in circles, unsure of where their responsibilities lay. The advice they got was no help. Orzech consulted with Polish Socialist Party leader Zygmunt Zaremba, who swore that his people would stay in Warsaw till the end and advised the Bund to do the same. Over at city hall, Mayor Stefan Starzynski told Alter and Erlich the opposite. As Jews and socialists, they were doubly dead when the Nazis entered the city. They should flee.

DAY THREE

The next morning, Alter and Erlich visited the Polish Socialist Party's headquarters on Warecka Street. Party secretary Kazimierz Puzak was eager to talk. A lifelong revolutionary who had survived six years of Siberian slave labor, Puzak had seen his share of trouble. He contemptuously dismissed the government's plans for a counteroffensive: a hare-brained scheme for the army to retreat to the Bug River, a hundred and fifty miles east, and restart the fight from there. "If Poland can't defend itself at the Vistula, God himself will be unable to help it at the Bug," he sneered. Unlike his friend Zaremba, Puzak realized the acute danger that the Jewish leaders faced. He urged Alter and Erlich to run.

The train's departure drew closer, but the pair refused to leave. Zaremba had called a city council meeting, and they wanted to hear him out. Erlich ordered a comrade to take his ticket.

At the central committee's final meeting, the mood was somber. After speaking with Puzak, Erlich and Alter were convinced that Warsaw would fall quickly, and that the Gestapo would consider the Bund's leadership a juicy catch. The central committee formed a plan. Top leaders would flee Warsaw, while the second tier stayed behind to reform the Bund as an underground organization, just as they had been in the days of the tsar. Alter wanted to lead this clandestine party. Having survived one world war already, he knew that escape was no guarantee of safety. "One hundred of us will leave here; after the war, perhaps ten will return. I have just as much chance of remaining alive in Warsaw," he said. Erlich insisted Alter was too famous to go underground. Reluctantly, Alter complied.

All around Warsaw, rank-and-file Bundists were making similar calculations. Should they stay or run? Around six hundred party members joined the exodus out of the capital. Others balked at the thought of abandoning their homes for the uncertainty of the road.

The sky was a perfect blue, the sort that portends disaster. Newspaper headlines screamed that the government had left Warsaw. In the Erlich apartment, the family filled their knapsacks. Henryk added an old photo of Sophia and their boys. Was it from Saint Petersburg, their long-lost capital, or Lublin, their first city of exile? Her memoirs do not say. She didn't go to her desk. All of her notes, poems, and manuscripts suddenly receded, as if into a void.

They were five people: Sophia, Henryk, their two sons, Alexander and Victor, and Alexander's wife, Shoshke. The family waited until dark, when pilots had a harder time spotting targets. At the threshold, Sophia did something that showed her experience as an itinerant revolutionary and refugee. She left the door open. She knew that, whatever happened, she would not be coming back.

The street was a human river. That night, Colonel Roman Umiastowski of the Warsaw Defense Command had ordered all military-aged men to set out for the right bank of the Vistula, where they would be mobilized into the army. It was an idiotic idea—there were no weapons there for these recruits—but the men heeded the call, as did many of their family members. Three hundred thousand people left Warsaw, on bicycles, on horseback, and on foot.

The Erlichs made their way to Praga, where the central committee had arranged for a truck to take them east. By the time they showed up, the truck had been seized by other refugees. Comrades procured a car with two empty seats for Sophia and Henryk. Sophia looked at Alexander and Shoshke. Both seemed too fragile to walk. She shoved the couple into the car. "Mama!" Alexander screamed. Her legs shook. They had to stay together, she thought. They could tolerate anything if they stayed together. She forced herself to stand still until the car drove away. Sophia and her men joined the crowds shuffling east. The footsteps on cobblestones reminded her of a funeral march.

ARTHUR ZYGIELBOJM

On September 8, just before midnight, Arthur Zygielbojm, a Bundist councilman from Lodz, arrived in Warsaw after a harrowing journey on foot. On one bucolic country road, the German bombers had strafed his group. He had been separated from his twenty-year-old son Józef in the chaos, and hoped the boy would find him later.

Though he worked in Lodz, Warsaw was the city of Zygielbojm's heart. One of a dozen children, he had been born into shtetl poverty and got his first job at age ten. His carpentry apprenticeship ended when he lost two fingers to a table saw, so he tried his luck as a glove maker. This trade sent him to Warsaw, where he reinvented himself. He cut his teeth in the labor movement and traded his humble wife for a gorgeous actress. As a writer, he found endless inspiration in Warsaw's antic streets, in the stab and jab of its municipal politics, in the lissome women he continued to chase. Now he found his beloved city shattered by bombardment, and his friends unmoored after their leaders' flight. At the offices of the Polish Socialist Party, Zygmunt Zaremba gave him an earful about the Bund's perceived desertion, then filled him in on the workers' brigades that he and his comrade Mieczyslaw "Mek" Niedzialkowski had formed to defend Warsaw.

Despite the evacuation of the government and the collapse of the army, the two men had convinced Mayor Starzynski not to surrender. The country's leaders may have abandoned them, but thanks to the Polish Socialist Party, the city would fight alone.

WORKERS' BRIGADES FOR THE DEFENSE OF WARSAW

Commanded by socialist infantry captain Marian Kenig, Zaremba's workers' brigades would lay mines, dig trenches, and fight alongside the 140,000 troops still in Warsaw. Thousands applied, even though the government provided them with little more than shovels and pickaxes.

Zygielbojm implored Zaremba to let him form Jewish battalions, but, still angry at the Bundist exodus, Zaremba refused. Instead, the Bund sent thousands of recruits to the Polish Socialist Party.

When he was not coordinating defense, Zygielbojm was at *Naye Folkstsaytung*'s offices, where the Bund published the city's last Yiddish paper. Their journalists instructed readers to dig wells and to collect broken glass to be melted into new windowpanes. In the announcements section, people inquired after laundry that fell from lines during bombardments and about relatives lost in the chaos. *Naye Folkstsaytung* ran a distribution center where fighters could request necessities; Bundists delivered them under sniper fire.

A tight little crew began to emerge: Zygielbojm, the hard-drinking bon vivant David Klin, the gentle engineer Abrasha Blum, the journalist Victor Shulman, and the refined teacher Sonia Nowogrodska, a frequent political prisoner whose husband Emanuel was fortuitously in New York when war began. These five activists would form the nucleus of an underground.

Warsaw filled with refugees, who camped out in abandoned ministries and on streets. Food grew short, and the lines at bakeries made easy targets for German planes. Sonia Nowogrodska organized a kitchen out of the Bund's headquarters at 26 Dluga Street, until a bomb hit their building. She set up a new kitchen around the corner.

Zygielbojm organized Tsukunft members into civil defense brigades. There was no water to put out fires, so they collected buckets of sand. They stood on rooftops with their little buckets, ready to smother incendiary bombs as they fell. Poles worked alongside them. Shrapnel does not distinguish on the basis of identity. In basements and on barricades, they were simply the people of Warsaw. The city became their country.

HENRYK ERLICH

Erlich's group spent nine days on the road, traversing highways jammed with the chaotic remnants of the Polish army. Nazi warplanes strafed them relentlessly. They slogged through mud, mosquitos, and sand. Their group had a single horse cart, which the group took turns riding in. Henryk refused to sit longer than his due.

Their group contained the brightest stars of the party. Viktor Alter, Bernard Goldstein, Shloyme Gilinsky, Shloyme Mendelson. Each shtetl greeted them as celebrities. Locals elbowed each other. *Can you believe it's the attorney Erlich? One of the top people in Poland! And here he is in Bereza Kartuska? In Maltsh?*

In tiny Miedzyrzec, thirty miles outside of Warsaw, the group heard that the capital had refused to surrender. Bernard Goldstein and Viktor Alter decided to turn back. The military had closed direct routes, so the pair took the long road, through Lublin. In the bombarded city, they managed to publish two issues of their newspaper before it was time to skip town. The pair decided to split up to increase their odds of reaching Warsaw. When Bernard hugged Alter goodbye, he didn't realize this was the last time he'd see his friend.

The rest of Erlich's group moved on. Their first night back on the road, the sky opened into an inferno. They ran into the woods to hide. Beyond the sparse trees they saw peasant cottages on fire. More bombs fell. They pressed themselves face down into the dirt. Union organizer Joseph Rothenberg noticed that Erlich remained standing. "An intense look had come over him. Was he concentrating on the vastness of the night, on the sky aflame with the crimson reflection of the fire?" But Erlich just told him that they had to help the peasants. He walked toward the burning cottages.

THE SIEGE

The Wehrmacht reached Warsaw's outskirts on September 15 and the city fell under siege. The next night, on the eve of Rosh Hashanah, the Luftwaffe pounded the Jewish quarter. Twenty blocks went up in flame.

The *Naye Folkstsaytung* editors moved into the office with their families. Like all of Warsaw, they were starving. Once, Sonia Nowogrodska managed to procure an onion from the soup kitchen. She divided it between four people. It was their only meal that day.

The city gasworks were shut to prevent an explosion, and electricity was cut, so Lazar Klug, head of the Jewish Printers' Union, set *Naye Folkstsaytung*'s type by hand. Every day, the crew cranked out ten thousand copies on a rotary press.

In one article, Zygielbojm described the newspaper's wartime ambience.

> The machinists work quickly, because who knows where a bomb will drop. Faster, faster. The street needs to hear the Bundist word. We work faster, with heart, and while we work, we crack jokes at Hitler's expense.
>
> Suddenly, BOOM BOOM BOOM. A bomb explodes nearby. Everything becomes still. We hide in corners . . . One of the printers gets up . . . He sings the refrain from one of Goldfaden's operettas:

Since bombs have bombldibombled
Never was there such a bomb,
Never was there such a bomb [as this].

Everyone laughs. We sing together, we set the copy, and the newspaper comes out at the appointed hour.

PINSK

On the night of September 16, the Erlichs' group reached Pinsk, a pretty little market town in the northeast. At this point, Warsaw was the sole part of western Poland not in Nazi hands. After their nearly two-hundred-fifty-mile journey, the group was beat. When they arrived at the house of the local Bund leader, they nearly collapsed on his porch. While someone went to fetch them drinks, their host turned on the radio. A voice emerged from the static. It was Vyacheslav Molotov, the Soviet minister of foreign affairs.

> It's been two weeks, and Poland has already lost all its industrial centers, most of the large cities and cultural centers. . . . The Polish state and her government have actually ceased to exist. . . .
>
> The Soviet government considers it as a sacred duty to give a helping hand to their Ukrainian and Byelorussian brothers living in Poland. . . . [and] ordered the high command of the Red Army to order troops to cross the border.

The Soviet Union was invading Poland.

COLLAPSE

Due to the German invasion, few Polish soldiers remained on the Russian border, so the Red Army entered with ease. That day, the entire national government, diplomatic corps, and military leadership abandoned Poland. An endless parade of official vehicles, including trucks filled with the country's gold reserves, crossed the little bridge into Romania. Marshal Edward Rydz-Smigly departed without even giving a final order to his army. The colonels had promised to build a blood-and-soil nation. They were now nothing more than refugees.

VOLKOVYSK

Since the war started, the mood amongst Volkovysk's Jews had been bleak. Nazi warplanes circled menacingly. The first victim had been the mother of the Bundist councilman Schlossberg; she was hiding beneath a bridge that the bombers hit. Soon, Sam Rothbort's hometown was filled with burned houses and desperate refugees.

The local nationalist leader, pharmacist Hugon Tyminski, was practically orgasmic. Poland would beat the Germans fast, Tyminski bragged. Then they'd deal with the Jews. His crew marched around with flags and patriotic hoots, smashing the windows of Jewish shops. Rumor had it that Tyminski and his friends had prepared a list of Jews to murder when the moment was ripe.

When news of the Russian invasion hit, the Polish army fled, and a mob descended on the Jewish neighborhood. They murdered seven Jews, including elderly Alexander Markov, and cheerful Itcheh, who always danced so well at weddings.

The night was long and vile. Shlomo Markus, son of the Bundist leatherworker Avram Markus, hid with his girlfriend, Nechama Schein, in a warehouse next to his father's home. From there, they might have heard the screams as Tyminski's friends plundered the Jewish neighborhood. With dawn came a miracle, at least by Shlomo and Nechama's reckoning. They heard the rumble of Soviet tanks.

Nechama would never forget her joy that day, despite everything that happened afterward. It was "as if we had conquered the world and everything in it," she later wrote. The Red Army's arrival didn't just halt Tyminski's pogrom. It promised protection from the Nazi advance. Nechama and Shlomo ran out to greet the Soviets. Nechama clambered up the tank's body to embrace the gun turret, tears streaming down her cheeks. Elsewhere in the Jewish neighborhood, Sam Rothbort's old comrade, the Bundist shoemaker Meir Zeleviansky, strode out with a Russian song on his lips. Spry as a kid, he climbed atop the Red Army tank, hugged its driver, and rode through the streets beside him, singing as if he had also fought and won. Perhaps he had, in his fashion. At sixty-some years old, Zeleviansky had seen Volkovysk change hands six times and be held by four regimes, three of which no longer existed. This time, he could support the winning side. Perhaps that's why he did what he did. He had lived long enough to know that all victories are temporary. Change is the only constant, so when one gets the chance to bring justice, they should take it.

Later that day, Volkovysk watched in astonishment as old Zeleviansky strapped a rifle to his back, walked to the pharmacy that belonged to Tyminski, and arrested its proprietor in the name of the Soviet Union. Tyminski was executed shortly afterward.

HENRYK ERLICH

It took the Red Army only a day to reach Pinsk. Locals trotted out to welcome their new bosses. There were even a few Bundists amongst the group.

Erlich's group and the rest of the Bund's central committee were still in Pinsk when the Red Army invaded. They spent the first week of the occupation locked inside a local Bundist leader's home. The inactivity galled them. Erlich was so stupefied by boredom he snuck out just to wait on breadlines. When the NKVD called a local comrade in for a friendly interrogation about the central committee, they knew it was time to leave.

The central committee decided to head for Vilna—all of them except Henryk Erlich. He chose to travel to Lublin, his hometown, which everyone believed had ended up in Soviet hands. No one could agree on why he went. His comrade Joseph Rothenberg wrote that Erlich wanted to visit his family before traveling to Vilna. His son Victor believed that his father intended to stay in Lublin, reckoning it easier to operate on familiar turf. Erlich had no illusions about his prospects under the Soviets, but his chances were still better with them than with the Nazis.

Whatever his intentions, Erlich decided to travel alone. He likely wanted to spare his family trouble. On September 30, Sophia hugged her husband goodbye at the Pinsk railway station, and he boarded a train west, toward his birthplace.

WARSAW

As September waned, Poland's capital seemed like it would hold out longer than the country.

Impatient with Warsaw's stubbornness, the Nazis redoubled their brutality. German siege guns pounded the city. Five-hundred-pound bombs fell on buildings, shattering them into an incoherence of scattered bricks. Dazed survivors poked through the wreckage. What could be salvaged? A tea kettle? A parakeet? A lover's body?

Parliament was gone. Belvedere Palace was gone. The Grand Theatre was gone. Only a single hospital still functioned. Polish socialists begged the British Labour Party for help. None came. Mayor Starzynski begged the French and British governments for help during his daily

Polish radio addresses. None came. The Paris of the East was burning, and the mermaid with the sword, the city's guardian, was nowhere to be found.

Workers' brigades tore up tramways and used the tracks to construct anti-tank barricades. When a Panzer tried to cross, the spikes flipped it upward to expose its weak underbelly, and Varsovians ran at it with Molotov cocktails fashioned with the rags of their ripped-up clothes. *Naye Folkstsaytung* shut down. Zygielbojm was on the barricades, alongside teamsters, adolescent boys, and women armed with kitchen knives.

On September 27, the end was imminent. There was no food, no water, no help. Hitler watched the battle from across the river. Mayor Starzynski and Major General Michal Tomaszewski called a meeting of every opposition party, from the Polish Socialist Party to the Endeks. They didn't think to invite the Bund, or any other representative of Poland's Jews. Together, these men created the political base of what would eventually become the Polish Home Army, the largest underground resistance force in occupied Europe. The next day Mayor Starzynski surrendered Warsaw to the Nazis. Only the Polish socialist leader Mek Niedzialkowski refused to sign. "The working class does not capitulate," he said.

HENRYK ERLICH

When the Nazis entered Warsaw, they tore through the city looking for Henryk Erlich. The Gestapo visited the *Naye Folkstsaytung* offices and the ruins of his apartment. They kidnapped other, random Henryk Erlichs on suspicion that they were him. The real Henryk Erlich was elsewhere, hidden in a safe house in the east.

Erlich never made it to Lublin, which had ended up on the Nazi side of the border. Instead, his train stopped in Brest-Litovsk, the last city in the Soviet zone. The city swarmed with Bundist refugees, and the Soviet secret police had already questioned several local leaders about Erlich's whereabouts.

When Bundist Leybetchke Berman turned up at Erlich's safe house, he was astonished at how dapper the leader looked. Erlich wore a neatly pressed blue suit, and his collar was iris white. This costume of ostentatious dignity contradicted the sadness in his eyes. Erlich paced, lighting one cigarette from the last. The claustrophobia was killing him. Except for brief nighttime walks, he couldn't leave his rooms.

The reason was obvious. Everyone knew that Viktor Alter had never made it back to Warsaw. He was in Kovel when the Soviets seized the city. Alongside a delegation of Polish socialist railway workers, Alter had presented the new authorities with a statement expressing hope that they would help Poland liberate itself from the Nazis. The Soviets arrested the entire group. With his own arrest seemingly imminent, Erlich decided his best bet would be to strike out for Bialystok, and from there to Vilna, where the rest of the central committee had fled.

Berman begged Erlich to put on rags, shave his beard, and blend in with the other refugees. Erlich refused. Hiding was beneath his dignity. Let the Soviets do what they would.

On the night of October 4, Berman and Erlich walked to the Brest-Litovsk railway station, where they hoped to catch the train to Bialystok. The station was lit like an interrogation room. Refugees crouched on the floor, chewing their last onions or picking lice out of their hair. All eyes turned to Erlich when he entered. He wore a sharp fedora and a tailored blue coat. His silver beard sparkled like betrayal. Berman went to the cashier to buy a ticket. Out of the corner of his eye, he saw a Jewish communist he knew from Warsaw walk up to Erlich, inspect his face, then disappear through a side door. Berman ran to Erlich's side.

"We have to run!" Berman whispered.

"I do not wish to run. I will not. I am not a criminal," Erlich responded.

Berman would have argued, but the look on Erlich's face shut him down. Five minutes later, the communist returned with a secret policeman and two Red Army soldiers. They led Erlich through a side door. The Bund's leader was under arrest.

Berman stayed all night in the station, hoping for Erlich's release. Occasionally, soldiers allowed him to visit his comrade in the back room. Erlich sat very straight. He smoked compulsively and answered his guards with the same cold dignity as always.

The last time Berman saw Erlich, a Red Army soldier was leading him to the bathroom, with his rifle pressed into Erlich's back. Berman noticed Erlich's unwrinkled suit, his handsome beard, the proud bearing of his head. Berman got on the next train out of the city.

CHAPTER 21

OCCUPATION

(October 1939–October 1940)

WARSAW

WHEN BERNARD GOLDSTEIN RETURNED TO WARSAW IN OCTOBER, HE could not believe the ruination. German bombs had leveled 10 percent of Warsaw's buildings and killed forty thousand of its people. Dazed survivors wandered between structures shorn of their façades. Every pane of glass was broken. The windows gaped like empty eye sockets. Walls leaned against each other for support, threatening to collapse into the dust of the Paris of the East. This was the price of resistance.

Bernard moved back into his old apartment on Nowolipie Street, where his brother was living after losing his own home during the siege. Outside, posters announced the Nazis' latest executions. Makeshift burial sites pocked city gardens. At the corners of Marszalkowska Street and Jerozolimskie Avenue, the cobblestones had been pulled up to make way for a mass grave of Warsaw's defenders, the workers who had fought beside Zaremba and Zygielbojm on the barricades. Residents blanketed it with flowers.

Immediately after they entered Warsaw, the Germans ordered Mayor Starzynski to supply twelve prominent hostages, to be shot if order broke down. Starzynski approached the Bundist councilwoman Esther Iwinska. When she put it to the party committee, Zygielbojm refused to let a woman go into Gestapo custody. He falsified Warsaw residency documents and took her place. The hostages didn't remain captive for long; the Germans released them as soon as they had secured control.

This was the last time the city stood together. The brotherhood of the siege faded quickly as Jews and Poles adjusted to their new places in the occupation hierarchy. With characteristic meticulousness, the Nazis stoked hatred between the two communities. They covered the walls with racist caricatures and filled their puppet press with stories about Jewish treachery. The Gestapo installed itself in the former Ministry of

Education on Szucha Avenue and staged spectacles where they forced Jews to strip and hand their clothes to Poles.

Many Poles appeared to approve, thought the Bundist David Klin. In fact, *Jude* seemed to be the first German word that some of his neighbors learned. "Jude!" barked the Polish kids when Jewish women lined up to get water at the Vistula. Wehrmacht soldiers pulled them from the queues by their hair. "Jude!" kids shouted at the Jews lined up for free bread on Dluga Street. The Wehrmacht clubbed the Jews with rifle butts.

Wehrmacht men strutted through ashes, hookers on their arms, their faces plump and pink. They liked to have fun. They mugged the Jews, smashed their skulls for laughs. They forced well-dressed Jewish girls to cut rabbis' beards while they took snapshots to send to their girlfriends in Munich. Why not? They were masters. The East was their playground.

On October 12, 1939, Hitler annexed Lodz and Poznan to the Reich. The rest of Poland would become a province, where half a million German "pioneers" could settle on dream plantations, served by Polish slaves. Poles of German extraction, the so-called Volksdeutsche, would have special privileges. Jews would be ghettoized in cities, starved, and murdered. This Nazi plan came straight from Western imperial projects in Africa and Asia. If, as Martinican philosopher Aimé Césaire later wrote, fascism was colonialism turned inward, then Poland would be the European ground zero for its most savage technologies of degradation, separation, and erasure.

JUDENRAT

Ten days after capitulation, the Gestapo marched into the kehillah building at 26 Grzybowska Street and arrested the interim chairman, the genteel Adam Czerniakow. Czerniakow was an engineer by trade and a lukewarm Zionist by conviction who had forgone his Palestine immigration certificate to serve Warsaw's Jewish community during the siege. After two days of torture, the Gestapo informed Czerniakow that he was now the "elder" of a mirror-world kehillah. To distinguish this institution from its predecessor, I'll use its German name: the Judenrat. Whereas the kehillah functioned as a communal charity, the Judenrat was a classic colonial device to implicate victims in their own oppression.

The Gestapo ordered Czerniakow to make a list of twenty-four Jews to serve as Judenrat members, with twenty-four more as alternates. Czerniakow requested a delegate from the Bund. Though the Bund rejected the Judenrat on principle, they had no choice but to comply. Because the Germans already knew Zygielbojm as a hostage, they decided he would be the sacrificial lamb.

THE UNDERGROUND

"The Bund decided." Even these words seem impossible. Most of their leaders had fled. The occupation banned newspapers, radios, gatherings, the very act of being outside after eight P.M. Yet, alone of all Jewish political parties, the Bund rebuilt within two weeks of Warsaw's surrender. They could do this because they came from the underground.

The men and women who founded the Bund in 1897 did so as criminals. They knew the insides of interrogation rooms, the rigors of conspiracy, the smell of bullets. Bundists hid weapons, built bombs, and fought on the barricades of the Revolution of 1905. They forged documents, incited mutinies, taped pamphlets to their bodies disguised as pregnant bellies. They assassinated cops and broke nationalists' kneecaps. When the tsar fell and the Bolsheviks booted them from Russia, the Bund relearned the lessons of the underground in Poland. This experience would serve them well.

That October, twenty Bundists met at a communal party kitchen, with bowls of soup set in front of them as alibis. Among them were Bernard Goldstein, Sonia Nowogrodska, Arthur Zygielbojm, Lazar Klug, and Abrasha Blum. They sketched out a strategy. They would build more tearooms and soup kitchens to serve as clandestine organizing hubs. They would secretly contact their prewar labor leaders, establish illegal trade unions, and set up an underground political organization. As for Bernard, he was too famous to wander the streets. He would lie low, see no one but trusted operatives, and stay locked in his apartment. Warsaw's legendary enforcer needed to disappear.

SOVIET VILNA

When Leybetchke Berman returned to Pinsk, he told Sophia Dubnova the news of her husband's arrest. The family decided to leave at once for Soviet-occupied Vilna. It was the largest city in northeast Poland, and they guessed that Henryk Erlich would wind up in its notorious Lukiskes prison. Sophia waited outside the prison with the rest of the wives, as she had during Henryk's last arrest, in 1921. When she got to the front of the queue, the dour officer refused to confirm or deny Henryk's incarceration. She quickly realized that further inquiries were dangerous.

Memory is long on the left, and the Soviet Union knew how to nurse a grudge. They had not forgotten their decades spent sparring with the Bund. They remembered how Vladimir Medem had walked out of the 1903 congress of the Russian Social Democratic Labor Party, and how Henryk Erlich led delegates out of the Smolny Institute to protest the Bolshevik seizure of power in 1917. Not to mention the obnoxious way that Mark Liber and Raphael Abramovich had tried to organize resistance to the newborn Soviet state. Even when Bundists joined the Communist Party, as many had in Ukraine during the civil war, the party never trusted them. During the purges of the 1930s, these Bundists-turned-communists ended up in mass graves.

In the first weeks of World War II, the Soviets rounded up hundreds of Bundist activists. The seventy-year-old leader Anna Rozental disappeared into Lukiskes, as did YIVO director Zalman Reisen, and every Bundist on the city council. Arrests gobbled up the Bund's leadership in Lviv. When the *Naye Folkstsaytung* writer Baruch Shefner visited Soviet-occupied Bialystok, he found buildings plastered with posters that read, DOWN WITH THE REPTILE TRAITORS OF THE POLISH SOCIALIST PARTY AND THE BUND.

The two thousand Bundists who fled into the Soviet zone learned to keep their heads down.

Borders were still fluid between the German and Soviet zones. If you had enough money, you could even leave Europe altogether, or try. Leaders sent smugglers back to Warsaw for their families. Shloyme Gilinsky's son Victor was five when his father paid a staggering price to get him and his mother out. "When we left it was sudden, after dark, in a canvas-covered truck. (I still have the pajamas I wore.) . . . It took us out of Warsaw and plunked us down on a road where we continued with horse and wagon," he told me in an email. But the Soviet zone was too dangerous for Bundists. In November, they breathed a sigh of relief when the Soviets granted Vilna to independent Lithuania. Gilinsky and, days later, his wife and son slipped over the border past Soviet guards and their howling dogs. It was a still winter night, and the guide who carried Victor told him, "Don't cough or we all die." He didn't.

In Lithuania, Bundists could focus on survival. "The sea overflowed and flooded Vilna," wrote the Bundist librarian Herman Kruk. "A place to lie down is a dream. A piece of bread is rare. A shirt—who thinks now of shirts?" The crème de la crème of Yiddish intelligentsia was crammed into classrooms and attics. Normal people were lucky for a patch of floor. In a dormitory on Sadowa Street, Zionists and Bundists fought the same ideological battles as always, if with a new wartime twist. The Bundists argued that they were not mere Jews who fled the Nazis but political refugees, like their brothers in the Polish Socialist Party, whose fate was tied to theirs. That year, they published a declaration: "Poland is our homeland, where we are entitled to equal citizenship rights, where our future lies. . . . Any other solutions offered, under present conditions, by Zionist or other Jewish groups, are wrong and utopian, as they always were."

The Bund scrambled to set up its own infrastructure. To stay with comrades, wrote Kruk, was better than "being jumbled up in a herd of faceless uprooted refugees." For money, they turned to three members whom the war had stranded in New York: Benjamin Tabachinski, Jacob Pat, and Emanuel Nowogrodski, whose wife, Sonia, helped lead the Warsaw underground. All of them now worked for the Jewish Labor Committee. The trio begged their comrades to leave Europe and even secured pricey British visas for two dozen party leaders. The leaders refused. They had abandoned Warsaw. How could they abandon the continent? From Lithuania, they could at least funnel support to their comrades under Nazi occupation.

They even managed to publish books. I own one: an anthology devoted to the recently deceased Arkady Kremer. Pati wrote the first essay. Amid reams of bland political hagiography, it stood out as an affectionate portrait of her flawed, infuriating beloved. He was not the stern man whose photo hung at party conferences. He was the friendless student in a Zavalne Street attic who had asked her with such bewitching rudeness, "Have you ever seen how poor children live?" and so embroiled her in a love triangle. Girl. Boy. Revolution.

She wrote about what happened after Arkady stepped down from leadership in 1906. She had not regretted their loss of status. For the first time since university, they were together. After years in Paris, the couple returned to Vilna in 1921, leaving their daughter, Vera, to her bohemian paradise. Arkady taught math for the TSYSHO schools. He never learned good Yiddish, and his students mocked his Russian accent. She wrote about his final illness, when old men whom he had radicalized back in tsarist times came over to argue politics, and he asked, "Why me? Do they think I'm something special?"

Pati had remained in Vilna after her husband's death. In the winter of 1939, she was seventy-two. Her health was shot, and her heart broken by her comrades' arrests, but she remained a revolutionary. She wrote to the Bundist pioneer John Mill in New York, "I believe that our holy idea will triumph, and I will remain faithful to my final breath."

WARSAW

Before they got started on the Jews in earnest, the Nazis murdered the Polish elite. In the first months of the occupation, Nazis killed forty-three thousand Poles, including doctors, priests, scholars, military men, and socialist politicians. The Gestapo arrested the Polish socialist leader Mek Niedzialkowski and hauled him in front of SS boss Heinrich Himmler for interrogation. The veteran radical looked over his glasses and said, "From you, I neither want nor demand anything. With you, I fight."

The Nazis wanted to remold Poles into obedient and stupid servants, unable to add numbers larger than five hundred. They shuttered all education institutions beyond tenth grade, banned Poles from libraries, burned Polish classics, and forbade the orchestras to play Chopin. They shipped thousands of Polish men to the Reich as slaves. Still, *The New York Times*'s anonymous German correspondent tried to strike a chipper note. "Today, Poland's society is dancing once more with undeniable grace and chic on the parquet floor," he wrote. Only the eight P.M. curfew marred the fun.

The correspondent said little about Warsaw's Jews, except that they were treated better there than in the provinces. He didn't note the cavalcade of humiliations.

Jew, you do not live in this nice apartment anymore. It's ours. You do not work for Christian firms. You do not work in slaughterhouses. You do not work in textiles. Your bank account is frozen. You ride in the yellow streetcar. You don't ride any streetcars. You walk in the gutter. You learn your place.

You will not eat from the soup kitchens. You will not take from breadlines. Our aid is for Aryans only. At Zygielbojm's urging, Mayor Starzynski protested this discrimination. On October 27, the Gestapo dragged him to their headquarters at Szucha Street. He was never seen again.

Jew, you will work for the Reich. We will make you productive, parasite. We will civilize you. Teach you what labor means. Patrols seized men and women off the streets to fill in the trenches by hand, to move stolen furniture, to bury the bodies of resistance members shot beside the ruined Parliament. Zygielbojm saw them at the Judenrat building afterward, "covered with mud and blood, their hands torn and bleeding, faces pale, breaking under the strain of witnessing the daily executions."

When Zygielbojm arrived at the Judenrat, a dead body often lay in the entrance—a poor Jew whose relatives could not afford the burial fee.

To survive, Jews depended on the same mutual aid societies that had helped them weather other repressive regimes. The richest of these was the Joint Distribution Committee, or Joint, an American funded charity that provided sixty thousand meals a day in Warsaw and worked hand in glove with the underground. Many activists got cover jobs with the Joint, including Bundists Sonia Nowogrodska and David Klin. The Bund ran their own mutual aid network out of the party's soup kitchens, which gave six hundred of their members meal tickets, financial support, and home employment.

Warsaw housing blocks turned themselves into mini societies. Building councils collected supplies for people sent to labor camps, set up poetry readings and children's play groups, took up food collections, and funded it all with voluntary taxes and benefit soirées.

With most workplaces shut, peddlers filled the streets. Fear of labor roundups kept Jewish adults inside, so they sent their children to sell black bread and onion, cookies baked from God knows what, hand-rolled cigarettes, and carbide lamps, indispensable since the power was out. Germans beat the kids, but they were nervy and had strong legs. They evaded the occupiers to provide for their families.

Zygielbojm watched one teenage soap-seller in Saxon Gardens. After Germans swiped her stock, she ran after them, shouting that she had a sick mother and a father killed by their bombs. Though they slapped her face and called her a kike, she kept chasing them, clawing at their uniforms, screaming at them to give her what belonged to her. One German punched her. She crumpled into the mud. When she got up, her lips were pressed together in a tight line. A trickle of blood ran down her chin.

"You only live once," she shouted in Polish. She slapped one German hard across the face. She kept fighting all the way to the Gestapo headquarters.

Naye Folkstsaytung was no more, of course. The Germans had seized their press, along with all the others in the city. But some farsighted Bundist had hidden a mimeograph machine in a party member's home on 67 Mila Street.

Marek Edelman worked the machine. He printed all night by a sputtering carbide lamp, running the paper between ink-coated cylinders, cursing the cramps in his hand. He ran off handbills in Yiddish and Polish by anonymous authors and handed them to girls he knew only by nickname, to be distributed throughout the country. That November, he would print the first issue of a new monthly newspaper. It spoke about Nazi repressions of Jews and of Poles, and about the socialist and democratic Europe that would come after the present nightmare.

ARTHUR ZYGIELBOJM

At the end of October, a Gestapo lieutenant stormed into the Judenrat building and ordered Adam Czerniakow, the reluctant "elder" of the

Judenrat, to assemble the members and their alternates in thirty minutes, on pain of death.

The Gestapo officer's jackboots shone, as did his vulpine smile. He lined the men in rows.

In front of a film crew brought in to document the moment, the Gestapo officer gestured at a map of Warsaw and announced that the city's 360,000 Jewish residents would be shoved into an area of the city smaller than New York's Central Park. The Judenrat had three days to execute this order. If they didn't, the alternates would be shot. The Gestapo led the twenty-four alternates into trucks, leaving the Judenrat alone.

The Bund's delegate to the Judenrat, Arthur Zygielbojm, stared at the paintings of the rabbis that decorated the conference room. These generations of wise men had no wisdom for the moment. Instead, he drew inspiration from his party's rebel past.

They couldn't go into a ghetto, Zygielbojm said. What would their people think? How could they face their kids? The men in that room were leaders. They needed to reject the Gestapo's order, whatever the consequences.

Terrified of collective punishment, the Judenrat refused to listen.

Rumor of the ghetto spread. By Monday, ten thousand desperate people had converged on the Judenrat. Zygielbojm went out to meet them. Two Bundists lifted him on their shoulders so he could address the crowd. He told the Jews to keep their heads up, refuse the order, and to resist, with their bare hands if necessary, anyone who tried to drag them from their homes. There was scattered applause, but also terror. Wouldn't this make things worse?

Afterward, Zygielbojm resigned from the Judenrat. He knew exactly what this meant. Yet he felt a strange sort of calm, one that he had felt since the Wehrmacht marched into Warsaw. "It is the total readiness to die which provides you with the indomitable strength to fight for life," he later wrote.

REFUGEES

Intra-German squabbles postponed the construction of Warsaw's ghetto, but each day, ghetto logic strangled the city's Jews. Stars marked the shops. Stars marked the arms. At first, some Poles showed support for Jews forced to wear armbands, but after a hellish winter, sympathy faded. Poles averted their eyes when their Jewish neighbors passed. They had their own problems.

At the start of November, two young men arrived at the Warsaw Judenrat from the tiny town of Sierpc. Their clothing was torn and bloodstained, and their faces taut with horror. They described how a militia of local Volksdeutsche had herded Sierpc's 1,700 Jews into the town square, forced them to strip, and savagely beat them, all while they ordered the Polish fireman's band to play a cheerful march. Robbed, tortured, crammed into airless trucks, and taken to the small town of Kutno, Sierpc's Jews were now being forcibly marched to Warsaw. The two young men had barely managed to escape.

Over the next months, seventy-eight thousand Jews arrived in Warsaw from the parts of Poland annexed to the Reich. They were driven out of their towns with nothing after mass rape, after relatives were burned alive in town squares, and after the theft of their last possessions. Hundreds of refugees walked from Lodz with their kids strapped to their backs and their fingers lost to frostbite. Zygielbojm met a Bundist woman who had been detained with her children in a concentration camp on Lodz's outskirts. Hundreds of women were "ordered to undress naked, perform calisthenics for the amusement of the German soldiers who brutally kicked and beat them. On the pretext of searching for hidden jewels, the women were sexually molested," he wrote. These internal refugees had been workers, intellectuals, shopkeepers, but in Warsaw, they had and were nothing. The Bund organized their displaced members by city, found them places to sleep, to launder their rags, to eat watery soup, to remember who they had been.

ARTHUR ZYGIELBOJM

Since he'd quit the Judenrat, Zygielbojm had lived an excruciating half existence. "The water began to boil and every minute the threat of catastrophe hung in the air," he later wrote. Death seemed to follow him. One afternoon, he dropped off a message for a Polish socialist comrade at a homeless shelter. The Gestapo arrested his comrade the next day. Zygielbojm blamed himself. He was too well-known to leave Warsaw illegally. He'd be caught, along with his helpers. At last, salvation came in the form of a corrupt Dutch consul who, for a hefty bribe, provided Zygielbojm with a visa. For protection, a Polish socialist worker would shadow him on his perilous journey out of Poland. From there, he would travel through Germany and onward to the Netherlands.

On his last night in Warsaw, Zygielbojm's friends threw him a farewell party at David Klin's apartment. One miraculously produced herring, another a bottle of wine. It could have been one of their prewar soirées. They stayed up all night evaluating the calamity that had befallen their country. Klin typed up six copies of their conclusions. Three would be smuggled abroad and three hidden in Poland, to be unearthed later. Before Zygielbojm left, Bernard embraced him. "So, my friend, tomorrow you'll be on your way. You're a lucky man and I'm certain you'll make it," he said. He told Zygielbojm not to forget them. At the doorstep, Zygielbojm realized he had no pen. Klin handed him his luxurious Pelikan fountain pen. A gift for the road.

JACOB CELEMENSKI

The Nazis divided Warsaw into zones for Poles, Jews, and German overlords, with the fanciest quarters their exclusive preserve. They forced Jews into sadistic labor camps from which they would return disabled and broken.

Nazis forbade most Jews to ride trains, so cities became islands. To communicate, the Bund used couriers. Since a man's status as a Jew could be revealed by pulling down his pants, most couriers were young women with light hair and button noses that let them pass as Poles. These couriers were born actresses, steel-tempered and cucumber cool. On smuggling missions, Klara Zachariasz of Tomaszow donned a swastika armband and flirtatiously asked Wehrmacht soldiers to carry her suitcases full of contraband. These exploits became legends.

One of the Bund's rare male couriers was the tailor Jacob Celemenski, whose brutish blond looks provoked a friend to tell him, "You not only look like a goy but also an antisemitic goy." He arrived in Warsaw in February 1940 to report on conditions in Krakow. Sitting in Bernard Goldstein's shabby quarters, he listened to the leaders explain their methods for organizing under the Nazi occupation. Bundists operated in five-member cells. Members of one cell would not know any details about other cells, in order to prevent them from disclosing information under torture. Each member swore loyalty to the death. Through an illegal radio transmitter, the Bund received foreign broadcasts, which they disseminated in their underground press. They set up what they called a socialist Red Cross to provide medical help, find safe houses, and aid comrades in concentration camps. Money from New York Bundists arrived sporadically through Vilna; the Gestapo caught two of the four couriers who made the trip. They also moved money through the hawala system, a means of transfer still used in war zones today. Someone in Warsaw would give the Bund a hundred dollars, after which the Bund's foreign committee would give a hundred dollars to the depositor's cousin in New York.

When the Nazis banned Jews from education, the Bund organized an expansive underground school system. They ran youth groups, choirs, sports. After the Nazis sealed their Bronislaw Grosser Library, Bundists tunneled into the building through an adjoining cellar and rescued the books. They organized secret lending libraries in members' apartments. Their representatives showed up in ransacked houses to tell the survivors to endure.

They even reopened the Medem Sanatorium. The sanatorium's children had been sent home at the start of the war, and the director, Shloyme Gilinsky, fled east with his family. When the Nazis invaded Miedzeszyn, they let Polish locals loot the buildings. The locals stripped it down to the windowpanes. The sanatorium's new director, Shloyme Abramson, swept up the broken glass and gathered the remaining teachers, and by November the sanatorium was back in business. Soon, it cared for two hundred orphans.

THE POLES

Through it all, the Bund remained close with the Polish Socialist Party. These bonds, born in street fights and prison cells, were now nurtured in safe houses where leaders of the two parties gave speeches garlanded with the phrases "joint struggle," "socialism," and "solidarity," and in the joint escapades, like Zygielbojm's flight from Poland.

The Polish Socialist Party was the only political group to tackle their own country's antisemitism. In one May Day proclamation, they swore that "the new Poland must repair the mistakes of the past. . . . The ordeals of the Jewish people of which we are the daily witness must teach us how to live in harmony with those who suffer the persecution of a common enemy."

Their words were a balm compared to the actions of other strata of society. In Warsaw, what had started as individual attacks grew into mass pogroms. At regular intervals, hundreds of Poles would invade Warsaw's Jewish neighborhood with crowbars and even guns, chant "Long live Poland without Jews," and bludgeon every person in their path. The German occupiers looked on with amusement. Jewish workers fought back, but they were no match for armed mobs reinforced by the Wehrmacht. Other Poles seldom intervened in the attacks. Where was the church? Silent. The Polish underground press sometimes warned Poles not to help in Nazi persecutions, but that was it. In Jewish memoirs of the time, I find stories of decency, of peasants who offered bread to deportees, of the Polish woman who warned Zygielbojm to "cover up [your star], sir, a pig is coming this way," when a Nazi approached, but these were exceptions.

GOOD FRIDAY

On March 22, a glittering, frosty Good Friday, the Nazis organized a tour de force of violence. They paid poor Polish youth four zlotys a day to storm Jewish Warsaw, cracking bones, breaking glass, and snatching whatever valuables they could. German cameramen documented the destruction.

After the pogrom stretched into a second day, then a third, men belonging to Bundist labor unions besieged the party's soup kitchens with demands to defend their neighborhoods. The Bund convened an emergency meeting in Bernard Goldstein's apartment to make a plan. They didn't want to provoke reprisals by killing the pogromists, so they armed themselves with pipes and brass knuckles rather than knives and guns. Teamsters, water carriers, coalmen, and slaughterhouse workers formed battle squads around the city. When the pogromists came, they were ready.

The battle lasted for hours, spilling from one neighborhood to the next, as Jewish workers and some Polish socialists joined in. Ambulances hauled the bloody pogromists away. Injured Jews had their wounds sewn up in private apartments.

The next day, the Germans called off the pogrom.

Later, the Bund would realize that the Nazis had staged the Good Friday pogrom with documentation as their primary purpose. When the images ran in Munich cinemas and glossy Berlin magazines, viewers would see three things. Subhuman Jews. Savage Poles. Civilized Germans, beneficently keeping the peace.

This propaganda only worked because enough Poles were willing to play their parts. After all, "Long live Poland without Jews!" was not a German chant. It came from the Nara boys whom Bundists once fought in Saxon Gardens. The Bund realized that racism was a fault line to be exploited by the occupier. "So-called Polish antisemitism is a betrayal of Poland, because it places a weapon in the hands of [the] enemies, because it permits the Nazis to execrate, besmirch and harm the coming Free and Just Poland," wrote the Bundist press. Again, they were Cassandras.

WALLS

In March, the Gestapo summoned the Judenrat chairman Czerniakow with a demand that the Judenrat pay for walls to encircle Warsaw's Jewish neighborhood. Protection from savage Poles, the officer said. The

Gestapo told the Poles the walls would protect them from typhus-spreading Jews. Twenty walls had gone up by June. They were eight feet high, topped with barbed wire, and coated with broken glass.

BRUSSELS

In April, Arthur Zygielbojm arrived in Brussels after a death-defying trip through the Reich. As a parting gift, in Aachen, by the Belgian border, the Gestapo whipped him for two hours straight. Worse than the torture, he had seen how average Germans—the wholesome teen boy, the buxom chick he flirted with—relished his country's destruction. He was rotten with hate. On April 6, in Brussels at the last futile meeting of the Labor and Socialist International, he calmly presented facts about the life of Jews in Poland. Though his words shocked the delegates, they did nothing but approve an anodyne May Day resolution, constructed to offend no one.

A few weeks later, the Nazis invaded Belgium. Zygielbojm fled across the border into France.

FRANCE

Hitler didn't stop at Belgium. The panzers that broke Poland now rolled over the Weygand Line, then the Somme. "When Paris ends the world ends," wrote the dissident Russian revolutionary Victor Serge, but cherry blossoms still sprinkled the Rive Gauche.

Like Victor Serge, the Bundists fled the German advance. They were used to exile. Here where I live is my country, they once said, but after five displacements, home just meant the ground beneath their feet. The Bund's stalwart archivist Franz Kursky packed his precious papers into twenty crates and tried to find a truck to take them south. When none came, he hid the crates as best he could and joined Raphael Abramovich, Arthur Zygielbojm, and the rest on the blasted road to the unoccupied zone.

They crowded into Marseilles. The Mediterranean port was now a massive encampment, with refugees shoved together in flophouses, abandoned buildings, in front of consulates where they begged for visas out of Europe. In this scramble for survival, Victor Serge noted that "we former revolutionaries are utterly beaten . . . and among us a squalid battle is beginning for places on the last lifeboat from the sinking ship." Political parties that once fought to change the world were now only useful as a means to help their members escape the continent. Hannah Arendt, Marc Chagall, Claude Lévi-Strauss, André Breton, and other art stars had a network run by American journalist Varian Fry to get them out. The leaders of defeated socialist movements, like the Spanish Republicans, the German social democrats, the Italian Anti-Fascists, and the Russian Mensheviks, all turned to the Jewish Labor Committee.

Back in New York, Nowogrodski and American Federation of Labor president William Green drew up lists of hundreds of socialist refugees and their families and presented these names to the immigration authorities to request emergency visas. The authorities dallied. The assistant secretary of state, Breckinridge Long, had little affection for refugees. A scion of confederate aristocracy and an admirer of *Mein Kampf*, Long took pride in making sure immigration quotas remained unfilled. He reflected popular sentiment. Americans didn't want Europe's trash. Father Coughlin demonized Jews on the radio. Members of the Christian Front beat them on the New York streets. In Congress, one Southern senator bellowed, "No living nation need permit its own conquest by unselected immigrants." Afraid of backlash, even American Jewish groups didn't ask for the immigration quotas to be lifted but instead lobbied for Jews to be permitted into Palestine, which neither Brits nor Palestinians would tolerate. Open borders might have saved the Jews of Europe, but they were not on offer, by anyone, anywhere on earth.

To learn how the Jewish Labor Committee fought their way through immigration bureaucracy, I sat for days in their archives at New York University and twirled the bobbins of microfiche like a wicked witch at her spinning wheel. On these slides, desperate telegrams appeared, begging for help for this old socialist stranded in Geneva, that stateless journalist trapped in a concentration camp in Gurs. For someone's mother. Someone's brother. Someone's wife.

My son. Stop. My friend. Stop. Karl Kautsky's widow. Stop. Not a communist. Stop. Name misspelled on visa. Stop. Uncle Pat. Stop. Abramovich. Stop.

Picture Raphael Abramovich as he was then, a small, gray man in Hotel Regina in Toulouse, surrounded by the remnants of his party. He had lost his revolution, then his country, then his oldest son to Stalin, but he could still argue in four languages about all the ways the leftist dream had gone so wrong. He was the Jewish Labor Committee's conduit to Mensheviks and Bundists in southern France. He stood on the endless lines at consulates, and rejected French comrades' prognostications of future victory with a cynicism he had learned from his own fugitive youth. At last, the visas came. The Jewish Labor Committee wired Abramovich five thousand dollars. Soon he and the rest of his comrades were crossing the Pyrenees on foot, lugging suitcases and scamming border guards, perhaps passing Walter Benjamin on the way. Then they were in Lisbon—he, Franz Kursky, Arthur Zygielbojm, and all the rest. Then they were on ships to New York.

SAM ROTHBORT

What of those who stayed? My mother takes another note from her shoebox, written to Sam in the swooping hand of his gallerist David Caz-Delbo. "My dear Sam Renoir," it begins, "I am in perfected agony. I am trying to paint but my thoughts are always with my family [in France and Poland]. . . . I am avoiding people and remain most of the time in my room or wandering in the park. . . . Let us hope that better times will come, and I will be able to see before I die my family."

The page is mottled with tears.

CHIUNE SUGIHARA

While Nazi Germany was invading France, the Soviet Union invaded Lithuania. After the Red Army took Vilna, Chaim Fizshitz, former head of the Bundist emigration bureau in Warsaw, presented the Soviets with a list of his comrades in need of exit visas. They threw him in the gulag. Other Bundists adopted fake names and hid themselves in the countryside, or in Kovno, where they were less likely to be recognized. Sophia and her sons split up to increase their chances of survival.

"Our only hope will lie in the frail web of understanding of one person for the pain of another," wrote the American novelist John Dos Passos, at the end of 1940, about the plight of refugees. This understanding struck the Japanese vice consul to Lithuania, Chiune Sugihara, in June of that year, when he looked out his embassy window in Kaunas to see it surrounded by mobs of Jews. A week before, the Dutch honorary consul Jan Zwartendijk had started to grant Dutch yeshiva students visas to the colony of Curaçao. Soon, rumors of the miraculous Dutch visas spread to both Bundists and ordinary Jewish refugees. The island was never their intended destination. The visas were in fact a ruse to enable their bearers to travel to Vladivostok, on the far eastern edge of Soviet territory, just across the sea from Japan. They would figure things out from there. After they had obtained their visas from Zwartendijk, refugees crowded in front of Sugihara's consulate in pursuit of Japanese transit visas, the final slips of paper that would allow them to escape the continent.

A career diplomat and expert on Russian affairs, Sugihara had little in common with the crowds outside his office. He didn't need it. He saw people desperate enough to kiss his shoes, and he decided that he didn't give a damn about his bosses in Tokyo. Ignoring requirements that he only grant visas to people with money, Sugihara calligraphed forms for twenty hours a day while his wife iced his arm so he could keep going. When the Japanese embassy closed three weeks later, he had produced papers for nearly three thousand people. Two hundred and fifty of them were Bundists, including Sophia Dubnova and her family.

Armed with false papers and dodgy visas, the Erlichs crossed into Russian territory. They were about to put to test a proposition tried by the Malian ruler Mansa Muhammad ibn Gao seven hundred years prior, when he set sail for the edge of the map to find out once and for all if the earth was round or flat. If the world was flat, then your way was barred. But if it was round, then you needed only to walk in the opposite direction to the one you had intended. Look neither right nor left. Let nothing stop you. Eventually, you would arrive wherever you wanted to go.

GAZA

As I write this passage I exchange text messages with my friend J. in Gaza. I worked with him nine years ago, when I reported from the besieged strip, and we kept in touch. Then came October 7 and the Israeli invasion that turned Gaza into a charnel house. J.'s father-in-law died because the blockade kept out his meds. J. lives with thirteen family members in a tent in Khan Yunis. Whenever he leaves a voice note, I hear the drones in the background.

My friends and I tried to help J. leave. For a while, the only way out of Gaza was to pay five thousand dollars a person to get on a list run by businessmen tied with Egyptian security. Impossibly, we raised the money. Some came from Victor Gilinsky, son of Medem Sanatorium director Shloyme Gilinsky, whom the Jewish Labor Committee bribed out of Europe back in 1941.

My inbox is full of requests from Gaza. "My name is X. I beg you, help us." There are too many to answer. Each is a universe of need, created by a state that claims the Holocaust as its justification. Two million people cannot crowdfund their way out of a killing cage, any more than the Jewish Labor Committee could pay enough bribes to save the Jews of Poland. It all comes down to who has motivated friends in wealthy countries. And often, even that isn't enough.

We raised the money. We brought the unmarked bills to Cairo, to give to J.'s relative. Then Israel invaded Rafah, sealing the border. J.'s family could not get out.

GHETTO

On October 12, Yom Kippur, loudspeakers announced the creation of a ghetto in Warsaw's Jewish neighborhood. The 113,000 Poles who lived in the neighborhood would leave their homes, as would 138,000 Jews and Christians of Jewish ancestry who lived outside it.

Most Poles didn't resist the ghetto but instead fought to tighten its boundaries and get more land for themselves. Priests and businessmen bickered over every street. A tumult of real estate swaps began, as rich Jews who lived outside the ghetto tried to exchange properties with poor Poles who lived within it.

Not every Polish group fell into this frenzy. After the announcement, the Polish Socialist Party's underground press wrote, "The burden of all wars and subjugation forever falls on the working man, regardless of nationality. How degradingly cynical is the fact that the walls of the ghetto being raised by Polish and Jewish laborers . . . are meant to become a barrier between them, as if different fates awaited them."

This was an idealistic statement, full of the sort of humanistic solidarity that both the Bund and the Polish Socialist Party excelled at. What followed would put it to the test.

CHAPTER 22

DIVIDED CITY

(October 1940–June 1941)

RAIN POUNDED WARSAW FOR THE LAST TWO WEEKS OF OCTOBER AS the Jews dragged the remnants of their lives into the ghetto. Weary convoys hauled their possessions from as far away as Praga. They herded shrieking kids, pushed their elderly parents in wheelbarrows, guided scrawny cows. Nurses carried their patients on stretchers; some died on the way. The Bund tried to cope. On Smocza Street, they set up a refreshment stand. They grabbed every wheeled conveyance they could and helped. Their militiamen protected the displaced.

For a few weeks, the Germans permitted Jews to go to their jobs and shops in other neighborhoods, until, on November 15, they locked the gates. From then on, there would be two Warsaws—the Aryan side, where life continued as it had since the occupation began, and the ghetto, a teeming microcosm of humanity in extremis.

"In its unfinished chain of crimes and atrocities committed in our country, the Hitlerite occupiers have added a new link: the living body of the Polish capital has been cut up by a shameful wall," wrote the Polish Socialist Party in their underground newspaper. For the brief time that the ghetto stayed open to visitors, hundreds of Poles arrived with food parcels for their friends. "The astounded gendarmes saw Aryans and arm-band wearers kissing each other at exit points," wrote sociologist and ghetto inmate Emanuel Ringelblum.

For other Poles, the ghetto fulfilled a cherished dream. At long last, they had Warsaw without Jews. "All houses vacated by Jews were immediately locked by the Germans and then, with all their contents, gratuitously given to Polish merchants and hucksters," wrote Marek Edelman.

HERITAGE TOURISM

The Nazis set most ghettos in towns' traditional Jewish neighborhoods. For this reason, when a Jewish traveler looks for her heritage in Eastern

Europe, she will by and large be walking through the places where her ancestors waited to be killed. This sets a certain tone for the trip.

Sometimes a ghetto will have been erased altogether, burned by its inmates, as it was in Bialystok, its old birzhes and synagogues now dumpster-filled alleyways behind Soviet apartment blocks. Sometimes, as in Krakow, it will be preserved in forensic detail, with a touristy Jewish restaurant and an antique store whose stock of Yiddish-inscribed baubles is enough to send a shudder down an observant shopper's spine. (I felt the same in Jaffa's souk, which Zionist militias ethnically cleansed of its Palestinian inhabitants in 1948—but I digress.)

In 2022, I spent six weeks traveling through the Bund's stomping grounds. I wanted to see how these activists lived. Instead, I felt only the heaviness of their murders. The cities, with their new names and strident nationalisms, had been cleansed of us so thoroughly that we only exist on commemorative plaques. In Eastern Europe I saw four things. A thousand-year civilization could be ended. It was irreversible. The place belonged to the grandchildren of the people who helped do it. It wasn't the grandchildren's fault. I sat in Ukraine with a new friend and told her how it disturbed me when I learned that Lviv had been one-third Jewish before World War II. "Things change," she responded kindly. Indeed, they do.

THE OTHER CITY

The Warsaw ghetto was fixed in the heart of the Jewish city, but with parts amputated. Neither the Gesia Cemetery nor the Grand Synagogue nor the Mirowska Square market made it within the walls. There were no gardens in the ghetto, hardly even a tree. What remained was half a million souls crushed together. There were more Jews in the ghetto than there were in Palestine.

People slept everywhere, in corners, hallways, cellars, curbs. The streets were so crowded it took an hour to walk five blocks. You shoved through peddlers, scammers, and feral skeletons who would snatch the bread out of your hands and eat it even while the crowd showered them in blows. The horses had all been slaughtered, so former professionals yoked themselves to rickshaws. *Riksha* in Yiddish.

Despite all manner of degradation, humans stubbornly resist their own erasure. They refuse the role that fascists have written for them. They mock their oppressors. They create and love.

There was high culture in the ghetto. Eighty members of the Warsaw Philharmonic and the Polish Radio Symphony Orchestra were ghetto inmates, as were the performers of the legendary Yiddish Art

Theatre. Grand concerts played in the old movie hall. There were art exhibits, and there was Hamlet.

There was mutual aid, from Aleynhilf, the Jewish self-help committee whose soup kitchens kept people from starvation, from the Joint, and from the thousand building committees that had emerged during the siege and now were the bedrock of hyperlocal organization. The Germans planned a population density of seven to a room, so each tenement became a universe. In the courtyards, the committees threw concerts to raise money for the families of men taken to labor camps. They might follow up with vaudeville, a clothing collection, a public meeting, or a lecture on I. L. Peretz. Marek Edelman watched his Tsukunft comrade, the gorgeous Pola Lipszyc, sing for the kids in a Krochmalna Street courtyard. "We'll do everything to make the world happy."

There was God. Underground synagogues, yeshivas, even a kosher butcher, as well as a church for Catholics of Jewish descent, tended to by one Father Godlewski.

There were quarrels. Squabbles. Beefs. You'd be the same if you were shoved cheek by jowl with your enemies. All the old battles continued. Competitive Yiddish and Hebrew cultural organizations fought over language politics. Following the party line from Hitler-allied Moscow, Jewish communists celebrated the fall of France as a victory over capitalism. The Orthodox pestered soup kitchens to keep kosher. The Bundists and the Zionists insulted each other in whatever mediums they had.

People got pleasure where they could. Brothels and pastry shops, yes, but also the lounge chairs that entrepreneurs dragged into a patch of sunlight, where girls could work on their tans. "Every dance is a protest against the occupier," wrote the sociologist Emanuel Ringelblum. "The mania for parties exceeds all limits. People say that every morning [at dawn] they see people going home from the dance halls . . . with balloons in their hands, half-drunk, singing in the street like in the good old days before the war."

There was the pretense of self-government, in the form of the Judenrat, which would administer the ghetto for their Nazi bosses. The Germans didn't use the word *ghetto* at first. They called it the Jewish "quarter," like the German or Polish "quarter," as if this quasi concentration camp was merely a neighborhood like any other. With typical perversion, the Nazis framed it as a gift. Walls equaled protection, they said. The Judenrat equaled autonomy. Its chairman, Adam Czerniakow, was now rebranded as a "mayor."

To enforce their dictates, the Germans created the Jewish Police Service. Each cop had nothing but a starred hat and a rubber truncheon, but membership in the force meant exemption from forced labor, so rich boys flocked to join. Their "chief" was a Catholic convert named Jozef Szerynski, who had been a colonel in the prewar force. The Jewish Police even had their own prison on Gesia Street. The Bund forbade its members from joining.

There were even tourists—buses full of gawping Wehrmacht soldiers, officers in onyx Mercedes—all keen to see the *untermenschen* up close. "Occasionally a young officer would pull out his revolver and shoot into the crowd. How amusing these scampering Jews were," wrote the famed hematologist Ludwik Hirszfeld, himself a ghetto inmate.

The ghetto quickly grew its own culture, a lexicon of songs, slang, jokes, and insults, all of them meticulously chronicled by Emanuel Ringelblum and his fellow scholars of the Oneg Shabbat archive, their attempt to create an anthropology of the apocalypse.

Ringelblum was a Zionist, so when he invited the Bund to contribute to his Oneg Shabbat project, they refused, citing ideological incompatibility. Instead, the Bund compiled their own archives to document Nazi crimes and their party's resistance and hid them in an apartment on Swietokrzyska Street. These archives have never been found.

BORDERS

The ghetto would never be sealed. Nazi aspirations didn't matter. Nor did the layers of German, Ukrainian, Polish, and Jewish guards. Man has never made a border that would not be crossed. Jews and Germans battled over the porousness of the enclosure. The ghetto became a shadow city whose paths could not be delineated on any map, a Lovecraftian architecture of bunkers, warrens, blind alleys, smuggling tunnels, holes concealed by removable bricks, passages bored between Jewish and Aryan houses. An Aryan tram rolled through a gate in the wall and down the Jewish boulevard. A Jewish bridge passed over the Aryan market. There was even a sort of stock exchange, a courthouse with one entrance on Lezno Street and the other outside the ghetto, in whose corridors Jews and Poles conspired for black market success. No wall could separate the two peoples of Warsaw, even if what drew them together was less affection than the cool logic of trade.

The Germans allotted Jews only 184 calories a day, so the vast majority of food needed to be smuggled in. Writer Rachel Auerbach called the smugglers "saints and heroes of our dark age," and they were the patrons of the ghetto's survival. Through the twenty-two official gates and the thousands more unofficial holes squeezed kids little older than toddlers. As the months passed, the kids kept squirming out to beg or thieve the Aryan side. Then there were the Poles who snuck over to the souk on Gesia Street where they could barter a potato for a wedding dress, some old flour for a golden ring. The deals were good, but even so, you can't besmirch their courage; in November, the Gestapo shot a Pole for smuggling in a sack of bread. There were the Jewish workers who lined up by the wall each day to join labor battalions that the Germans organized to work outside the ghetto—the jobs were shit, but it was a chance to find some food in the Polish city. Then there were the professional smugglers, the porters and gangsters of Bernard's old milieu, who moved their cargo in corpse wagons, tram cars, and trucks while corrupt guards pretended not to see. It was not just food. Poles brought in raw materials, and ghetto Jews became geniuses of manufacture. They set up home workshops to churn out commodities that their Polish partners smuggled to the Aryan city: cigarette holders, wooden-soled slippers with cardboard tops, aluminum spoons made from the wrecks of planes, mattresses, rag rugs, dyed linens, toys assembled by six-year-olds, and twenty-five thousand brushes a day. The ghetto, against all odds, became self-sufficient.

Top smugglers spent lavishly at the new cabarets that catered to the ghetto elite. At Café Sztuka, run by the showgirl turned informant Madame Machno, at the brothel Britannia, or at A la Fourchette, they enjoyed performances by the aristocracy of Warsaw's prewar nightlife. There, exquisite Vera Gran sang "Her First Ball" while the pianist Wladyslaw Szpilman accompanied her with a buoyant legato. The poet Wladyslaw Szlengel satirized ghetto life in his weekly sketch show. Society girls fought for the chance to work as taxi dancers. At the cabarets, smugglers, Judenrat members, and Gestapo informants sat next to German occupiers, who liked to go slumming in the ghetto for a bit of kinky frisson. They blew thousands of zlotys a night, at a time when people had already begun to die of starvation. At tables set with crystal, they ate duck till the fat slicked their chins, drank till they puked, and stepped over the corpses on their way out. Models and bottles.

THE PARTY

Since his Nowolipie Street apartment fell within the ghetto's boundaries, Bernard Goldstein didn't need to move. He grew a thick beard to hide his famous scar and stayed inside as much as possible. Couriers kept him apprised on the party's underground activities. To kill time, he played cards with Abrasha Blum and scrawny, sarcastic Marek Edelman.

A childhood friend of Bernard's son Janek, Edelman had grown up around the Goldstein home, filching Bernard's cigarettes and worshiping the old fighter as a hero.

In the ruins of bombed-out buildings, Marek taught kids to sing the SKIF's anthem: *We are young, and the world is open.* When Marek led his charges home, through the rubble and the smoke of burning trash, they sang together. "In all the filth that lay about, the hunger, the humiliation and waste of every kind of human feeling . . . we managed to give these children a little joy," he later wrote.

"In order to defend ourselves against the feeling of helplessness that engulfed us, we tried to rebuild and strengthen all the prewar institutions, to create at least the illusion of a life that used to be," Bernard Goldstein wrote. The Bund turned their former schools and newspaper offices into party kitchens and tea halls, which served as meeting points for activists and for illicit schools. They ran libraries out of couriers' briefcases. Ghetto residents sought stories of other holocausts—one favorite was *The Forty Days of Musa Dagh*, an epic born of the Armenian genocide.

The Bund's most important arm was its youth movement, Tsukunft. Energetic teenagers whose futures had crumbled in a matter of months, Tsukunft activists had less time for theoretical disputes than their elders. Their overwhelming concern was for ghetto youth like themselves.

In the courtyards, Tsukunft assembled groups to read the party press, discuss the French Revolution, and collect necessities for refugees. They set up job co-ops that served as safe havens from forced labor roundups. They issued a pamphlet to honor the anniversary of the Paris Commune. It began with a Victor Hugo quote: "In the grave is the corpse. The idea lives." These hungry youths risked their lives for poetry readings. I think of all the plump pundits in America who claim that art is a frivolity to which the poor are indifferent. For the Tsukunft kids, art was as vital as bread.

The Bund ran secret printshops in the basement of the *Naye Folkstsaytung* building, in the old Bund club, and in comrades' apartments. Their newspapers' names changed constantly to evade the Gestapo, and they were distributed by five-person cells. Each copy of their newspaper had at least twenty readers; it was passed house to house, to be read aloud to groups of neighbors. The most important rule: "Shut up! . . . Loose lips are an offense against the movement."

The papers, with their sixteen single-spaced pages and their crudely drawn covers, are reminiscent of the hectographs Pati Kremer printed three generations before. The news they published was always bad. Most of Western Europe had fallen under Nazi rule. The Luftwaffe pummeled London. Field Marshal Rommel's tanks rolled toward Palestine.

In their op-eds, Bundists agitated against the ghetto elites with headlines like "The Masses Pay—the Rich Rule" and "What Happened to the Bread?" They dreamed big. "We stand fast in favor of a free, independent, socialist Poland in a voluntary federation of socialist republics in Europe," Maurycy Orzech wrote.

They wrote in a grandiose manner I recognized from my great-grandfather's pronouncements. When my grandmother Ruth married, Sam could not afford catering, so he bragged instead about serving raisins made from "succulent rubaiyat grapes" grown in his own "orchard"—in truth, his Brooklyn backyard. I imagined that this was Sam's own style, but I now realize it was the idiom of the Jewish working class that he came from. They all used words to bridge the chasm between their meager means and their glorious aspirations.

The underground press was costly and dangerous. Activists flirted with starvation just to afford ink. If they were caught, they could expect torture at best. Despite this, each Jewish party used their press to launch attacks on other Jews.

Even in the ghetto, Bundists clashed with Zionists—"prisoners of the ideology of statehood," in the words of Marek Edelman.

In *Neged Hazerem*, the newspaper of Zionist youth movement Hashomer Hatzair, writers excoriated the Bund for their rejection of a Jewish state. "Upon reading the Bund's small periodical, our hearts are filled with pity for the masses in whose eyes the eternal scattering of the Jews is idyllic. . . . The [Bund's] tremendous and victorious party didn't grant—nor can it do so—any spiritual support during these terrible days."

When Zionist youth cut a deal to work on Polish farms, Bundist papers called it a betrayal of their homeland. These youth replaced Polish men whom Nazis kidnapped for slave labor, and every farm job they took made it easier for Nazis to deport their fellow citizens. The Zionists rolled their eyes. On the farms, they had milk and potatoes. Besides, what had their fellow Polish citizens ever done for them?

WARSAW

We are surrounded by mighty walls. There is no way out. Every wall seems to mock you as you approach it: You'll go no farther, and everything on my other side is hidden from you now and forevermore. . . . But those walls and the people who built them

> and stand behind them are mistaken. . . . Today we know that even when they wish to isolate us, thousands of fibers connect us with all the workers . . . on the other side. Our thoughts are with them, and we are fully confident that they are with us.

So wrote the Bundist newspaper *Voice of Youth* that winter.

Bundists put their hopes in their Polish comrades, old friends like Antoni Zdanowski, who had accompanied Viktor Alter to the Spanish front lines and shared a prison cell with Bernard Goldstein back in the days of the tsar.

Bundists who could pass as Poles began to sneak over to the other side of the wall to join them.

Polish Warsaw was repressed and hungry, but in comparison to the ghetto, it was a paradise, with parks, fresh vegetables, and apartments that housed less than seven people to a room. But it was dangerous too. An industry of professional blackmailers had sprung up to prey on Jews passing as Aryans. These blackmailers would latch on to a prospective victim—sometimes an old acquaintance, sometimes a stranger—and threaten to expose her unless she paid her savings. Once the victim was sucked dry, the blackmailer might turn her over to the Gestapo anyway.

A new vocabulary emerged for Jews on the Aryan side. Safe houses were called *melinas*. Once blackmailers showed up, a melina was considered "burned" and had to be abandoned. A Jew could have a Good Face: blond, snub-nosed, and happy. Or she could have a Bad Face: dark, hook-nosed, tragic. Physiognomy was destiny. If you had a good face, you could live in the open; girls with good faces often got jobs as maids. But woe to Jews with bad faces. They hid away in basements or attics, at the mercy of landlords who might throw them out on a whim.

One of the first Bundists to sneak out was David Klin, whose cultivated Polish, stolid blond mien, and job for the Joint Distribution Committee gave him the best chance of survival. The Polish Socialist Party provided Klin with the directions to an underground meeting point. Klin showed up at a vegetable shop on Czerniakowska Street and asked the salesgirl for directions to an avenue that no longer existed. She ushered him through a hidden door, into a forgery lab where operatives manufactured passports, travel permits, and certificates attesting to impeccable Aryan birth. The Polish socialists provided these false papers to Bundist leaders, along with money, underground newspapers, and communiqués from the government-in-exile to be shared inside the ghetto. Polish socialist leaders had themselves smuggled into the ghetto to meet with their Bundist comrades. They risked their lives escorting the Bundists out.

All of this must have assured the Bund that they were right to remain internationalists, that their salvation lay in multiethnic solidarity.

In December, the Bund's *Voice of Youth* ran on its cover a picture of two hands shaking through a hole in the ghetto wall. "All men are brothers, whether yellow, black, brown or white," read the headline. "Talk of peoples, colors and races is a bunch of nonsense."

When they launched a new Polish paper out of David Klin's safe house, they took its title from an old slogan of the country's independence movement. *For Your Freedom and Ours.*

ARTHUR ZYGIELBOJM

On January 17, 1941, the Jewish Labor Committee threw a grand conference at Carnegie Hall to congratulate themselves on their rescue of European socialists, 308 of whom were in attendance. Friedrich Adler, secretary of the Labor and Socialist International, was there, along with Menshevik Raphael Abramovich; the Bund's Noyakh Portnoy; Julius Deutsch, the former commander of Red Vienna's Schutzbund; and the elegantly dressed Arthur Zygielbojm. After a coast-to-coast lecture tour about the persecution of Polish Jews, Zygielbojm had settled in New York, working as an editor at a Yiddish newspaper. Archivist Lucy Dawidowicz remembered him as a debonair man "who enjoyed frivolous pursuits. . . . His reputation as a skirt-chaser spread quickly from office to office." He did not seem like the hero she expected from the stories she had heard about his defiant stand against the creation of the Warsaw ghetto.

On the podium, the Jewish Labor Committee officials gave stirring homilies to antifascist solidarity. Union boss David Dubinsky thanked State Department secretary Breckinridge Long, who had rubber-stamped his comrades' visas. Dubinsky didn't mention Long's flamboyant racism, nor his obsessive efforts to keep less-connected refugees out of America. After many years in the corridors of power, Dubinsky knew when to hold his tongue.

I wonder what Zygielbojm felt when he sat in the audience. Did he try the wine? Was the chicken juicy, or did it taste like ash? Did his eyes linger on the ladies, or were their faces replaced by the people he'd left behind?

SOPHIA DUBNOVA

A few weeks later, three more of the Jewish Labor Committee's beneficiaries disembarked in Moscow: Sophia Dubnova, her son Victor, and her now daughter-in-law Iza, who had managed to meet up with them in Vilna. It had been two decades since Sophia left her homeland. For all the oceans of ink she spent on nostalgic poetry, she never imagined these would be the circumstances of her return.

Despite the cold, the trio took the opportunity to play tourist, visiting the treacly social-realist canvases at the Tretyakov Gallery and catching a performance at the Moscow State Jewish Theatre. In his memoirs, Victor Erlich recalled the Lenin mausoleum. "Thousands of shabbily dressed pilgrims were slowly filing past the mummified leader under the watchful eyes of the stone-faced guards." He does not mention if they joined the lines. I let myself imagine that they did. Sophia Dubnova could have looked down at the preserved remains of her Exileland acquaintance, whose revolution had driven her and Henryk from their country, and wondered at the absurdity of how their lives had ended up. She a refugee. Henryk a prisoner. Lenin a dummy in a box.

She only knew one person in Moscow: her brother, Yasha, who was now a mathematics professor. Should she contact him? Or would that get him in trouble? When she finally called, she pretended to be a family friend. When he showed up at their dingy hotel, he chided her for her trick.

"I wanted to make it easier for you not to show up if it was truly inconvenient," Sophia explained.

"I don't think they can do much more to me than they've already done," Yasha responded. His wife, a communist true believer, had been arrested in the purges.

A few days later, the Erlichs boarded the Trans-Siberian Railway. It took three weeks to cross the continent. Outside the window, the world unfurled like an endless strip of white. The NKVD searched them in frigid Vladivostok. Then they were on a fishing boat, crammed far over capacity with a hundred refugees, crossing the churning Sea of Japan.

They were nauseous and wobbly when the boat pulled into the port of Tsuruga. As Sophia dragged herself onto the deck, her eyes settled on an incredible sight. What stopped her was not just the pagodas that lined the shimmering bay, nor the women in their exuberant kimonos, nor even the brilliance of the azure sky. It was the infinity of pink, of such fragile freshness that it must have reminded her of her youth in Paris, of the soft evenings she walked with Henryk by the Seine, of everything she thought she'd left behind. Beauty. No other word but that. It was springtime. The cherry trees were in bloom.

WARSAW

Winter had been brutal in the Warsaw ghetto. Five thousand people were dying each month. Their families left their naked corpses on the street to avoid burial costs.

There was neither food nor fuel. All most people had to eat was bread full of sawdust, "spit out soup" made from unprocessed oats, and vile little fish called stinkies. Typhus tore through crowded tenements.

At the end of April, the Nazis ordered mass roundups to provide workers for labor camps. At their order, Jewish Police snatched ghetto youth to clear marshes or dig holes in conditions of such lurid sadism that they came back disabled or dead. The Bund's newspaper reported on the horrors of these camps and berated the Jewish Police, rich boys "with clean hands," for their collaboration.

In early May, the Gestapo caught one of the Tsukunft's newspaper distributors, a teenage metalworker named Alter Bas. In a letter that Bas smuggled out of Pawiak Prison, he described how the interrogators had torn out his fingernails. "Be well. Be careful. I'll perish here," he finished. His arrest terrified his Tsukunft comrades. Had they been infiltrated?

One afternoon, Maurycy Orzech, head of the Bundist Artisans' Union, was walking down a ghetto street when he saw a Jewish Policeman bludgeoning a woman. He punched the policeman in the face. The cop went down. Orzech got on top and pummeled the cop, to the approving hoots of the crowd, until more cops hauled him to Pawiak Prison. No one seemed capable of getting him out.

Soon afterward, two young Jewish men showed up at Bernard's building at Nowolipie Street and asked the janitor to see the ledger book. They lingered on the letter *G*. Not liking their looks, the janitor rushed upstairs to warn Bernard, who was hosting his usual card game with Abrasha Blum. Bernard glanced out the window and saw a few people milling outside. Gestapo agents, no doubt. He decided to flee.

He ran into the courtyard, squeezed himself through a hole into the adjoining schoolyard, then scaled the wall to drop himself into the courtyard of a friend's building. As he landed, he must have felt every day of his fifty-two years.

Ten minutes later, Gestapo agents raided his apartment. In the wreckage, they left a note demanding he report to their headquarters the next morning. When he didn't show, they arrested his nephew Jacob in his place. Despite his pleas, the party would not allow Bernard to give himself up to save Jacob's life. Bernard was too important, they argued. The Gestapo tortured Jacob to death in their basement. Nothing could quiet Bernard's shame.

After a few days at his friend's place, Bernard's comrades dressed him in a long black capote and a velvet kashket. In the mirror, he looked every inch the pious Hasid. Armed Bundists tailed the "rabbi" to the first of his hideouts. From then on, Bernard Goldstein would live in a series of locked rooms in apartments whose residents were sworn to silence.

Bernard only broke the rules once, when he was hiding at his comrade Manya Wasser's apartment. Ten people shared the flat, among them a teenage girl who organized underground Bundist kindergartens. One day, the girl knocked on Bernard's door. Flushed with embarrassment, she asked his advice. She was in love with a comrade named Kostek, and he with her, but the two were virgins. Did Bernard think it was wrong if they had sex before the Nazis killed them all?

"You're breaking no law. Take your sweetheart and be happy," he responded awkwardly. He wondered why she had come to him. She said nothing. As he felt her expectant eyes, he laughed at his own stupidity. With Bernard in the apartment, she couldn't bring her boyfriend over, but she had nowhere else to be alone. "Send Kostek to me," he told her.

The next day, Bernard told Kostek that he wanted him to stop by periodically to deliver reports on party printing presses. When Kostek showed up, Bernard was nowhere to be found. Instead, Kostek's girlfriend was there to greet him.

JACOB CELEMENSKI

In June, the Bund's courier Celemenski entered the Warsaw ghetto in the guise of a utilities inspector. He had a new Polish name, Czeslaw, a sharp suit, and several sets of fake documents provided by the Polish Socialist Party. To keep his cover, he learned to ignore suffering, to stride about with God-granted arrogance. If a Jewish friend called out his name, he would bark at them with such contempt that he could barely live with himself afterward.

By the end of 1940, the Nazis had set up Jewish ghettos in most towns and cites in occupied Poland. As in Warsaw, they had herded Jews inside walled-off neighborhoods, where they subjected them to a brutal regime of starvation, forced labor, and terror. Celemenski had spent months traveling between these ghettos, trying to organize Bundist delegates to come to Warsaw for a conference. By the time he arrived back in the capital, everything had fallen apart. Orzech was in jail and Bernard in hiding. The ghetto had grown too dangerous to consider anything like a conference. Their desire to see one another still held, however, and once the Bund managed to bribe Orzech out of prison, they called a meeting of the central committee.

Celemenski told the committee about what he had witnessed in his odyssey around Poland. Through his words, the six leaders traveled the battered outposts of their network. He described the arguments over whether to enter the Judenrat. While the central committee rejected the institution, in the town of Piotrkow-Trybunalski, the Bund ran the Judenrat, to seemingly good effect, and in other cities, Bundists wondered which tactic was right. In Miedzyrzec, an illegal brush maker's cooperative gave him 25,000 zlotys for shtetls in need. In Lublin, he found the Bundist councilwoman Bella Shapiro working as a waitress at the party soup kitchen and guarding her orphaned twin nephews like pearls. She was arrested shortly after his visit. In Bedzin, he met the Bundist pioneer Yitzchok Mordechai Pesachson, whose daughter had just been grabbed in a manhunt. "Every town must go to battle, no surrender," Pesachson told Celemenski, cracking his knuckles as he spoke. "We must hit back with arms or bare fists." Later that day, Celemenski visited a teenage Bundist who had just been released by the Gestapo. The boy took off his shirt to show the mangled flesh of his back. Everywhere Celemenski met young people who wanted to take up arms.

As Celemenski spoke, he took for granted the existence of these Jewish communities. They might have been starved, caged, and tortured, but they lived, and so the Bund lived with them. He could not imagine their absence.

With the conference canceled, the Bund's central committee came up with a new mission for Celemenski. He would deliver aid to the cities he visited, but this time, for safety, the Bund's newspapers would be dropped off beforehand by Jadwiga Wisniewska, a Polish actress who worked as a courier for the Polish Socialist Party.

Jadwiga was an attractive blonde, with something histrionic in her voice. She copied Celemenski's list of addresses onto a slip of tissue paper that she concealed in her gold lipstick case. The next day, she departed to Czestochowa with the newspapers. Celemenski would catch up with her.

When Celemenski reached his safe house in Czestochowa, there were no papers waiting for him. In fact, Jadwiga had never shown up.

In Piotrkow-Trybunalski, his next stop, Celemenski learned the reason for Jadwiga's absence. On the way to Czestochowa, Gestapo officers had blockaded her railway car and searched every passenger. Wisely, she had left her suitcase on the other side of the car. At first, the Gestapo was about to pin it on another traveler. Then they saw the lipstick case.

The Nazi undid the case's latch, opened the top, and shook out the roll of tissue paper with its list of names. "I'm an actress," Jadwiga swore. The Nazi removed the cap from the lipstick tube. He turned the base. The lipstick emerged. He held it next to Jadwiga's lips. A perfect match.

The Gestapo hunted down the names on that list concealed in Jadwiga's lipstick case. They made arrests in Krakow, in Piotrkow-Trybunalski, in Czestochowa, where they clamped the party librarian's breasts in a bathroom door until she passed out. Most of those arrested activists joined Jadwiga at a year-old concentration camp near the city of Oswiecim in southeast Poland. It is better known by its German name: Auschwitz.

CHAPTER 23

BARBAROSSA

(June 1941–July 1942)

VOLKOVYSK

LIFE IN SOVIET-OCCUPIED VOLKOVYSK HAD NOT GONE BADLY FOR THE Bundist Avram Markus. Of course, some things took getting used to. The Soviets banned all political parties, and nationalized Avram's little leather tannery—not that a good Marxist like himself believed in private enterprise in the first place. And he must have done a double take every time he crossed Broad Street, which the town's new masters had renamed in honor of Lenin. On the other hand, things were looking up for his son Shlomo. Avram might have argued with Shlomo in the past, but the boy's holier-than-thou communism had finally paid off. If the Poles had refused to recognize Shlomo's medical degree, the Russians had no such compunction. Formerly unemployed, Shlomo Markus now headed Volkovysk's Jewish hospital. He was an important man who traveled between villages on a horse provided by the party. His girlfriend, Nechama Schein, got a similarly respectable job at the state bank. The couple tried to ignore the cattle cars chugging to gulags out east, full of anyone who disagreed with the new order.

Though the Soviet occupation spelled the end of Avram Markus's political career, it did have upsides. "Because there was no longer any antisemitism in the city, Jews breathed more freely," *The Volkovysk Memorial Book* recounted. The book didn't say how the town's Christian residents felt about this change of affairs as their formerly submissive neighbors got jobs with the new regime, became policemen, and started to act disconcertingly like equals.

Around the middle of June, Markus began to notice German planes. They flew in quick circles before they skittered westward. Like everyone else in Volkovysk, he and the old Bundist shoemaker Zeleviansky argued as to their meaning. And what to make of the Russian tanks that had passed through Ostroger Street toward the German border, or of the new airstrip the Russians were building in the nearby shtetl of Rosh?

On June 22, explosions interrupted Avram Markus's breakfast. He looked at his wife, Fruma, then out the window. The sounds were coming from Rosh. The couple ran outside, where, crowded together with their anxious neighbors, they saw a convoy of Soviet automobiles coming from Rosh. German bombers had hit the airstrip, destroying every plane. Volkovysk residents turned on their radios to hear Foreign Minister Molotov announce that Nazis had attacked the Soviet Union. He called on citizens to defend their fatherland. At the same time, the Red Army began to flee toward Minsk.

The next day, German incendiary bombs hit Broad and Grodno Streets, the Tiferet Bakhurim Synagogue, and the Talmud Torah school. "Entire streets were ringed with fire," *The Volkovysk Memorial Book* said. People hid in basements, only to be crushed by rubble, or they ran into fields, where German planes gunned them down. Dozens of people died in the bombardment, including my distant relative Joseph Beckenstein. I imagine Sam Rothbort's watercolors. The edges blacken and curl.

Shlomo Markus worked in the hospital till the early hours of the morning. An endless stream of victims came in, mutilated, burned, twitching in shock. They were the people he grew up with.

When Shlomo came home, he told Nechama he was staying. He couldn't abandon his patients. She protested that, as communists, they would be first up against the wall when the Nazis came. He spelled out a plan. The party had given him a horse. She and her sister would ride to Minsk, where they'd find each other when things settled down. Nechama packed a bag with Shlomo's most precious possession, his medical degree.

Around noon, Nechama and her sister rode through the teeming streets. Yesterday's Soviet conquerors were absconding in wagons, in private cars, on stolen bicycles, their frenzied flight like that of wasps from a burning nest. As she tried to lead her horse between the blasts, Nechama was probably too distracted to notice someone else hitting the road. Amidst soldiers packed into a Red Army truck sat the old Bundist shoemaker Zeleviansky, who had arrested the pharmacist Tyminski on the first day of the Soviet occupation and so taken revenge on behalf of Volkovysk's Jews. Though he was Sam Rothbort's age, Zeleviansky had thrown in his lot with younger men. He didn't know what the future would hold, only that his hometown was not in it.

LITHUANIA

As the Wehrmacht tore through Soviet territory, they were followed by the Einsatzgruppen, mobile death squads assigned to bring about the final solution to the Jewish question. Their first massacre of Jews came days after the invasion's start, in the small Lithuanian town of Gargzdai. Gargzdai's Lithuanians didn't object. In Ukraine and across the Baltics, Soviet rule had hardened opinions amongst people who already considered Jews synonymous with communists. When the Germans showed up, local patriotic partisans immediately morphed into Nazi henchmen. When the next Gargzdai massacre came, Lithuanians would do it themselves.

Kovno fell to the Nazis on June 25. On that day, Lithuanian partisans stormed the rickety-rack Slobodka suburb, tied its famous rabbi to a chair, placed his head on a holy book, and sawed through his neck. Lithuanians herded dozens more Jewish men into a nearby garage and bludgeoned them to death with crowbars while the crowd hooted like they were at a football match. The star perpetrator took time to pose for photos and then, accordion in hand, climbed atop his victims' bodies and sang the national anthem. Kovno is now known as Kaunas. It is a nice little city these days, with many outdoor restaurants. It even has a marketing slogan: "It's Kaunastic!"—a clumsy play on the word fantastic. I noted their awkward efforts to court Jewish tourists, but when I walked past Slobodka's shanties, I had to stop myself from throwing up. The only thing that lifted my mood was a bright little dosa shop that an Indian immigrant had opened. I bought five packs of cigarettes to support him. *Only you can fix this place,* I thought. *It needs new blood. Please, bring your cousins.*

PATI KREMER

Nazi bombs pounded Vilna. The walls shook in the fine old tenement on Kwaszelna Street where Pati Kremer lived alone. She had heard about the trucks headed east, filled with commissars' wives and other party bigwigs. Even her friends were skipping town. As for her, at seventy-four, she had no more energy to run. She heard a knock on her door. Her friend, the Bundist librarian Herman Kruk, stood shaking on her threshold. He wanted to evacuate, but his papers were a mess, and the Soviets forbade him to leave the city. She soothed him like a little boy. As the floor rumbled, the pair discussed their futures. A year of Soviet arrests had just about finished the Bund in Vilna. They were no longer an organization, just a few cowed comrades, with their party treasury hidden in Pati's apartment. The Nazi invasion promised worse, but perhaps it presented an opportunity.

The Bund was born in Vilna, in 1897 as the party of Jewish workers. These workers would need them to weather whatever horrors lay ahead.

Thanks to an unlucky arrest, Pati Kremer had missed the Bund's founding conference. Decades later, she would preside over its final Vilna incarnation.

EASTERN FRONT

Vilna fell on June 23. Minsk on June 24. Riga on June 27. Sophia's father, the famed historian Simon Dubnov, still lived in Riga. Old and sick, he had rejected his American friends' offers of visas, believing his place was with his people. Weeks later, a Latvian collaborator herded Dubnov toward Riga's newly minted ghetto. Dubnov moved too slowly. The Latvian shot him in the back.

VOLKOVYSK

The Nazis took Volkovysk on June 28. In the first days, German automobiles careened through the streets, their passengers shooting out windows at random. The yellow stars and race laws soon followed, but since their bombs had destroyed the Jewish neighborhood, Germans didn't need to delineate a ghetto. Survivors were already crowded in New Alley, the only street where houses still stood.

Nationalist ringleader Tyminski was dead, but his friends remained, and they were eager to share their lists of targets with the town's new overlords. Guided by these tips, the Gestapo locked Jews and communists in the White prison, which had held political prisoners since tsarist times, then put them on buses to the Mayak forest.

Mayak's pits swallowed two hundred people the first week, including the local Bundist leader Avram Markus, his wife, and their daughter.

SOPHIA DUBNOVA

Sophia Dubnova's ship, the *Heian Maru*, docked in Seattle in August 1941.

After a few hours bobbing in the port, they had their first local contact when a representative of the local Association of Polish Catholic Women boarded the ship. The biddy walked amongst the refugees, squinting at their faces, then sighed with disappointment at all the "little Jews" on board. "I was told there were Poles on the ship," she groaned.

Without U.S. visas, the Erlichs could not disembark, so they boarded a tiny boat to Vancouver. After two years of war, the wealth of North America awed them. Chocolate milkshakes? Miracle of miracles. After they made their way to Montreal, Jewish socialists fêted them like royalty. Sophia and Victor addressed mass rallies in a Yiddish neither would ever master. She waited for messages from her son Alexander, who had already reached New York. He was trying to get them visas.

Sophia Dubnova would be one of 1,300 people whom the Jewish Labor Committee saved from Europe, using networks born in tsarist Russia half a century before. Her timing was impeccable. Shortly after the Erlichs' arrival, Canada closed its door to Jewish refugees. In the government's eyes, Jews were arrogant con men who thought themselves too good to work in Canadian cobalt mines, pushy jerks whose only aim was to import more of their worthless ilk from Europe. The three thousand whom Canada had already admitted were quite enough. From now on, refugees would be Aryan only.

On September 8, the Wehrmacht cut the last road to Petrograd, which had been renamed again and was now Leningrad. Sophia's beloved city was under siege. The Red Army scrambled toward the Russian steppes, abandoning western Ukraine to Nazi rule.

This was the state of Soviet defense on September 23, when a telegram appeared in *The Forward*.

> We continue the common struggle against fascism and for socialism. Convey our greetings to our comrades and friends.
>
> —VIKTOR ALTER AND HENRYK ERLICH.
> HOTEL METROPOLE. MOSCOW.

HENRYK ERLICH

Henryk Erlich had spent the last two years in Soviet prisons. After his arrest, the NKVD had shipped him from Brest-Litovsk to Moscow's Lubyanka prison. Each night, guards dragged him out for an interrogation. Shockingly, they didn't beat him. Instead, foul-mouthed dullards shone bright lights in his eyes and barked that he was a fascist spy and a henchman of the recently assassinated Leon Trotsky. Sometimes, they brought in people he knew, detained comrades or Warsaw communists who had foolishly traveled to the workers' paradise. Each witness recited an improbable lie. Erlich tried to explain himself, to argue his innocence. It didn't work.

As the highest-ranking Polish politician in Soviet custody, Erlich was quite the catch. Once, the NKVD chief Lavrentiy Beria even dropped in to observe an interrogation.

Some months into his imprisonment, Erlich asked his jailors for permission to write the history of the Bund. He probably reckoned that his own story was over; he told cellmates that the Soviets would never set him free. In partitioned Poland, enemies hunted his comrades. What would remain of the cause to which he had given his life? Nothing, unless someone left a record. He knew the NKVD would preserve whatever he wrote. Imagining a juicy confession, Erlich's jailers agreed. Every day, guards led him to a little room with a desk and writing supplies and left him to his memories.

Over 252 lucid, detailed pages, Erlich told the history of the Bund in Poland. He didn't write to save himself. That was impossible. Instead, he wrote to preserve the memory of his party. Even an enemy archive held the possibility of survival. Erlich would have known that no empire lasts forever, and that eventually every government must fall. One day, new hands might open dusty boxes. His words might speak to the future.

Erlich wrote about how the Bund had always sought peace between Poland and Soviet Russia, and he had even gone to jail for it, but he rebuked the Comintern, whose social fascism theory had enabled the rise of Hitler. He showed how early persecutions of socialists led inexorably to the fratricidal bloodbath of the Moscow show trials. "The fact of my arrest and custody (and is it only mine?) must also serve me, unfortunately, as confirmation of those darker sides of the Soviet policy that we have always criticized," he wrote. (Over these lines a secret policeman later scrawled, "Trotskyism!")

Erlich closed: "I do not feel any guilt, neither for myself nor for my party."

This was not the abject self-denunciation his jailors expected, but despite their fury, Erlich refused to alter his text. When they handed him a prewritten confession, he coldly dropped it in the trash. The interrogator blustered and shoved a gun into Erlich's face. Guards chucked him into a punishment cell.

That summer, three NKVD men frog-marched Erlich into a truck packed with fellow prisoners, then shoved them all into a boxcar. This was the start of a torturous five-day journey to the southwestern city of Saratov. Sun beat the train's metal roof, turning the car into a sweatbox. Prisoners ate only salted herring. Tormented by thirst, they fought over sips of water.

On the first day, Erlich recognized a face across the boxcar. He squeezed through the prisoners, laid a hand on the man's shoulder, and whispered: "Comrade Finesilver?"

At first, Abraham Finesilver didn't recognize the emaciated man "with a head of sparse gray hair and a face of such velvety-soft expression in the deepest eyes," but he knew the voice, which had soared over

Warsaw crowds each May Day. "Comrade Erlich," he answered. He began to cry.

On the second day, the boxcar pulled into a station, and the prisoners heard the impossible sound of children's laughter. One prisoner pressed his face to the window. Across the tracks, he saw a train so crowded that some passengers sat on the roofs.

"Who are you?" he shouted.

"Civilians from Minsk!" they hollered back.

Through the window, a guard whacked the prisoner in the face with his rifle butt. He fell, spitting blood and teeth.

As an act of solidarity, one of the Minsk evacuees began to read aloud from his newspaper. His booming voice carried into the cattle car. This is how Erlich learned that Hitler had invaded the Soviet Union. He permitted himself a moment of satisfaction. He had predicted it.

In Saratov, guards threw Erlich into a solitary cell. At night, he talked to himself. He pretended that he was back in his father-in-law's summer house in Riga, with Sophia and the boys. Had his enemies caught them, or had they made it out?

At his sham trial, Erlich tried to give a speech, like he had at the Second Congress of the Soviets, back in 1917, but the judge cut him short. The verdict was prewritten. Death penalty. "This court has no right to try me!" Erlich shouted. Guards dragged him to his execution cell.

Death row prisoners were not permitted newspapers, so Erlich didn't know about the negotiations between the Soviet Union and the Polish government-in-exile that followed the German invasion, nor about the deal to free all Polish citizens imprisoned in the Soviet Union. Neither did he know that, thanks to a campaign led by Bundist refugees in New York City, he and Viktor Alter were international causes célèbres. When Polish prime minister–in–exile Wladyslaw Sikorski presented the Soviets with a list of eight VIP prisoners, it included the two men's names.

The first inkling Erlich got of the new political reality came when a jovial NKVD major showed up at his cell to congratulate him. Thanks to the beneficence of the Soviet Union, Erlich's sentence had been commuted to a mere ten years of hard labor, the grinning major said. These ten years had also been commuted. In a few days, Erich would be in Moscow. The major stuck out his hand for Erlich to shake.

The NKVD released Erlich on September 12, 1941, and brought him to Moscow's luxurious Hotel Metropole. He bathed, put in a state-provided set of dentures, and trimmed his famous silver beard. The next day, Viktor Alter joined him.

BABI YAR

At the end of September, Nazis and their Ukrainian collaborators murdered almost the entire Jewish population of Kyiv. They lined thirty-three thousand naked humans at the edge of the Babi Yar ravine, then shot them all in the head. Ukrainians resold their clothes. Nearly eighty years later, in the midst of the full-scale Russian invasion, I was on the back of a Ukrainian friend's motorcycle, part of a convoy of bikers returning from the Borodyanka displaced persons camp, and they stopped at Babi Yar to split up. It was just a park to them, banal with familiarity, but I asked for a moment to walk around. The ravine seemed large as an ocean bed. It was calmed with grass, topped by a Soviet monument. When I closed my eyes, I could see nothing but the bodies in the pit. My friend hugged me. I felt dramatic—silly, even. Why shouldn't it be a park? What were they supposed to do? Declare the land off limits? All land is watered with blood.

VIKTOR ALTER AND HENRYK ERLICH

Viktor Alter seemed shockingly buoyant after his two years' imprisonment, if much thinner and rather aged. Unlike Erlich, he had not tried to explain anything to his interrogators. Why should he justify himself to *them*? From the first, he maintained a sardonic silence. He went on a series of hunger strikes, just as he had during his previous stay in a Soviet prison, but the state had changed since 1919. Guards strapped him to a chair, shoved a tube down his nose, and pumped slop directly into his stomach, then locked him in a punishment cell, designed so that a prisoner could neither sit nor stand nor lie down. Alter didn't break. Eventually they acceded to his demand for pencil and paper, which he used to write a treatise on non-Newtonian physics. His hobby, he said. He asked them to send it to a scientific institute for evaluation.

Now Alter was back among the living, his big body slouched in the booth at the Metropole Hotel. He laughed uproariously at the absurdity of it all. It was pretty funny, wasn't it? One day, he and Erlich are in their death cells, and the next, they're surrounded by flunkies in Moscow's finest fleshpot.

The Soviets appeared to need Alter and Erlich. A few days after their release, an NKVD bigwig named Colonel Volkovysky stopped by their hotel suite. Volkovysky was a loquacious sort, gossipy, full of apologies for the injustice of their imprisonment. The Soviet Union would make it up to them later. But enough about the past. With Hitler advancing toward Moscow, it was time for old rivals to unite. Alter and Erlich were influential men, Volkovysky said, with important roles to play in the war against the Nazis. What did they think about helming a Jewish antifascist committee?

As envisioned by the Soviet Union, the Jewish Antifascist Committee would mobilize American Jews to pressure their government to enter the war. Eager to do more to aid their comrades trapped under Nazi occupation, Alter and Erlich proposed additional responsibilities for the prospective committee. It could make antifascist propaganda, enlist anti-Nazi fighters, and help Jews in the camps and ghettos of occupied Europe.

After two years of prison stasis, Alter and Erlich yearned to return to the fray, but they wrote their proposal with full knowledge as to the nature of their newfound friends. Erlich knew Volkovysky's oily compliments had no more substance than the verdict the judge had so recently handed him. All this could disappear like a mirage.

EVACUATION

In the middle of October, the Wehrmacht reached the suburbs of Moscow. Stalin ordered the government to move six hundred miles east to the old trading city of Kuybyshev, formerly called Samara. The politburo, the ministries, and the embassies were evacuated, along with the preserved corpse of Vladimir Lenin, which would spend the rest of the war in a rural schoolhouse. Alter and Erlich joined the elite exodus from the capital.

SOPHIA DUBNOVA

At last, Sophia Dubnova received the letter she had been waiting for since Henryk Erlich's telegram appeared in *The Forward*. It had traveled a great distance, carried in a Polish diplomatic pouch from Moscow to the Bund's New York headquarters, brought to her son Alex's Upper West Side apartment, then mailed to her refuge in Montreal:

> Sophie, my love, my dearest children . . . I was brimful of tenderest love for all of you and of the boundless gratitude for what you had given me. . . . In defiance of common sense, I didn't believe that I would never see you again. . . .

Henryk Erlich didn't dwell on what he'd suffered. The important thing was that he was back. He had a future. He might even come to New York.

WARSAW

The Bund had always said that eastern Europe was their homeland, but what had their homeland become? Who were their eastern European neighbors? Were their socialist friends mere exceptions, or were they harbingers of a decent future?

"We have been physically separated from Polish society with walls and barbed wire. . . . We effectively no longer share a cultural, economic or social life like we did in 'the before times,'" wrote the Bund's Polish paper, *For Your Freedom and Ours*. "Out there, we don't truly know what the position of the Polish masses is toward the Jewish masses. Some say there is a rise in antisemitism. Others read thousands of stories that bear witness to the opposite," to the concern that Polish workers felt for the sufferings of their fellow Jewish citizens.

They could not "close their eyes to the fact that the ceaseless, focused antisemitic agitation fomented by the Germans is carving permanent marks in the minds and souls of the Poles." They were painfully aware of the way Polish police, and even many ordinary people, gleefully turned in Jewish fugitives. They read articles in the underground press that described Jews as harmful foreigners worthy of expulsion and merely objected to the gore of Nazi methods. Yet despite all this, the Bund insisted on their ideal of Hereness. "Poland was never a hotel," said their party press. It was not an Egypt to escape.

The Bund refused to forget themselves. In October, two thousand Warsaw ghetto inmates took part in celebrations for the party's forty-fourth anniversary. When one of their founders, Noyakh Portnoy, died that same month in New York exile, Tsukunft raised money for a Polish gravesite where, after the war, "the remains of our dear grandfather will rest."

In their press, the Bund commemorated lost Polish socialist friends, like the politician Norbert Barlicki and the intellectual Kazimierz Czapinski. Both had been murdered in Auschwitz. They promoted the theories of Sigmund Freud and urged young Jews to read the Indian writer Rabindranath Tagore, to look at his country's independence struggle and find resonances with their own fight. They turned their fierce analytical lens on France and England. Both powers shared blame for Nazi victories, wrote *Voice of Youth*. "They disregarded Japan's acts of plunder in China and those of Italy in Abyssinia. [They] gazed with equanimity at Germany's resurgence under Hitlerism. . . . The famous 'nonintervention' policy helped strangle Red Spain."

Foreshadowing the Martinican philosopher Aimé Césaire, Bundists described how the Nazi slaughter was an extrapolation of what Europe had inflicted on the world. "It is the Hitlerites' attempt to invoke the colonial methods of extermination that the European imperialists adopted in the previous centuries . . . and apply them to weak and small peoples [of Europe]."

When the Nazis wanted to reduce them to bodies, they held most fiercely to critical thought, humanism, and love.

"We must declare a fight to the death against the indifference growing within us. Before the world finishes off Nazism in battle, we must win a victory of morality. . . . We must oppose brutality with active empathy, the debasement of man with a defense of his dignity, and the madness of racism with the brotherhood of peoples," wrote the Bundist Ignacy Samsonowicz in an open letter to a Polish comrade, published in *For Your Freedom and Ours.*

> I stand in the death district and look upon its people. Poles. Workers. Brothers of this same shared earth. They build this terrible tomb. . . . I know powers from hell construct these walls, not Polish workers who are also enslaved. And I know one day, these same Poles will tear down these walls beside us . . . and form a New Life, a New City, equally happy for everyone.
>
> After all, the workers of Paris built the Bastille at the kings' command, and those same workers smashed it into dust.

VIKTOR ALTER AND HENRYK ERLICH

Kuybyshev groaned under the weight of evacuated ambassadors, apparatchiks, and VIPs. It was a city of wood shacks, ringed with hastily built armament factories. Its unpaved streets were arranged like lines on graph paper beneath an endless sky. In winter, temperatures fell forty degrees below zero. Theaters played Chekhov, but the audience's feet were wrapped in rags. Their boots were needed by soldiers at the front.

In Kuybyshev, Viktor Alter relished his return to life. He was eager to read, to talk, to dive back into the fight. He would pause in the middle of a meal, soup spoon hovering in the air, just to win a point of debate. He spoke his mind, writing to British comrades that the NKVD was the essence of counterrevolution. He lived like he was free.

It was different for Henryk Erlich. Ksawery Pruszynski, a conservative writer who worked for the Polish embassy, sometimes shared dinner with the pair. Erlich seemed much older than Alter, "restrained, pensive, and terribly lonely," with a look of "placid pessimism" in his eyes. Once, Pruszynski spotted Erlich at the Kuybyshev theater. The Bundist leader stood alone near the entrance, "meditating, completely alien to his surroundings." His face brought to mind the old group portraits taken at congresses of exiled revolutionaries in Geneva.

History held few surprises for Henryk Erlich. He had been in and out of jail, seen an empire fall, participated in one revolution and been the victim of a second. He had lost two countries and been condemned to death. A believer in humane, democratic socialism, he had watched Europe collapse into irrational slaughter despite the entreaties of intellectuals like himself. Yet he still tried. This was the world. There was no other. It was worth fighting for.

In Kuybyshev, Alter and Erlich befriended Stanislaw Kot, the liberal historian who served as Poland's ambassador to the Soviet Union. The three men worked to arrange the release of Polish prisoners. It was too late for some—elderly Bundist pioneer Anna Rozental was already dead—but the Soviets freed dozens more Bundists and Polish socialists thanks to their efforts. Alter and Erlich organized aid for the Jewish refugees, and urged Jewish men to enlist in the new Polish army that General Wladyslaw Anders was raising in Buzuluk.

Jews flocked to join Anders's Army, as it was known. Many of them had no military motives and just wanted a hot meal and a modicum of safety after having survived the gulag. Their arrival infuriated the general. He had never put much stock in Jewish military competence, and after seeing how some Polish Jews welcomed Soviet troops in 1939, he was inclined to tar them all as traitors. (Anders didn't ask himself why Jews might have preferred Soviet to Nazi rule.) Anders ordered his enlistment offices to rudely reject Jewish applicants. Meanwhile, a group of Revisionist Zionists tried to sell Anders on the idea of a Jewish army, which could conquer Palestine when the war was done, and rid Poland of its Jewish problem forever.

After hearing troubling reports from Jews of mistreatment in Buzuluk, Alter and Erlich set up a meeting with Anders. They opposed the Revisionists' plan for a Jewish army, but also the racism they saw festering in Anders's ranks. After Anders described how Jews welcomed the Soviets, Alter shouted, "Those are isolated incidents!" When the pair requested Anders set up a spokesman for Jewish affairs, Anders refused, then threw them out of his office. (Later, after countless reports of discrimination and mistreatment, most of Anders's Jewish soldiers deserted when his army got to Palestine.)

At Kuybyshev's ratty Grand Hotel, Alter and Erlich were surrounded by released friends, Polish intellectuals, and handlers from the NKVD.

Mostly, they plotted to get out. They kept in constant touch with the English ambassador Stafford Cripps and wrote polite letters to Stalin and Beria, asking to be sent abroad. Erlich needed rest. Hunger tormented him, no matter how much he ate. He could barely climb a flight of stairs. Polish socialist ministers in London had nominated him for a post in the government-in-exile, but he longed to go to New York. Let Alter take London. He needed to see his family.

On December 4, just after midnight, Alter, Erlich, and a friend sat in the Grand Hotel dining room, warming themselves with cups of tea. That morning, their NKVD handler had told them to expect a reply to their request to leave Russia. When the hotel employee entered to tell Alter he was wanted at the telephone, no one had to ask who was calling.

Alter returned immediately and told Erlich to get his coat and join him. He said they'd be back in an hour.

They never returned.

LONDON

In March 1942, Arthur Zygielbojm sailed for London to serve as a delegate to the Polish government-in-exile. His inclusion came at the suggestion of the Polish Socialist Party.

Zygielbojm didn't have an easy time amongst the exiled politicians in London, whose policies were only slightly better than those of the prewar government. Prime Minister Wladyslaw Sikorski saw little use for Jews in his country, telling British foreign secretary Anthony Eden, "It is quite impossible . . . for Poland to continue to maintain 3.5 million Jews after the war. Room for them must be found elsewhere." At various times, his cabinet included two Endeks, the OZON racist Adam Koc, the notorious pogromist Józef Haller, and Stanislaw Stronski, who had helped incite the murder of Poland's first president. Soon after Zygielbojm arrived, Endek politician Zofia Zaleska introduced a proposal to deport any surviving Polish Jews to a special homeland that would be established elsewhere. Zygielbojm's fellow Jewish delegate, Zionist Ignacy Schwarzbart, meekly suggested that this homeland be set up in Palestine.

Only Zygielbojm and one Polish Socialist representative voted against the proposal. "The Jewish population has a fatherland. That fatherland is Poland, just as it is the fatherland of the Polish masses," Zygielbojm wrote in protest. The fatherland disagreed.

JUDENREIN

Horrific news came from the Jerusalem of Lithuania. That winter, a Polish boy scout arrived in the Warsaw ghetto from Vilna. Once inside the ghetto, he told contacts in Zionist youth movements that Nazis and their Lithuanian collaborators had murdered a third of the city's Jews in the Ponar forest, then buried their bodies in pits. Through couriers, Bernard Goldstein asked a Polish union buddy to confirm the rumors. After his return, Bundists smuggled the friend into the ghetto. In Bernard's Gesia Street safe house, his friend told him that the massacres went far beyond Vilna. Whole towns in eastern Poland were now *judenrein*—the Nazi term for "clean of Jews."

In early February, a Jewish chemist with the pseudonym of Yakov Grojanowski brought an even more shattering report to the ghetto. At a camp in the village of Chelmno, Nazis had applied their German efficiency to the mechanics of mass murder. Instead of tiresome shootings, they herded Jews into the backs of sealed trucks, which they then pumped full of poison gas. Nazis had forced Grojanowski to bury the bodies. "The execution lasts fifteen minutes, accompanied by the roar of the motor which is set in operation to drown out the screams and groans of the tortured defenseless victims," the Bundist press reported.

Few people wanted to believe them. Who could believe in the industrialized destruction of an entire people? Of course, it had happened in the past. Only thirty-six years before, in what is now Namibia, German colonists had butchered the Herero and Nama peoples in desert concentration camps. But that was far away. And even if some massacres took place in eastern Poland, the ghetto inmates doubted the same could happen in Warsaw, the biggest Jewish city in Europe. They clung to hope.

LEON FEINER

That winter, another Bundist leader showed up in Warsaw: the lawyer Leon Feiner, who had spent months languishing in Lida prison, at the tender mercies of the NKVD.

The Soviets had arrested Feiner during an attempted crossing into independent Lithuania. When he told his interrogators that, before the war, he had often defended communists in court, they only laughed and called him a fascist dog. The verdict came down: enemy of the people. The judge sentenced Feiner to death.

The Nazis came, the guards fled, and the prisoners broke out of their cells. Feiner walked the three hundred miles to Warsaw. When he turned up at a Polish socialist friend's doorstep, he was barefoot, bloody, and covered in lice. A few months later, David Klin smuggled Feiner into the ghetto. Bernard couldn't recognize his old friend. The Feiner of his memories was an incorrigible dandy and champion skier. This Feiner was a battered old man.

The party installed Feiner on the Aryan side. He had one task—getting guns. The submissive deaths of Chelmno's Jews filled the Bundists with shame. Vowing resistance, they resurrected their old militia with the help of a left-wing faction of the Polish Socialist Party. Five hundred fighters stood at the ready, under Bernard Goldstein's leadership. They believed they would take part in the liberation of Warsaw.

"The acquisition of arms became the one goal toward which we strained every sinew of our organization," Bernard Goldstein wrote. "How much time we had we didn't know, but we knew we didn't have enough." To liberate anything, they needed guns. For that, they needed the Home Army.

THE POLISH HOME ARMY

By early 1942, scattered Polish resistance groups had coalesced into the powerful Home Army, led by Colonel Stefan Rowecki and under the tenuous control of the Polish government-in-exile. The Home Army had hidden weapons caches, and hundreds of thousands of soldiers. They derailed trains, planted typhus-infected lice in Nazi shirt collars, and illicitly published *Information Bulletin*, the most popular newspaper in the country. Their symbol, a conjoined *P* and *W* that resembled an anchor, was scribbled everywhere in Aryan Warsaw. These letters stood for *Polska Walczaca* ("Fighting Poland").

The Home Army ruthlessly enforced its decrees over Polish society, shooting Gestapo informants and publishing blacklists of collaborators. A Pole who violated their boycott of German newspapers could expect a brick to the head. But as of 1942, the Home Army didn't punish blackmailers who hunted Jews in Aryan Warsaw, nor the Polish police who returned Jews to the ghetto.

Rowecki himself sympathized with Jews under Nazi occupation; he wrote horrified cables to the government-in-exile about the extermination campaign in the East. But he also knew his country. Many Poles had taken over Jewish property that they were disinclined to return, and many more equated all Jews with treacherous communists. (Even the

Home Army's own newspaper sometimes indulged in this accusation.) Many Poles bristled when exiled Polish politicians in London spoke about Jewish equality.

The Home Army's political bureau didn't include a single Jewish party, only a two-person "Jewish Department" that consisted of a Polish lawyer and his Jewish wife. Feiner tried to persuade them to give him weapons. He came up empty-handed.

ANTEK ZUCKERMAN AND CELINA LUBETKIN

Another group of Warsaw ghetto inmates was also contemplating insurrection: the Zionist youth activists at Dror.

Dror was a pioneering movement, in the parlance of the day, that dreamed of building agricultural communes in a Palestine they imagined to be more-or-less empty. To prepare themselves, they had set up training farms in Poland where, when they were not tilling the land, they studied Marx, learned Hebrew, and worshipped Joseph Stalin. Believing toil meant redemption, they worked to harden their muscles for the future Jewish state. Unlike the Bund, Dror was a movement by and for the young. This fact is important. Young people perceive unprecedented events more clearly than their elders, since, at such moments, experience only clouds the vision. Dror had no middle-aged leaders to hold them back.

In the Warsaw ghetto, Dror's leaders were Zivia "Celina" Lubetkin and Yitzhak "Antek" Zuckerman. Twenty-six and twenty-five respectively, Celina and Antek were lovers. They were also hardened operatives who had abandoned their families to organize behind Nazi lines. (Lithuanians had murdered Antek's parents in the Ponar forest.) Unlike many activists, Celina and Antek grasped that the Chelmno gas vans were early steps toward a mechanized slaughter of Europe's entire Jewish population. A genocide.

They could only fathom one response to this extermination: united, armed resistance. They needed the sort of weapons that only the Polish underground could provide. Only one Jewish group had these contacts: the Bund, their enemies.

THE MEETING

On March 23, seven delegates from the ghetto's leftist parties met at the Bund's soup kitchen on Orla Street to discuss resistance. Abrasha Blum and Maurycy Orzech were the Bundist representatives.

Neither Blum nor Orzech left an account of the meeting, so I rely here on testimony by Antek Zuckerman and the left-wing Zionist Hirsch Berlinski, both of whom considered Bundists their enemies. Keep this in mind as you read what follows.

Antek opened the meeting with information about the mass murder of Vilna's Jews. He appealed to the delegates to forget their differences in the face of extermination and come together to form a combat group.

Orzech shot Antek a withering look. "You're still a very young man, and your evaluation of the situation is too hasty," Orzech said—or so Antek remembered. Berlinski also recalled Orzech's icy mood, the way he bristled at sharing space with ideological opponents. "Were it not for the conditions in the ghetto, we would not be sitting around the table with the present political composition," Orzech said—at least by Berlinksi's telling.

Orzech explained that Jews were not the only victims, and that the Nazis also gassed Poles in Auschwitz. Sooner or later, the Poles would rise up, and on that day, the Bund's militia would rise with them. "We have to wage our struggle together for a better world, for the redemption of mankind," Orzech declared. He ended by telling the delegates that the entire meeting had been pointless.

In his memoirs, Antek reviled Orzech for his refusal. How could he ask Jews to wait for some far-off Polish uprising? Why did he care about ideological differences when, within a few months, most of the ghetto would be dead? I try to see it from the Bund's perspective. Their party had spent the last twenty years working with Polish socialists to build a future in their shared homeland. They had pledged their loyalty to a socialist movement, which they expected would protect them in turn. What could have seemed more delusional than some vague proposal for Jews to rise up on their own? Jews had no guns, and no support from the Aryan city. Before they managed to kill a single Nazi, the Germans would burn them alive. And the kids advancing this plan were not just any kids but representatives of an ideology that the Bund had loathed since its inception.

Without the Bund's help, a Jewish combat organization was dead on arrival.

CATS

That spring, Bernard Goldstein noted new arrivals to the Warsaw ghetto—thousands of beautifully dressed Czech and German Jews. They came with engraved leather luggage and blistering contempt for their trashy Polish brethren. So loud, so dirty, and that Yiddish! They gave everyone a bad name. German Jews knew their purgatory was temporary. After the war they'd go back to their nice apartments in Berlin. Many were Christian—Aryan except for a grandmother who had converted from Judaism. Some even had sons in the Wehrmacht.

"We called them cats," a survivor friend told me. In Polish, the phrase "I had" is *miałem*, pronounced "meow-em." I had a factory. I had a brass bed stand. I had a box at the opera. I had German friends. I had a country. Meow, meow, meow, meow, meow.

BERNARD GOLDSTEIN

Before dawn on April 18, Bernard Goldstein tossed in his narrow bed. He seldom slept through the night. When he closed his eyes, his mind ran through a rosary of horrors. His nephew's death in the Gestapo basement. His fault. The teens rounded up for labor camps. He couldn't protect them.

He woke up in a sweat. Was it a bullet? Or was that only a dream? Outside, a searchlight glared on the wall of the Gesia prison. He heard two shots and saw two silhouettes fall. Then it was dark and silent.

He didn't know when he fell asleep, only that when his eyes opened, it was light. Downstairs, two Jews scrubbed blood off the pavement.

That night, Gestapo men had invaded the ghetto with a list of sixty activists to kill. Guided by Jewish Police, the Gestapo pulled each activist from their bed and shot them on the sidewalk. Bodies stayed where they fell.

Polish socialists had warned Maurycy Orzech about a potential raid, but only Sonia Nowogrodska and the printer Lazar Klug managed to get his message and to escape. The Bund lost ten comrades.

A few days later, Adam Czerniakow summoned Orzech to the Judenrat office, to tell him the executions were a punishment for the Bund's underground activities. He begged the Bund to stop issuing its newspaper. Orzech refused. He reminded Czerniakow about the gas vans in Chelmno, proof that the Germans would kill them no matter how obediently they behaved.

More executions came. Two weeks later, the Gestapo killed sixty people, many of them printers for the underground press. They brought Bundist printer Moishe Sklar back from Pawiak for a curbside execution. When friends found Sklar's body, they saw that the Gestapo had cut his flesh into strips, burned holes through his feet, and crushed his penis. A Jewish Policeman stole the shoes off his corpse.

The Bundist press warned the ghetto that these murders were not random. They were terrorism, meant to paralyze the people into submission. Privately, Bundist leaders vowed resistance until death. They begged their Polish socialist friends for weapons. None came.

LONDON

At the start of May, a Home Army courier arrived in London, carrying two letters from Leon Feiner, the elegant lawyer who was now the Bund's agent on the Aryan side of Warsaw.

In the first letter, addressed to the Polish government-in-exile, Feiner described how Germans and their Lithuanian henchmen were systematically murdering the entire Jewish population of eastern Poland, using bullets and poison gas. (He also documented the murders of Roma.) Feiner criticized the antisemitism or complicit silence of most of the underground press but praised the Polish socialists. He insisted on the Bund's future in a free Poland.

The second letter, addressed to Arthur Zygielbojm, was intended for public distribution. Feiner estimated that the Germans had already murdered seven hundred thousand Polish Jews, and millions more faced "immediate annihilation." He demanded that Allied governments declare that German prisoners of war, and even German citizens who lived in their countries, would be killed if the annihilation of Jews continued.

Zygielbojm tried everything to publicize the Bund's report. He sent it to Prime Minister Sikorski and the British government. He placed an article in *The Telegraph* and read it on the BBC. On July 2, *The New York Times* printed a small item, of the sort it now runs about similar far-flung genocides. Thanks to the Bund, Americans read about the final solution at their breakfast tables. Then they turned the page.

WARSAW

In May, German film crews arrived to make a documentary about Jewish life in the Warsaw ghetto. The directors forced well-dressed girls to kick starving beggars. They stood a plump smuggler's wife next to a bald wretch in a potato sack. In the shuttered Jewish ritual bath, they ordered Hasidim to mime sex with young girls. They set up a floor show at Café Sztuka, sat artists down at the well-stocked tables, and made them applaud the showgirls till their palms bled. They ordered Judenrat chairman Czerniakow to insult a crowd of rabbis. "Wave your hands," they commanded. "Jews wave their hands!" They brought a menorah to his apartment and lit all the candles, to give it the proper Jewish ambience. Their cameras caressed every detail.

That same month, Nazis started to ship Poles to a slave labor camp near a small village fifty miles northeast of the capital. There, they ordered the Poles to build something. They would not explain its purpose.

BY THE END OF July, Warsaw's Jews had spent nearly two years inside a ghetto. A hundred thousand of them were dead. Every day, the Gestapo rounded up young men for their sadistic work camps. Germans gunned down Jews for any reason, or none. The once proud community kitchens had so little food they could only prolong starvation.

All the while, the Bund's old guard kept up their talk about working-class solidarity and the need to maintain ideological distinctions. The youth began to drift away. They couldn't understand why the leaders had refused to join a united combat group. Who cared if their fellow fighters were communists or Zionists? No one was going to Moscow. Palestine might as well have been Mars. The ghetto was their country. Did the leaders really think they had more in common with walled-off Polish workers than with Jewish teens dying before their eyes?

TISH B'AV

Rumors circulated that the Germans wanted to deport Warsaw's Jews to worksites in the East. The Judenrat denied it, but a blanket of anxiety fell, thick and paralyzing. Ghetto inmates whispered that maybe the order would only apply to the people in refugee hostels, or the smugglers in Gesia prison. Each treasured a wild hope that she would survive.

July 22 was Tisha b'Av, the day when Jews mourn the destruction of the temple in Jerusalem. A young Bundist named Vladka Peltel was in her mother's home when her neighbor burst in to tell them about the posters.

"The street was thick with people, streaming from every doorway as news spread from house to house, jostling and elbowing to get close enough to read the notices pasted on the wall. Each, it seemed, was consumed by the need to see the notices with his own eyes," Vladka wrote.

> By order of the German authorities, all the Jews of Warsaw, regardless of age or sex, will be deported. Only those employed in German workshops, the Judenrat, the Jewish Police, and the Jewish hospital will be exempt. . . . Those failing to comply with this edict will be liable for death.

Gina Klepfisz

CHAPTER 24

BOXCAR

(July 1942–January 1943)

THE GREAT AKTION

IT WAS DRIZZLING ON JULY 22, 1942, WHEN THE NAZIS BEGAN TO liquidate the Warsaw ghetto.

Deportations followed their own satanic rhythm. The Jewish Police, supervised by SS men and their Latvian, Lithuanian, and Ukrainian helpers, would surround a building, bash down the doors, and force the residents into the courtyard. Anyone who couldn't walk, they carried. Once in the courtyard, SS men inspected the Jews' documents to decide who stayed and who went. Henchmen shoved those marked for deportation into waiting horse carts. As the carts began to roll, those inside threw notes onto the pavement for their relatives. "I love you. Save me."

Carts went to a collection point at Stawki Square, next to the train tracks. History calls it by its German name, the Umschlagplatz. There, thousands of people stood packed like cattle in a factory farm. There was no food and no water. There were also no toilets, so they sat in their own shit. "In this crowded square all the continually nursed illusions collapse," Marek Edelman wrote. "This is the moment of revelation, that soon the worst, the unthinkable, the thing one would not believe to the very last moments, is about to happen."

In the morning and the afternoon, Jews were forced into the boxcars. One hundred people to a boxcar. Thirty boxcars a shift. Six thousand people a day.

The Germans assured the ghetto that they would spare workers in their factories. The ghetto believed them. Everyone hunted for a work card, paying Germans handsomely for their enslavement.

"All of us felt that active resistance and obstruction of the deportations were the only possible course," Bernard Goldstein wrote. "The ghetto had no right to sacrifice sixty thousand human beings so that survivors might continue their slave existence a little longer." The first night, activists embarked on a flurry of meetings, at least one of which was attended by a Polish socialist. They knew they couldn't launch an uprising alone and unarmed, but they could forge work passes and pull their comrades from the boxcars. They would save one another while they found weapons and persuaded the ghetto to act.

The next afternoon, representatives from various political movements met at the offices of the Jewish self-help group Aleynhilf at 25 Nowolipki Street. Abrasha Blum and Maurycy Orzech represented the Bund. The party had instructed them to urge their fellow representatives toward a united resistance.

Two Zionist youth movements—Dror and Hashomer Hatzair—had the same idea. Dror's general secretary, Antek Zuckerman, who had clashed with Orzech several months earlier, continued advancing his idea of a united Jewish combat group. He reminded the activists that the Jewish Police were only armed with rubber clubs, which were hardly better than the sticks and rocks that littered the ghetto. Any organized group could take them. They just needed the will.

This time, Blum and Orzech agreed with him, but Antek's words shocked the other delegates. Rebellion meant mass suicide, Labor Zionist Ignacy Schiper warned, not just for the participants but for the entire ghetto. Orthodox leader Zisha Friedman counseled faith in God. The majority voted against organized resistance.

The meeting ended at twilight. Blum was lingering on the corner of Nowolipki Street, chatting with Marek Edelman, when a comrade, Berek Sznajdmil, ran up with shocking news. Unable to endure the upcoming deportation of the ghetto's children, Judenrat chairman Adam Czerniakow had swallowed cyanide.

"Did he leave a note?" Edelman asked. He had, Berek said, but it was nothing special.

GINA KLEPFISZ

At first, Bundists, communists, and left-wing Zionists tried to make a committee to organize resistance, but roundups soon made communication between the groups impossible, as each activist fought to keep their immediate circle alive. In their underground newspaper, the Bund urged defiance. Maurycy Orzech wrote, "Do not believe you are being sent to work. . . . You are being led to your deaths. This is the devilish continuation of the extermination campaign which has already been carried out in the provinces. Resist! Fight tooth and nail! Do not report to the Umschlagplatz!"

In late July, Nazis offered the starving ghetto inmates an enticement. Anyone who volunteered for deportation would get three kilograms of bread and one kilogram of marmalade. The Bund's best fighters went like this. Big men, teamsters and porters who had once made nationalists weep, now lined up meekly at the collection point. They were not afraid of work, and why would the Germans feed them only to kill them the next day?

As the seizures spread, the Bund fought to keep their members alive. They set up workshops to counterfeit employment documents like those assigned to the Judenrat and Aleynhilf, whose workers were exempt from deportation, which they distributed amongst their comrades. Even these cards caused more guilt. Every Bundist who survived meant that someone else would end up in a boxcar.

The old Jewish hospital sat beside the Umschlagplatz. A clinic still functioned, as if to maintain the illusion that people were being deported to work. Nurses circulated in their crisp white uniforms. They were permitted to go into the Umschlagplatz, and sometimes they could snatch a person out. There were many Bundists amongst the hospital staff, including Gina Klepfisz. Before the war, Gina had stitched up wounded Tsukunft fighters after brawls at the university, while her brother Michal fought the nationalists with his fists. Both brother and sister were Morgenstern athletes. Photos show Gina in a tie, her hair cropped and slicked. A glamorous, ideal butch.

When the deportations started, Gina had put on her starched dress, clean like nothing else around her, and made her way to the hospital. From the windows overlooking the Umschlagplatz, she tried to spot her comrades. When she saw one, she grabbed a doctor's smock, shoved her way into the scrum, and before anyone could see, put the smock on her friend's back. Thus dressed, he could leave with her. She had to work fast. Nurses still risked being shoved into the boxcars. These rescues had their own moral agony. A rescuer could only save a few people each day. The rest went into the boxcars.

In one roundup, the Germans took Gina's parents. She could not manage to save them.

ZALMAN FRIEDRICH

When cheerful letters began to arrive from relatives sent away on the boxcars, the ghetto deluded itself as to their significance. They wanted to believe the letters were real, that their relatives were alive. The Bund knew better, but to convince the ghetto, they needed proof. They smuggled blond Zalman Friedrich to the Aryan side of the city, where Polish socialists provided him with a railway worker's uniform and information on the movements of the ghetto boxcars. He followed their trail about fifty-four miles east, to Sokolow Podlaski. There, railway men told him that the Germans had built a new spur, heading toward a village called Treblinka. Twice a day, boxcars packed with Jews went in that direction. They always returned empty. In the Sokolow Podlaski market, Friedrich spotted a naked, blood-soaked man, his face rendered unrecognizable from beatings. It was an old comrade, the nephew of the Soviet ambassador to America. He had just escaped from the Treblinka death camp.

VLADKA PELTEL

The Bund's past mocked its present. One night, in one crowded hideout, Vladka Peltel listened to her former teacher reminisce about Red Vienna, which she had visited during the Workers' Olympiad in 1931. The teacher spoke about how she carried the Bund's banner down the Ringstrasse, and how the Viennese children cheered as she passed.

Her memories infuriated the others. They had also believed in universal brotherhood, in a world without exploitation and war, but now such sentiments seemed like cruel jokes.

"Where are they now, your noble-hearted Austrians?" one of her companions sneered.

The teacher insisted that Austrians were not all monsters, that they didn't know the atrocities done in their name.

A few days later, she was deported to Treblinka.

SONIA NOWOGRODSKA

Locked together in a comrade's attic, Bernard Goldstein and Sonia Nowogrodska listened helplessly to their city's murder. Through Jacob Celemenski, news came of the liquidation of the Medem Sanatorium. Before the deportation, teachers told the older children to flee into the forest, but peasants caught them and handed them over. The younger kids kicked and bit as the Nazis loaded them into trucks; their teachers accompanied them to Treblinka. Afterward, Poles looted the sanatorium. The geese and rabbits the children raised went straight into the peasants' soup pots.

Bernard and Sonia had passports listing them as a married couple, and fake work permits they didn't trust. They passed the time discussing their own deaths. As she spoke, Sophia dealt herself games of solitaire. Her hands were steady as she matched up the cards.

Sometimes she said they should give themselves up to the Umschlagplatz. Only scum remained in the ghetto, she told her former student Marek Edelman. The good people had gone to Treblinka, leaving only selfish, amoral brutes. What right did she have to stay? Her place was with Jewish workers, wherever they went. "If I shall be with them, then, perhaps, they will not forget that they are human beings," she said.

MARMALADE

After a year spent begging every contact in the Polish underground, the Bund finally seemed on the verge of getting guns. A Polish socialist friend told Maurycy Orzech that the underground had diverted a railway car full of German rifles to the Warsaw station, where it sat, ready for the Bund to loot. Maurycy slipped over to the Aryan side to arrange the theft. He told Marek to wait for his call at Sonia Nowogrodska's old apartment, one of the only places in the ghetto with a working phone line. He would call the morning of August 13.

Marek waited in Sonia's empty flat. He was hungry, and the light glittered tauntingly on a jar of marmalade that sat on the kitchen shelf. Hours passed. The sun moved west. He waited for the phone to ring. He heard a clamor from the window. Outside, Nazis drove a crowd of Jews toward the Umschlagplatz. Marek saw Sonia Nowogrodska among them.

Only one photo remains of Sonia in the ghetto. She is thin and intelligent looking. She wears a silly fedora. Her suit is so sleek it makes her armband seem like a fashion statement.

It was afternoon when they loaded Jews straight into boxcars. Marek knew he could not save her. After the sun set, he ate the marmalade.

The telephone never rang.

CAULDRON

Bernard Goldstein ran from one hiding spot to the next. Old acquaintances saved his life a thousand times. The workers he had unionized hid him in their factories. A thief he once threatened gave him precious bread. He crouched beneath rag piles, stood in the closet of the Jewish hospital, squeezed beneath the floorboards of an abandoned building, crammed into a cubbyhole to find a young woman, warm and soft, who clung to him like he was life. In a Niska Street attic, the rats kept him awake. He didn't mind. "They were friends—rats. . . . We were not so far apart. I too, lying hidden in my own burrow, was a hateful and hunted animal."

On September 6, six weeks after they started their deportations, the Germans forced the last hundred thousand ghetto Jews into a single block for a two-day selection that prisoners nicknamed "the cauldron." Documents meant nothing anymore. All that mattered was a numbered slip of paper. Anyone without one went into the boxcars. "The chances of receiving [one] were almost nil, but the mere fact that such chances did exist was sufficient to confuse people, to cause their attention to converge solely on the means of securing the numbered slip," Marek Edelman wrote. Numbed by horror, even young Bundists followed the herd. When the Germans surrounded their workshop, the Tsukunft member Vladka Peltel's comrades decided to rebel. Henoch Russ mounted a chair and called on his fellow workers to stay at their posts, and resist anyone who tried to drag them out. There was an awkward silence. A supervisor ordered them down to the courtyard. The workers streamed out. Vladka and her friends followed.

BIRTHDAY

The mass deportations ended on September 21, 1942. They had taken most of Warsaw's Bundists with them. Despite their people's decimation, the Bund managed to publish their newspaper a week later, with Zalman Friedrich's report on the Treblinka death camp. They implored their readers to face the truth.

> Every Jew should know the fate of those resettled. The same fate awaits the remaining few left in Warsaw. The conclusion is: Don't let yourself be taken! Run away! . . . Help one another! Take care of the children! . . . We must survive so that we can demand a reckoning for the tortured brothers and sisters. . . .

That night was Yom Kippur. It had been exactly forty-five years since the Bund's creation.

BERNARD GOLDSTEIN

Bernard walked through the streets without recognition. Stores gaped obscenely. Possessions lay strewn around the ravaged courtyards. Survivors scurried like mice.

Only fragments remained of the largest Jewish city in Europe. Where were the Krochmalna brides and Yankl Scarface? The showgirls of Qui Pro Quo? The worshippers at the thieves' synagogue? The Seven Lions of Praga? The Yiddish actresses who painted a new face each night? Where were the slaughterhouse workers, the commies, the black hats, the housewives, the hacks, the brats who followed Khaskele Hunchback to the forest on bright spring days and returned tan and sleepy to their mothers?

Gone.

CROSSING

That autumn, Abrasha Blum ordered Bernard Goldstein to leave the ghetto. Inside, he was a burden. Outside, he could convince Polish socialists to get them guns. Comrades would sneak him onto a work gang headed to the Okecie airport. He could run from there.

Dressed in his white hospital uniform, Marek Edelman led Bernard to the assembly point at 51 Mila Street. Bernard's beard made him look older, and his feet were so swollen he could barely walk. He examined the sloppy kid he'd known since childhood and thought about how their roles had switched. Two years before, Bernard had been the Bund's strongman, and Marek had walked behind him like an acolyte. Now Marek gently led him by the arm. At the assembly point, the supervisor, a former Morgenstern athlete, pressed a bribe into the SS man's palm. He looked the other way while Bernard joined the workers on a wagon. As soon as they crossed the gate, he saw a truck with the blond Bundist Zalman Friedrich in the back. At Friedrich's signal, Bernard jumped off the wagon, pulled himself up into the truck's passenger seat, and ripped the Star of David from his arm.

It was an exquisite fall day in Aryan Warsaw. The sun shone across the ornate balconies of Wolska Street, and the oak leaves flamed in Titian red. The cafés were packed. Passengers hung off the sides of street cars. Pretty girls ran errands. Their heels were vertiginous, and they set their hats elegantly off-kilter atop meticulously waved blond hair.

This was his city. Every alleyway had known his feet. The police chief had feared him. Tabloids had fêted him. Workers had shaken his hand. Bernard Goldstein stared at the rushing river of humanity. He felt nothing at all.

THE ARYAN SIDE

Twenty thousand Jews hid on the Aryan side of Warsaw, in conditions of abject fear.

The Polish city was more hostile than ever. Some of it was due to Nazi propaganda, but the hatred had a material base. Many Poles had profited from Jewish persecution. Their debts to Jewish lenders were canceled. They were given Jewish stores as trustees. There was a glut of nice apartments after their Jewish owners went into the ghetto. Who would want to give that up? The deportations to Treblinka did little to increase Polish sympathy. The seeming passivity of the Jews disgusted them. Even the underground press berated the victims for failing to fight back. These articles didn't mention that the Polish underground refused to give Jews weapons.

At Bernard's first meeting on the Aryan side, Orzech and Feiner filled him in on their comrades' conditions. Unable to find refuge, many Bundists slept in cemeteries or bombed-out ruins. After the raid on Medem Sanatorium, Arthur Zygielbojm's wife, Manya, had wandered the countryside with her young son until finally returning to the ghetto in desperation.

To save other comrades from Manya's fate, the Bund relied on couriers like Adina Blady. Once a doctor at the Bersohn and Bauman Children's Hospital, Adina had poisoned her young patients to spare them from Treblinka. On the Aryan side, she and her former co-worker Marisha Feinmesser found melinas for fugitive Jews. The pair rented dozens of rooms under a panoply of fake names, using elaborate pretexts and eye-popping bribes—even enduring sexual molestation from one of their Polish helpers. They had no choice. Melinas meant survival.

Through it all, the Bund continued to give, as well as receive, solidarity. In addition to the telegrams they sent abroad about their people's extermination, they sent others to call for Indian independence and demand the release of Mahatma Gandhi, arrested in August for his Quit India campaign.

This humanism in the context of a genocide amazes me. If anything sustained it, it was perhaps the help that Polish socialists gave. Though they failed to provide the Bund with weapons, Polish socialists still risked their lives to save their comrades. At a time when Nazis punished such aid with the executions of entire families, Polish socialists hid Bundists in their humble homes. When she fled to the Aryan side, Gina Klepfisz, the Bundist nurse who saved her comrades at the Umschlagplatz, found refuge with two old acquaintances, the Polish socialist sisters Anna Wachalska and Maria Sawicka. Like Gina, Maria was an athlete; as a sprinter for the Polish Socialist Party's sports club, she had even traveled to Red Vienna with the Bund for the Workers' Olympiad. She and Gina had been friends since their teenage years. They grew closer now—so close that, decades later, Maria asked the Klepfisz family if she could be buried in Gina's grave. The women shared a single bed.

SOPHIA DUBNOVA

In October 1942, the Erlichs disembarked at New York City's Pennsylvania Station. In the three years since they set out from Warsaw, they had nearly circumnavigated the globe. Viktor Alter's sister Esther Iwinska was there to embrace them. "America is ruled by old women," she said, a grin lighting up her usually acerbic face.

The Erlichs moved into a dingy apartment near Columbia University, amidst their fellow socialist refugees. Like the rest of the New York Bundists, they fought to learn what had happened to Alter and Erlich. But the leads were drying up. Fiorello La Guardia, Eleanor Roosevelt, Albert Einstein, and Clement Attlee in the U.K. all made inquiries, which turned up nothing. When Polish ambassador Stanislaw Kot tried to intervene, the Soviets told him Alter and Erlich were Soviet citizens and thus none of his business.

THE WARSAW GHETTO

After the deportations stopped, twenty-five Tsukunft members gathered in a Franciszkanska Street apartment near the brush factory to scream out their grief. They were the first generation raised in independent Poland. The beneficiaries of the Bund's social infrastructure, they grew up as a family. They had marched together on May Day, read Sholem Aleichem at the TSYCHO schools, learned to ice-skate at the Morgenstern sports clubs, had their first hookups at Bundist summer camps, fought nationalist students in the Tsukunft militia. They had been raised on an ethos of universalist socialism and physical resistance, to believe in the better and more beautiful tomorrow.

All of this was gone. They had lost their families, their sweethearts, and most of their comrades. The Bund's adult leaders were dead or hiding in Aryan Warsaw. The youth were on their own, with no more elders to restrain them. This best explains the choice that they made. They no longer cared about political doctrines or ideological spats, not when they had seen the Umschlagplatz. They would join the Zionists in a suicidal act of rebellion.

THE JEWISH COMBAT ORGANIZATION

The Jewish Combat Organization—*Zydowska Organizacja Bojowa*, known by its Polish initials, ZOB—was founded by Antek Zuckerman,

Celina Lubetkin, and their Dror comrades just after the Great Aktion began. They had not managed to accomplish much. They made one ally—the People's Guard, a communist paramilitary that the Soviets created inside Poland after the Nazis invaded the Soviet Union—but it was a small group, with few weapons to share. The People's Guard gave the ZOB several pistols, which they used to wound the Jewish Police chief. They also burned down warehouses filled with looted property. But their actions frightened other ghetto inmates, who worried about German retaliation. When the ZOB hung copies of their manifestos, other Jews beat them up. The Gestapo found their guns without trying, and most of the young people they sent to join partisan groups in nearby forests were caught and shot. By October, they were so ashamed of their failure that they wanted to set the whole ghetto on fire. Eventually, Antek prevailed upon his comrades to stay alive a bit longer. If they had to die, they ought to take some Germans with them.

This left them in the same position as the Bund's militia. To fight, they needed guns, which only the Polish underground could provide. Though the Home Army had hundreds of machine guns and over seven thousand small arms hidden around Warsaw, they were loath to share them with the Jewish resistance. The Home Army had a solid strategy: shun open confrontation with the Germans and instead build up strength until Allied troops were close enough to support them in an uprising. General Rowecki claimed that a ghetto revolt would be premature and doomed to failure. Yet even as he said this, he swore to protect Poles from Nazi extermination. "If the occupiers decide to direct the same methods they are using against the Jews against the Polish people, they will meet with ferocious resistance," the Home Army's newspaper promised. Jews might have been Polish citizens, but they were not Poland's responsibility.

After they finally made contact with the Home Army in October, the ZOB concocted a serious-sounding body called the Jewish National Committee in order to look legitimate. They just needed to convince the Bundists to join them.

This was not an easy task. For decades, the Bund had been loath to team up with other Jewish political groups, preferring instead to work with non-Jewish parties like the Mensheviks or the Polish Socialists, whom they found to be more natural ideological bedfellows. After the mass deportation of the Warsaw ghetto, young Bundists no longer saw the wisdom of this plan, but their elders outside the ghetto still held fast to old political distinctions. There was also a more banal obstacle to unity. Bundists and Zionists had disliked each other since childhood. In a ghetto blighted with informers, they wanted to fight alongside their friends. The Bundists bickered, until Tsukunft leader Henoch Russ cast the deciding vote for unity.

In late October, the Bund joined the ZOB, with Marek Edelman as their commander. (The Jewish National Committee was a step too far, so the Bund cooked up a coordinating committee to be a bureaucratic condom between themselves and the Zionists.)

Even then, unity only went so far. The ZOB would have nothing to do with the ghetto's *other* resistance group, the right-wing Zionist ZZW. Some bridges are too far to cross.

After the deportations, the Germans cut the ghetto into enclaves, which Jews were forbidden to cross between. The ZOB split these enclaves into twenty wards. Parties made their own combat units, each comprised of a commander and five fighters armed with knives, axes, and brass knuckles. The ZOB units would operate autonomously, allowing each unit to fight alone if communication broke down. For the mostly ceremonial role of commander in chief, the ZOB elected a tough, grandiose boy named Mordechai Anielewicz, a member of the left-wing Zionist youth movement Hashomer Hatzair whose mother once sold rotten fish down by the river. They picked him because he wanted it so much.

Bundist battle squads assigned themselves to the brush factory, where four thousand Jews manufactured camouflage for military trains. Admission was tough. The Bund only accepted fighters who had their own weapons, and whom the party had known before the war. They chauvinistically rejected women, until one Tsukunft member threatened to quit if his girlfriend couldn't fight alongside him.

The ZOB's first act was to rid the ghetto of collaborators. Fighters shot Jakub Lejkn, second in command of the Jewish Police, and Israel Fuerst, a liaison with the Gestapo. Afterward, they posted communiqués to explain the executions. Their posters warned the ghetto not to trust the occupiers who had murdered their families. Nazism "throws a boat to the next victim before slaughtering him. . . . Do not delude yourself and let yourself be deluded. . . . Prepare yourself to defend your lives."

When German guards arrested three Bundists who had beaten a sadistic foreman in Hallman's factory, Bundist Gabriel Frishdorf led a raid to free his men. These acts of defiance transformed the ZOB into legends. Bakers baked them bread, leatherworkers made them holsters, and ladies turned over their jewelry to fund the cause.

In December the Home Army finally gave the ZOB ten revolvers. Despite the ZOB's pleas, no more guns arrived. Rowecki didn't believe that Jews would use them.

JAN KARSKI

That October, Home Army courier Jan Karski met two Jewish leaders in a ruined villa on the outskirts of Warsaw. One was the Zionist Adolf Berman, and the other was the Bundist Leon Feiner.

At first, Feiner's appearance shocked Karski. With his silver whiskers, ruddy face, and bespoke suit, he looked exactly like a Polish aristocrat. "Our entire people are being destroyed," he said, pressing his hands to the table. "A few may be saved, perhaps, but three million Polish Jews are doomed. This cannot be prevented by any force in Poland, neither the Polish nor the Jewish underground. Place this responsibility on the shoulders of the Allies." Feiner described the deportations, and the Bund's report on Treblinka.

The two leaders told Karski to demand that the world try to halt the extermination, that they execute Germans in Allied countries or pay bribes to rescue Jews. Anything but sit and watch them die. When Karski asked them what to tell Jewish leaders in the West, Feiner gripped his arm so tightly that it ached. His eyes were no longer those of a Polish aristocrat but of a shattered survivor.

"Tell them that there are moments when we hate them all . . . because they are safe 'there' and do not rescue us. Because they don't do enough. . . . Let the Jewish leaders, then, do something that will force the other world to believe us. . . . We are all dying here; let them die too. . . . Let them crowd the offices of Churchill and others, let them proclaim a fast before the doors of the mightiest and not retreat until they believe us, until they will take some action to rescue those of our people who are still alive."

Before Karski left, Feiner handed him a report he had written at the height of the Great Aktion, describing the Nazi extermination campaign that had already consumed over 1.2 million human lives. It was the first major Jewish report on the Holocaust.

ARTHUR ZYGIELBOJM

Arthur Zygielbojm's London post as a Bund delegate for the Polish government-in-exile had not been easy, but he tried his hardest. He sent death camp testimonies to indifferent bigwigs. He appealed to international law. He gave speeches at PEN clubs, union rallies, coal mines, and synagogues. He organized petitions, wrote essays, let labor politicians use him in their factional squabbles just to get their ear. He convened conferences. He gave broadcasts on the BBC. "It will actually be a shame . . . to belong to the human race if steps are not taken to halt the greatest crime in human history," he cried when news broke about the use of poison gas in Chelmno. Afterward, England's chief Rabbi suggested a polite day of prayer and mourning. Zygielbojm could have puked. British Jews should smash up the streets, he replied, like his people in Warsaw would have done if British Jews were being butchered. The respectable British Jews did no such thing.

After all the fake reports of German atrocities that the British media put out during World War I, the British public was skeptical of Zygielbojm's claims. Exiled German socialists worried he would make all Germans look bad. At the foreign office, top diplomat Frank Roberts refused to accept the idea that Hitler treated Jews worse than other peoples under Nazi occupation. All Zygielbojm could do was send cash. Thanks to his efforts, that October, Home Army parachutists brought five thousand dollars to Bundist leaders hiding on the Aryan side of Warsaw.

The Polish Home Army courier Jan Karski arrived in London in November, with a microfilm copy of Feiner's report hidden inside his hollowed-out fake teeth. On December 2, Karski met Arthur Zygielbojm at the bustling Stratton House, where the Polish Ministry of the Interior was headquartered. Zygielbojm had a hard, skeptical face. Karski imagined he had started life out as a street cleaner.

"My dear man. I am a Jew. Tell me what you know about the Jews of Poland," Zygielbojm demanded. He sat tensely, staring into the distance.

Karski pulled no punches about Feiner's report, nor about the horrors he had witnessed when Feiner snuck him into the ghetto. When Karski repeated some British naysaying, Zygielbojm jumped up in rage. "Don't tell me what is said and done here. . . . I came to you to hear about what is happening there! What they want there!"

In the underground, comrades nicknamed Karski "the tape recorder" for his faculty of reproducing words in all their emotional cadence. He began to speak. Or rather, Leon Feiner spoke through him.

> There are moments when we hate them all; we hate them because they are safe "there" and do not rescue us. Because they don't do enough . . . Let them do something that will force the other world to believe us. . . . Let them proclaim a fast before the doors of the mightiest and not retreat until they believe us. . . .
>
> We are all dying here; let them die too.

Zygielbojm sprung back as if he had been slapped. It was impossible to have this sort of public hunger strike in England, he explained. Police would carry him off to an asylum long before he could starve himself to death. After a few moments, he calmed himself down enough to ask Karski for details. How did Feiner look? What was he wearing? Was he nervous? What was the ghetto like?

When the time was up, Zygielbojm looked at Karski as if he were one of his lost Warsaw friends. . . . "I'll do everything they demand if only I'm given a chance," he said. "You believe me, don't you?"

After Karski visited British and American leaders, their countries' spokesmen issued ferocious denunciations of Nazi atrocities. This was cold comfort to Arthur Zygielbojm. Words didn't save anyone, he knew, even though they were all anyone would offer. The guilt ate him alive.

Zygielbojm tried harder. He distributed hundreds of copies of Feiner's report to British politicians, celebrities, and journalists, to little result. He cabled Winston Churchill. Churchill's underlings blew him off. He met with Deputy Prime Minister Stanislaw Mikolajczyk, to demand the Home Army use their guns to defend Polish Jews. Mikolajczyk told him this went against the Home Army's strategy of waiting for the right moment to rise up against the Germans, and that the very suggestion was treasonous.

Every day that passed, Nazis murdered more of the world he came from. As he told BBC listeners, "I am aware right now that perhaps I am a representative of a community of the dead."

CONTRABAND

Everyone told Gina Klepfisz not to get the operation. You can survive ulcers, they said. But she had always been athletic, strong enough to pull people out of boxcars. She didn't want to be weak. She checked herself into a Catholic hospital under the name of Kazimiera Juzwiak. Afterward, an infection developed. A father confessor prattled in Latin at her deathbed.

Did she have anything to confess? he asked.

"I am a Jew," she spat back.

As her niece, the poet Irena Klepfisz, later wrote, "Such a will to be known can alter history."

On December 5, comrades buried Gina at the Catholic Brodno cemetery, with her Polish pseudonym engraved on the tombstone. They were Bundists and Polish socialists.

Tsukunft member Vladka Peltel attended Gina's funeral. She had snuck out of the ghetto that morning, with a map of the Treblinka death camp hidden inside her shoe. A few days later, she met Leon Feiner in a convent restaurant on Sewerynow Street. Feiner gave Vladka her missions. Befriend Poles. Find melinas for women and children. Assist Jews in hiding. Get weapons. When Vladka bought her first revolver, she couldn't even tell if it worked until she showed it to Bernard Goldstein. It was legit, he told her. She turned it over in her hands, like a jewel.

With the help of Polish socialist friends, the Bund bought stolen guns from the guards at army dumps, from demoralized German soldiers returned from the Battle of Stalingrad, and from Poles who worked at arms factories. They also had contacts in the underworld, like pickpocket king Roman Kowalski, aka the Tsar of Venice, who refused payment for weapons out of loyalty to his Jewish fellow thieves.

Each weapon had to be smuggled into the ghetto. Dressed as a Polish peddler, Vladka concealed revolvers in boxes of nails and hid metal files in potato sacks. (Prisoners used files to saw through barred boxcar windows.) In Feiffer's factory, which adjoined the ghetto, she repackaged dynamite into smaller parcels, then bribed the guard not to notice. She paid a smuggler to use his ladder, tied a kerchief around her arm in lieu of an armband, and dropped over the wall. Despite everything, she was always relieved to be back inside. "I was among my own," she wrote.

CHILDREN

Everyone knew the end was near, and they needed to smuggle out their children. It was hard to find them placements. Most Poles didn't want to hide kids, who might reveal their identities with a clumsy phrase and get their host families murdered. Polish families sometimes mistreated their charges, or stole the money meant to maintain them. And there was the pain of separation.

Gina Klepfisz's brother—the handsome, athletic engineer Michal Klepfisz—was a new father when the deportations began in the Warsaw ghetto. In 1942, he left his one-year-old daughter, Irena, outside a Catholic orphanage. He had to watch from a distance as the brides of Christ took away his only child. He never saw her again. Once, he tried to speak to the Mother Superior, to give her chocolates for his daughter. The Mother Superior told him that if he ever came back, she would throw Irena out on the street.

MORDECHAI ANIELEWICZ

The Home Army's ten revolvers were hardly sufficient, but they were a start. They let the ZOB kill snitches and save arrested comrades. As a show of force, the ZOB planned a public demonstration. On January 21, fighters would take over several streets in the central ghetto, hang wreathes and banners to commemorate the fallen, and light a bonfire in

Muranow Square. They would also arrest any Jewish Policeman they could catch. In advance of the demonstration, they published a manifesto calling on Jews to resist. "Our slogan must be—all are ready to die as human beings."

The demonstration would never take place. On January 18, 1943, just before sunrise, Nazis entered the ghetto for a new round of roundups. They banged doors, demanding Jews come out. Instead, the ghetto inmates retreated to their hiding places.

The raid took the ZOB by surprise, catching most of their members away from their arms caches. Only the kids from Mordechai Anielewicz's Zionist Hashomer Hatzair youth group were prepared. They wandered outside, guns and hand grenades hidden beneath their clothing, and allowed themselves to be taken. I say kids, not fighters, because that's what they were. Most had never fired a gun. The kids wove themselves through a column of Jews headed toward the Umschlagplatz. At the corner of Mila and Zamenhof, it was now or never. Someone shouted, "Fire." Seventeen-year-old Margalit Landau pulled a grenade from beneath her dress and threw it at a German. The kids, now fighters, began to shoot.

CHAPTER 25

REVOLT

(January 1943–May 1943)

HALINKA

FOR A FEW SECONDS, THE GERMANS WERE PARALYZED. HOW DID JEWS get guns? In the shock, Mordechai Anielewicz managed to wrestle a weapon away from a German soldier. He dove behind some rubble, firing wildly, until a hand popped out from a bunker and pulled him to safety. The trance broke. The Germans gunned down the deportation column.

For the next three days, clashes raged around the ghetto. In the Schutz factory, Bundist Avram Feiner died trying to grab a German's carbine. Germans caught Boruch Peltz's Bundist battle squad unarmed and herded them to the Umschlagplatz. There, Peltz implored the Jews not to enter the boxcars. The commandant shot them all.

Of all January's victims, I think first of a fourteen-year-old girl named Halinka Kipman, whose name I found in journalist Janina Bauman's youthful ghetto memoir *Winter in the Morning*. Few facts remain about Halinka's life. Her parents were doctors. She went to a Bundist school. She was pretty. She slept with her boyfriend. Girls gossiped that she was a slut.

She tried to seize joy where she could.

Janina Bauman spent the January revolt huddled behind a wardrobe. When she went outside afterward, she found Halinka's body, dark hair spread over the bloodstained snow, and her handsome boyfriend beside her. "I cried for them, and hated myself, a righteous virgin, hiding like a coward while others fought and died," Janina wrote.

This chapter is dedicated to Halinka.

THE JEWISH COMBAT ORGANIZATION

As Frantz Fanon wrote, "violence is a dis-intoxicating force." The gains of the January revolt were not military—the ZOB was only able to steal seven weapons—so much as psychological. The ghetto learned that defiance was possible. German supermen could bleed.

The ZOB fighters became the ghetto's kings. They raided the Gesia Street jail and liberated its prisoners. They levied taxes on anyone who still had money, and kidnapped or shot those who would not pay. They robbed the Judenrat treasury, hauling off cash in a soup vat. They clashed with the right-wing Zionists of the ZZW, who they considered little more than Mussolini-style fascists. At one meeting between the groups, a ZZW fighter shoved a pistol into Marek Edelman's face and demanded to be given control of the rebellion. When the ZZW tried to muscle in on a ZOB robbery, it ended in a shootout.

No matter how just their cause, when a group militarizes, they are faced with impossible moral choices. Once, ZOB fighters caught a boy of thirteen eavesdropping on a meeting. Was he a spy? Or just a curious potential applicant, like he claimed? Whatever the truth, the ZOB shot him. It was too dangerous to keep him alive.

MICHAL KLEPFISZ

January's unplanned revolt had another effect. It raised the ZOB's status in the eyes of Home Army leadership. General Rowecki sent another shipment of guns into the ghetto. He no longer doubted that Jews would use them.

How many guns? Polish and Jewish sources differ, but according to Marek Edelman, the ZOB received forty-nine revolvers, five hundred bullets, fifty grenades, and one machine gun. The rest was either stolen in transit or simply never sent.

On the Aryan side, Bundists plotted to get more weapons. They could afford to pay. In addition to ghetto robberies, the Bund had another source of funds—the Jewish Labor Committee. But money didn't help if they couldn't find honest sellers.

The situation inspired Bundist engineer Michal Klepfisz to think back to his university studies. He brought out an old chemistry textbook and read the part about what happens when you mix potash, hydrochloric acid, cyanide, sugar, and gasoline. The promised results seemed tantalizing. He tested the recipe in a deserted lime kiln on his landlord's property. He threw the bottle. The glass shattered. The liquid burst into flame.

In an abandoned church, a Home Army officer helped Klepfisz refine his skills with explosives, teaching him to manufacture grenades, land mines, pipe bombs filled with shrapnel, and souped-up Molotov cocktails. Klepfisz used this knowledge to create bomb factories inside the ghetto, with chemicals provided by the Polish Socialist Party.

In rooms silent as sanctums, teenagers stirred vats of incendiary liquids, then transferred them into old vodka bottles to be weighed, measured, and lined up. A single misstep and the house could blow. Marek Edelman sometimes saw Klepfisz astride the wall on Parysowski Square, passing down enormous packages of benzene and potassium chloride while the smugglers kept their respectful distance. The stockpiles accumulated.

STEFAN MACHAI

Someone was watching the Bundists in Aryan Warsaw. Melinas burned. SS men showed up at the homes of the Polish families hiding their comrades' kids. When blackmailers raided Vladka Peltel's apartment, she barely blustered her way out. The Gestapo caught Michal Klepfisz at the end of January and put him on a boxcar to Treblinka. He took a file hidden beneath his clothes and sawed through the window bars, then pulled himself through and jumped from the moving train. A guard shot him in the ankle as he ran.

The losses were too numerous to be coincidental, and the party began to suspect Klepfisz's old friend Stefan Machai, a working-class Polish socialist who let Klepfisz hide in his apartment. No one wanted to believe it. Klepfisz had known Machai for years, since their days working together in a metal factory. He had done a lot for the Bund, sheltering activists in his basement and hustling to get them guns. But Machai had changed over the last few months. Maybe it was the weapons trade, where contacts with the underworld were inevitable. He drank too much. He quit his backbreaking job as a rickshaw puller, bought bespoke suits, and stayed out late gorging himself at Warsaw nightspots with friends he refused to talk about. He wouldn't say where he got his cash.

Machai knew the most sensitive details about the Bund's underground operations in Aryan Warsaw. He was their only possible betrayer.

After Klepfisz limped back to Warsaw, the Bund cut off contact with Machai, except for an anonymous letter to warn him what happened to snitches. Jacob Celemenski wanted to ask the Home Army to shoot him. The Gestapo saved them the trouble.

THE JEWISH COMBAT ORGANIZATION

The Nazis knew that Jews would resist new deportations, so they turned to trickery. In March, they appointed the German industrialist Walter

Toebbens to convince the ghetto's forty thousand remaining workers to voluntarily load themselves onto the boxcars. With honied words and unctuous posters, Toebbens described a bucolic labor camp near Lublin, where workers and their families could live peacefully till the war's end. Thanks to a poster campaign by the ZOB, no one believed him. When the Germans tried to "evacuate" the brush factory, the Bund's stronghold, not a single worker had showed up. That night, the ZOB's battle squads torched German warehouses. When the Germans asked the Judenrat for help, the chairman told them he was powerless against the fighters.

It was a gorgeous spring in the Warsaw ghetto. The chestnut trees were blooming. Girls in flimsy pink blouses sunbathed on Muranow Square. Everyone who could was buying guns.

The ghetto was alive with the sound of digging as its inmates hurried to build bunkers. Entire tenements chipped in to hire engineers to create these hiding spots. The best bunkers had radios, water wells, hookups to the city's power grid, dried food supplies, and weapons caches. When the Germans entered, Jews would retreat into their underground city.

In their barracks, fighters disassembled and reassembled their precious guns. They aimed, then pretended to shoot. They were very young. Most were under twenty. The youngest was only thirteen. They knew that they would die, so they tried to suck the last drops of sweetness out of life. They had vodka, and they had each other. Marek Edelman remembered a beautiful Tsukunft girl he would not name, "who knew how to make scrambled eggs with ham, and also how to caress . . . to give herself to one boy at nine o'clock in the evening. And another at midnight." Fighters longed for the battle that would crown their lives.

The ZOB built fortifications, lay mines, and dug tunnels into the sewer system. They cut passageways between attics and between courtyards, so their couriers could move invisibly. They filled lightbulbs with corrosive acid. They set up observation posts and patrols. Tailors at Roerich's garment factory smuggled out extra German uniforms. In one of her trips into the ghetto, Vladka Peltel tried on an SS cap for her friend. The two girls dissolved into giggles.

The ZOB coordinated with the Home Army. When the Germans invaded, Polish fighters agreed to blow up part of the ghetto wall at Bonifraterska Street, allowing for a mass escape.

In February, the Bundist underground sent a final radio message to Arthur Zygielbojm, telling him that the Nazis planned to liquidate the Warsaw ghetto. "Alert the whole world. Appeal to the pope for official intervention and to the allies to declare German war prisoners as hostages. . . . Only you can save us. The responsibility with regards to history will rest on you."

HENRYK ERLICH AND VIKTOR ALTER

While fighters prepared ersatz hand grenades inside the Warsaw ghetto, the rest of the world was riveted by the Battle of Stalingrad. After six months of combat, the Red Army had turned the destroyed city into a death trap for the German invaders. At the start of February, the Soviets retook the ruins, at the cost of a million lives. It was the first blow to Nazi invincibility.

The New York Bund had not forgotten about Henryk Erlich and Viktor Alter, but it seemed like everyone else had given up. The Polish government-in-exile wrote them off as a lost cause. No matter how many telegrams American Federation of Labor chairman William Green sent the Soviet ambassador, Maxim Litvinov, he received only noncommittal non-answers.

Amidst mass sympathy for the Soviet Union, Ambassador Litvinov finally saw fit to answer Green's queries about Alter and Erlich. In a letter dated February 23, 1943, he informed Green that the two leaders had been shot as Nazi collaborators that past December. A few weeks later, the Soviets sent the Polish embassy a bill for Alter and Erlich's stay at the Metropole Hotel in Moscow.

Sophia Dubnova would never learn what really happened to her husband. Secret policemen entombed his story in envelopes stamped with the words PRESERVE FOREVER, which languished until the Soviet Union collapsed in 1991. The next year, Sophia's niece, a retired Moscow editor named Victoria Dubnova, fought through KGB bureaucracy to discover the truth about Alter and Erlich's deaths.

After their arrests, the NKVD locked Alter and Erlich in solitary confinement in the Kuybyshev prison, where they were known only by their numbers, 41 and 42. They were charged with no crimes and received no interrogations. Stalin had no more use for them. After he signed their arrest warrants, they simply disappeared. The NKVD shot Viktor Alter in February 1943, a week before Litvinov's letter. After his death, they burned his possessions.

The NKVD did not execute Henryk Erlich. He was sixty years old. His health was broken from multiple imprisonments. He knew he would never see the sky again. On May 15, 1942, Sophia Dubnova's husband, an intellectual, musically gifted, and affectionate father from Lublin, hung himself from the bars of his cell.

AFTERLIVES

The Bund protested the executions, of course. They published an open letter in *The New York Times* and an editorial in *The New Republic*. Jewish workers smashed the Soviet embassy's windows in Manhattan. In Mexico City, communists and Bundists brawled at a memorial for Erlich and Alter. But their outrage had little effect. The Soviets were the heroes of Stalingrad, and the realities of wartime geopolitics muted the Bund's supporters. Former Bundist Sidney Hillman refused to attend a rally at New York's Mecca Temple to condemn Alter and Erlich's executions. Even in the Vilna ghetto, when Pati Kremer chaired a memorial meeting for Alter and Erlich, she didn't condemn the Soviet Union. She couldn't. In nearby forests, Red Army partisans had begun to set up bases, and they gave guns to Jewish fighters.

"Martyrs never die." I've never believed this phrase, which sounds like the sort of sentence one might embroider on a throw pillow. Martyrs die just like everyone else. Viktor Alter was dead, and so was Henryk Erlich.

Martyrs survive in the memories of the living. After their deaths, the names of the Bund's two leaders floated around the camps and ghettos of occupied Poland, where they combined into a code word used to tell imprisoned comrades that help was on the way.

Shaindel Kirsch was a skinny girl with a crippled arm who once belonged to the Bundist tailors' union. Then the war came, and the Germans killed her family. In 1943, they shipped her to Blizyn concentration camp to work as a sewing slave. One autumn day, a trash man sidled up and told her to wait that night by the barbed wire fence for a secret message. She waited for hours in the frigid darkness, until she saw a slip of paper flutter downward. Who threw it she didn't know. She snatched the paper without looking and hurried back to her barracks. When she read its contents, she began to shake.

> Put down what members of our family are held in Camp Blizyn. Money is forthcoming. You shall be well supplied—Henyrk Viktorovich

Only later would she recognize the names as those of her party's murdered leaders, but she understood the instructions well enough. One night by the fence a few weeks later, unknown hands tossed her a package filled with cash. With it, Shaindel and four comrades bribed their way out of the camp, bought guns, and fled into the forest.

PASSOVER

When operatives on the Aryan side called the ZOB central command in the first hours of April 19 to say that thousands of men were massing outside the ghetto walls for the long-awaited liquidation, they were ready. Michal Klepfisz and Zalman Friedrich had just smuggled a last shipment of explosives over the ghetto wall.

At two A.M., the ZOB's battle squads mobilized. ZZW fighters and unaffiliated "wildcat" groups took their positions. Sentries ran from house to house alerting the civilians, who gathered their valuables and retreated to their bunkers. The ghetto fell silent.

From balconies and windows, the fighters watched the Nazis goose-step down Nalewki Street, singing a cheerful march. Edelman had taken care to dress well that night, in a red angora sweater and two leather bandoliers, crossed like Pancho Villa. As he saw the convoy enter the ghetto, he imagined the Germans' thoughts. With the ghetto quiet, it must have seemed like the rebel Jews had lost their spirit, "as if those few immature boys had at last realized that there was no point in attempting the unfeasible, that they understood that the Germans had more rifles than there were rounds for all their pistols," he later wrote.

Fighters showered the Germans with Molotov cocktails.

While one group of Germans scattered on Nalewki Street, fighters barricaded another group into the intersection of Zamenhof and Mila. The fighters were Bundists, Zionists, and communists, but that didn't matter. What mattered were their pistols, and the little explosives they had been manufacturing all spring. They threw bombs. They fired. Their sole machine gun let out sporadic shots. A German tank rolled toward the intersection. A girl tossed her Molotov cocktail. Flame spread on the chassis. The crew screamed as they burned. The girl laughed. Her face was rosy from the fire.

More battles raged at Nalewki and Gesia, and in Muranow Square. The result was the same. Flabbergasted and unprepared, Germans fled from Jewish guerrillas. By afternoon, they had retreated entirely from the ghetto.

The fighters walked through the blood-slick streets. Aryan supermen lay with their guts out, their bones broken, their eyes still open in disbelief. The fighters kissed one another, then whooped with joy, in voices they could not recognize. They stripped the bodies of weapons.

COMRADES

The Polish underground press covered the uprising with admiration, even as they chided other Jews for having allowed themselves to be "dragged to their deaths without putting on a fight." They didn't mention the Home Army's unwillingness to give them guns until it was too late. Many papers urged Varsovians to do their "Christian" duty and help ghetto escapees. Even the fascist *Polska* admitted that the Germans "stood helpless before a small group of revolting Jews."

The Polish underground might have praised the ghetto fighters, but did they help them when it mattered?

Despite their Soviet backing, the People's Guard militia was tiny and poorly armed, but they were the only partisan group where Poles and Jews fought as equals, and they followed Moscow's order to encourage anti-Nazi revolts. The People's Guard gave the ghetto a few more guns from their meager arsenal and made several attacks on the wall. The ghetto fighters thought they tried their best.

The fighters felt differently about the Home Army. In memoirs written decades after the events, their words burn with anguished disappointment. Before the uprising, the Home Army had given the ZOB fifty guns, most of them pistols that the Polish officers knew were lousy for street fighting. More guns might have come if the Gestapo had not caught the ZOB's liaison Aryeh Wilner in March. As per protocol, the Home Army cut off Wilner's comrades. The flow of arms stalled, until Antek Zuckerman managed to make contact a week before the uprising. Once the revolt began, Home Army fighters kept their promise and tried to blow up the ghetto wall, but Polish police tipped off the Germans. Two teenage Home Army fighters died in the ensuing shootout. Similar attempts ended in failure.

Yet, even as they provided aid, the Home Army never committed to the Jewish fighters. Rowecki and Warsaw general Antoni Chrusciel both refused to meet Antek at the height of the uprising. Another Home Army leader told Antek that the ghetto was a nest of communists.

The truth was this: the government-in-exile didn't judge April 1943 to be an opportune moment for rebellion. The Americans had not yet landed in Europe. The Red Army was hundreds of miles away. If Warsaw rose up, no one would help them, and Nazis would destroy the city. Prime Minister Sikorski said as much to Rowecki in an April 27 telegram. It was fine to aid Jews, but the uprising must not be allowed to spread to Aryan Warsaw.

The Bund's friends in the Polish Socialist Party sympathized with their fighters but came to similar conclusions. Sociologist Emanuel Ringelblum quoted an unnamed Polish socialist: "[The ghetto fighters] ought to be supplied with arms, but active cooperation is impossible. . . . The Party must choose the right moment for the struggle, and not let itself be deflected by sentiment, however noble."

On the first day of the uprising, Bundists on the Aryan side decided to grab their guns and throw grenades at the Nazis marching toward the ghetto gates. Jacob Celemenski hurried to a safe house on Slowackiego Street to coordinate with the Polish Socialist Party. After he tapped out the code, two activists opened the door. He knew them to be brave, compassionate people, but that afternoon, they only offered him excuses. Unfortunately, their party's battle squads weren't ready. Unfortunately, they had no guns. Unfortunately, the Nazis would retaliate. Unfortunately. Unfortunately. Unfortunately. Bernard Goldstein's Polish comrades similarly refused to organize street protests or go on strike in solidarity.

The Polish Socialist Party and the Bund were comrades. They had gone to jail together, marched together, struck together, punched fascists together, and manned the barricades together during the siege of Warsaw. When the Germans occupied their country, Polish socialists forged documents for Bundists, rescued their kids, hid their fighters, even went to Auschwitz for distributing their party press. After the great deportation had ended, Polish socialists helped found Zegota, the only official council to aid Jews that would ever exist in occupied Europe. As the ghetto burned, Zegota's Polish socialist chairman, Julian Grobelny, searched its perimeter for fugitives to help, all while weeping for his valiant friends who fought inside.

I once thought that the Polish Socialist Party betrayed the Bund. The truth was sadder than that. The ghetto revolt revealed the hard limits of even the strongest solidarity. Polish socialists were willing to die for their Bundist friends. They *did* die for their Bundist friends. They would not sacrifice the Poles of Warsaw.

JURGEN STROOP

The ghetto uprising humiliated Nazi military command in Warsaw, especially the aristocratic *obergruppenführer* Ferdinand von Sammern-Frankenegg, who had already been disgraced by January's resistance. His bosses quickly demoted him. His replacement, the monocle-sporting Jurgen Stroop, had already proven his ruthlessness by exterminating the Jews of Lviv. In Warsaw, Stroop ensconced himself in the luxurious

Hotel Bristol. To unwind after a long day of liquidation, he sipped burgundy, puffed Egyptian cigarettes, and ordered the bloodiest of steaks.

On the second day of the uprising, Stroop sent three hundred SS men to the gate of the brush factory area, territory of the Bundist battle squads. When they passed Swietojerska Street, a ZOB fighter pressed two wires together, detonating a land mine. The ground exploded. Nazis flew upward in fragments, Übermenschen reduced to a cascade of severed limbs.

Two SS men with white rags limped forward to request a fifteen-minute truce to collect their wounded. The fighters answered them with bullets. Criminals, Stroop sniffed. This was against the rules.

THE FISH AND THE SEA

Imperial armies have a hard time invading urban enclaves. Architecture undoes their advantages. IEDs explode beneath their armored vehicles. They lose themselves in dark tenements and unmapped alleyways. Guerrillas spring from rooftops and tunnel networks and shoot, only to disappear. Invaders fight an enemy that is nowhere and everywhere.

"The guerrilla is the fish. The people are the sea," said the general Efraín Ríos Montt, who committed a genocide against the indigenous Maya people of Guatemala. "If you cannot catch the fish, you have to drain the sea." The ghetto was not Guatemala, nor was it the casbah of Algiers, nor Vietnam. Long before the battle started, Nazis doomed both sea and fish. Yet General Stroop came to conclusions that prefigured those of Ríos Montt. At Hotel Bristol, he laid out a strategy. He would not fight rebels head-on. Instead, he would exterminate them with fire.

On the third day of the uprising, the Nazis began to burn the Warsaw ghetto. Their flamethrowers started on Mila, Zamenhof, Nalewki, and the brushworks, then went house to house. Howitzers thundered. German planes dropped incendiary bombs.

In revenge, the ZOB torched the German workshops. They destroyed the furniture factory, the mattress factory. The tailors' workshops went up in smoke. Fire rose in pillars, in a massive auto-da-fé. Black smoke filled the air of northern Warsaw. The sky glowed a demonic red.

Glass shattered. Beams broke. The pavement melted into tarry sludge. With the streets impassable, Bundist courier Tobcia Dawidowicz ran messages between factories, balanced like a tightrope walker on the burning joists.

The bunkers were fuller than anyone intended. The air boiled, its oxygen depleted by too many lungs. Above ground, the Germans hunted

Jews' hiding spots with bloodhounds, then pumped them full of chlorine gas. If survivors emerged, Nazis forced them to strip, then dragged them to the Umschlagplatz.

On the fourth day of the uprising, the Nazi propaganda department brought a press junket to view subdued sections of the ghetto. After showing the embedded journalists the charred corpses of the rebels, the jolly German comms officer took them out for beers. They had to "burn out this nest of revolt completely," the comms officer declared. He banged his fist on the table for emphasis.

MICHAL KLEPFISZ

Eyes burning, wet handkerchiefs wrapped over their mouths, the ZOB fought house by house, stairwell by stairwell, sometimes hand to hand. Women fought alongside men. "They were not human—perhaps devils or goddesses," said Jurgen Stroop. They feigned defeat, then pulled grenades from their underwear when SS officers got too close.

Nazis cornered Michal Klepfisz's battalion in an attic near the brush factory. It was dark. A German machine gun peeking out behind a chimney kept his fighters pinned. Grenade in hand, Klepfisz charged the machine gun. It went quiet. His comrades escaped. A few days later, Marek Edelman returned to bury his body. It had two rows of bullet holes across the stomach.

INFERNO

Fighters moved by night, dressed in stolen German uniforms, their feet wrapped in rags to muffle their footsteps. They laid land mines and tried to pick off isolated patrols. Bunkers caved in. The ground collapsed beneath their feet. They pulled desperate civilians from the earth and led them to temporary safety.

They had dreamed of facing their enemy in battle. Instead, they burned like ants beneath the magnifying glass of a sadistic child.

FOR YOUR FREEDOM AND OURS

On April 23, the Bundist writer Ignacy Samsonowicz appealed to Warsaw's Polish population in the name of the Jewish Combat Organization.

> Poles, Citizens, Soldiers of Freedom,
>
> . . . Amidst the smoke of fires, dust and blood of the murdered Warsaw ghetto—we, prisoners of the ghetto, send you sincere

fraternal greetings. We know that with heartfelt pain and tears of sympathy . . . you are looking on at this war, which for many days we are carrying out with a vicious invader.

Know that every threshold of the ghetto has been and continues to be a fortress, that we may perish in this struggle but never surrender. Like you, we breathe with desire for revenge for all the crimes of our common foe.

The battle is being waged for your freedom, and ours!

A BEAUTIFUL WARSAW SUNDAY

"The workers of Paris built the Bastille at the kings' command, and those same workers smashed it into dust," wrote Samsonowicz in 1941, in his love letter to proletarian solidarity. Where were the workers of Warsaw as their neighbors burned alive?

On the eve of the uprising, Polish sentiments toward Jews had reached a low point. The Nazis had just revealed to them a Soviet massacre of three thousand Polish officers in the Katyn forest in 1939. Of course, Nazi newspapers blamed it on the Jews. Despite this, many Poles admired the ghetto's defiance. A few said it was a good thing that Warsaw was rid of its Jewish problem, but most were sympathetic, even the racists. They shed a tear, then went about their day.

There was a merry-go-round outside the ghetto walls. The Jews burned while the Polish children whirled beneath the flaming sky. Two years later, in his work "Campo dei Fiori," the poet Czeslaw Milosz would describe the smell of smoke, and how the ghetto's ash floated over the wall to coat the Aryan city.

This wind from the burning houses
blew open the girls' skirts
And the happy throngs laughed
On a beautiful Warsaw Sunday.

SEWER

On May Day, the Bundist fighters buried their dead, then lined up to sing "The Internationale."

There was no more food. The wells were clogged with rubble. They had little ammo with which to fight. Germans set fire to their hideouts, broke into their bunkers with pneumatic drills, and pumped their breathing vents with chlorine gas.

Most of the ghetto's Bundists were dead. Germans pushed Tsukunft leader Henoch Russ into a boxcar bound for Majdanek. Anna Braude Heller, the indomitable head doctor of Bersohn and Bauman Children's Hospital, burned alive in a bunker, as did the printer Lazar Klug. Wounded by a grenade, Berek Sznajdmil waved his pistol at his comrades. "Keep fighting!" he shouted, then shot himself in the head.

With the ghetto reduced to ashes, the ZOB decided to flee. Zalman Friedrich and a daring teenage Zionist named Kazik Rotem crawled through the ZZW's tunnel on Bonifraterska Street to find help on the Aryan side. Vladka Peltel brought the pair to Leon Feiner and Antek Zuckerman, to figure out how to rescue the surviving fighters.

There was only one way to escape: the sewers. But they offered only the slimmest chance of salvation. In those labyrinthine death traps, fugitives slogged through fermented shit up to their collarbones, only to get lost, collapse of thirst, and drown. Antek knew the Home Army had maps of the sewer system, but they refused to share them with the ghetto fighters. Such maps had military uses and the Home Army didn't trust the Jews.

MILA 18

On May 8, bloodhounds discovered the ZOB's command post at 18 Mila Street. It was a vast bunker, owned by a mob boss named Shmuel Asher, supplied with power, water, even vodka from the Aryan side. It was meant for 30 gangsters, but Shmuel Asher had invited 120 ZOB fighters to stay, among them commander Mordechai Anielewicz and their liaison to the Home Army, Aryeh Wilner, whom friends had just bribed out of Gestapo torture chambers. When the Germans found the bunker, they sealed the exits and pumped in chlorine gas. A few fighters managed to escape, but most stayed trapped in the bunker, amidst the poison and the heat. They wouldn't surrender. Aryeh Wilner told them what would happen if they did. Some took cyanide tablets. The rest used their guns. Anielewicz shot his beloved, Mira Fuchrer, then turned his pistol on himself. Two weeks before his death, he had sent a final letter out of the ghetto, asking for weapons. He described the uprising as "the dream of my life."

That night, Marek Edelman and Celina Lubetkin left their bunker at 30 Franciszkanska Street to check on Anielewicz. They picked through an apocalyptic wasteland. With every step, the ground threatened to collapse beneath their feet. Near the ruined bunker at 18 Mila Street, the pair discovered fifteen wounded survivors huddled underneath a building's hatchway. They told Edelman and Lubetkin about the bunker's end. Edelman was furious. Anielewicz had no right to kill himself. "You have to fight to the end," he later wrote. "Maybe suicide is a fine symbol, but you don't sacrifice your life for symbols."

Lubetkin and Edelman led the surviving fighters to a bunker at 22 Franciszkanska Street, which had a tunnel to the sewer system. Giving up hope for Kazik and Zalman's return from the Aryan side, Edelman ordered Abrasha Blum to find an escape route through the sewers.

The rest waited in the stifling dark. They lay mostly naked on the wooden planks, breathing in each other's breaths. All the phone lines had been burned, so they could not communicate with the outside world. Sometimes they bickered. Yiddish or Hebrew? Socialism or Zionism? Sometimes they reminisced about the battle they had fought. These starving youth, armed only with pistols and homemade bombs, had launched the first urban revolt in occupied Europe. Sometimes, they just waited to die.

KAZIK ROTEM

Kazik refused to give up efforts to rescue his comrades, even after the Home Army declined to help. Through some communist contacts, he arranged for a truck to pick up survivors at a predetermined time on a street corner a few miles outside the ghetto. Then he and a communist fighter cooked up a plan to get back in.

For guides, Kazik and the communist found a gullible pair of sewer workers. Pretending to be a Polish criminal, Kazik fed them tall tales of treasures hidden within the ghetto, promising the workers a share of the loot if they led them through the sewers. As soon as they went underground, Kazik pressed his gun to a worker's head. They crawled through slime for hours, Kazik goading the workers forward with threats and swigs from a bottle of vodka. Once past the ghetto walls, the communist kept his gun trained on the workers while Kazik climbed out to look for their comrades.

It was dark when Kazik pulled himself out of the sewer. He staggered through the rubble, past piles of corpses, until he reached the ruined bunker at 30 Franciszkanska Street. All the fighters were dead, he thought. He sat in the rubble and contemplated his weapon. A great relief filled him. His job was done. He could join his beloveds. The Germans would come at sunrise. He could shoot a few before he went.

Then something intervened. Call it God, or chance, or the dialectical forces of history, but somehow, in the interlocking hellscape of the Warsaw sewer system, Abrasha Blum's group ran into Kazik's communist comrade and told him about the ZOB's improbable survival. After finding Kazik, the group hurried to the bunker at 22 Franciszkanska Street.

The bunker inhabitants prepared for their exit. All except for two teenage sex workers, who had joined the fighters a few days before. Edelman refused to take them along. It was nothing personal, he later said. He just didn't know them well enough.

Sixty-two fugitives lowered themselves into the intestinal tract of Warsaw.

ARTHUR ZYGIELBOJM

While Michal Klepfisz threw himself against a machine gun, while teenage girls pulled the grenades from their underwear and hurled them at SS officers, while Anielewicz smothered in a bunker alongside his girlfriend and mobsters and poets, while the last surviving fighters of the Warsaw ghetto prepared to escape through miles of human shit . . . British and Americans dignitaries were hobnobbing in Bermuda at a lavish conference, pretending to care about refugees. Though the United States and the United Kingdom had resentfully organized this Caribbean convening in response to mass Jewish protests, it explicitly didn't focus on Jewish refugees. The two powers preferred to ignore the fact that Jews (never mind Roma) were targeted for extermination. Instead, delegates mulled over the problem of refugees, Jewish and not, who were lucky enough to be in neutral countries.

In the lead-up to the conference, the Bund's New York committee called for all democratic countries to open their borders to refugees, and to rescue Jews still trapped under Nazi occupation. America and Britain had no such intentions. The Bermuda conference had one goal. The two powers wanted to look like they were doing something, while continuing to do nothing.

Dignitaries sipped cocktails, posed on the white sand beaches, smoked cigars, and, mostly, said no. No, they would not approach Hitler to release death camp prisoners. No, Britain would not accept more Jews, nor let them into the countries it colonized—especially not Palestine. No, the United States would not lift its immigration quotas; its resources were quite exhausted from "caring" for Japanese Americans in internment camps. The two powers resolved to organize an impotent bureaucratic body and issue a declaration on the postwar repatriation of refugees. This was a theoretical concern. It was by no means assured that any Jews would be left in Europe to repatriate by the time the war was done.

The Bermuda conference was the final blow for Arthur Zygielbojm.

Nothing he tried had worked. The Polish government-in-exile didn't listen to him. The British government did nothing. He detested the Zionists, whose views he characterized as "another 100,000 Jews murdered. Give more money for Palestine," but he still tried to coordinate with them to protest the genocide. His Bundist comrades in New York were absorbed in ideological bickering and wanted to replace him with someone else. All the while, desperate messages arrived from his comrades in Warsaw.

On May 11, Zygielbojm listened to the Polish underground radio declare the murders of the last Jews in the Warsaw ghetto. He probably guessed his wife and his son were among them. The next night, in his Paddington apartment, he swallowed poison. Before he did, he wrote three letters.

The first, to Prime Minister Sikorski, contains these words:

> I wish to express my strongest protest against the inactivity with which the world is looking on and permitting the extermination of the Jewish people. I know how little human life is worth, especially today. But as I was unable to do anything with my life, perhaps by my death I shall contribute to destroying the indifference of those who are able and should act. . . . My comrades in the Warsaw ghetto have fallen with guns in their hands. . . . I wasn't given the chance to die like them, together with them. But I belong with them, in their mass graves.

A second was to his brother in South Africa. "I cry into the dead of night: Oh, deaf world, save them save them! The sky is cold and silent like the people down below."

In his final letter, to his comrades in New York, he said goodbye.

> I have a debt to pay to all I left behind. . . . I thank you all for all the happiness you gave me during the long years we lived, worked, and fought together.
>
> I love you all. Long live the Bund.

CHAPTER 26

ASHES

(May 1943–January 1945)

WARSAW

WHILE ZYGIELBOJM'S CORPSE LAY IN HIS PADDINGTON APARTMENT, forty ghetto fighters pulled themselves up from the sewers into Aryan Warsaw. Crowds goggled at the shit-smeared skeletons, but the weapons they carried persuaded onlookers to stay quiet.

The truck Kazik arranged idled at the intersection. The fighters ran into the back. They had no time to wait. They could already smell the cool Lomianki woods, just outside the city. The truck filled. There was no more space for the comrades who remained in the sewer. "We have to get them," Celina screamed, pointing her gun at Kazik. "Another truck's coming," he swore.

The truck sped off with the ghetto fighters. They left the others behind.

LEGEND

On May 16, Stroop declared the liquidation of the Warsaw ghetto complete. To celebrate, he ordered his men to dynamite the Great Synagogue on Tlomackie Street. As he pressed the charge, he saw the "rainbow burst of colors, the fiery explosion [that] soared above the clouds, an unforgettable tribute to our triumph over the Jews."

No one knows how many Nazis died in the doomed uprising. Stroop claimed sixteen, but that number contradicts the carnage he described in his report and in later testimony. The hundreds claimed by Marek Edelman seem equally unlikely. No one knows how many Jews died either, as the Nazi numbers don't add up, and they never excavated the bunkers where they murdered most of their victims. For months afterward, survivors hid in the ghetto's ruins, kept alive by Polish helpers.

The Nazis tried to minimize the revolt. In Germany, they painted it as the work of Poles, and in Poland, as the work of Soviets. Meanwhile, across the world, the uprising resonated as a symbol, though no one agreed on what it represented. For some, it was a cry of the human spirit. First Lady Eleanor Roosevelt wrote in a telegram to the Bund's New York committee: "It is trite perhaps, to say what is true, that [the ghetto fighters] died for all of us, that we must live for them." When W.E.B. Du Bois visited the ghetto's ruins in 1949, he described the fighters' "deliberate sacrifice in life for a great ideal in the face of the fact that the sacrifice might be completely in vain" as something that reinforced his commitment to universalist socialism. For others, it had a more exclusive meaning. Communists claimed the revolt as communist, and Polish socialists saw it as part of "the legend of Fighting Poland." In Palestine, Zionist leadership rebranded the ghetto fighters as proto-Israelis, ignoring their eastern European birth and political diversity. Palestinians too have found the uprising to be a powerful example of armed resistance, though Arabic media generally airbrushes out the Zionist politics of many of the fighters. In Arabic, it is called the Warsaw Ghetto Intifada.

The revolt's most important audience was Jews trapped inside the charnel house of occupied Poland. Afterward, Jews rose up at Sosnowiec, in Trawniki labor camp, even in Treblinka and Sobibor. In Bialystok, near my great-grandmother's Lunna Wola, the resistance burned the ghetto themselves. When the liquidation came, young women set fire to the factories of their enslavement. Fighters attacked the ghetto walls with homemade benzene bombs, in a futile attempt to break through into freedom.

In the Vilna ghetto, Warsaw's revolt inspired the poet Hirsch Glick to write an anthem for the resistance:

Never say this is the final road for you,
Though leadened skies may cover over days of blue.
As the hour that we longed for is so near,
Our step beats out the message—we are here!

When the Nazis liquidated the Vilna ghetto a few months later, Glick and hundreds of other partisans fled through the sewers. Their guide was the Bundist engineer Shmuel Kaplinski, who had worked on the sewer system before the war. They brought their song with them into the forest. Not everyone made it out. Nazis set up three gallows at the ghetto gates, from which they hung three fighters. Bundist courier Asya Big dangled between her boyfriend and a communist. The poet Avrom Sutzkever described the way her body swayed, slim and graceful as a cornstalk.

The Germans shipped the stronger Jews to labor camps in Estonia.

The Lithuanians rounded up the rest and marched them to the Ponar forest.

PATI KREMER

Pati Kremer waits in a Ponar trench with her comrades. Her fey beauty has long since vanished, first from the rigors of her impoverished exile, then from age, and finally from starvation. Her hair is sparse. Furrows run down her cheeks. Pati Kremer was born in 1867 in Vilna. She has fought for the workers since she was fifteen, when she tried to teach ungrateful seamstresses how to read in Novgorod. In Vilna, she helped found the Bund. She translated Marx into Yiddish. She tapped out codes in prison. She crossed borders without a passport, harangued strikers, smuggled pamphlets, wandered continents. After her husband's death, she had lived the quiet life of an editor, until the Soviets arrested the Bund's best activists, and the Nazis came, and it fell on her to resurrect her movement.

When the Lithuanians forced them into the ghetto, Pati Kremer saw the streets strewn with discarded books. This could not stand. Straight as a queen, she collected her treasures. The kids followed her. They knew who she was.

In the ghetto, she wrote poetry of great romance, about a life of questionably useful sacrifice. When the Bundists celebrated May Day, they hung her husband's photo on the wall. Her comrades saved her life, and she saved their souls in turn. When the Tsukunft kids defied the Bund's leaders and joined the Zionist Abba Kovner's partisans, she helped them hide their weapons. She slept soundly through the night.

The ghetto grew smaller. The Jerusalem of Lithuania disappeared into the trenches of Ponar.

Death is not glorious. It is pain, then nothing. There was no grand moral, just the dissolution of an irreplaceable self. Survivors tell me how much they hate sentimental portrayals of the Holocaust. They can't stand the dishonesty. They'll pardon me. This story is true.

The Ponar forest. The freezing women. The drunk Lithuanians. The pit, deep and wet like a wound. Here where I live is my country. It may have spit me out and offered me to demons, but it is mine all the same.

"Let's sing 'The Oath,'" says Pati Kremer. "Then death will not seem so terrible."

The women sing.

Eighty years later, I walk to the Ponar death site. It is a lonely hike from the train station. Lithuanians take their dogs there sometimes, but otherwise, only the occasional tour group visits. On the way, I pick flowers for Pati Kremer. I walk by the trenches where they forced Jews to wait, and to the pits where the dead bodies fell. Which pit was Pati Kremer's? Any and all. I choose one and climb to the bottom. The forest echoes around me. I say Pati Kremer's name and play a song on my phone. The Yiddish lyrics are old and dark like the pines.

> *Heaven and earth will hear us,*
> *the bright stars will bear witness,*
> *an oath of blood, an oath of tears—*
> *We swear, we swear, we swear!*

WARSAW

Despite their international renown, the ghetto fighters found no respite in occupied Poland. The first betrayals came while they were still in the Lomianki forest. Bundist Zalman Friedrich escorted four ill comrades to a nearby village, where a peasant agreed to rent them a room. Once paid, the peasant immediately ratted them out to the authorities. Before their executions, Polish police paraded the heroes of the Warsaw ghetto through neighboring villages on a horse cart, with insulting placards hung around their necks. The remaining fighters tried to join with local partisans, but even socialist Home Army units refused to accept them. Partisans needed to melt into the peasant population, and most peasants refused to shelter Jews.

They found few melinas in Aryan Warsaw. Germans imposed the death penalty on anyone who failed to report hidden Jews, and few Poles wanted to take the risk. The battered ghetto fighters found themselves at the mercy of thousands of blackmailers. A few weeks after the revolt, the Gestapo caught Bundist fighter Velvel Rozowski while he scrambled to raise money to pay off blackmailers. Other blackmailers tipped off the Gestapo about the whereabouts of Tsukunft leader Abrasha Blum. Blum tried to escape through a window using tied-together bedsheets as a rope. The rope snapped. His legs shattered. The Gestapo murdered him in their basement on Szucha Avenue.

TWO DEATHS

Two deaths worsened the fortunes of the Jewish resistance. At the end of June, the Gestapo captured the Home Army's General Stefan Rowecki. For all his flaws, Rowecki was competent and fair-minded, and he armed the ghetto fighters in the end. His replacement, the aristocratic Endek Bronislaw Bor-Komorowski, more closely resembled the OZON leaders who led interwar Poland off a cliff. In defiance of the government-in-exile, Bor-Komorowski refused to aid ghetto fighters, and he would not accept a single Jewish partisan unit into the Home Army. To the good general, Jewish partisans were merely commie criminals. In September, he ordered his commanders to execute them on sight. The next March, Bor-Komorowski welcomed a Nazi-collaborationist paramilitary called the National Armed Forces into the Home Army.

Shortly after Rowecki's arrest, Prime Minister Sikorski's plane crashed on his way back from the Middle East. After Sikorski's death, the government-in-exile lurched further to the right. Indicative of this shift is a memo, written that July by Endek politician Roman Knoll, the director of foreign affairs. "In the Homeland . . . the feeling is such that the return of the Jews to their jobs and workshops is completely out of the question." Since Poles had taken Jewish property, they would regard the return of Jews "as an invasion, to be resisted by physical force." To avoid any unpleasantness, Jews should be sent to a "closed area" in the east before being deported. In other words, a ghetto.

ADINA BLADY

In Warsaw, the surviving Bundists scrambled from one precarious hideout to another, from tenement to closet to stinking bunker, always aware that the city would just as soon have them dead.

"Our tasks now come down to this: to keep alive the remnants who have survived . . . so there will be some reserve for the future and witnesses to this crime," wrote Leon Feiner in his November report to the government-in-exile. The Bundists organized help for three thousand Jews hidden in Aryan Warsaw. Their couriers, Adina Blady and Marisha Feinmesser, created their operations center. The two women painted their lips, undid extra buttons on their sundresses, and flirted audaciously until they scored an apartment in a former courthouse at 24 Miodowa Street. It was the only place where people locked in claustrophobic melinas could freely meet their friends. The Bund stored their fake passports, their illicit party newspapers, and sacks of cash parachuted in by the Home Army. They shared this money with Zionist ghetto fighters, whose comrades in Palestine gave them nothing until the last months of the war.

Once a month, Adina refreshed the cash pile. She dressed carefully for her mission. One pair of panties beneath her garter belt, another pair on top. Two blouses, the one underneath bound with a belt. A false-bottomed shopping basket, de rigueur for women smugglers. Smile. Always Smile.

At a Zegota safe house on Senatorska Street, Adina shoved bills between her layers of lingerie. She walked carefully back to her apartment. If they stopped her, she was done. Once home, Adina spread the money on her bed. She divided it into piles. Each pile was for a courier, who would then pay rent for between fifty and a hundred hidden humans.

Over the next few days, Adina would distribute money to the people on her list, running to beat the curfew. "In one flat after another I saw the same thing: pale faces, sad eyes, hands stretched out for those few zlotys, a signature on a small card, and on my way," she wrote. She reassured the isolated, brought books for the smart kids, told the desperate that the war would end. She kept her people sane. She carried out her duties numbly. A few weeks after the ghetto fell, the Germans took her lover, Stefan, and since then, she had not felt anything at all.

When she returned to 24 Miodowa Street, she lay out a bottle of vodka and two glasses. When Marisha returned from her rounds, the two women drank and drank.

The couriers' greatest achievement was to set up the ZOB headquarters at 18 Lezno Street. Marisha Feinmesser dressed up as a bougie bride, eager to make her dream home. Maria Sawicka played her sister-in-law. The two sweet-talked the landlord, promising to pay an astronomical rent if he permitted them to renovate. Fancy ladies like them deserved the best. Their "workers," a Bundist and a Polish socialist, built a fake wall in the back room, with a small door hidden behind a laundry basket. At various times, Bernard Goldstein, Celina Lubetkin, Antek Zuckerman, and Marek Edelman lived behind that wall, squeezed between guns, gold bars, and the Bund's archives.

In their melinas, young people drank, starved, celebrated the rare chicken dinner, fucked, and fell in love. They had little else to do. Bernard got drunk one night, tried to dance, and broke his leg. Six weeks in a cast, in a claustrophobic underground hideout. Adina Blady became his lover around this time. She admired the old fighter but didn't love him—that part of her had died with her boyfriend's arrest. She saw their affair as something akin to charity. Bernard was miserable, and he wanted her so much.

When the fighter men impregnated fighter women, Adina found them unanesthetized abortions, and held their hands so they didn't scream. She does not mention anyone holding her hand during her own abortion, only Bernard's fury that she wouldn't give birth to his child.

THE WAR

Despite everything, Bundists still imagined themselves part of a mighty socialist movement. In September, they used an illegal radio to send greetings from their Warsaw safe house to the Swiss Social Democratic Party's annual congress. "Those of us who will remain alive after the present bloody deluge will continue . . . together with you, organized workers of democratic Switzerland, our mutual struggle for a new world devoid of class distinction and race hatred." They held surreptitious May Day celebrations. On the Bund's forty-sixth anniversary, they gathered at 24 Miodowa Street to mark their party's birthday. "Little by little, almost in whispers, we recalled the days when such celebrations had been held in vast halls before huge audiences of workers with appropriate songs, music, speeches, and fluttering flags," wrote Vladka Peltel.

With secret radios and smuggled microfilm, Bundists followed the progress of the war. By the summer of 1944, they could finally imagine an end. Allied bombers pounded Berlin. Mussolini had been deposed. Americans, Brits, and Charles de Gaulle's Free French forces fought their way up the Italian peninsula. Most of these Free French were not Frenchmen at all but troops from North Africa, among them a young Algerian football player named Ahmed Ben Bella.

VOLKOVYSK

After the largest tank battle in history, at Kursk, the Soviets rolled through Ukraine and into Poland. The Red Army liberated Volkovysk in July 1944. There was little left to liberate. The Nazis had murdered twenty-nine thousand people in the town's vicinity, including prisoners of war, communists, Polish intellectuals, and almost all the area's Jews. Bombs had erased Sam's old neighborhood. Germans had desecrated the cemetery where his mother was buried, using its headstones to reinforce a bridge. In 2008, the municipal government ran sewer lines through what was left. Of the many sights recorded in Sam's memory paintings, only the chalk cliffs remain.

Except for the old shoemaker Zeleviansky, who disappeared with the Red Army, none of Volkovysk's Bundists survived. Nazis shot the Bundist councilman Shepsel Ravitzky in an early massacre. Berel Falkovitch, the bridle maker, was killed in Treblinka, as was Tsukunft member Tzipa Pashinker, and activist Chana Irmess. Chana's husband, Yaakov Rubinstein, who proudly posed with his students beneath the banner WE ARE THE FUTURE, was murdered in Auschwitz. Only one person connected to

Volkovysk's Bund managed to evade the Nazis: the communist son of Bundist newspaper editor Avram Markus. In spring 1942, Shlomo Markus escaped the Zhetl ghetto to join the partisans. Five months later, while he was on a food procurement run in a nearby village, Germans surrounded his group. He saved his last bullet for himself.

As far as I can tell, every member of Sam's extended family who remained in Volkovysk was murdered in the Holocaust. Only one received the dignity of an individual story. A talented musician in his thirties, Gershon Beckenstein played in the Auschwitz orchestra with the number 942670 tattooed on his arm. A cellblock friend testified that Gershon died just before the camp's evacuation, but the musician's name appears in the Buchenwald archives, in January 1945. Buchenwald rebelled that April. Perhaps.

As for Rose, Sam's self-sacrificing wife, the mother of his four children—she had left her whole family in Lunna Wola. I have a picture sent by her niece, curly-haired Golda. "May it be an eternal memento," Golda wrote on the back. Where did Golda go? Unknown. The only information I found about Rose's family comes from testimonies collected by the Yad Vashem Holocaust Remembrance Center in Jerusalem. In 1942, five Kravitzes from Lunna Wola arrived at Auschwitz via the Kelbasin transit camp. All of them ended up in the gas chambers.

Rose was not a religious woman, but for the rest of her life, she lit one candle on Friday night, as her own heterodox sort of Kaddish.

THE RED ARMY

A few days after they freed Volkovysk, the Red Army liberated Vilna, with the help of Jewish partisans. After the battle, Zionists, Bundists, and communists posed together for photos, as if they had never been enemies. The guys wore leather jackets like Bolshevik commissars. The girls paired jackboots with summer blouses. Their smiles could dazzle diamonds. Nine months before, the Bundist engineer Shmuel Kaplinski had led many of these kids through the sewers to a perilous life in the forest. They returned to their hometown as conquerors.

At the end of July, the Soviets set up a provisional government in Lublin, which included Polish socialists and three Bundists: Leo Finkelstein, Grisza Jaszunski, and Michael Schuldenfrei. Stalin might have killed Alter and Erlich, but some Bundists were willing to let bygones be bygones. Here where they lived was their country, and its future would be decided by the Soviets.

WARSAW

Varsovians could hear the Russian guns. Illicit Soviet radio dispatches urged them to rebellion, but even more convincing were the lines of vehicles filled with Germans fleeing west. On July 31, Red Army tanks entered Praga.

The Bund's central committee met at Ignacy Samsonowicz's apartment to discuss the Soviet arrival. The meeting had barely started when Samsonowicz's lover burst in with news from her Home Army friends. The Warsaw uprising had begun.

The Bundists had no question about what to do next. They would fight alongside their fellow Polish citizens. The twenty-two surviving ZOB fighters thought the same and immediately issued a proclamation. "Join the Insurrection. On the Battlefield We Will Achieve Victory for a Free, Independent, Strong and Just Poland." Under gunfire, Leon Feiner made his way to the Polish Socialist Party's field headquarters on Zurawia Street, to meet Zygmunt Zaremba and insist the Polish underground publish their call to battle.

The fighting began in the working-class Zoliborz district and spread throughout the city. Everyone took part, from socialist workers' militias to the fascist National Armed Forces, to the Soviet-backed People's Guard. In the courtyard of Ignacy Samsonowicz's building, Bernard Goldstein and Jacob Celemenski tore up the cobblestones to build barricades. It could have been the siege of Warsaw. No, the Revolution of 1905. The next morning Celemenski and Samsonowicz crawled through a tunnel to 20 Wspolna Street, where the Polish Socialist Party was raising a militia. They enlisted under fake Polish names and didn't tell anyone that they were Jews.

This was wise. During the uprising, dozens of Jews emerged from hiding only to be murdered by their Polish fellow citizens. The ghetto fighter Jerek Grasberg left his bunker to join the rebellion, only to be shot by the Home Army. Bundists Marek Edelman and Julek Fiszgrund narrowly escaped the same fate. Some Poles robbed survivors and threw them out of their hiding places on the ludicrous charge that they were German spies. The Home Army rejected Jews, forcing ZOB fighters to join the pro-Soviet People's Guard.

Warsaw fought on the assumption that the Russians would save them. The Russians had no such plans. The Red Army set up camp in Praga but didn't cross the river. Instead, they waited, as close as Brooklyn is to Manhattan, and let the Nazis bring in reinforcements to crush the rebellion. Stalin didn't like the Home Army and was happy to see them and the Germans kill each other off, saving him the trouble. The Red Army watched while the Paris of the East burned like last year's ghetto. I imagine that sometimes they smelled the smoke, and that pieces of ash floated across the Vistula. Over their vodka, perhaps, the Red Army soldiers laughed on those beautiful Warsaw Sundays.

FRANCE

Paris was liberated in August 1944. The men who had fought their way through the South of France were largely colonial troops—Senegalese, Maghrebi, or Martinican, like the young Frantz Fanon—but this would not do for Free French commander Charles de Gaulle's self-image. He wanted it to seem like the French had freed themselves, so he shipped the Black African soldiers home before they could reach the capital. When there were not enough white Free Frenchmen to fill the brigade that would take Paris, he added Algerians, Syrians, and Spaniards. In blown-out photographs, they would look pale enough.

Some Bundists had fought in the French resistance, run relief for Comité de la rue Amelot, and died in Gestapo prisons. Others survived precariously in the South of France. When these activists returned to Paris, they discovered their party's archives had been abandoned in a warehouse with other unwanted loot.

Later that year, in the city of lights, Vera Dobrinksy posed for her painter husband. She had met Isaac when she was a sculpture student at the Colarossi Academy, and the pair had immediately hit it off. Perhaps it was because they both traced their roots to Vilna. The two artists had shacked up in a studio on Rue d'Odessa, close to their friend the famous painter Chaïm Soutine, and plunged into Montparnasse bohemia. Vera could have drunk the world like an apéritif at Café du Dome. Then the Nazis came and sent them fleeing for the South of France. When they returned, most of their artwork had been destroyed, Soutine was dead from a botched ulcer operation, and many of their friends had been gassed.

For her portrait, Vera wore a red kimono and tied her hair into a chignon. She had a lovely fairy face, if one marred by sadness. I recognized it instantly. It was the face of her mother, Pati Kremer, when she stepped out of a Vilna train station at the end of the nineteenth century, ready to remake the world.

WARSAW

Nazi planes pounded Warsaw, engulfing whole neighborhoods in fire. the Archcathedral of Saint John crumbled. The exquisite Old Town

Square burned. Flames devoured the ZOB headquarters at 18 Lezno Street, with their sacks of cash, gold bars, and party archives. In their apartment at 24 Miodowa Street, the Bundist couriers Adina Blady and Marisha Feinmesser set up a field hospital for wounded fighters. As the fire grew closer, they evacuated patients through tunnels beneath the building. They had to leave behind anyone they couldn't move. One was the Polish socialist Janek Kulikowski, who had hidden Bundist fugitives and bought grenades for the ghetto uprising. He burned alive in the flames.

As the uprising dragged on, the Polish mood turned bitter. Old whispers started again. "Jews made the war." "Jews made the rebellion." "Jews brought this on our heads." As hunger spread, Poles refused Jews ration cards and threw them out of soup kitchens. When the Bund appealed to the Polish Socialist Party and the Home Army to denounce the racism, they got nowhere. When *Monitor Polski*, the official newspaper of the government-in-exile, printed a communiqué overturning Nazi laws, they conveniently forgot to retract the laws concerning Jews. After the Bund barraged them with complaints, they corrected this oversight, but only in the finest print.

When Bundist leaders met at Ignacy Samsonowicz's apartment on Zurawia Street, their mood was bleak. They could no longer communicate with the three thousand Jews under their care. Leon Feiner was gravely ill with pneumonia. The partisan Hannah Fryshdorf, widow of a ghetto fighter, was nine months pregnant when she escaped from a Gestapo raid and found her people. Bernard Goldstein delivered her son in a filthy basement, "while all around her the world flamed and crackled and paid no heed."

After two months, General Bor-Komorowski surrendered. Warsaw lay in rubble, and two hundred thousand Poles were dead. The Nazis gave survivors three days to "evacuate" to a transit camp in Pruszkow.

Most Polish fighters took off their armbands and mingled with the civilians. Few Jews could do the same. If their faces didn't betray them, a blackmailer might. Many of the Bund's activists prepared to hide. On Vladka Peltel's last visit to Samsonowicz's apartment, she found Leon Feiner and Salo Fishgrund counting out stacks of American dollars, the only currency accepted on the black market. Jews in their network would need money to buy food and guns. But the party didn't know their people's whereabouts. Were they even alive? Or had they died on the barricades, been buried alive in their bunkers, or been shot by their brothers in the Polish Home Army?

Bundists with good faces, like Vladka Peltel and Jacob Celemenski, tried to sneak through German lines and disappear into the countryside. Others like Bernard Goldstein joined the thousands of Jews who hid in basements to wait for liberation. They endured months of disease, starvation, and madness below ground, while above, the Germans blew up their city block by block. Bernard and his comrades moved from place to place, leaving by night to forage food. They caught dysentery and were slowly starving to death. One night, in December, when he was almost too weak to move, Bernard heard voices outside his cellar. He pointed his revolver at the door.

"Who's there?" asked a Polish voice. A gun barrel pushed through the doorway.

"Friends," he answered.

"Amtcho?" the voice asked. It was a shibboleth, its meaning clear to both parties. *Are you a Jew?*

"Yes," Bernard answered.

The door burst open. The stranger threw his arms around Bernard's neck and hugged him furiously, then kissed his filthy cheeks. It was Yulek, son of a Praga teamster. Bernard had organized his dad's union, back when the Bund were kings.

Yulek brought Bernard and his friends to a bunker full of a cross-section of the sort of Warsaw Jews whom he might have known in another lifetime. The bunker inhabitants burned his lice-infested clothes, fed him, and returned him slowly back to life. Three weeks later, one of the bunker's patrols reported an extraordinary sound. They heard Russian voices in central Warsaw. A few days later, another patrol confirmed the news. The Red Army was marching through the center of the city. Bernard began to weep. He embraced the thug next to him. The group wriggled from their burrow. They were free.

At first Bernard could not see. He was unaccustomed to the sunlight. He blinked. His eyes focused. The landscape resembled the surface of the moon. On Marszalkowska Street, he watched the Red Army parade their tanks through the sepulcher that once had been his city. He could barely recognize a thing. Even the Jewish cemetery on Gesia Street had been pillaged, the graves dug up, the ground littered with skulls missing their gold teeth.

Living skeletons walked uneasily amidst the rubble. Later, he heard a Pole whisper, "Still so many Jews?"

CHAPTER 27

SCATTER

(1945–1948)

THE BUNDISTS EMERGED INTO A POSTWAR WORLD THAT HAD LITTLE room for them. Some of their comrades had barely survived Auschwitz. Others were prisoners in work camps in Soviet Central Asia, or refugees scattered from Buenos Aires to Shanghai. The war had left the Bund's leadership split between America and Poland, just as the iron curtain was about to fall. The anti-Soviet Bundists in New York would soon find themselves on a collision course with the Lublin Bundists, whose country's future lay with the Soviet Union.

The world that they came from was gone. Once, thousands of Jewish communities had lain like lace across the map of eastern Europe. They had made the "here" in the party's concept of Hereness. These places had burned, along with their inhabitants. The Nazis murdered 90 percent of Polish Jews—and one-third of the Jews on earth.

Another chapter was about to close. After the Soviets took Warsaw, Leon Feiner's friends could see he was facing the end. The elegant lawyer had spent the uprising nearly paralyzed with pneumonia. Friends took him to Lublin, where hospitals still functioned. Doctors diagnosed him with terminal blood cancer. The Polish Bund's first postliberation conference took place around Feiner's deathbed. In the statement they published afterward, they gave their support to the Soviet-backed government. The only dissenter was Bernard Goldstein.

BERNARD GOLDSTEIN

"Still alive?"

This was the question that greeted many Jews who made their way back from the death camps. It was often followed by an exasperated sigh, as if to say, *I thought they'd finished you off.*

The Endek politician Roman Knoll had been correct in 1943 when he said that many Poles would view the return of Jews as an invasion. "There is no place for a Jew in the countryside and towns today," since

Poles had taken over their businesses, said the Polish underground leader Jerzy Braun in July 1945. "What they take for anti-Semitism is only economic law." Jews who tried to reclaim their property faced hostility, if not violence. Many were killed for the crime of having survived.

"The returning Jews were made to feel that they were superfluous, that every piece of bread they ate was food taken from the mouths of their betters," Bernard Goldstein wrote. Even Yiddish became dangerous. When Bernard chatted with a friend in their native language, a passerby insulted them, then reported him to the police. At the station, the cop warned the two men that it was "inadvisable" to provoke Poles. Bernard's Polish communist friends were sympathetic but did nothing. They had bigger fish to fry.

Like all occupiers, Soviets quickly made themselves hated in Poland. They looted homes, stripped the factories of Lodz and hauled them back to Russia, and hunted down members of the Home Army. A nationalist insurgency rose against them. Called cursed soldiers, these partisans combined anticommunism with a genocidal loathing of the country's few remaining Jews. It was the same thing, after all. A Jew was a commie. A commie was a Jew. Nationalists murdered over a thousand Jews in the war's aftermath. When Marek Edelman traveled by train, he saw dead Jews at many stations, their bodies covered with newspapers. Sometimes their pants had been pulled down; nationalists had checked to see if men were circumcised before killing them.

Within months of liberation, tens of thousands of Jews fled for American-occupied Europe. One of them was Bernard Goldstein. The racism had disgusted him, but political repression was the final straw. The Left has a long memory, and the communists had passed a death sentence against him in prewar Warsaw. The walls closed in. Acquaintances transformed into snitches. When the NKVD brought Bernard in for a chat, the interrogator lay a gun on the table to intimidate him. At Bundist meetings, Bernard denounced his party's acceptance of the Soviet occupiers, only to see his "comrades" taking notes for the police. After the war, he had expected to rebuild his party in a country purified by shared suffering. Instead, he found bigots, morons, and stool pigeons. He felt like he was suffocating. Anyone he met with risked arrest. To avoid incriminating others, he locked himself in his room.

"This was not the liberation for which . . . I had degraded myself to the level of the meanest animal in order to remain alive," he later wrote. With a fake passport, he made his way to a Czech displaced persons' camp, and from there to New York City. He spent the rest of his life in the Bronx, as an honorary grandfather to his comrades' children. There, he at last fulfilled the dream he shared with his best friend, Shloyme Mendelson, back in Warsaw, and became a writer, penning two volumes of memoirs that survive as thrilling testaments to his party's heyday. As Naguib Mahfouz wrote, "Home is not where you are born. It is where all your attempts at escape cease."

Bernard Goldstein died in 1959. He is buried in Mount Carmel Cemetery in Queens, on the honor walk of Yiddish socialists, not far from his onetime cellmate Vladimir Medem. Someone has paid for the perpetual care of his grave. Whenever I visit, I take a teaspoon of dirt for a small act of necromancy. I go home, light a candle in front of his portrait, and ask the old hooligan for permission to tell his story.

JACOB PAT

In Poland's ruins, Bundists did what they had always done and threw themselves into activity. They joined the Central Committee of Polish Jews, an umbrella organization of the country's surviving Jewish groups, and pledged loyalty to the Soviet-backed government, the only defense Jews had against attacks by the nationalist paramilitaries. They set up workers' cooperatives and encouraged Jews to go into heavy industry. They resurrected their institutions: Tsukunft, SKIF, *Folkstsaytung*, the Morgenstern sport club, the orphanages, libraries, soup kitchens, old age homes, summer camps, and drama clubs that made up their prewar world. They even opened up a summer resort called the El Dorado.

Bundists scoured the country for their comrades' hidden children. It was not easy to get them back. After three years together, Polish protectors often loved these children like their own, and it was a grave trauma to split them apart. Bundists brought Zalman Friedrich's daughter Elzunia to America, where she was raised by affluent party comrades. At twenty-six, she died of an overdose.

In their public proclamations, the Bund's leaders thundered against emigration, but they had a hard time convincing Jews to stay in their families' graveyard. "Most of the members want to emigrate to America and join the comrades who are already there," Tsukunft's Warsaw secretary, Avraham Zilberstein, wrote to a Bundist in New York. Hereness felt like resignation.

The Bundist Jacob Pat realized the same when he returned to Poland in 1946 to distribute aid for the Jewish Labor Committee. In his hometown, Bialystok, where the Bund won fifteen thousand votes in the prewar municipal elections, the party had only twenty-three members left. He met stubborn, traumatized people who eked out livings in threadbare cooperative workshops, under constant threat from their Polish fellow citizens. Almost everyone wanted to leave. "You can smell the ships here," one of Pat's interlocutors told him. It didn't matter to them whether they sailed for America or for Palestine.

Pat's memoir gives a single glimpse of the bonds that once tied Bundists to the Here of Poland. At a newly opened Jewish community center in the Silesian town of Dzierzoniow, Pat heard the melody of "The Blue Danube." Inside, hundreds of young people waltzed. They were Poles and Jews. The dancers demanded one song after the next. They whirled, their feet light, and girls clung to their partners' shoulders. Pat stared at the numbers on their arms.

At the Polish Socialist Party's clubhouse next door, the young secretary poured Pat a whisky. He spoke of solidarity, of the brotherhood of peoples. He rolled up his sleeve to show the number on his arm.

The secretary raised a glass. He toasted his friends, socialist resistance fighters who had been shot by the Gestapo. "Bolek, Antek, Zdzislaw—let's drink to their memory! Let's drink to the memory of our Jewish comrades! Let's drink to our brave dead!" Then he looked at Pat as if to seek forgiveness. "Brother, believe me. We socialists are not guilty in all this. I mean . . . the Jews and the other things. Believe me, I am ashamed of what is happening in our country."

The secretary spoke across a chasm carved by genocide, and when I first read his words in 2018, I could not imagine myself in his place. He was a Pole. I am a Jew. My tribalism precluded understanding. But two years into the annihilation of Gaza, I feel only empathy for him, along with my own inadequacy. What had I done to stop this genocide, still live-streamed on our smartphone screens? Not enough. The secretary had also tried to stop mass slaughter. His sacrifices were far graver than anything I could comprehend. Yet it didn't work. If we also fail, what chasm will we look across to seek forgiveness?

The secretary's sentences trailed off, until all that was left was a supplication. "Comrade . . . Brother . . . We socialists . . . Believe me . . ."

KIELCE

The final blow fell in July 1946, in the southeastern city of Kielce, when a Polish boy came home late. He blamed the Jews, as one did, saying that they had locked him in the basement of a communal apartment building, where they planned to make matzoh from his blood. It didn't matter that this building had no basement. Polish mobs slaughtered forty-two young Jewish residents. Cops and soldiers joined in. When Marek Edelman traveled to Kielce on an ambulance train, feathers from torn duvets still floated in the air, like they did after pogroms in my great-grandfather's day. Everything smelled like burning meat.

After Kielce, the Bund demanded that Polish government "eradicate antisemitism and arrest its disseminators." At the same time, they tried to persuade Jews that the pogrom was just a speed bump, that this country was still their home. Few believed them. Hundreds of Bundists asked the Jewish Labor Committee to get them visas to America.

They joined the flood out of Poland. Zionist smuggling networks crisscrossed the country, helping Jews flee to American-occupied Germany and, from there, to Palestine. One of their most charismatic representatives was Antek Zuckerman, founder of the Jewish Combat Organization. After everything he'd seen, Antek had even less respect for the Bund's ideology of Hereness, which he damned as a self-destructive delusion. Anyone could see that Jews had no future without a state. Antek's wife, Celina, had already left for Palestine, where she gave birth to their child. He joined her there in 1948. The two heroes of the uprising spent the rest of their lives on a kibbutz for ghetto fighters like them, built on the ruins of a Palestinian village, ethnically cleansed by Zionist militias that became the IDF.

DISPLACED PERSONS

The collapse of the Third Reich created a new category of human, the displaced person, or DP. When the war ended, there were eighty thousand concentration camp inmates and nine million forced laborers inside Germany, the vast majority of them not Jews. Americans hastily threw up camps to accommodate them. Most were shit-encrusted hellholes, where Jews bunked next to Nazi collaborators on the principle that people with the same passport ought to get along.

The first Bundists in these camps were survivors of the death factories, like the courier Jacob Celemenski, whom Nazis arrested as a Pole after the Warsaw Uprising. After a joyful encounter with a cellblock full of Bundists in the Bergen-Belsen DP camp, Celemenski rode the rails through ruined Germany in search of his surviving comrades. He eventually discovered that 1,200 Bundists had made their homes in the archipelago of waiting. Some of them imagined that they'd go home to help rebuild their communities in Poland. Others deduced the impossibility of return.

The barbed wire that circled the first camps came down in 1946. At the request of Jewish groups, Americans allowed Jews to live in separate camps, away from the Nazi collaborators. Conditions remained grim.

There was no work and barely enough food. People lived in flimsy shacks, eleven to a room. It was limbo, if not hell.

On June 1, 1946, 150 of those Bundists who had been "dispersed and shoved aside all over Germany" gathered in the Feldafing DP camp in Bavaria for a three-day conference to figure out what came next. They decided to run for the survivors' committees that constituted camp self-governance. It seemed like a natural step. After all, a mere six years back, they had dominated the kehillahs and city councils in Poland.

Times had changed. Immediately after the armistice, Zionist youth leaders, teachers, doctors, soldiers of Britain's Jewish Legion, and fighters from the Haganah and Irgun paramilitaries had all arrived from Palestine to win over the survivors, and they quickly converted the camps into their territory. When the Bund's old enemy, Jewish Agency head David Ben-Gurion, visited the camps, many DPs greeted him as a hero. Zionist emissaries were organized, well funded, and had friends in the U.S. military, who didn't want a mass influx of Jews into America. They quickly seized control of camp administrations, which gave out travel passes, jobs, and extra rations.

While most of these emissaries cared deeply about survivors, their arrival had a more self-interested motive. For the Jewish Agency, the 360,000 Jewish DPs were not traumatized individuals hoping to rebuild their lives. They were "human material," in Ben-Gurion's words, to fight for a Jewish state. With World War II over, the war for Palestine was about to begin anew. Jewish DPs formed an invaluable demographic resource, while their suffering increased sympathy for the Zionist cause.

"Along came the missionaries from the Holy Land, to gather the flock onto the path of righteousness," wrote the Bundist DP Moshe Ajzenbud, a machinist and aspiring fiction writer, in one of his fiery dispatches to the party press. "They act as lords of the camp. The Zionists have convinced the world that survivors form one united front."

Zionists thwarted efforts to settle Jewish refugees anywhere other than Palestine and branded Jews as deserters if they signed up for immigration to other countries. They even resorted to sabotage. Bundists in the Bindermichl camp claimed that Zionists smashed a school built to train furriers for jobs in Canada, leaving behind graffiti denouncing deserters.

In this atmosphere, Bundists were marginalized, intimidated, or simply erased. The Central Committee of Liberated Jews, which represented survivors in the DP camps, even denied that Bundists still existed. In the words of one survivor, his comrades lived like hidden Jews in the days of the Spanish Inquisition.

The Zionist press mocked Bundists for their stubbornness. As one article incredulously put it, "Bundists who were strung up on the same pine that grew in the soil they wished to hold on to forever . . . who saw their theory of exilic existence refuted in the most horrible way . . . pop up again and publicly declare 'Follow us.' "

In displaced persons camps, Bundist survivors tried to keep their spirits up. They organized libraries, theater troupes, and field trips to nearby palaces. They released a calligraphed bulletin of their activities. They set up cooperatives and posed with red flags in the woods. None of it worked. The Bundists had no jobs, no way to get money except the black market. They lived surrounded by the Germans who had murdered their families. "Can you call it living, the physical act of breathing? Or by medical examination the beating of a pulse?" asked the Bundist Anke Zilberstein. "Can we today as an uprooted people, who don't take any active part in society, call our state anything else but vegetative?" The movement they built had been decimated, as had the Polish world of their birth. They had lost the context that gave meaning to their lives.

WARSAW

In November 1947, the Bund's flag went up in German DP camps, in a Shanghai social club, and at a Roman union hall. It was their fiftieth anniversary. In New York's Manhattan Center, five thousand people watched the young courier Vladka Peltel hand the party's banner to seventy-eight-year-old John Mill, the last surviving Bundist pioneer. At Warsaw's Gesia Street cemetery, Bundists unveiled a memorial for the ghetto fighters. Carved from red stone, a man who resembled Michal Klepfisz emerged from fire, a homemade grenade in his fist.

Despite this celebration, the Polish Bund was in its final days. Only a fragment remained of what had once been the largest Jewish community in Europe. Cold War geopolitics had already forced the Polish Bund to formally separate from the Bund run by their comrades in New York, but this renunciation would not be enough to save them. After rigged elections that year, the Soviet-backed government decided it was done with democratic charades. The government forced the Polish Socialist Party to merge with the communists and arrested its recalcitrant leaders. Kazimierz Puzak, who had warned Alter and Erlich to flee Warsaw, died in Rawicz prison. Antoni Zdanowski, Alter's travel buddy on the Madrid front line, was tortured to death by the secret police. The Bund was next. Under extreme pressure, the party voted to dissolve itself in 1949. Some members disappeared into private life. Others, including most of Tsukunft's leadership, smuggled themselves out of Poland.

Marek Edelman stayed, despite harassment by the secret police. Someone had to look after the dead. He became a prominent heart surgeon. As an older man, he took part in the Solidarity movement that, in 1989, would lead to the dissolution of his country's dictatorship. "To be a Jew means always being with the oppressed, never with the oppressors," Edelman wrote. For this reason, he never became a Zionist. Though he was fêted across the world, Israel never forgave him. When Prime Minister Yitzhak Rabin traveled to Poland to commemorate the fiftieth anniversary of the ghetto uprising, the uprising's commander was not permitted to speak. Edelman died in 2009. At his funeral, mourners sang the Bund's anthem over his coffin. He received no honors from the Jewish state.

CONSCRIPTION

"The future of the Jewish community in Palestine . . . cannot be built upon latent or open war against the Arab majority of the country as well as against the Arab countries surrounding Palestine," warned the *Bund Bulletin* in 1947. "However, such a state of affairs would be the inevitable result of the creation of a Jewish state." At the end of 1947, the United Nations approved a partition plan for Palestine, which granted Jews, who were a only a third of the population, 56 percent of the land. Palestinian leadership understandably rejected this offer. The next day, the Haganah sent out mobilization notices to all military-aged men and women, and community leaders in Arab countries similarly began to recruit fighters. As the Jewish Agency's leader, David Ben-Gurion, wrote at the time, the future borders of a Jewish state would be "determined by force." Secretly, Ben-Gurion and his generals began to plan for the realization of their long-held dream—the mass expulsion of the Arab population of Palestine.

The Haganah had money from American Jews and would soon get weapons from Soviet-backed Czechoslovakia, but still worried about their numerical disadvantage; Palestinians outnumbered them three to two. In March 1948, David Ben-Gurion approved a draft for Jewish refugees in Europe. They were not Israeli citizens, as Israel didn't exist, nor were they all Zionists. The Haganah claimed them as fighters merely because they were Jews, "citizens of Israel who are prevented from reaching Israel, but citizens of Israel nonetheless," in the words of the Haganah officer Nahum Shadmi, who led the effort.

The draft was not a popular success. Most Zionist true believers were already in Palestine, and the Jews who remained in the camps were more interested in building homes somewhere stable than signing up as cannon fodder for a place they'd never been. "Most Jewish refugees, who had been through the hell of the ghetto, slavery, and death camps under the Nazis, Soviet forced-labor camps, and other disasters yearn for some quiet place," wrote the Bundist correspondent Moshe Ajzenbud. A report from the Zionist youth movement Gordonia put it in harsher terms. "The corruption of these [Polish] Jews is so great that they are totally uninterested" in going to fight in Palestine. Instead, hundreds had registered for American visas.

When appeals to patriotism failed, Zionists turned to stronger inducements. On March 30, the Congress of Survivors in the American occupation zone of Germany resolved that "draft dodgers" would be "removed from all social and political life."

This enforcement went into immediate effect. Camp administrations fired non-Zionist employees, levied fines, threw people out of apartments, and denied them their meager supplemental rations. They published blacklists to publicly shame draft dodgers, targeting Bundists with a special cruelty. In the Eschwege camp, Bundists complained that they were fired from jobs and denied medical treatment. In Neu Freimann, Bundist art teacher Jacob Celnik lost his job after he refused to register for the draft. And in Grugliasco, near Turin, Bundists claimed that after a Zionist-led smear campaign, the camp committee's Bundist chairman, Jacob Freidman, was stripped of his position, then his housing and rations, and finally reported to the Italian police as a criminal. Unable to catch him, police instead locked his brother in a concentration camp.

In the end, Zionists imposed the draft by force. It was shocking, said the Bundist newspaper *Unzer Shtime*, "that Jews, the standard victims of Fascism and terrorism, would be capable of the kinds of violence Zionists in the camps exercise toward their Bundist and other non-Zionist political rivals." Hundreds of affidavits attested to the attacks. Bundists and other non-Zionist Jews told stories of night raids and mob beatings. Bundists in the Bad Reichenhall camp claimed Zionists publicly whipped a draft dodger, then took photos to frighten others into compliance. In a camp near Ulm, Germany, Zionists beat the elderly fathers of sons who avoided the draft. Conscription continued until April 1949, at which point recruits from DP camps made up a third of the new Israeli army.

In his last article written before his death in 1948, Bernard Goldstein's best friend Shloyme Mendelson condemned the "totalitarian" methods that Zionism used to repress Jewish dissent. "What a bitter irony that after the utter destruction brought upon the Jewish people by Fascism, the latter's methods of terror are now triumphant in Jewish life. . . . It is as if the slaughterer had infected his victims with his germs during the slaughter."

Bundist camp chapters tried to protect their members. They collected testimonies about abuse, noting names and dates for verification, then shared their reports with the party press and visiting Bundist delegates. In Austria, Bundists appealed for help from the Socialist Party of Austria.

Even as Bundist DPs tried to resist conscription, they battled to free their members from the camps. Because of the Bund's connections with the American labor movement, hundreds of DPs applied for membership, hoping to net U.S. visas. The Bund tried to guide their members through the labyrinth of training programs, bureaucratic loopholes, and registration lists. At camp meetings, Bundists demanded free immigration to all countries, despite the rage it inspired in Zionist audiences, who wanted them to focus on Palestine. On the First of May, Bundist DPs didn't just march for socialism. They marched for their freedom of movement. They screamed for the borders to fall.

When a Bundist dignitary visited from New York, the greatest gift he could bring was a visa.

REFUGE

"Had the gates to America opened wide after the war, it may well be that the masses of Jews would have flowed to America and only a minority would have come here," said Ben-Gurion shortly after the creation of Israel. The Bund agreed. For over a decade, their New York leadership had begged the United States to grant visas to Jewish refugees. In 1947, they excoriated the world that indifferently watched Hitler's victims languish in DP camps. They petitioned the UN to accept the displaced.

"Even Hitler's unparalleled massacre of six million of our kin could not eradicate from our souls the faith in true international socialism. Our comrades are unbroken in their spirit and are resolved to do their share in the worldwide fight for our and everybody's freedom. . . . Unfortunately, we do not meet an adequate response from other peoples," said the Bundist leader Emanuel Sherer at a convention of the Socialist Party of America in New York. "Again and again, we hear in this country the call for opening the doors of Palestine to the Jewish DP. But what about the doors of this great country? It is indeed a very painful blow to those directly concerned—but it is to no lesser extent a shame to our civilization—that this elemental demand for opening the gates of *all* countries to the uprooted and displaced victims of the most horrible Nazi cruelties is still not fulfilled."

That year, the Bund reconstituted itself as an international organization, with its base now in New York City. At their first conference they called for a secular, democratic Palestine, with cultural autonomy and constitutionally protected equal rights, and said that Zionists must "renounce the goal of an independent Jewish state."

Despite their supplications, despite their connections with the labor movement and with officials in the former Roosevelt administration, the Bundists could only get American visas for a sliver of their membership. After the war, the country wanted nothing to do with Jews like them. When Congress tried to pass a bill to accept two hundred thousand survivors, Georgia Democrat E. E. Cox denounced "the scum of all Europe—an aggregation of loafers [and] revolutionists . . . [who] will join those who are gnawing away at the foundation of our constitutional government." When the bill finally passed in 1948, it banned 90 percent of Jewish survivors, because they had taken wartime refuge in the Soviet Union.

The camps closed. The Bundists scattered. The lucky ones got visas for refugee communities in Melbourne and Johannesburg, Paris and Montevideo. Others were not so lucky. In the years after the Holocaust, hundreds of Bundist survivors left for Palestine. Their party had given them fairy tales. Zionists offered a place where they could rebuild their lives.

SOLIDARITY

In 1948, Bundist Leivik Hodes wrote that his party's philosophy depended on their fundamental faith in solidarity.

> [This] belief in mankind is not popular today. In these last years we have all seen it become deeply debased, despoiled, and spat on. But if man is at heart a beast, no amount of running away will help.
>
> The Bund had always put its cards on socialism, which means a better future for all humanity . . . If the dream of socialism becomes true, then there is no one to run from; if the dream dissipates, like so many other of mankind's better dreams, then there is nowhere to run to. The mirage of a little "statelet" surrounded by enemies is no amulet against anti-Semitism and extermination. . . .
>
> . . . The remnants of the Jewish masses lurch through the camps, wander around homeless, or float like splinters on the

> foaming waves of the stormy post-war world. But with every day it becomes clearer that the pathway to healing these wounds leads . . . not through increasing the number of uprooted refugees, but through building and rebuilding. . . .

Such solidaristic principles found fewer adherents after the Holocaust. "Deeply grieved and shaken by the murder of six million of their brethren, the masses of the Jewish people became enveloped by strong nationalist tendencies, which . . . fanned by skillful Zionist propaganda, caused among the Jews a psychosis of Zionist and Messianic illusions," the Bund's coordinating committee wrote in 1948. For many Jews, the Holocaust seemed to confirm the Zionist prognosis. Jews couldn't survive as a minority in the diaspora. Existence meant having a state.

Jews were hardly alone in thinking this way. Oppression seldom breeds compassion, and a genocide is not a school for personal growth. History is full of stories of traumatized refugees who were radicalized by movements that promised them redemption through violence. That many survivors became Zionists is not exceptional. It is human and banal.

And yet.

In social justice circles, it's said that an oppressed group can't be racist, because racism requires power. If a group is powerless, they can be as bigoted as they like. Jews have been powerless for most of our history. The rituals of our religion are those of a powerless people, and we have hated with a powerless hate. On Purim we make noise to celebrate not just Haman's death but the murder of our enemies, the people of Amalek, down to the last man, woman, and child. For a long time, this was just an expression of impotent emotion. Theater, in the Aristotelian sense. Catharsis. We weren't going to do anything about it. It's not like we had an army.

This is fine when a group is powerless, but power is a fluid thing. Jews now have an army, and those once-impotent fantasies about destroying Amalek have transformed into white phosphorus bombs dropped on Gaza, into torture camps and mass graves full of cancer patients, shot with their catheters still in.

Zionism has been many things, but among them, it was once the ideology of some of the most powerless people on earth. In 1942, young Zionists in the Warsaw ghetto founded the Jewish Combat Organization. Exactly five years after the ghetto revolt, on the eve of Passover 1948, Zionist paramilitaries ethnically cleansed fifteen thousand Palestinians from Haifa.

Was it the same Zionism in the Warsaw ghetto as in Haifa? And what does this say about the ideologies of other oppressed people today?

Maybe it's this. An oppressed people's beliefs are not benign just because they lack power. Beliefs are good or bad on their own merits, because nothing stays the same. Demographics change. Empires weaken. Insurgents take charge. Without a clear set of ethics that respects human life, today's victims transform into tomorrow's killers. Oppressed becomes oppressor the moment the power flips.

PALESTINE

Ben-Gurion announced the state of Israel in May 1948, with the support of the Soviet Union and the United States. In the attacks that preceded the declaration, and in the war that followed, Zionist militias violently expelled over 750,000 Palestinians from their homes. The Bund demanded the right of return for these refugees, but Israel had no such intention. For Israel to exist, Palestine could not. The IDF tortured Palestinians who tried to return or shot them as "infiltrators." Their property became booty for the new Israeli state.

"It appears that 2,000 years of suffering and of untold hardships caused by the misery of numerous deportations were entirely forgotten as soon as circumstances caused a fraction of the Jewish population to be placed in a position of self-government," wrote the Bund in the *Bulletin* in September 1948. "True to its Zionist self, the Jewish Government of the State of Israel appears ready to forfeit the moral rights of the Jewish DPs in Europe and elsewhere by refusing to permit the Arab refugees to return to their homes in Palestine."

Despite Israel's best efforts, these Palestinians refused to disappear.

"At present, when more than half a million Arab displaced persons are demanding permission to return to their former homes . . . how the State of Israel could cope with a Jewish immigration of any scope without the 'miracle' of the vanished Arabs is beyond anybody's imagination. Yet the Arab refugee problem remains most urgent," wrote the Bund in the *Bulletin* in June 1949. In 1951, the *Bund Bulletin* ran a story about the hundreds of thousands of Palestinian refugees in camps in neighboring countries, "prevented from returning to their homesteads and villages and whose property is as good as confiscated by the conqueror." Themselves veterans of countless exiles, these Bundists saw the Nakba for what it was: the foundational crime of the Zionist endeavor. Born of another people's violent dispossession, Israel had yoked itself into an ever-worsening cycle of repression and resistance. Its own violence would poison it, and the cancer would metastasize, until there was nothing else left.

CHAPTER 28

HOME

(1949–present)

SOPHIA DUBNOVA

A WOMAN EMERGES FROM THE FILTHY WATERS OF THE HUDSON. ONCE copper, she has greened with age. At her base are some verses penned by a Jewish poet over a century ago to welcome pogrom survivors. Time has given these words an ironic lilt.

She was never supposed to be here. Native to France, she had been destined for Egypt, but something brought her to New York. Call it God, or chance, or the dialectical forces of history. Whatever it was, she's here. Here she remains, her torch thrust upward into the smoke-choked sky. "Mother of exiles," as the Jewish poet called her, in a name truer than her official one. She is a fitting symbol for the city where so many exiled Bundists made their homes.

Among these exiles was Sophia Dubnova, who passed the rest of her life in Manhattan's Upper West Side, not far from my mother's apartment. During her New York years, Sophia published prolifically, including a volume of poetry, a biography of her beloved historian father, and a delicious memoir that I relied on to write this book. Though she was Bundist royalty, she refused to confine herself to the role of Henryk Erlich's widow. There were too many battles to be fought, right here in her newfound country. In the 1960s, she threw herself into the civil rights movement, though by then, her vision was so bad that she sometimes picketed the wrong shops. She died in 1986, at age 101, engaged and lucid to the last. Shortly before her death, she told her grandson Henry she had a confession to make. She was no longer a socialist but an anarchist.

Both of Sophia's sons became professors. The eldest, Alexander, taught economics at Columbia University in New York City. There, he became close to another refugee—a brilliant Palestinian critic by the name of Edward Said. Over email, Said's daughter, Najla, recalled a moment in 1981, when she was only seven. She and her father ran into Erlich in front of his building. Erlich wore a pin for Solidarity, the Polish trade-union movement that would help bring down the country's dictatorship. "My dad explained to me right then and there what *solidarity* meant," Najla told me. "I learned that big important word because of [Alexander Erlich]." She had occasion to remember this story in 2024, when students protesting Israel's genocide in Gaza set up a solidarity encampment on the lawn of Columbia University, right below her father's former office.

THE BUND

Alexander Erlich was one of the people who tried to steward the Bund through the second half of the twentieth century. By 1950, the once mighty movement had been reduced to small communities of Holocaust survivors scattered across the globe. Exhausted, traumatized, and with most of their loved ones dead, these Bundists turned to each other. They were all they had. They moved into the same apartment buildings, got jobs at the same garment factories, intermarried, and became family. They worked together to compile histories of their party—fat Yiddish volumes that I used to write this book.

But they would never again hold political power. There would be no more grand marches for May Day, no fiery election campaigns. Those days were gone. When the tiny Bund branch in Tel Aviv tried to run for the Knesset, they could not even raise enough money to get on the ballot. In America, Bundists set up socialist Sunday schools and a summer camp for their children, but they fell out of touch with the political and cultural zeitgeist. The Soviet Union's murder of their leaders pushed these Bundists into a reactive anticommunism, even while, during the McCarthy years, they lived in terror of being deported as communists. As the decades wore on, their opposition to Zionism grew tepid, but the mere fact that such opposition continued was enough to relegate them to the margins of Jewish life. In one letter I found, from 1978, the writer Irving Howe complained about an incident at Columbia University, where he debated Edward Said about Israel. When it came time for questions, a little old Bundist with a thick Yiddish accent sprang up. "He let loose an attack upon Zionists, Israelis, etc. which would have been shocking if it had come from an Arab. . . . I felt somehow ashamed that a fellow Jew, and a socialist at that, would talk this way," Howe wrote.

Stubbornly, the Bund persisted, but membership shrank each year. This was probably inevitable. For all its notions of transnational Hereness, the Bund's ideology grew from the twisted streets of the former

Pale of Settlement. It was a movement for the Jewish masses of eastern Europe. Those masses were gone, and the Bund was lost without them.

One treasure remained from their murdered homeland: Yiddish, the language of the Jewish Street. This the Bundists would not lose. While the postwar period's combination of the Soviet gulag, Western assimilation, and Israeli hegemony squeezed their party into political irrelevance, Bundists nurtured the Yiddish tongue. The composer Gustav Mahler once said that tradition is not the worship of ashes but the preservation of fire. Bundists guarded the glowing coals. They were politically spent. By the 1980s, little was left of their party but a dwindling number of old people with faded red banners, ghosts in a legion hall for Veterans of Lost Causes. But their efforts with Yiddish would help launch a linguistic revival, complete with music, poetry, and international festivals. At these defiant celebrations of diasporic creativity, their party's songs would once again be sung. Through art, they planted the seeds of their own rediscovery.

The Bund's Worldwide Organizing Committee dissolved around 2003, but affiliated groups survive in Australia and France. In August 2018, when someone pasted a swastika on an advertisement in Melbourne, it was immediately covered by a sticker for the organization my great-grandfather had joined in 1898.

SAM ROTHBORT

Though he died before I was born, I grew up surrounded by reminders of my great-grandfather. It was not just the thousands of his paintings, sculptures, watercolors, and mosaics that filled my great-aunt's house in Brooklyn but the very presence of Grandpa Sam himself, as if his personality had been too vivid to allow him to be rendered a ghost. From my great-aunt Ida and my mother, I knew his story.

"Without art you're dead!" Sam liked to say. Each day, he got up and made his work. His paintings would never get the grand museum retrospectives or high auction prices of his more socially adept contemporaries, but he remained an artist till his final breath. When times were good, he sold paintings to high society and received newspaper profiles lauding him as the next Cézanne. When times were bad, he foraged his materials from the trash. He shunned the institutions that shunned him, spreading his paintings on his front lawn every morning for his Rothbort Home Museum of Direct Art. He grew sunflowers, ate black bread baked from flour he ground himself, and drank the water from a well he dug in his backyard. (He didn't trust the tap.) He exchanged letters with

Isaac Bashevis Singer. He loved his Rose. He made art with his son, the brilliant, tormented Lawrence, who was murdered in 1963. Despite his share of tragedies, Sam was a happy man.

While Sam sometimes attended Jewish socialist meetings, he was not an activist. He belonged to no American party I know of, confining his political work to writing letters to President Eisenhower, which he thought hastened the end of the Korean War. He was a long way from the boy who helped shoot two police officers in the Volkovysk market square.

But though he had traveled far from his origins, he still kept up with his comrades. In a shoebox of old Yiddish documents sent by a second cousin, I found the program for the fiftieth-anniversary banquet of Workmen's Circle branch 100—formerly the Volkovysk Revolutionary Union, which Sam had joined in 1904 as a young exile in New York. I found Sam's name on the seating chart, next to others I recognized as belonging to fellow Volkovysk Bundists.

Like him, they had Americanized their names and traded their black peasant blouses for respectable suits and frocks, but despite these New World disguises, they retained flickers of their rebel pasts. All of them bore memories of strikes and jailbreaks and smuggled pamphlets, of windows smashed in the dead of night, of the idealistic quest for a better and more beautiful world. All of them had raised the red flag in the woods and sang "The Oath," the Bund's anthem.

Heaven and earth will hear us,
the bright stars will bear witness,
an oath of blood, an oath of tears—
We swear, we swear, we swear!

Perhaps they sang it that night.

Sam Rothbort was a singular man, but he was still formed by the revolutionary commitments of his youth. As I researched this book, I learned to recognize the traces of Bundism he carried within him. His benign lawlessness. His contempt for money. The welcome he gave to my Puerto Rican father. His lack of ties to Israel. The two embracing children he carved in stone, who, he wrote "have not yet been misled by false theories of race creed or color." His bohemian humanism, big enough to take in the world.

The Bund shaped Sam's life, and then through him, it shaped mine. As I traveled the world, I held these lessons tight. Sam taught me what it meant to live as an artist, in defiance of authority's indifference or repression. He made me the woman who I am.

On traditional Jewish New Year's cards, the old year is represented as an aged man shuffling off into the horizon, before the arrival of the fat New Year's baby. Sam always rejected this metaphor. "I prefer the human idea of history repeating," he wrote. "Years are not loaves of bread; we can't slice them: they roll together in Time's rolling wheel." From a marble block, he sculpted the old year hugging the New Year's baby to his cheek. The past is not dead, Sam knew. It holds tight to our eternal present, sometimes invisibly, but ready to be reclaimed by those who need it.

I finish this book beneath a portrait of my great-grandfather.

Sam Rothbort in his elder years

POSTSCRIPT: HISTORY NEVER ENDS

IN 1938, HENRYK ERLICH WROTE, "IF A JEWISH STATE SHOULD ARISE in Palestine, its spiritual climate will be: eternal fear of the external enemy (Arabs); eternal struggle for every bit of ground with the internal enemy (Arabs) . . . Is this a climate in which freedom, democracy, and progress can grow? Indeed, is it not the climate in which reaction and chauvinism ordinarily flourish?"

Erlich killed himself four years later, as Zionists like to remind me on social media. People who met him in prison say that he remained a Bundist till the end. Time after time in party hagiographies, I read the same story. In gulags, in concentration camps, on the execution block, the Bundist would leave his final testimony. "I die knowing that I was right." The Bundist periodicals kept the same line, even as they faded into irrelevance. I die knowing that I was right.

I was right. Sure, you were. That and $2.90 will get you to Coney Island. What could be stupider than to keep insisting you were right when the whole world says otherwise, when your enemies are triumphant, when even your kids forsake you?

And yet.

History keeps moving. No victory is final. Neither is any defeat.

In 2023, after a massacre led by Hamas, Israel began a genocide in Gaza. On social media, Palestinians exposed the violence that has continued since the beginning of the Nakba, with every house that settlers steal, every gang rape in an Israeli prison camp, every crater carved by Israeli bombs. Around the world, people organized, marched, fundraised and got dragged off to jail to denounce Israel's crimes. Many of them were Jews. In March 2025, Jewish Voices for Peace even staged a sit-in inside Trump Tower, right below the gold-plated escalator where Trump announced his first presidential campaign. I was there with them.

Well-heeled representatives of institutional Jewish life condemned those of us who protested the genocide. A good Jew was a Zionist, they claimed. We were self-hating tokens, traitors to our people. We had not learned the lessons of history.

History, though, is never settled. Bodies rot, but ideas remain. They resurface like land mines or buried gold.

Or like pages scribbled by a doomed man for his enemies' archive, in hopes of reaching the future.

In 2018, five years before Israel's war on Gaza, long-dead Bundists' words began to circulate on social media. In part, this was because of my article for *The New York Review of Books*. The Bund's ideas found an audience. They had a moral clarity and toughness that attracted young Jews seeking a heritage beyond the Israeli state. After 2023, this rediscovery reached a fever pitch. The Bund's anti-Zionism, which had so marginalized them during the long decades of Israeli communal dominance, would lead a new generation to embrace them. In Berlin, in New York, and even in their birthplace, Vilna, young people have raised the Bund's banner in support of Hereness, of democratic socialism, and of Palestinian liberation.

"I was right," said the man as he went to the gallows. Sometimes, with the distance of years, he looks less like a fool.

Instead, he resembles a prophet.

"OKAY, THEY WERE RIGHT," one friend told me after he finished my manuscript. "Right and dead. What's the big lesson you want us to take away from that? After all, the Bund failed."

"Lost," I answered, more sharply than I meant.

"What's the difference between failed and lost?" he responded.

"Failure is what happens to those overcome by their own faults and errors. To lose is to succumb to greater force."

Here, I confess a secret. I didn't just write this book out of scholarly devotion. I had a hidden hope. By studying the Bund's story, I wanted to find out if there was some way that my people, the Jews of eastern Europe, could have saved themselves.

The more I wrote, the more I realized the wrongness of my premise. Though individuals escaped in various ways, there was no way out for eastern European Jews as a collective. Not as long as they were fighting alone. No small minority could have rescued themselves from the horrors of the twentieth century. Despite astounding feats of heroism, cunning, and creativity, they couldn't hold Hitler back, nor the intractable hatred of so many of their Christian neighbors. This Bund could not change the balance of force. Neither could any other Jewish group in eastern Europe, whether assimilationist or Zionist, capitalist or communist, Hasidic or Christian convert. Six million scattered humans can't defeat vast armies of organized killers.

The accusation of failure isn't one we should level against the Bund, or any other Jewish group of that place and time. It's for the Western world of which they were such a precarious part. It was the West, after all, that hypocritically paid lip service to freedom and humanity while hewing to the crude doctrines of might. The true failures were the democracies who played nice with Hitler in the early years, then shut their doors to Jewish refugees who fled from the hell they helped enable. The failures were the British and American diplomats who hobnobbed in Bermuda while the ghetto burned.

The Western world failed the Jews of Europe when they refused to provide the basic solidarity that the historical moment demanded—the solidarity upon which the Bund's humanism relied. This betrayal allowed Zionism to present itself as the only possible salvation. If the world came down to strong predators and weak victims, Zionism at least offered Jews the possibility of strength.

But Zionism is ethnonationalism. Like all ethnonationalisms, it required mass murder to clear the land to build its dream. On this haunted territory, oppressed became oppressors. Seventy-odd years after they stuck their state upon another people's ruin, the inheritors of Zion would liquidate their very own ghetto in Gaza beside the sea.

For ethnonationalism, this is what winning means.

So why did I write this book about the Bund—who lost, who were failed—and not about victorious killers?

Because I am sick of monsters—whether they belong to my group or any other. Because I know that we all have the capacity to be victims and tormenters, as well as bystanders, staring blankly at a burning wall. Because I want off the samsara wheel of atrocity, and the Bund's demand of solidarity across difference is the only way to get there.

Such solidarity is fragile and frequently betrayed, but it is all we have. It is the only thing that can save us.

There is no other earth, after all. We are trapped together on this one. It belongs to all of us, as inheritance and prison. It is Egypt *and* the promised land.

I return to *do'ikayt*—Hereness, a doctrine created by the godless Jews of the diaspora, written with mongrel words in Hebrew letters, then spread by itinerant troublemakers carrying forged passports, whose fundamental demand was the right to stay. What does Hereness mean in our age of blood-soaked mass displacement? An attempt, I believe, to find the self in exile, to square homeland with the freedom to leave.

Sam made another painting, titled *Without Passport.* It shows two men and a woman in a moonlit forest, dragged off by the tsarist police. They were most likely Jews who lacked the internal passport that would allow them to travel outside the Pale of Settlement. But they had tried anyway. Was this a betrayal of Hereness? Or was the Here within them, in their act of illicit movement? Did their defiance taste like home?

I like to think that, later that night, Sam and his comrades sawed through the bars of the trio's jail cell window. They would have shimmied out, the couple perhaps pausing for a kiss amidst the frigid stillness of the forest, then gone on, past a border blurred by snowfall, going wherever they wanted to go.

ACKNOWLEDGMENTS

Like all books, *Here Where We Live Is Our Country* was a collective endeavor. I am indebted to too many people to list. I apologize for my inevitable elisions.

Thank you to my editor, Chris Jackson, a legend in his field, who stood by me as this book grew into something far bigger than I had imagined, and to the wonderful Greg Mollica and Hiab Debessai. Thank you to my valiant agent, Alice Whitwham, and to the wise, incisive editorial counsel of Miriam Elder. I am grateful to the Dorothy and Lewis B. Cullman Center for Scholars and Writers at the New York Public Library, for giving me the room and stipend I needed to finish this project. Thank you to the New America Foundation and the Puffin Foundation for their support.

This book involved research in eight languages on four continents. Thank you to translators and researchers Ethan Fraenkel, Sophie Hurwitz, Egina Manachova, and Lesia Prokopenko. Thank you to Lukas Hermsmeier and Arikia Millikan for helping me track down an obscure volume of socialist history in Berlin, and to Zach Smerin for filling me in on the postwar Polish Bund. Thank you to Sasha Slansky for saving me with the endnotes.

My favorite editor, Matt Seaton, commissioned my first article on the Bund for *The New York Review of Books*. He didn't know he was changing my life.

Archives are how the past speaks to the present, and so I must thank all the archivists I relied on. Thank you to Lyudmila Sholokhova, queen of New York Public Library's Dorot Collection, and to Leo Greenbaum, boss of YIVO's Bund archives. Thank you to the keepers of the Melbourne Bund archives and to those of the Jewish Historical Institute in Warsaw, to the overlords of the Tamiment Library, to the Yiddish Book Center, and to Hy Wolfe, who despite all odds continues to run the CYCO Yiddish bookstore in Queens. I must also thank the teachers at YIVO who taught me Yiddish and thus opened the linguistic doorway to the Bund's world.

I would never have written this book if not for the descendants of Bundists who shared their stories. Thank you to Fay Rosenfeld, Sheva Zucker, Mark and Henry Erlich, Victor Gilinsky, Brian Gocial, and Mimi Erlich (honor to her memory). Bundist scholar Jack Jacobs was profoundly generous with his knowledge. Thank you to Marvin Zuckerman for translating Bernard Goldstien's story into English and for singing me radical anthems in California parking lots. Above all, I thank my queen Irena Klepfisz. I'm sorry for leaving all those curse words in.

Thank you to Madeleine Atkins Cohen, whose translation of Leivik Hodes would provide a moral touchstone for the book.

Thank you to all of those who were with me during my travels: beautiful Zuzana Hertzberg, Gabi von Seltmann, Paula Sawicka, Anna Grechishkina (a heroic Ukrainian soldier who held my hand at Babi Yar), and to the Yiddish singers of Lviv. I would also like to thank Omar Hamilton and Yasmin El-Rifae, who invited me to speak about the Bund in Ramallah at the Palestine Festival of Literature, and who are the embodiments of the sort of solidarity that I hope to champion in this book.

I am indebted to Najla Said for her memories of Alexander Erlich.

This book was shaped by long, whisky-fueled conversations. Thank you to Mike Dawson, Rozina Ali, May Jeong, Natasha Lennard, Asad Dandia, Nermeen Shaikh, Murtaza Hussain, Azmat Khan, Sharif Abdel Kouddous, Morgan Bassichis, Raghu Karnad, Eleanor Saitta, Seth Anziska, Mark Mazower, Mohammed El-Kurd, Ibtisam Azem, Marisa Mazria-Katz, Sinan Antoon, Nikos Boulos, Hazem Jamjoum, Simone Zimmerman, Sarah Leonard, Max Fractal, Budour Hassan, Katia Zagoritou, Mahdi Sabbagh, Tareq Baconi, Sara Yasin, Camille Sojit-Pejcha, Caroline Caldwell, Jason Stanley, V, and my dear Naomi Klein. To everyone who talked with me till dawn about the horrors of the last century while trying to fight against the horrors of our present one, thank you. Thank you to Fred, my love.

To my great-aunt Ida, for preserving Sam's legacy.

To my father, who told me to question authority and be interesting.

To my mother, who taught me to make art. You are this book's co-creator and animating spirit. There is no work without you.

To the people of Palestine.

GLOSSARY OF POLITICAL PARTIES AND ARMED MOVEMENTS

Narodniks: populist revolutionary movement in tsarist Russia.

People's Will: populist revolutionary terrorist group that assassinated Tsar Alexander II.

Emancipation of Labor group: Marxist revolutionary group founded by Russian exiles in Switzerland.

Black Hundreds: a collection of violent, racist, and ultranationalist terrorist groups that supported Tsar Nicholas II.

Russian Social Democratic Labor Party (RSDLP): Marxist revolutionary party founded by the Bund and Russian revolutionary groups. In 1903, the party split into **Mensheviks** and **Bolsheviks.**

Socialist Revolutionary Party (the SRs): populist, socialist underground political party in tsarist Russia. Popular among the peasantry and known for its assassinations of tsarist officials.

Polish Socialist Party (PPS): started as an underground political party in the tsarist empire devoted to Polish independence and socialism, it became a legal political party in independent Poland.

National Democratic Party (the Endeks): antisemitic right-wing Polish political party.

National Radical Camp (the Naras): a racist right-wing Polish political party with a violent armed wing.

Falanga: racist, right-wing Polish armed youth movement.

Camp of National Unity (OZON): official government-backed political movement in Poland between 1935 and 1939.

Poale Tsion: left-wing Zionist political party.

Betar: right-wing Zionist armed youth movement founded by Vladimir Jabotinsky.

The Jewish Agency for Palestine: unofficial governing body of Jews in Palestine under the British Mandate from 1929 onward.

Haganah: left-wing Zionist militia in Mandate Palestine that was integrated into the Israel Defense Forces in 1948.

Irgun: right-wing Zionist militia in Mandate Palestine created by followers of Jabotinsky.

Jewish Labor Committee: committee founded by former Bundists in New York in 1934, devoted to rescuing European labor leaders from fascist countries.

Polish Home Army: underground resistance army in Nazi-occupied Poland, controlled by the Polish government-in-exile.

Jewish Combat Organization (*Zydowska Organizacja Bojowa*, or **ZOB**): armed Jewish resistance movement in the Warsaw ghetto, formed by left-wing Zionists, Bundists, and communists.

Jewish Military Union (*Zydowski Zwiazek Wojskowy*, or **ZZW**): right-wing Zionist resistance movement in the Warsaw ghetto.

People's Guard: pro-Soviet underground resistance militia in Nazi-occupied Poland.

BUNDIST TERMS

Birzhe: in tsarist Russia, a street that served as a gathering place for workers, where revolutionaries freely operated and organized.

Folkstsaytung (renamed ***Naye Folkstsaytung*** in 1926): main Bundist periodical in Poland from 1921–1939.

Tsukunft ("Future"): movement for Bundist teenagers in interwar Poland.

SKIF (Socialist Children's Union): Bundist movement for Jewish children in interwar Poland.

YAF (*Yidishe Arbeter Froy*, or **Jewish Working Women**): Bundist women's movement in interwar Poland.

Morgenstern ("Morning Star"): Bundist athletic club in interwar Poland.

TSYSHO (Central Yiddish School System): Bundist-dominated network of Yiddish-language schools in interwar Poland.

Medem Sanatorium: Bundist sanatorium for poor children at risk of tuberculosis.

NOTES

CHAPTER ONE: ORIGINS

5 **sculpt a communist fist:** Samuel Rothbort, *Out of Wood and Stone* (Stuyvesant House, 1952), 34.
5 **"Everyone makes mistakes":** Isaac Babel, *Odessa Tales* (Pushkin Press, 2019).
8 **wrote his policies:** Robert F. Byrnes, "Pobedonostsev's Conception of the Good Society: An Analysis of His Thought After 1880," *The Review of Politics* 13, no. 2 (April 1951), 186.
9 **"Be a man in the streets":** Judah Leib Gordin, "Awake My People!," 1866.
10 **Narodniks abandoned the cities:** Orlando Figes, *A People's Tragedy: The Russian Revolution, 1891–1924* (Jonathan Cape, 1996), 85–86.
10 **Pogromists beat:** Peled, *Class and Ethnicity in the Pale*, 18–19.
11 **the new tsar brought back:** Peled, *Class and Ethnicity in the Pale*, 24.
11 **the Narodnik terrorist group People's Will:** Lucy Dawidowicz, *The Golden Tradition: Jewish Life and Thought in Eastern Europe* (Holt, Rinehart and Winston, 1967), 406.
11 **"socialist-minded Russian students":** Dawidowicz, *The Golden Tradition*, 410.
12 **Volkovysk was a picturesque stop:** Jacob Solomon Berger, *The Volkovysk Memorial Book: The Trilogy*, vol. 1 (Volkovysk Yizkor Book Committee, 2002), 7.
12 **Jews made up:** Berger, *Volkovysk Memorial Book*, vol. 1, 12.
12 **Volkovysk's houses were wooden:** Berger, *Volkovysk Memorial Book*, vol. 1, 13.
13 **they found a mammoth tusk:** Berger, *Volkovysk Memorial Book*, vol. 1, 222.
13 **A baker's son:** "Er Foraybikt Der Shtetl," *Forverts*, May 4, 1968, 3.
13 **She married at twelve:** Samuel Rothbort, untitled poem, Samuel Rothbort Archives, Private Collection of Janice Caban.
13 **He molded the dough:** Rothbort, *Out of Wood and Stone*, 9.
14 **bout of smallpox:** Rothbort, *Out of Wood and Stone*, 21.
14 **"Search me," Sam bluffed:** Rothbort, *Out of Wood and Stone*, 57.
14 **"fearful poetry and strange beauty":** Samuel Rothbort Archives, Private Collection of Janice Caban.
14 **An army garrison was quartered:** Berger, *Volkovysk Memorial Book*, vol. 1, 275–76.
14 **a traditional religious school:** Berger, *Volkovysk Memorial Book*, vol. 1, 281.
14 **hidden beneath his desk:** Berger, *Volkovysk Memorial Book*, vol. 1, 281.
15 **By the end of 1892:** R. Robbins, *Famine in Russia* (Columbia University Press, 1975), 171.
15 **troupes of boy singers:** "Er Foraybikt Der Shtetl," *Forverts*, May 4, 1968, 3.
15 **a less glamorous apprenticeship:** Berger, *Volkovysk Memorial Book*, vol. 1, 220.
15 **Karl Kautsky:** Jack Jacobs, "Marxism and Anti-Semitism: Kautsky's Perspective," *International Review of Social History* 30, no. 3 (1985): 400–430.
15 **Kept out of the best-paying jobs:** Peled, *Class and Ethnicity in the Pale*, 26–28, 116.
15 **tsarist employment law:** Inna Shtakser, *The Making of Jewish Revolutionaries in the Pale of Settlement* (Palgrave Macmillan, 2014), 24.
16 **in the Bloch tannery:** Samuel Rothbort, "The Ghetto Pillow," Samuel Rothbort Archives, Private Collection of Janice Caban.
16 **Many tanners died by forty:** Ezra Mendelsohn, *Class Struggle in the Pale: The Formative Years of the Jewish Workers' Movement in Tsarist Russia* (Cambridge University Press, 1970), 24.
16 **"Siberian plague":** For a description of tanners' lives and diseases, see Sophia Dubnova-Erlich, *Garber-Bund un Bershter-Bund* (Kultur-lige, 1937).
16 **studying Talmudic law:** Berger, *Volkovysk Memorial Book*, vol. 1, 220.
16 **When his voice cracked:** Rothbort, *Out of Wood and Stone*, 31.

CHAPTER TWO: THE PARTY

19 **Pati Srednitskaya returned:** Y. Sh. Hertz, *Doyres Bundistn*, vol. 1 (Farlag Unser Tsait, 1956), 131.
19 **When Pati was fifteen:** Hertz, *Doyres Bundistn*, vol. 1, 130.
20 **A few years later:** *Arkady: Zamlbukh Tsum Ondenk fun Grinder fun "Bund" Arkady Kremer* (Unzer Tsait, 1942), 31.
20 **the tiny attic on Zavalne Street:** *Arkady: Zamlbukh Tsum Ondenk fun Grinder fun "Bund" Arkady Kremer*, 32.

20 **Arkady was a provincial tutor's son:** *Arkady: Zamlbukh Tsum Ondenk fun Grinder fun "Bund" Arkady Kremer,* 35.

20 **tutoring yeshiva boys:** *Arkady: Zamlbukh Tsum Ondenk fun Grinder fun "Bund" Arkady Kremer,* 39–41.

21 **Arkady refused to inform:** *Arkady: Zamlbukh Tsum Ondenk fun Grinder fun "Bund" Arkady Kremer,* 43.

21 **she was arrested as a terrorist:** Hertz, *Doyres Bundistn,* vol. 1, 131.

22 **the couple ensconced themselves in a garret:** *Arkady: Zamlbukh Tsum Ondenk fun Grinder fun "Bund" Arkady Kremer,* 48, 55.

22 **They met John Mill:** Hertz, *Doyres Bundistn,* vol. 1, 132.

22 **then Liuba Levinson joined their reading:** Rebekka Denz, "Bundistinnen: Frauen Im Allgemeinen Jüdischen Arbeiterbund ("Bund") Dargestellt Anhand Der Jiddischen Biographiensammlung 'Doires Bundistn'" (Potsdam University, 2009); Hertz, *Doyres Bundistn,* vol. 1, 155.

22 **this clique accepted Arkady:** Henry J. Tobias, *The Jewish Bund in Russia from Its Origins to 1905* (Stanford University Press, 1972), 11–13, 22–23.

22 **The rules were strict:** *Arkady: Zamlbukh Tsum Ondenk fun Grinder fun "Bund" Arkady Kremer* (Unzer Tsait, 1942), 125–26.

22 **Pati opened a dental office:** Hertz, *Doyres Bundistn,* vol. 1, 133.

23 **the Vilna Group devoted itself:** Tobias, *The Jewish Bund in Russia,* 16–17.

23 **three quarters of Jewish workers:** See Zvi Gitelman, *The Emergence of Modern Jewish Politics: Bundism and Zionism in Eastern Europe* (University of Pittsburgh Press, 2003), 12. According to Gitelman, in 1926, nine years after the Pale of Settlement was formally abolished, three quarters of Jews in the Soviet Union spoke Yiddish as a native language.

23 **Only Pati and Shmuel Gozhansky:** Hertz, *Doyres Bundistn,* vol. 1, 133.

23 **Jews fetishized books:** Shtakser, *The Making of Jewish Revolutionaries in the Pale of Settlement,* 32–34.

23 **gave these workers a chance:** Jonathan Frankel, *Prophecy and Politics: Socialism, Nationalism, and the Russian Jews, 1862–1917* (Cambridge University Press, 1981), 180.

23 **Surplus value:** Naomi Shepherd, *A Price Below Rubies: Jewish Women as Rebels and Radicals* (Harvard University Press, 1993), 144.

23 **Pati helped workers:** Hertz, *Doyres Bundistn,* vol. 1, 132.

24 **Peppering their speech:** Shtakser, *The Making of Jewish Revolutionaries,* 35; Tobias, *The Jewish Bund in Russia,* 21, 29.

24 **Mostly, they'd created hipsters:** *Arkady: Zamlbukh Tsum Ondenk fun Grinder fun "Bund" Arkady Kremer,* 52; Peled, *Class and Ethnicity in the Pale,* 41; Israel Getzler, *Martov: A Political Biography of a Russian Social Democrat* (Cambridge University Press, 2003), 21–22.

24 **For decades, Jewish workers:** Y. Sh. Hertz, *Di Geshikhte fun Bund* (Unzer Tsayt Farlag, 1981), 73; Tobias, *The Jewish Bund in Russia,* 19.

24 **The first strikes:** Gregory Aronson, "Der Bund in Rusland," *Unser Tsait,* XVII (November-December 1957), 16.

24 **They created mutual aid funds:** Clive Gilbert, *A Revolution in Jewish Life: The History of the Jewish Workers' Bund* (The Jewish Socialists' Group, 1987), 11.

24 **That's why an 1894 May Day speech:** Julius Martov, *The Turning Point in the History of the Jewish Labor Movement, Union of Russian Social Democrats* (Maison Hengel, 1900); Hertz, *Di Geshikhte fun Bund,* 73.

24 **sensitive writer:** Getzler, *Martov,* 20

24 **They could not:** Koppel Pinson, "Arkady Kremer, Vladimir Medem, and the Ideology of the Jewish 'Bund,'" *Jewish Social Studies* 7, no. 3 (July 1945), 239.

25 **Tuers like Pati:** Hertz, *Doyres Bundistn,* vol. 1, 132–33.

25 **After that, the workers:** Tobias, *The Jewish Bund in Russia,* 27.

25 **spread across the Pale of Settlement:** Tobias, *The Jewish Bund in Russia,* 39.

25 **In cities across the Pale:** Tobias, *The Jewish Bund in Russia,* 35.

25 **A slim pamphlet in his native Russian:** Arkady Kremer, "On Agitation," in *Marxism in Russia: Key Documents 1879–1906,* ed. Neil Harding (Cambridge University Press, 2008), 192–205.

26 **illegal educational circles:** Kremer, "On Agitation," 202–3.

26 **"make them realize the need to unite":** Getzler, *Martov,* 22–23.

26 **Kremer held that illegal educational circles:** Peled, *Class and Ethnicity in the Pale, 37.*

27 **its most influential reader:** Vladimir Lenin, *What Is to Be Done? Burning Questions of Our Movement* (International Publishers, 1929), 33.

27 **Unreformed, Martov resolved:** Getzler, *Martov,* 29–31.

27 **Plekhanov's call:** Tobias, *The Jewish Bund in Russia,* 63–64.

28 **Invitations arrived:** Tobias, *The Jewish Bund in Russia,* 65.

28 **Police arrested Pati Kremer:** Hertz, *Doyres Bundistn,* vol. 1, 133.

28 **Despite his wife's arrest, Arkady Kremer:** *Arkady: Zamlbukh Tsum Ondenk fun Grinder fun "Bund" Arkady Kremer,* 57; Hertz, *Di Geshikhte fun Bund,* 113.

28 **"Jewish workers suffer":** Pinson, "Arkady Kremer, Vladimir Medem," 245.

28 **Next March:** Harold Shukman, "Relations Between the Jewish Bund and the RSDLP, 1897–1903," Oxford University (1961), 30.

28 **They entered the RSDLP:** Bernard K. Johnpoll, *The Politics of Futility: The General Jewish Workers Bund of Poland, 1917–1943* (Cornell University Press, 1967), 26; Peled, *Class and Ethnicity in the Pale,* 50–51; Tobias, *The Jewish Bund in Russia,* 76–79.

28 **police seized the Bund's printing presses:** Tobias, *The Jewish Bund in Russia*, 82–83.
28 **As they led him off:** *Arkady: Zamlbukh Tsum Ondenk fun Grinder fun "Bund" Arkady Kremer*, 29.
29 **had reduced the RSDLP:** Shukman, "Relations Between the Jewish Bund and the RSDLP," 36–39.
29 **a tough, Yiddish-speaking proletariat:** Tobias, *The Jewish Bund in Russia*, 86.
29 **illicit handbills, and newspapers:** Myron Perlman, "In the Ranks of Liberation: The Jewish Workers' Bund," marxists.org/subject/jewish/ch-bund.pdf, accessed July 9, 2025; Tobias, *The Jewish Bund in Russia*, 158.
29 **a young tutor named Chaim Nemzer:** Berger, *Volkovysk Memorial Book*, vol. 1, 70.
29 **ignore the rats:** Rothbort, *Out of Wood and Stone*, 21.
29 **"He should kill me":** Shtakser, *The Making of Jewish Revolutionaries*, 43–44.
29 **Apprentices loathed:** Berger, *Volkovysk Memorial Book*, vol. 1, 69–70.
30 **Strikes had a standard choreography:** a description of a similar strike is provided in Hersh Mendel, *Memoirs of a Jewish Revolutionary* (Pluto Press, 1989) 54–56.
30 **When the boss brought in strikebreakers:** Berger, *Volkovysk Memorial Book*, vol. 1, 70.
30 **Abandoning his rebellious son:** "He Perpetuates the Shtetl," unlabeled article found in papers of Janice Caban.
30 **the pastries might be fried in pig fat:** Shtakser, *The Making of Jewish Revolutionaries*, 43.
31 **a note Sam Rothbort had written:** Samuel Rothbort papers, private collection of Janice Caban.
31 **After the strike:** Berger, *Volkovysk Memorial Book*, vol. 1, 71.
32 **The underground offered these girls:** Shtakser, *The Making of Jewish Revolutionaries*, 47–48.
32 **They made a library:** Berger, *Volkovysk Memorial Book*, vol. 1, 71.
32 **They met in the Zamkov forest:** Berger, *Volkovysk Memorial Book*, vol. 1, 72.
32 **Heaven and Earth will hear us:** Sh. An-sky, "Di Shvue," The Yosl and Chana Mlotek Yiddish Song Collection at the Worker's Circle, yiddishsongs.org/di-shvue.
32 **On Sabbath nights:** Berger, *Volkovysk Memorial Book*, vol. 1, 21.

CHAPTER THREE: QUESTIONS OF IDENTITY

35 **had him baptized:** *Vladimir Medem: The Life and Soul of a Legendary Jewish Socialist*, translated and edited by Samuel A. Portnoy (Ktav Publishers, 1979), 5.
35 **"My Jewish origin":** Medem, *Vladimir Medem*, 3.
35 **He grew into a pious:** Medem, *Vladimir Medem*, 8–12.
35 **Reading from a Hebrew bible:** Medem, *Vladimir Medem*, 59.
35 **Medem entered medical school:** Medem, *Vladimir Medem*, 105–9.
35 **Medem eavesdropped on:** Medem, *Vladimir Medem*, 113–15.
35 **Cossack troops broke up:** Medem, *Vladimir Medem*, 119–23.
36 **Medem was exiled back to Minsk:** Medem, *Vladimir Medem*, 125.
36 **On Friday nights:** Medem, *Vladimir Medem*, 134.
36 **That winter, the Bund got in touch:** Medem, *Vladimir Medem*, 146–49.
36 **He joined the editorial board:** Medem, *Vladimir Medem*, 159–60.
36 **His comrades might have nicknamed him:** Medem, *Vladimir Medem*, 177.
37 **In 1901, police rounded up:** Medem, *Vladimir Medem*, 194; "Vladimir Medem" in *Leksikon fun Der Nayer Yidisher Literature*, Congress for Jewish Culture, congressforjewishculture.org/people/2815/Medem-Vladimir-July-30-1879-January-9-1923, accessed July 10, 2025.
37 **In an 1881 letter:** Samuel Baron, *Plekhanov: Father of Russian Marxism* (Stanford University Press, 1963), 67.
37 **Medem arrived in Exileland:** Medem, *Vladimir Medem*, 206–12.
38 **"No Russians!":** Medem, *Vladimir Medem*, 218.
38 **Incurable kidney disease:** Medem, *Vladimir Medem*, xix, 238.
38 **He also rejoined the underground:** Medem, *Vladimir Medem*, 223.
38 **Launched in 1898:** Tobias, *The Jewish Bund in Russia*, 92–94.
38 **Within a few years:** Tobias, *The Jewish Bund in Russia*, 244.
38 **After meticulously gluing the pages:** John Mill, "Vladimir Medem in Oyslandishn Komitet fun 'Bund,'" *Vladimir Medem: tsum tsvantsikstn yortsayt* (Amerkikaner reprezentants fun algemeynem Yidishn arbeter Bund in Poyln, 1943), 124–29.
38 **When, after two years imprisonment:** *Arkady: Zamlbukh Tsum Ondenk fun Grinder fun "Bund" Arkady Kremer*, 57.
38 **In 1902, they arranged for Pati:** Hertz, *Doyres Bundistn*, vol. 1, 134.
38 **"What happened to all the money":** *Arkady: Zamlbukh Tsum Ondenk fun Grinder fun "Bund" Arkady Kremer*, 58.
39 **Bearing the Ottoman script:** Correspondance, Section Juive de la Federation Socialiste Ouvriere-Salonique, 1913, The Bund Foreign Committee Records, RG 1401, box 4, folder 149, YIVO Institute for Jewish Research.
39 **postmarked from Constantinople:** Letter from T. I. Kahan, resident of Jaffa, on the socialist group Hatikva in Constantinople, The Bund Foreign Committee Records, RG 1401, box 39, YIVO Institute for Jewish Research.
41 **"A people destined":** Giuseppe Mazzini, *Life and Writings of Joseph Mazzini* (Smith & Elder, 1890), 276.
41 **Zionism grew alongside it:** Naomi Klein developed the concept of Zionism as a doppelgänger to European nationalism in Naomi Klein, *Doppelganger: A Trip into the Mirror World* (Farrar, Straus and Giroux, 2023).

41 **"The working men have no country":** Karl Marx and Fredrich Engels, *The Communist Manifesto* (Monthly Review Press, 1964), 90.
41 **founded the Bund as an internationalist:** Joshua Zimmerman, *Poles, Jews and the Politics of Nationality* (University of Wisconsin Press, 2004) 41.
41 **His co-founder John Mill:** Zimmerman, *Poles, Jews and the Politics of Nationality*, 42–43; Johnpoll, *The Politics of Futility*, 27.
42 **national cultural autonomy:** Roni Gechtman, "Kossovskii, Vladimir," *The YIVO Encyclopedia of Jews in Eastern Europe*, encyclopedia.yivo.org/article/2108, accessed July 13, 2025.
42 **Son of an aspiring Hebrew-language poet:** Hertz, *Doyres Bundistn*, vol. 1, 196.
42 **Traumatized by his experience:** Hertz, *Doyres Bundistn*, vol. 1, 199–200; Peled, *Class and Ethnicity in the Pale*, 54.
42 **Liber and Medem grew close:** Medem, *Vladimir Medem*, 275–76.
42 **As a schoolboy:** Raphael Abramovich, *In tsvey revolutsyes: Di geshikhte fun a dor*, vol. 1 (Arbeter Ring, 1944), 26–27.
42 **expulsion from university in Riga:** Abramovich, *In tsvey revolutsyes*, vol. 1, 52–53.
42 **broadly similar:** Peled, *Class and Ethnicity in the Pale*, 58.
42 **"Social Democracy and the National Question":** Vladimir Medem, *Di Sotsial-Demokratie un Di Nastionale-Frage*, translated by James Conway for the private archives of Brian Gocial.
43 **"Solidarity of the entire nation":** Pinson, "Arkady Kremer, Vladimir Medem," 249.
44 **one of my prized possessions:** Y. Sh. Hertz. *Der Bund in Bilder:1957–1897* (Unzer Tsayt Farlag, New York), 21.
44 **Lekert made his name in 1902:** Hirsz Abramowicz, *Profiles of a Lost World: Memoirs of East European Jewish Life Before World War II* (Wayne State University Press, 1999), 132.
44 **Bundists showered him with flyers:** Hertz, *Di Geshikhte fun Bund*, vol. 1, 235.
44 **Instead he bought a pistol:** Sholom Levine, "The Martyrdom of Hirsch Leckert," *Jewish Life*, May 1948, 14–17; Hertz, *Di Geshikhte fun Bund*, vol. 1, 237–38.
45 **"Vengeance for a shameful insult":** Tobias, *The Jewish Bund in Russia*, 153
45 **Volkovysk Bundists robbed the government:** Berger, *Volkovysk Memorial Book*, vol. 1, 72.

CHAPTER FOUR: RIVALRIES OF EXILE

46 **in the shadow of a pogrom:** For the definite description of Kishinev's global significance in 1903 and the years that followed, see Steven Zipperstein, *Pogrom: Kishinev and the Tilt of History* (Liveright Publishing Corporation, 2018).
47 **historians later proved this letter:** Zipperstein, *Pogrom*, 95.
47 **In the German city of Karlsruhe:** Medem, *Vladimir Medem*, 268.
47 ***Iskra*, the punchy new newspaper:** Getzler, *Martov*, 47–48.
47 **Lenin saw this as a recipe for failure:** Peled, *Class and Ethnicity in the Pale*, 99–100.
47 **Lenin had long yearned to subordinate the Bund:** Tobias, *The Jewish Bund in Russia*, 185.
47 **Lenin decided to shape:** Shukman, "Relations Between the Jewish Bund and the RSDLP," 112–13.
48 **When Medem finally met Lenin:** Medem, *Vladimir Medem*, 227–28.
48 **its fifth congress:** Medem, *Vladimir Medem*, 281–82.
48 **sole representatives of the Jewish proletariat:** Peled, *Class and Ethnicity in the Pale*, 66–67.
48 **that tiny discussion group:** Medem, *Vladimir Medem*, 268–71.
48 **Medem again crossed Trotsky's path:** Pinson, "Arkady Kremer, Vladimir Medem," 250.
48 **Other Jewish revolutionaries disagreed:** Peled, *Class and Ethnicity in the Pale*, 97.
49 **Black poet Amiri Baraka wrote:** "Black Dada Nihilimus" by Amiri Baraka, *Somebody Blew Up America & Other Poems* (House of Nehesi, 2014).
49 **He saw no point:** Jonathan Frankel, *Prophecy and Politics*, 231.
49 **"However perfect the organization":** Getzler, *Martov*, 57.
49 **It was a cage:** There is a fascinating discussion of these tensions in Zvi Y. Gitelman, *Jewish Nationality and Soviet Politics: The Jewish Sections of the CPSU, 1917–1930*, 35. For more on Martov's feelings about Jewish vs. all-Russian organizing, see Getzler, *Martov*, 59–62.
49 **Russian Social Democratic Labor Party's second congress:** Brian Pearce, *1903—Second Congress of the Russian Social-democratic Labour Party* (New Park Publications, 1978), marxists.org/history/international/social-democracy/rsdlp/1903/foreword.htm.
49 **was infested with fleas:** Leon Trotsky, *My Life: An Attempt at an Autobiography* (Charles Scribner's Sons, 1930), 138.
50 **Everything had been stacked against them:** Tobias, *The Jewish Bund in Russia*, 207.
50 **overwhelmingly the largest revolutionary group:** Medem, *Vladimir Medem*, 26.
50 **the delegates fled to London:** Medem, *Vladimir Medem*, 285–86.
51 **dragged on for six weeks:** Tobias, *The Jewish Bund in Russia*, 216.
51 **When the vote came:** Medem, *Vladimir Medem*, 289.
51 **a "piece of flesh":** Medem, *Vladimir Medem*, 290.
51 **"Lenin had bared his teeth":** Medem, *Vladimir Medem*, 291.
51 **"masters of the situation":** Tobias, *The Jewish Bund in Russia*, 219.
52 **the Dreyfus affair:** Peled, *Class and Ethnicity in the Pale*, 19.

52 **Stripped of their land:** Rashid Khalidi, *The Hundred Years' War on Palestine: A History of Settler Colonialism and Resistance, 1917–2017* (Metropolitan Books, 2020), 9.
52 **"our hardest struggle":** Frankel, *Prophecy and Politics*, 141.
52 **"the most evil enemy":** Tobias, *The Jewish Bund in Russia*, 251.
52 **The Bund banned Zionists from membership:** Peled, *Class and Ethnicity in the Pale*, 57.
53 **suffering from mass hypnosis:** Medem, *Vladimir Medem*, 292–96.
53 **Price for von Plehve's acquiescence:** Medem, *Vladimir Medem*, 297; Tobias, *The Jewish Bund in Russia*, 248.
53 **"We are not strangers here":** Tobias, *The Jewish Bund in Russia*, 252.
53 **In 1906, *the American Jewish Yearbook* published:** "From Kishinew to Bialystok: A Table of Pogroms from 1903 to 1906," *American Jewish Yearbook*, vol. 8 (American Jewish Committee), 1906–1907, berdichev.org/pogroms.html.
53 **these self-defense groups pose:** Hertz, *Der Bund in Bilder*, 37.
53 **two hundred of these youth:** Tobias, *The Jewish Bund in Russia*, 228.
53 **The pogromists only managed to kill:** "From Kishinew to Bialystok."
54 **"Killing a European":** Jean-Paul Sartre, "Preface" in Franz Fanon, *The Wretched of the Earth* (Grove Press, 2004), lv.
54 **During Easter:** Tobias, *The Jewish Bund in Russia*, 226–29, 314–15, 340.
54 **fighters "asked" wealthy Jews:** Shtakser, *The Making of Jewish Revolutionaries*, 144.
54 **knives, whips, handguns, and metal bats:** see Shtakser, *The Making of Jewish Revolutionaries*, 133, for a list of Bundist self-defense groups and weapons.
54 **pension application of one Naum L'vovich:** Shtakser, *The Making of Jewish Revolutionaries*, 184.

CHAPTER FIVE: THE GOLDEN LAND

57 **the nation's first Arabic newspaper:** "Another Daily Newspaper," *The New York Times*, July 8, 1898, 3.
58 **so-called New York City Race Riot:** Saidiya Hartman, *Wayward Lives, Beautiful Experiments* (W. W. Norton, 2019), 167–68.
58 **Harris Rotbarth, once Reb Hersch:** *New York City Directory, 1904–1905* (Trow Directory, Printing and Bookbinding Company, 1905).
59 **Sam wrote some doggerel:** Samuel Rothbort archives, Private Collection of Janice Caban.
59 **was home to 290,000 Jews:** Tony Michels, *A Fire in Their Hearts: Yiddish Socialists in New York* (Harvard University Press, 2005), 92.
59 **two drunk marines:** "Two Marines on a Rampage," *Brooklyn Eagle*, April 19, 1904, 22.
60 **Sam began to draw the town:** "Harriet Semegram Barry's Oral History," The Yiddish Book Center, yiddishbookcenter.org/collections/oral-histories/interviews/woh-fi-0001194/harriet-semegram-barry-2019.
60 **"The nearby little river":** Samuel Rothbort papers, Private Collection of Janice Caban.
60 **"From the margins of Europe":** Michels, *A Fire in Their Hearts*, 10.
60 **also toiled in the shops:** Michels, *A Fire in Their Hearts*, 28.
60 **the Russian Colony:** Michels, *A Fire in Their Hearts*, 27.
60 **encounters with their exiled German neighbors:** Michels, *A Fire in Their Hearts*, 29.
60 **It organized trade unions:** Michels, *A Fire in Their Hearts*, 51–52.
60 **a strike by New York Jews:** Michels, *A Fire in Their Hearts*, 51.
61 **In 1886, radicals shipped copies:** Michels, *A Fire in Their Hearts*, 66.
61 **inspiration for their own, underground:** Frankel, *Prophecy and Politics*, 199.
61 **"erase all boundaries":** Michels, *A Fire in Their Hearts*, 22.
61 **soapbox speakers at Rutgers Square:** Michels, *A Fire in Their Hearts*, 89.
61 **There were strikes by butchers, bricklayers:** "Meat Strikers to Tie Up New York Plants," *New York Times*, August 9, 1904, 1;"Brick Layers' Strike Officially Called Off; Outcome Hailed as a Victory for Arbitration Agreement. Over $1,000,000 in Wages Lost. Peace Precipitated by Formal Charge Entered Against the Union by Employers' Board," *New York Times*, April 7, 1904, 2; "Elevator Workers Join the Strikers," *New York Times*, April 2, 1904, 14; "No Big Policeman Can Scare Striking Misses," *New York Times*, November 17, 1904, 7.
61 **In April 1904, on Orchard Street:** "Violence in Strike of Asphalt Workers," *New York Times*, April 9, 1904, 2.
61 **In July, fifty thousand:** "Over 50,000 Idle in Clothing Strike," *New York Times*, July 3, 1904, 16.
61 **Then, in August, forty thousand:** "Building Strikes Hit Forty Thousand Men," *New York Times*, April 17, 1904, 1.
61 **Banned all Jews from membership:** *One Union: A History of the International Union of Painters & Allied Trades, 1887–2003* (Aspatore, 2004), 87–88.
62 **In December 1903, Arkady Kremer:** *Arkady: Zamlbukh Tsum Ondenk fun Grinder fun "Bund" Arkady Kremer*, 60–61.
62 **Arkady met with small groups:** *Arkady: Zamlbukh Tsum Ondenk fun Grinder fun "Bund" Arkady Kremer*, 60–61; Tobias, *The Jewish Bund in Russia*, 241.
62 **London set up the Bund's:** Gordon Goldberg, *Meyer London: A Biography of the Socialist New York Congressman, 1871–1926* (McFarland & Company, 2013), 46.

62 **Liuba drew herself a bath:** Hertz, *Doyres Bundistn,* vol. 1, 156.
62 **On November 11, 1903:** YIVO Landsmanshaftn Collections, Wolkovisker Rayoner Branch 100, Workmen's Circle, RG 1400, 106.
62 **Elected a board:** "Farayns-Barikhtn," *Forverts,* November 27, 1903, 8.
63 **held a masquerade ball:** "Page 8 Advertisements, Column 4," *Forverts,* November 4, 1904, 8.
63 **At a masquerade:** this description of the Volkovysk Revolutionary Union's masquerade ball is based on a masquerade ball described by Michels, *A Fire in Their Hearts,* 108–9.
63 **"Von Plehve dead!":** "Plehve Gehargt!" *Forvertz,* July 28, 1905, 1.
63 **The Jewish Labor Bund held weekly picnics:** "Page Two Advertisements," *Forverts,* July 28, 1904.
63 **The tsar's nuts:** "Gantz Yurop Fret-Zikh," *Forverts,* July 29, 1904, 1.
64 ***A Bloodbath:*** "A Blut-Bad!" *Forverts,* January 23, 1905, 1.

CHAPTER SIX: REVOLUTIONARY PREQUEL

65 **Vladimir Medem was blasé:** Medem, *Vladimir Medem,* 344.
65 **Gapon had advised the authorities:** Abraham Ascher, *The Revolution of 1905: A Short History* (Stanford University Press, 2004), 27.
66 **160,000 Saint Petersburg workers walked out:** Ascher, *The Revolution of 1905,* 28.
66 **as an atheist and a Marxist:** Medem, *Vladimir Medem, 344.*
66 **"The Great Day has come!":** Tobias, *The Jewish Bund in Russia,* 296.
66 **strikes wracked the Pale of Settlement:** Tobias, *The Jewish Bund in Russia,* 296; Frankel, *Prophecy and Politics,* 145.
66 **the Bund's thirty thousand members:** Tobias, *The Jewish Bund in Russia,* 140.
67 **The Russian Social Democratic Labor Party:** Ascher, *The Revolution of 1905,* 61–62.
67 **hold a conference in Riga:** Hertz, *Geshikhte fun Bund: Volume Two,* 257–58.
67 **rich neighborhoods we never dared enter:** Frank Wolff, *Yiddish Revolutionaries in Migration: The Transnational History of the Jewish Labour Bund* (Haymarket Books, 2022), 67.
68 **in the Polish town of Krynki:** D. Rabin, "Krynki, the tannery town, in creativity and struggle," *Memorial Book of Krynki,* at jewishgen.org/yizkor/krynki/kry068.html, accessed July 13, 2025; Tobias, *The Jewish Bund in Russia,* 297.
68 **Russian uprising electrified New York:** "Revolution Party Here Hails News with Joy," *New York Times,* January 23, 1905, 2.
68 **Morris Winchevsky read the latest dispatches:** "East Side Excitement," *New York Tribune,* January 23, 1905, 2.
68 **Jenny Horowitch dissolved into tears:** "Revolution Party Here Hails News with Joy," *New York Times,* January 23, 1905, 2.
68 **In the Brooklyn neighborhood of Brownsville:** "Cheers in Brownsville for Russian Terrorists," *Brooklyn Daily Eagle,* January 28, 1905, 3.
69 **twenty Bundists gathered in Dvinsk:** Hertz, *Geshikhte fun Bund,* vol. 2, 239–44; Tobias, *The Jewish Bund in Russia,* 300–302.
69 **Friends of the Bund branch:** Wolff, *Yiddish Revolutionaries in Migration,* 359–60.
69 **Abramovich recalled a shtetl rabbi:** Abramovich, *In tsvey revolutsyes,* vol. 1, 202–3.
70 **They pinned their hopes on the army:** Tobias, *The Jewish Bund in Russia,* 317–18.
70 **thousands of Bundist pamphlets:** Aleksander Łaniewski, "Bund w guberni grodzieńskiej podczas rewolucji 1905 roku. Zarys problematyki" (Institute of History of the Polish Academy of Sciences, 2018), 81.
70 **the party proclaimed a general strike:** Hertz, *Di Geshikhte fun Bund,* vol. 2, 188.
70 **Matzoh balls:** Hertz, *Di Geshikhte fun Bund,* vol. 2, 231–32.
70 **She seized a brief break:** *Arkady: Zamlbukh Tsum Ondenk fun Grinder fun "Bund" Arkady Kremer,* 61–62.
70 **56 Orchard Street:** "Farains-Barikhtn," *Forverts,* November 27, 1903, 8.
71 **about smuggled guns:** Hoover Institution, Okhrana Files, Outgoing Dispatches, Volume 1887, Document 261.
71 **officers had ordered five men shot:** "5 Soldatn Dershosn In Volkovysk," *Forverts,* April 1, 1905, 1.
71 **Volkovysk Revolutionary Union held a special meeting:** "Barikhtn un Notitsn," *Forverts,* April 28, 1905, 8.
71 **police spread rumors:** Hertz, *Di Geshikhte fun Bund,* vol. 2, 193, 197–98.
72 **In the Grodno:** Łaniewski, "Bund w guberni grodzieńskiej podczas rewolucji 1905 roku. Zarys problematyki," 81.
72 **In Ukraine, they created parallel organizations:** Hertz, *Di Geshikhte fun Bund,* vol. 2, 197, 222–26.
72 **Cossacks shot three workers:** "Troops Fire on Populace," *Brooklyn Daily Eagle,* May 28, 1905, 1.
72 **members of the Little Bund:** Hertz, *Di Geshikhte fun Bund,* vol. 2, 205–7.
72 **Despite the prohibitions of older activists:** Jack Jacobs, *Bundist Counterculture in Interwar Poland* (Syracuse University Press, 2009), 29–34.
72 **On March 27:** Hertz, *Di Geshikhte fun Bund,* vol. 2, 205–7.
73 **By May 30, thirty-five thousand people:** "Hospital Stormed at Lodz," *New York Times,* May 31, 1905, 2.
73 **On June 18:** *Rewolucja 1905. Przewodnik Krytyki Politycznej* (Wydawnictwo Krytyka Polityczna, 2009), 60–61; Hertz, *Geshikhte fun Bund,* vol. 2, 206.
73 **by the time the chaos stopped:** "Deadly Rioting at Lodz," *New York Times,* June 20, 1905, 2.
73 **Within a few hours:** Hertz, *Geshikhte fun Bund,* vol. 2, 206–7.
73 **Fortified by looted liquor:** "Lodz a Shambles," *New York Times,* June 25, 1905, 1–2.

74 **workers began building barricades:** Hertz, *Geshikhte fun Bund,* vol. 2, 208–9.
74 **The three parties proclaimed:** Hertz, *Di Geshikhte fun Bund,* vol. 2, 206–8.
74 **"The fury of the mob":** "Hospital Stormed at Lodz," *New York Times,* May 31, 1905, 2.
74 **"Every alley must be a fortress,":** Hertz, *Di Geshikhte fun Bund,* vol. 2, 204.
74 **Beneath constant gunfire, government sappers:** "Several Hundred Slain?" *New York Times,* June 25, 1905, 2.
74 **witnesses watched them snatch baubles:** "Lodz a Shambles," *New York Times,* June 25, 1905, 1–2.
74 **Cossacks gunned down:** "Barricades Stormed by Troops in Warsaw," *New York Times,* June 27, 1905, 1.
74 **prisons overflowed with Jewish socialists:** "Riots and Bloodshed Throughout Russia," *New York Times,* June 28, 1905, 1.
74 **authorities killed 561 people:** "Lodz in State of Siege; Victims over 200," *The Brooklyn Daily Eagle,* June 26, 1905, 1.
74 **the party sent their top orator:** Hertz, *Doyris Bundistn,* vol. 1, 363–65.
75 **when girls in Popov's factory:** Weinberg, *The Revolution of 1905 in Odesa: Blood on the Steps* (Indiana University Press, 1993), 34.
75 **She was literary and romantic:** Sophia Dubnova-Erlich, *Bread and Matzoh* (Hermitage, 2004), 116.
75 **and a long nose:** Abramovich, *In tsvey revolutsyes,* vol. 1, 200–201.
75 **Esther had been tortured to death:** Hertz, *Doyris Bundistn,* vol. 1, 366–77.
75 **workers in the Peresyp industrial district:** Weinberg, *The Revolution of 1905 in Odesa: Blood on the Steps,* 127–28.
75 **Soon, to move between neighborhoods:** Weinberg, *The Revolution of 1905 in Odesa,* 129–31. Hertz, *Geshikhte fun Bund: Volume Two,* 212.
75 **A battleship named *Potemkin:*** Weinberg, *The Revolution of 1905 in Odesa, 132.*
75 **where they hoped to contact:** Constantine Feldmann, *The Revolt of the Potemkin* (Leonaur Books, 2021), 31.
76 **Lipshitz mounted the Bund's platform:** Hertz, *Doyris Bundistn,* vol. 1, 364–65.
76 **two Mensheviks and a Bundist:** Feldmann, *The Revolt of the Potemkin,* 34–36.
76 **Tens of thousands of people:** Feldmann, *The Revolt of the Potemkin,* 52–53.
76 **historian Robert Weinberg sketches:** Weinberg, *The Revolution of 1905 in Odesa,* 139.
76 **they set upon him:** Feldmann, *The Revolt of the Potemkin,* 50.
76 **His script identifies the orator:** Sergei Eisenstein, *The Battleship Potemkin* (Classical Film Scripts) (Lorrimer, 1968).
76 **people started to loot:** Weinberg, *The Revolution of 1905 in Odesa,* 135–36; Feldmann, *The Revolt of the Potemkin,* 53.
77 **putrid corpse of Vakulenchuk:** Feldmann, *The Revolt of the Potemkin,* 49.
77 **They aimed for the opera house:** Feldmann, *The Revolt of the Potemkin,* 59–60.
77 **finally surrendered in Romania:** Feldmann, *The Revolt of the Potemkin,* 87–88.
77 **tsarist officials blamed:** Weinberg, *The Revolution of 1905 in Odesa,* 139–40.

CHAPTER SEVEN: REACTION

78 **As Raphael Abramovich traveled:** Tobias, *The Jewish Bund in Russia,* 309.
79 **Medem sat down at the piano:** Medem, *Vladimir Medem,* 345–46.
79 **"When strikes involve millions of workers":** S. An-Sky, *In Shtrom,* quoted in Jonathan Frankel, *Crisis, Revolution and Russia's Jews* (Cambridge University Press, 2008), 87.
79 **"A mighty new crack":** Henry J. Tobias and Charles E. Woodhouse, "Revolutionary Optimism and the Practice of Revolution: The Jewish Bund in 1905," *Jewish Social Studies* 47, no. 2 (Spring 1985), 143.
80 **police opened fire on protesters:** Jonathan Frankel, *Prophecy and Politics,* 149.
80 **Even Volkovysk got a martyr:** Berger, *Volkovysk Memorial Book,* vol. 1, 73.
80 **pogroms broke out in 690 towns:** Frankel, *Prophecy and Politics,* 135; Hertz, *Geshikhte fun Bund,* vol. 2, 287.
80 **In Odesa, the pogrom began:** Weinberg, *The Revolution of 1905 in Odesa,* 165–68.
81 **City Governor Dimitri Niedhardt:** Weinberg, *The Revolution of 1905 in Odesa,* 176.
81 **According to historian Robert Weinberg:** Weinberg, *The Revolution of 1905 in Odesa,* 71.
81 **Blood-smeared Russian mothers:** "Fearful Scenes at Odessa," *Brooklyn Daily Eagle,* November 4, 1905, 1.
81 **young woman named Nadezhda Grinfeld:** Hertz, *Doyris Bundistn,* vol. 1, 360–61; Hertz, *Geshikhte fun Bund,* vol. 2, 290.
81 **dragging captive pogromists back:** Weinberg, *The Revolution of 1905 in Odesa,* 171–72.
81 **Twenty-two Bundists died fighting the mobs:** *Die Judenpograme in Russland,* Zionist Organization, 1910.
81 **eight hundred Odesa Jews:** Jeffrey Veidlinger, *In the Midst of Civilized Europe* (Metropolitan Books, 2021), 35; Victor Sebestyen, *Lenin: The Man, the Dictator, and the Master of Terror* (Pantheon Books, 2017), 176.
81 **"pogroms exist only":** Tobias, *The Jewish Bund in Russia,* 235.
81 **Pogromists rampaged under police protection:** Tobias and Woodhouse, "Revolutionary Optimism," 144.
81 **multitudinous Black Hundreds groups:** Sebestyen, *Lenin,* 176.
82 **He personally pardoned every Dubrovin follower:** Richard Wortman, "Nicholas II and the Revolution," in *The Revolution of 1905 and Russia's Jews,* ed. Stefani Hoffman and Ezra Mendelsohn (University of Pennsylvania Press, 2008), 41.

82 **"nine-tenths of the revolutionaries [were] Jews":** Sebestyen, *Lenin,* 176.

82 **"The Jewish people have been persecuted":** "Note and Comment," *New York Age,* November 23, 1905, 4.

82 **"no nation has yet interfered":** "The Turk and Other Sinners," *New York Age,* November 30, 1905, 4.

82 **"The civilized world has never witnessed anything":** "Jews Worse Off Than We," *New York Age,* December 7, 1905, 8.

82 **"The crime of the century is being committed":** "Jews Worse Off Than We," *New York Age,* December 7, 1905, 8.

83 **Trotsky had smuggled himself back:** Isaac Deutscher, *The Prophet Armed: Trotsky, 1879–1921* (Oxford University Press, 1954), 117–24.

83 **dramatically tore it to shreds:** Leon Trotsky, *1905* (Random House, 1971), 116–17.

83 **boarded trains packed with political exiles:** Abramovich, *In tsvey revolutsyes,* vol. 1, 231–34.

84 **He imagined the lakes:** Medem, *Vladimir Medem,* 356–58.

84 **She'd gotten pregnant:** Vladimir Medem, *A Lebnsveg* (Gina Medem bukh-ķomiţeţ, 1950), 204–5.

84 **Medem and his comrade Vladimir Kossovsky:** Medem, *Vladimir Medem,* 360–64.

85 **a twenty-seven-year-old playwright named A. Vayter:** "A Vayter" in *Leksikon fun Der Nayer Yidisher Literature,* Congress for Jewish Culture, congressforjewishculture.org/people/4686/Vayter-A, accessed July 10, 2025.

85 **thousands of Jews and Christians marched:** Dubnova-Erlich, *Bread and Matzoh,* 114–15.

85 **on his first day in Vilna:** Medem, *Vladimir Medem,* 364–65.

86 **In cities throughout the Pale:** Tobias, *The Jewish Bund in Russia,* 307; Hertz, *Geshikhte fun Bund,* vol. 2, 316.

86 **They forced bosses to close early:** Frankel, *Prophecy and Politics,* 147–48.

86 **Bundists set up courts:** Tobias, *The Jewish Bund in Russia,* 309.

86 **they commandeered the synagogues:** For a fascinating fictionalization of this practice, see Frankel, *Crisis, Revolution and Russia's Jews,* 78–79.

86 **Medem savored his first days in Vilna:** Medem, *Vladimir Medem,* 366–67.

87 **police had padlocked the building:** Medem, *Vladimir Medem,* 368.

87 **"This time we're not alone":** Tobias and Woodhouse, "Revolutionary Optimism," 145.

87 **the party dispatched Medem:** Medem, *Vladimir Medem,* 369–70.

88 **A coachman explained it to Abramovich:** Abramovich, *In tsvey revolutsyes,* vol. 1, 242–43.

88 **On Monday, December 4, 1905:** "Great Demonstration of Mourning by Jews," *Brooklyn Daily Eagle,* December 5, 1905, 1.

89 **"For many Jews inclined to socialism":** Medem, *Vladimir Medem,* 352.

89 **Historian Simon Dubnov described:** Frankel, *Prophecy and Politics,* 136.

90 **"I cannot but emphasize":** Frankel, *Prophecy and Politics,* 146.

90 **One hundred twenty-five thousand Jews:** Cowen Report—European Investigation Entry No. 9; File No. 51411/056.

90 **turning Brownsville into a boomtown:** "Building in Brownsville: Contractors Pushing Work in Anticipation of Great Influx of Jews from Russia," *Brooklyn Daily Eagle,* December 23, 1905, 12.

90 **Arrests dogged them:** Łaniewski, "Bund w guberni grodzieńskiej podczas rewolucji 1905 roku. Zarys problematyki," 83, 89.

90 **The governor of their district decried:** Łaniewski, "Bund w guberni," 100.

90 **even managed a costume ball:** "Mitings, Lekshurs," *Forverts,* October 3, 1906, 2.

90 **It was on a list:** "Far Di Strikende Rifer Makher," *Forverts,* April 27, 1907, 8.

CHAPTER EIGHT: INTERREGNUM

93 **"I have been struck":** Naomi Klein, "Preface," in Alaa Abd el-Fattah, *You Have Not Yet Been Defeated: Selected Writings 2011–2019* (Seven Stories Press, 2022), 37.

93 **a decade after he had launched:** *Arkady: Zamlbukh Tsum Ondenk fun Grinder fun "Bund" Arkady Kremer,* 62.

93 **Frustrated young people:** Frankel, *Prophecy and Politics,* 152.

94 **this number had plummeted to 609:** Joshua Meyers, "The Bund by the Numbers: The Ebbs and Flows of a Jewish Radical Party," *In geveb* (May 2020), ingeveb.org/blog/the-bund-by-the-numbers, accessed Jun 10, 2025.

94 **Medem had not imagined things going like this:** Medem, *Vladimir Medem,* 385–88.

94 **They set up unions:** Johnpoll, *The Politics of Futility,* 34.

94 **With most of his friends abroad:** Medem, *Vladimir Medem,* 440–49.

95 **saw a poster for an appearance by Saharat:** Gina Medem, "On the Other Side of the Fight: Fragments from Medem's Personal Life," *Di Tsukunft,* March 1923, 147–50.

95 **most of the larger party's energy:** Medem, *Vladimir Medem,* 457–62.

95 **His kidney disease worsened:** Medem, *A Lebnsveg,* 195.

96 **the recently Jewish neighborhood of Williamsburg:** "New Hebrew Quarter over New Bridge," *New York Tribune,* April 3, 1904, A1.

96 **At night, in mansions still coated:** "Er Foraybikt Der Shtetl," *Forverts,* May 4, 1968, 3.

96 **from *lunas,* an old Baltic word for mud:** Emil Majuk, *Shtetl Routes, Travels Through the Forgotten Continent* (Shtetl Routes, 2018), 518.

97 **attacked the Lunna post office:** Łaniewski, "Bund w guberni," 96.

97 **He thought of an afternoon:** Rothbort, *Out of Wood and Stone,* 36–37.

97 **Sam was climbing forty-foot extension ladders:** Rothbort, *Out of Wood and Stone,* 72.

97 **"the beautiful classic disappeared":** Rothbort, *Out of Wood and Stone*, 27.
97 **the pair sat at a café:** Medem, *A Lebnsveg*, 195–96.
97 **She ran into Medem again:** Medem, *Vladimir Medem*, 465; Medem, *A Lebnsveg*, 199.
98 **"give so much to the world":** Medem, *A Lebnsveg*, 196.
98 **"You're too young to end up a nurse":** Medem, *A Lebnsveg*, 201–2.
98 **Inevitably, his kidney disease attacked:** Medem, *A Lebnsveg*, 203.
98 **the party sent Medem to Vienna:** Medem, *Vladimir Medem*, 481–84.
99 **the Bund was on the rise again:** Joshua Meyers, "The Bund by the Numbers: The Ebbs and Flows of a Jewish Radical Party," *In geveb* (May 2020), ingeveb.org/blog/the-bund-by-the-numbers, accessed June 10, 2025.
99 **She gave him an ultimatum:** Medem, *Vladimir Medem*, 499.
99 **Abramovich warned Medem:** Medem, *Vladimir Medem*, 494.
99 **He and Gina boarded a train:** Medem, *Vladimir Medem*, 495.
100 **The failed 1905 revolution:** Michaels, *A Fire in Their Hearts*, 155–56.
100 **With fifty-nine thousand members:** Michaels, *A Fire in Their Hearts*, 180.
100 **swallowed up radical grouplets:** YIVO's Landsmanshaftn Collections, Wolkovisker Rayoner Branch 100, Workmen's Circle, RG 1400, 106.
100 **Okhrana sent secret agents:** "Find that Evalenko Was a Russian Spy," *New York Times*, October 13, 1910, 1.
100 **the Bund's annual summer picnic:** Wolff, *Yiddish Revolutionaries in Migration*, 230–31.
100 **Thousands marched on the anniversary:** "Red Sunday Parade Was a Mild Affair," *New York Times*, January 23, 1906, 6.
100 **People packed lecture halls to see:** "Maxime Comes Here to Aid Revolution," *New York Times*, April 20, 1906, 20.
100 **when a white mob attacked:** Wolff, *Yiddish Revolutionaries in Migration*, 242.
101 **Street parades marked May Day:** Wolff, *Yiddish Revolutionaries in Migration*, 241.
101 **In the 1912 presidential election:** "Socialist Party Membership by States 1904–1940," Mapping American Social Movements Project, from depts.washington.edu/moves/SP_map-members.shtml, retrieved July 13, 2025.
101 **Jewish districts in New York:** Michaels, *A Fire in Their Hearts*, 218.
101 **"Don't worry about Goldfogle's pathetic":** "London Voters: You'll Assuredly Be Protected," *Forvertz*, November 3, 1914.
101 **fifty thousand people gathered:** Annie Polland, "Socialist Elected!" *HuffPost*, November 4, 2014, huffpost.com/entry/socialist-elected_b_6101022.
101 **It was the first skyscraper:** Sam Kestenbaum, "The Forward Building: From Labor Citadel to Luxury Condos," *The Forward*, April 16, 2016, forward.com/culture/338587/the-forward-building-from-labor-citadel-to-luxury-condos.
101 **A *Forward* writer spotted many Bundists:** "Der Historisher Obend In Idishen Kvartel," *Forverts*, November 5, 1914, 1.
102 **When London arrived at four A.M.:** "To Teach Congress Socialism," *Brooklyn Citizen*, November 29, 1914, 14.
102 **Paints came before shoes:** Rothbort, *Out of Wood and Stone*, 37.
102 **Sam joined Local 992 in Brownsville:** Sam Rothbort personal papers, Private Collection of Janice Caban.
102 **he took newly arrived Bundists:** "Zikhoroynes Vegn Berl Botvinik," *Forverts*, October 2, 1965, 6.
102 **He made his living painting murals:** Rothbort, *Out of Wood and Stone*, 66.
102 **he wondered how such delicate wings:** Rothbort, *Out of Wood and Stone*, 27.

CHAPTER NINE: COLLAPSE

104 **Medem crossed the border without incident:** Medem, *Vladimir Medem*, 495–500.
105 **a barely educated young Bundist:** Bernard Goldstein, *Twenty Years with the Jewish Labor Bund: A Memoir of Interwar Poland* (Purdue University Press, 2016), 16.
105 **Until one balmy afternoon:** Medem, *Vladimir Medem*, 506.
106 **The Bund's 1914 statement:** Hertz, *Di Geshikhte fun Bund*, vol. 3, 15.
107 **Bundists fled Austria for neutral countries:** Hertz, *Di Geshikhte fun Bund*, vol. 3, 18.
107 **Take the Kremers:** *Arkady: Zamlbukh Tsum Ondenk fun Grinder fun "Bund" Arkady Kremer*, 63–64.
107 **The military drafted:** Jeffrey Veidlinger, *In the Midst of Civilized Europe* (Metropolitan Books, 2021) 37.
107 **police rounded up leaders:** Hertz, *Di Geshikhte fun Bund*, vol. 3, 19.
107 **Within months, over two hundred thousand people:** Hertz, *Di Geshikhte fun Bund*, vol. 3, 9.
107 **they had as little as twelve hours:** Gil Ribak, *Gentile New York: The Images of Non-Jews Among Jewish Immigrants* (Rutgers University Press, 2012), 134.
107 **"Go to Palestine":** Veidlinger, *In the Midst of Civilized Europe*, 39.
107 **They were disgorged into towns:** Veidlinger, *In the Midst of Civilized Europe*, 40.
108 **They marched into the provinces:** Veidlinger, *In the Midst of Civilized Europe*, 37.
108 **Jews were fired from their government jobs:** Veidlinger, *In the Midst of Civilized Europe*, 38–39.
108 **The poet S. An-sky:** S. An-sky, *1915 Diary of S. An-sky, a Russian Jewish Writer at the Eastern Front* (Indiana University Press, 2016), 25.
108 **A Jew communicated with the Austrians:** Veidlinger, *In the Midst of Civilized Europe*, 38.
108 **In Volkovysk, survivors told S. An-sky:** S. An-sky, *The Enemy at His Pleasure: A Journey Through the Jewish Pale of Settlement During World War I* (Metropolitan Books, 2002), 272.

108 **Austrian Jews fled en masse:** Veidlinger, *In the Midst of Civilized Europe*, 39.
108 **the Bund tried to protest:** Hertz, *Di Geshikhte fun Bund*, vol. 3, 19–20.
108 **In free Geneva:** Hertz, *Di Geshikhte fun Bund*, vol. 3, 11.
108 **They set up tea houses:** Hertz, *Di Geshikhte fun Bund*, vol. 3, 33.
108 **Long-standing German communities:** Hertz, *Di Geshikhte fun Bund*, vol. 3, 34.
108 **When Yiddish schools sprang up:** Hertz, *Di Geshikhte fun Bund*, vol. 3, 36.
108 **Despite their socialist, secular ideology:** Hertz, *Di Geshikhte fun Bund*, vol. 3, 58, 60.
109 **Despite his hopes, the war:** Medem, *Vladimir Medem*, 510–11.
109 **When the soldiers filed past:** Medem, *Vladimir Medem*, 513.
109 **When Medem arrived in Orel prison:** Medem, *Vladimir Medem*, 515.
109 **"One became a minuscule element":** Medem, *Vladimir Medem*, 521.
110 **He was one of thirty-five:** Medem, *Vladimir Medem*, 523–24.
110 **He listened to his cellmates' stories:** Medem, *Vladimir Medem*, 527–34.
110 **"Style can become":** Edmund White, *Genet: A Biography* (Random House, 1994), 189.
110 **Fellow prisoners described him:** Wolff, *Yiddish Revolutionaries in Migration*, 60; Medem, *Vladimir Medem*, 552–56.
111 **"The fight against tsarist reaction":** Hertz, *Di Geshikhte fun Bund*, vol. 3, 15.
111 **In May, 1915:** Medem, *Vladimir Medem*, 542–43; "Protses fon Bundistn In Varshe" *Forverts*, May 26, 1915, 8.
111 **Thanks to Gina's bribes:** Medem, *Vladimir Medem*, 554.
111 **Medem and his cellmates:** Medem, *Vladimir Medem*, 564–65; "Der Berimter Bundist Medem Vemen Di Daitshen Hoben Geratevet fun Katorge," *Forverts*, August 14, 1915, 1.

CHAPTER TEN: REVOLUTIONARY ECSTASIES

114 **Sophia Dubnova began the year:** Dubnova-Erlich, *Bread and Matzoh*, 178.
114 **only to be expelled:** Dubnova-Erlich, *Bread and Matzoh*, 83–84.
114 **smuggled pamphlets between cities:** Dubnova-Erlich, *Bread and Matzoh*, 107–9.
114 **incited mutiny:** Dubnova-Erlich, *Bread and Matzoh*, 120–30.
114 **She spent the halcyon year:** Dubnova-Erlich, *Bread and Matzoh*, 149–59.
114 **Taverne du Panthéon:** Roberta Reeder, *Anna Akhmatova: Poet & Prophet* (Allison & Busby, 1995), 32.
114 **The Bund once chose her:** Dubnova-Erlich, *Bread and Matzoh*, 154–55.
114 **She'd met Henryk Erlich:** Samuel Portnoy, ed., *Henryk Erlich and Victor Alter: Two Heroes and Martyrs of Jewish Socialism* (Ktav Publishing House, 1990), 10–11.
114 **First arrested at twenty:** Portnoy, ed., *Henryk Erlich and Victor Alter*, 8.
114 **They wandered the Left Bank together:** Dubnova-Erlich, *Bread and Matzoh*, 158–59.
115 **She wore a gray overcoat:** Dubnova-Erlich, *Bread and Matzoh*, 164.
115 **they settled in Saint Petersburg:** Portnoy, ed., *Henryk Erlich and Victor Alter*, 12–15.
115 **Henryk was in and out:** Dubnova-Erlich, *Bread and Matzoh*, 169.
115 **the Bund became close:** Johnpoll, *The Politics of Futility*, 35.
115 **gather the pages of whatever speech:** Hertz, *Di Geshikhte fun Bund*, vol. 3, 64; Dubnova-Erlich, *Bread and Matzoh*, 170.
115 **dated the right-wing Zionist:** Dubnova-Erlich, *Bread and Matzoh*, 91–95.
115 **dressed in lavish costumes:** Dubnova-Erlich, *Bread and Matzoh*, 165.
115 **Sophia had made a name for herself:** Dubnova-Erlich, *Bread and Matzoh*, 171–73.
116 **The Germans advanced, taking Lublin:** Portnoy, ed., *Henryk Erlich and Victor Alter*, 16.
116 **The *Chronicle* office:** Dubnova-Erlich, *Bread and Matzoh*, 174–75, 177.
116 **Henryk busied himself:** Hertz, *Di Geshikhte fun Bund*, vol. 3, 63.
116 **"Not everything can be foretold":** Reeder, *Anna Akhmatova*, 63.
116 **She watched the crowds gather:** Dubnova-Erlich, *Bread and Matzoh*, 178.
117 **a gathering of leftist activists:** Alexander Kerensky and Robert Browder, *The Russian Provisional Government 1917: Documents* (Stanford University Press, 1961), 32.
117 **Desperate reports piled up:** Kerensky and Browder, *Russian Provisional Government 1917*, 40.
117 **he ran to the center gate:** Alexander Kerensky, *The Kerensky Memoirs: Russia and History's Turning Point* (Cassell, 1966), 196.
117 **That afternoon, in room 12:** Kerensky and Browder, *Russian Provisional Government 1917*, 70; Hertz, *Di Geshikhte fun Bund*, vol. 3, 87; Orlando Figes, *A People's Tragedy: The Russian Revolution, 1891–1924* (Jonathan Cape, 1996), 324–25; N. N. Sukhanov, *The Russian Revolution 1917: A Personal Record* (Princeton University Press, 1984), 39.
117 **declared themselves the Temporary Executive Committee:** Figes, *A People's Tragedy: The Russian Revolution, 1891–1924*, 327–28.
118 **When dawn came:** Sukhanov, *The Russian Revolution 1917*, 64–65, 73–74.
118 **When Erlich woke up:** Sukhanov, *The Russian Revolution 1917*, 44–46.
118 **Chaos defined Erlich's first days:** Sukhanov, *The Russian Revolution 1917*, 83–85.
119 **Military deserters wandered:** Figes, *A People's Tragedy*, 330.
119 **Among their first catches:** Figes, *A People's Tragedy*, 328–29; Sukhanov, *The Russian Revolution 1917*, 57.
119 **marched him at gunpoint to Tauride:** Sukhanov, *The Russian Revolution 1917*, 52.
119 **"Almost a million men":** "East Side Rejoices Wildly over News of Czar's Fall," *New York Tribune*, March 17, 1917, 4.

119 **In Café Monopole:** "East Side Throngs Toast Fall of House of Romanoff," *New York Tribune,* March 18, 1917, 1.
119 **Crowds smashed every window:** Kenneth Ackerman, *Trotsky in New York: A Radical on the Eve of Revolution* (Counterpoint, 2017), 186.
119 **"I was a Russian prisoner":** "East Side Rejoices Wildly over News of Czar's Fall."
119 **Journalists besieged the offices:** Ackerman, *Trotsky in New York,* 186.
119 **jotted down quotes:** "East Side Throngs Toast Fall of House of Romanoff."
120 **In *The New York Age:*** James W. Johnson, "Russian Democracy and the Jews," *New York Age,* March 22, 1917, 4.
120 **Henryk moved into Tauride Palace:** Dubnova-Erlich, *Bread and Matzoh,* 179.
120 **Sophia woke up to banging:** Dubnova-Erlich, *Bread and Matzoh,* 180–81.
120 **Sophia often braved the snowdrifts:** Dubnova-Erlich, *Bread and Matzoh,* 180.
121 **with countless Bundists among the leaders:** Hertz, *Di Geshikhte fun Bund,* vol. 3, 109–11.
121 **I think of Leivik Hodis:** Leivik Hodis, *Biografie un Shriftn* (Unzer Tsayt Farlag, 1952), 16–18.
122 **Twenty Bundists joined a band:** "100,000 Exiles of Siberia Race to Freedom on 50,000 Sledges," *New York Tribune,* April 4, 1917, 6.
122 **At New York rallies in support:** Ackerman, *Trotsky in New York,* 194.
122 **the largest voluntary reverse migration:** Michaels, *A Fire in Their Hearts,* 218.
122 **He had made good use:** Johnpoll, *The Politics of Futility,* 41–43.
122 **soup kitchens:** "A. Ring Shikt $1000 Tsu Medem Far Varshever Folks-Kikh," *Forverts,* June 17, 1916, 1; "Ar. Ring Shikt $2000 Tsum Barimten Bundist Medem," *Forverts,* April 21, 1916, 1.
122 **Medem soon found the limits:** *Vladimir Medem: tsum tsvantsikstn yortsayt* (Amerkikaner reprezentants fun algemeynem Yidishn arbeter Bund in Poyln, 1943), 106.
122 **As punishment, the Germans locked him:** "Iz Medem Arestirt in Varshe?" *Forverts,* February 27, 1917, 1.
123 **Party membership exploded:** Gitelman, *Jewish Nationality and Soviet Politics,* 72.
123 **new Bundist branches sprang up:** Hertz, *Di Geshikhte fun Bund,* 103.
123 **On March 22, 1917, the provisional government:** Kerensky and Browder, *Russian Provisional Government 1917,* 1823.
123 **The *New York Tribune* reported:** "Petrograd Academy Opened to Six Hundred Jews," *New York Tribune,* May 22, 1917.
123 **From their commandeered office:** "Yom Tovdige Minuten," *Forverts,* July 29, 1917, 5.
123 **the Bund sent a communiqué:** "Russian Jews' Bund Greets Jews Here," *New York Times,* April 21, 1917, 8.
124 **million Petrograd residents:** "Ilya Orlov: On the Field of Mars," *The Russian Reader,* Nov. 13, 2014, therussianreader.com/2014/11/13/ilya-orlov-field-of-mars.
124 **Sophia saw S. An-sky:** Dubnova-Erlich, *Bread and Matzoh,* 181–82.
124 **Beneath banners reading:** Arye Gelbard, *Der jüdische Arbeiter-Bund Russlands im Revolutionsjahr 1917* (Europaverlag, 1982), 19–20.
124 **They teased one another:** Hertz, *Geshikhte fun Bund,* vol. 3, 92.
124 **a younger face, that of Mark Liber:** Hertz, *Doyris Bundistn,* vol. 1, 216.
124 **Kronstadt sailors carried him:** Dubnova-Erlich, *Bread and Matzoh,* 184.
124 **"His talent was created":** "Yom Tovdige Minuten," *Forverts,* July 29, 1917, 5.
125 **Should their party participate:** Hertz, *Geshikhte fun Bund,* vol. 3, 95.
125 **the Bund resolved to sit:** Gitelman, *Jewish Nationality and Soviet Politics,* 82–83.
125 **imprisoned party activists:** Hertz, *Der Bund in Bilder,* 76.
126 **he proposed a resolution:** Hertz, *Geshikhte fun Bund,* vol. 3, 95.
126 **the country's eight hundred Russian political exiles:** Raphael Abramovich, *The Soviet Revolution, 1917–1939* (International Universities Press, 1962), 25–26.
126 **On April 9, 1917, Vladimir Lenin:** Vladimir Lenin, *Collected Works,* vol. 24 (Foreign Languages Pub. House, 1970), 27.
126 **Erlich joined his fellow representatives:** Henryk Erlich, "Lenin, Reminiscences and Impressions," in Portnoy, ed., *Henryk Erlich and Victor Alter,* 274–75.
127 **Lenin turned his back:** E. Crankshaw, "When Lenin Returned," *The Atlantic,* October 1, 1954, theatlantic.com/magazine/archive/1954/10/when-lenin-returned/303867, retrieved October 9, 2021.

CHAPTER ELEVEN: REVOLUTIONARY DISCONTENTS

128 **Walking beside her husband:** Dubnova-Erlich, *Bread and Matzoh,* 185.
129 **The boy first saw Lenin:** Dubnova-Erlich, *Bread and Matzoh,* 184–85.
129 **over half a million people went on strike:** Figes, *A People's Tragedy,* 367.
129 **Peasants itched to evict:** see Figes, *A People's Tragedy,* 364, for a description of peasant redistribution of land.
129 **Back in Switzerland, Bundist Raphael Abramovich:** Abramovich, *In tsvey revolutsyes,* vol. 2, 12–13.
130 **At last, the great day arrived:** Abramovich, *In tsvey revolutsyes,* vol. 2, 16–21.
130 **Henryk Erlich stepped forward:** Abramovich, *In tsvey revolutsyes,* vol. 2, 23.
130 **In Petrograd, Abramovich quickly found himself:** Abramovich, *In tsvey revolutsyes,* vol. 2, 48–49.
130 **They appointed him as editor:** Abramovich, *In tsvey revolutsyes,* vol. 2, 49.
131 **He lobbied relentlessly for peace:** Gitelman, *Jewish Nationality and Soviet Politics,* 87.
131 **Within weeks of Abramovich's arrival:** Abramovich, *In tsvey revolutsyes,* vol. 2, 80–81.
132 **Abramovich could not help but marvel:** Abramovich, *In tsvey revolutsyes,* vol. 2, 61–62.

132 **They marched through Petrograd:** Abramovich, *In tsvey revolutsyes,* vol. 2, 87–88.
132 **with five hundred thousand people:** Alexander Rabinowitch, "Demonstration, Petrograd, 18 June 1917," in *From Communism to Anti-Communism: Photographs from the Boris Souvarine Collection at the Graduate Institute, Geneva* (Graduate Institute Publications, 2017).
132 **In the sea of Cyrillic signage:** Abramovich, *In tsvey revolutsyes,* vol. 2, 84–85.
133 **he listened incredulously:** Erlich, "Lenin, Reminiscences and Impressions," in Portnoy, ed., *Henryk Erlich and Victor Alter,* 279.
133 **The tour, which began:** Abramovich, *The Soviet Revolution, 1917–1939,* 50.
133 **French papers called him:** Hertz, *Di Geshikhte fun Bund,* vol. 3, 154.
133 **the press smeared them:** "Russian Delegates Reach London," *New York Times,* July 25, 1917, 3.
133 **the French and British governments:** Abramovich, *The Soviet Revolution,* 51.
133 **where the debacle of Kerensky's offensive:** Figes, *A People's Tragedy,* 408.
134 **If only he could lie:** Portnoy, ed., *Henryk Erlich and Victor Alter,* 19.
135 **When Abramovich saw Litvak:** Abramovich, *In tsvey revolutsyes,* vol. 2, 122–23.
135 **Financial contributors were in the back:** A. Litvak, *Dos Revolutsyonere Rusland* (Tsenṭral-ferband fun "Bund" in ferlag fun der Idisher sotsyalisṭisher federatsye in Ameriḳa, 1917), 128.
135 **"the revolution's far-flung children":** Litvak, *Dos Revolutsyonere Rusland,* 1.

CHAPTER TWELVE: DENOUEMENT

136 **with 3,500 local members:** Nikolai Stashkevich, *The October Revolution in Byelorussia* (Voice of the Motherland Library, 1979), 105.
136 **They ran the local soviet:** Stashkevich, *The October Revolution in Byelorussia,* 10.
136 **controlled the central bureau:** Stashkevich, *The October Revolution in Byelorussia,* 51.
136 **the Bundist Aron Vaynshteyn:** Gitelman, *Jewish Nationality and Soviet Politics,* 85–86.
136 **Abramovich began the five-hundred-mile journey:** Abramovich, *In tsvey revolutsyes,* vol. 2, 140–41.
136 **Streets swarmed with refugees:** Elissa Bemporad, "Minsk," in *The YIVO Encyclopedia of Jews in Eastern Europe,* YIVO Institute for Jewish Research, 2025, yivoencyclopedia.org/article.aspx/minsk.
136 **the city felt like a celebration:** for a description of the Jubilee, see Abramovich, *In tsvey revolutsyes,* vol. 2, 140–45.
136 **Singers serenaded them:** "Di Yubelteg in Minsk," *Der Veker,* no. 36, October 1917.
136 **every party, except the Bolsheviks:** Gelbard, *Der jüdische Arbeiter-Bund Russlands,* 88.
136 **At a soirée for leaders:** for a description of the Jubilee, see Abramovich, *In tsvey revolutsyes,* vol. 2, 140–45.
137 **"We were always democratic":** Hertz, *Di Geshikhte fun Bund,* vol. 3, 139.
137 **the Bund's jubilee had collapsed:** Gitelman, *Jewish Nationality and Soviet Politics,* 86.
137 **There were violent strikes:** Figes, *A People's Tragedy,* 462; John Reed, *Ten Days that Shook the World* (Boni & Liveright, 1922), 25–26.
137 **Bolsheviks swept the municipal elections:** Figes, *A People's Tragedy,* 457–59.
138 **In *Workers' Voice,* Abramovich warned:** Raphael Abramovich, "Di Politishe Lage," *Arbeter Shtime,* October 27, 1917, 1.
138 **Later, Abramovich would bemoan:** Abramovich, *In tsvey revolutsyes,* vol. 2, 157–60.
139 **top Bolshevik Felix Dzerzhinsky lounged:** Abramovich, *In tsvey revolutsyes,* vol. 2, 162–63.
139 **Liber's sister, who died of tuberculosis:** Felix Dzerzhinsky, *Prison Diaries and Letters* (Foreign Languages Publishing House, 1959), 183.
139 **at the Smolny buffet:** Abramovich, *In tsvey revolutsyes,* vol. 2, 148–49.
139 **Dzerzhinsky icily rejected Abramovich's requests:** Abramovich, *In tsvey revolutsyes,* vol. 2, 163.
139 **took a second to appreciate:** Abramovich, *In tsvey revolutsyes,* vol. 2, 164.
140 **The Soviet's old chairman:** Reed, *Ten Days that Shook the World,* 87.
140 **A frail figure fought his way:** Reed, *Ten Days that Shook the World,* 89.
140 **The Soviet unanimously accepted:** Vladimir Brovkin, *The Mensheviks After October* (Cornell University Press, 1987), 17–18.
140 **Henryk Erlich got the final word:** Reed, *Ten Days that Shook the World,* 93–94.
140 **an error Abramovich bemoaned:** Abramovich, *In tsvey revolutsyes,* vol. 2, 167–68.
140 **"eyes snapping behind thick glasses":** Reed, *Ten Days that Shook the World,* 93–94.
141 **Erlich and the rest:** Reed, *Ten Days that Shook the World,* 97–98.

CHAPTER THIRTEEN: AFTER OCTOBER

143 **"The Coup!":** "Der Oyfshtand," *Arbeter Shtime,* November 26, 1917, 1.
143 **crazy escapade by Lenin and Trotsky:** David Zaslovsky, "Reb Lenin's 'Sotsial Revolutsie,'" *Arbeter Shtime,* November 26, 1917, 2.
143 **One day Sophia received:** Dubnova-Erlich, *Bread and Matzoh,* 100–104.
144 **At home, Sophia returned:** Dubnova-Erlich, *Bread and Matzoh,* 188.
144 **A new slogan went up:** Gitelman, *Jewish Nationality and Soviet Politics,* 100.
144 **150,000 Jews demonstrated:** "Russian Jews Grateful," *The New York Times,* December 13, 1917, 5.
144 **The Bund chose Raphael Abramovich:** Abramovich, *In tsvey revolutsyes,* vol. 2, 186–89.
145 **All the Bund had to show:** Hertz, *Di Geshikhte fun Bund,* vol. 3, 168.
145 **campaign to discredit the election results:** Figes, *A People's Tragedy,* 509.
145 **they put Petrograd and Moscow:** Figes, *A People's Tragedy,* 513–14.

145 ***Workers' Gazette*, where Henryk Erlich was co-editor:** Portnoy, ed., *Henryk Erlich and Victor Alter*, 1.
145 **sent detachments of sailors:** Brovkin, *The Mensheviks After October*, 106.
145 **They were preparing an attack:** Brovkin, *The Mensheviks After October*, 45.
145 **Martov argued that they could:** Brovkin, *The Mensheviks After October*, 46–47.
146 **To intimidate delegates:** Abramovich, *In tsvey revolutsyes*, vol. 2, 201.
146 **Machine guns pointed threateningly:** Abramovich, *The Soviet Revolution*, 127.
146 **Sophia marched alongside Henryk:** Dubnova-Erlich, *Bread and Matzoh*, 189.
146 **Bolshevik forces killed twenty-one people:** Abramovich, *The Soviet Revolution*, 128.
147 **"The best among the Russian people":** Maxim Gorky, *Untimely Thoughts: Essays on Revolution, Culture and the Bolsheviks, 1917–1918* (Paul S. Eriksson, 1968), 124.
147 **but it horrified the leaders:** Veidlinger, *In the Midst of Civilized Europe*, 48, 51–52.
147 **If the Bolsheviks would shut down:** Veidlinger, *In the Midst of Civilized Europe*, 57.
147 **the Law of National-Personal Autonomy:** Veidlinger, *In the Midst of Civilized Europe*, 58–59.
147 **even voting against Ukrainian independence:** Gitelman, *Jewish Nationality and Soviet Politics*, 157; Hertz, *Di Geshikhte fun Bund*, vol. 3, 173–74, 178.
147 **Many Jews viewed Ukrainians:** Veidlinger, *In the Midst of Civilized Europe*, 12–13.
147 **many Ukrainians viewed Jews:** Figes, *A People's Tragedy*, 77–79.
147 **When the Rada's minister:** Veidlinger, *In the Midst of Civilized Europe*, 49–51.
148 **When Moishe Rafes:** Gitelman, *Jewish Nationality and Soviet Politics*, 157.
148 **"We will slaughter all the yids":** Veidlinger, *In the Midst of Civilized Europe*, 67–68.
148 **condemned the Russians:** Gitelman, *Jewish Nationality and Soviet Politics*, 167.
148 **Three weeks later, Haidamaks:** Veidlinger, *In the Midst of Civilized Europe*, 70.
148 **The Germans took over railroads:** Wlodizmierz Medrzecki, "Germany and Ukraine between the Start of the Brest-Litovsk Peace Talks and Hetman Skoropads'kyi's Coup," *Harvard Ukrainian Studies* vol. 23, no. 1–2 (1999): 47–71.
148 **hauled away Ukraine's famous black earth:** Veidlinger, *In the Midst of Civilized Europe*, 70.
149 **Rebellion grew against the Germans:** Veidlinger, *In the Midst of Civilized Europe*, 76.
149 **On the afternoon of April 28:** Veidlinger, *In the Midst of Civilized Europe*, 74–75.
149 **Bundists ran candidates for local soviets:** Hertz, *Di Geshikhte von Bund*, vol. 3, 193; Brendan McGeever, *Antisemitism and the Russian Revolution* (Cambridge University Press, 2019), 44.
149 **Writing grew harder for Henryk Erlich:** Dubnova-Erlich, *Bread and Matzoh*, 191.
149 **"Bonapartist clubs that gather together":** Brovkin, *The Mensheviks After October*, 206.
149 **Erlich's neighbor whispered:** Dubnova-Erlich, *Bread and Matzoh*, 191.
150 **The hetman blamed the Jews:** Abramson, *A Prayer for the Government. Ukrainians and Jews in Revolutionary Times, 1917–1920* (Harvard University Press, 1999), 101.
150 **Kyiv soon filled:** Figes, *A People's Tragedy*, 555–56.
150 **cutting Bolshevik stars into the corpses:** Figes, *A People's Tragedy*, 678.
150 **the Bundist leader Vladimir Kossovsky:** McGeever, *Antisemitism and the Russian Revolution*, 47.
151 **"The summer was dusty and torrid":** Dubnova-Erlich, *Bread and Matzoh*, 192.
151 **The Cheka arrested:** Vladimir Brovkin, *Dear Comrades: Menshevik Reports on the Bolshevik Revolution and the Civil War* (Hoover Institution Press, 1991), 118.
151 **and in Vitebsk they publicly executed:** Hertz, *Di Geshikhte fun Bund*, vol. 3, 195–97.
151 **"the persecution of socialists":** Brovkin, *Dear Comrades*, 218.
151 **she and Henryk contemplated:** Dubnova-Erlich, *Bread and Matzoh*, 191–92.
151 **They would stay in Lublin:** Victor Erlich, *Child of a Turbulent Century* (Northwestern University Press, 2006), 6.
151 **On the freight train west:** Dubnova-Erlich, *Bread and Matzoh*, 193–94, 197.

CHAPTER FOURTEEN: THE CHAOS

155 **Artists in the glittery Abraham & Straus:** Michael Lisicky, "The Inside Story of Iconic Brooklyn Emporium Abraham & Straus at the Dawn of the 20th Century," *The Brownstoner*, brownstoner.com/history/abraham-straus-brooklyn-department-store-history-michael-lisicky-book-excerpt.
155 **like the evocatively named Golden Rooster:** "Weiss for June 10, 1919," Case #260086, Bureau Section Files, 1909–21 (National Archives Microfilm Publication M1085, roll 948); Investigative Reports of the Bureau of Investigation 1908–1922.
155 **In my mother's shoebox we found:** Samuel Rothbort Archives, Private Collection of Janice Caban.
156 **a hunter of German spies:** "New Hunter of Spies in New York District," *New York Times*, March 31, 1918, 52.
156 **the "slacker raids" of September 1918:** "60,187 Men Taken in Slacker Raids," *New York Times*, September 8, 1918, 9.
156 **Sam stood at Local Board 75:** *U.S., World War I Draft Registration Cards, 1917–1918* [database online], Provo, Utah: Ancestry.com Operations Inc, 2005, ancestry.com/imageviewer/collections/6482/images/005262925_02646?pId=12019050.
156 **She hated the overstuffed:** Dubnova-Erlich, *Bread and Matzoh*, 195–98.
156 **With money provided:** Johnpoll, *The Politics of Futility*, 1–43, 49.
156 **The Bundist Emanuel Nowogrodski:** Emanuel Nowogrodski, *The Jewish Labor Bund in Poland 1915–1939* (Shengold Books, 2001), 15.

157 **When Medem arrived at the Erlich home:** Dubnova-Erlich, *Bread and Matzoh,* 196.
157 **"We are in greater need":** Portnoy, ed., *Henryk Erlich and Victor Alter,* 23.
157 **revolutionary bank robber:** Richard Watt, *Bitter Glory: Poland and Its Fate, 1918–1939* (Simon and Schuster, 1979), 36.
157 **longtime acquaintance of the Bund:** Zimmerman, *Poles, Jews, and The Politics of Nationality,* 27.
157 **"I took the red tram of socialism":** "Józef Piłsudski (1867–1935)," *Ministry of Foreign Affairs,* June 16, 2025, archive.org/web/20060213175243/http://poland.gov.pl/Jozef,Pilsudski,(1867-1935),1972.html.
157 **he invited the Bund to join:** Hertz, *Di Geshikhte fun Bund,* vol. 4, 16.
157 **The Bund declined:** Johnpoll, *The Politics of Futility,* 73.
158 **"the worst enemies" of Poland:** Johnpoll, *The Politics of Futility,* 47.
158 **National Democrats, an economically conservative:** Johnpoll, *The Politics of Futility,* 12, 46.
158 **Erlich joined the Lublin Soviet:** Hertz, *Di Geshikhte fun Bund,* vol. 4, 21–22.
158 **"For the first time in my life":** Dubnova-Erlich, *Bread and Matzoh,* 196–98.
158 **The Bund sent Henryk Erlich:** Johnpoll, *The Politics of Futility,* 80.
159 **When Polish troops took Lviv:** Veidlinger, *In the Midst of Civilized Europe,* 83–86.
159 **over a thousand pogroms:** Veidlinger, *In the Midst of Civilized Europe,* 4.
160 **Sophia joined Henryk in Warsaw:** Dubnova-Erlich, *Bread and Matzoh,* 199.
160 **In one article, Medem described:** Vladimir Medem, *Fun Mayn Notis-bukh* (Drukaria O Rom, 1920), 95–97.
160 **supervised union work:** Goldstein, *Twenty Years with the Jewish Labor Bund,* 18.
161 **Sophia strove to convey the beauty:** Dubnova-Erlich, *Bread and Matzoh,* 201.
161 **posters went up around Kyiv:** Veidlinger, *In the Midst of Civilized Europe,* 88.
161 **Bernard Goldstein led their fighters:** Goldstein, *Twenty Years with the Jewish Labor Bund,* 9.
161 **Born in an impoverished shtetl:** Bernard Goldstein, *The Stars Bear Witness* (Viking Press, 1949), 3–6.
161 **spoke in a mangled mixture:** Marek Edelman, *Tambien hubo amor en el gueto* (Galaxia Gutenberg, 2013), 17.
161 **Bernard spent the next decade:** Goldstein, *Twenty Years with the Jewish Labor Bund,* 3–6.
162 **Bernard's two hundred fighters:** Goldstein, *Twenty Years with the Jewish Labor Bund,* 9.
162 **The Directorate barely controlled its own troops:** Veidlinger, *In the Midst of Civilized Europe,* 102–4.
162 **Berdichev's Bundist mayor, David Lipetz:** McGeever, *Antisemitism and the Russian Revolution,* 142–43, 152–55.
163 **troops led by Ivan Semesenko:** Veidlinger, *In the Midst of Civilized Europe,* 147–49.
163 **"In order to deflect the attention":** Nowogrodski, *The Jewish Labor Bund in Poland,* 27.
163 **Two victims were Bundists:** Hertz, *Di Geshikhte von Bund,* vol. 4, 43.
163 **After Erlich denounced the Pinsk pogrom:** Nowogrodski, *The Jewish Labor Bund in Poland,* 302–3.
163 **his soldiers murdered eighty-five:** Anna Cichopek-Gajraj and Glenn Dynner, "Pogroms in Modern Poland, 1918–1946," in *Pogroms: A Documentary History* (Oxford University Press, 2021), 196; Veidlinger, *In the Midst of Civilized Europe,* 182.
163 **Polish legionnaires broke down the door:** "A Vayter" in *Leksikon fun Der Nayer Yidisher Literature,* Congress for Jewish Culture, congressforjewishculture.org/people/4686/Vayter-A, accessed July 10, 2025; Hertz, *Geshikhte von Bund,* vol. 3, 44.
163 **"The Polish Army brings Liberty":** Norman Davies, *White Eagle, Red Star* (Pimlico, 2003), 51.
164 **They published antipogrom leaflets:** McGeever, *Antisemitism and the Russian Revolution,* 123.
164 **After a second pogrom:** Veidlinger, *In the Midst of Civilized Europe,* 197.
164 **In February 1919, in Kyiv:** Hertz, *Di Geshikhte fun Bund,* vol. 3, 210.
164 **The Kombund would ally:** Abramson, *A Prayer for the Government,* 149.
164 **Rafes saw as the only force:** McGeever, *Antisemitism and the Russian Revolution,* 151.
164 **"For us there is no other way":** Gitelman, *Jewish Nationality and Soviet Politics,* 175.
165 **"I do not imagine any social democracy":** Hertz, *Doyris Bundistn,* vol. 1, 375.
165 **Cheka stormed Berdichev's Bundist cultural club:** Anna Rozental, "Froien–geshtaltn in 'Bund'," *Naye Folkstzeitung,* November 19, 1937, posenlibrary.com/frontend/female-figures-in-the-bund-by-anna-rozental; Jack Jacobs, "The General Jewish Workers' Bund," *The Cambridge History of Socialism* (Cambridge University Press, 2022), 152–71.
165 **"I know that people with opinions":** Hertz, *Doyris Bundestn,* vol. 1, 375.
165 **at the Bund's Twelfth Congress:** Hertz, *Di Geshikhte fun Bund,* vol. 3, 225.
165 **A majority of delegates:** Jacobs, "The General Jewish Workers' Bund," 152–71.
166 **When she announced her faction's decision:** Gitelman, *Jewish Nationality and Soviet Politics,* 193.
166 **Their decision was the last straw:** Johnpoll, *The Politics of Futility,* 102.
166 **Rather than capitulate:** Hertz, *Di Geshikhte fun Bund,* vol. 3, 227.
166 **"The existing government demands":** Brovkin, *Dear Comrades,* 197.
166 **Social Democratic Bund committee in Mogilev:** Brovkin, *Dear Comrades,* 221.
166 **More arrests of Bundist leaders:** Johnpoll, *The Politics of Futility,* 103; Hertz, *Di Geshikhte fun Bund,* vol. 3, 238.
166 **The Social Democratic Bund issued:** Hertz, *Di Geshikhte fun Bund,* vol. 3, 237.
166 **On May Day of 1920:** Goldstein, *Twenty Years with the Jewish Labor Bund,* 31–33.
166 **Pilsudski returned to Warsaw:** Davies, *White Eagle, Red Star,* 109.
167 **"his long legs were like girls":** Isaac Babel, "My First Goose," *Collected Stories* (Penguin Books, 1998), 119.

167 **On July 8, 1920:** Johnpoll, *The Politics of Futility*, 98.
167 **Newspapers smeared the Bund:** Johnpoll, *The Politics of Futility*, 99; Portnoy, ed., *Henryk Erlich and Victor Alter*, 28.
167 **the government banned the party:** Goldstein, *Twenty Years with the Jewish Labor Bund*, 47.
167 **Soldiers smashed their union halls:** Goldstein, *Twenty Years with the Jewish Labor Bund*, 35.
167 **Sympathetic printers typeset their newspapers:** Goldstein, *Twenty Years with the Jewish Labor Bund*, 53–54.
167 **Police sealed Warsaw's Jewish districts:** Davies, *White Eagle, Red Star*, 163.
167 **They arrested hundreds of Bundists:** Johnpoll, *The Politics of Futility*, 99.
167 **Sophia was with her maid:** Dubnova-Erlich, *Bread and Matzoh*, 202–3.
168 **"unfurl the Red Banner of Revolution":** Davies, *White Eagle, Red Star*, 153.
168 **the Polish army hunted draft dodgers:** Davies, *White Eagle, Red Star*, 193.
168 **The police caught Henryk Erlich:** Goldstein, *Twenty Years with the Jewish Labor Bund*, 49–50.
168 **In Sophia's Warsaw:** Dubnova-Erlich, *Bread and Matzoh*, 204.
168 **blank brick walls of Mokotow prison:** Goldstein, *Twenty Years with the Jewish Labor Bund*, 50.
168 **Sophia knew what to do:** Dubnova-Erlich, *Bread and Matzoh*, 204.
168 **The Polish army took Volkovysk:** "Poles Beaten by Ukrainians Near Lemberg," *New York Tribune*, February 21, 1919, 3.
168 **In April 1920, after rumors:** "Porgromen Oyf Yidn In Panavetsh, Volkovysk Un a R Gantze Ray Andere Shtedt," *Forverts*, April 19, 1920, 1.
168 **a group of Volkovysk immigrants:** Berger, *Volkovysk Memorial Book*, vol. 1, 35–36.
169 **Around two hundred thousand Jews were murdered:** Veidlinger, *In the Midst of Civilized Europe*, 313.
170 **"the world's foremost problem":** Henry Ford, "The International Jew: The World's Foremost Problem," *The Dearborn Independent*, November 1920, 8–15.
170 **The venerable *New York Times* listed:** "New York Reds Potent in Russia," *New York Times*, February 18, 1918, 4.
170 **Even if Jews fled Soviet Russia:** Veidlinger, *In the Midst of Civilized Europe*, 313–14.
170 **young Nazi newspaper editor Alfred Rosenberg:** Veidlinger, *In the Midst of Civilized Europe*, 324–25.
170 **From her dining room table Sophia:** Dubnova-Erlich, *Bread and Matzoh*, 204–5.
170 **The government threatened Erlich:** "Bundist Erlich Vet Krign Biz 8 Yor For Belongn Tsum Bund," *Forverts*, October 31, 1920, 1.
170 **When Sophia visited her husband:** Dubnova-Erlich, *Bread and Matzoh*, 206–7.

CHAPTER FIFTEEN: THE COMMUNIST ROMANCE

172 **Poland emerged from the war:** Watt, *Bitter Glory*, 79–80.
173 **ads for handguns:** "Meldungen," *Naye Folktsaytung*, May 13, 1935, 6.
173 **In 1919, Argentine police arrested Wald:** Hertz, *Doyris Bundestn*, vol. 3, 279–80.
173 **a blistering indictment:** "Di Tsivilizirte Americaner Darf Zikh Shemen," *Naye Folktsaytung*, July 7, 1928, 3, 1.
173 **Activist Yonia Fain recalled:** Josh Waletzky, *What Can We Do About China?* [Video], January 27, 2024, vimeo.com/907096583/20ed87ddc4?ts=0.
173 **The Bund created a youth movement:** Jack Jacobs, *Bundist Counterculture in Interwar Poland* (Syracuse University Press, 2009), 9–13.
173 **Bundist teachers dominated:** Nathan Cohen, "The Bund's Contribution to Yiddish Culture in Poland Between the Two World Wars," in Jack Jacobs, *Jewish Politics in Eastern Europe: The Bund at 100* (New York University Press, 2001), 116.
173 **"filled [a child's] small brain":** Johnpoll, *The Politics of Futility*, 50.
174 **bit off an enemy's nose:** Benny Mer, "Why Smocza?" *K-Larevue*, June 16, 2025, k-larevue.com/en/why-smocza.
174 **the Bund tapped Bernard Goldstein:** Goldstein, *Twenty Years with the Jewish Labor Bund*, 23.
174 **Seven Lions of Praga:** Goldstein, *Twenty Years with the Jewish Labor Bund*, 27–29.
174 **child bagel hawkers:** Goldstein, *Twenty Years with the Jewish Labor Bund*, 130.
174 **At the thieves' synagogue:** Goldstein, *Twenty Years with the Jewish Labor Bund*, 101–9.
174 **Jewish and Polish slaughterhouse workers:** Goldstein, *Twenty Years with the Jewish Labor Bund*, 138–39.
175 **When Bundist writer Moyshe Olgin:** Gennady Estraikh, *Transatlantic Russian Jewishness: Ideological Voyages of the Yiddish Daily* Forverts *in the First Half of the Twentieth Century* (Academic Studies Press, 2020), 81.
175 **"I wish that more radical":** Joshua Rubenstein, "Leon Trotsky, a Revolutionary and a Jew in Spite of Himself," Lecture, YIVO, New York, NY, November 5, 2017.
175 **the Bund's Krakow convention:** Johnpoll, *The Politics of Futility*, 12, 83–91.
175 **The main dissenter was Vladimir Medem:** Goldstein, *Twenty Years with the Jewish Labor Bund*, 42–43; Nowogrodski, *The Jewish Labor Bund in Poland*, 30.
175 **"The day is not far off":** Vladimir Medem, "On Terror," *Dissent*, Spring 1975.
175 **When Medem failed:** Johnpoll, *The Politics of Futility*, 12, 95.
175 **he asked American garment unions:** Goldstein, *Twenty Years with the Jewish Labor Bund*, 44.
175 **the Twenty-one Conditions:** Johnpoll, *The Politics of Futility*, 104–5.
176 **the Bund dispatched an envoy:** Nowogrodski, *The Jewish Labor Bund in Poland*, 33–34.
176 **"Comrades, what this has cost":** Gitelman, *Jewish Nationality and Soviet Politics*, 212.

176 **The Comintern sent X:** Nowogrodski, *The Jewish Labor Bund in Poland*, 38–41.
176 **Clinging to hope, the Bund sent:** Johnpoll, *The Politics of Futility*, 110.
176 **"the Cary Grant of labor":** Erlich, *Child of a Turbulent Century*, 39.
177 **Alter had joined the Bund:** *Soviet Russia Arrests Henryk Ehrlich and Victor Alter, Noted Polish Socialist Leaders* (American Delegation of the General Jewish Workers Bund of Poland, 1942).
177 **He studied engineering in Belgium:** Majer Bogdanski, "Purged from History," *Jewish Socialist*, October–December 1991; Portnoy, ed., *Henryk Erlich and Victor Alter*, 44–46, 53.
177 **When Alter and Wasser arrived:** Nowogrodski, *The Jewish Labor Bund in Poland*, 46–47.
177 **he tried to help:** Portnoy, ed., *Henryk Erlich and Victor Alter*, 46–47.
177 **In December 1921:** Johnpoll, *The Politics of Futility*, 113.
178 **the labor movement was the front line:** Goldstein, *Twenty Years with the Jewish Labor Bund*, 63–64; Johnpoll, *The Politics of Futility*, 118.
178 **Bernard Goldstein organized:** Leonard Rowe, "Jewish Self Defense," in *Studies on Polish Jewry 1918–1939*, ed. Joshua Fishman (YIVO Institute, 1974), 109–16; Goldstein, *Twenty Years with the Jewish Labor Bund*, 65–69.
178 **Most importantly, Bernard created a culture:** Nowogrodski, *The Jewish Labor Bund in Poland*, 222–25.
178 **their first ever election campaign:** Goldstein, *Twenty Years with the Jewish Labor Bund*, 77; Johnpoll, *The Politics of Futility*, 129.
178 **Endeks won 40 percent of deputies:** Watt, *Bitter Glory: Poland and Its Fate*, 189.
179 **the liberal populist Gabriel Narutowicz:** Darek Makowski, "Killed by an Artist: The Story of the First President of Poland," June 16, 2025, culture.pl/en/article/killed-by-an-artist-the-story-of-the-first-president-of-poland; Paul Brykczynski, "Political Murder and the Victory of Ethnic Nationalism in Interwar Poland," PhD diss., University of Michigan, 2013.
179 **Endek leader Roman Dmowski fulminated:** "Anti-semites Urge the Expulsion of Jews From Poland," The Jewish Telegraphic Agency, Feburary 27, 1923.
179 **"a wholesome struggle":** The Jewish Telegraphic Agency Inc. to Daily News, "Hooligans Smash Synagogue Windows in Posen; Molest Jews," April 13, 1923.
179 **Attacks ravaged Jewish communities:** "Mob in Warsaw Maims and Loots," *New York Times*, April 7, 1923, 6; Jewish Telegraphic Agency Inc., to Daily News, "Hooligans Smash Synagogue Windows."
179 **When Jewish parliamentarians tried:** "Storm in Polish Assembly," *New York Times*, April 19, 1923, 10.
179 **The government targeted the Bund:** Johnpoll, *The Politics of Futility*, 124–26.
179 **shutting down *Folkstsaytung*:** Goldstein, *Twenty Years with the Jewish Labor Bund*, 143–44.
179 **On May Day 1923:** The Jewish Telegraphic Agency Inc. to Daily News, "Warsaw Jewish Labor Abstain from May Day Celebrations," May 1, 1923.
179 **flanked by a thousand militiamen:** Goldstein, *Twenty Years with the Jewish Labor Bund*, 145–46.
180 **Congress passed the Emergency Quota Act:** Veidlinger, *In the Midst of Civilized Europe*, 329–30.
180 **"filthy, un-American, and often dangerous":** Dennis Wepman, *Immigration: From the Founding of Virginia to the Closing of Ellis Island* (New York City, Facts on File, 2002), 242.
180 **The party, he wrote, "was cemented":** Johnpoll, *The Politics of Futility*, 122.
180 **He would always be their prince:** "Vladimir Medem," *Forverts*, January 10, 1923, 4.
180 **Medem died of nephritis:** "Genose Vladimir Medem Zehr Krank," *Forverts*, January 3, 1923, 1.
180 **Over his coffin, Baruch Charney Vladeck:** The Jewish Telegraphic Agency, "Medem Funeral Attended by Thousands," January 16, 1923.

CHAPTER SIXTEEN: ENEMY OF ZION

181 **Three thousand political prisoners:** "Say Terror Reigns in Polish Republic," *New York Times*, June 1, 1924, 65.
181 **they turned away Jewish applicants:** Nowogrodski, *The Jewish Labor Bund in Poland*, 255–56.
182 **According to Borochov:** Ber Borochov, "The National Question and the Class Struggle," quoted in Johnpoll, *The Politics of Futility*, 19.
182 **To back up this dubious point:** Frankel, *Prophecy and Politics*, 341.
182 **Ben-Gurion had spent:** Tom Segev, *A State at Any Cost* (Farrar, Straus and Giroux, 2019), 49.
183 **sometimes kidnapped and sexually tortured:** Hillel Cohen, *Year Zero of the Arab-Israeli Conflict 1929* (Brandeis University Press, 2015), 209.
183 **a Jewish-only labor union:** Frankel, *Prophecy and Politics*, 385–86. See also Zachary Lockman, *Arab and Jewish Workers in Palestine, 1906–1948* (University of California Press, 1996).
183 **"The Jewish revolt was only terrifying":** Frankel, *Prophecy and Politics*, 166.
183 **In 1923, he wrote an essay:** Vladimir Jabotinsky, "The Iron Wall," first published in Russian under the title "O Zheleznoi Stene" in *Rassvyet*, November 4, 1923.
184 **"Jewish Endek":** Daniel Kupfert Heller, *Jabotinsky's Children* (Princeton University Press, 2017), 62.
184 **"Zionism drew its vital juices":** Nowogrodski, *The Jewish Labor Bund in Poland*, 189.
184 **even apolitical Jews turned up:** The Jewish Telegraphic Agency Inc. to Jewish Daily Bulletin, "Desire to Emigrate to Palestine Increases in Poland," January 1, 1924.
184 **He chronicled the trip:** Victor Alter, *Der Emes Vegn Palestine* (Di Velt, 1925).
184 **he heard American tourists hee-haw:** Alter, *Der Emes Vegn Palestine*, 8.
184 **On a boat ride:** Alter, *Der Emes Vegn Palestine*, 10.
184 **Alter had a typical European attitude:** Alter, *Der Emes Vegn Palestine*, 15–17.
185 **"There is almost no relation":** Alter, *Der Emes Vegn Palestine*, 48.

185 **Musa Kazim Pasha al-Husseini:** see: Michael Provence, *The Last Ottoman Generation and the Making of the Modern Middle East* (Cambridge University Press, 2017).

185 **"The immigrants dumped upon the country":** Esco Foundation for Palestine, *Palestine: A Study of Jewish, Arab, and British Policies,* vol. 1 (Yale University Press, 1947), 286.

185 **"Palestine will be a free country":** Alter, *Der Emes Vegn Palestine,* 49–52.

185 **"We feel this is our country":** Alter, *Der Emes Vegn Palestine,* 60–61.

186 **Palestine was Arab:** Alter, *Der Emes Vegn Palestine,* 63.

186 **"It's because they hope":** Alter, *Der Emes Vegn Palestine,* 61.

186 **Nationalists continued their attempts:** The Jewish Telegraphic Agency Inc., to Jewish Daily Bulletin, "Spread Propaganda to Renew Economic Boycott in Poland," December 2, 1924.

186 **uniting Jewish trade unions:** Goldstein, *Twenty Years with the Jewish Labor Bund,* 83–87.

186 **They created campaigns:** Nowogrodski, *The Jewish Labor Bund in Poland,* 255–75; The Jewish Telegraphic Agency Inc. to Jewish Daily Bulletin, "Jewish Workers in Poland Demand Right to Work," April 4, 1926.

186 **party decided to publish:** The Jewish Telegraphic Agency Inc. to Jewish Daily Bulletin, "Orthodox and Sabbath Violators Fight Battle on Warsaw Streets," December 31, 1923; The Jewish Telegraphic Agency Inc. to Jewish Daily Bulletin, "Bundists Deplore Orthodox Hooliganism," December 27, 1923; Goldstein, *Twenty Years with the Jewish Labor Bund,* 149–51.

187 **Henryk Erlich ran a raucous campaign:** Hertz, *Di Geshikhte fun Bund,* vol. 3, 117.

187 **women were not allowed to vote:** The Jewish Telegraphic Agency Inc. to JTA Bulletin, "Jewish Women in Warsaw Declare Strike Against Lack of Suffrage," June 13, 1924.

187 **his party opposed circumcision:** Nowogrodski, *The Jewish Labor Bund in Poland,* 85.

187 **a Bundist delegate threw a chair:** The Jewish Telegraphic Agency Inc. to JTA Bulletin, "Warsaw Kehillah Council Closes Session Because of Fighting Among Members," March 12, 1926.

187 **Bundist women founded their own organization:** Jacobs, *Bundist Counterculture in Interwar Poland,* 89–92.

187 **In the summer:** Nowogrodski, *The Jewish Labor Bund in Poland,* 166.

187 **Bundist workers gathered:** Goldstein, *Twenty Years with the Jewish Labor Bund,* 209.

187 **the Medem Sanatorium:** "Ernste Un Komishe Pasenrung In Der Alter Haym," *Forverts,* August 13, 1924, 5.

187 **Inspired by Rousseau's ideas on education:** Conversation with Victor Gilinsky.

187 **respite for kids who lived:** Jacobs, *Bundist Counterculture in Interwar Poland,* 69.

187 **Medem Sanatorium didn't beat children:** Jacobs, *Bundist Counterculture in Interwar Poland,* 71–72.

188 **They observed Jewish holidays:** Jacobs, *Bundist Counterculture in Interwar Poland,* 67, 74.

188 **the Bund released a film:** *Mir kumen on,* Alexsander Ford, 1935.

CHAPTER SEVENTEEN: HERE WHERE WE LIVE IS OUR COUNTRY

189 **On May 12, 1926:** Watt, *Bitter Glory: Poland and Its Fate, 1918–1939,* 224; The Jewish Telegraphic Agency Inc. to JTA Bulletin, "Pilsudski Brings Coup in Poland to Successful Conclusion," May 18, 1926, jta.org/archive/pilsudski-brings-coup-in-poland-to-successful-conclusion.

189 **From his apartment on Nowolipie Street:** Goldstein, *Twenty Years with the Jewish Labor Bund,* 159.

189 **At the *Folkstsaytung* office:** Johnpoll, *The Politics of Futility,* 147.

189 **Alter grabbed Erlich:** Portnoy, ed., *Henryk Erlich and Victor Alter,* 53.

189 **To support the coup:** Jewish Telegraphic Agency Inc. to JTA Bulletin, "Pilsudski Brings Coup in Poland,"

189 **Bundists lined up:** Johnpoll, *Politics of Futility,* 147–48.

190 **The Bund gave Pilsudski their support:** Johnpoll, *Politics of Futility,* 150.

190 ***The Bund in Pictures:*** Y. Sh. Hertz, *Der Bund in Bilder: 1897–1957* (Unzer Tsayt Farlag, 1958).

190 **Bundist-dominated TSYSHO school:** Cohen, "The Bund's Contribution to Yiddish Culture in Poland between the Two World Wars," in *Jewish Politics in Eastern Europe: The Bund at 100,* ed. Jack Jacobs (New York University Press, 2001), 117.

190 **to night schools for Jewish workers:** Goldstein, *Twenty Years with the Jewish Labor Bund,* 215.

190 **In the words of Victor Gilinsky:** Conversation with Victor Gilinsky.

190 **the Bund created SKIF:** Jack Jacobs, *Bundist Counterculture in Interwar Poland* (Syracuse University Press, 2009), 37.

191 **"We are young":** Leivik Hodis, *Biografie un Shriftn* (Unzer Tsayt Farlag, 1952), 26.

191 **Marek Edelman:** Witold Beres and Krzysztof Burnetko, *Marek Edelman: Being on the Right Side* (Beres Media, 2016), 39.

191 **There were Polish and German children:** Jacobs, *Bundist Counterculture in Interwar Poland,* 70.

191 **the Bund founded their sports club:** Jacobs, *Bundist Counterculture in Interwar Poland,* 50; Roni Gechtman, "Socialist Mass Politics Through Sport: The Bund's Morgnshtern in Poland, 1926–1939," *Journal of Sport History* 26, no. 2 (1999): 326–52; Hertz, *Der Bund in Bilder,* 133; Goldstein, *Twenty Years with the Jewish Labor Bund,* 175–82.

191 **In summer, they rented pools:** Gechtman, "Socialist Mass Politics Through Sport."

191 **In April 1927, Morgenstern took over:** Goldstein, *Twenty Years with the Jewish Labor Bund,* 179–80.

191 **On their first May Day:** Goldstein, *Twenty Years with the Jewish Labor Bund,* 281–83.

192 **In October, the Bund celebrated:** Hertz, *Der Bund in Bilder,* 94; Victor Erlich, *Child of a Turbulent Century* (Northwestern University Press, 2006), 33.

192 **the famous basement cabaret:** "Qui Pro Quo," October 7, 2020, culture.pl/en/artist/qui-pro-quo.

192 **Nigerian jazz percussionist August Agbola O'Browne:** Nicholas Boston, "August Browne: The Nigeria-Born Man Who Joined the Polish Resistance," BBC World News, October 2, 2020, bbc.com/news/world-africa-54337607.

192 **the Association of Jewish Writers and Journalists:** Shachar Pinsker, *A Rich Brew: How Cafés Created Modern Jewish Culture* (New York University Press, 2018), 73–80.

192 **the diva Ida Kaminska:** Michael C. Steinlaug, "Kaminski Family," *The Yivo Encyclopedia of Jews in Eastern Europe,* yivoencyclopedia.org/article.aspx/Kaminski_Family.

193 **get a ham sandwich by Tabachinsky's:** Portnoy, *Bad Rabbi,* 88.

193 **by Fat Yosl's tavern:** Goldstein, *Twenty Years with the Jewish Labor Bund,* 235–38; Wojciech Rodak, "Towarzysz Bernard: Pięść Warszawskiego Bundu," Warsaw Ghetto Museum, 1943.pl/artykul/towarzysz-bernard-piesc-warszawskiego-bundu.

193 **was parceled out to the Polish military veterans:** Mikalaj Bychowcew and Renata Hawrylik-Kuklinska, *Wolkowysk: miasto trzech narodow* (Rozpisani.pl, 2020), 13.

193 **The volunteer fire brigade:** Berger, *The Volkovysk Memorial Book,* vol. 1, 89–93, 97–98.

193 **uses the word *squatters:*** Berger, *Volkovysk Memorial Book,* vol. 1, 277.

193 **ran their newspaper:** *Der Volkovysker Veker,* July 8, 1927.

193 **against the town's Zionist elite:** "Di Balebatim Vayzn, Voz Zay Kenen," *Der Volkovysker Veker,* July 15, 1927, 2.

193 **passed by Kanoval home:** Berger, *Volkovysk Memorial Book,* vol. 1, 336.

194 **their neighbor Moshe Rutchik's house:** Berger, *Volkovysk Memorial Book,* vol. 3, 14–15.

194 **found a patron:** Hamilton Easter Field, "Brooklyn Art Exhibitions," *Brooklyn Daily Eagle,* March 21, 1920, 89.

194 **"My feeling is that the antipathy":** Hamilton Easter Field, "Samuel Rothbort, by the Editor," *The Arts,* June–July 1921.

194 **"Rothbort, you don't know":** Samuel Rothbort, "Rothbort on Rothbort," *David's Art Expo,* davidsartexpo.com/samuel-rothbort-s-autobiography.

195 **In 1924, he moved the family:** "Er Foraybikt Der Shtetl," *Forverts,* May 4, 1968, 3.

195 **On a stained lunch counter:** Rothbort, *Out of Wood and Stone,* 22.

195 **He sculpted the prophets:** Rothbort, *Out of Wood and Stone,* 25.

195 **amidst stunted birch trees:** Rothbort, *Out of Wood and Stone,* 26.

195 **"The day is not far off":** Vladimir Medem, "On Terror," 190.

195 **a new theory called social fascism:** Lea Haro, "Entering a Theoretical Void: The Theory of Social Fascism and Stalinism in the German Communist Party," *Critique* 39, no. 4 (December 2011): 565.

196 **Poland's Jewish communists escalated:** Mendel, *Memoirs of a Jewish Revolutionary* (Pluto Press, 1989), 274.

196 **they enlisted the underworld:** Goldstein, *Twenty Years with the Jewish Labor Bund,* 71–73.

196 **cross-eyed pimp Simkhe Macz:** Goldstein, *Twenty Years with the Jewish Labor Bund,* 167.

196 **Communists broke into:** Goldstein, *Twenty Years with the Jewish Labor Bund,* 215–16.

196 **Once, a gang stormed:** Goldstein, *Twenty Years with the Jewish Labor Bund,* 202.

196 **Communists in Bundist-led unions:** Goldstein, *Twenty Years with the Jewish Labor Bund,* 189–90.

196 **Bernard tried to speak:** Goldstein, *Twenty Years with the Jewish Labor Bund,* 198–99.

196 **and sent fanatical teenagers:** Goldstein, *Twenty Years with the Jewish Labor Bund,* 205–7.

196 **Another communist tried to assassinate:** Goldstein, *Twenty Years with the Jewish Labor Bund,* 200.

196 **communists would murder several Bundist workers:** Johnpoll, *Politics of Futility,* 173.

196 **They even shot up Medem Sanatorium:** Goldstein, *Twenty Years with the Jewish Labor Bund,* 222–23.

197 **On New Year's Day, 1929:** Daniel Kupfert Heller, *Jabotinsky's Children* (Princeton University Press, 2017), 68–69.

197 **a hundred thousand Jews had immigrated:** "Demographics of Historic Palestine Prior to 1948," Canadians for Justice and Peace in the Middle East, June 2022, cjpme.org/fs_007.

197 **Jabotinsky fixated on East Jerusalem's:** Mary Ellen Lundsten, "Wall Politics: Zionist and Palestinian Strategies in Jerusalem, 1928," *Journal of Palestine Studies* 8, no. 1 (Autumn 1978): 3–27.

197 **on the Jewish mourning day:** For the preeminent history of the 1929 Palestine riots, see Cohen, *Year Zero for the Arab-Israeli Conflict: 1929.*

198 **These murders set off a worldwide explosion:** Nowogrodski, *The Jewish Labor Bund in Poland,* 195.

198 **Days after the riots, Jabotinsky:** Heller, *Jabotinsky's Children,* 85.

198 **Protests against the Palestine riots:** "3,000 Jews Parade in Poland," *New York Times,* August 29, 1929, 4.

198 **street mobs chanted, "Jabotinsky was right":** Berger, *Volkovysk Memorial Book,* vol. 3, 35.

198 **The Bund refused to join:** Nowogrodski, *Jewish Labor Bund in Poland,* 195.

198 **"an enemy of the Jews":** Nowogrodski, *Jewish Labor Bund in Poland,* 194.

198 **was not a Jewish party but:** Henryk Erlich, "Mir, Di Araber," *Naye Folkstsaytung,* June 21, 1929, 3.

198 **In 1928, *Naye Folkstsaytung* covered:** "Arabisher Congres in Palistine," *Naye Folkstsaytung,* July 27, 1928, 5.

199 **The Bund had no problem with emigration:** The Jewish Telegraphic Agency Inc. to JTA Bulletin, "Jewish Labor Delegates Clash in Offering Views to Migration Congress," June 27, 1926.

199 **They even ran a bureau:** Y. Sh. Hertz, *Di Geshikhte fun Bund,* vol. 5 (Unzer Tsayt Farlag, 1981), 101.

199 **Days after the riots:** Nowogrodski, *Jewish Labor Bund in Poland,* 195.

199 **The Bund said the same:** "Likvidirn Dem Tsionism," *Naye Folkstsaytung,* September 1, 1929, 5.

200 **In one piece reprinted:** "A Shtim Fon An Araber Vegn Di Palistiner Blutike Kampfn," *Naye Folkstsaytung,* September 1, 1929, 2.

200 **In "Who Are the Arabs":** "Freylekher Vinkl," *Naye Folkstsaytung*, September 6, 1929, 8.

200 **In 1929, Bundist speakers toured:** Nowogrodski, *Jewish Labor Bund in Poland*, 196.

200 **When the Bundist leader G. Zeibert:** "Jewish Socialist Attacks Zionism," *New York Times*, November 29, 1929, 16.

200 **The Bund even published:** Y. Khmurner, *Vos Lernen Unz Di Geshenishn In Palestine* (Tsentral Komitet Fun Bund in Poilin, 1929).

200 **In a statement sent:** "Der Entfer Fon Der Algemener Arbeter Organizatsie In Eretz-Yisroel," *Haynt*, September 15, 1929, 8.

201 **In Vilna, Zionists vowed:** "Vayterdige Begrisungen Tsum 'Haynt,'" *Haynt*, November 10, 1929, 4.

201 **and hooligans attacked a Bundist:** "Tsionistisher Khooliganizm," *Naye Folkstsaytung*, September 1, 1929, 4.

201 **In Warsaw, the Zionist daily *Haynt*:** "Di Shande Fon Bundizm," *Haynt*, September 26, 1929.

201 **They called for Bundists to be expelled:** "Bund Un Kolel-Yisroel," *Haynt*, October 7, 1929, 4.

201 ***Haynt* began a jeremiad:** Yuu Nishimura, "On the Cultural Front: The Bund and the Yiddish Secular School Movement in Interwar Poland," *East European Jewish Affairs* 43, no. 3 (2013): 265–81, DOI:10.1080/13501674.2013.852805.

201 **Furious at the challenge:** "Opposition Chiefs Arrested in Poland," *New York Times*, September 11, 1930, 6.

201 **"instituted a de facto dictatorship":** Goldstein, *Twenty Years with the Jewish Labor Bund*, 192.

201 **His government viciously repressed the Left:** "Polish Police Quell Red Demonstration," *New York Times*, January 23, 1930, 4; "Red Ousted from Sejm," *New York Times*, January 11, 1930, 11.

201 **Bernard planned his marches:** Goldstein, *Twenty Years with the Jewish Labor Bund*, 280.

201 **repression drew The Polish Socialist Party:** Eli Tzur, "The Bund and the PPS," American Association For Polish-Jewish Studies, aapjstudies.org/index.php?id=114, accessed June 16, 2025.

202 **Bernard touchily declined:** Goldstein, *Twenty Years with the Jewish Labor Bund*, 287–88.

202 **it meant that Henryk Erlich:** Goldstein, *Twenty Years with the Jewish Labor Bund*, 267.

202 **The Bund's city councilwoman:** Goldstein, *Twenty Years with the Jewish Labor Bund*, 237.

202 **If the butcher stole meat:** Goldstein, *Twenty Years with the Jewish Labor Bund*, 245.

202 **Did some rich kid marry:** Goldstein, *Twenty Years with the Jewish Labor Bund*, 261–63.

202 **When a landlord tried to evict:** Goldstein, *Twenty Years with the Jewish Labor Bund*, 268–69.

202 **The Bund launched a campaign:** Goldstein, *Twenty Years with the Jewish Labor Bund*, 231–32.

202 **sharpsters like Puny Hannah:** Portnoy, *Bad Rabbi*, 121–24.

202 **Comrade Bernard recruited local delinquents:** Leonard Rowe, "Jewish Self Defense: A Response to Violence," in *Studies on Polish Jewry: 1919–1939*, ed. Joshua A. Fishman (YIVO Institute for Jewish Research, 1974), 133–34.

202 **a crooked-shouldered militiaman:** Goldstein, *Twenty Years with the Jewish Labor Bund*, 241–43.

203 **Each day, furious women:** Goldstein, *Twenty Years with the Jewish Labor Bund*, 253–57.

203 **when a group of communists:** Goldstein, *Twenty Years with the Jewish Labor Bund*, 264.

203 **three hundred athletes:** Gechtman, "Socialist Mass Politics Through Sport."

204 **inspire the Bund's own youth militia:** Rowe, "Jewish Self Defense," 144.

204 **All of this weighed on Bernard:** Goldstein, *Twenty Years with the Jewish Labor Bund*, 289.

204 **A hundred thousand workers:** "Die Arbeiterolympiade 1931," *Arbeitsport*, June 16, 2025, arbeitersport.at/de/1919-1934-neue-zeit/manifestation-demonstration-arbeiterolympiade, accessed October 11, 2025.

204 **Bernard crashed with a railway worker:** Goldstein, *Twenty Years with the Jewish Labor Bund*, 290–91.

204 **At the opening ceremony:** "Die Arbeiterolympiade 1931."

204 **the French and German athletes:** Paula Arnold, "The Vienna Olympiad as Sign of Good Will," *Baltimore Sun*, August 29, 1931, 7.

204 **white-clad Czechs:** "80,000 Athletes in Vienna," *New York Times*, July 24, 1931, 21.

204 **Yiddish banner high:** Gechtman, "Socialist Mass Politics Through Sport."

204 **Congress of the Labor and Socialist International:** Julius Braunthal, *History of the International: Volume 2, 1914–1943* (Frederick A. Praeger Publishers, 1967), 362.

205 **German Social Democratic Party chairman:** Sozialistische Arbeiter-Internationale, *Vierter Kongress der Sozialistischen Arbeiter-Internationale, Wien, 25. Juli bis 1. August 1931, Berichte und Verhandlungen* (Verlag des Sekretariats der SAI, 1932), 577–80.

205 **After the congress, Bernard Goldstein:** Goldstein, *Twenty Years with the Jewish Labor Bund*, 292.

205 **It started that fall semester:** "Jewish Law Students Attacked in Warsaw," *New York Times*, November 3, 1931, 34; "162 Hurt in Attack on Jewish Traders," *New York Times*, November 4, 1931, 26.

205 **The next day, Endeks:** "Warsaw University Closed After Fight," *New York Times*, November 5, 1931, 18.

206 **Within a week, riots forced:** "Poor Storm Offices of Warsaw Charities," *New York Times*, April 2, 1931, 4; "Report Grave State of Jews in Poland," *New York Times*, October 5, 1931, 4.

206 **The riots spread:** "Polish Riots Spread," *New York Times*, November 13, 1931, 10; David G. Roskies, "Legend of Max Weinreich," *Tablet*, January 27, 2023, tabletmag.com/sections/arts-letters/articles/legend-max-weinreich-yiddish.

206 **In Lowicz, a small town:** "Polish Teachers Lead Anti-Jewish Raiders," *New York Times*, November 16, 1931, 2.

206 **They demolished Jewish graves:** Jerzy Shapiro, "Anti-Semitic Riots Turn to a Boycott," *New York Times*, November 22, 1931, 12.

206 **After a rock killed:** Rowe, "Jewish Self Defense," 118.
206 **they confined themselves to expelling:** "New Attacks on Jews in Many Polish Towns," *New York Times*, November 21, 1931, 9.
206 **To combat the riots, Bernard:** Goldstein, *Twenty Years with the Jewish Labor Bund*, 297.
206 **When nationalist students tried:** "Warsaw Jews Form Self-Defense Unit," *New York Times*, November 8, 1931, 13.
206 **When the University of Warsaw reopened:** "Anti-Semitic Riots Die Down in Poland," *New York Times*, November 28, 1931, 20.
206 **At student restaurants:** "Jewish Students Shunned in Poland," *New York Times*, November 26, 1931, 12.
206 **nationalist youth donned uniforms:** "Jewish Trade Ban Slumps in Poland," *New York Times*, December 23, 1931, 10.
206 **Nationalist newspapers:** "Anti-Semitic Riots Turn to a Boycott," *New York Times*, November 22, 1930, 12.
206 **Endek politicians:** "Polish Nationalists Favor Jewish Curb," *New York Times*, November 24, 1931, 7.
206 **In the summer of 1932:** Erlich, *Child of a Turbulent Century*, 23.
206 **She had been in the city:** Dubnova-Erlich, *Bread and Matzoh*, 218–20.
206 **The newly legalized Brownshirts:** "Storm Troops Legal Today," *New York Times*, June 14, 1932, 9.
207 **fought the communist Red Front Fighters:** "Nazi-Red Rows Add Four to Death Toll," *New York Times*, June 24, 1932, 12; "Nazi Uniform Riots Cause Two Deaths," *New York Times*, June 22, 1932, 6.
207 **By mid-July, these political clashes:** "Nazi Blames the Left," *New York Times*, July 20, 1932, 7.
207 **communists and social democrats regarded:** Braunthal, *History of the International: Volume II: 1914–1943*, 379; Rosa Leviné-Meyer, *Inside German Communism: Memoirs of Party Life in the Weimar Republic* (Pluto, 1977), 171.
207 **After the July elections:** The Jewish Telegraphic Agency Inc. to JTA Bulletin, "Jews Breathe More Freely as Nazi Party Fails to Secure Majority; Emphasize That Fight for Jewish Rig," August 2, 1932.
207 **In their smuggled proclamations:** "Mensheviki Appeal to Russian Labor," *New York Times*, February 12, 1928, 60.
207 **In Grunewald, a leafy Berlin suburb:** Dubnova-Erlich, *Bread and Matzoh*, 236.
207 **Sophia and Victor returned:** Erlich, *Child of a Turbulent Century*, 31.
207 **A thousand nationalist students:** "Bans Curb on Jews in Polish Colleges," *New York Times*, March 5, 1932, 4.
207 **"Revenge yourselves on the Jews!":** "Article 4—No Title," *New York Times*, November 11, 1932, 7.
207 **young Bundists and Polish Socialists:** "Two Clash Victims Honored in Lwow," *New York Times*, December 1, 1932, 7.
207 **the police it shut down:** "Policemen in Warsaw Quell Demonstration," *New York Times*, December 3, 1932, 7.
207 **Worse violence broke out in Lviv:** "Police Fight 1,000 in Polish Rioting," *New York Times*, November 14, 1932, 6.
207 **One of the gangsters stabbed:** "30 Hurt in Poland in Anti-Semitic Riot," *New York Times*, November 29, 1932, 7; "Youth Slain in Polish Riot," *New York Times*, November 28, 1932, 7.
207 **Sixty thousand Christians:** "Two Clash Victims Honored in Lwow," *New York Times*, November 30, 1932, 7.
207 **The cause turned out:** "Rioting at Funeral of Youth in Lwow," *New York Times*, November 30, 1932, 5.
207 **After that, the city exploded:** "Youth Slain in Polish Riot," *New York Times*, November 28, 1932, 7.
208 **Nationalist student riots spread:** The Jewish Telegraphic Agency Inc. to Jewish Daily Bulletin, "News Brief," December 6, 1932; "Two Clash Victims Honored in Lwow," *New York Times*, December 1, 1932, 7.
208 **"After Hitler, our turn!":** C.L.R. James, *World Revolution 1917–1936* (Purnell and Sons, 1937), marxists.org/archive/james-clr/works/world/ch12.htm#n25.
208 **The social democrats decided:** Braunthal, *History of the International: Volume II: 1914–1943*, 381–82.

CHAPTER EIGHTEEN: DANGEROUS SOLIDARITIES

209 **On the night of February 28:** "Untergetsunden Dem Reichstag," *Naye Folkstsaytung*, March 1, 1933, 1.
209 **The government banned the leftist press:** "Hitler Intensifies Drive on Left," *New York Times*, March 2, 1933, 1.
209 **68 Lindenstrasse, where the Bund had its archives:** Marek Web, "Between New York and Moscow: The Fate of the Bund Archives," in *Jewish Politics in Eastern Europe: The Bund at 100*, ed. Jack Jacobs (Palgrave Macmillan, 2001), 248.
210 **He titled a chapter of his memoir:** Franz Kursky, *Gezamlte Shriftn* (Farlag Der Veker, 1952), 160.
210 **Storm troopers made the laws:** Frederick T. Birchall, "3 More Americans Attacked in Reich," *New York Times*, March 10, 1933, 13.
210 **They could beat a socialist parliamentarian:** "Charge Terrorism by Nazi Troopers," *New York Times*, March 15, 1933, 10.
210 **Thanks to a last-minute intervention:** Web, "Between New York and Moscow: The Fate of the Bund Archives," 249.
210 **In Paris, *The New York Times*:** "German Fugitives Tell of Atrocities at Hands of Nazis," *New York Times*, March 20, 1933, 1.
210 **Polish Jews beseeched their consulate:** "Poles in Germany Ask Warsaw's Aid," *New York Times*, March 13, 1933, 6.

226 **When Jabotinsky spoke in Vilna:** "Jewish Bund Attack on Vladimir Jabotinsky," Zionism and Israel Information Center, zionism-israel.com/hdoc/bund_jabo.htm, accessed June 23, 2025.

226 **British police beat:** Michael Provence, *The Last Ottoman Generation and the Making of the Modern Middle East* (Cambridge University Press, 2017), 212.

226 **when 164,000 new Jewish immigrants:** Gudrun Krämer, *A History of Palestine: From the Ottoman Conquest to the Founding of the State of Israel* (Princeton University Press, 2008), 240.

226 **In 1936, Palestinians declared:** See Ghassan Kanafani, *The Revolution of 1936–1939 in Palestine: Background, Details, and Analysis* (1804 Books, 2023).

227 **As Henryk Erlich wrote:** "Nayn, mir zaynen nisht kayn atoh bekhartonu-folk" [No, we are not a chosen people], *Naye Folkstsaytung*, May 1933, translated by Vera Szabó.

227 **Placed the ultimate blame:** "Araber Vegn Der-Radio Redė Fon Hoykh-Komand Harold Mekmikal," *Naye Folkstsaytung*, August 14, 1935, 3.

227 ***Naye Folkstsaytung* wrote in 1937:** Melzer, *No Way Out*, 140.

227 **To illustrate the reality:** "Un Dem Fremdn Zolstu Nisht Narn," *Naye Folkstsaytung*, August 27, 1935, 4.

227 **briefly joined a Betar youth group:** Heller, *Jabotinsky's Children*, 192.

228 **Bernard Goldstein stood:** Goldstein, *Twenty Years with the Jewish Labor Bund*, 367–68.

228 **Black smoke filled:** "Paraders Are Bombed on May Day at Warsaw," *New York Times*, May 2, 1937, 1.

228 **To avenge Avram Shenker's murder:** Goldstein, *Twenty Years with the Jewish Labor Bund*, 369–70.

228 **That year's hit song:** "Polish Tangos: The Unique Interwar Soundtrack to Poland's Independence," *Culture.pl*, culture.pl/en/article/polish-tangos-the-unique-interwar-soundtrack-to-polands-independence.

228 **Several Bundists enlisted:** Aleksander Szurek, *The Shattered Dream* (Eastern European Monographs, 1989), 234.

228 **including Beniak Livshitz:** Y. Sh. Hertz, *Doyres Bundistn*, vol. 2 (Unzer Tsayt Farlag, 1956), 463.

228 **Ali Abdel Khaleq:** Abraham Nevine, "Liberating Palestine in Spain: Novel on Palestinian Arab Volunteers in the IB," *The Volunteer*, February 17, 2023, albavolunteer.org/2023/02/liberating-palestine-in-spain-novel-on-palestinian-arab-volunteers-in-the-ib/.

229 **Baghdadi Jew Setty Abraham Horresh:** Chris Brooks, "Iraqi Volunteers in Spain," *The Volunteer*, August 5, 2019, albavolunteer.org/2019/08/iraqi-volunteers-in-spain/.

229 **Mack Coad:** "Biography: Coad, Mack," The Abraham Lincoln Brigade Archives, alba-valb.org/volunteers/mack-coad/.

229 **As he wrote in his book:** Johnpoll, *Politics of Futility*, 218.

229 **Alter and Zdanowski crossed:** "Przez Ludową Hiszpanię—Rozmowa z Tow. Antonim Zdanowskim," *Lewico.pl*, lewicowo.pl/przez-ludowa-hiszpanie-rozmowa-z-tow-antonim-zdanowskim.

229 **In anarchist Barcelona:** Julius Deutsch and Victor Alter, *Hiszpania W Ogniu; Rok Wojny Domowej* (Myśli Socjalistycznej, 1937), 29–31.

229 **Alter's nephew, a leftist radio engineer:** Comunicado: Victor Iwinski. Originally from The Russian State Archive of Socio-Political History. Moscow, Russia. Preserved in the digital archives of Stowarzyszenie Ochotnicy Wolności.

229 **Abramovich's son, the journalist Mark Rein:** "The Case of Mark Rein," *Socialist Appeal*, October 23, 1937.

229 **In Valencia, Zdanowski and Alter:** "Przez Ludową Hiszpanię—Rozmowa z Tow. Antonim Zdanowskim."

229 **One afternoon, a shell exploded:** "Przez Ludową Hiszpanię—Rozmowa z Tow. Antonim Zdanowskim."

230 **One night, Alter sat:** Deutsch and Alter, *Hiszpania W Ogniu; Rok Wojny Domowej*, 59.

230 **he traversed the country:** Deutsch and Alter, *Hiszpania W Ogniu; Rok Wojny Domowej*, 75.

230 **When he got back to Warsaw:** Alexander Erlich, "The Life of Victor Alter," in *Henryk Erlich and Victor Alter*, ed. Portnoy, 51.

230 **when three hundred Morgenstern athletes:** Gechtman, "Socialist Mass Politics Through Sport."

230 **At Warsaw City Hall:** Goldstein, *Twenty Years with the Jewish Labor Bund*, 270.

230 **Nationalists descended on Saxon Gardens:** "Hundreds of Jews Attacked in Warsaw," *New York Times*, September 23, 1937, 12.

230 **Naras rigged an IED:** "18 in Warsaw Hurt by Anti-Jewish Bomb," *New York Times*, September 28, 1937, 11.

230 **The government banned newspapers:** "Hundreds of Jews Attacked in Warsaw," *New York Times*, September 23, 1937, 12.

230 **The Bund plastered Warsaw:** Fishman, ed., *Studies on Polish Jewry: 1919–1939*, 528.

230 **On the evening of September 26:** Goldstein, *Twenty Years with the Jewish Labor Bund*, 383–84.

231 **A few nights later:** Rowe, "Jewish Self Defense," 124; Goldstein, *Twenty Years with the Jewish Labor Bund*, 384–85.

231 **In October 1937:** " 'Ghetto' Created in Polish Colleges," *New York Times*, October 6, 1937, 7.

232 **"This first attempt to institute":** "Fishman, ed., *Studies on Polish Jewry: 1919–1939*, 289–90.

232 **Erlich and Alter met:** Gertrud Pickhan, " 'That Incredible History of the Polish Bund Written in a Soviet Prison': The NKVD Files on Henryk Erlich and Wiktor Alter," *Polin: Studies in Polish Jewry, Volume 10: Jews in Early Modern Poland*, ed. Gershon David Hundert (Liverpool University Press, 1997), 263.

232 **even expelled them:** "Polish Jews Picketed," *New York Times*, November 18, 1937, 4.

232 **Polish socialist students:** Oskar Lange, "Ghetto Benches in Polish Universities," *New York Times*, March 20, 1938, 66.

232 **With Polish socialist support, the Bund:** "Jewish Students Strike," *New York Times*, October 15, 1937, 2.

232 **Polish socialists gave fiery speeches:** "Jews of Poland Strike," *New York Times*, October 20, 1937, 13.

232 **As *The Nation*'s correspondent:** Johnpoll, *Politics of Futility*, 216.
232 **the Erlich apartment became:** Dubnova-Erlich, *Bread and Matzoh*, 235.
232 **Bernard Goldstein smuggled himself:** Goldstein, *Twenty Years with the Jewish Labor Bund*, 376.
233 **On November 17, 1937:** Nowogrodski, *Jewish Labor Bund in Poland*, 169.
233 **delegates from the Polish Socialist Party:** Piotr Wróbel, "The Bund and the PPS, 1897–1939," in *Jewish Politics in Eastern Europe*, ed. Jacobs, 166.
233 **spoke about the brutal poverty:** Henryk Erlich, "Manifesto of the General Jewish Workers' Union (Bund) in Poland," in *Henryk Erlich and Victor Alter*, ed. Portnoy, 235.

CHAPTER NINETEEN: THE EVE

235 **Mexico found them culturally unsuitable:** Gisela Argote, "The Jewish Migration to Mexico During Nazi Germany," *Pathways: A Journal of Humanistic and Social Inquiry* 1, no. 3 (February 2021): 5.
235 **Australia didn't want to:** "Speech by Lt. Colonel Thomas W. White (Australia) in the Public Session on July 7, 1938, 3.30pm, p. 2/2," *Closed Borders: The International Conference on Refugees in Évian 1938*, evian1938.de/en/australia/.
235 **Even the American Jewish Committee:** Haim Genizi, "The American Jewish Committee and the Admission of Nazi Collaborators into the United States, 1948–1950," Yad Vashem: The World Holocaust Remembrance Center, yadvashem.org/articles/academic/american-jewish-committee-and-admission-of-nazi-collaborators.html#footnoteref3_5c9ddzf.
235 **the poet W. H. Auden wrote:** W. H. Auden, "Refugee Blues," 1939.
236 **His mother, Tsipie, had died:** Y. Sh. Hertz, *Doyres Bundistn*, vol. 3 (Unzer Tsayt Farlag, 1956), 352.
236 **Afterward, Marek went a little crazy:** Hanna Krall, *Shielding the Flame: An Intimate Conversation with Dr. Marek Edelman, the Last Surviving Leader of the Warsaw Ghetto Uprising* (Henry Holt, 1986), 39.
236 **Marek didn't walk near Theater Square:** Beres and Burnetko, *Marek Edelman*, 40–41.
236 **Trzeciak was an admirer of Hitler:** "Antysemita W Sutannie—Ksiądz Stanisław Trzeciak," lekcjareligii.pl/ksiadz-stanislaw-trzeciak.html.
236 **They only caught Marek twice:** Beres and Burnetko, *Marek Edelman*, 44.
236 **The Falanga newspaper incited:** "Polacy! Kupujcie Tylko w Firmach Chrześcijańskich," *Falanga*, April 14–17, 1938, 14, Catholic University of Lublin Archive, dlibra.kul.pl/Content/39099/41835.pdf.
236 **Now funded by Christian merchants':** Melzer, *No Way Out*, 45.
236 **In Volkovysk, pharmacist Hugon Tyminski's followers:** Berger, *Volkovysk Memorial Book*, vol. 1, 325.
236 **On May Day, a nationalist bomb:** "Day Is Tragic in Poland," *New York Times*, May 2, 1938, 3.
236 ***Thirteen Theses on the Jewish Question:*** Zimmerman, *Polish Underground and the Jews, 1939–1945*, 19; Melzer, *No Way Out*, 29–31.
237 **Bund attempted to make their own:** Melzer, *No Way Out*, 101–4.
237 **After Polish foreign minister Józef Beck:** Zimmerman, *Polish Underground and the Jews, 1939–1945*, 19.
237 **"Zionism, in point of fact":** Henryk Erlich, "Is Zionism a Liberating Democratic Movement?" in *Henryk Erlich and Victor Alter*, ed. Portnoy, 258–63.
237 **"The Zionists regard themselves":** Antony Polonsky, "The New Jewish Politics and Its Discontents," in *The Emergence of Modern Jewish Politics: Bundism and Zionism in Eastern Europe*, ed. Zvi Gitelman (University of Pittsburgh Press, 2003), 37.
238 **"If a Jewish state should arise":** Erlich, "Is Zionism a Liberating Democratic Movement?" 258–63.
238 **I found a faded poster:** "Val-Komitet fon Bund," Folder 517: Volkovysk, YIVO Center for Jewish Research.
238 **For the Histadrut's chief:** Yoav Gelber, "Zionist Policy and the Fate of European Jewry (1939–1942)," in *The Nazi Holocaust, Part 8: Bystanders to the Holocaust, Volume 2*, ed. Michael Robert Marrus (Walter de Gruyter, 2011), 582–83.
239 **According to historian Seth Anziska:** Seth Anziska, "One of Those Extremists," *London Review of Books*, July 13, 2023, lrb.co.uk/the-paper/v45/n14/seth-anziska/one-of-those-extremists.
239 ***Naye Folkstsaytung* knew:** Hodes Leivik, "Di Rikht-Linien Fon Evian," *Naye Folkstsaytung*, August 7, 1938, 3.
239 **That August, the Bundist Jacob Pat:** Yakov Pat, "A par teg in Berlin," *Naye Folkstsaytung*, August 19, 1938, 5.
240 **The Labor and Socialist International collapsed:** Braunthal, *History of the International: Volume II: 1914–1943*, 489–91.
240 **The Polish government had refused:** Pickhan, " 'That Incredible History,' " 262.
240 **To the tabloids:** Goldstein, *Twenty Years with the Jewish Labor Bund*, 370.
240 **To Chief Runge:** Goldstein, *Stars Bear Witness*, 16.
240 **That fall, Bernard got a tip:** Goldstein, *Twenty Years with the Jewish Labor Bund*, 387–89.
241 **Afraid that Germany might deport:** Lucy Dawidowicz, *The War Against the Jews: 1933–1945* (Random House, 1986), 100.
241 **Inside Germany, Polish embassy staff:** Melzer, *No Way Out*, 122.
241 **Poland's ambassador to Germany:** Melzer, *No Way Out*, 143.
241 **the Gestapo began to round up:** "Germany Deports Jews to Poland," *New York Times*, October 29, 1938, 1, 3; Dawidowicz, *War Against the Jews*, 100.
242 **Jews caught queuing:** "Polish Jews Leaders Plead for Refugees," *New York Times*, November 16, 1938, 7.
242 **Machine guns sprayed them:** Jerzy Shapiro, "Nazi Guns Forced Jews into Poland," *New York Times*, November 1, 1938, 17.

242 **thousands of deportees camped:** "Ousted Jews Find Refuge in Poland After Border Stay," *New York Times,* October 31, 1938, 1, 3; "Poland Bars Jews Deported by Reich," *New York Times,* November 2, 1938, 13; Melzer, *No Way Out,* 125.

242 **The Bund formed a help committee:** "Haynt Hoybn Zikh An In Berlin Unterhandlungen," *Naye Folkstsaytung,* November 2, 1938, 1.

242 **When *Naye Folkstsaytung* reported:** Anne-Christin Klot, "Journalism as a Weapon: Jewish Journalists from Warsaw and the Production of Knowledge During Hitler's Rise to Power in 1933 and the November Pogroms in 1938," in *New Perspectives on Kristallnacht,* ed. Steven J. Ross, Wolf Gruner, and Lisa Ansell (Purdue University Press, 2019).

242 **They raised funds, brought in doctors:** "Tsvishn di aroysgeshikte yidn fun Daytshland," *Naye Folkstsaytung,* November 20, 1938; "Hilf Far Di Aroysgeshikhte Yidn Fun Daytshland," *Naye Folkstsaytung,* November 4, 1938, 1.

243 ***Naye Folkstsaytung* covered "the horrifying pogrom":** "Der Shrekhtlekher Pogrom In Daytshland," *Naye Folkstsaytung,* November 13, 1938, 1.

243 **about the one-billion-Reichsmark fine:** "Pogromen Oyf Yidn In Daytshland," *Naye Folkstsaytung,* November 11, 1938, 1.

243 **A week after Kristallnacht, Henryk Erlich:** Henryk Erlich, "In Der Finsterer Nakht," *Naye Folkstsaytung,* November 18, 1938, 3.

243 **In the late thirties, Sam Rothbort:** "Harriet Semegram Barry's Oral History," The Yiddish Book Center, yiddishbookcenter.org/collections/oral-histories/interviews/woh-fi-0001194/harriet-semegram-barry-2019.

244 **"We struck back at every action":** Goldstein, *Stars Bear Witness,* 31.

244 **This love shone when:** Goldstein, *Twenty Years with the Jewish Labor Bund,* 392–93.

244 **They had won victories:** Nowogrodski, *Jewish Labor Bund in Poland,* 171; Melzer, *No Way Out,* 107–10.

244 **OZON representatives issued plans:** "Poles to Get Bill Restricting Jews," *New York Times,* December 5, 1938, 10.

245 **As Camus wrote later:** Albert Camus, *L'Espagne libre* (Calmann-Lévy, 1946), 9.

245 **young Warsaw Bundist Beniak Livshitz:** Y. Sh. Hertz, *Doyres Bundistn,* vol. 2, 462.

245 **Hitler invaded what was left:** Watt, *Bitter Glory,* 393.

245 **On April 28, Hitler told:** Watt, *Bitter Glory,* 400.

246 **Historian Rashid Khalidi estimates:** Rashid Khalidi, *The Hundred Years' War on Palestine* (Profile Books, 2020), 12.

246 **SS *St. Louis* departed from Hamburg:** "Voyage of the St. Louis," *Holocaust Encyclopedia,* United States Holocaust Museum, encyclopedia.ushmm.org/content/en/article/voyage-of-the-st-louis, accessed June 16, 2025.

246 **In *Naye Folkstsaytung,* Leivik Hodes wrote:** Hodis, *Biographie un Shriftn,* 111–13.

247 **Jews gave generously:** Melzer, *No Way Out,* 159–60.

247 **The pro-government newspaper *Gazeta Polska:*** Wynot, " 'A Necessary Cruelty,' " 1057.

247 **They threw the Bundist city councilman:** Pickhan, " 'That Incredible History,' " 263–64.

247 **That summer, they swept:** Melzer, *No Way Out,* 109.

247 **Even in little Volkovysk:** Berger, *Volkovysk Memorial Book,* vol. 3, 60.

247 **Morgenstern was the most popular:** Jacobs, *Bundist Counterculture in Interwar Poland,* 60.

247 **A hundred thousand workers:** *Jewish Labor Bund: 1897–1957* (International Jewish Labor Bund, 1958), 9.

247 **Eighty years later:** Email exchange with Victor Gilinsky.

247 **Every evening, Marek Edelman:** Beres and Burnetko, *Marek Edelman,* 36.

247 **Morgenstern soccer teams:** Gechtman, "Socialist Mass Politics Through Sport."

247 **Viktor Alter's wife:** "Jean Alter Obituary," *Legacy.com,* legacy.com/us/obituaries/dailycamera/name/jean-alter-obituary?id=46853117, accessed June 16, 2025.

247 **In July, Bernard Goldstein:** Goldstein, *Twenty Years with the Jewish Labor Bund,* 395–96.

248 **Erlich denounced the pact:** Johnpoll, *Politics of Futility,* 226.

248 **The government called the Bund's office:** Goldstein, *Twenty Years with the Jewish Labor Bund,* 396.

248 **"United, Strong and Ready!":** Fishman, ed., *Studies on Polish Jewry: 1919–1939,* 101.

248 **raised fortunes for the Air Force:** Fishman, ed., *Studies on Polish Jewry: 1919–1939,* 101.

248 **"At the hour when the country's":** The Jewish Telegraphic Agency Inc. to JTA Bulletin, "Polish Jews Join in Defense Work; Many Dig Trenches, Work on Sabbath," August 29, 1939.

249 **the writers at *Naye Folkstsaytung* noted:** *Naye Folkstsaytung,* August 30, 1939.

CHAPTER TWENTY: INVASION

253 **On September 1, Warsaw's Yiddish daily:** *Haynt,* September 1, 1939.

253 **1.8 million German troops:** Zimmerman, *Polish Underground and the Jews, 1939–1945,* 38.

253 **and striking sixty cities:** David Klin, *À cache-cache avec la mort: Un résistant juif à Varsovie de 1939 à 1945* (Éditions Le Manuscrit, 2017), 33.

253 **In *Naye Folkstsaytung,* Henryk Erlich:** Portnoy, ed., *Henryk Erlich and Victor Alter,* 71.

253 **with tricolors and union jacks:** "Scenes in Warsaw During First Few Days After Hitler Declared War and Sent Troops into Poland," *New York Times,* September 17, 1939, 46.

253 **They burned their documents:** Aviva Ravel, *Faithful unto Death: The Story of Arthur Zygielbojm* (Arthur Zygielbojm Branch, Workmen's Circle, 1980), 50.

253 **The luxury shops:** For vivid visuals of Warsaw during the siege, see Aleksandra Janiszewska, *The Colors of War: The Siege of Warsaw in Julien Bryan's Color Photographs* (Karta Center, 2010).

254 **The mix of lies and truth:** Klin, *À cache-cache avec la mort*, 35.

254 ***Naye Folkstsaytung*'s correspondent Pinkhos Schwartz:** Daniel Blatman, *For Our Freedom and Yours: The Jewish Labor Bund in Poland, 1939–1949* (Vallentine Mitchell, 2003), 2–3; letter from Maurycy Orzech to Emanuel Nowogrodski, September 28, 1939.

254 **But how could they fight:** Goldstein, *Stars Bear Witness*, 27.

254 **Orzech consulted with Polish Socialist Party:** Letter from Maurycy Orzech to Emanuel Nowogrodski, September 28, 1939.

254 **Over at city hall:** Letter from Maurycy Orzech to Emanuel Nowogrodski, September 28, 1939.

254 **The next morning, Alter and Erlich:** Blatman, *For Our Freedom and Yours*, 3–4; letter from Maurycy Orzech to Emanuel Nowogrodski, September 28, 1939.

255 **Alter wanted to lead:** Lucjan Blit, "Henryk Erlich and Victor Alter in Soviet Russia," in *Henryk Erlich and Victor Alter*, ed. Portnoy, 89–91.

255 **Around six hundred party members:** Blatman, *For Our Freedom and Yours*, 4.

255 **Newspaper headlines screamed:** Blit, "Henryk Erlich and Victor Alter in Soviet Russia," 90.

255 **In the Erlich apartment:** Dubnova-Erlich, *Bread and Matzoh*, 246–47.

255 **That night, Colonel Roman Umiastowski:** J. Biskupska, *Survivors: Warsaw Under Nazi Occupation* (Cambridge University Press, 2022), 35–36.

255 **The Erlichs made their way:** Dubnova-Erlich, *Bread and Matzoh*, 247.

256 **On September 8, just before midnight:** Ravel, *Faithful unto Death*, 47–48.

256 **One of a dozen children:** For Zygielbojm's pre-war biography, see Ravel, *Faithful unto Death*, 13–44.

256 **in the lissome women:** For an account of Zygielbojm's womanizing, see Lucy Dawidowicz, *From That Place and Time: A Memoir, 1938–1947* (W. W. Norton, 1989), 216.

256 **Zygmunt Zaremba gave him an earful:** Letter from Arthur Zygielbojm to Emanuel Nowogrodski, February 10, 1940, private collection of Brian Gocial.

256 **fight alongside the 140,000 troops:** "Robotnicza Brygada Obrony Warszawy We Wrszeszniu 1939 Roku," PolskieRadio24.pl., September 6, 2023, polskieradio.pl/39/156/artykul/1498966,robotnicza-brygada-obrony-warszawy-we-wrzesniu-1939-roku.ho.

257 **Instead, the Bund sent thousands:** Letter from Arthur Zygielbojm to Emanuel Nowogrodski, February 10, 1940, private collection of Brian Gocial; Zygmunt Zaremba, *Obrona Warszawy: wrzesień 1939 roku* (Komitet Zagraniczny PPS, 1941), 15.

257 **When he was not coordinating defense:** Johnpoll, *Politics of Futility*, 227–28.

257 **Their journalists instructed:** "Di Lage Oyf Di Frontn," *Naye Folkstsaytung*, September 16, 1939, 1, 2; "Meldungen," *Naye Folkstsaytung*, September 9, 1939, 1, 2; "Perzonen, Gezukht dorkh Kiruvim," *Naye Folkstsaytung*, September 9, 1939, 1, 2, all Centralna Biblioteka Judaistyczna.

257 **fighters could request necessities:** Ravel, *Faithful unto Death*, 51.

257 **A tight little crew began to emerge:** Klin, *À cache-cache avec la mort: Un résistant juif à Varsovie de 1939 à 1945*, 37–38; letter from Arthur Zygielbojm to Emanuel Nowogrodski, February 10, 1940, private collection of Brian Gocial.

257 **Warsaw filled with refugees:** Biskupska, *Survivors*, 32.

257 **Sonia Nowogrodska organized a kitchen:** Klin, *À cache-cache avec la mort*, 38–40.

257 **Zygielbojm organized Tsukunft members:** Ravel, *Faithful unto Death*, 49.

257 **they collected buckets of sand:** Emmanuel Ringelblum, *Polish-Jewish Relations During the Second World War* (Yad Vashem, 1974), 26.

257 **Erlich's group spent nine days:** Erlich, *Child of a Turbulent Century*, 52.

257 ***Can you believe it's the attorney:*** Portnoy, ed., *Henryk Erlich and Victor Alter*, 84.

258 **In tiny Miedzyrzec:** Goldstein, *Stars Bear Witness*, 28–29; Portnoy, ed., *Henryk Erlich and Victor Alter*, 72.

258 **Their first night back on the road:** Portnoy, ed., *Henryk Erlich and Victor Alter*, 82.

258 **on the eve of Rosh Hashanah:** Klin, *À cache-cache avec la mort*, 43.

258 **The *Naye Folkstsaytung* editors moved:** Klin, *À cache-cache avec la mort*, 43–44.

258 **The city gasworks were shut:** Goldstein, *Stars Bear Witness*, 32.

258 **Every day, the crew cranked out:** Klin, *À cache-cache avec la mort*, 43.

258 **In one article, Zygielbojm described:** "Zayt Bombes Hobn Zikh Gebamblt," *Naye Folkstsaytung*, September 16, 1939, translation of the operetta by Marvin Zuckerman.

259 **On the night of September 16:** Erlich, *Child of a Turbulent Century*, 54.

259 **It was Vyacheslav Molotov:** "The Speech on Radio of the Chairman of the Soviet of People's Comissars of the U.S.S.R. Comrade V. M. Molotov September 17, 1939," October 1939, histdoc.net/history/molotov_radio_17091939.html.

259 **That day, the entire national government:** Zimmerman, *Polish Underground and the Jews, 1939–1945*, 38.

260 **Since the war started, the mood:** Berger, *Volkovysk Memorial Book*, vol. 1, 328–29.

260 **The night was long and vile:** Berger, *Volkovysk Memorial Book*, vol. 3, 62.

260 **the Bundist shoemaker Meir Zeleviansky:** Berger, *Volkovysk Memorial Book*, vol. 1, 329.

261 **There were even a few Bundists:** Erlich, *Child of a Turbulent Century*, 54.

261 **His comrade Joseph Rothenberg:** Portnoy, ed., *Henryk Erlich and Victor Alter*, 93.

261 **His son Victor believed:** Erlich, *Child of a Turbulent Century*, 55.

261 **The Grand Theatre was gone:** "Polish Radio Thanks Nazis for Razing Ugly Buildings," *New York Times,* September 10, 1939, 46.
261 **Polish socialists begged the British Labour Party:** "Defiant Warsaw Still Repels Foe," *New York Times,* September 21, 1939, 6.
261 **Mayor Starzynski begged:** "Defiant Warsaw Still Repels Foe."
262 ***Naye Folkstsaytung* shut down:** Blatman, *For Our Freedom and Yours,* 7–8.
262 **adolescent boys:** "Defiant Warsaw Still Repels Foe," 6.
262 **Mayor Starzynski and Major General Michal Tomaszewski:** Zimmerman, *Polish Underground and the Jews, 1939–1945,* 49.
262 **Only the Polish socialist leader Mek:** Johnpoll, *Politics of Futility,* 228.
262 **When the Nazis entered Warsaw:** Goldstein, *Stars Bear Witness,* 33.
262 **The real Henryk Erlich was elsewhere:** Portnoy, ed., *Henryk Erlich and Victor Alter,* 73–78.
262 **Viktor Alter had never made it:** Portnoy, ed., *Henryk Erlich and Victor Alter,* 72–73.
263 **Berman begged Erlich:** Portnoy, ed., *Henryk Erlich and Victor Alter,* 73–78.

CHAPTER TWENTY-ONE: OCCUPATION

264 **When Bernard Goldstein returned:** Goldstein, *Stars Bear Witness,* 30.
264 **German bombs had leveled 10 percent:** "Phoenix from the Ashes: A Short Story of Warsaw That Was Destroyed and Rebuilt," The Warsaw Rising Museum, April 26, 2024, 1944.pl/en/article/phoenix-from-the-ashes.-a-short-story-of-warsaw,5482.html.
264 **Bernard moved back:** Goldstein, *Stars Bear Witness,* 33.
264 **At the corners of Marszalkowska Street:** Jan Karski, *Story of a Secret State* (Houghton Mifflin Company, 1944), 52.
264 **Bundist councilwoman Esther Iwinska:** Ravel, *Faithful unto Death,* 53; Goldstein, *Stars Bear Witness,* 32.
264 **The Gestapo installed itself:** Ravel, *Faithful unto Death,* 62.
265 **Many Poles appeared to approve:** Klin, *À cache-cache avec la mort,* 47; Goldstein, *Stars Bear Witness,* 34.
265 **as Martinican philosopher Aimé Césaire:** See Aimé Césaire, *Discourse on Colonialism* (Monthly Review Press, 2001).
265 **arrested the interim chairman:** Ravel, *Faithful unto Death,* 55–56.
265 **Judenrat was a classic colonial device:** Dawidowicz, *War Against the Jews,* 119.
266 **Because the Germans already knew Zygielbojm:** Klin, *À cache-cache avec la mort,* 52.
266 **the Bund rebuilt within two weeks:** Johnpoll, *Politics of Futility,* 228–30.
266 **That October, twenty Bundists met:** Ravel, *Faithful unto Death,* 54.
266 **tearooms and soup kitchens:** Dawidowicz, *War Against the Jews,* 265.
266 **establish illegal trade unions:** Johnpoll, *Politics of Futility,* 228–30.
266 **As for Bernard:** Goldstein, *Stars Bear Witness,* 43; letter from Arthur Zygielbojm to Emanuel Nowogrodski, February 10, 1940, private collection of Brian Gocial.
266 **the dour officer refused:** Erlich, *Child of a Turbulent Century,* 55.
267 **the Soviets rounded up hundreds:** Camille Huysmans, "Memorial Meeting in London for the Executed Henryk Erlich and Victor Alter," *The Ghetto Speaks,* no. 12, June 1, 1943, 8.
267 **The seventy-year-old leader Anna Rozental:** Blatman, *For Our Freedom and Yours,* 17.
267 **YIVO director Zalman Reisen:** Herman Kruk, *The Last Days of the Jerusalem of Lithuania: Chronicles from the Vilna Ghetto and the Camps* (Yale University Press, 2002), xxxix.
267 **Arrests gobbled up the Bund's leadership:** Jacob Celemenski, *Elegy for My People* (Jacob Celemenski Memorial Trust, 2000), 6.
267 **down with the reptile traitors:** Gennady Estraikh, *Transatlantic Russian Jewishness: Ideological Voyages of the Yiddish Daily* Forverts *in the First Half of the Twentieth Century* (Academic Studies Press, 2020), 255.
267 **The two thousand Bundists who fled:** Blatman, *For Our Freedom and Yours,* 15.
267 **Shloyme Gilinsky's son Victor:** Email from Victor Gilinsky, March 13, 2024.
267 **"The sea overflowed and flooded Vilna":** Kruk, *Last Days of the Jerusalem of Lithuania,* 28–32.
267 **The Bundists argued:** Blatman, *For Our Freedom and Yours,* 25.
268 **That year, they published a declaration:** Dawidowicz, *War Against the Jews,* 267.
268 **To stay with comrades, wrote Kruk:** Kruk, *Last Days of the Jerusalem of Lithuania,* 32.
268 **For money, they turned:** Blatman, *For Our Freedom and Yours,* 121–22; Collomp, *Résister au Nazisme,* 95.
268 **even secured pricey British visas:** Collomp, *Résister au Nazisme,* 97; Blatman, *For Our Freedom and Yours,* 20.
268 **They even managed to publish:** Kruk, *Last Days of the Jerusalem of Lithuania,* 45.
268 **Pati wrote the first essay:** *Arkady: Zamlbukh Tsum Ondenk Fun Grinder Fun "Bund" Arkady Kremer,* 65–70.
268 **the couple returned to Vilna:** Y. Sh. Hertz, *Doyres Bundistn,* vol. 1, 134.
268 **She wrote to the Bundist pioneer:** Y. Sh. Hertz, *Doyres Bundistn,* vol. 1, 136.
268 **Nazis killed forty-three thousand Poles:** Zimmerman, *Polish Underground and the Jews, 1939–1945,* 48.
269 **The veteran radical looked:** Karski, *Story of a Secret State,* 130.
269 **unable to add numbers:** Zimmerman, *Polish Underground and the Jews, 1939–1945,* 48.
269 **banned Poles from libraries:** Ludwik Hirszfeld, *The Story of One Life* (University of Rochester Press, 2010), 179.

269 **Still, *The New York Times*'s:** "Visitor Finds Life in Warsaw Easier," *New York Times,* January 14, 1940, 34.
269 **At Zygielbojm's urging, Mayor Starzynski:** Klin, *À cache-cache avec la mort,* 51.
269 **bury the bodies of resistance members:** Klin, *À cache-cache avec la mort,* 60.
269 **Zygielbojm saw them:** Ravel, *Faithful unto Death,* 61.
269 **provided sixty thousand meals a day:** "Gives 60,000 Meals Daily," *New York Times,* February 25, 1940, 34.
270 **The Bund ran their own:** Zygielbojm letter to Nowogrodski, Febuary 10, 1940, private Collection of Brian Gocial.
270 **Building councils collected supplies:** Yisrael Gutman, *The Jews of Warsaw: Ghetto, Underground, Revolt* (Indiana University Press, 1982), 45–46.
270 **they sent their children:** Goldstein, *Stars Bear Witness,* 38–42.
270 **Zygielbojm watched one teenage soap-seller:** Ravel, *Faithful unto Death,* 76.
270 **The Germans had seized:** Johnpoll, *Politics of Futility,* 229.
270 **Marek Edelman worked the machine:** Beres and Burnetko, *Marek Edelman,* 58.
271 **The Bund's delegate to the Judenrat:** Ravel, *Faithful unto Death,* 81–85.
271 **Rumor of the ghetto spread:** Dawidowicz, *War Against the Jews,* 204–5; Goldstein, *Stars Bear Witness,* 36–38.
271 **ten thousand desperate people:** Johnpoll, *Politics of Futility,* 231–32.
271 **"It is the total readiness":** Ravel, *Faithful unto Death,* 174.
271 **At first, some Poles:** Gutman, *Jews of Warsaw,* 30.
271 **two young men arrived:** Ravel, *Faithful unto Death,* 71–72.
272 **the Polish fireman's band:** "Jews' Plight Held Critical in Poland," *New York Times,* December 10, 1939, 56.
272 **Zygielbojm met a Bundist woman:** Ravel, *Faithful unto Death,* 72.
272 **The Bund organized their displaced members:** Klin, *À cache-cache avec la mort,* 49.
272 **"The water began to boil":** Ravel, *Faithful unto Death,* 93–94.
272 **a Polish socialist comrade:** Ravel, *Faithful unto Death,* 95, 98.
272 **On his last night in Warsaw:** Klin, *À cache-cache avec la mort,* 69–71; Goldstein, *Stars Bear Witness,* 38.
273 **"So, my friend, tomorrow":** Ravel, *Faithful unto Death,* 95–96.
273 **Klara Zachariasz of Tomaszow:** Celemenski, *Elegy for My People,* 78.
273 **"You not only look":** Celemenski, *Elegy for My People,* 11.
273 **Sitting in Bernard Goldstein's shabby quarters:** Celemenski, *Elegy for My People,* 14–15.
273 **Each member swore loyalty:** Dawidowicz, *War Against the Jews,* 265, 277.
273 **Money from New York Bundists:** Blatman, *For Our Freedom and Yours,* 20.
273 **They also moved money:** Goldstein, *Stars Bear Witness,* 50.
273 **organized an expansive underground school system:** Johnpoll, *Politics of Futility,* 229–30.
274 **After the Nazis sealed:** Goldstein, *Stars Bear Witness,* 49.
274 **Their representatives showed up:** Ravel, *Faithful unto Death,* 89.
274 **They even reopened the Medem Sanatorium:** Letter from Arthur Zygielbojm to Emanuel Nowogrodski, February 10, 1940, private collection of Brian Gocial; Hayyim Solomon Kazdan, *Medem-Sanatorye-bukh* (Ha-menorah, 1971), 67–68.
274 **Through it all, the Bund remained close:** Letter from Arthur Zygielbojm to Emanuel Nowogrodski, February 10, 1940, private collection of Brian Gocial.
274 **leaders of the two parties:** Celemenski, *Elegy for My People,* 24–25.
274 **In one May Day proclamation:** Karski, *Story of a Secret State,* 128.
274 **Jewish workers fought back:** Ringelblum, *Polish-Jewish Relations During the Second World War,* 52; Celemenski, *Elegy for My People,* 16–18.
274 **Other Poles seldom intervened:** Ringelblum, *Polish-Jewish Relations During the Second World War,* 37.
274 **Where was the church:** Ringelblum, *Polish-Jewish Relations During the Second World War,* 52.
274 **The Polish underground press sometimes warned:** Zimmerman, *Polish Underground and the Jews, 1939–1945,* 72.
274 **the Polish woman who warned Zygielbojm:** Ravel, *Faithful unto Death,* 102.
275 **On March 22, a glittering, frosty:** Klin, *À cache-cache avec la mort,* 63–64; Goldstein, *Stars Bear Witness,* 51–54.
275 **Teamsters, water carriers, coalmen:** Beres and Burnetko, *Marek Edelman,* 60.
275 **"So-called Polish antisemitism":** Beres and Burnetko, *Marek Edelman,* 65.
276 **Twenty walls had gone up:** Gutman, *Jews of Warsaw,* 50–51.
276 **In April, Arthur Zygielbojm arrived:** Ravel, *Faithful unto Death,* 162; letter from Arthur Zygielbojm to Emanuel Nowogrodski, February 10, 1940, private collection of Brian Gocial.
276 **the buxom chick:** Ravel, *Faithful unto Death,* 128–29.
276 **he calmly presented:** Ravel, *Faithful unto Death,* 165.
276 **they did nothing:** Braunthal, *History of the International: Volume II: 1914–1943,* 491.
276 **"When Paris ends the world ends":** Victor Serge, *Memoirs of a Revolutionary* (1963; repr. New York Review Books, 2012), 416.
276 **The Bund's stalwart archivist:** Web, "Between New York and Moscow: The Fate of the Bund Archives," 249.
276 **"we former revolutionaries are utterly beaten":** Serge, *Memoirs of a Revolutionary,* 422.
277 **American journalist Varian Fry:** Collomp, *Résister au Nazisme,* 116.
277 **The leaders of defeated socialist movements:** Collomp, *Résister au Nazisme,* 104–12.

277 **Back in New York, Nowogrodski and:** Wyman, *Paper Walls,* 138; Collomp, *Résister au Nazisme,* 104.
277 **admirer of *Mein Kampf*:** "Those Eighteen Terrible Months," Antisemitism: The Fight in World War Two America Podcast, National World War II Museum, New Orleans, nationalww2museum.org/war/podcasts/antisemitism-fight-wwii-america/episode-4-those-terrible-18-months.
277 **Father Coughlin demonized Jews:** Collomp, *Résister au Nazisme,* 43–44.
277 **In Congress, one Southern senator bellowed:** Wyman, *Paper Walls,* 11.
277 **Afraid of backlash, even American Jewish:** Wyman, *Paper Walls,* 37.
277 **in Hotel Regina in Toulouse:** Collomp, *Résister au Nazisme,* 274, 106.
277 **He was the Jewish Labor Committee's:** Raphael Abramovich, "Genose Abramovich Dertsaylt Vi Azoy Er Hot Zikh Aroysgeratavet Fun Frankraykh," *Forverts,* September 11, 1940, 2–3; Raphael Abramovich, "Genose Abramovich Dertsaylt Vi Azoy Er Hot Zikh Aroysgeratavet Fun Frankraykh," *Forverts,* September 12, 1940, 3, 8; Raphael Abramovich, "Genose Abramovich Dertsaylt Vi Azoy Er Hot Zikh Aroysgeratavet Fun Frankraykh," *Forverts,* September 13, 1940; Raphael Abramovich, "Genose Abramovich Dertsaylt Vi Azoy Er Hot Zikh Aroysgeratavet Fun Frankraykh," *Forverts,* September 14, 1940, 3; Raphael Abramovich, "Di Tragishe Nacht Ven Frankraykh Hot Zikh Undergegebn," *Forverts,* September 16, 1940.
278 **Chaim Fizshitz:** Blatman, *For Our Freedom and Yours,* 27.
278 **Sophia and her sons:** Erlich, *Child of a Turbulent Century,* 63.
279 **Sugihara calligraphed forms for twenty hours:** Hillel Levine, *In Search of Sugihara: The Elusive Japanese Diplomat Who Risked His Life to Rescue 10,000 Jews from the Holocaust* (Free Press, 1996), 4.
279 **Armed with false papers:** Erlich, *Child of a Turbulent Century,* 67–70.
279 **whom the Jewish Labor Committee bribed out:** Collomp, *Résister au Nazisme,* 106–7.
279 **the Jewish Labor Committee could pay enough:** Frank Wolff, *Yiddish Revolutionaries in Migration: The Transnational History of the Jewish Labor Bund* (Haymarket Books, 2022), 382.
280 **The 113,000 Poles:** "Daily Life in The Warsaw Ghetto," Imperial War Museums, iwm.org.uk/history/daily-life-in-the-warsaw-ghetto, accessed July 1, 2025; Gutman, *Jews of Warsaw,* 60.
280 **Most Poles didn't resist:** Gutman, *Jews of Warsaw,* 56–58.
280 **"The burden of all wars":** Gutman, *Jews of Warsaw,* 56.

CHAPTER TWENTY-TWO: DIVIDED CITY

281 **The Bund tried to cope:** Goldstein, *Stars Bear Witness,* 65–67.
281 **"In its unfinished chain":** Zimmerman, *Polish Underground and the Jews, 1939–1945,* 80.
281 **"The astounded gendarmes saw Aryans":** Ringelblum, *Polish-Jewish Relations During the Second World War,* 89.
281 **"All houses vacated by Jews":** Beres and Burnetko, *Marek Edelman,* 67.
282 **There were more Jews:** Mooli Brog, "From the Top of Masada to the Bottom of the Ghetto," in *Myth and Memory: Transfigurations of Israeli Consciousness,* ed. David Ohana and Robert Wistrich (Van Leer Institute Press, 1996), 203–27.
282 **People slept everywhere:** Goldstein, *Stars Bear Witness,* 65.
282 **Eighty members of the Warsaw Philharmonic:** Brzezinski, *Isaac's Army,* 113.
283 **there was Hamlet:** Marek Edelman, *The Guardian: Edelman Speaks,* translated by E. P. Kulawiec, unpublished manuscript courtesy of Paula Sawicka, 16.
283 **whose soup kitchens:** Gutman, *Jews of Warsaw,* 103–4.
283 **The Germans planned a population density:** Gutman, *Jews of Warsaw,* 60.
283 **Marek Edelman watched his Tsukunft comrade:** Edelman, *Guardian,* 16.
283 **tended to by one Father Godlewski:** Edelman, *Guardian,* 17.
283 **Jewish communists celebrated:** Gutman, *Jews of Warsaw,* 129.
283 **lounge chairs that entrepreneurs dragged:** Gutman, *Jews of Warsaw,* 111.
283 **"Every dance is a protest":** Beres and Burnetko, *Marek Edelman,* 82.
283 **Germans created the Jewish Police:** Gutman, *Jews of Warsaw,* 86–90.
284 **The Bund forbade its members:** Goldstein, *Stars Bear Witness,* 68.
284 **"Occasionally a young officer":** Ludwik Hirszfeld, *The Story of One Life* (University of Rochester Press, 2010), 193.
284 **they refused, citing ideological incompatibility:** Samuel Kassow, *Who Will Write Our History?* (Vintage, 2009), 148.
284 **Instead, the Bund compiled:** Edelman, *Guardian,* 16, 100.
284 **a Lovecraftian architecture of bunkers:** Goldstein, *Stars Bear Witness,* 75–79.
284 **A Jewish bridge passed over:** Goldstein, *Stars Bear Witness,* 81.
284 **Writer Rachel Auerbach called:** Jan Darsa, *The Jews of Poland* (Facing History and Ourselves National Foundation, Inc., 1998), 155.
285 **souk on Gesia Street:** Ringelblum, *Polish-Jewish Relations During the Second World War,* 74.
285 **the Gestapo shot a Pole:** Ringelblum, *Polish-Jewish Relations During the Second World War,* 80.
285 **There were the Jewish workers:** Hirszfeld, *Story of One Life,* 194.
285 **Then there were the professional smugglers:** Gutman, *Jews of Warsaw,* 68–69.
285 **Poles brought in raw materials:** Joseph Kermish, *To Live with Honor and Die with Honor* (Yad Vashem, 1986), 146–51; Ringelblum, *Polish-Jewish Relations During the Second World War,* 65.
285 **the new cabarets:** John and Bogdana Carpenter, "Introduction to the Work of Wladyslaw Szlengel," *Manhattan Review* 15, no. 2 (Fall–Winter 2012–2013); Goldstein, *Stars Bear Witness,* 70, 91.

285 **at the brothel Britannia:** Beres and Burnetko, *Marek Edelman*, 81.
285 **There, exquisite Vera Gran sang:** Janusz Kowalczyk, "Wiera Gran," *Culture.pl*, April 2013, culture.pl/en/artist/wiera-gran.
285 **Since his Nowolipie Street apartment:** Goldstein, *Stars Bear Witness*, 86.
286 **Marek taught kids to sing:** Edelman, *Guardian*, 15.
286 **"In order to defend ourselves":** Goldstein, *Stars Bear Witness*, 85.
286 **party kitchens and tea halls:** General Jewish Workers' Union "Bund" in Poland, *In di yorn fun Yidishn hurbn di shtim fun untererdishn Bund*, 14.
286 **They ran libraries out of couriers':** Dawidowicz, *War Against the Jews*, 258.
286 **In the courtyards, Tsukunft assembled:** Blatman, *For Our Freedom and Yours*, 47.
286 **They issued a pamphlet:** Dawidowicz, *War Against the Jews*, 272.
286 **The Bund ran secret printshops:** General Jewish Workers' Union "Bund" in Poland, *In di yorn fun Yidishn hurbn di shtim fun untererdishn Bund*, 332.
286 **The most important rule:** Dawidowicz, *War Against the Jews*, 269–70.
287 **In their op-eds, Bundists agitated:** Dawidowicz, *War Against the Jews*, 272–73.
287 **"We stand fast in favor":** General Jewish Workers' Union "Bund" in Poland, *In di yorn fun Yidishn hurbn di shtim fun untererdishn Bund*, 19.
287 **"prisoners of the ideology":** Edelman, *Guardian*, 16.
287 **In *Neged Hazerem:*** Joseph Kermish and Tikva Fatal-Knaani, eds., *The Jewish Underground Press in Warsaw*, vol. 2 (Yad Vashem Publications, 2017), 69.
287 **When Zionist youth cut a deal:** Gutman, *Jews of Warsaw*, 140.
287 **On the farms, they had milk:** Yitzhak Zuckerman, *A Surplus of Memory: Chronicle of the Warsaw Ghetto Uprising* (University of California Press, 1993), 67.
287 **"We are surrounded by mighty walls":** Blatman, *For Our Freedom and Yours*, 46.
288 **old friends like:** Goldstein, *Stars Bear Witness*, 48; Johnpoll, *Politics of Futility*, 232.
288 **An industry of professional blackmailers:** Klin, *À cache-cache avec la mort*, 64–65.
288 **a melina was considered "burned":** Ringelblum, *Polish-Jewish Relations During the Second World War*, 119.
288 **One of the first Bundists to:** Klin, *À cache-cache avec la mort*, 90–91.
289 **When they launched a new Polish:** Beres and Burnetko, *Marek Edelman*, 91.
289 **On January 17, 1941, the Jewish Labor:** Catherine Collomp, "The Jewish Labor Committee, American Labor, and the Rescue of European Socialists, 1934–1941," *International Labor and Working-Class History*, no. 68; Collomp, *Résistir au Nazisme*, 127–30.
289 **Archivist Lucy Dawidowicz remembered him:** Dawidowicz, *From That Place and Time*, 216.
289 **the Jewish Labor Committee's beneficiaries disembarked:** Erlich, *Child of a Turbulent Century*, 72–77.
290 **pulled into the port of Tsuruga:** Erlich, *Child of a Turbulent Century*, 77–78.
291 **"spit out soup":** Beres and Burnetko, *Marek Edelman*, 82.
291 **The Bund's newspaper reported:** *Biulitan*, April 14, 1941; *Biulitan*, May 16, 1941.
291 **"Be well. Be careful":** Celemenski, *Elegy for My People*, 46–47.
291 **His arrest terrified his Tsukunft comrades:** Blatman, *For Our Freedom and Yours*, 97.
291 **One afternoon, Maurycy Orzech:** Celemenski, *Elegy for My People*, 91; Goldstein, *Stars Bear Witness*, 71.
291 **Soon afterward, two young Jewish men:** Celemenski, *Elegy for My People*, 94; Goldstein, *Stars Bear Witness*, 94.
292 **Bernard only broke the rules:** Goldstein, *Stars Bear Witness*, 96–97.
292 **In June, the Bund's courier Celemenski:** Celemenski, *Elegy for My People*, 45–47, 95.
293 **He described the arguments:** Celemenski, *Elegy for My People*, 52.
293 **in the town of Piotrkow-Trybunalski:** Celemenski, *Elegy for My People*, 68–72.
293 **In Miedzyrzec, an illegal brush maker's:** Celemenski, *Elegy for My People*, 48.
293 **the Bundist councilwoman Bella Shapiro:** Celemenski, *Elegy for My People*, 61–63.
293 **In Bedzin, he met the Bundist pioneer:** Celemenski, *Elegy for My People*, 39–40.
293 **dropped off beforehand by Jadwiga Wisniewska:** Celemenski, *Elegy for My People*, 96–97, 100–103.
293 **Celemenski learned the reason:** Celemenski, *Elegy for My People*, 79–80.

CHAPTER TWENTY-THREE: BARBAROSSA

295 **nationalized Avram's little leather tannery:** Berger, *Volkovysk Memorial Book*, vol. 1, 330.
295 **the town's new masters had renamed:** Bychowcew and Hawrylik-Kuklinska, *Wolkowysk*, 228.
295 **Shlomo Markus now headed:** Berger, *Volkovysk Memorial Book*, vol. 3, 62.
295 **"there was no longer any antisemitism":** Berger, *Volkovysk Memorial Book*, vol. 1, 331.
295 **new airstrip the Russians were building:** Berger, *Volkovysk Memorial Book*, vol. 1, 331–32.
296 **the Tiferet Bakhurim Synagogue:** Bychowcew and Hawrylik-Kuklinska, *Wolkowysk*, 57.
296 **"Entire streets were ringed with fire":** Berger, *Volkovysk Memorial Book*, vol. 1, 335.
296 **my distant relative Joseph Beckenstein:** Berger, *Volkovysk Memorial Book*, vol. 1, 333.
296 **Shlomo Markus worked in the hospital:** Berger, *Volkovysk Memorial Book*, vol. 3, 62.
296 **sat the old Bundist shoemaker Zeleviansky:** Berger, *Volkovysk Memorial Book*, vol. 3, 422.
297 **the small Lithuanian town of Gargzdai:** Blatman, *For Our Freedom and Yours*, 90.
297 **Lithuanian partisans stormed:** Ephraim Oshry, *Annihilation of Lithuanian Jewry* (Judaica Press, 1995), 3.
297 **the Bundist librarian Herman Kruk:** Kruk, *Last Days of The Jerusalem of Lithuania*, 46–48, 309–10.

298 **Weeks later, a Latvian collaborator:** Dubnova-Erlich, *Bread and Matzoh*, 252.
298 **Nazis took Volkovysk on June 28:** Berger, *Volkovysk Memorial Book*, vol. 1, 338–42.
298 **local Bundist leader Avram Markus:** Berger, *The Volkovysk Memorial Book*, vol. 1, 341.
298 **Sophia Dubnova's ship, the *Heian Maru*:** Erlich, *Child of a Turbulent Century*, 81.
299 **Jews were arrogant con men:** Piotr Długołęcki, ed., *Confronting the Holocaust: Documents on the Polish Government-in-Exile's Policy Concerning Jews 1939–1945* (Polski Instytut Spraw Miedzynadowowych, 2022), 263–64.
299 **a telegram appeared in *The Forward*:** "Bafrite Firer Fon Yidishe Sotsialisten In Poiln Rufn Tsu Gemeynzamen Gegn Nazis," *Forverts*, September 21, 1941, 1.
299 **Erlich tried to explain himself:** Pickhan, " 'That Incredible History,' " 248, 251–54.
299 **the NKVD chief Lavrentiy Beria:** Johnpoll, *Politics of Futility*, 238.
299 **Some months into his imprisonment:** Abraham Finesilver, "With Comrade Erlich in Soviet Prisons," in *Henryk Erlich and Victor Alter*, ed. Portnoy, 119; Pickhan, " 'That Incredible History,' " 257–72.
300 **they handed him a prewritten confession:** Finesilver, "With Comrade Erlich in Soviet Prisons," 122.
300 **At first, Abraham Finesilver didn't recognize:** Finesilver, "With Comrade Erlich in Soviet Prisons," 123.
301 **At night, he talked to himself:** Erlich, *Child of a Turbulent Century*, 84–85.
301 **campaign led by Bundist refugees:** Blatman, *For Our Freedom and Yours*, 71; Portnoy, ed., *Henryk Erlich and Victor Alter*, 165.
301 **The NKVD released Erlich:** Lucan Way, "Exhuming the Buried Past: In the KGB Files," *The Nation*, March 1, 1993.
302 **he maintained a sardonic silence:** Portnoy, ed., *Henryk Erlich and Victor Alter*, 237; Pickhan, " 'That Incredible History,' " 254–55.
302 **Alter was back among the living:** Portnoy, ed., *Henryk Erlich and Victor Alter*, 182, 179.
302 **an NKVD bigwig named Colonel Volkovysky:** Johnpoll, *Politics of Futility*, 238; Erlich, *Child of a Turbulent Century*, 87.
303 **the Jewish Antifascist Committee:** "A Call to Arms," *The Ghetto Speaks*, no. 3, September 1, 1942, 3.
303 **Dubnova received the letter:** Erlich, *Child of a Turbulent Century*, 84–85.
304 **"We have been physically separated":** "Who in Poland Is Helping Hitler," *Za Nasza I Wasza Wolność*, no. 7, October 1941.
304 **"close their eyes":** Quoted in Beres and Burnetko, *Marek Edelman*, 108.
304 **They were painfully aware:** Beres and Burnetko, *Marek Edelman*, 73, 91.
304 **"Poland was never a hotel":** Kermish and Fatal-Knaani, eds., *Jewish Underground Press in Warsaw*, vol. 2, 78.
304 **In October, two thousand Warsaw ghetto:** Blatman, *For Our Freedom and Yours*, 45.
304 **"the remains of our dear grandfather":** Henokh Rus, *Book of Minutes of the Underground Youth Organization "Tsukunft" in the Warsaw Ghetto, January 1941–July 1942*, unpublished manuscript and translation, courtesy of Brian Gocial.
304 **Norbert Barlicki:** "Norberd Berlinski, Herman Liberman," *Tsayt-Frage*, no. 3, December 1941.
304 **intellectual Kazimierz Czapinski:** "Kazhimiezh Tchapinski," *Tsayt-Frage*, no. 3, December 1941.
304 **theories of Sigmund Freud:** "Zigmund Froyd," *Tsayt-Frage*, no. 3, December 1941.
304 **Indian writer Rabindranath Tagore:** "Rabindranat Tagore," *Tsayt-Frage*, no. 3, December 1941.
304 **"They disregarded Japan's acts":** Kermish and Fatal-Knaani, eds., *The Jewish Underground Press in Warsaw*, vol. 2, 237.
305 **"It is the Hitlerites' attempt":** Kermish and Fatal-Knaani, eds. *The Jewish Underground Press in Warsaw*, vol. 2, 634.
305 **"We must declare a fight":** Beres and Burnetko, *Marek Edelman*, 96–98, 100.
305 **Their boots were needed:** "Kuibyshow and Why It Became the USSR Capital," *The Argus Week-end Magazine*, May 2, 1942, 3, trove.nla.gov.au/newspaper/article/11974382.
305 **Viktor Alter relished his return:** Blatman, *For Our Freedom and Yours*, 78–80.
305 **Ksawery Pruszynski, a conservative writer:** Ksawery Pruszyński, "Two Men," in *Henryk Erlich and Victor Alter*, ed. Portnoy, 156–60.
306 **no military motives:** Długołęcki, ed., *Confronting the Holocaust*, 253.
306 **Anders ordered his enlistment offices:** Israel Gutman, "Jews in General Anders' Army in the Soviet Union," Yad Vashem, yadvashem.org/articles/academic/jews-anders-army.html.
306 **Meanwhile, a group of Revisionist Zionists:** Długołęcki, ed., *Confronting the Holocaust*, 253.
306 **troubling reports from Jews:** Blit, "Henryk Erlich and Victor Alter in Soviet Russia," 103.
306 **"Those are isolated incidents!":** Długołęcki, ed., *Confronting the Holocaust*, 254.
306 **threw them out of his office:** Gutman, "Jews in General Anders' Army."
306 **when his army got to Palestine:** "Jewish Soldiers in the Polish Army," *The Ghetto Speaks*, no. 18, December 1, 1943, 5.
307 **They kept in constant touch:** Erlich, *Child of a Turbulent Century*, 85–89; Blit, "Henryk Erlich and Victor Alter in Soviet Russia," 107.
307 **Polish socialist ministers in London:** "Poilishe Sotsialisten Nominirn 'Bund'-Firer Erlich Als Mitglid Fon Golus-Regirung," *Forverts*, September 25, 1941, 8.
307 **His inclusion came:** Johnpoll, *Politics of Futility*, 243.
307 **"It is quite impossible":** Zimmerman, *Polish Underground and the Jews, 1939–1945*, 47.
307 **Endek politician Zofia Zaleska:** Johnpoll, *Politics of Futility*, 244–50; "Opposition to Anti-Semitic Motion of the Polish National Council in London," *The Ghetto Speaks*, no. 5, November 1, 1942, 2–3.

307 **"The Jewish population has a fatherland":** "Protest fun Algemaynem Idishn Arbeiter Bund Kegnr dem Anti-Semisishn Bashlus fun Poylishn Natsional-Rat Vegn a Idisher Milukhe," *Unzer Tsait*, July 1942, 2.
308 **Yakov Grojanowski:** Blatman, *For Our Freedom and Yours*, 90.
308 **"The execution lasts fifteen minutes":** Dawidowicz, *War Against the Jews*, 296.
308 **months languishing in Lida prison:** Hertz, *Doyres Bundistn*, vol. 2, 82.
309 **he turned up at a Polish socialist:** Goldstein, *Stars Bear Witness*, 98–99.
309 **The party installed Feiner:** Goldstein, *Stars Bear Witness*, 88.
309 **"The acquisition of arms became":** Johnpoll, *Politics of Futility*, 251.
309 **Five hundred fighters:** Edelman, *Guardian*, 25.
309 **take part in the liberation:** Beres and Burnetko, *Marek Edelman*, 114.
309 **A Pole who violated their boycott:** Karski, *Story of a Secret State*, 259.
309 **didn't punish blackmailers:** Goldstein, *Stars Bear Witness*, 209–10.
309 **Rowecki himself sympathized with Jews:** Zimmerman, *Polish Underground and the Jews, 1939–1945*, 103.
309 **Many Poles had taken over:** Gutman, *Jews of Warsaw*, 73.
310 **sometimes indulged in this accusation:** Zimmerman, *Polish Underground and the Jews, 1939–1945*, 134.
310 **two-person "Jewish Department":** Zimmerman, *Polish Underground and the Jews, 1939–1945*, 123.
310 **Feiner tried to persuade them:** Blatman, *For Our Freedom and Yours*, 95.
310 **Only one Jewish group had:** Zuckerman, *Surplus of Memory*, 166.
310 **On March 23, seven delegates:** Dawidowicz, *War Against the Jews*, 296–97.
311 **Antek opened the meeting:** Zuckerman, *Surplus of Memory*, 172–75.
311 **"You're still a very young man":** Arnon Rubin, "Facts and Fictions About the Rescue of the Polish Jewry During the Holocaust," United States Holocaust Museum Memorial Claims Conference, Tel Aviv, Israel, 2002, 2.
311 **"Were it not for the conditions":** Gutman, *Jews of Warsaw*, 169.
311 **Without the Bund's help:** Zuckerman, *Surplus of Memory*, 171–75.
311 **Bernard Goldstein noted new arrivals:** Goldstein, *Stars Bear Witness*, 104–5.
312 **Before dawn on April 18, Bernard:** Goldstein, *Stars Bear Witness*, 100.
312 **Polish socialists had warned Maurycy Orzech:** Celemenski, *Elegy for My People*, 107.
312 **More executions came:** Beres and Burnetko, *Marek Edelman*, 118; Blatman, *For Our Freedom and Yours*, 99.
312 **Bundist printer Moishe Sklar:** Goldstein, *Stars Bear Witness*, 102.
312 **The Bundist press warned:** Johnpoll, *Politics of Futility*, 241; Beres and Burnetko, *Marek Edelman*, 118.
313 **begged their Polish socialist friends:** Goldstein, *Stars Bear Witness*, 108.
313 **a Home Army courier:** Zimmerman, *Polish Underground and the Jews, 1939–1945*, 144.
313 **In the first letter:** "Mass Slaughter of Jews in Poland," *The Ghetto Speaks*, no. 2, August 1, 1942, 1–3.
313 **The second letter:** Zimmerman, *Polish Underground and the Jews, 1939–1945*, 144–47; Lucy Dawidowicz, *A Holocaust Reader* (Behram House, 1976), 316.
313 **Zygielbojm tried everything:** Michael Fleming, "Zygielbojm in London: Labor, the Holocaust, and the Politics of Memory," in *Essays Commemorating Szmul Zygielbojm*, ed. Michael Fleming (PUNO Press, 2018), 66–74.
313 **sent it to Prime Minister Sikorski:** "Memorandum to General Wladyslaw Sikorski," *The Ghetto Speaks*, no. 8. February 1, 1943, 8.
313 **the British government:** "Appeal to President Franklin D. Roosevelt and Prime Minister Winston Churchill," *The Ghetto Speaks*, no. 7, January 1, 1943, 5.
313 **read it on the BBC:** "A Special Broadcast by Szmul Zygielbojm," *The Ghetto Speaks*, no. 8, February 1, 1943, 7.
313 **On July 2, *The New York Times*:** "Allies Are Urged to Execute Nazis," *New York Times*, July 2, 1942, 6; Beres and Burnetko, *Marek Edelman*, 148.
313 **In May, German film crews arrived:** Przemysław Batorski, "The Germans Shoot a Film in the Warsaw Ghetto," Emanuel Ringelbaum Jewish Historical Institute, jhi.pl/en/articles/may-1942-the-germans-shoot-a-film-in-the-warsaw-ghetto,5173-; Hirszfeld, *Story of One Life*, 234; Beres and Burnetko, *Marek Edelman*, 118; Goldstein, *Stars Bear Witness*, 91–92.
314 **Nazis started to ship Poles:** Biskupska, *Survivors*, 119.
314 **A young Bundist named Vladka Peltel:** Vladka Meed, *On Both Sides of the Wall* (United States Holocaust Memorial Museum, 1993), 13.

CHAPTER TWENTY-FOUR: BOXCAR

316 **Carts went to a collection point:** Gutman, *Jews of Warsaw*, 217.
316 **"This is the moment":** Brzezinski, *Isaac's Army*, 180.
316 **"All of us felt that active resistance":** Goldstein, *Stars Bear Witness*, 111; Blatman, *For Our Freedom and Yours*, 102.
316 **The first night:** Beres and Burnetko, *Marek Edelman*, 127–29.
316 **attended by a Polish socialist:** Marek Edelman, *The Ghetto Fights* (American Representation of the General Jewish Workers' Union of Poland, 1946), 56.
317 **Aleynhilf at 25 Nowolipki Street:** "Warsaw Ghetto—Grosaktion Summer 1942," Holocaust Historical

Society, holocausthistoricalsociety.org.uk/contents/naziseasternempire/warsawghettogrosaktionsummer1942.html, accessed July 1, 2025; Beres and Burnetko, *Marek Edelman*, 129.

317 **Dror's general secretary, Antek Zuckerman:** Zuckerman, *Surplus of Memory*, 193; Zivia Lubetkin *In the Days of Destruction and Revolt* (Ghetto Fighters' House, 1981), 106; Blatman, *For Our Freedom and Yours*, 102.

317 **chatting with Marek Edelman:** Beres and Burnetko, *Marek Edelman*, 125.

317 **Bundists, communists, and left-wing Zionists:** Dawidowicz, *War Against the Jews*, 302–3.

317 **Maurycy Orzech wrote, "Do not believe":** Goldstein, *Stars Bear Witness*, 112.

318 **Big men, teamsters and porters:** Ringelblum, *Polish-Jewish Relations During the Second World War*, 160; Beres and Burnetko, *Marek Edelman*, 138.

318 **They set up workshops to counterfeit:** Meed, *On Both Sides of the Wall*, 22–23.

318 **Before the war, Gina had:** Rowe, "Jewish Self Defense," 146.

318 **while her brother Michal fought:** "Michael Klepfisz," *The Ghetto Speaks*, no. 14, August 1, 1943, 7.

318 **From the windows overlooking:** Beres and Burnetko, *Marek Edelman*, 139.

319 **Twice a day, boxcars packed:** Goldstein, *Stars Bear Witness*, 118; "Warsaw Ghetto—Grosaktion Summer 1942," Holocaust Historical Society, holocausthistoricalsociety.org.uk/contents/naziseasternempire/warsawghettogrosaktionsummer1942.html, accessed July 1, 2025.

319 **Vladka Peltel listened to her former teacher:** Meed, *On Both Sides of the Wall*, 51.

319 **she was deported to Treblinka:** Meed, *On Both Sides of the Wall*, 54.

319 **Locked together in a comrade's attic:** Goldstein, *Stars Bear Witness*, 127–28.

319 **liquidation of the Medem Sanatorium:** Johnpoll, *Politics of Futility*, 242.

319 **Afterward, Poles looted the sanatorium:** Celemenski, *Elegy for My People*, 119.

319 **Bernard and Sonia had passports:** Goldstein, *Stars Bear Witness*, 120.

319 **They passed the time discussing:** Goldstein, *Stars Bear Witness*, 129.

319 **Only scum remained in the ghetto:** Edelman, *Ghetto Fights*, 64.

320 **A Polish socialist friend told Maurycy:** Beres and Burnetko, *Marek Edelman*, 133; Edelman, *Guardian*, 25.

320 **Nazis drove a crowd of Jews:** Goldstein, *Stars Bear Witness*, 130–31.

320 **Marek knew he could not:** Edelman, *Guardian*, 26–27; Brzezinski, *Isaac's Army*, 182–83.

320 **Bernard Goldstein ran from one hiding:** Goldstein, *Stars Bear Witness*, 120–51.

320 **"They were friends—rats":** Goldstein, *Stars Bear Witness*, 149.

320 **Germans forced the last hundred thousand:** Edelman, *Ghetto Fights*, 135; Gutman, *Jews of Warsaw*, 211.

321 **"The chances of receiving [one] were":** Edelman, *Ghetto Fights*, 65.

321 **Tsukunft member Vladka Peltel's comrades:** Meed, *On Both Sides of the Wall*, 70.

321 **They implored their readers:** Dawidowicz, *War Against the Jews*, 310.

321 **Bernard walked through the streets:** Goldstein, *Stars Bear Witness*, 151–53.

322 **Marek Edelman led Bernard:** Goldstein, *Stars Bear Witness*, 159–63.

322 **The Polish city was more hostile:** Ringelblum, *Polish-Jewish Relations During the Second World War*, 194, 197.

323 **Even the underground press berated:** Ringelblum, *Polish-Jewish Relations During the Second World War*, 162.

323 **At Bernard's first meeting:** Goldstein, *Stars Bear Witness*, 169–70.

323 **Adina had poisoned her young patients:** Adina Blady-Szwajger, *I Remember Nothing More: The Warsaw Children's Hospital and the Jewish Resistance* (Collins Harvill, 1990), 57.

323 **The pair rented dozens of rooms:** Celemenski, *Elegy for My People*, 126.

323 **even enduring sexual molestation:** Jacob Pat, *Ashes and Fire* (International Universities Press, 1947), 174; Blady-Szwajger, *I Remember Nothing More*, 126.

323 **call for Indian independence:** "The Jewish Masses of Poland Express Their Solidarity with the Anti-Fascist World," *The Ghetto Speaks*, no. 5, November 1, 1942, 4.

323 **demand the release of Mahatma Gandhi:** "The Underground Jewish Labor Movement of Poland Demands Release of Mohandas Gandhi," *The Ghetto Speaks*, no. 9, March 1, 1943, 6.

323 **Polish socialists hid Bundists:** Celemenski, *Elegy for My People*, 147.

323 **the Polish socialist sisters:** Polish Center for Holocaust Research (Centrum Badan nad Zagłąda Żydów), Sawicka, Marysia, getto.pl/en/People/S/Sawicka-Marysia-Unknown.

323 **Maria asked the Klepfisz family:** Conversation with Irena Klepfisz.

324 **In October 1942, the Erlichs disembarked:** Erlich, *Child of a Turbulent Century*, 103.

324 **they fought to learn:** Blatman, *For Our Freedom and Yours*, 86.

324 **When Polish ambassador Stanislaw Kot:** *Soviet Russia Arrests Henryk Ehrlich and Victor Alter. Noted Polish Socialist Leaders* (American Delegation of the General Jewish Workers' Union of Poland, 1942), 3.

324 **The Jewish Combat Organization—*Zydowska Organizacja Bojowa:*** Dawidowicz, *Holocaust Reader*, 367; Lubetkin, *In the Days of Destruction and Revolt*, 115–17; Blatman, *For Our Freedom and Yours*, 103.

325 **The People's Guard gave the ZOB:** Edelman, *Guardian*, 31.

325 **Though the Home Army had:** Ringelblum, *Polish-Jewish Relations During the Second World War*, 173.

325 **they were loath to share them:** Ringelblum, *Polish-Jewish Relations During the Second World War*, 162.

325 **that a ghetto revolt would be premature:** Zimmerman, *Polish Underground and the Jews, 1939–1945*, 171.

325 **"If the occupiers decide to direct":** Zimmerman, *Polish Underground and the Jews, 1939–1945*, 161.

325 **most of the young people:** Lubetkin, *In the Days of Destruction and Revolt*, 119.

325 **Eventually, Antek prevailed:** Lubetkin, *In the Days of Destruction and Revolt*, 122.

326 **they wanted to fight alongside their friends:** Beres and Burnetko, *Marek Edelman*, 144–45.
326 **In late October, the Bund joined:** Zuckerman, *Surplus of Memory*, 223.
326 **The Jewish National Committee was:** Blatman, *For Our Freedom and Yours*, 104; Lubetkin, *In the Days of Destruction and Revolt.* 134–35.
326 **the right-wing Zionist ZZW:** Zuckerman, *Surplus of Memory*, 225–26.
326 **Germans cut the ghetto into enclaves:** Edelman, *Guardian*, 136.
326 **the ZOB split these enclaves:** Dawidowicz, *War Against the Jews*, 317; Edelman, *Ghetto Fights*, 106.
326 **mother once sold rotten fish:** Krall, *Shielding the Flame*, 4.
326 **he wanted it so much:** Beres and Burnetko, *Marek Edelman*, 144.
326 **Bundist battle squads assigned:** Gutman, *Jews of Warsaw*, 269.
326 **The Bund only accepted fighters:** Edelman, *Guardian*, 37.
326 **They chauvinistically rejected women:** Celemenski, *Elegy for My People*, 142–43.
326 **The ZOB's first act:** Ringelblum, *Polish-Jewish Relations During the Second World War*, 167.
326 **Afterward, they posted communiqués:** Dawidowicz, *Holocaust Reader*, 358.
326 **Their posters warned:** Dawidowicz, *Holocaust Reader*, 355.
326 **When German guards arrested three Bundists:** Edelman, *Ghetto Fights*, 72.
326 **In December the Home Army finally:** Zimmerman, *Polish Underground and the Jews, 1939–1945*, 179; Beres and Burnetko, *Marek Edelman*, 146–47.
326 **Despite the ZOB's pleas:** Ringelblum, *Polish-Jewish Relations During the Second World War*, 284–87.
326 **no more guns arrived:** Gutman, *Jews of Warsaw*, 299.
326 **Rowecki didn't believe:** Zimmerman, *Polish Underground and the Jews, 1939–1945*, 197–98.
327 **Home Army courier Jan Karski met:** Karski, *Story of a Secret State*, 320–34.
327 **"Tell them that there are moments":** "What 'X' Requested Me to Tell the Jews of the Free Countries," *The Ghetto Speaks*, no. 9, March 1, 1943, 1; "Authentic Report from Poland Describing the Wholesale Annihilation of Poland's Jews," *The Ghetto Speaks*, no. 8, February 1, 1943, 1.
327 **Feiner handed him a report:** Zimmerman, *Polish Underground and the Jews, 1939–1945*, 155.
327 **Arthur Zygielbojm's London post:** Ravel, *Faithful unto Death*, 167–72. For a comprehensive account of Zygielbojm's activities, see Fleming, "Zygielbojm in London," 66–74, 83–90.
327 **"It will actually be a shame":** Thomas Wood and Stanislaw Jankowski, *Karski: How One Man Tried to Stop the Holocaust* (Texas Tech University Press, 1994), 152.
328 **top diplomat Frank Roberts:** Tony Kushner, "Too Little, Too Late? Reflections on Britain's Holocaust Memorial Day," *Journal of Israeli History* 23, no. 1 (2006): 116–29.
328 **Home Army parachutists:** Zimmerman, *Polish Underground and the Jews, 1939–1945*, 172.
328 **On December 2, Karski met:** Karski, *Story of a Secret State*, 334–38.
328 **There are moments when we hate:** "What 'X' Requested Me to Tell," 1.
328 **Zygielbojm sprung back:** Karski, *Story of a Secret State*, 334–38.
329 **This was cold comfort:** Dawidowicz, *From That Place and Time*, 231.
329 **He distributed hundreds of copies:** Blatman, *For Our Freedom and Yours*, 139–46.
329 **He cabled Winston Churchill:** "Appeal to President Franklin D. Roosevelt and Prime Minister Winston Churchill," *The Ghetto Speaks*, no. 7, January 1, 1943, 5.
329 **Churchill's underlings blew him off:** "Assurance Given by the British Government," *The Ghetto Speaks*, no. 9, March 1, 1943, 6–7.
329 **As he told BBC listeners:** Halina Taborska, "'I Cannot Be Silent and I Cannot Live': The Szmul Zygielbojm Warsaw Monument on the Memorial Route to the Struggle and Martyrdom of the Jews, 1940–1943," in *Essays Commemorating Szmul Zygielbojm*, ed. Fleming, 30.
329 **She checked herself into a Catholic:** Celemenski, *Elegy for My People*, 139.
329 **As her niece, the poet Irena Klepfisz:** Irena Klepfisz, "Solitary Acts," *Her Birth and Later Years: New and Collected Poems, 1971–2021* (Wesleyan University Press, 2022).
329 **On December 5, comrades buried Gina:** Celemenski, *Elegy for My People*, 79–81.
329 **They were Bundists and Polish socialists:** "Funeral of Warsaw Ghetto Resister Gina (Regina) Klepfisz in the Brodno Catholic Cemetery. Most of the People in Attendance are Jews in Hiding or Poles Who Are Helping Them," photograph no. 17996, United States Holocaust Museum, December 1942, collections.ushmm.org/search/catalog/pa1064735.
329 **Tsukunft member Vladka Peltel:** Meed, *On Both Sides of the Wall*, 85.
330 **When Vladka bought her first revolver:** Meed, *On Both Sides of the Wall*, 95.
330 **pickpocket king Roman Kowalski:** Wojciech Rodak, "Tajemnice 'Cara z Wenecji': Jak Król pomagał warszawskim Żydom," Warsaw Ghetto Museum, October 24, 2022, 1943.pl/artykul/tajemnice-cara-z-wenecji-jak-krol-polswiatka-pomagal-warszawskim-zydom/.
330 **smuggle out their children:** Meed, *On Both Sides of the Wall*, 106.
330 **Most Poles didn't want to hide:** Ringelblum, *Polish-Jewish Relations During the Second World War*, 141.
330 **Once, he tried to speak:** Conversation with Irena Klepfisz.
330 **the ZOB planned a public demonstration:** Gutman, Jews of Warsaw, 304.
331 **Only the kids from Mordechai Anielewicz's:** Zuckerman, *Surplus of Memory*, 282; Gutman, *Jews of Warsaw*, 313.

CHAPTER TWENTY-FIVE: REVOLT

332 **Bundist Avram Feiner died:** Meed, *On Both Sides of the Wall*, 121.
332 **Germans caught Boruch Peltz's:** Celemenski, *Elegy for My People*, 156.

332 **a fourteen-year-old girl named:** "Given name: Halinka, Family name: Kipman," Centrum Badan nad Zagłądą Żydów (Polish Center for Holocaust Research), getto.pl/en/People/K/Kipman-Halinka-Unknown.

332 **Janina Bauman's youthful ghetto memoir:** Janina Bauman, *Winter in the Morning: A Young Girl's Life in the Warsaw Ghetto and Beyond, 1939–1945* (Virago Press, 1986), 95.

332 **"violence is a dis-intoxicating force":** Adam Shatz, *The Rebel's Clinic: The Revolutionary Lives of Frantz Fanon* (Macmillan, 2024), 155.

332 **The gains of the January revolt:** Gutman, *Jews of Warsaw*, 315.

333 **They raided the Gesia Street jail:** Johnpoll, *Politics of Futility*, 254.

333 **They levied taxes on anyone:** Beres and Burnetko, *Marek Edelman*, 159–60.

333 **They robbed the Judenrat treasury:** Lubetkin, *In the Days of Destruction and Revolt*, 167.

333 **hauling off cash:** Zuckerman, *Surplus of Memory*, 317.

333 **They clashed with the right-wing:** Edelman, *Guardian*, 32–33.

333 **Once, ZOB fighters caught:** Beres and Burnetko, *Marek Edelman*, 162.

333 **according to Marek Edelman, the ZOB:** Zimmerman, *Polish Underground and the Jews, 1939–1945*, 203; Beres and Burnetko, *Marek Edelman*, 150.

333 **The situation inspired Bundist engineer Michal:** Meed, *On Both Sides of the Wall*, 124–26.

333 **In an abandoned church:** Zimmerman, *Polish Underground and the Jews, 1939–1945*, 207.

333 **pipe bombs filled with shrapnel:** Zuckerman, *Surplus of Memory*, 293.

334 **In rooms silent as sanctums:** Meed, *On Both Sides of the Wall*, 138.

334 **Marek Edelman sometimes saw Klepfisz:** Beres and Burnetko, *Marek Edelman*, 171.

334 **The Gestapo caught Michal Klepfisz:** Goldstein, *Stars Bear Witness*, 174–75.

334 **He took a file hidden beneath:** Conversation with Irena Klepfisz.

334 **Klepfisz's old friend Stefan Machai:** Meed, *On Both Sides of the Wall*, 127–32.

335 **the brush factory, the Bund's stronghold:** Johnpoll, *Politics of Futility*, 254.

335 **That night, the ZOB's battle squads:** Goldstein, *Stars Bear Witness*, 185.

335 **he was powerless:** Dawidowicz, *Holocaust Reader*, 347.

335 **It was a gorgeous spring:** Beres and Burnetko, *Marek Edelman*, 156.

335 **the sound of digging:** Emmanuel Ringelblum, *Notes from the Warsaw Ghetto: The Journal of Emmanuel Ringelblum* (Schocken Books, 1974), 340–43.

335 **fighters disassembled and reassembled:** Meed, *On Both Sides of the Wall*, 106–8.

335 **The youngest was only thirteen:** Beres and Burnetko, *Marek Edelman*, 179.

335 **Marek Edelman remembered:** Beres and Burnetko, *Marek Edelman*, 176.

335 **The ZOB built fortifications:** Goldstein, *Stars Bear Witness*, 187.

335 **dug tunnels into the sewer system:** Goldstein, *Stars Bear Witness*, 182.

335 **They cut passageways:** Edelman, *Guardian*, 153.

335 **In one of her trips:** Meed, *On Both Sides of the Wall*, 137.

335 **In February, the Bundist underground:** Dawidowicz, *War Against the Jews*, 335.

336 **No matter how many telegrams:** Johnpoll, *Politics of Futility*, 239.

336 **In a letter dated February 23:** "The First Authentic Statement About the Execution of Henryk Erlich and Victor Alter," *The Ghetto Speaks*, no. 10, April 1, 1943, 1; Johnpoll, *Politics of Futility*, 239–40.

336 **the Soviets sent the Polish embassy:** Blatman, *For Our Freedom and Yours*, 86.

336 **The next year, Sophia's niece:** Lucan Way, "Exhuming the Buried Past: In the KGB Files," *The Nation*, March 1, 1993.

336 **After his death, they burned:** Blatman, *For Our Freedom and Yours*, 85.

336 **The NKVD did not execute Henryk Erlich:** Johnpoll, *Politics of Futility*, 239; Erlich, *Child of a Turbulent Century*, 95–97.

337 **They published an open letter:** "Reaction of the American Press," *The Ghetto Speaks*, no. 10, April 1, 1943, 8–10.

337 **Jewish workers smashed the Soviet embassy's:** Kruk, *Last Days of the Jerusalem of Lithuania*, 481.

337 **In Mexico City, communists and Bundists:** Aribert Reimann, "Local Brawls and Global Confrontation: Transnational Political Violence Among the Exiled Lett in Mexico City During 1943," PhD dissertation, University of Cologne, 2017.

337 **wartime geopolitics muted the Bund's supporters:** Erlich, *Child of a Turbulent Century*, 89–92.

337 **Even in the Vilna ghetto:** Kruk, *Last Days of the Jerusalem of Lithuania*, 498.

337 **the names of the Bund's two leaders:** Celemenski, *Elegy for My People*, 152.

337 **Shaindel Kirsch was a skinny girl:** Pat, *Ashes and Fire*, 206–9.

338 **Michal Klepfisz and Zalman Friedrich:** Meed, *On Both Sides of the Wall*, 142.

338 **Sentries ran from house to house:** "The Last Passover in the Warsaw Ghetto," YouTube video, Yad Vashem, March 21, 2013, yadvashem.org/yv/en/exhibitions/warsaw_ghetto_testimonies/last_passover.asp.

338 **the fighters watched the Nazis goose-step:** Dawidowicz, *Holocaust Reader*, 375; Edelman, *Ghetto Fights*, 75.

338 **singing a cheerful march:** Lubetkin, *In the Days of Destruction and Revolt*, 181.

338 **in a red angora sweater:** Beres and Burnetko, *Marek Edelman*, 167.

338 **"as if those few immature boys":** Edelman, *Ghetto Fights*, 75.

338 **fighters barricaded another group:** Beres and Burnetko, *Marek Edelman*, 169.

338 **Aryan supermen lay:** Lubetkin, *In the Days of Destruction and Revolt*, 181–82.

339 **even as they chided other Jews:** Biuletyn Informacyjny, quoted in " 'The Yids Are Burning!': Poles' Reaction to the Uprising in the Warsaw Ghetto," *Polin Polish Righteous*, sprawiedliwi.org.pl/en/about-the-righteous/poles-reaction-to-the-uprising-in-the-warsaw-ghetto-1943.

339 **Many papers urged Varsovians:** Biuletyn Informacyjny, quoted in " 'The Yids Are Burning!' "

339 **Even the fascist *Polska* admitted:** "Polish Fascist Describes the Battle of the Ghetto of Warsaw," *The Ghetto Speaks*, no. 16, October 1, 1943, 5.

339 **made several attacks on the wall:** Ringelblum, *Polish-Jewish Relations During the Second World War*, 180.

339 **The ghetto fighters thought:** Beres and Burnetko, *Marek Edelman*, 177.

339 **had given the ZOB fifty guns:** Gutman, *Jews of Warsaw*, 360.

339 **caught the ZOB's liaison:** Meed, *On Both Sides of the Wall*, 95; Zimmerman, *Polish Underground and the Jews, 1939–1945*, 204; Lubetkin, *In the Days of Destruction and Revolt*, 171; Beres and Burnetko, *Marek Edelman*, 153.

339 **Home Army fighters kept their promise:** Zimmerman, *Polish Underground and the Jews, 1939–1945*, 215.

339 **Similar attempts ended in failure:** Zimmerman, *Polish Underground and the Jews, 1939–1945*, 217.

339 **Rowecki and Warsaw general Antoni Chrusciel:** Zimmerman, *Polish Underground and the Jews, 1939–1945*, 222; Zuckerman, *Surplus of Memory*, 361.

339 **Another Home Army leader told Antek:** Zuckerman, *Surplus of Memory*, 359; Lubetkin, *In the Days of Destruction and Revolt*, 196.

339 **the government-in-exile didn't judge April 1943:** Beres and Burnetko, *Marek Edelman*, 247.

339 **Prime Minister Sikorski said as much:** Zimmerman, *Polish Underground and the Jews, 1939–1945*, 221.

339 **the Polish Socialist Party sympathized:** Blatman, *For Our Freedom and Yours*, 107.

340 **Sociologist Emanuel Ringelblum quoted:** Ringelblum, *Polish-Jewish Relations During the Second World War*, 183.

340 **On the first day of the uprising:** Meed, *On Both Sides of the Wall*, 140–42.

340 **Jacob Celemenski hurried to a safe house:** Celemenski, *Elegy for My People*, 158–59.

340 **Bernard Goldstein's Polish comrades:** Goldstein, *Stars Bear Witness*, 193–94.

340 **Zegota's Polish socialist chairman, Julian Grobelny:** Marcin Urynowicz, "The Story of Julian Grobelny," POLIN Museum of the History of Polish Jews, sprawiedliwi.org.pl/en/stories-of-rescue/story-julian-grobelny.

340 **In Warsaw, Stroop ensconced:** Kazimierz Moczarski, *Conversations with an Executioner* (Prentice-Hall, 1981), 118.

341 **The ground exploded:** Lubetkin, *In the Days of Destruction and Revolt*, 186.

341 **"The guerrilla is the fish":** Vincent Bevins, *The Jakarta Method: Washington's Anticommunist Crusade and the Mass Murder Program That Shaped Our World* (PublicAffairs, 2020), 227.

341 **Their flamethrowers started:** Dawidowicz, *Holocaust Reader*, 377.

341 **In revenge, the ZOB torched:** "Polish Fascist Describes," 3.

341 **Bundist courier Tobcia Dawidowicz ran:** Celemenski, *Elegy for My People*, 165.

342 **Nazis forced them to strip:** Moczarski, *Conversations with an Executioner*, 151.

342 **the Nazi propaganda department brought:** "Polish Fascist Describes," 4–5.

342 **"They were not human":** Beres and Burnetko, *Marek Edelman*, 170.

342 **pulled grenades from their underwear:** Lubetkin, *In the Days of Destruction and Revolt*, 215.

342 **Nazis cornered Michal Klepfisz's battalion:** Goldstein, *Stars Bear Witness*, 191.

342 **their feet wrapped in rags:** Dawidowicz, *Holocaust Reader*, 378.

342 **They pulled desperate civilians:** Dawidowicz, *War Against the Jews*, 337–39.

342 **led them to temporary safety:** Lubetkin, *In the Days of Destruction and Revolt*, 201–2.

342 **On April 23, the Bundist writer Ignacy Samsonowicz:** Dawidowicz, *Holocaust Reader*, 359. Marek Edelman identifies the declaration's author as Ignacy Samsonowicz. See Edelman, *Guardian*, 20.

343 **Nazi newspapers blamed it:** Beres and Burnetko, *Marek Edelman*, 159.

343 **many Poles admired the ghetto's defiance:** Ringelblum, *Polish-Jewish Relations During the Second World War*, 178.

343 **There was a merry-go-round:** Beres and Burnetko, *Marek Edelman*, 172.

343 **in his work "*Campo dei Fiori*":** Czesław Miłosz, "Campo dei Fiori," translated by Adam Gillon, *The Fiddlehead*, no. 24, Fall 1959.

343 **On May Day, the Bundist fighters:** Edelman, *Ghetto Fights*, 82–83.

343 **Germans pushed Tsukunft leader Henoch Russ:** Interview with Brian Gocial, relative of Henoch Russ.

344 **Anna Braude Heller, the indomitable head:** Hertz, *Doyres Bundistn*, vol. 2, 143.

344 **as did the printer Lazar Klug:** Hertz, *Doyres Bundistn*, vol. 2. 69.

344 **Wounded by a grenade, Berek Sznajdmil:** Celemenski, *Elegy for My People*, 166.

344 **Zalman Friedrich and a daring teenage:** Zuckerman, *Surplus of Memory*, 366; Lubetkin, *In the Days of Destruction and Revolt*, 238–39.

344 **Zalman Friedrich and a daring teenage:** Zuckerman, *Surplus of Memory*, 360; Lubetkin, *In the Days of Destruction and Revolt*, 196.

344 **On May 8, bloodhounds discovered:** Lubetkin, *In the Days of Destruction and Revolt*, 190–91.

344 **pumped in chlorine gas:** Lubetkin, *In the Days of Destruction and Revolt*, 231–33.

344 **Two weeks before his death:** "The Last Letter from Ghetto Revolt Commander Mordecai Anielewicz, Warsaw," April 23, 1943, Documents on the Holocaust, Selected Sources on the Destruction of the Jews of Germany and Austria, Poland and the Soviet Union, Yad Vashem, Jerusalem, 1981, Document no. 145.

345 **"You have to fight":** Beres and Burnetko, *Marek Edelman*, 188–89.

345 **Lubetkin and Edelman led:** Beres and Burnetko, *Marek Edelman*, 192.
345 **They lay mostly naked:** Lubetkin, *In the Days of Destruction and Revolt*, 209.
345 **All the phone lines:** Lubetkin, *In the Days of Destruction and Revolt*, 207.
345 **Yiddish or Hebrew:** Lubetkin, *In the Days of Destruction and Revolt*, 218.
345 **Sometimes they reminisced:** Lubetkin, *In the Days of Destruction and Revolt*, 216–17.
345 **Kazik refused to give up:** Lubetkin, *In the Days of Destruction and Revolt*, 240; Beres and Burnetko, *Marek Edelman*, 195.
345 **It was dark when Kazik pulled:** Simha Rotem, *Memoirs of a Warsaw Ghetto Fighter: The Past Within Me* (Yale University Press, 1994), 52.
346 **except for two teenage sex workers:** Beres and Burnetko, *Marek Edelman*, 196.
346 **Sixty-two fugitives lowered themselves:** Beres and Burnetko, *Marek Edelman*, 196.
346 **the Bund's New York committee:** "Memorandum on the Bermuda Conference," *The Ghetto Speaks*, no. 11, May 1, 1943, 2–4.
346 **Dignitaries sipped cocktails:** David Wyman, *The Abandonment of the Jews: America and the Holocaust, 1941–1945* (Pantheon, 1984), 108–23.
346 **their resources were quite exhausted:** Wyman, *Abandonment of the Jews*, 106.
347 **as "another 100,000 Jews murdered":** David Rosenberg, "The Struggle to Memorialize Zygielbojm in London," in *Essays Commemorating Szmul Zygielbojm*, ed. Michael Fleming, 8.
347 **but he still tried to coordinate:** Blatman, *For Our Freedom and Yours*, 147–50.
347 **All the while, desperate messages:** Zimmerman, *Polish Underground and the Jews, 1939–1945*, 226.
347 **On May 11, Zygielbojm listened:** Fleming, "Zygielbojm in London," 91.
347 **The first, to Prime Minister Sikorski:** Dawidowicz, *From That Place and Time*, 242.
347 **A second was to his brother:** " 'The Sky Is Cold and Silent Like the People Down Below': Farewell Letters from Shmuel Zygielbojm," Emanuel Ringelblum Jewish Historical Institute, jhi.pl/en/articles/farewell-letters-from-shmuel-zygielbojm,3296, accessed June 22, 2025.
347 **In his final letter:** "Szmul Zygielbojm's Parting Words to His Closest Friends," *The Ghetto Speaks*, no. 15, September 1, 1943, 7–8.

CHAPTER TWENTY-SIX: ASHES

348 **forty ghetto fighters pulled themselves up:** This description is pieced together from eyewitness accounts by Marek Edelman, Shima Rotem, and Celina Lubetkin. See Edelman, *Guardian*, 47; Lubetkin, *In the Days of Destruction and Revolt*, 252; Beres and Burnetko, *Marek Edelman*, 199; Rotem, *Memoirs of a Warsaw Ghetto Fighter*, 55–57.
348 **On May 16, Stroop declared:** Moczarski, *Conversations with an Executioner*, 164.
348 **Stroop claimed sixteen:** Dawidowicz, *Holocaust Reader*, 120.
348 **that number contradicts the carnage:** Moczarski, *Conversations with an Executioner*, 137.
348 **For months afterward:** Beres and Burnetko, *Marek Edelman*, 207.
348 **kept alive by Polish helpers:** Goldstein, *Stars Bear Witness*, 205.
348 **they painted it as the work:** Jurgen Stroop, *The Stroop Report: The Jewish Quarter of Warsaw Is No More!* (Pantheon Books, 1979), 48.
348 **in Poland, as the work:** "Polish Fascist Describes," 4; Gutman, *Jews of Warsaw*, 429.
349 **First Lady Eleanor Roosevelt wrote:** "To the Madness of the Brave—Glory," *The Ghetto Speaks*, no. 23, April 1, 1944, 2.
349 **When W.E.B. Du Bois visited:** W.E.B. Du Bois, "The Negro and the Warsaw Ghetto," *Jewish Life*, May 1952.
349 **Communists claimed the revolt as communist:** Marci Shore, "Children of the Revolution: Communism, Zionism, and the Berman Brothers," *Jewish Social Studies* 10, no. 3 (Spring–Summer 2004; New Series); Marci Shore, "The Jewish Hero History Forgot," *New York Times*, April 18, 2013.
349 **Polish socialists saw it:** "Towarzysze i obywatele" [Comrades and citizens], *WRN*, May 7, 1943, quoted in Maciej Żuczkowski, "The Press of the Polish Socialist Party—Freedom, Equality, and Independence and the Jews During World War II," *Polish-Jewish Studies*, vol. 1, 2020, 558.
349 **Trawniki labor camp:** "Excerpt from Report 'B,' " *The Ghetto Speaks*, no. 24, April 1, 1944, 3–4.
349 **the resistance burned the ghetto themselves:** Szymon Datner, "The Fight and the Destruction of Ghetto Białystok," The Landsmanschaft of Białystok and the Surrounding Area, Yehud, Israel, 1945, jwmww2.org/userfiles/file/GhettoBiaystok.pdf, accessed October 12, 2025.
349 **In the Vilna ghetto, Warsaw's revolt:** Hirsh Glik, "Zog Nit Keyn Mol" (lyrics), 1943, translated by Roslyn Bresnick Perry, The Yosl and Chana Mlotek Yiddish Song Collection at the Workers Circle, yiddishsongs.org/zog-nit-keyn-mol/.
349 **Their guide was the Bundist engineer:** Abraham Sutzkever and Justin D. Cammy, *From the Vilna Ghetto to Nuremberg: Memoir and Testimony* (McGill-Queen's University Press, 2021), 140.
349 **Bundist courier Asya Big:** Sutzkever and Cammy, *From the Vilna Ghetto to Nuremberg*, 179; Blatman, *For Our Freedom and Yours*, 110–14.
350 **After her husband's death:** Y. Sh. Hertz, *Doyres Bundistn*, vol. 1, 134.
350 **Pati Kremer saw the streets:** Y. Sh. Hertz, *Doyres Bundistn*, vol. 1, 136.
350 **In the ghetto, she wrote poetry:** Y. Sh. Hertz, *Doyres Bundistn*, vol. 1, 137.
350 **Her comrades saved her life:** Kruk, *Last Days of the Jerusalem of Lithuania*, xliv–xlv, 123.
350 **she helped them hide their weapons:** Y. Sh. Hertz, *Doyres Bundistn*, vol. 1, 137.
350 **"Let's sing 'The Oath':** Y. Sh. Hertz, *Doyres Bundistn*, vol. 1, 137.

351 **Bundist Zalman Friedrich:** Meed, *On Both Sides of the Wall,* 157–58.

351 **Home Army units refused to accept them:** Meed, *On Both Sides of the Wall,* 157; Ringelblum, *Polish-Jewish Relations During the Second World War,* 221.

351 **Germans imposed the death penalty:** Zimmerman, *Polish Underground and the Jews, 1939–1945,* 223; Ringelblum, *Polish-Jewish Relations During the Second World War,* 234.

351 **the Gestapo caught Bundist fighter:** Beres and Burnetko, *Marek Edelman,* 217–18.

351 **Tsukunft leader Abrasha Blum:** Meed, *On Both Sides of the Wall,* 167.

352 **Bor-Komorowski refused to aid ghetto fighters:** Zimmerman, *Polish Underground and the Jews, 1939–1945,* 249–51.

352 **he would not accept a single:** Zimmerman, *Polish Underground and the Jews, 1939–1945,* 255.

352 **Jewish partisans were merely commie criminals:** Zimmerman, *Polish Underground and the Jews, 1939–1945,* 245.

352 **In September, he ordered his commanders:** Ringelblum, *Polish-Jewish Relations During the Second World War,* 219.

352 **Bor-Komorowski welcomed a Nazi-collaborationist paramilitary:** Ringelblum, *Polish-Jewish Relations During the Second World War,* 310.

352 **Endek politician Roman Knoll:** Joanna Michlic, *Poland's Threatening Other: The Image of the Jew from 1880 to the Present* (University of Nebraska Press, 2006), 183.

352 **In Warsaw, the surviving Bundists:** Beres and Burnetko, *Marek Edelman,* 221.

352 **"Our tasks now come down":** Dawidowicz, *War Against the Jews,* 340; Zimmerman, *Polish Underground and the Jews, 1939–1945,* 359.

352 **three thousand Jews hidden:** Goldstein, *Stars Bear Witness,* 225.

352 **Their couriers, Adina Blady:** Blady-Szwajger, *I Remember Nothing More,* 104–5.

352 **apartment in a former courthouse:** Celemenski, *Elegy for My People,* 126.

352 **The Bund stored their fake passports:** Pat, *Ashes and Fire,* 167.

352 **their illicit party newspapers:** Celemenski, *Elegy for My People,* 201.

352 **They shared this money with Zionist:** Beres and Burnetko, *Marek Edelman,* 222.

352 **Once a month, Adina refreshed:** Blady-Szwajger, *I Remember Nothing More,* 106–9.

353 **Marisha Feinmesser dressed up:** Pat, *Ashes and Fire,* 169–71.

353 **hidden behind a laundry basket:** Celemenski, *Elegy for My People,* 196.

353 **At various times, Bernard Goldstein:** Beres and Burnetko, *Marek Edelman,* 221.

353 **Adina Blady became his lover:** Blady-Szwajger, *I Remember Nothing More,* 147–48.

353 **Adina found them unanesthetized abortions:** Blady-Szwajger, *I Remember Nothing More,* 148.

354 **In September, they used an illegal radio:** "We Who Are About to Die Greet You," *The Ghetto Speaks,* no. 19, January 1, 1944, 6.

354 **They held surreptitious May Day celebrations:** Celemenski, *Elegy for My People,* 200–201.

354 **"Little by little, almost in whispers":** Meed, *On Both Sides of the Wall,* 189.

354 **With secret radios and smuggled microfilm:** Goldstein, *Stars Bear Witness,* 235.

354 **The Red Army liberated Volkovysk:** "Pripet Center Won," *New York Times,* July 15, 1944, 1.

354 **using its headstones:** Bychowcew and Hawrylik-Kuklinska, *Wolkowysk,* 60.

354 **In 2008, the municipal government:** "Belarus: Jewish Cemetery at Volkovysk Dug Up for Water and Sewer Pipelines," *Samuel Gruber's Jewish Art and Monuments,* October 21, 2009, samgrubersjewishartmonuments.blogspot.com/2009/10/belarus-jewish-cemetery-at-volkovysk.html.

354 **Bundist councilman Shepsel Ravitzky:** Berger, *Volkovysk Memorial Book,* vol. 1, 427.

354 **Berel Falkovitch, the bridle maker:** Berger, *Volkovysk Memorial Book,* vol. 1, 419.

354 **Tsukunft member Tzipa Pashinker:** Berger, *Volkovysk Memorial Book,* vol. 1, 448.

354 **activist Chana Irmess:** Berger, *Volkovysk Memorial Book,* vol. 1, 412.

354 **Chana's husband, Yaakov Rubinstein:** Berger, *Volkovysk Memorial Book,* vol. 1, 412.

355 **In spring 1942, Shlomo Markus:** Berger, *Volkovysk Memorial Book,* vol. 3, 62–63.

355 **Gershon Beckenstein played:** Berger, *Volkovysk Memorial Book,* vol. 1, 422. More information came through correspondence with Marta Bolek of the Bureau for Former Prisoners Archive State Museum Auschwitz-Birkenau, February 6, 2024. "BBW.89.2024. Beckenstein G. (personal detail unknown), was deported to KL Auschwitz on January 28, 1943 in transport directed by the RSHA from Ghetto Wolkowysk. He was registered as prisoner no. 94270. Last entry in files: on October 27, 1944. There is no information about his further fate. Source of information: list of transports incoming to KL Auschwitz, list of members of the camp orchestra (encl.), bonus letters."

355 **the musician's name appears:** Personal file of BECKENSTEIN, GERSZON, born on 20-May-1911. DocID: 5497989. Arolsen Archives, collections.arolsen-archives.org/en/document/5497989.

355 **In 1942, five Kravitzes:** Shoah Names DB, search criteria: kravitz, lunna. *Yad Vashem: The World Holocaust Remembrance Center.* Retrieved July 22, 2025. collections.yadvashem.org/en/names/search-results/kravitz,%20luna?page=1.

355 **Nine months before, the Bundist engineer:** Sutzkever and Cammy, *From the Vilna Ghetto to Nuremberg,* 140.

355 **At the end of July:** Blatman, *For Our Freedom and Yours,* 167.

356 **lines of vehicles filled with Germans:** Lubetkin, *In the Days of Destruction and Revolt,* 265.

356 **The Bund's central committee:** Celemenski, *Elegy for My People,* 206.

356 **immediately issued a proclamation:** Lubetkin, *In the Days of Destruction and Revolt,* 267.

356 **Under gunfire, Leon Feiner:** Celemenski, *Elegy for My People,* 206.

356 **The fighting began in the working-class:** Cyryl Ryzak, "The Warsaw Uprising Was a Fight to Define Poland's Future," *Jacobin*, August 1, 2021, jacobin.com/2021/08/warsaw-uprising-poland-factions-right-nationalism-kaczynski-communists-jews-home-army.
356 **In the courtyard of Ignacy Samsonowicz's:** Celemenski, *Elegy for My People*, 207.
356 **The next morning Celemenski:** Celemenski, *Elegy for My People*, 208.
356 **During the uprising, dozens of Jews:** Beres and Burnetko, *Marek Edelman*, 231.
356 **Bundists Marek Edelman and Julek Fiszgrund:** Beres and Burnetko, *Marek Edelman*, 227.
356 **Some Poles robbed survivors:** Meed, *On Both Sides of the Wall*, 256; Celemenski, *Elegy for My People*, 211.
356 **forcing ZOB fighters to join:** Beres and Burnetko, *Marek Edelman*, 228; Lubetkin, *In the Days of Destruction and Revolt*, 268.
357 **largely colonial troops:** Ken Chen, "In the Zone of Nonbeing," *The Nation*, June 3, 2024.
357 **he shipped the Black African soldiers:** Roger Cohen, "Macron Honors African Soldiers Who Helped Liberate France in World War II," *New York Times*, August 15, 2024.
357 **he added Algerians, Syrians, and Spaniards:** Mike Thompson, "Paris Liberation Made 'Whites Only,'" BBC Radio 4, April 6, 2009, news.bbc.co.uk/2/hi/europe/7984436.stm.
357 **Some Bundists had fought:** Henri Minczeles, "La résistance du Bund en France pendant l'Occupation," *Le Monde Juif* 2, no. 154 (1995): 138–53.
357 **they discovered their party's archives:** Web, "Between New York and Moscow: The Fate of the Bund Archives," 249.
357 **Vera Dobrinksy posed:** Isaac Dobrinsky, *Vera, femme de l'artiste*, oil on canvas, inscribed with authentication by Vera Dobrinsky "Paris, 1944" on the back, bonhams.com/auction/26977/lot/51/isaac-dobrinsky-ukrainian-1891-1973-vera-femme-de-lartiste-painted-in-1930-unframed.
357 **The two artists had shacked up:** Nadine Nieszawer, Deborah Princ, Arthur Princ, and Boris Princ, *Histoire des Artistes Juifs de l'École de Paris: Stories of Jewish Artists of the School of Paris* (Les Étoiles Editions, 2020), 116–17.
358 **Flames devoured the ZOB headquarters:** Beres and Burnetko, *Marek Edelman*, 223.
358 **Polish socialist Janek Kulikowski:** Celemenski, *Elegy for My People*, 219.
358 **Old whispers started again:** Celemenski, *Elegy for My People*, 219.
358 **When *Monitor Polski*:** Goldstein, *Stars Bear Witness*, 244.
358 **When Bundist leaders met:** Celemenski, *Elegy for My People*, 209.
358 **They could no longer communicate:** Meed, *On Both Sides of the Wall*, 259.
358 **Leon Feiner was gravely:** Meed, *On Both Sides of the Wall*, 259.
358 **The partisan Hannah Fryshdorf:** Celemenski, *Elegy for My People*, 175.
358 **Bernard Goldstein delivered her son:** Goldstein, *Stars Bear Witness*, 248.
358 **On Vladka Peltel's last visit:** Meed, *On Both Sides of the Wall*, 259.
358 **Others like Bernard Goldstein:** Goldstein, *Stars Bear Witness*, 251–52.
359 **"Who's there?":** Goldstein, *Stars Bear Witness*, 267–69.
359 **They heard Russian voices:** Goldstein, *Stars Bear Witness*, 273–74.
359 **skulls missing their gold teeth:** Meed, *On Both Sides of the Wall*, 263.
359 **Later, he heard a Pole whisper:** Goldstein, *Stars Bear Witness*, 277.

CHAPTER TWENTY-SEVEN: SCATTER

360 **took place around Feiner's deathbed:** David Slucki, *The International Jewish Labor Bund After 1945: Towards a Global History* (Rutgers University Press, 2012), 58; Hertz, *Doyres Bundistn*, vol. 2, 87.
360 **they gave their support:** Blatman, *For Our Freedom and Yours*, 168.
360 **"Still alive?":** Jan Tomasz Gross, *Fear: Anti-Semitism in Poland After Auschwitz: An Essay in Historical Interpretation* (Random House, 2006), 36.
360 **"There is no place":** D. Libionka, "Kwestia żydowska" w Polsce w ocenie Delegata Rządu RP i KG ZWZ-AK w latach 1942–1944," paper presented at a conference in Lublin in 2006, 15–16.
361 **"The returning Jews were made":** Goldstein, *Stars Bear Witness*, 277.
361 **Bernard's Polish communist friends:** Goldstein, *Stars Bear Witness*, 278.
361 **Nationalists murdered over a thousand:** Beres and Burnetko, *Marek Edelman*, 258.
361 **When Marek Edelman traveled:** Beres and Burnetko, *Marek Edelman*, 281.
361 **Within months of liberation:** Blatman, *For Our Freedom and Yours*, 179.
361 **"This was not the liberation":** Goldstein, *Stars Bear Witness*, 285.
361 **an honorary grandfather:** Conversation with Irena Klepfisz.
362 **pledged loyalty:** Blatman, *For Our Freedom and Yours*, 172–73.
362 **They set up:** "Bund Youth Movement of Poland Resists Communist Coercion," *Jewish Labor Bund Bulletin*, April–May 1949, 2; Blatman, *For Our Freedom and Yours*, 185.
362 **They resurrected their institutions:** Slucki, *International Jewish Labor Bund*, 63–65.
362 **Bundists scoured the country:** Beres and Burnetko, *Marek Edelman*, 270–78.
362 **Zalman Friedrich's daughter Elzunia:** Beres and Burnetko, *Marek Edelman*, 271–78.
362 **"Most of the members want":** Blatman, *For Our Freedom and Yours*, 178.
362 **The Bundist Jacob Pat realized:** Pat, *Ashes and Fire*, 76.
363 **"You can smell the ships":** Pat, *Ashes and Fire*, 11.
363 **At a newly opened Jewish community:** Pat, *Ashes and Fire*, 143–46.
363 **When Marek Edelman traveled:** Beres and Burnetko, *Marek Edelman*, 279–80.
364 **After Kielce, the Bund demanded:** Blatman, *For Our Freedom and Yours*, 181.

364 **Hundreds of Bundists asked:** Blatman, *For Our Freedom and Yours,* 182.
364 **They joined the flood:** Blatman, *For Our Freedom and Yours,* 179.
364 **Zionist smuggling networks crisscrossed:** Beres and Burnetko, *Marek Edelman,* 288–89; Zeev Mankowitz, *Life Between Memory and Hope: The Survivors of the Holocaust in Occupied Europe* (Cambridge University Press, 2002), 17.
364 **Antek had even less respect:** Zuckerman, *Surplus of Memory,* 652.
364 **built on the ruins:** "Welcome To al-Sumayriyya," *Palestine Remembered,* palestineremembered.com/Acre/al-Sumayriyya/index.html, accessed July 12, 2025.
364 **there were eighty thousand concentration camp:** Mankowitz, *Life Between Memory and Hope,* 11.
364 **Most were shit-encrusted hellholes:** Yosef Grodzinsky, *In the Shadow of the Holocaust* (Common Courage Press, 2004), 39–40.
364 **the courier Jacob Celemenski:** Celemenski, *Elegy for My People,* 231–34.
364 **1,200 Bundists had made their homes:** Mankowitz, *Life Between Memory and Hope,* 19.
364 **Some of them imagined:** Mankowitz, *Life Between Memory and Hope,* 27.
365 **People lived in flimsy shacks:** Grodzinsky, *In the Shadow of the Holocaust,* 143.
365 **On June 1, 1946, 150 of:** Grodzinsky, *In the Shadow of the Holocaust,* 133–35.
365 **They decided to run:** Grodzinsky, *In the Shadow of the Holocaust,* 134.
365 **Haganah and Irgun paramilitaries:** Grodzinsky, *In the Shadow of the Holocaust,* 167.
365 **They quickly seized control:** Mankowitz, *Life Between Memory and Hope,* 47.
365 **which gave out travel passes:** Grodzinsky, *In the Shadow of the Holocaust,* 152.
365 **their suffering increased sympathy:** Grodzinsky, *In the Shadow of the Holocaust,* 147.
365 **"Along came the missionaries":** Grodzinsky, *In the Shadow of the Holocaust,* 136, 139.
365 **branded Jews as deserters:** Grodzinsky, *In the Shadow of the Holocaust,* 135.
365 **Bundists in the Bindermichl camp:** "Nationalism on the Warpath: A New Wave of Zionist Terror," *Jewish Labor Bund Bulletin,* July 1948, 4.
365 **The Central Committee of Liberated Jews:** Grodzinsky, *In the Shadow of the Holocaust,* 157.
365 **In the words of one survivor:** Grodzinsky, *In the Shadow of the Holocaust,* 134.
365 **The Zionist press mocked Bundists:** Mankowitz, *Life Between Memory and Hope,* 74.
366 **Bundist survivors tried to keep:** Slucki, *International Jewish Labor Bund,* 50–51.
366 **They released a calligraphed bulletin:** "Eksekutif fun Di Bundishe Groupn In Daytshland: Biulitin No. 3," Folder 1552, "Records of the Displaced Persons Camps in Germany," Record Group 294.2, YIVO Institute for Jewish Research Archives, New York.
366 **"Can you call it living":** Slucki, *International Jewish Labor Bund,* 50–51.
366 **In November 1947, the Bund's flag:** "Bund Anniversary Rally in New York," *Jewish Labor Bund Bulletin,* February 1948, 2.
366 **a Roman union hall:** "Displaced Persons Camps and Centers in Italy," Folder 369.1, Record Group 294.3, YIVO Institute for Jewish Research Archives, New York.
366 **Only a fragment remained:** Slucki, *International Jewish Labor Bund,* 57.
366 **forced the Polish Bund to formally separate:** Blatman, *For Our Freedom and Yours,* 194.
366 **Kazimierz Puzak, who had warned:** Zygmunt Zaremba, "Kazimierz Pużak: A Sketch of His Biography, 1950," lewicowo.pl/kazimierz-puzak-szkic-zyciorysu.
366 **Antoni Zdanowski, Alter's travel buddy:** "Stalin's Agents Assassinate Polish Socialist," *Labor Action,* April 12, 1948, 1.
366 **the party voted to dissolve itself:** Blatman, *For Our Freedom and Yours,* 213–14; Beres and Burnetko, *Marek Edelman,* 292.
366 **most of Tsukunft's leadership:** Slucki, *International Jewish Labor Bund,* 72.
367 **despite harassment by the secret police:** Beres and Burnetko, *Marek Edelman,* 263–66.
367 **As an older man, he took part:** Edelman, *Guardian,* 73.
367 **"To be a Jew means":** Selma James, *Our Time Is Now: Sex, Race, Class, and Caring for People and Planet* (PM Press, 2021), 188.
367 **the uprising's commander was not permitted:** Itzhak Luden, "I Am the Guardian of the Jewish Graves," *Jewish Currents,* October 7, 2015, jewishcurrents.org/marek-edelman-the-heroic-anti-hero.
367 **"The future of the Jewish community":** "Statement on Palestine and Zionism Issued by the New York Bund Organization, 1947," *Jewish Labor Bund Bulletin,* February 1948, 6.
367 **sent out mobilization notices:** Grodzinsky, *In the Shadow of the Holocaust,* 174.
367 **As the Jewish Agency's leader, David Ben-Gurion:** Ilan Pappé, *The Ethnic Cleansing of Palestine* (Oneworld Publications, 2006), 36–37.
367 **"citizens of Israel who are prevented":** Grodzinsky, *In the Shadow of the Holocaust,* 170. Additional description is available in Shay Hazkani, *Dear Palestine: A Social History of the 1948 War* (Stanford University Press, 2021), 42–45.
368 **"Most Jewish refugees":** Grodzinsky, *In the Shadow of the Holocaust,* 193.
368 **A report from the Zionist youth:** Grodzinsky, *In the Shadow of the Holocaust,* 194.
368 **resolved that "draft dodgers":** Grodzinsky, *In the Shadow of the Holocaust,* 191.
368 **Camp administrations fired:** Grodzinsky, *In the Shadow of the Holocaust,* 199.
368 **In Neu Freimann:** Grodzinsky, *In the Shadow of the Holocaust,* 205.
368 **And in Grugliasco:** "The Case of Jakob Friedman," *Jewish Labor Bund Bulletin,* July 1948, 5.
368 **It was shocking:** Grodzinsky, *In the Shadow of the Holocaust,* 207.
368 **Bundists in the Bad Reichenhall:** "Nationalism on the Warpath," 4.

368 **Zionists beat the elderly fathers:** Grodzinsky, *In the Shadow of the Holocaust*, 199.
368 **Conscription continued until April 1949:** Hazkani, *Dear Palestine*, 47–48.
368 **In his last article written before:** S. Mendelson, "Bundism, Zionism and the Jewish State," *Unser Tsayt*, January–February 1948.
369 **Bundist camp chapters tried to protect:** YIVO records of Displaced Persons Camps in Germany. Folder 1552: Bund. Page 10. YIVO Center for Jewish Research, New York.
369 **They collected testimonies:** YIVO records of Displaced Persons Camps in Germany. Folder 1552: Bund. Page 12. YIVO Center for Jewish Research, New York.
369 **In Austria, Bundists appealed:** "Nationalism on the Warpath," 4.
369 **they battled to free their members:** Slucki, *International Jewish Labor Bund*, 48–49.
369 **Because of the Bund's connections:** Slucki, *International Jewish Labor Bund*, 48–49.
369 **On the First of May, Bundist DPs:** "Oyfruf! Zol Lebn Der 1 Mai!" Folder 1552, "Records of the Displaced Persons Camps in Germany," 20, Record Group 294.2, YIVO Institute for Jewish Research Archives, New York; "Eksekutif fun Di Bundishe Groupn In Daytshland: Biulitin No. 3," Folder 1552, "Records of the Displaced Persons Camps in Germany," Record Group 294.2, YIVO Institute for Jewish Research Archives, New York.
369 **"Had the gates to America opened":** Tom Segev, *A State at Any Cost* (Farrar, Straus and Giroux, 2019), 346.
369 **In 1947, they excoriated the world:** "The First World Conference of the Jewish Labor Bund: Summarized Report," *Jewish Labor Bund Bulletin*, October 1947, 3.
369 **They petitioned the UN:** "One Year After the World Conference of the Bund in Brussels," *Jewish Labor Bund Bulletin*, May 1948, 7.
369 **"Even Hitler's unparalleled massacre":** "Address by Dr. E Scherer at Reading," *Jewish Labor Bund Bulletin*, June 1948, 3.
370 **At their first conference they called:** *Ṭezn un maṭeryaln tsu der ṿelṭ-ḳonferents fun bundishe organizatsyes un grupes Brisel, Mai 1947* (American Representation of the Bund in New York, 1947).
370 **"renounce the goal of an independent":** New York Bund Organization, "Statement on Palestine and Zionism," *Jewish Labor Bund Bulletin*, 1948, 7.
370 **"the scum of all Europe":** Eleanor Roosevelt, "My Day," June 12, 1948, Eleanor Roosevelt Papers, www2.gwu.edu/~erpapers/myday/displaydoc.cfm?_y=1948&_f=md000991.
370 **it banned 90 percent:** David Nasaw, "America Denied Refugees After the End of World War II—Just as We Are Today," *Time*, September 17, 2020, time.com/5889460/american-history-war-on-immigrants, accessed July 3, 2025.
370 **hundreds of Bundist survivors left for:** Slucki, *International Jewish Labor Bund*, 193.
370 **In 1948, Bundist Leivik Hodes:** Madeleine Atkins Cohen, "On the Frontiers of a Divided World," *Yiddishkayt*, August 12, 2014, yiddishkayt.org/border-lessons/, accessed July 3, 2025.
371 **"Deeply grieved and shaken":** "Statement," *Jewish Labor Bund Bulletin*, August–September 1948, 1.
371 **the Holocaust seemed to confirm:** Mankowitz, *Life Between Memory and Hope*, 54.
372 **"It appears that 2,000 years":** "Arab Refugees," *Jewish Labor Bund Bulletin*, August–September 1948, 4.
372 **"when more than half a million":** "New Immigrants in Israel," *Jewish Labor Bund Bulletin*, June 1949, 3.
372 **"prevented from returning to their homesteads":** "Third Anniversary of Israel," *Jewish Labor Bund Bulletin*, March–May 1951, 4.

CHAPTER TWENTY-EIGHT: HOME

373 **her vision was so bad:** Conversation with Mark Erlich.
373 **she told her grandson Henry:** Conversation with Henry Erlich.
373 **Over email, Said's daughter, Najla:** Conversation over Instagram with Najla Said.
374 **They worked together to compile:** Wolff, *Yiddish Revolutionaries in Migration*, 185.
374 **tiny Bund branch in Tel Aviv:** The Tel Aviv Bund ran on a platform of Yiddish language rights and Jewish-Palestinian solidarity. See Slucki, *International Jewish Labor Bund*, 200–201. For more on Bundists in Israel, see Eran Torbiner's documentary *Bunda'im*.
374 **during the McCarthy years, they lived:** Conversation with Irena Klepfisz.
374 **the writer Irving Howe complained:** Letter from Irving Howe to Motl Zelmanowicz, February 28, 1978, Melbourne Bund Archives.
375 **The Bund's Worldwide Organizing Committee:** Slucki, *International Jewish Labor Bund*, 43.
375 **groups survive in Australia and France:** The Medem Library continues in Paris as a Yiddish cultural center. In Melbourne, Australia, there still exists an active Bund branch founded by Holocaust survivors, which maintains a SKIF youth group. It is primarily concerned with Yiddish culture.
375 **he foraged his materials:** Rothbort, *Out of Wood and Stone*, 28.
376 **He made art with his son:** "Er Foraybikt Der Shtetl," *Forverts*, May 4, 1968, 3; "How to Succeed as an Artist: Get Murdered," *Sunday News*, March 1, 1964, 2.
376 **"have not yet been misled":** Undated letter from Samuel Rothbort to Albert Barry. Private collection of Janice Caban.
377 **"I prefer the human idea":** Rothbort, *Out of Wood and Stone*, 83.

SELECTED BIBLIOGRAPHY

ARCHIVAL COLLECTIONS

Bund Archives, YIVO Institute for Jewish Research, New York, New York.
Bund Foreign Committee Records, YIVO Institute for Jewish Research, New York, New York.
Displaced Persons Camps Collection, YIVO Institute for Jewish Research, New York, New York.
Jewish Labor Committee Records, Tamiment Library and Robert F. Wagner Labor Archives, New York University, New York, New York.
Landsmanshaftn Collection, YIVO Institute for Jewish Research, New York, New York.
Melbourne Bund Archive, The Jewish Labour Bund, Melbourne, Australia.
Okhrana records 1883–1917, Hoover Institution Library and Archives, Stanford University, Stanford, California.
Records of the Workmen's Circle, YIVO Institute for Jewish Research, New York, New York.
The Communist International Archives, The Russian State Archive for Social and Political History, Moscow, Russia.
The Ringelblum Archive, The Jewish Historical Institute, Warsaw, Poland.
The Samuel Rothbort Papers, personal archives of Janice Caban, New York, New York.

INTERVIEWS

Henry Erlich
Irena Klepfisz
Jack Jacobs
Janice Caban
Mark Erlich
Marvin Zuckerman
Mimi Erlich
Najla Said
Paula Sawicka
Victor Gilinsky
Zenon Neumark

NEWSPAPERS AND PERIODICALS

Arbeter Shtime. Petrograd, Russia, 1917.
Falanga. Warsaw, Poland, 1938.
The Forward.
Haynt. Warsaw, Poland, 1929.
Naye Folkstsaytung. Warsaw, Poland, 1927–1939.
Robotnik. Warsaw, Poland, 1933.
The Brooklyn Daily Eagle.
The Ghetto Speaks. New York, 1942–1945.
The Jewish Labor Bund Bulletin. New York, 1947–1951.
The New York Age.
The New York Times.
The New York Tribune.
Volkovysker Veker. Volkovsyk, Poland, 1929.

DISSERTATIONS AND THESES

Denz, Rebekka. "Bundistinnen: Frauen Im Allgemeinen Jüdischen Arbeiterbund ("Bund") Dargestellt Anhand Der Jiddischen Biographiensammlung 'Doires Bundistn.' " Potsdam University, 2009.
Langer, Jacob. "Corruption and the Counterrevolution: The Rise and Fall of the Black Hundred." Duke University, 2007.
Łaniewski, Aleksander. "Bund w guberni grodzieńskiej podczas rewolucji 1905 roku. Zarys problematyki." Institute of History of the Polish Academy of Sciences, 2018.

Shukman, H. "The Relations Between the Jewish Bund and the RSDRP, 1897–1903." University of Oxford, 1961.

ARTICLES

Berlin, George. "The Jewish Labor Committee and American Immigration Policy in the 1930's." In *Studies in Jewish Bibliography, History, and Literature in Honor of I. Edward Kiev*, edited by Charles Berlin. Ktav Publishing House, 1971.

Collomp, Catherine. "The Jewish Labor Committee, American Labor, and the Rescue of European Socialists, 1934–1941." *International Labor and Working-Class History, No. 68, Labor in Postwar Central and Eastern Europe.* Cambridge University Press. Fall 2005.

Du Bois, W.E.B. "The Negro and the Warsaw Ghetto." *Jewish Life.* May 1952.

Hickey, Michael C. "Revolution on the Jewish Street: Smolensk, 1917." *Journal of Social History* 31, no. 4 (1998): 823–50.

Klot, Anne-Christin. "Journalism as a Weapon: Jewish Journalists from Warsaw and the Production of Knowledge During Hitler's Rise to Power in 1933 and the November Pogroms in 1938." In *New Perspectives on Kristallnacht*, edited by Steven J. Ross, Wolf Gruner, and Lisa Ansell. Purdue University Press, 2019.

Kozłowska, Magdalena. " 'Did You Teach Us to Do Otherwise?': Young Women in the Tsukunft Youth Movement in Interwar Poland and Their Role Models." *Aspasia*, Volume 14, 2020.

Medrzecki, Wlodizmierz. "Germany and Ukraine Between the Start of the Brest-Litovsk Peace Talks and Hetman Skoropads'kyi's Coup." *Harvard Ukrainian Studies* 23, no. 1–2 (1999): 47–71.

Meyers, Joshua. "The Bund by the Numbers: The Ebbs and Flows of a Jewish Radical Party." *In geveb.* 2020.

Pickhan, Getrud. " 'That Incredible History of the Polish Bund Written in a Soviet Prison': The NKVD Files on Henryk Erlich and Wiktor Alter." In *Polin: Studies in Polish Jewry Volume 10: Jews in Early Modern Poland*, edited by Gershon David Hundert. Liverpool University Press, 1997.

Pinson, Koppel. "Arkady Kremer, Vladimir Medem, and the Ideology of the Jewish 'Bund.'" *Jewish Social Studies* 7, no. 3 (1945): 233–64.

Richie, Alexandra. *The Invasion of Poland.* The National WWII Museum of New Orleans. October 17, 2023. nationalww2museum.org/war/articles/invasion-poland-september-1939.

Tobias, Henry, and Charles Woodhouse. "Revolutionary Optimism and the Practice of Revolution: The Jewish Bund in 1905." *Jewish Social Studies* 47, no. 2 (1985): 135–50.

BOOKS

Abd el-Fattah, Alaa. *You Have Not Yet Been Defeated: Selected Writings, 2011–2019.* Fitzcarraldo Editions, 2021.

Abramovich, Raphael. *In tsvey revolutsyes: Di geshikhte fun a dor.* Arbeter Ring, 1944.

———. *The Soviet Revolution, 1917–1939.* International Universities Press, 1962.

Abramowicz, Hirsz. *Profiles of a Lost World: Memoirs of East European Jewish Life Before World War II.* Wayne State University Press, 1999.

Abramson, Henry. *A Prayer for the Government: Ukrainians and Jews in Revolutionary Times, 1917–1920.* Harvard University Press, 1999.

Ackerman, Kenneth. *Trotsky in New York: A Radical on the Eve of Revolution.* Counterpoint, 2017.

Alter, Viktor. *Der Emes Vegn Palestine.* Farlag Di Velt, 1925.

Alter, Viktor, and Julius Deutsch. *Hiszpania w Ogniu; Rok Wojny Domowej.* Myśli Socjalistycznej, 1937.

An-Sky, S. *1915 Diary of S. An-sky, a Russian Jewish Writer at the Eastern Front.* Indiana University Press, 2016.

———. *The Enemy at His Pleasure: A Journey Through the Jewish Pale of Settlement During World War I.* Metropolitan Books/Henry Holt, 2002.

Arkady: Zamlbukh Tsum Ondenk Fun Grinder Fun "Bund" Arkady Kremer. Unzer Tsayt, 1942.

Ascher, Abraham. *The Mensheviks in the Russian Revolution.* Cornell University Press, 1976.

———. *The Revolution of 1905: A Short History.* Stanford University Press, 2004.

Barkan, Elazar, Elizabeth Cole, and Kai Struve, eds. *Shared History—Divided Memory: Jews and Others in Soviet Occupied Poland, 1939–1941.* Leipziger Universitätsverlag, 2007.

Baron, Samuel. *Plekhanov: The Father of Russian Marxism.* Stanford University Press, 1963.

Bauman, Janina. *Winter in the Morning: A Young Girl's Life in the Warsaw Ghetto and Beyond, 1939–1945.* Virago Press, 1986.

Belyakova, Zoia. *The Romanov Legacy: The Palaces of St. Petersburg.* Hazar Publishing, 1994.

Beres, Witold, and Krzysztof Burnetko. *Marek Edelman: Being on the Right Side.* Beres Media, 2016.

Berger, Jacob Solomon. *The Volkovysk Memorial Book: The Trilogy.* Volkovysk Yizkor Book Committee, 2002.

Biskupska, J. *Survivors: Warsaw Under Nazi Occupation.* Studies in the Social and Cultural History of Modern Warfare. Cambridge University Press, 2022.

Blady-Szwajger, Adina. *I Remember Nothing More: The Warsaw Children's Hospital and the Jewish Resistance.* Collins Harvill, 1990.

Blatman, Daniel. *For Our Freedom and Yours: The Jewish Labor Bund in Poland, 1939–1949.* Vallentine Mitchell, 2003.

Bojcun, Marko. *The Workers' Movement and the National Question in Ukraine: 1897–1918.* Brill, 2021.

Bor-Komorowski, Tadeusz. *The Secret Army: The Memoirs of General Bor-Komorowski.* Frontline Books, 2011.

Braunthal, Julius. *History of the International: Volume II: 1914–1943.* Frederick A. Praeger Publishers, 1967.

Brossat, Alain, and Sylvie Klingberg. *Revolutionary Yiddishland: A History of Jewish Radicalism*. Verso Books, 1983.
Brovkin, Vladimir. *Dear Comrades: Menshevik Reports on the Bolshevik Revolution and the Civil War*. Hoover Institute Press, 1991.
———. *The Mensheviks After October*. Cornell University Press, 1987.
Brykenzynski, Paul. *Primed for Violence: Murder, Antisemitism, and Democratic Politics in Interwar Poland*. University of Wisconsin Press, 2016.
Bushnell, John. *Mutiny amid Repression: Russian Soldiers in the Revolution of 1905–1906*. Indiana University Press, 1985.
Bychowcew, Mikalaj, and Renata Hawrylik-Kuklinska. *Wolkowysk: miasto trzech narodow*. Rozpisani.pl, 2020.
Celemenski, Jacob. *Elegy for My People*. Jacob Celemenski Memorial Trust, 2000.
Collomp, Catherine. *Résister au Nazisme: Le Jewish Labor Committee, New York, 1934–1945*. CNRS Éditions, 2016.
Collomp, Catherine, and Bruno Groppo, eds. *An American in Hitler's Berlin: Abraham Plotkin's Diary, 1932–1933*. University of Illinois Press, 2009.
Darsa, Jan. *The Jews of Poland*. Facing History and Ourselves National Foundation, 1998.
Davies, Norman. *White Eagle, Red Star*. MacDonald & Co., 1972.
Dawidowicz, Lucy. *From That Place and Time: A Memoir, 1938–1947*. W. W. Norton, 1989.
———. *The Golden Tradition: Jewish Life and Thought in Eastern Europe*. Holt, Rinehart, and Winston, 1967.
———. *A Holocaust Reader*. Behram House, 1976.
———. *The War Against the Jews: 1933–1945*. Random House, 1986.
Deutscher, Isaac. *The Prophet Armed: Trotsky, 1879–1921*. Oxford University Press, 1954.
Długołęcki, Piotr, ed. *Confronting the Holocaust: Documents on the Polish Government-in-Exile's Policy Concerning Jews, 1939–1945*. Polski Instytut Spraw Miedzynadowowych, 2022.
Dubnova-Erlich, Sophia. *Bread and Matzoh*. Translated by Alan Shaw. Hermitage, 2004.
———. *Garber-Bund un Bershter-Bund*. Kultur-lige, 1937.
———. "Scorched Hearth." *An Anthology of Jewish-Russian Literature: Volume One*. Edited by Maxim D. Shrayer. M. E. Sharpe, 2007.
———. "A Shtetl." *An Anthology of Jewish-Russian Literature: Two Centuries of Dual Identity in Prose and Poetry*. Vol. 1 Edited by Maxim D. Shrayer. M. E. Sharpe, 2007.
Edelman, Marek. *The Guardian: Edelman Speaks*. Translated by E. P. Kulawiec. Unpublished manuscript. From the archives of Paula Sawicka.
Edelman, Marek. *The Ghetto Fights*. American Representation of the General Jewish Workers' Union of Poland, 1946.
———. *También hubo amor en el gueto*. Galazia Gutenberg, 2013.
Erlich, Victor. *Child of a Turbulent Century*. Northwestern University Press, 2006.
Esco Foundation for Palestine. *Palestine: A Study of Jewish, Arab, and British Policies*. Volume 1. Yale University Press, 1947.
Estraikh, Gennady. *Transatlantic Russian Jewishness: Ideological Voyages of the Yiddish Daily* Forverts *in the First Half of the Twentieth Century*. Academic Studies Press, 2020.
Feingold, Henry. *The Politics of Rescue*. Rutgers University Press, 1970.
Feldmann, Constantine. *The Revolt of the Potemkin*. Leonaur Books, 2021.
Figes, Orlando. *A People's Tragedy: The Russian Revolution, 1891–1924*. Jonathan Cape, 1996.
Fleming, Michael, ed. *Essays Commemorating Szmul Zygielbojm*. PUNO Press, 2018.
Frankel, Jonathan. *Jewish Politics and the Russian Revolution of 1905*. Tel Aviv University, 1982.
———. *Prophecy and Politics: Socialism, Nationalism, and the Russian Jews, 1862–1917*. Cambridge University Press, 1981.
Garlinski, Jozef. *Fighting Auschwitz*. Fawcett, 1975.
Gelbard, Arye. *Der jüdische Arbeiter-Bund Russlands im Revolutionsjahr 1917*. Europaverlag, 1982.
Getzler, Israel. *Martov: A Political Biography of a Russian Social Democrat*. Cambridge University Press, 2003.
Gitelman, Zvi. *The Emergence of Modern Jewish Politics: Bundism and Zionism in Eastern Europe*. University of Pittsburgh Press, 2003.
———. *Jewish Nationality and Soviet Politics: The Jewish Sections of the CPSU, 1917–1930*. Princeton University Press, 1972.
Goldberg, Gordon. *Meyer London: A Biography of the Socialist New York Congressman, 1871–1926*. McFarland & Company, 2013.
Goldelman, Soloman. *Jewish National Autonomy in Ukraine 1917–1920*. Ukrainian Research and Information Institute, 1968.
Golder, Frank. *Documents of Russian History: 1914–1917*. Peter Smith, 1964.
Goldstein, Bernard. *The Stars Bear Witness*. Viking Press, 1949.
———. *Twenty Years with the Jewish Labor Bund: A Memoir of Interwar Poland*. Purdue University Press, 2016.
Gorky, Maxim. *Untimely Thoughts: Essays on Revolution, Culture, and the Bolsheviks, 1917–1918*. Paul S. Eriksson, 1968.
Grodzinksy, Yosef. *In the Shadow of the Holocaust*. Common Courage Press, 2004.
Gross, Jan Tomasz. *Fear: Anti-Semitism in Poland After Auschwitz: An Essay in Historical Interpretation*. Random House, 2006.

Gutman, Yisrael. *The Jews of Warsaw: Ghetto, Underground, Revolt.* Indiana University Press, 1982.
Hagan, William. *Anti Jewish Violence in Poland, 1914–1920.* Cambridge University Press, 2018.
Haimson, Leopold, ed. *The Making of Three Russian Revolutionaries.* Cambridge University Press, 1987.
Harding, Neil, ed. *Marxism in Russia: Key Documents 1879–1906.* Cambridge University Press, 2008.
Hartman, Saidiya. *Wayward Lives, Beautiful Experiments.* W. W. Norton, 2019.
Hazkani, Shay. *Dear Palestine: A Social History of the 1948 War.* Stanford University Press, 2021.
Heller, Celia. *On the Edge of Destruction: Jews and Poland Between the Two World Wars.* Columbia University Press, 1977.
Heller, Daniel Kupfert. *Jabotinsky's Children.* Princeton University Press, 2017.
Hertz. Y. Sh. *Der Bund in Bilder: 1897–1957.* Unzer Tsayt Farlag, 1958.
———. *Di Geshikhte Fun Bund: Volumes One–Five.* Unzer Tsayt Farlag, 1981.
———. *Doyres Bundistn.* Unzer Tsayt Farlag, 1956.
Hirszfeld, Ludwik. *The Story of One Life.* University of Rochester Press, 2010.
Hodis, Leivik. *Biografie un Shriftn.* Unzer Tsayt Farlag, 1952.
Hoffman, Stefani, and Ezra Mendelsohn, eds. *The Revolution of 1905 and Russia's Jews.* University of Pennsylvania Press, 2008.
Howe, Irving. *World of Our Fathers: The Journey of the East European Jews to America and the Life They Found and Made.* Open Road Media, 2017.
Jacobs, Jack. "Bundist Anti-Zionism in Interwar Poland." In *Rebels Against Zion: Studies on the Jewish Left Anti-Zionism,* edited by August Grabski. Zydowski Instytut Historyczyny im. Emanuela Ringelbluma, 2011.
Jacobs, Jack. *Bundist Counterculture in Interwar Poland.* Syracuse University Press, 2009.
———, ed. *Jewish Politics in Eastern Europe: The Bund at 100.* NYU Press, 2001.
James, C.L.R. *World Revolution 1917–1936.* Purnell and Sons, 1937.
Janiszewska, Aleksandra, ed. *The Colors of War: The Siege of Warsaw in Julien Bryan's Color Photographs.* Karta Center, 2010.
Jewish Labor Bund: 1897–1957. The International Jewish Labor Bund, 1958.
Johnpoll, Bernard K. *The Politics of Futility: The General Jewish Workers Bund of Poland, 1917–1943.* Cornell University Press, 1967.
Kanafani, Ghassan. *The 1936–39 Revolt in Palestine.* Tricontinental Society, 1980.
Karski, Jan. *Story of a Secret State.* Houghton Mifflin Company, 1944.
Kerensky, Alexander. *The Kerensky Memoirs: Russia and History's Turning Point.* Cassell, 1966.
Kerensky, Alexander, and Robert Browder. *The Russian Provisional Government 1917: Documents.* Stanford University Press, 1961.
Kermish, Joseph, and Tikva Fatal-Knaani, eds. *The Jewish Underground Press in Warsaw: Volume Two.* Yad Vashem Publications, 2017.
Khalidi, Rashid. *The Hundred Years War on Palestine.* Profile Books, 2020.
Khmurner, Y. *Vos Lernen Unz Di Geshenishn In Palestine.* Tsentral Komitet Fun Bund in Poilin, 1929.
Klin, David. *À cache-cache avec la mort: Un résistant juif à Varsovie de 1939 à 1945.* Éditions Le Manuscrit, 2017.
Krall, Hanna. *Shielding the Flame.* Henry Holt & Company, 1986.
Krämer, Gudrun. *A History of Palestine: From the Ottoman Conquest to the Founding of the State of Israel.* Princeton University Press, 2008.
Lenin, Vladimir. *Collected Works: Volume 24.* Foreign Languages Pub. House, 1970.
———. *Lenin Collected Works, Volume 19, 20.* Progress Publishers, 1977.
———. *What Is to Be Done? Burning Questions of Our Movement.* International Publishers, 1929.
Leviné-Meyer, Rosa. *Inside German Communism: Memoirs of Party Life in the Weimar Republic.* Pluto Press, 1977.
Litvak, A. *Dos Reyolutsyonere Rusland.* Tsenṭral-ferband fun "Bund" in ferlag fun der Idisher sotsyalisṭisher federatsye in Ameriḳa, 1917.
———. *Geklibene Shriftn.* Unzer Tsayt Farlag, 1945.
Lubetkin, Zivia. *In the Days of Destruction and Revolt.* Ghetto Fighters' House, 1981.
Mankowitz, Zeev. *Life Between Memory and Hope: The Survivors of the Holocaust in Occupied Europe.* Cambridge University Press, 2002.
Marcus, Joseph. *Social and Political History of the Jews in Poland, 1919–1939.* Mouton Publishers, 1983.
Martov, Julius. *The Turning Point in the History of the Jewish Labor Movement, Union of Russian Social Democrats.* Maison Hengel, 1900.
McGeever, Brendan. *Antisemitism and the Russian Revolution.* Cambridge University Press, 2019.
Medem, Gina. *A Lebnsveg.* Gina Medem bukh-ḳomiṭeṭ, 1950.
Medem, Vladimir. *Fun Meyn Notits Bukh.* Drukarnia O. Rom, 1920.
———. *Vladimir Medem: The Life and Soul of a Legendary Jewish Socialist.* Ktav Publishers, 1979.
Meed, Vladka. *On Both Sides of the Wall.* The United States Holocaust Memorial Museum, 1993.
Melzer, Emanuel. *No Way Out: The Politics of Polish Jewry, 1935–1939.* Hebrew Union College Press, 1997.
Mendel, Hersh. *Memoirs of a Jewish Revolutionary.* Pluto Press, 1989.
Mendelsohn, Ezra. *Class Struggle in the Pale: The Formative Years of the Jewish Worker's Movement in Tsarist Russia.* Cambridge University Press, 1970.
Mendelsohn, Shloyme. *The Polish Jews Behind the Nazi Ghetto Walls.* Yiddish Scientific Institute, 1942.
Michels, Tony. *A Fire in Their Hearts: Yiddish Socialists in New York.* Harvard University Press, 2005.

Michlic, Joanna. *Poland's Threatening Other: The Image of the Jew from 1880 to the Present.* University of Nebraska Press, 2006.

Moczarski, Kazimierz. *Conversations with an Executioner.* Prentice-Hall, 1981.

Neumark, Zenon. *Hiding in the Open: A Young Fugitive in Nazi-Occupied Poland.* Vallentine Mitchell, 2008.

Nieszawer, Nadine. *Artistes Juifs de L'École de Paris: 1905–1939.* Somogy Éditions d'Art, 2015.

Nowicki, Ron. *Warsaw: The Cabaret Years.* Mercury House, 1992.

Nowogrodski, Emanuel. *The Jewish Labor Bund in Poland, 1915–1939.* Translated by Paula Sawicka. Shengold Books, 2001.

One Union: A History of the International Union of Painters and Allied Trades, 1887–2003. Aspatore, 2004.

Pappé, Ilan. *The Ethnic Cleansing of Palestine.* Oneworld Publications, 2006.

Pearce, Brian. *1903—Second Congress of the Russian Social-democratic Labour Party.* New Park Publications, 1978.

Pinsker, Shachar. *A Rich Brew: How Cafés Created Modern Jewish Culture.* New York University Press, 2018.

Polonsky, Anthony. "The Bund in Polish Political Life, 1935–1939." In *Essential Papers on Jews and the Left,* edited by Ezra Mendelsohn. New York University Press, 1997.

Portnoy, Samuel, ed. and trans. *Henryk Erlich and Victor Alter: Two Heroes and Martyrs of Jewish Socialism.* Ktav Publishers, 1990.

Pruszynski, Xavier. *Russian Year: The Notebook of an Amateur Diplomat.* Roy Publishers, 1944.

Rabinowitch, Alexander. *The Bolsheviks Come to Power.* Haymarket Books, 2017.

———. *Prelude to Revolution: The Petrograd Bolsheviks and the July 1917 Uprising.* Indiana University Press, 1968.

Rafes, Moshe, and A. Kirzhnits. *Der Yidisher Arbeter.* Tsenṭraler farlag far di felḳer fun F.S.S.R., 1926.

Ravel, Aviva. *Faithful unto Death: The Story of Arthur Zygielbaum.* Arthur Zygielbaum Branch, Workmen's Circle, 1980.

Reed, John. *Ten Days That Shook the World.* Boni & Liveright, 1922.

Reeder, Roberta. *Anna Akhmatova: Poet and Prophet.* Allison & Busby, 1995.

Rewolucja 1905. Przewodnik Krytyki Politycznej. Wydawnictwo Krytyka Polityczna, 2009.

Ribak, Gil. *Gentile New York: The Images of Non-Jews Among Jewish Immigrants.* Rutgers University Press, 2012.

Rich, J. C. *60 Years of the Jewish Daily Forward.* Forward Association, 1957.

Ringelblum, Emmanuel. *Notes from the Warsaw Ghetto: The Journal of Emmanuel Ringelblum.* Schocken Books, 1974.

———. *Polish-Jewish Relations During the Second World War.* Yad Vashem, 1974.

Rotem, Simha (Kazik). *Memoirs of a Warsaw Ghetto Fighter: The Past Within Me.* Yale University Press, 1994.

Rothbort, Samuel. *Out of Wood and Stone.* Stuyvesant House, 1952.

Rowe, Leonard. "Jewish Self Defense: A Response to Violence." In *Studies on Polish Jewry: 1919–1939,* edited by Joshua A. Fishman. YIVO Institute for Jewish Research. New York, 1974.

Russ, Henokh. "Book of Minutes of the Underground Youth Organization 'Tsukunft' in the Warsaw Ghetto: January 1941–January 1942." Translated by Mark Nowogrodski. From the personal archives of Brian Gocial.

Sebestyen, Victor. *Lenin: The Man, the Dictator, and the Master of Terror.* Pantheon Books, 2017.

Segev, Tom. *A State at Any Cost.* Farrar, Straus and Giroux, 2019.

———. *One Palestine, Complete: Jews and Arabs Under the British Mandate.* Holt Paperbacks, 1999.

Serge, Victor. *Memoirs of a Revolutionary.* New York Review Books, 2012. Originally published in 1963.

Shandler, Jeffrey, ed. *Awakening Lives: The Autobiographies of Jewish Youth in Poland Before the Holocaust.* Yale University Press, 2002.

Shepherd, Naomi. *A Price Below Rubies: Jewish Women as Rebels and Radicals.* Harvard University Press, 1993.

Shtakser, Inna. *The Making of Jewish Revolutionaries in the Pale of Settlement.* Palgrave Macmillan, 2014.

Silberfarb, Moses. *The Jewish Ministry and Jewish National Autonomy in Ukraine.* Aleph Press, 1993.

Slezkine, Yuri. *The Jewish Century.* New edition. Princeton University Press, 2019.

Slucki, David. *The International Jewish Labor Bund After 1945: Towards a Global History.* Rutgers University Press, 2012.

Sozialistische Arbeiter-Internationale (SAI). *Vierter Kongress der Sozialistischen Arbeiter-Internationale. Wien, 25. Juli bis 1. August 1931. Berichte und Verhandlungen.* Verlag des Sekretariats der SAI, 1932.

Stashkevich, Nikolai. *The October Revolution in Byelorussia.* Voice of the Motherland Library, 1979.

Steinberg, Mark. *The Russian Revolution, 1905–1921.* Oxford University Press, 2017.

Sukhanov, N. N. *The Russian Revolution 1917: A Personal Record.* Princeton University Press, 1984.

Sutzkever, Abraham, and Justin Cammy. *From the Vilna Ghetto to Nuremberg: Memoir and Testimony.* McGill-Queen's University Press, 2021.

Szurek, Alexander. *The Shattered Dream.* Eastern European Monographs, Boulder. Distributed by Columbia University Press, 1989.

Ṭezn un maṭeryaln tsu der velṭ-ḳonferents fun bundishe organizatsyes un grupes Brisel, Mai 1947. Ameriḳaner reprezenṭants fun Bund in Nyu-Yorḳ, 1947.

Tobias, Henry J. *The Jewish Bund in Russia from Its Origins to 1905.* Stanford University Press, 1972.

Trotsky, Leon. *1905.* Random House, 1971.

———. *History of the Russian Revolution.* Haymarket Books, 2008.

———. *My Life: An Attempt at an Autobiography.* Charles Scribner's Sons, 1930.

Ury, Scott. *Barricades and Banners: The Revolution of 1905 and the Transformation of Warsaw Jewry.* Stanford University Press, 2012.

Veidlinger, Jeffrey. *In the Midst of Civilized Europe.* Metropolitan Books, 2021.

Vladimir Medem Tsum tsvantsikstn yortsayt. American Representation of the General Jewish Workers' Union of Poland, 1943.

Watt, Richard M. *Bitter Glory: Poland and Its Fate, 1918 to 1939.* Simon and Schuster, 1979.

Weinberg, Robert. *The Revolution of 1905 in Odessa: Blood on the Steps.* Indiana University Press, 1993.

Wolff, Frank. *Yiddish Revolutionaries in Migration: The Transnational History of the Jewish Labour Bund.* Haymarket Books, 2022.

Wyman, David S. *The Abandonment of the Jews: America and the Holocaust, 1941–1945.* Pantheon, 1984.

———. *Paper Walls: America and the Refugee Crisis, 1938–1941.* University of Massachusetts Press, 1968.

Zaremba, Zygmunt. *Obrona Warszawy: wrzesień 1939 roku.* Komitet Zagraniczny PPS, 1941.

———. *Wojna I Konspiracja.* B. Swiderski, 1957.

Zarembina, Natalia. *Oboz smierci: The Camp of Death.* Edipresse Ksiazki, 2005.

Zimmerman, Joshua. *Poles, Jews, and the Politics of Nationality: The Bund and the Polish Socialist Party in Late Tsarist Russia, 1892–1914.* University of Wisconsin Press, 2004.

———. *The Polish Underground and the Jews, 1939–1945.* Cambridge University Press, 2015.

Zipperstein, Steven. *Pogrom: Kishinev and the Tilt of History.* Liveright Publishing Corporation, 2018.

Zuckerman, Yitzhak. *A Surplus of Memory: Chronicle of the Warsaw Ghetto Uprising.* University of California Press, 1993.

INDEX

Page numbers in *italics* indicate illustrations.

ABOUT THE AUTHOR

Molly Crabapple got her start drawing at underground burlesque shows and became a journalist on the front lines of Occupy Wall Street. She has reported with words and art from Ukraine, Syria, Lebanon, Gaza, Greek refugee camps, the U.S.-Mexican border, and Puerto Rico after Hurricane Maria, for places like *The New York Times, The New York Review of Books, The Paris Review, Vanity Fair, Rolling Stone,* and *The New Yorker.* Her work has been nominated for a National Book Award and has won two Emmys. She's done animations with AOC and Jay-Z, and her work is in the permanent collection of the Museum of Modern Art. She was a 2020 New America fellow, and a 2024 Cullman Center fellow at the New York Public Library.

ABOUT THE TYPE

This book was set in Walbaum, a typeface designed in 1810 by German punch cutter J. E. (Justus Erich) Walbaum (1768–1839). Walbaum's type is more French than German in appearance. Like Bodoni, it is a classical typeface, yet its openness and slight irregularities give it a human, romantic quality.